ENCE
VOICES

JOHN SOMER
Kansas State Teachers College

JOSEPH COZZO

LITERARY EXPERIENCE

public and private voices

SCOTT, FORESMAN AND COMPANY
Glenview, Illinois   London

To
Connie

ACKNOWLEDGMENTS

——Sophocles, *Antigone:* From *Three Theban Plays* of Sophocles, translated by Theodore Howard Banks. Copyright © Theodore Howard Banks, 1956. Reprinted by permission of Oxford University Press, Inc. ——William Shakespeare, *Romeo and Juliet:* From *The Complete Works of Shakespeare* by Hardin Craig. Copyright 1951 by Scott, Foresman and Company. ——Henrik Ibsen, *Hedda Gabler:* From *Hedda Gabler and Other Plays* by Henrik Ibsen, translated by Una Ellis-Fermor. Copyright 1950. Reprinted by permission of Penguin Books Ltd. ——John M. Synge, *The Playboy of the Western World:* Copyright 1907, renewed 1935 by the Executors of the Estate of John M. Synge. Reprinted from *The Complete Works of John M. Synge,* by permission of Random House, Inc. ——Tennessee Williams, *The Glass Menagerie:* From *Six Modern American Plays.* Copyright 1945 by Tennessee Williams and Ewina D. Williams. Reprinted by permission of Random House, Inc. ——William Shakespeare, "I. From fairest creatures we desire increase; II. When forty winters shall besiege thy brow; XII. When I do count the clock that tells the time; XVIII. Shall I compare thee to a summer's day?; XIX. Devouring Time, blunt thou the lion's paws; XXIX. When, in disgrace with fortune and men's eyes; XXX. When to the sessions of sweet silent thought; XXXV. No more be grieved at that which thou hast done; XLII. That thou hast her, it is not all my grief; LV. Not marble, nor the gilded monuments; LXV. Since brass, nor stone, nor earth, nor boundless sea; LXVIII. Thus is his cheek the map of days outworn; LXXIII. That time of year thou mayst in me behold; LXXXVI. Was it the proud full sail of his great verse; XCIV. They that have power to hurt and will do none; XCV. How sweet and lovely dost thou make the shame; CVI. When in the chronicle of wasted time; CXVI. Let me not to the marriage of true minds; CXXVII. In the old age black was not counted fair; CXXIX. The expense of spirit in a waste of shame; CXXX. My mistress' eyes are nothing like the sun; CXXXVIII. When my love swears that she is made of truth; CXLIV. Two loves I have of comfort and despair; CXLVI. Poor soul, the centre of my sinful earth; CXLVII. My love is as a fever, longing still; CLII. In loving thee thou know'st I am forsworn": From *The Complete Works of Shakespeare* by Hardin Craig. Copyright 1951 by Scott, Foresman and Company. ——Emily Dickinson, "613: They shut me up in Prose; 501: This World is not Conclusion; 1400: What mystery pervades a well!; 1068: Further in Summer than the Birds; 1593: There came a Wind like a Bugle; 519: 'Twas warm–at first–like Us; 547: I've seen a Dying Eye; 465: I heard a Fly buzz–when I died; 712: Because I could not stop for Death; 670: One need not be a Chamber–to be Haunted; 258: There's a certain Slant of light; 280: I felt a Funeral, in my Brain; 341: After great pain, a formal feeling comes; 822: This Consciousness that is aware; 508: I'm ceded–I've stopped being Theirs; 326: I cannot dance upon my Toes; 675: Essential Oils–are wrung; 1129: Tell all the Truth but tell it slant; 1071: Perception of an object costs; 290: Of Bronze–and Blaze; 451: The Outer–from the Inner; 328: A Bird came down the Walk; 1261: A Word dropped careless on a Page; 1651: A Word made Flesh is seldom": Reprinted by permission of the publishers and the Trustees of Amherst College from Thomas H. Johnson, Editor, *The Poems of Emily Dickinson,* Cambridge, Mass.: The Belknap Press of Harvard University Press, Copyright 1951, 1955, by The President and Fellows of Harvard College. ——Thomas Hardy, "Channel Firing": Reprinted with permission of The Macmillan Company from *Collected Poems* by Thomas Hardy. Copyright 1924 by The Macmillan Company; "Convergence of the Twain": Reprinted with permission of The Macmillan Company from *Collected Poems* by Thomas Hardy. Copyright 1924 by The Macmillan Company. ——A. E. Housman, "Terence, This Is Stupid Stuff": From "A Shropshire Lad." From *The Collected Poems of A. E. Housman.*

PREFACE

Literary Experience: Public and Private Voices is a combined edition of *Dramatic Experience: The Public Voice, Poetic Experience: Public Poems and Private Visions*, and *Narrative Experience: The Private Voice*.

The most significant characteristic of this text is that it suggests an answer to the persistent problem of organization without distorting the study of literature. Too often texts emphasize secondary considerations rather than the literature itself; they superimpose an order on the material which may be improper or even alien to it. The triumph of criticism, for example, has almost made the study of literature secondary. *Literary Experience*, however, clarifies an order which is inherent in the nature of the individual genres. As the section titles suggest, there is an established movement from the oldest and most public literary experience to the newest and most private.

Drama, the most public of literary expressions, is also one of the oldest. Consequently, any study of this genre must acknowledge its historical heritage as well as its technical variety. *Literary Experience* contains plays representative of the major periods of dramatic excellence in Western civilization which also serve to emphasize various successful approaches to dramatic expression. Both comic and tragic elements have been included, and all five plays have been successfully performed and received by audiences for years. They easily lend themselves to classroom analysis, and as a consequence, the teacher has been provided with a collection of eminently teachable plays illustrating both the historical and technical aspects of the drama.

Poetry stands as a median between the public voice of drama and the private voice of fiction, and shares elements of both. Poetry can be an open, public expression, celebrating the common experience of a people, or it can share the inward, meditative qualities of a confession, following the poet as he sculpts his private, individual vision. It can compel with a grand swelling of musical lyricism or it can shock with the velocity of an electrified image. *Literary Experience* contains examples of all these qualities of expression: dramatic, narrative, didactic, lyrical, imagistic — public and private verse. The poems are listed in chronological order and are distinguished in three ways. First, they are the most favored, and consequently the most representative, of their respective periods. Second, the works of five major poets, William Shakespeare, John Donne, William Blake, Emily Dickinson, and William Butler Yeats, are presented in depth, making possible a serious study of their "private" poetic visions. Enough of these poems are included to reveal the author's private symbology and philosophy. Third, the modern selections seek to combine works which illustrate the experimentation *and* conventionality in contemporary poetry as a kind of addition to, and resumé of, previous movements.

The short story, the most private of literary expressions, is certainly the newest, so that a historical study is not truly relevant. The most distinctive characteristic of a short story is its unique, meditative communication with a single reader. Frank O'Connor in *The Lonely Voice* argues that even the definition of a short story depends upon the state of alienation of its characters, rather than its length. A valid approach to the short story, then, is to study it on its own terms, both psychological and problematical. In order to facilitate this study, stories in this text have been arranged according to the approximate age of the protagonist, following him from youth to old age.

Interpretive apparatus in the book has been purposely avoided to minimize opposing approaches between editor and teacher and to free the individual pieces from serving any one critical system. Only the works themselves have been arranged to suggest an approach for study. An alternate table of contents, following the text, provides an additional, technical approach. Finally, information necessary for the understanding of a work, which cannot be ascertained in a dictionary, has been supplied in footnotes.

JS
JC

CONTENTS

Sophocles DRAMATIC EXPERIENCE

ANTIGONE 3

William Shakespeare

ROMEO AND JULIET 35

Henrik Ibsen

HEDDA GABLER 118

John Millington Synge

THE PLAYBOY OF THE WESTERN WORLD 184

Tennessee Williams

THE GLASS MENAGERIE 228

English Lyrical Ballads POETIC EXPERIENCE

The Twa Corbies 295
Edward 296
Sir Patrick Spens 297

Christopher Marlowe

The Passionate Shepherd to His Love 300

Sir Walter Raleigh

The Nymph's Reply to the Shepherd 301

Edmund Spenser

from *Amoretti*

XXXI. *Ah! why hath Nature to so hard a heart*
302
LXXIX. *Men call you fair, and you do credit
it* 302

William Shakespeare: Cycle of Conflict

SONNETS

I. *From fairest creatures we desire increase*
304
II. *When forty winters shall besiege thy brow*
305
XII. *When I do count the clock that tells the
time* 305

XVIII. *Shall I compare thee to a summer's day?* 306

XIX. *Devouring Time, blunt thou the lion's paws* 306

XXIX. *When, in disgrace with fortune and men's eyes* 307

XXX. *When to the sessions of sweet silent thought* 307

XXXV. *No more be grieved at that which thou hast done* 308

XLII. *That thou hast her, it is not all my grief* 308

LV. *Not marble, nor the gilded monuments* 309

LXV. *Since brass, nor stone, nor earth, nor boundless sea* 309

LXVIII. *Thus is his cheek the map of days outworn* 310

LXXIII. *That time of year thou mayst in me behold* 310

LXXXVI. *Was it the proud full sail of his great verse* 310

XCIV. *They that have power to hurt and will do none* 311

XCV. *How sweet and lovely dost thou make the shame* 312

CVI. *When in the chronicle of wasted time* 312

CXVI. *Let me not to the marriage of true minds* 313

CXXVII. *In the old age black was not counted fair* 313

CXXIX. *The expense of spirit in a waste of shame* 314

CXXX. *My mistress' eyes are nothing like the sun* 314

CXXXVIII. *When my love swears that she is made of truth* 315

CXLIV. *Two loves I have of comfort and despair* 315

CXLVI. *Poor soul, the centre of my sinful earth* 316

CXLVII. *My love is as a fever, longing still* 316

CLII. *In loving thee thou know'st I am forsworn* 317

John Donne: From Eros to Agape

Community 318
Song (Go and catch a falling star) 319
The Apparition 320
A Valediction: Of Weeping 320
The Flea 321
The Sun Rising 322
A Valediction: Forbidding Mourning 323
The Ecstasy 324
The Canonization 327
HOLY SONNETS
  VII. *At the round earth's imagined corners,*
    blow 328
   X. *Death be not proud, though some have*
    called thee 329
  XIII. *What if this present were the world's last*
    night? 329
  XIV. *Batter my heart, three-personed God; for*
    You 330

Ben Jonson

Come, My Celia 331
Still to Be Neat 331

Robert Herrick

Delight in Disorder 333
Upon Julia's Clothes 333
Corinna's Going A-Maying 334

Andrew Marvell

To His Coy Mistress 336

John Milton

On His Having Arrived at the Age of Twenty-Three
338
On His Blindness 338

Alexander Pope

from *An Essay on Man*
  from *Epistle I. Of the Nature and State of Man,*
    With Respect to the Universe 340
  from *Epistle II. Of the Nature and State of Man*
    with Respect to Himself, as an Individual
    345

Thomas Gray

    Elegy Written in a Country Churchyard 346

Robert Burns

    To a Mouse 350
    Auld Lang Syne 351

William Blake: Innocence and Experience

    To Spring 353
    To Autumn 353
    The Blossom 354
    Ah! Sun-flower 354
    The Sick Rose 355
    The Lamb 355
    The Tyger 356
    The Fly 357
    Song (My silks and fine array) 357
    The Divine Image 358
    from *Songs of Innocence*
        The Chimney Sweeper 359
    from *Songs of Experience*
        The Chimney Sweeper 360
    The Garden of Love 360
    I Asked a Thief to Steal Me a Peach 360
    London 361
    The Clod and the Pebble 362
    A Poison Tree 362
    Mad Song 363
    Are Not the Joys of Morning Sweeter 363
    O Lapwing, Thou Fliest Around the Heath
        364
    Thou Hast a Lap Full of Seed 364
    Preface to Milton 364

William Wordsworth

    Composed upon Westminster Bridge 366
    The World Is Too Much with Us 366

Samuel Taylor Coleridge

    Kubla Khan 368

George Noel Gordon, Lord Byron

    She Walks in Beauty 370
    When a Man Hath No Freedom 370

Percy Bysshe Shelley

>   *Ode to the West Wind*   372
>   *Ozymandias*   375

John Keats

>   *To Autumn*   376
>   *Ode on a Grecian Urn*   377

Alfred, Lord Tennyson

>   *Ulysses*   379
>   *The Eagle: A Fragment*   381

Robert Browning

>   *Porphyria's Lover*   382
>   *My Last Duchess*   383
>   *Meeting at Night*   385

Matthew Arnold

>   *Dover Beach*   386

Walt Whitman

>   *Out of the Cradle Endlessly Rocking*   388
>   *When I Heard the Learn'd Astronomer*   393

Emily Dickinson: Aesthetics of Estrangement

>   613: *They shut me up in Prose*   394
>   501: *This World is not Conclusion*   394
>   1400: *What mystery pervades a well!*   395
>   1068: *Further in Summer than the Birds*   396
>   1593: *There came a Wind like a Bugle*   396
>   519: *'Twas warm — at first — like Us*   397
>   547: *I've seen a Dying Eye*   397
>   465: *I heard a Fly buzz — when I died*   398
>   712: *Because I could not stop for Death*   398
>   670: *One need not be a Chamber — to be Haunted*
>   399
>   258: *There's a certain Slant of light*   400
>   280: *I felt a Funeral, in my Brain*   400
>   341: *After great pain, a formal feeling comes*   401
>   822: *This Consciousness that is aware*   401
>   508: *I'm ceded — I've stopped being Theirs*   402
>   326: *I cannot dance upon my Toes*   402
>   675: *Essential Oils — are wrung*   403
>   1129: *Tell all the Truth but tell it slant*   403

1071: *Perception of an object costs*   404
290: *Of Bronze—and Blaze*   404
451: *The Outer—from the Inner*   405
328: *A Bird came down the Walk*   405
1261: *A word dropped careless on a Page*   406
1651: *A Word made Flesh is seldom*   406

Gerard Manley Hopkins

God's Grandeur   407
Pied Beauty   407
Spring and Fall   408

Thomas Hardy

Channel Firing   409
The Convergence of the Twain   410

A. E. Housman

Terence, This Is Stupid Stuff   412

Rupert Brooke

Heaven   415

Wilfred Owen

Dulce et Decorum Est   417

William Butler Yeats: The Dominion of the Imagination

Down by the Salley Gardens   418
Adam's Curse   418
The Fascination of What's Difficult   420
A Dialogue of Self and Soul   420
Crazy Jane Talks with the Bishop   422
The Lake Isle of Innisfree   423
The Wild Old Wicked Man   423
Why Should Not Old Men Be Mad?   425
The Song of Wandering Aengus   426
Sailing to Byzantium   426
Easter, 1916   428
The Second Coming   430
Leda and the Swan   431
Lapis Lazuli   432

Robert Frost

Birches   434
Once by the Pacific   435

T. S. Eliot

    The Love Song of J. Alfred Prufrock   437
    Journey of the Magi   441

William Carlos Williams

    The Yachts   443
    Spring and All   444
    The Red Wheelbarrow   445

Ezra Pound

    In a Station of the Metro   446
    The River-Merchant's Wife: A Letter   446
    Ancient Music   447

H. D. (Hilda Doolittle)

    Hymn   448

Claude McKay

    America   449

Edna St. Vincent Millay

    Spring   450
    Siege   450

E. E. Cummings

    anyone lived in a pretty how town   452
    if i have made, my lady, intricate   453

Wallace Stevens

    Thirteen Ways of Looking at a Blackbird   454
    Sunday Morning   456

W. H. Auden

    O Where Are You Going   460
    Mundus et Infans   460

Theodore Roethke

    The Waking   463
    My Papa's Waltz   463

Kenneth Patchen

    O When I Take My Love Out Walking   465

Robert E. Hayden

    The Diver   466

Dylan Thomas

> *The Force That through the Green Fuse Drives the Flower* 468
> *Do Not Go Gentle into That Good Night* 469

Gwendolyn Brooks

> from *The Children of the Poor*
> #4: *First fight. Then fiddle. Ply the slipping string* 470

Lawrence Ferlinghetti

> *The Pennycandystore* 471

Alan Dugan

> *Tribute to Kafka for Someone Taken* 472

James Dickey

> *The Performance* 473

Leonard E. Nathan

> *Fall's Girl* 475

Lucien Stryk

> *The Cannery* 476
> *The Pit* 476

Gary Snyder

> from *Myths & Texts (Hunting)*
> #8 *"this poem is for deer"* 478

LeRoi Jones

> *An Agony. As Now.* 480

James Joyce   **NARRATIVE EXPERIENCE**

> ARABY 485

Graham Greene

> THE BASEMENT ROOM 490

Nathaniel Hawthorne

> MY KINSMAN, MAJOR MOLINEUX 510

Ralph Ellison

> FLYING HOME 525

Ernest Hemingway

> SOLDIER'S HOME 541

James Baldwin
      SONNY'S BLUES 547

Mary McCarthy
      "CRUEL AND BARBAROUS TREATMENT" 573

William Faulkner
      DRY SEPTEMBER 583

John Cheever
      TORCH SONG 593

Anton Chekhov
      GOOSEBERRIES 606

Flannery O'Connor
      A GOOD MAN IS HARD TO FIND 615

Leo Tolstoy
      THE DEATH OF IVAN ILYCH 628

Alternate Contents   **673**
Index of Authors and Titles   **676**
Index of First Lines of Poems   **679**

DRAMATIC EXPERIENCE
the public voice

CONTENTS

Sophocles
>ANTIGONE   3

William Shakespeare
>ROMEO AND JULIET   35

Henrik Ibsen
>HEDDA GABLER   118

John Millington Synge
>THE PLAYBOY OF THE WESTERN WORLD   184

Tennessee Williams
>THE GLASS MENAGERIE   228

Sophocles

496?–406 B.C.

ANTIGONE

translated by Theodore Howard Banks

CHARACTERS

CREON, *King of Thebes, brother of Jocasta, the mother and wife of Oedipus*

EURYDICE, *Queen of Thebes, wife of Creon*

HAEMON, *son of Creon*

ANTIGONE
ISMENE } *daughters of Oedipus and Jocasta*

TIRESIAS, *a prophet*

BOY, *attendant of Tiresias*

GUARD

MESSENGER

CHORUS *of Theban Elders*

ATTENDANTS

3

SCENE: *Courtyard of the royal palace at Thebes. Daybreak.*

(*Enter* ANTIGONE *and* ISMENE.)

ANTIGONE. Dear sister! Dear Ismene! How many evils
  Our father, Oedipus, bequeathed to us!
  And is there one of them—do you know of one
  That Zeus has not showered down upon our heads?
  I have seen pain, dishonor, shame, and ruin,
  I have seen them all, in what we have endured.
  And now comes this new edict by the King
  Proclaimed throughout the city. Have you heard?
  Do you not know, even yet, our friends are threatened?
  They are to meet the fate of enemies.   10
ISMENE. Our friends, Antigone? No, I have heard
  Nothing about them either good or bad.
  I have no news except that we two sisters
  Lost our two brothers when they killed each other.
  I know the Argive army fled last night,
  But what that means, or whether it makes my life
  Harder or easier, I cannot tell.
ANTIGONE. This I was sure of. So I brought you here
  Beyond the palace gates to talk alone.
ISMENE. What is the matter? I know you are deeply troubled.   20
ANTIGONE. Yes, for our brothers' fate. Creon has given
  An honored burial to one, to the other
  Only unburied shame. Eteocles
  Is laid in the earth with all the rites observed
  That give him his due honor with the dead.
  But the decree concerning Polyneices
  Published through Thebes is that his wretched body
  Shall lie unmourned, unwept, unsepulchered.
  Sweet will he seem to the vultures when they find him,
  A welcome feast that they are eager for.   30
  This is the edict the good Creon uttered
  For your observance and for mine—yes, mine.
  He is coming here himself to make it plain
  To those who have not heard. Nor does he think it
  Of little consequence, because whoever
  Does not obey is doomed to death by stoning.
  Now you can show you are worthy of your birth,
  Or bring disgrace upon a noble house.

---

2. OEDIPUS, Oedipus killed his father and married his mother, not knowing who they were. Antigone, Ismene, Polyneices, and Eteocles were the children of this incestuous relationship. Antigone suggests that even the children have been punished for these sins.

ISMENE. What can I do, Antigone? As things are,
   What can I do that would be of any help?   40
ANTIGONE. You can decide if you will share my task.
ISMENE. What do you mean? What are you planning to do?
ANTIGONE. I intend to give him burial. Will you help?
ISMENE. To give him burial! Against the law?
ANTIGONE. He is our brother. I will do my duty.
   Yours too, perhaps. I never will be false.
ISMENE. Creon forbids it! You are too rash, too headstrong.
ANTIGONE. He has no right to keep me from my own.
ISMENE. Antigone! Think! Think how our father perished
   In scorn and hatred when his sins, that he   50
   Himself discovered, drove him to strike blind
   His eyes by his own hand. Think how his mother,
   His wife—both names were hers—ended her life
   Shamefully hanging in a twisted noose.
   Think of that dreadful day when our two brothers,
   Our wretched brothers, fought and fell together,
   Each slayer and each slain. And now we too,
   Left all alone, think how in turn we perish,
   If, in defiance of the law, we brave
   The power of the commandment of a king.   60
   O think Antigone! We who are women
   Should not contend with men; we who are weak
   Are ruled by the stronger, so that we must obey
   In this and in matters that are yet more bitter.
   And so I pray the dead to pardon me
   If I obey our rulers, since I must.
   To be too bold in what we do is madness.
ANTIGONE. I will not urge you. And I would not thank you
   For any help that you might care to give me.
   Do what you please, but I will bury him,   70
   And if I die for that, I shall be happy.
   Loved, I shall rest beside the one I loved.
   My crime is innocence, for I owe the dead
   Longer allegiance than I owe the living.
   With the dead I lie forever. Live, if you choose,
   Dishonoring the laws the gods have hallowed.
ISMENE. No, I dishonor nothing. But to challenge
   Authority—I have not strength enough.
ANTIGONE. Then make that your excuse. I will go heap
   The earth above the brother that I love.   80
ISMENE. O Sister, Sister! How I fear for you!
ANTIGONE. No, not for me. Set your own life in order.
ISMENE. Well then, at least, tell no one of your plan.

Keep it close hidden, as I too will keep it.
ANTIGONE. Oh! Publish it! Proclaim it to the world!
   Then I will hate you less than for your silence.
ISMENE. Your heart is hot for deeds that chill the blood.
ANTIGONE. I know that I give pleasure where I should.
ISMENE. Yes, if you can, but you will try in vain.
ANTIGONE. When my strength fails, then I shall try no longer.   90
ISMENE. A hopeless task should never be attempted.
ANTIGONE. Your words have won their just reward: my hatred
   And the long-lasting hatred of the dead.
   But leave me and the folly that is mine
   To undergo the worst that can befall me.
   I shall not suffer an ignoble death.
ISMENE. Go then, Antigone, if you must go.
   And yet remember, though your act is foolish,
   That those who love you do so with all their hearts.
                    (*Exeunt* ANTIGONE *and* ISMENE. *Enter* CHORUS.)
CHORUS.
   Sunbeam, eye of the golden day, on Thebes the seven-gated,   100
      On Dircé's streams you have dawned at last, O fairest of light.
      Dawned on our foes, who had come enflamed by the quarrel
         of Polyneices,
      Shone on their glittering arms, made swifter their headlong
         flight.
         From Argos they came with their white shields flashing,
         Their helmets, crested with horsehair, agleam:
         An army that flew like a snow-white eagle
            Across our borders with shrilling scream.

   Above our roofs it soared, at our gates with greedy jaws it was
         gaping;
      But before their spears tasted our blood, and before our
         circle of towers
      Felt the flame of their torches, they turned to flight. The foes
         of the Theban dragon   110
         Found the surge and clamor of battle too fierce for their
            feebler powers.
         For Zeus, who abhors a proud tongue's boasting,
            Seeing their river of armor flow
         Clashing and golden, struck with his lightning
            To silence the shout of our foremost foe.
      He crashed to the earth with his torch, who had scaled the top
         of our ramparts.

110. THEBAN DRAGON, the builders of Thebes sprang from the dragon teeth that
Cadmus had planted.

Raging in frenzy against us, breathing tempestuous hate,
Raging and threatening in vain. And mighty Ares, our ally,
  Dealing havoc around him, apportioned to other foemen their
    fate.
    For at seven portals, their seven leaders,   120
      Down to the earth their bronze arms threw
    In tribute to Zeus, the lord of the battle;
      Save the fated brothers, the wretched two,
    Who went to their common doom together,
      Each wielding a spear that the other slew.

Now glorious Victory smiles upon jubilant Thebes rich in
    chariots.
Let us give free rein to our joy, forgetting our late-felt war;
Let us visit in night-long chorus the temples of all the immortals,
  With Bacchus, who shakes the land in the dances, going
    before.
    But behold! The son of Monoeceus approaches,   130
      Creon, the new-crowned King of the land,
    Made King by new fortunes the gods have allotted.
      What step has he pondered? What has he planned
    To lay before us, his council of elders,
      Who have gathered together at his command?

(*Enter* CREON.)
CREON. Elders of Thebes, our city has been tossed
  By a tempestuous ocean, but the gods
  Have steadied it once more and made it safe.
  You, out of all the citizens, I have summoned,
  Because I knew that you once reverenced   140
  The sovereignty of Laius, and that later,
  When Oedipus was King and when he perished,
  Your steadfast loyalty upheld his children.
  And now his sons have fallen, each one stained
  By his brother's blood, killed by his brother's hand,
  So that the sovereignty devolves on me,
  Since I by birth am nearest to the dead.
  Certainly no man can be fully known,
  Known in his soul, his will, his intellect,
  Until he is tested and has proved himself   150
  In statesmanship. Because a city's ruler,
  Instead of following the wisest counsel,
  May through some fear keep silent. Such a man
  I think contemptible. And one whose friend
  Has stronger claims upon him than his country,

Him I consider worthless. As for me,
I swear by Zeus, forever all-beholding,
That I would not keep silence, if I saw
Ruin instead of safety drawing near us;
Nor would I think an enemy of the state   160
Could be my friend. For I remember this:
Our country bears us all securely onward,
And only while it sails a steady course
Is friendship possible. Such are the laws
By which I guard the greatness of the city,
And kindred to them is the proclamation
That I have made to all the citizens
Concerning the two sons of Oedipus:
Eteocles, who has fallen in our defence,
Bravest of warriors, shall be entombed   170
With every honor, every offering given
That may accompany the noble dead
Down to their rest. But as for Polyneices,
He came from exile eager to consume
The city of his fathers with his fire
And all the temples of his father's gods,
Eager to drink deep of his kindred's blood,
Eager to drag us off to slavery.
To this man, therefore, nothing shall be given.
None shall lament him, none shall do him honor.   180
He shall be left without a grave, his corpse
Devoured by birds and dogs, a loathsome sight.
Such is my will. For never shall the wicked
Be given more approval than the just,
If I have power to stop it. But whoever
Feels in his heart affection for his city
Shall be rewarded both in life and death.
CHORUS. Creon, son of Menoeceus, it has pleased you
So to pass judgment on our friend and foe.
And you may give commands to all of us,   190
The living and the dead. Your will is law.
CREON. Then see that this command is carried out.
CHORUS. Sir, lay that burden on some younger man.
CREON. Sentries have been assigned to guard the body.
CHORUS. Then what additional duty would you give us?
CREON. Never to countenance the disobedient.
CHORUS. Who is so stupid as to long for death?
CREON. Death is indeed the punishment. Yet men
Have often been destroyed by hope of gain.

(Enter GUARD.*)*

GUARD. My Lord, I cannot say that I have hurried,   200
  Or that my running has made me lose my breath.
  I often stopped to think, and turned to go back.
  I stood there talking to myself: "You fool,"
  I said, "Why do you go to certain death?"
  And then: "You idiot, are you still delaying?
  If someone else tells Creon, you will suffer."
  I changed my mind this way, getting here slowly,
  Making a short road long. But still, at last,
  I did decide to come. And though my story
  Is nothing much to tell, yet I will tell it.   210
  One thing I know. I must endure my fate,
  But nothing more than that can happen to me.
CREON. What is the matter? What is troubling you?
GUARD. Please let me tell you first about myself.
  I did not do it. I did not see who did.
  It is not right for me to be punished for it.
CREON. You take good care not to expose yourself.
  Your news must certainly be something strange.
GUARD. Yes, it is strange—dreadful. I cannot speak.
CREON. Oh, tell it, will you? Tell it and go away!   220
GUARD. Well, it is this. Someone has buried the body,
  Just now, and gone—has sprinkled it with dust
  And given it other honors it should have.
CREON. What are you saying? Who has dared to do it?
GUARD. I cannot tell. Nothing was to be seen:
  No mark of pickaxe, no spot where a spade
  Had turned the earth. The ground was hard and dry,
  Unbroken—not a trace of any wheels—
  No sign to show who did it. When the sentry
  On the first watch discovered it and told us,   230
  We were struck dumb with fright. For he was hidden
  Not by a tomb but a light coat of dust,
  As if a pious hand had scattered it.
  There were no tracks of any animal,
  A dog or wild beast that had come to tear him.
  We all began to quarrel, and since no one
  Was there to stop us, nearly came to blows.
  Everyone was accused, and everyone
  Denied his guilt. We could discover nothing.
  We were quite willing to handle red-hot iron,   240
  To walk through fire, to swear by all the gods
  That we were innocent of the deed itself,

And innocent of taking any part
In planning it or doing it. At last
One of us spoke. We trembled and hung our heads,
For he was right; we could not argue with him,
Yet his advice was bound to cause us trouble.
He told us all this had to be reported,
Not kept a secret. We all agreed to that.
We drew lots for it, and I had no luck.   250
I won the prize and was condemned to come.
So here I stand, unwilling, because I know
The bringer of bad news is never welcome.
CHORUS. Sir, as he spoke, I have been wondering.
Can this be, possibly, the work of gods?
CREON. Be silent! Before you madden me! You are old.
Would you be senseless also? What you say
Is unendurable. You say the gods
Cared for this corpse. Then was it for reward,
Mighty to match his mighty services,   260
That the gods covered him? He who came to burn
Their pillared temples and their votive offerings,
Ravage their land, and trample down the state.
Or is it your opinion that the gods
Honor the wicked? Inconceivable!
However, from the first, some citizens
Who found it difficult to endure this edict,
Muttered against me, shaking their heads in secret,
Instead of bowing down beneath the yoke,
Obedient and contented with my rule.   270
These are the men who are responsible,
For I am certain they have bribed the guards
To bury him. Nothing is worse than money.
Money lays waste to cities, banishes
Men from their homes, indoctrinates the heart,
Perverting honesty to works of shame,
Showing men how to practice villainy,
Subduing them to every godless deed.
But all those men who got their pay for this
Need have no doubt their turn to pay will come.   280
(*To the* GUARD.) Now, you. As I still honor Zeus the King,
I tell you, and I swear it solemnly,
Either you find the man who did this thing,
The very man, and bring him here to me,
Or you will not just die. Before you die,
You will be tortured until you have explained
This outrage; so that later when you steal

You will know better where to look for money
And not expect to find it everywhere.
Ill-gotten wealth brings ruin and not safety.   290
GUARD. Sir, may I speak? Or shall I merely go?
CREON. You can say nothing that is not offensive.
GUARD. Do I offend your hearing or your heart?
CREON. Is it your business to define the spot?
GUARD. The criminal hurts your heart, and I your ears.
CREON. Still talking? Why, you must have been born talking!
GUARD. Perhaps. But I am not the guilty man.
CREON. You are. And what is more you sold yourself.
GUARD. You have judged me, sir, and have misjudged me, too.
CREON. Be clever about judging if you care to.   300
But you will say that treachery leads to sorrow
Unless you find the man and show him to me.

(*Exit* CREON.)

GUARD. Finding him is the best thing that could happen.
Fate will decide. But however that may be,
You never are going to see me here again.
I have escaped! I could not have hoped for that.
I owe the gods my thanks for guarding me.   (*Exit* GUARD)

CHORUS.
Many the marvelous things; but none that can be
    More of a marvel than man! This being that braves
With the south wind of winter the whitened streaks of the sea,   310
    Threading his way through the troughs of engulfing waves.
And the earth most ancient, the eldest of all the gods,
    Earth, undecaying, unwearied, he wears away with his toil;
Forward and back with his plowshare, year after year, he plods,
    With his horses turning the soil.

Man in devising excels. The birds of the air,
    That light-minded race, he entangles fast in his toils.
Wild creatures he catches, casting about them his snare,
    And the salt-sea brood he nets in his woven coils.
The tireless bull he has tamed, and the beast whose lair   320
    Is hidden deep in the wilds, who roams in the wooded hills.
He has fitted a yoke that the neck of the shaggy-maned horse will
        bear;
    He is master of all through his skills.
He has taught himself speech, and wind-like thought, and the lore
    Of ruling a town. He has fled the arrows of rain,
The searching arrows of frost he need fear no more,
    That under a starry sky are endured with pain.

Provision for all he has made—unprovided for naught,
   Save death itself, that in days to come will take shape.
From obscure and deep-seated disease he has subtly wrought   330
   A way of escape.

Resourceful and skilled, with an inconceivable art,
   He follows his course to a good or an evil end.
When he holds the canons of justice high in his heart
   And has sworn to the gods the laws of the land to defend,
Proud stands his city; without a city is he
   Who with ugliness, rashness, or evil dishonors the day.
Let me shun his thoughts. Let him share no hearthstone with me,
   Who acts in this way!

CHORUS. Look there! Look there! What portent can this be?   340
   Antigone! I know her, it is she!
   Daughter of Oedipus a prisoner brought?
   You defied Creon? You in folly caught?

(Enter GUARD *with* ANTIGONE.*)*
GUARD. She did it. Here she is. We caught this girl
   As she was burying him. Where is the King?
CHORUS. Leaving the palace there, just as we need him.

(Enter CREON.*)*
CREON. Why do you need my presence? What has happened?
GUARD. My Lord, no one should take a solemn oath
   Not to do something, for his second thoughts
   Make him a liar. I vowed not to hurry back.   350
   I had been battered by your storm of threats.
   But when a joy comes that exceeds our hopes,
   No other happiness can equal it.
   So I have broken my vow. I have returned,
   Bringing this girl along. She was discovered
   Busy with all the rites of burial.
   There was no casting lots, no, not this time!
   Such luck as this was mine and no one else's.
   Now sir, take her yourself, examine her,
   Convict her, do what you like. But as for me,   360
   I have the right to a complete acquittal.
CREON. This is the girl you caught? How? Where was she?
GUARD. Burying the dead man, just as I have told you.
CREON. Do you mean that? Or have you lost your mind?
GUARD. Your order was that he should not be buried.
   I saw her bury him. Is that all clear?

CREON. How was she seen? You caught her in the act?
GUARD. This was what happened. When we had gotten back,
   With your threats following us, we swept away
   The dust that covered him. We left him bare,   370
   A rotting corpse. And then we sat to windward,
   Up on the hillside, to avoid the stench.
   All of us were alert, and kept awake
   Threatening each other. No one could get careless.
   So the time passed, until the blazing sun
   Stood at the zenith, and the heat was burning.
   Then suddenly the wind came in a blast,
   Lifting a cloud of dust up from the earth,
   Troubling the sky and choking the whole plain,
   Stripping off all the foliage of the woods,   380
   Filling the breadth of heaven. We closed our eyes
   And bore the affliction that the gods had sent us.
   When it had finally stopped, we saw this girl.
   She wailed aloud with a sharp, bitter cry,
   The cry a bird gives seeing its empty nest
   Robbed of its brood. And she too, when she saw
   The naked body, was loud in her lament
   And cursed the men who had uncovered him.
   Quickly she sprinkled him with dust, and then
   Lifting a pitcher, poured out three libations   390
   To do him honor. When we ran and caught her,
   She was unterrified. When we accused her
   Both of her earlier and her present act,
   She made no effort to deny the charges.
   I am part glad, part sorry. It is good
   To find that you yourself have gotten clear,
   But to bring trouble on your friends is hard.
   However, nothing counts except my safety.
CREON (to ANTIGONE). You there. You, looking at the ground. Tell me.
   Do you admit this or deny it? Which?   400
ANTIGONE. Yes, I admit it. I do not deny it.
CREON (to GUARD). Go. You are free. The charge is dropped.

                               (*Exit* GUARD.)
                               Now you,

   Answer this question. Make your answer brief.
   You knew there was a law forbidding this?
ANTIGONE. Of course I knew it. Why not? It was public.
CREON. And you have dared to disobey the law?
ANTIGONE. Yes. For this law was not proclaimed by Zeus,
   Or by the gods who rule the world below.
   I do not think your edicts have such power

That they can override the laws of heaven,   410
Unwritten and unfailing, laws whose life
Belongs not to today or yesterday
But to time everlasting; and no man
Knows the first moment that they had their being.
If I transgressed these laws because I feared
The arrogance of man, how to the gods
Could I make satisfaction? Well I know,
Being a mortal, that I have to die,
Even without your proclamations. Yet
If I must die before my time is come,   420
That is a blessing. Because to one who lives,
As I live, in the midst of sorrows, death
Is of necessity desirable.
For me, to face death is a trifling pain
That does not trouble me. But to have left
The body of my brother, my own brother,
Lying unburied would be bitter grief.
And if these acts of mine seem foolish to you,
Perhaps a fool accuses me of folly.
CHORUS. The violent daughter of a violent father,   430
She cannot bend before a storm of evils.
CREON (*to* ANTIGONE). Stubborn? Self-willed? People like that, I tell
    you,
Are the first to come to grief. The hardest iron,
Baked in the fire, most quickly flies to pieces.
An unruly horse is taught obedience
By a touch of the curb. How can you be so proud?
You, a mere slave? (*To* CHORUS.) She was well schooled already
In insolence, when she defied the law.
And now look at her! Boasting, insolent,
Exulting in what she did. And if she triumphs   440
And goes unpunished, I am no man—she is.
If she were more than niece, if she were closer
Than anyone who worships at my altar,
She would not even then escape her doom,
A dreadful death. Nor would her sister. Yes,
Her sister had a share in burying him.
(*To* ATTENDANT.) Go bring her here. I have just seen her, raving,
Beside herself. Even before they act,
Traitors who plot their treason in the dark
Betray themselves like that. Detestable!   450
(*To* ANTIGONE.) But hateful also is an evil-doer
Who, caught red-handed, glorifies the crime.
ANTIGONE. Now you have caught me, will you do more than kill me?

CREON. No, only that. With that I am satisfied.
ANTIGONE. Then why do you delay? You have said nothing
  I do not hate. I pray you never will.
  And you hate what I say. Yet how could I
  Have won more splendid honor than by giving
  Due burial to my brother? All men here
  Would grant me their approval, if their lips   460
  Were not sealed up in fear. But you, a king,
  Blessed by good fortune in much else besides,
  Can speak and act with perfect liberty.
CREON. All of these Thebans disagree with you.
ANTIGONE. No. They agree, but they control their tongues.
CREON. You feel no shame in acting without their help?
ANTIGONE. I feel no shame in honoring a brother.
CREON. Another brother died who fought against him.
ANTIGONE. Two brothers. The two sons of the same parents.
CREON. Honor to one is outrage to the other.   470
ANTIGONE. Eteocles will not feel himself dishonored.
CREON. What! When his rites are offered to a traitor?
ANTIGONE. It was his brother, not his slave, who died.
CREON. One who attacked the land that he defended.
ANTIGONE. The gods still wish those rites to be performed.
CREON. Are the just pleased with the unjust as their equals?
ANTIGONE. That may be virtuous in the world below.
CREON. No. Even there a foe is never a friend.
ANTIGONE. I am not made for hatred but for love.
CREON. Then go down to the dead. If you must love,   480
  Love them. While I yet live, no woman rules me.
CHORUS. Look there. Ismene, weeping as sisters weep.
  The shadow of a cloud of grief lies deep
  On her face, darkly flushed; and in her pain
  Her tears are falling like a flood of rain.

(*Enter* ISMENE *and* ATTENDANTS.)
CREON. You viper! Lying hidden in my house,
  Sucking my blood in secret, while I reared,
  Unknowingly, two subverters of my throne.
  Do you confess that you have taken part
  In this man's burial, or deny it? Speak.   490
ISMENE. If she will recognize my right to say so,
  I shared the action and I share the blame.
ANTIGONE. No. That would not be just. I never let you
  Take any part in what you disapproved of.
ISMENE. In your calamity, I am not ashamed
  To stand beside you, beaten by this tempest.

ANTIGONE. The dead are witnesses of what I did,
    To love in words alone is not enough.
ISMENE. Do not reject me, Sister! Let me die
    Beside you, and do honor to the dead.   500
ANTIGONE. No. You will neither share my death nor claim
    What I have done. My death will be sufficient.
ISMENE. What happiness can I have when you are gone?
ANTIGONE. Ask Creon that. He is the one you value.
ISMENE. Do you gain anything by taunting me?
ANTIGONE. Ah, no! By taunting you, I hurt myself.
ISMENE. How can I help you? Tell me what I can do.
ANTIGONE. Protect yourself. I do not grudge your safety.
ISMENE. Antigone! Shall I not share your fate?
ANTIGONE. We both have made our choices: life, and death.   510
ISMENE. At least I tried to stop you. I protested.
ANTIGONE. Some have approved your way; and others, mine.
ISMENE. Yet now I share your guilt. I too am ruined.
ANTIGONE. Take courage. Live your life. But I long since
    Gave myself up to death to help the dead.
CREON. One of them has just lost her senses now.
    The other has been foolish all her life.
ISMENE. We cannot always use our reason clearly.
    Suffering confuses us and clouds our minds.
CREON. It clouds your mind. You join in her wrong-doing.   520
ISMENE. How is life possible without my sister?
CREON. Your sister? You have no sister. She is dead.
ISMENE. Then you will kill the wife your son has chosen?
CREON. Yes. There are other fields that he can plow.
ISMENE. He will not find such an enduring love.
CREON. A wicked woman for my son? No, never!
ANTIGONE. O Haemon, Haemon! How your father wrongs you!
CREON. You and your marriage! Let me hear no more!
CHORUS. You are unyielding? You will take her from him?
CREON. Death will act for me. Death will stop the marriage.   530
CHORUS. It seems, then, you have sentenced her to death.
CREON. Yes. And my sentence you yourselves accepted.
    Take them inside. From now on, they are women,
    And have no liberty. For even the bold
    Seek an escape when they see death approaching.

                            (*Exeunt* ANTIGONE, ISMENE, *and* ATTENDANTS.)

CHORUS.
    Blessèd the life that has no evil known,
    For the gods, striking, strike down a whole race—
        Doomed parent and doomed child both overthrown.
    As when the fierce breath of the winds of Thrace

Across the darkness of the sea has blown   540
A rushing surge; black sand from deep below
   Comes boiling up; wind-beaten headlands moan,
Fronting the full shock of the billow's blow.

The race of Oedipus, from days of old,
To long dead sorrows add new sorrows' weight.
   Some god has sent them sufferings manifold.
None may release another, for their fate
   Through generations loosens not its hold.
Now is their last root cut, their last light fled,
   Because of frenzy's curse, words overbold,   550
And dust, the gods' due, on the bloodstained dead.

O Zeus, what human sin restricts thy might?
Thou art unsnared by all-ensnaring sleep
   Or tireless months. Unaging thou dost keep
Thy court in splendor of Olympian light.
   And as this law was true when time began,
Tomorrow and forever it shall be:
   Naught beyond measure in the life of man
         From fate goes free.

For hope, wide-ranging, that brings good to some,   560
To many is a false lure of desire
   Light-minded, giddy; and until the fire
Scorches their feet, they know not what will come.
   Wise is the famous adage: that to one
Whom the gods madden, evil, soon or late,
   Seems good; then can he but a moment shun
         The stroke of fate.

But Haemon comes, of your two sons the last.
Is his heart heavy for the sentence passed
   Upon Antigone, his promised bride,   570
And for his hope of marriage now denied?

(*Enter* HAEMON.)
CREON. We soon shall know better than seers could tell us.
   My son, Antigone is condemned to death.
   Nothing can change my sentence. Have you learned
   Her fate and come here in a storm of anger,
   Or do you love me and support my acts?
HAEMON. Father, I am your son. Your greater knowledge
   Will trace the pathway that I mean to follow.

My marriage cannot be of more importance
Than to be guided always by your wisdom.   580
CREON. Yes, Haemon, this should be the law you live by!
In all things to obey your father's will.
Men pray for children round them in their homes
Only to see them dutiful and quick
With hatred to requite their father's foe,
With honor to repay their father's friend.
But what is there to say of one whose children
Prove to be valueless? That he has fathered
Grief for himself and laughter for his foes.
Then, Haemon, do not, at the lure of pleasure,   590
Unseat your reason for a woman's sake.
This comfort soon grows cold in your embrace:
A wicked wife to share your bed and home.
Is there a deeper wound than to find worthless
The one you love? Turn from this girl with loathing,
As from an enemy, and let her go
To get a husband in the world below.
For I have found her openly rebellious,
Her only out of all the city. Therefore,
I will not break the oath that I have sworn.   600
I will have her killed. Vainly she will invoke
The bond of kindred blood the gods make sacred.
If I permit disloyalty to breed
In my own house, I nurture it in strangers.
He who is righteous with his kin is righteous
In the state also. Therefore, I cannot pardon
One who does violence to the laws or thinks
To dictate to his rulers; for whoever
May be the man appointed by the city,
That man must be obeyed in everything,   610
Little or great, just or unjust. And surely
He who was thus obedient would be found
As good a ruler as he was a subject;
And in a storm of spears he would stand fast
With loyal courage at his comrade's side.
But disobedience is the worst of evils.
For it is this that ruins cities; this
Makes our homes desolate; armies of allies
Through this break up in rout. But most men find
Their happiness and safety in obedience.   620
Therefore we must support the law, and never
Be beaten by a woman. It is better

To fall by a man's hand, if we must fall,
Than to be known as weaker than a girl.
CHORUS. We may in our old age have lost our judgment,
And yet to us you seem to have spoken wisely.
HAEMON. The gods have given men the gift of reason,
Greatest of all things that we call our own.
I have no skill, nor do I wish to have it,
To show where you have spoken wrongly. Yet   630
Some other's thought, beside your own, might prove
To be of value. Therefore it is my duty,
My natural duty as your son, to notice,
On your behalf, all that men say, or do,
Or find to blame. For your frown frightens them,
So that the citizen dares not say a word
That would offend you. I can hear, however,
Murmurs in darkness and laments for her.
They say: "No woman ever less deserved
Her doom, no woman ever was to die   640
So shamefully for deeds so glorious.
For when her brother fell in bloody battle,
She would not let his body lie unburied
To be devoured by carrion dogs or birds.
Does such a woman not deserve reward,
Reward of golden honor?" This I hear,
A rumor spread in secrecy and darkness.
Father, I prize nothing in life so highly
As your well-being. How can children have
A nobler honor than their father's fame   650
Or father than his son's? Then do not think
Your mood must never alter; do not feel
Your word, and yours alone, must be correct.
For if a man believes that he is right
And only he, that no one equals him
In what he says or thinks, he will be found
Empty when searched and tested. Because a man
Even if he be wise, feels no disgrace
In learning many things, in taking care
Not to be over-rigid. You have seen   660
Trees on the margin of a stream in winter:
Those yielding to the flood save every twig,
And those resisting perish root and branch.
So, too, the mariner who never slackens
His taut sheet overturns his craft and spends
Keel uppermost the last part of his voyage.

Let your resentment die. Let yourself change,
For I believe—if I, a younger man,
May have a sound opinion—it is best
That men by nature should be wise in all things.   670
But most men find they cannot reach that goal;
And when this happens, it is also good
To learn to listen to wise counselors.
CHORUS. Sir, when his words are timely, you should heed them.
And Haemon, you should profit by his words.
Each one of you has spoken reasonably.
CREON. Are men as old as I am to be taught
How to behave by men as young as he?
HAEMON. Not to do wrong. If I am young, ignore
My youth. Consider only what I do.   680
CREON. Have you done well in honoring the rebellious?
HAEMON. Those who do wrong should not command respect.
CREON. Then that disease has not infected her?
HAEMON. All of our city with one voice denies it.
CREON. Does Thebes give orders for the way I rule?
HAEMON. How young you are! How young in saying that!
CREON. Am I to govern by another's judgment?
HAEMON. A city that is one man's is no city.
CREON. A city is the king's. That much is sure.
HAEMON. You would rule well in a deserted country.   690
CREON. This boy defends a woman, it appears.
HAEMON. If you are one. I am concerned for you.
CREON. To quarrel with your father does not shame you?
HAEMON. Not when I see you failing to do justice.
CREON. Am I unjust when I respect my crown?
HAEMON. Respect it! When you trample down religion?
CREON. Infamous! Giving first place to a woman!
HAEMON. But never to anything that would disgrace me.
CREON. Each word you utter is a plea for her.
HAEMON. For you, too, and for me, and for the gods.   700
CREON. You shall not marry her this side of death.
HAEMON. Then if she dies, she does not die alone.
CREON. What! Has it come to this? You threaten me?
HAEMON. No. But I tell you your decree is useless.
CREON. You will repent this. You! Teaching me wisdom!
HAEMON. I will not call you mad. You are my father.
CREON. You woman's slave! Your talk will not persuade me.
HAEMON. Then what you want is to make all the speeches.
CREON. So. Now by all the gods in heaven above us,
One thing is certain: you are going to pay   710

For taunting and insulting me. (*To* ATTENDANTS.) **Bring out**
That hated object. Let her die this moment,
Here, at her bridegroom's feet, before his eyes.
HAEMON. No, you are wrong. Not at my feet. And never
Will you set eyes upon my face again.
Rage, rave, with anyone who can bear to listen.   (*Exit* HAEMON.)
CHORUS. Sir, he is gone; his anger gives him speed.
Young men are bitter in their agony.
CREON. Let him imagine more than man can do,
Or let him do more. Never shall he save   720
These two girls; they are going to their doom.
CHORUS. Do you intend to put them both to death?
CREON. That was well said. No, not the innocent.
CHORUS. And the other? In what way is she to die?
CREON. Along a desolate pathway I will lead her,
And shut her, living, in a rocky vault
With no more food than will appease the gods,
So that the city may not be defiled.
Hades, who is the only god she worships,
May hear her prayers, and rescue her from death.   730
Otherwise she will learn at last, though late,
That to revere the dead is useless toil.   (*Exit* CREON.)
CHORUS.
None may withstand you, O love unconquered,
    Seizing the wealth of man as your prey,
In the cheek of a maiden keeping your vigil,
    Till night has faded again to day.
You roam the wilds to men's farthest dwellings,
    You haunt the boundless face of the sea.
No god may escape you, no short-lived mortal
    From the madness that love inflicts may flee.   740

You twist our minds until ruin follows.
    The just to unrighteous ways you turn.
You have goaded kinsman to strive with kinsman
    Till the fires of bitter hatred burn.
In the eyes of a bride you shine triumphant;
    Beside the eternal laws your throne
Eternal stands, for great Aphrodite,
    Resistless, works her will on her own.

But now I too am moved. I cannot keep
    Within the bounds of loyalty. I weep   750
When I behold Antigone, the bride,
    Near the room where all at last abide.

(Enter ANTIGONE, *guarded.)*

ANTIGONE.

    See me, my countrymen! See with what pain
I tread the path I shall not tread again,
Looking my last upon the light of day
    That shines for me no more.
Hades, who gives his sleep to all, me, living, leads away
    To Acheron's dark shore.
Not mine the hymeneal chant, not mine the bridal song,
    For I, a bride, to Acheron belong.   760

CHORUS.

    Glorious, therefore, and with praise you tread
The pathway to the deep gulf of the dead.
You have not felt the force of fate's decrees,
Struck down by violence, wasted by disease;
But of your own free will you choose to go,
Alone of mortals, to the world below.

ANTIGONE.

    I know how sad a death she suffered, she
Who was our guest here, Phrygian Niobe.
Stone spread upon her, close as ivy grows,
    And locked her in its chains.   770
Now on her wasted form, men say, fall ceaselessly the snows,
    Fall ceaselessly the rains;
While from her grieving eyes drop tears, tears that her bosom
        steep.
And like hers, my fate lulls me now to sleep.

CHORUS.

    She was a goddess of the gods' great race;
Mortals are we and mortal lineage trace.
But for a woman the renown is great
In life and death to share a godlike fate.

ANTIGONE.

    By our fathers' gods, I am mocked! I am mocked! Ah! why,
You men of wealth, do you taunt me before I die?   780
O sacred grove of the city! O waters that flow
    From the spring of Dircé! Be witness; to you I cry.
What manner of woman I am you know
And by what laws, unloved, unlamented, I go
    To my rocky prison, to my unnatural tomb.
        Alas, how ill-bestead!

---

767. NIOBE, a Phrygian princess married to Amphion, king of Thebes, whose
children were killed by Apollo and Artemis. Later she was turned into a rock
on Mt. Sipylus and when the snow melted on the mountain, tears appeared to
flow from the rock

No fellowship have I; no others can share my doom,
Neither mortals nor corpses, neither the quick nor the dead.

CHORUS.

You have rushed forward with audacious feet
And dashed yourself against the law's high seat.   790
That was a grievous fall, my child, and yet
In this ordeal you pay your father's debt.

ANTIGONE.

You have touched on the heaviest grief that my heart can hold:
Grief for my father, sorrow that never grows old
For our famous house and its doom that the fates have spun.
My mother's bed! Ah! How can its horrors be told?
My mother who yielded her love to one
Who was at once my father and her son.
Born of such parents, with them henceforth I abide,
Wretched, accursed, unwed.   800
And you, Polyneices, you found an ill-fated bride,
And I, the living, am ruined by you, the dead.

CHORUS.

A pious action may of praise be sure,
But he who rules a land cannot endure
An act of disobedience to his rule.
Your own self-will you have not learned to school.

ANTIGONE.

Unwept, unfriended, without marriage song,
Forth on my road I miserable am led;
I may not linger. Not for long
Shall I, most wretched, see the holy sun.   810
My fate no friend bewails, not one;
For me no tear is shed.

(*Enter* CREON.)

CREON. Do you not know that singing and lamentation
Would rise incessantly as death approached,
If they could be of service? Lead her away!
Obey my orders. Shut her in her grave
And leave her there, alone. Then she can take
Her choice of living in that home, or dying.
I am not stained by the guilt of this girl's blood,
But she shall see the light of day no longer.   820

ANTIGONE. O tomb! O cavern! Everlasting prison!
O bridal-chamber! To you I make my way
To join my kindred, all those who have died
And have been greeted by Persephone.
The last and far most miserable of all,

I seek them now, before I have lived my life.
Yet high are the hopes I cherish that my coming
Will be most welcome to my father; welcome,
Mother, to you; and welcome to you, Brother.
For when you died I ministered to you all,   830
With my own hands washed you and dressed your bodies,
And poured libations at your graves. And now,
Because I have given to you, too, Polyneices,
Such honors as I could, I am brought to this.
And yet all wise men will approve my act.
Not for my children, had I been a mother,
Not for a husband, for his moldering body,
Would I have set myself against the city
As I have done. And the law sanctions me.
Losing a husband, I might find another.   840
I could have other children. But my parents
Are hidden from me in the underworld,
So that no brother's life can bud and bloom
Ever again. And therefore, Polyneices,
I paid you special honor. And for this
Creon has held me guilty of evil-doing,
And leads me captive for my too great boldness.
No bridal bed is mine, no bridal song,
No share in the joys of marriage, and no share
In nursing children and in tending them.   850
But thus afflicted, destitute of friends,
Living, I go down to the vaults of death.
What is the law of heaven that I have broken?
Why should I any longer look to the gods,
Ill-fated as I am? Whose aid should I invoke,
When I for piety am called impious?
If this pleases the gods, then I shall learn
That sin brought death upon me. But if the sin
Lies in my judges, I could wish for them
No harsher fate than they have decreed for me.   860
CHORUS. Still the storm rages; still the same gusts blow,
    Troubling her spirit with their savage breath.
CREON. Yes. And her guards will pay for being slow.
ANTIGONE. Ah! With those words I have drawn close to death.
CREON. You cannot hope that you will now be freed
    From the fulfillment of the doom decreed.
ANTIGONE.
    O Thebes, O land of my fathers, O city!
    O gods who begot and guarded my house from of old!
        They seize me, they snatch me away!

Now, now! They show no pity.   870
They give no second's delay.
You elders, you leaders of Thebes, behold me, behold!
The last of the house of your kings, the last
See what I suffer. See the doom
That is come upon me, and see from whom,
Because to the laws of heaven I held fast.

                                   (*Exeunt* ANTIGONE *and* GUARDS.)

CHORUS.
    This likewise Danaë endured:
The light of heaven she changed for a home brass-bound,
    In a tomb-like chamber close immured.
And yet, O my child, her race was with honor crowned,   880
    And she guarded the seed of Zeus gold-showered.
But naught from the terrible power of fate is free.
    Neither war, nor city walls high-towered,
Nor wealth, nor black ships beaten by the sea.

    He too bowed down beneath his doom,
The son of Dryas, swift-angered Edonian king,
    Shut fast in a rocky prison's gloom.
How he roused the god with his mad tongue's mocking sting,
    As his frenzy faded, he came to know;
For he sought to make the god-filled maenads mute,   890
    To quench the Bacchic torches' glow,
And angered the Muses, lovers of the flute.

By the double sea and the dark rocks steely blue
    The beach of Bosporus lies and the savage shore
Of Thracian Salmydessus. There the bride
    Of Phineus, whose fierce heart no mercy knew,
Dealt his two sons a blow that for vengeance cried;
    Ares beheld her hand, all stained with gore,
Grasping the pointed shuttle that pierced through
    Their eyes that saw no more.   900

In misery pining, their lot they lamented aloud,
    Sons of a mother whose fortune in marriage was ill.
From the ancient line of Erechtheus her blood she traced;
    Nurtured in caves far-distant and nursed in cloud,

---

877. DANAË, a princess shut in a bronze tower by her father, Acrisius, king of
Argos, because it was prophesied that he would be killed by her son. Zeus appeared to her in the form of a golden rainshower and she conceived a son,
Perseus, who did kill Acrisius. 886. SON OF DRYAS, Lycurgus, a Thracian king,
who opposed the Dionysiac religion and was imprisoned by Dionysus.

Daughter of Boreas, daughter of gods, she raced
  Swift as a steed on the slope of the soaring hill.
And yet, O child, O child, she also bowed
  To the long-lived fates' harsh will.

(*Enter* TIRESIAS *and* BOY.)

TIRESIAS. Elders of Thebes, we have come to you with one
  Finding for both the pathway that we followed,   910
  For in this fashion must the blind be guided.
CREON. What tidings, old Tiresias, are you bringing?
TIRESIAS. I will inform you, I the seer. Give heed.
CREON. To ignore your counsel has not been my custom.
TIRESIAS. Therefore you kept Thebes on a steady course.
CREON. I can bear witness to the help you gave.
TIRESIAS. Mark this. You stand upon the brink of ruin.
CREON. What terrible words are those? What do you mean?
TIRESIAS. My meaning is made manifest by my art
  And my art's omens. As I took my station   920
  Upon my ancient seat of augury,
  Where round me birds of every sort come flocking,
  I could no longer understand their language.
  It was drowned out in a strange, savage clamor,
  Shrill, evil, frenzied, inarticulate.
  The whirr of wings told me their murderous talons
  Tore at each other. Filled with dread, I then
  Made trial of burnt sacrifice. The altar
  Was fully kindled, but no clear, bright flame
  Leaped from the offering; only fatty moisture   930
  Oozed from the flesh and trickled on the embers,
  Smoking and sputtering. The bladder burst,
  And scattered in the air. The folds of fat
  Wrapping the thigh-bones melted and left them bare.
  Such was the failure of the sacrifice,
  That did not yield the sign that I was seeking.
  I learned these things from this boy's observation;
  He is my guide as I am guide to others.
  Your edict brings this suffering to the city,
  For every hearth of ours has been defiled   940
  And every altar. There the birds and dogs
  Have brought their carrion, torn from the corpse
  Of ill-starred Polyneices. Hence, the gods
  Refuse our prayers, refuse our sacrifice,
  Refuse the flame of our burnt-offerings.
  No birds cry clearly and auspiciously,
  For they are glutted with a slain man's blood.

Therefore, my son, consider what has happened.
All men are liable to grievous error;
But he who, having erred, does not remain   950
Inflexible, but rather makes amends
For ill, is not unwise or unrewarded.
Stubborn self-will incurs the charge of folly.
Give to the fallen the honors he deserves
And do not stab him. Are you being brave
When you inflict new death upon the dead?
Your good I think of; for your good I speak,
And a wise counselor is sweet to hear
When the advice he offers proves of value.

CREON. Old man, all of you shoot your arrows at me   960
Like archers at a target. You have used
Even the art of prophecy in your plotting.
Long have the tribe of prophets traded in me,
Like a ship's cargo. Drive whatever bargain
May please you, buy, sell, heap up for yourself
Silver of Sardis, gold of India. Yet
I tell you this: that man shall not be buried,
Not though the eagles of Zeus himself should bear
The carrion morsels to their master's throne.
Not even from the dread of such pollution   970
Will I permit his burial, since I know
There is no mortal can defile the gods.
But even the wisest men disastrously
May fall, Tiresias, when for money's sake
They utter shameful words with specious wisdom.

TIRESIAS. Ah! Do men understand, or even consider—

CREON. Consider what? Doubtless some platitude!

TIRESIAS. How precious beyond any wealth is prudence.

CREON. How full of evil is the lack of prudence.

TIRESIAS. Yet you are sick, sick with that same disease.   980

CREON. I will not in reply revile a prophet.

TIRESIAS. You do. You say my prophecy is false.

CREON. Well, all the race of seers are mercenary.

TIRESIAS. And love of base wealth marks the breed of tyrants.

CREON. Are you aware that you address your King?

TIRESIAS. I made you King by helping you save Thebes.

CREON. Wise in your art and vicious in your acts.

TIRESIAS. Do not enrage me. I should keep my secret.

CREON. Reveal it. Speak. But do not look for profit.

TIRESIAS. You too will find no profit in my words.   990

CREON. How can you earn your pay? I will not change.

TIRESIAS. Then know this. Yes, be very sure of it.

Only a few more times will you behold
The swift course of the chariot of the sun
Before you give as payment for the dead
Your own dead flesh and blood. For you have thrust
A living soul to darkness, in a tomb
Imprisoned without pity. And a corpse,
Belonging to the gods below you keep
Unpurified, unburied, unrevered.   1000
The dead are no concern either of yours
Or of the gods above, yet you offend them.
So the avengers, the destroyers, Furies
Of Hades and the gods, lurking in ambush,
Wait to inflict your sins upon your head.
Do you still think my tongue is lined with silver?
A time will come, and will not linger coming,
That will awaken in your house the wailing
Of men and women. Hatred shakes the cities,
Hatred of you. Their sons are mangled corpses,   1010
Hallowed with funeral rites by dogs or beasts
Or birds who bear the all-polluting stench
To every city having hearth or altar.
You goaded me, and therefore like an archer
I shoot my angry arrows at your heart,
Sure arrows; you shall not escape their sting.
Boy, lead me home. Let him expend his rage
On younger men, and let him learn to speak
With a more temperate tongue, and school his heart
To feelings finer than his present mood.   1020

(*Exeunt* TIRESIAS *and* BOY.)

CHORUS. Sir, he is gone, with fearful prophecies.
      And from the time that these dark hairs have whitened,
      I have known this: never has he foretold
      Anything that proved false concerning Thebes.
CREON. I also know it well, and it dismays me.
      To yield is bitter. But to resist, and bring
      A curse upon my pride is no less bitter.
CHORUS. Son of Menoeceus, listen. You must listen.
CREON. What should I do? Tell me, I will obey.
CHORUS. Go. Free the girl. Release her from the cavern,   1030
      And build a tomb for the man you would not bury.
CREON. So that is your advice—that I should yield?
CHORUS. Sir, you should not delay. The gods are swift
      In cutting short man's folly with their curse.
CREON. How hard it is to change! Yet I obey.
      I will give up what I had set my heart on.

No one can stand against the blows of fate.
CHORUS. Go. Go yourself. These things are not for others.
CREON. I will go this moment. Guards there! All of you!
 Take up your axes. Quick! Quick! Over there.   1040
 I imprisoned her myself, and I myself
 Will set her free. And yet my mind misgives me.
 Never to break the ancient law is best.   (*Exit* CREON.)
CHORUS.
  Thou art known by many a name.
  O Bacchus! To thee we call.
  Cadmean Semele's glory and pride,
 Begotten of Zeus, whose terrible lightnings flame,
   Whose thunders appall.
 Bacchus, thou dost for us all in thy love provide.
  Over Icaria thou dost reign,   1050
  And where the worshippers journey slow
  To the rites of Eleusis, where mountains shield
 The multitudes crossing Demeter's welcoming plain.
 Thou makest this mother-city of maenads thine own,
  A city beside the rippling flow
 Of the gentle river, beside the murderous field
  Where the teeth of the dragon were sown.

  In the torches' wind-blown flare
  Thou art seen, in their flicker and smoke.
  Where the two-fold peaks of Parnassus gleam,   1060
 Corycian nymphs, as they move through the ruddy glare,
   Thee, Bacchus, invoke.
 They move in their dance beside the Castalian stream.
  O Bacchus, guardian divine!
  Down from the slopes of Nysa's hills
  Where a mantle of ivy covers the ground,
 From headlands rich with the purple grape and the vine,
 Thou comest to us, thou comest. O be not long!
  Thy triumph the echoing city fills.
 The streets are loud with thy praises; the highways resound, 1070
  Resound with immortal song.

 Thou honorest highly our Theban city,
  Thou, and thy mother by lightning slain.
 Our people sicken. O Bacchus have pity!
  Across the strait with its moaning wave,
 Down from Parnassus, come thou again!
  Come with thy healing feet, and save!

O thou who leadest the stars in chorus,
  Jubilant stars with their breath of fire,
Offspring of Zeus, appear before us!   1080
  Lord of the tumult of night, appear!
With the frenzied dance of thy maenad choir,
  Bacchus, thou giver of good, draw near!

(*Enter* MESSENGER.)
MESSENGER. You of the house of Cadmus and Amphíon,
  No man's estate can ever be established
  Firmly enough to warrant praise or blame.
  Fortune, from day to day, exalts the lucky
  And humbles the unlucky. No one knows
  Whether his present lot can long endure.
  For Creon once was blest, as I count blessings;   1090
  He had saved this land of Cadmus from its foes;
  He was the sovereign and ruled alone,
  The noble father of a royal house.
  And now, all has been lost. Because a man
  Who has forfeited his joy is not alive,
  He is a living corpse. Heap, if you will,
  Your house with riches; live in regal pomp.
  Yet if your life is unhappy, all these things
  Are worth not even the shadow of a vapor
  Put in the balance against joy alone.   1100
CHORUS. What new disaster has the King's house suffered?
MESSENGER. Death. And the guilt of death lies on the living.
CHORUS. The guilt of death! Who has been killed? Who killed him?
MESSENGER. Haemon is killed, and by no stranger's hand.
CHORUS. He killed himself? Or did his father kill him?
MESSENGER. He killed himself, enraged by his murderous father.
CHORUS. Tiresias! Now your prophecy is fulfilled.
MESSENGER. Consider, therefore, what remains to do.
CHORUS. There is the Queen, wretched Eurydice.
  Perhaps mere chance has brought her from the palace;   1110
  Perhaps she has learned the news about her son.

(*Enter* EURYDICE.)
EURYDICE. Thebans, I heard you talking here together
  When I was on my way to greet the goddess,
  Pallas Athene, and to pray to her.
  Just as I loosed the fastening of the door,
  The words that told of my calamity
  Struck heavily upon my ear. In terror
  I fell back fainting in my women's arms.

But now, repeat your story. I shall hear it
As one who is not ignorant of grief.   1120
MESSENGER. My Lady, I will bear witness to what I saw,
And will omit no syllable of the truth.
Why should I comfort you with words that later
Would prove deceitful? Truth is always best.
Across the plain I guided my Lord Creon
To where unpitied Polyneices lay,
A corpse mangled by dogs. Then we besought
Hecate, goddess of the roads, and Pluto
To moderate their wrath, and to show mercy.
We washed the dead with ceremonial water.   1130
Gathering the scattered fragments that remained,
With fresh-cut boughs we burned them. We heaped up
A mound of native earth above his ashes.
Then we approached the cavern of Death's bride,
The rock-floored marriage-chamber. While as yet
We were far distant, someone heard the sound
Of loud lament in that unhallowed place,
And came to tell our master. As the King
Drew near, there floated through the air a voice,
Faint, indistinct, that uttered a bitter cry.   1140
The King burst out in anguish: "Can it be
That I, in my misery, have become a prophet?
Will this be the saddest road I ever trod?
My son's voice greets me. Quickly, slaves! Go quickly!
When you have reached the sepulcher, get through
The opening where the stones are wrenched away,
Get to the mouth of the burial chamber. Look,
See if I know his voice—Haemon's, my son's—
Or if I am deluded by the gods."
We followed our despairing master's bidding   1150
And in the farthest recess of the tomb
We found Antigone, hanging, with her veil
Noosed round her neck. And with her we found Haemon,
His arms flung round her waist, grieving aloud
For his bride lost in death, his ruined marriage,
His father's deeds. But when his father saw him,
Creon cried piteously and going in,
Called to him brokenly: "My son, my son,
What have you done? What are you thinking of?
What dreadful thing has driven you out of your mind?   1160
Son, come away. I beg you. I beseech you."
But Haemon glared at him with furious eyes
Instead of answering, spat in his face,

And drew his sword. His father turned to fly
So that he missed his aim. Immediately,
In bitter self-reproach, the wretched boy
Leaned hard against his sword, and drove it deep
Into his side. Then while his life yet lingered,
With failing strength he drew Antigone close;
And as he lay there gasping heavily,   1170
Over her white cheek his blood ebbed away.
The dead lie clasped together. He is wedded,
Not in this world but in the house of Death.
He has borne witness that of all the evils
Afflicting man, the worst is lack of wisdom.   (*Exit* EURYDICE.)
CHORUS. What does that mean? Who can interpret it?
   The Queen has gone without a single word.
MESSENGER. It startles me. And yet I hope it means
   That hearing these dreadful things about her son,
   She will not let herself show grief in public   1180
   But will lament in private with her women.
   Schooled in discretion, she will do no wrong.
CHORUS. How can we tell? Surely too great a silence
   Is no less ominous than too loud lament.
MESSENGER. Then I will enter. Perhaps she is concealing
   Some secret purpose in her passionate heart.
   I will find out, for you are right in saying
   Too great a silence may be ominous.

                (*Exit* MESSENGER. *Enter* CREON *with* ATTENDANTS,
                    carrying the body of HAEMON *on a bier.*)
CHORUS. Thebans, look there! The King himself draws near,
   Bearing a load whose tale is all too clear.   1190
   This is a work—if we dare speak our thought—
   That not another's but his own hands wrought.
CREON.
    O, how may my sin be told?
   The stubborn, death-fraught sin of a darkened brain!
    Behold us here, behold
   Father and son, the slayer and the slain!
    Pain, only pain
   Has come of my design.
    Fate struck too soon; too soon your spirit fled.
    My son, my young son, you are lying dead   1200
   Not for your folly, but for mine, for mine.
CHORUS. Sir, you have come to learn the right too late.
CREON.
    My lesson has been bitter and complete.
   Some god has struck me down with crushing weight,

Filling my heart with cruelty and hate,
　　Trampling my happiness beneath his feet.
　　　Grief, bitter grief, is man's fate.

(*Enter* MESSENGER.)

MESSENGER (*indicating* HAEMON). Your load is heavy, Sir, but there
　　is more.
　　That is the burden you are bearing now.
　　Soon you must bear new woe within your house.　　　　　　　1210
CREON. And what worse misery can follow this?
MESSENGER. Your wife is dead, a mother like her son.
　　Poor woman, by her own hand she has died.
CREON.
　　　By her own hand she died.
　　Death, spare me! Can you never have your fill?
　　　Never be satisfied?
　　Herald of evil, messenger of ill,
　　　Your harsh words kill,
　　They smite me now anew.
　　　My wife is dead—You tell me my wife is dead.　　　　　　1220
　　　Death after death is heaped upon my head.
　　Speak to me, boy. Is what you tell me true?
MESSENGER. It is no longer hidden. Sir, look there.

(*The body of* EURYDICE *is disclosed through the palace doors.*)

CREON.
　　　Another horror that makes blind mine eyes!
　　What further agony has fate in store?
　　My dead son's body in my arms I bore,
　　　And now beside him his dead mother lies.
　　　　I can endure no more.
MESSENGER. There at the altar with a keen-edged knife
　　She stabbed herself; and as her eyes were darkened,　　　　1230
　　She wailed the death of Megareus, her son,
　　Who earlier had met a noble fate;
　　She wailed for Haemon; then, with her last breath,
　　You, as the slayer of your sons, she cursed.
CREON.
　　　I am shaken with terror, with terror past belief.
　　Is there none here to end my anguish? None?
　　　No sword to pierce me? Broken with my grief,
　　So steeped in agony that we are one.
MESSENGER. Sir, as she died, she burdened you with guilt,
　　Charging you with the death of both your sons.　　　　　　1240

1231. MEGAREUS, killed during the siege of the city.

CREON. And by what act of violence did she die?
MESSENGER. Hearing the shrill lament for Haemon's fate,
  Deep in her heart she drove the bright blade home.
CREON (*to* HAEMON).
    I am your slayer, I alone.
    I am guilty, only I.
    I, and none other, must atone.
    Lead me away. The truth I own.
    Nothing is left, except to die.
CHORUS. If anything can be good, those words are good.
  For when calamity has come upon us,   1250
  The thing that is the briefest is the best.
CREON.
    Draw near me, death! O longed for death, draw near!
  Most welcome destiny, make no delay.
    To tell me my last hour, my last breath, is here.
  I have no wish to see another day.
CHORUS. Such things are yet to come. We are concerned
  With doing what must needs be done today.
  The future rests in other hands than ours.
CREON. That is my whole desire. That is my prayer.
CHORUS. No. Do not pray. Men must accept their doom.   1260
CREON.
    My life's work there before me lies.
  My folly slew my wife, my son.
    I know not where to turn mine eyes.
  All my misdeeds before me rise.
    Lead me away, brought low, undone.   (*Exit* CREON.)

CHORUS.
    The crown of happiness is to be wise.
  Honor the gods, and the gods' edicts prize.
  They strike down boastful men and men grown bold.
  Wisdom we learn at last, when we are old.   1269

William Shakespeare

1564–1616

ROMEO AND JULIET

edited and annotated by HARDIN CRAIG

CHARACTERS

ESCALUS, *prince of Verona*
PARIS, *a young nobleman, kinsman to the prince*
MONTAGUE⎫ *heads of two houses at variance*
CAPULET ⎭ *with each other*
OLD MAN, *cousin to Capulet*
ROMEO, *son to Montague*
MERCUTIO, *kinsman to the prince, and friend to Romeo*
BENVOLIO, *nephew to Montague, and friend to Romeo*
TYBALT, *nephew to Lady Capulet*
FRIAR LAURENCE⎫ *Franciscans*
FRIAR JOHN ⎭
BALTHASAR, *servant to Romeo*
SAMPSON⎫ *servants to Capulet*
GREGORY ⎭
PETER, *servant to Juliet's nurse*
ABRAHAM, *servant to Montague*
APOTHECARY
THREE MUSICIANS
PAGE *to Paris; another* PAGE; *an* OFFICER

LADY MONTAGUE, *wife to Montague*
LADY CAPULET, *wife to Capulet*
JULIET, *daughter to Capulet*
NURSE *to Juliet*
CITIZENS *of Verona; several* MEN *and* WOMEN, *relations to both houses;* MASKERS, GUARDS, WATCHMEN, *and* ATTENDANTS

CHORUS

35

SCENE: *Verona; Mantua.*

PROLOGUE

Two households, both alike in dignity,
  In fair Verona, where we lay our scene,
From ancient grudge break to new mutiny,
  Where civil blood makes civil hands unclean.
From forth the fatal loins of these two foes
  A pair of star-cross'd lovers take their life;
Whose misadventured piteous overthrows
  Do with their death bury their parents' strife.
The fearful passage of their death-mark'd love,
  And the continuance of their parents' rage,   10
Which, but their children's end, nought could remove,
  Is now the two hours' traffic of our stage;
The which if you with patient ears attend,
What here shall miss, our toil shall strive to mend.

ACT I

SCENE 1: *Verona. A public place.*

(*Enter* SAMPSON *and* GREGORY, *of the house of Capulet, armed with swords and bucklers.*)

SAMPSON. Gregory, o' my word, we'll not carry coals.

GREGORY. No, for then we should be colliers.

SAMPSON. I mean, an we be in choler, we'll draw.

GREGORY. Ay, while you live, draw your neck out o' the collar.

SAMPSON. I strike quickly, being moved.

GREGORY. But thou art not quickly moved to strike.

SAMPSON. A dog of the house of Montague moves me.   10

GREGORY. To move is to stir; and to be valiant is to stand: therefore, if thou art moved, thou runn'st away.

SAMPSON. A dog of that house shall move me to stand: I will take the wall of any man or maid of Montague's.

PROLOGUE. 3. *mutiny*, state of discord. 6. *star-cross'd*, thwarted by destiny. Shakespeare shows in this play particularly, and throughout his plays generally, the current belief in the power of the stars. The idea blends with that of divine providence. 9. *fearful*, full of fear. *passage*, progress. 12. *two hours' traffic of our stage*. This line is one of a small number of references which enable us to tell the length of time occupied by a Shakespearean play. If the time was nearer two hours than three, the play must have been rapidly recited, with little loss of time between scenes. The bareness of the stage and the lack of a curtain would have contributed to the speed of presentation.

GREGORY. That shows thee a weak slave; for the weakest goes to the wall.

SAMPSON. True; and therefore women, being the weaker vessels, are ever thrust to the wall: therefore I will push Montague's men from the wall, and thrust his maids to the wall.

GREGORY. The quarrel is between our masters and us their men.

SAMPSON. 'Tis all one, I will show myself a tyrant: when I have fought with the men, I will be cruel with the maids, and cut off their heads.

GREGORY. The heads of the maids?

SAMPSON. Ay, the heads of the maids, or their maidenheads; take it in   29
what sense thou wilt.

GREGORY. They must take it in sense that feel it.

SAMPSON. Me they shall feel while I am able to stand: and 'tis known I am a pretty piece of flesh.

GREGORY. 'Tis well thou art not fish; if thou hadst, thou hadst been poor John. Draw thy tool; here comes two of the house of the Montagues.

SAMPSON. My naked weapon is out: quarrel, I will back thee.   40

GREGORY. How! turn thy back and run?

SAMPSON. Fear me not.

GREGORY. No, marry; I fear thee!

SAMPSON. Let us take the law of our sides; let them begin.

GREGORY. I will frown as I pass by, and let them take it as they list.

SAMPSON. Nay, as they dare. I will bite my thumb at them; which is a disgrace to them, if they bear it.   50

(Enter ABRAHAM *and* BALTHASAR.)

ABRAHAM. Do you bite your thumb at us, sir?

SAMPSON. I do bite my thumb, sir.

ABRAHAM. Do you bite your thumb at us, sir?

SAMPSON *(aside to* GREGORY). Is the law of our side, if I say ay?

GREGORY. No.

SAMPSON. No, sir, I do not bite my thumb at you, sir, but I bite my thumb, sir.

GREGORY. Do you quarrel, sir?

ABRAHAM. Quarrel, sir! no, sir.   60

SAMPSON. If you do, sir, I am for you: I serve as good a man as you.

ABRAHAM. No better.

ACT I, SCENE 1.   This scene serves to give us the atmosphere of the whole play, an atmosphere of feud. Sampson is a stupid bully, Gregory a merry one. 1. *carry coals,* endure insults. 4. *choler,* one of the four humors, productive of anger. 10. *moves,* incites. 15. *take the wall,* take the side of the walk nearest the wall, an act of discourtesy. 37. *poor John,* hake salted and dried—a poor kind of food. 42. *Fear,* mistrust. 43. *marry,* mild oath. 47. *list,* please. 48. *bite my thumb,* an insulting gesture.

SAMPSON. Well, sir.

GREGORY. Say 'better:' here comes one of my master's kinsmen.

SAMPSON. Yes, better, sir.

ABRAHAM. You lie.

SAMPSON. Draw, if you be men. Gregory, remember thy swashing blow.

(*They fight.*) 70

(*Enter* BENVOLIO.)

BENVOLIO. Part, fools!
Put up your swords; you know not what you do.

(*Beats down their swords.*)

(*Enter* TYBALT.)

TYBALT. What, art thou drawn among these heartless hinds?
Turn thee, Benvolio, look upon thy death.

BENVOLIO. I do but keep the peace: put up thy sword,
Or manage it to part these men with me.

TYBALT. What, drawn, and talk of peace! I hate the word,
As I hate hell, all Montagues, and thee:
Have at thee, coward!   (*They fight.*)

(*Enter several of both houses, who join the fray; then enter*
CITIZENS, *with clubs.*)

FIRST CITIZEN. Clubs, bills, and partisans! strike! beat them down!   80
Down with the Capulets! down with the Montagues!

(*Enter* CAPULET *in his gown, and* LADY CAPULET.)

CAPULET. What noise is this? Give me my long sword, ho!

LADY CAPULET. A crutch, a crutch! why call you for a sword?

CAPULET. My sword, I say! Old Montague is come,
And flourishes his blade in spite of me.

(*Enter* MONTAGUE *and* LADY MONTAGUE.)

MONTAGUE. Thou villain Capulet,—Hold me not, let me go.

LADY MONTAGUE. Thou shalt not stir a foot to seek a foe.

(*Enter* PRINCE, *with* ATTENDANTS.)

PRINCE. Rebellious subjects, enemies to peace,
Profaners of this neighbour-stained steel,—
Will they not hear? What, ho! you men, you beasts,   90
That quench the fire of your pernicious rage

70. *swashing*, crushing. 73. *drawn*, with drawn sword. *heartless hinds*, cowardly menials. Tybalt's spirit is irreconcilable throughout. 79. *Have at thee*, I shall attack thee, defend thyself. 80. *Clubs, bills, and partisans*, a rallying cry of London apprentices. *Bills* and *partisans* were long-handled spears with cutting blades. 83. *crutch*, i.e., a crutch would befit him better than a sword.

With purple fountains issuing from your veins,
On pain of torture, from those bloody hands
Throw your mistemper'd weapons to the ground,
And hear the sentence of your moved prince.
Three civil brawls, bred of an airy word,
By thee, old Capulet, and Montague,
Have thrice disturb'd the quiet of our streets,
And made Verona's ancient citizens
Cast by their grave beseeming ornaments,   100
To wield old partisans, in hands as old,
Canker'd with peace, to part your canker'd hate:
If ever you disturb our streets again,
Your lives shall pay the forfeit of the peace.
For this time, all the rest depart away:
You, Capulet, shall go along with me:
And, Montague, come you this afternoon,
To know our further pleasure in this case,
To old Free-town, our common judgement-place.
Once more, on pain of death, all men depart.   110

(*Exeunt all but* MONTAGUE, LADY MONTAGUE,
and BENVOLIO.)

MONTAGUE. Who set this ancient quarrel new abroach?
   Speak, nephew, were you by when it began?
BENVOLIO. Here were the servants of your adversary,
   And yours, close fighting ere I did approach:
   I drew to part them: in the instant came
   The fiery Tybalt, with his sword prepared,
   Which, as he breathed defiance to my ears,
   He swung about his head and cut the winds,
   Who nothing hurt withal hiss'd him in scorn:
   While we were interchanging thrusts and blows,   120
   Came more and more and fought on part and part,
   Till the prince came, who parted either part.
LADY MONTAGUE. O, where is Romeo? saw you him to-day?
   Right glad I am he was not at this fray.
BENVOLIO. Madam, an hour before the worshipp'd sun
   Peer'd forth the golden window of the east,
   A troubled mind drave me to walk abroad;
   Where, underneath the grove of sycamore
   That westward rooteth from the city's side,
   So early walking did I see your son: 130
   Towards him I made, but he was ware of me

102. *Canker'd . . . canker'd,* corroded . . . malignant. 109. *Free-town,* Villa
Franca in Brooke's poem *Romeus and Juliet.* 111. *set . . . abroach,* reopened.
119. *nothing,* not at all. *withal,* with this.

And stole into the covert of the wood:
I, measuring his affections by my own,
That most are busied when they're most alone,
Pursued my humour not pursuing his,
And gladly shunn'd who gladly fled from me.
MONTAGUE. Many a morning hath he there been seen,
With tears augmenting the fresh morning's dew,
Adding to clouds more clouds with his deep sighs;
But all so soon as the all-cheering sun   140
Should in the furthest east begin to draw
The shady curtains from Aurora's bed,
Away from light steals home my heavy son,
And private in his chamber pens himself,
Shuts up his windows, locks fair daylight out
And makes himself an artificial night:
Black and portentous must this humour prove,
Unless good counsel may the cause remove.
BENVOLIO. My noble uncle, do you know the cause?
MONTAGUE. I neither know it nor can learn of him.   150
BENVOLIO. Have you importuned him by any means?
MONTAGUE. Both by myself and many other friends:
But he, his own affections' counsellor,
Is to himself—I will not say how true—
But to himself so secret and so close,
So far from sounding and discovery,
As is the bud bit with an envious worm,
Ere he can spread his sweet leaves to the air,
Or dedicate his beauty to the sun.
Could we but learn from whence his sorrows grow,   160
We would as willingly give cure as know.

(*Enter* ROMEO.)
BENVOLIO. See, where he comes: so please you, step aside;
I'll know his grievance, or be much denied.
MONTAGUE. I would thou wert so happy by thy stay,
To hear true shrift. Come, madam, let's away.
                                        (*Exeunt* MONTAGUE *and* LADY.)
BENVOLIO. Good morrow, cousin.
ROMEO.   Is the day so young?
BENVOLIO. But new struck nine.
ROMEO.   Ay me! sad hours seem long.

---

133. *affections*, wishes, inclination. 135. *humour*, mood, whim. 143. *heavy*, sad.
151. *means*, agency. 155. *close*, secret, private. 157. *envious*, malicious. 163.
denied, refused. 165. *shrift*, confession. 166. *morrow*, morning. *cousin*, any
relative not belonging to one's immediate family.

Was that my father that went hence so fast?
BENVOLIO. It was. What sadness lengthens Romeo's hours?
ROMEO. Not having that, which, having, makes them short.   170
BENVOLIO. In love?
ROMEO. Out—
BENVOLIO. Of love?
ROMEO. Out of her favour, where I am in love.
BENVOLIO. Alas, that love, so gentle in his view,
  Should be so tyrannous and rough in proof!
ROMEO. Alas, that love, whose view is muffled still,
  Should, without eyes, see pathways to his will!
  Where shall we dine? O me! What fray was here?
  Yet tell me not, for I have heard it all.   180
  Here's much to do with hate, but more with love.
  Why, then, O brawling love! O loving hate!
  O any thing, of nothing first create!
  O heavy lightness! serious vanity!
  Mis-shapen chaos of well-seeming forms!
  Feather of lead, bright smoke, cold fire, sick health!
  Still-waking sleep, that is not what it is!
  This love feel I, that feel no love in this.
  Dost thou not laugh?
BENVOLIO.   No, coz, I rather weep.   189
ROMEO. Good heart, at what?
BENVOLIO.   At thy good heart's oppression.
ROMEO. Why, such is love's transgression.
  Griefs of mine own lie heavy in my breast,
  Which thou wilt propagate, to have it prest
  With more of thine: this love that thou hast shown
  Doth add more grief to too much of mine own.
  Love is a smoke raised with the fume of sighs;
  Being purged, a fire sparkling in lovers' eyes;
  Being vex'd, a sea nourish'd with lovers' tears:
  What is it else? a madness most discreet,
  A choking gall and a preserving sweet.   200
  Farewell, my coz.
BENVOLIO.   Soft! I will go along;
  An if you leave me so, you do me wrong.
ROMEO. Tut, I have lost myself; I am not here;

---

168. *Was . . . fast.* This line is matter of fact, not sentimental like Romeo's other utterances. See also 179.   174. *favour*, good will, liking.   176. *proof*, experience. 181–188. *Here's . . . this.* These lines, abounding in paradoxical phrases called oxymoron, such as *loving hate, cold fire*, are characteristic of artificial love poetry. They indicate Romeo's sentimentality.   193. *propagate*, increase.

This is not Romeo, he 's some other where.
BENVOLIO. Tell me in sadness, who is that you love.
ROMEO. What, shall I groan and tell thee?
BENVOLIO.   Groan! why, no:
  But sadly tell me who.
ROMEO. Bid a sick man in sadness make his will:
  Ah, word ill urged to one that is so ill!
  In sadness, cousin, I do love a woman.   210
BENVOLIO. I aim'd so near, when I supposed you loved.
ROMEO. A right good mark-man! And she's fair I love.
BENVOLIO. A right fair mark, fair coz, is soonest hit.
ROMEO. Well, in that hit you miss: she'll not be hit
  With Cupid's arrow; she hath Dian's wit;
  And, in strong proof of chastity well arm'd,
  From love's weak childish bow she lives unharm'd.
  She will not stay the siege of loving terms,
  Nor bide the encounter of assailing eyes,
  Nor ope her lap to saint-seducing gold: 220
  O, she is rich in beauty, only poor,
  That when she dies with beauty dies her store.
BENVOLIO. Then she hath sworn that she will still live chaste?
ROMEO. She hath, and in that sparing makes huge waste,
  For beauty starved with her severity
  Cuts beauty off from all posterity.
  She is too fair, too wise, wisely too fair,
  To merit bliss by making me despair:
  She hath forsworn to love, and in that vow
  Do I live dead that live to tell it now.   230
BENVOLIO. Be ruled by me, forget to think of her.
ROMEO. O, teach me how I should forget to think.
BENVOLIO. By giving liberty unto thine eyes;
  Examine other beauties.
ROMEO.   'Tis the way
  To call hers exquisite, in question more:
  These happy masks that kiss fair ladies' brows
  Being black put us in mind they hide the fair;
  He that is strucken blind cannot forget
  The precious treasure of his eyesight lost:
  Show me a mistress that is passing fair,   240
  What doth her beauty serve, but as a note

---

208. *sadness,* seriousness. 212. *fair,* beautiful. 213. *fair,* clear, distinct. 218.
stay, withstand. 222. *store.* She will die without children and therefore her
beauty will die with her. 225. *starved,* allowed to die. 235. *in question more,*
into greater consideration. 240. *passing,* surpassingly.

Where I may read who pass'd that passing fair?
Farewell: thou canst not teach me to forget.
BENVOLIO. I'll pay that doctrine, or else die in debt.   (*Exeunt.*)

SCENE 2: *A street.*

(*Enter* CAPULET, PARIS, *and* SERVANT.)
CAPULET. But Montague is bound as well as I,
  In penalty alike; and 'tis not hard, I think,
  For men so old as we to keep the peace.
PARIS. Of honourable reckoning are you both;
  And pity 'tis you lived at odds so long.
  But now, my lord, what say you to my suit?
CAPULET. But saying o'er what I have said before:
  My child is yet a stranger in the world;
  She hath not seen the change of fourteen years;
  Let two more summers wither in their pride,   10
  Ere we may think her ripe to be a bride.
PARIS. Younger than she are happy mothers made.
CAPULET. And too soon marr'd are those so early made.
  The earth hath swallow'd all my hopes but she,
  She is the hopeful lady of my earth:
  But woo her, gentle Paris, get her heart,
  My will to her consent is but a part;
  An she agree, within her scope of choice
  Lies my consent and fair according voice.
  This night I hold an old accustom'd feast,   20
  Whereto I have invited many a guest,
  Such as I love; and you, among the store,
  One more, most welcome, makes my number more.
  At my poor house look to behold this night
  Earth-treading stars that make dark heaven light:
  Such comfort as do lusty young men feel
  When well-apparell'd April on the heel
  Of limping winter treads, even such delight
  Among fresh female buds shall you this night
  Inherit at my house; hear all, all see,   30

244. *pay that doctrine,* give that instruction.
SCENE 2.   4. *reckoning,* estimation, repute.   8. *stranger in the world.* Capulet's
reluctance is largely a matter of manners.   17. *My . . . part.* This is also a conventional statement, since Capulet has no idea of letting Juliet have her way.
18. *An,* if. *scope,* limit.

And like her most whose merit most shall be:
Which on more view, of many mine being one
May stand in number, though in reckoning none.
Come, go with me. (*To* SERVANT, *giving a paper*.) **Go**, sirrah,
    trudge about
Through fair Verona; find those persons out
Whose names are written there, and to them say,
My house and welcome on their pleasure stay.   37

(Exeunt CAPULET and PARIS.)

SERVANT. Find them out whose names are written here! It is written,
    that the shoemaker should meddle with his yard, and the tailor with
    his last, the fisher with his pencil, and the painter with his nets; but
    I am sent to find those persons whose names are here writ, and can
    never find what names the writing person hath here writ. I must
    to the learned.—In good time.   45

(*Enter* BENVOLIO *and* ROMEO.)

BENVOLIO. Tut, man, one fire burns out another's burning,
    One pain is lessen'd by another's anguish;
    Turn giddy, and be holp by backward turning;
    One desperate grief cures with another's languish:
    Take thou some new infection to thy eye,   50
    And the rank poison of the old will die.
ROMEO. Your plaintain-leaf is excellent for that.
BENVOLIO. For what, I pray thee?
ROMEO.   For your broken shin.
BENVOLIO. Why, Romeo, art thou mad?
ROMEO. Not mad, but bound more than a madman is;
    Shut up in prison, kept without my food,
    Whipp'd and tormented and—God-den, good fellow.
SERVANT. God gi' god-den. I pray, sir, can you read?
ROMEO. Ay, mine own fortune in my misery.   60
SERVANT. Perhaps you have learned it without book: but,
    I pray, can you read any thing you see?
ROMEO. Ay, if I know the letters and the language.
SERVANT. Ye say honestly: rest you merry!
ROMEO. Stay, fellow; I can read.   (*Reads.*)
    'Signior Martino and his wife and daughters;

32–33. *Which . . . none.* Capulet may mean that his daughter will lose her
identity by being swallowed up in a number of others. He is punning on the
saying, "one is no number." The Arden editor places a comma after *of* and
dashes after *many* and *one.* He explains *reckoning* to mean "estimation" (as in
line 4, above), with wordplay, i.e., "counting heads." 34. *sirrah,* customary form
of address to servants. 48. *holp,* helped. 51. *rank,* corrupt. 57. *God-den,* good
evening. *fellow,* usual term for a servant.

County Anselme and his beauteous sisters; the lady widow of
Vitruvio; Signior Placentio and his lovely nieces; Mercutio and his
brother Valentine; mine uncle Capulet, his wife, and daughters; my
fair niece Rosaline; Livia; Signior Valentio and his cousin Tybalt;
Lucio and the lively Helena.'   74
A fair assembly: whither should they come?
SERVANT. Up.
ROMEO. Whither?
SERVANT. To supper; to our house.
ROMEO. Whose house?
SERVANT. My master's.   80
ROMEO. Indeed, I should have asked you that before.
SERVANT. Now I'll tell you without asking: my master is the great rich
   Capulet; and if you be not of the house of Montagues, I pray, come
   and crush a cup of wine. Rest you merry!   (*Exit.*)
BENVOLIO. At this same ancient feast of Capulet's
   Sups the fair Rosaline whom thou so lovest,
   With all the admired beauties of Verona:
   Go thither; and, with unattainted eye,   90
   Compare her face with some that I shall show,
   And I will make thee think thy swan a crow.
ROMEO. When the devout religion of mine eye
   Maintains such falsehood, then turn tears to fires;
   And these, who often drown'd could never die,
   Transparent heretics, be burnt for liars!
   One fairer than my love! the all-seeing sun
   Ne'er saw her match since first the world begun.
BENVOLIO. Tut, you saw her fair, none else being by,
   Herself poised with herself in either eye: 100
   But in that crystal scales let there be weigh'd
   Your lady's love against some other maid
   That I will show you shining at this feast,
   And she shall scant show well that now shows best.
ROMEO. I'll go along, no such sight to be shown,
   But to rejoice in splendour of mine own.   (*Exeunt.*)

SCENE 3: *A room in Capulet's house.*

(*Enter* LADY CAPULET *and* NURSE.)
LADY CAPULET. Nurse, where's my daughter? call her forth to me.

---

86. *crush a cup of wine*, drink a cup of wine. Cf. "crack a bottle."   87. *ancient*,
customary.   89. *admired*, wondered at.   90. *unattainted*, impartial.   95. *these*, i.e.,
these eyes.

NURSE. Now, by my maidenhead, at twelve year old,
   I bade her come. What, lamb! what, ladybird!
   God forbid! Where 's this girl? What, Juliet!

(*Enter* JULIET.)
JULIET. How now! who calls?
NURSE.   Your mother.
JULIET.   Madam, I am here.
   What is your will?
LADY CAPULET. This is the matter:—Nurse, give leave awhile,
   We must talk in secret:—nurse, come back again;
   I have remember'd me, thou 's hear our counsel.
   Thou know'st my daughter 's of a pretty age.   10
NURSE. Faith, I can tell her age unto an hour.
LADY CAPULET. She 's not fourteen.
NURSE.   I'll lay fourteen of my teeth,—
   And yet, to my teen be it spoken, I have but four,—
   She is not fourteen. How long is it now
   To Lammas-tide?
LADY CAPULET.   A fortnight and odd days.
NURSE. Even or odd, of all days in the year,
   Come Lammas-eve at night shall she be fourteen.
   Susan and she—God rest all Christian souls!—
   Were of an age: well, Susan is with God;
   She was too good for me: but, as I said,   20
   On Lammas-eve at night shall she be fourteen;
   That shall she, marry; I remember it well.
   'Tis since the earthquake now eleven years;
   And she was wean'd,—I never shall forget it,—
   Of all the days of the year, upon that day:
   For I had then laid wormwood to my dug,
   Sitting in the sun under the dove-house wall;
   My lord and you were then at Mantua:—
   Nay, I do bear a brain:—but, as I said,
   When it did taste the wormwood on the nipple   30
   Of my dug and felt it bitter, pretty fool,
   To see it tetchy and fall out with the dug!
   'Shake' quoth the dove-house: 'twas no need, I trow,
   To bid me trudge:

SCENE 3. 7. *give leave*, leave us. 9. *thou's*, thou shalt. 13. *teen*, sorrow. 15.
Lammas-tide, August 1. 23. *'Tis . . . years*. It has been thought that Shakespeare
was alluding in this line to a famous earthquake in 1580 and was, therefore,
writing in 1591. 29. *bear a brain*. The nurse prides herself on her memory.
31. *fool*, term of endearment. 32. *tetchy*, fretful. 33. *trow*, believe.

And since that time it is eleven years;
For then she could stand alone; nay, by the rood,
She could have run and waddled all about;
For even the day before, she broke her brow:
And then my husband—God be with his soul!
A' was a merry man—took up the child: 40
'Yea,' quoth he, 'dost thou fall upon thy face?
Thou wilt fall backward when thou hast more wit;
Wilt thou not, Jule?' and, by my holidame,
The pretty wretch left crying and said 'Ay.'
To see, now, how a jest shall come about!
I warrant, an I should live a thousand years,
I never should forget it: 'Wilt thou not, Jule?' quoth he;
And, pretty fool, it stinted and said 'Ay.'
LADY CAPULET. Enough of this; I pray thee, hold thy peace.   49
NURSE. Yes, madam: yet I cannot choose but laugh,
To think it should leave crying and say 'Ay.'
And yet, I warrant, it had upon it brow
A bump as big as a young cockerel's stone;
A parlous knock; and it cried bitterly:
'Yea,' quoth my husband, 'fall'st upon thy face?
Thou wilt fall backward when thou comest to age;
Wilt thou not, Jule?' it stinted and said 'Ay.'
JULIET. And stint thou too, I pray thee, nurse, say I.
NURSE. Peace, I have done. God mark thee to his grace!
Thou wast the prettiest babe that e'er I nursed: 60
An I might live to see thee married once,
I have my wish.
LADY CAPULET. Marry, that 'marry' is the very theme
I came to talk of. Tell me, daughter Juliet,
How stands your disposition to be married?
JULIET. It is an honour that I dream not of.
NURSE. An honour! were not I thine only nurse,
I would say thou hadst suck'd wisdom from thy teat.
LADY CAPULET. Well, think of marriage now; younger than you,
Here in Verona, ladies of esteem,   70
Are made already mothers: by my count,
I was your mother much upon these years
That you are now a maid. Thus then in brief:
The valiant Paris seeks you for his love.
NURSE. A man, young lady! lady, such a man

---

40. *A'*, he. 43. *holidame,* same as "halidom," a relic or holy thing. 48. *stinted,*
ceased.

As all the world—why, he 's a man of wax.
LADY CAPULET. Verona's summer hath not such a flower.
NURSE. Nay, he 's a flower; in faith, a very flower.
LADY CAPULET. What say you? can you love the gentleman?
  This night you shall behold him at our feast;   80
  Read o'er the volume of young Paris' face
  And find delight writ there with beauty's pen;
  Examine every married lineament
  And see how one another lends content,
  And what obscured in this fair volume lies
  Find written in the margent of his eyes.
  This precious book of love, this unbound lover,
  To beautify him, only lacks a cover:
  The fish lives in the sea, and 'tis much pride
  For fair without the fair within to hide: 90
  That book in many's eyes doth share the glory,
  That in gold clasps locks in the golden story;
  So shall you share all that he doth possess,
  By having him, making yourself no less.
NURSE. No less! nay, bigger; women grow by men.
LADY CAPULET. Speak briefly, can you like of Paris' love?
JULIET. I'll look to like, if looking liking move:
  But no more deep will I endart mine eye
  Than your consent gives strength to make it fly.   99

(*Enter a* SERVANT.)
SERVANT. Madam, the guests are come, supper served up, you called, my young lady asked for, the nurse cursed in the pantry, and every thing in extremity. I must hence to wait; I beseech you, follow straight.
LADY CAPULET. We follow thee. (*Exit* SERVANT.) Juliet, the county stays.   105
NURSE. Go, girl, seek happy nights to happy days.   (*Exeunt.*)

SCENE 4: *A street.*

(*Enter* ROMEO, MERCUTIO, BENVOLIO, *with five or six*
  MASKERS, TORCH-BEARERS, *and others.*)

76. *a man of wax*, such as one would picture in wax, i.e., handsome. 83. *married*, harmonized into mutual helpfulness (Hudson). 86. *margent*, commentary or marginal gloss. 89. *fish lives in the sea*. The figure of speech is of the binding of a book; since fishskins were used to cover books, this "unbound lover" is yet to be made complete. 97–99. *I'll . . . fly.* Juliet's attitude is one of proper obedience. 105. *county*, count.

ROMEO. What, shall this speech be spoke for our excuse?
  Or shall we on without apology?
BENVOLIO. The date is out of such prolixity:
  We'll have no Cupid hoodwink'd with a scarf,
  Bearing a Tartar's painted bow of lath,
  Scaring the ladies like a crow-keeper;
  Nor no without-book prologue, faintly spoke
  After the prompter, for our entrance:
  But let them measure us by what they will;
  We'll measure them a measure, and be gone.   10
ROMEO. Give me a torch: I am not for this ambling;
  Being but heavy, I will bear the light.
MERCUTIO. Nay, gentle Romeo, we must have you dance.
ROMEO. Not I, believe me: you have dancing shoes
  With nimble soles: I have a soul of lead
  So stakes me to the ground I cannot move.
MERCUTIO. You are a lover; borrow Cupid's wings,
  And soar with them above a common bound.
ROMEO. I am too sore enpierced with his shaft
  To soar with his light feathers, and so bound,   20
  I cannot bound a pitch above dull woe:
  Under love's heavy burden do I sink.
MERCUTIO. And, to sink in it, should you burden love;
  Too great oppression for a tender thing.
ROMEO. Is love a tender thing? it is too rough,
  Too rude, too boisterous, and it pricks like thorn.
MERCUTIO. If love be rough with you, be rough with love;
  Prick love for pricking, and you beat love down.
  Give me a case to put my visage in:
  A visor for a visor! what care I   30
  What curious eye doth quote deformities?
  Here are the beetle brows shall blush for me.
BENVOLIO. Come, knock and enter; and no sooner in,
  But every man betake him to his legs.
ROMEO. A torch for me: let wantons light of heart
  Tickle the senseless rushes with their heels,

SCENE 4. 1. *speech.* The older fashion was for maskers to be preceded by a messenger with a set speech, but *the date is out* for *such prolixity.* 4. *hood-wink'd,* blindfolded. 5. *Tartar's painted bow.* Tartar's bows are said to have resembled the old Roman bow with which Cupid was pictured. 6. *crow-keeper,* scarecrow. 10. *measure . . . measure,* perform a dance. 11. *ambling,* walking affectedly; used contemptuously of dancing. 21. *pitch,* height. 30. *visor,* a mask, for an ugly masklike face. 31. *quote,* take notice of. 36. *rushes.* Rushes were used for floor coverings.

For I am proverb'd with a grandsire phrase;
I'll be a candle-holder, and look on.
The game was ne'er so fair, and I am done.

MERCUTIO. Tut, dun 's the mouse, the constable's own word: 40
If thou art dun, we'll draw thee from the mire
Of this sir-reverence love, wherein thou stick'st
Up to the ears, Come, we burn daylight, ho!

ROMEO. Nay, that 's not so.

MERCUTIO.   I mean, sir, in delay
We waste our lights in vain, like lamps by day.
Take our good meaning, for our judgement sits
Five times in that ere once in our five wits.

ROMEO. And we mean well in going to this mask;
But 'tis no wit to go.

MERCUTIO.   Why, may one ask?

ROMEO. I dream'd a dream to-night.

MERCUTIO.   And so did I.   50

ROMEO. Well, what was yours?

MERCUTIO.   That dreamers often lie.

ROMEO. In bed asleep, while they do dream things true.

MERCUTIO. O, then, I see Queen Mab hath been with you.
She is the fairies' midwife, and she comes
In shape no bigger than an agate-stone
On the fore-finger of an alderman,
Drawn with a team of little atomies
Athwart men's noses as they lie asleep;
Her waggon-spokes made of long spinners' legs,
The cover of the wings of grasshoppers,   60
The traces of the smallest spider's web,
The collars of the moonshine's watery beams,
Her whip of cricket's bone, the lash of film,
Her waggoner a small grey-coated gnat,
Not half so big as a round little worm
Prick'd from the lazy finger of a maid;
Her chariot is an empty hazel-nut

38. *candle-holder*, an allusion to the proverb "A good candle-holder (i.e., a mere onlooker) is a good gamester." 40. *dun's the mouse*, a common phrase usually taken to mean "keep still." *Dun* (l. 41) alludes to a Christmas game, "Dun is in the mire," in which a heavy log was lifted by the players. 42. *sir-reverence*, corruption of "save-reverence" (*salve-reverentia*), an apology for something improper. 47. *five wits*, the five faculties, usually given as common wit, imagination, fantasy, judgment, and reason. 53. *Queen Mab*, a name of Celtic origin for the fairy queen. Mercutio's famous speech interested the audience, no doubt, but has little connection with plot or character. 57. *atomies*, tiny creatures. 63. *film*, gossamer thread. 64. *waggoner*, coachman. 65. *worm*. This alludes to an ancient and no doubt useful superstition that "worms breed in the fingers of the idle."

Made by the joiner squirrel or old grub,
Time out o' mind the fairies' coachmakers.
And in this state she gallops night by night   70
Through lovers' brains, and then they dream of love;
O'er courtiers' knees, that dream on court'sies straight,
O'er lawyers' fingers, who straight dream on fees,
O'er ladies' lips, who straight on kisses dream,
Which oft the angry Mab with blisters plagues,
Because their breaths with sweetmeats tainted are:
Sometime she gallops o'er a courtier's nose,
And then dreams he of smelling out a suit;
And sometime comes she with a tithe-pig's tail
Tickling a parson's nose as a' lies asleep,   80
Then dreams he of another benefice:
Sometime she driveth o'er a soldier's neck,
And then dreams he of cutting foreign throats,
Of breaches, ambuscadoes, Spanish blades,
Of healths five-fathom deep; and then anon
Drums in his ear, at which he starts and wakes,
And being thus frighted swears a prayer or two
And sleeps again. This is that very Mab
That plats the manes of horses in the night,
And bakes the elf-locks in foul sluttish hairs,   90
Which once untangled much misfortune bodes:
This is the hag, when maids lie on their backs,
That presses them and learns them first to bear,
Making them women of good carriage:
This is she—
ROMEO.   Peace, peace, Mercutio, peace!
Thou talk'st of nothing.
MERCUTIO.   True, I talk of dreams,
Which are the children of an idle brain,
Begot of nothing but vain fantasy,
Which is as thin of substance as the air
And more inconstant than the wind, who wooes   100
Even now the frozen bosom of the north,
And, being anger'd, puffs away from thence,
Turning his face to the dew-dropping south.
BENVOLIO. This wind, you talk of, blows us from ourselves;

70. *state*, pomp, dignity. 73. *straight*, immediately. 77. *Sometime*, from time to time, sometimes. 78. *suit*, a request or plea at court. 79. *tithe-pig's tail*. This alludes to the tenth pig given the parson as a church tax. 85. *anon*, by and by. 89. *plats the manes of horses*, an allusion to the familiar superstition of "witches stirrups," tangles in the manes of horses. 93. *learns*, teaches. 98. *vain*, empty, foolish. *fantasy*, imagination.

Supper is done, and we shall come too late.

ROMEO. I fear, too early: for my mind misgives
Some consequence yet hanging in the stars
Shall bitterly begin his fearful date
With this night's revels and expire the term
Of a despised life closed in my breast   110
By some vile forfeit of untimely death.
But He, that hath the steerage of my course,
Direct my sail! On, lusty gentlemen.

BENVOLIO. Strike, drum.   (*Exeunt.*)

SCENE 5: *A hall in Capulet's house.*

(MUSICIANS *waiting. Enter* SERVINGMEN, *with napkins.*)

FIRST SERVINGMAN. Where 's Potpan, that he helps not to take away? He
shift a trencher? he scrape a trencher!

SECOND SERVINGMAN. When good manners shall lie all in one or two
men's hands and they unwashed too, 'tis a foul thing.

FIRST SERVINGMAN. Away with the joint-stools, remove the court-cupboard, look to the plate. Good thou, save me a piece of marchpane;
and, as thou lovest me, let the porter let in Susan Grindstone and
Nell. Antony, and Potpan!   11

SECOND SERVINGMAN. Ay, boy, ready.

FIRST SERVINGMAN. You are looked for and called for, asked for and
sought for, in the great chamber.

SECOND SERVINGMAN. We cannot be here and there too. Cheerly, boys;
be brisk awhile, and the longer liver take all.

(*Enter* CAPULET, *with* JULIET *and others of his house,*
meeting the GUESTS *and* MASKERS.)

CAPULET. Welcome, gentlemen! ladies that have their toes
Unplagued with corns will have a bout with you.
Ah ha, my mistresses! which of you all   20
Will now deny to dance? she that makes dainty,
She, I'll swear, hath corns; am I come near ye now?
Welcome, gentlemen! I have seen the day
That I have worn a visor and could tell
A whispering tale in a fair lady's ear,
Such as would please: 'tis gone, 'tis gone, 'tis gone:
You are welcome, gentlemen! Come, musicians, play.
A hall, a hall! give room! and foot it, girls.

108. *date,* time.   109. *expire,* (transitive), bring to an end.
SCENE 5.   2. *trencher,* wooden dish or plate.   7. *joint-stools,* stools, properly
those made by a joiner.   8. *court-cupboard,* sideboard.   9. *marchpane,* cake
made from sugar and almonds.   21. *makes dainty,* hesitates from affectation to
dance.

(Music plays, and they dance.)

More light, you knaves; and turn the tables up,
And quench the fire, the room is grown too hot.   30
Ah, sirrah, this unlook'd-for sport comes well.
Nay, sit, nay, sit, good cousin Capulet;
For you and I are past our dancing days:
How long is 't now since last yourself and I
Were in a mask?
SECOND CAPULET.   By 'r lady, thirty years.
CAPULET. What, man! 'tis not so much, 'tis not so much:
'Tis since the nuptial of Lucentio,
Come pentecost as quickly as it will,
Some five and twenty years; and then we mask'd.
SECOND CAPULET. 'Tis more, 'tis more: his son is elder, sir;   40
His son is thirty.
CAPULET.   Will you tell me that?
His son was but a ward two years ago.
ROMEO. *(to a* SERVINGMAN*)*. What lady is that, which doth enrich the
    hand
Of yonder knight?
SERVINGMAN. I know not, sir.
ROMEO. O, she doth teach the torches to burn bright!
It seems she hangs upon the cheek of night
Like a rich jewel in an Ethiope's ear;
Beauty too rich for use, for earth too dear!
So shows a snowy dove trooping with crows,   50
As yonder lady o'er her fellows shows.
The measure done, I'll watch her place of stand,
And, touching hers, make blessed my rude hand.
Did my heart love till now? forswear it, sight!
For I ne'er saw true beauty till this night.
TYBALT. This, by his voice, should be a Montague.
Fetch me my rapier, boy. What dares the slave
Come hither, cover'd with an antic face,
To fleer and scorn at our solemnity?
Now, by the stock and honour of my kin,   60
To strike him dead I hold it not a sin.
CAPULET. Why, how now, kinsman! wherefore storm you so?
TYBALT. Uncle, this is a Montague, our foe,

29. *turn the tables up.* Tables were probably made of hinged leaves and placed on trestles. They were put aside for dancing.   42. *ward,* a minor under guardianship.   46-55. *O . . . night.* Romeo's love is love at first sight, a type of love provided for in Elizabethan psychological doctrine and, no doubt, in life.   49. *dear,* precious.   57. *Fetch me my rapier.* This speech of Tybalt's is in immediate contrast to the happy sentiment of Romeo's speech.   58. *antic,* fantastic.   59. *fleer,* to look mockingly.

A villain that is hither come in spite,
To scorn at our solemnity this night.
CAPULET. Young Romeo is it?
TYBALT.   'Tis he, that villain Romeo.
CAPULET. Content thee, gentle coz, let him alone;
  He bears him like a portly gentleman;
  And, to say truth, Verona brags of him
  To be a virtuous and well govern'd youth: 70
  I would not for the wealth of all the town
  Here in my house do him disparagement:
  Therefore be patient, take no note of him:
  It is my will, the which if thou respect,
  Show a fair presence and put off these frowns,
  An ill-beseeming semblance for a feast.
TYBALT. It fits, when such a villain is a guest:
  I'll not endure him.
CAPULET.   He shall be endured:
  What, goodman boy! I say, he shall: go to;
  Am I the master here, or you? go to.   80
  You'll not endure him! God shall mend my soul!
  You'll make a mutiny among my guests!
  You will set cock-a-hoop! you'll be the man!
TYBALT. Why, uncle, 'tis a shame.
CAPULET.   Go to, go to;
  You are a saucy boy: is 't so, indeed?
  This trick may chance to scathe you, I know what:
  You must contrary me! marry, 'tis time.
  Well said, my hearts! You are a princox; go:
  Be quiet, or—More light, more light! For shame!
  I'll make you quiet. What, cheerly, my hearts!   90
TYBALT. Patience perforce with wilful choler meeting
  Makes my flesh tremble in their different greeting.
  I will withdraw: but this intrusion shall
  Now seeming sweet convert to bitter gall.   (*Exit.*)
ROMEO (*to* JULIET). If I profane with my unworthiest nand
    This holy shrine, the gentle fine is this:
  My lips, two blushing pilgrims, ready stand
    To smooth that rough touch with a tender kiss.
JULIET. Good pilgrim, you do wrong your hand too much,

68. *portly,* an excellent bearing. 74. *respect,* regard. 79. *goodman boy,* a belittling ironical epithet. Capulet has a spirit more reconcilable than that of Tybalt. *go to,* expression of impatience. 83. *cock-a-hoop,* complete disorder. 91. *Patience perforce,* patience upon compulsion; *patience* is a general word for self-control 94. *convert,* change (to).

Which mannerly devotion shows in this;   100
  For saints have hands that pilgrims' hands do touch,
    And palm to palm is holy palmers' kiss.
ROMEO. Have not saints lips, and holy palmers too?
JULIET. Ay, pilgrim, lips that they must use in prayer.
ROMEO. O, then, dear saint, let lips do what hands do;
  They pray, grant thou, lest faith turn to despair.
JULIET. Saints do not move, though grant for prayers' sake.
ROMEO. Then move not, while my prayer's effect I take.
  Thus from my lips, by yours, my sin is purged.   109
JULIET. Then have my lips the sin that they have took.
ROMEO. Sin from my lips? O trespass sweetly urged!
  Give me my sin again.
JULIET.   You kiss by the book.
NURSE. Madam, your mother craves a word with you.
ROMEO. What is her mother?
NURSE.   Marry, bachelor,
  Her mother is the lady of the house,
  And a good lady, and a wise and virtuous:
  I nursed her daughter, that you talk'd withal;
  I tell you, he that can lay hold of her
  Shall have the chinks.
ROMEO.   Is she a Capulet?
  O dear account! my life is my foe's debt.   120
BENVOLIO. Away, be gone; the sport is at the best.
ROMEO. Ay, so I fear; the more is my unrest.
CAPULET. Nay, gentlemen, prepare not to be gone;
  We have a trifling foolish banquet towards.
  Is it e'en so? why, then, I thank you all;
  I thank you, honest gentlemen; good night.
  More torches here! Come on then, let 's to bed.
  Ah, sirrah, by my fay, it waxes late:
  I'll to my rest.   (*Exeunt all but* JULIET *and* NURSE.)
JULIET. Come hither, nurse. What is yond gentleman?
NURSE. The son and heir of old Tiberio.   131
JULIET. What 's he that now is going out of door?
NURSE. Marry, that, I think, be young Petrucio.
JULIET. What 's he that follows there, that would not dance?
NURSE. I know not.

95–108. *If . . . take.* These lines are in the form of a sonnet. They afford an
example of Shakespeare's early exuberance in poetic style. 99. *pilgrim.* Romeo
was masquerading as a pilgrim or palmer. 112. *by the book,* according to rule.
119. *chinks,* money. 120. *my foe's debt,* due to my foe, at his mercy. 124.
foolish, insignificant. *banquet,* dessert. *towards,* in preparation. 128. *fay,* faith.

JULIET. Go, ask his name: if he be married,
  My grave is like to be my wedding bed.
NURSE. His name is Romeo, and a Montague;
  The only son of your great enemy.
JULIET. My only love sprung from my only hate!   140
  Too early seen unknown, and known too late!
  Prodigious birth of love it is to me,
  That I must love a loathed enemy.
NURSE. What 's this? what 's this?
JULIET.   A rhyme I learn'd even now
  Of one I danced withal.   (*One calls within* 'JULIET.')
NURSE.   Anon, anon!
  Come, let's away; the strangers all are gone.   (*Exeunt.*)

ACT II

PROLOGUE

(*Enter* CHORUS.)
CHORUS. Now old desire doth in his death-bed lie,
  And young affection gapes to be his heir;
  That fair for which love groan'd for and would die,
  With tender Juliet match'd, is now not fair.
  Now Romeo is beloved and loves again,
  Alike bewitched by the charm of looks,
  But to his foe supposed he must complain,
  And she steal love's sweet bait from fearful hooks:
  Being held a foe, he may not have access
  To breathe such vows as lovers use to swear;   10
  And she as much in love, her means much less
  To meet her new-beloved any where:
  But passion lends them power, time means, to meet,
  Tempering extremities with extreme sweet.   (*Exit.*)

ACT II, PROLOGUE.   10. *use to swear,* are in the habit of swearing.   13.
passion, feeling of love.

SCENE 1: *A lane by the wall of Capulet's orchard.*

(*Enter* ROMEO.)

ROMEO. Can I go forward when my heart is here?
  Turn back, dull earth, and find thy centre out.

(He climbs the wall, and leaps down within it.)

(*Enter* BENVOLIO *and* MERCUTIO.)

BENVOLIO. Romeo! my cousin Romeo!

MERCUTIO.   He is wise;
  And, on my life, hath stol'n him home to bed.

BENVOLIO. He ran this way, and leap'd this orchard wall:
  Call, good Mercutio.

MERCUTIO.   Nay, I'll conjure too.
  Romeo! humours! madman! passion! lover!
  Appear thou in the likeness of a sigh:
  Speak but one rhyme, and I am satisfied;
  Cry but 'Ay me!' pronounce but 'love' and 'dove;'   10
  Speak to my gossip Venus one fair word,
  One nick-name for her purblind son and heir,
  Young Adam Cupid, he that shot so trim,
  When King Cophetua loved the beggar-maid!
  He heareth not, he stirreth not, he moveth not;
  The ape is dead, and I must conjure him.
  I conjure thee by Rosaline's bright eyes,
  By her high forehead and her scarlet lip,
  By her fine foot, straight leg and quivering thigh
  And the demesnes that there adjacent lie,   20
  That in thy likeness thou appear to us!

BENVOLIO. An if he hear thee, thou wilt anger him.

MERCUTIO. This cannot anger him: 'twould anger him
  To raise a spirit in his mistress' circle
  Of some strange nature, letting it there stand
  Till she had laid it and conjured it down;
  That were some spite: my invocation
  Is fair and honest, and in his mistress' name

SCENE 1. 2. *dull earth,* Romeo himself. *thy centre,* Juliet. The figure of speech is that of man as a microcosm or little world. 6. *conjure,* utter incantation. 12. *purblind,* completely blind. 13. *Adam,* Upton's conjecture; Qq and F: *Abraham.* It is thought that *Adam* may refer to Adam Bell, a famous archer in the old ballads; *Abraham* is a form of "abram" or "auburn," which would refer to Cupid's flaxen hair. 14. *King Cophetua,* reference to the ballad *King Cophetua and the Beggar Maid.* 16. *ape,* used as a term of endearment. 20. *demesnes,* regions. 22. *An if,* if. 25. *strange,* belonging to another person. 27. *spite,* injury. 28. *honest,* chaste.

I conjure only but to raise up him.

BENVOLIO. Come, he hath hid himself among these trees,   30
   To be consorted with the humorous night:
   Blind is his love and best befits the dark.

MERCUTIO. If love be blind, love cannot hit the mark.
   Now will he sit under a medlar tree,
   And wish his mistress were that kind of fruit
   As maids call medlars, when they laugh alone.
   O, Romeo, that she were, O, that she were
   An open et cætera, thou a poperin pear!
   Romeo, good night: I'll to my truckle-bed;
   This field-bed is too cold for me to sleep: 40
   Come, shall we go?

BENVOLIO.   Go, then; for 'tis in vain
   To seek him here that means not to be found.   (*Exeunt.*)

SCENE 2: *Capulet's orchard.*

(*Enter* ROMEO.)

ROMEO. He jests at scars that never felt a wound.

                         (JULIET *appears above at a window.*)
   But, soft! what light through yonder window breaks?
   It is the east, and Juliet is the sun.
   Arise, fair sun, and kill the envious moon,
   Who is already sick and pale with grief,
   That thou her maid art far more fair than she:
   Be not her maid, since she is envious;
   Her vestal livery is but sick and green
   And none but fools do wear it; cast it off.
   It is my lady, O, it is my love!   10
   O, that she knew she were!
   She speaks, yet she says nothing: what of that?
   Her eye discourses; I will answer it.
   I am too bold, 'tis not to me she speaks:
   Two of the fairest stars in all the heaven,
   Having some business, do entreat her eyes

31. *consorted,* associated. *humorous,* moist; also, influenced by humor or mood.
34. *medlar,* the fruit of the *Mespilus germanica,* edible only when partly decayed.
38. *poperin,* variety of pear; derived from the Flemish town *Poperinghe* in
Flanders.   39. *truckle-bed,* a bed on casters to be shoved under a standing bed.
40. *field-bed,* large bed; here, the ground.
SCENE 2.   There is no break in the action. Romeo must have been standing on
the front stage behind some obstruction to represent the garden wall. He speaks
at once, then turns to observe Juliet.   13. *discourses,* speaks.

To twinkle in their spheres till they return.
What if her eyes were there, they in her head?
The brightness of her cheek would shame those stars,
As daylight doth a lamp; her eyes in heaven   20
Would through the airy region stream so bright
That birds would sing and think it were not night.
See, how she leans her cheek upon her hand!
O, that I were a glove upon that hand,
That I might touch that cheek!

JULIET.   Ay me!

ROMEO.   She speaks:
O, speak again, bright angel! for thou art
As glorious to this night, being o'er my head,
As is a winged messenger of heaven
Unto the white-upturned wondering eyes
Of mortals that fall back to gaze on him   30
When he bestrides the lazy-pacing clouds
And sails upon the bosom of the air.

JULIET. O Romeo, Romeo! wherefore art thou Romeo?
Deny thy father and refuse thy name;
Or, if thou wilt not, be but sworn my love,
And I'll no longer be a Capulet.

ROMEO (aside). Shall I hear more, or shall I speak at this?

JULIET. 'Tis but thy name that is my enemy;
Thou art thyself, though not a Montague.
What's Montague? it is nor hand, nor foot,   40
Nor arm, nor face, nor any other part
Belonging to a man. O, be some other name!
What's in a name? that which we call a rose
By any other name would smell as sweet;
So Romeo would, were he not Romeo call'd,
Retain that dear perfection which he owes
Without that title. Romeo, doff thy name,
And for that name which is no part of thee
Take all myself.

ROMEO.   I take thee at thy word:
Call me but love, and I'll be new baptized;   50
Henceforth I never will be Romeo.

JULIET. What man art thou that thus bescreen'd in night
So stumblest on my counsel?

---

17. *spheres*, transparent concentric shells supposed to carry the heavenly bodies
with them in their revolution around the earth.   30. *mortals*, human beings.
46. *owes*, owns.   53. *counsel*, secret thought.

ROMEO.   By a name
  I know not how to tell thee who I am:
  My name, dear saint, is hateful to myself,
  Because it is an enemy to thee;
  Had I it written, I would tear the word.
JULIET. My ears have not yet drunk a hundred words
  Of that tongue's utterance, yet I know the sound:
  Art thou not Romeo and a Montague?   60
ROMEO. Neither, fair saint, if either thee dislike.
JULIET. How camest thou hither, tell me, and wherefore?
  The orchard walls are high and hard to climb,
  And the place death, considering who thou art,
  If any of my kinsmen find thee here.
ROMEO. With love's light wings did I o'erperch these walls;
  For stony limits cannot hold love out,
  And what love can do that dares love attempt;
  Therefore thy kinsmen are no let to me.
JULIET. If they do see thee, they will murder thee.   70
ROMEO. Alack, there lies more peril in thine eye
  Than twenty of their swords: look thou but sweet,
  And I am proof against their enmity.
JULIET. I would not for the world they saw thee here.
ROMEO. I have night's cloak to hide me from their sight;
  And but thou love me, let them find me here:
  My life were better ended by their hate,
  Than death prorogued, wanting of thy love.
JULIET. By whose direction found'st thou out this place?
ROMEO. By love, who first did prompt me to inquire;   80
  He lent me counsel and I lent him eyes.
  I am no pilot; yet, wert thou as far
  As that vast shore wash'd with the farthest sea,
  I would adventure for such merchandise.
JULIET. Thou know'st the mask of night is on my face,
  Else would a maiden blush bepaint my cheek
  For that which thou hast heard me speak tonight.
  Fain would I dwell on form, fain, fain deny
  What I have spoke: but farewell compliment!
  Dost thou love me? I know thou wilt say 'Ay,'   90
  And I will take thy word: yet, if thou swear'st,
  Thou mayst prove false; at lovers' perjuries,
  They say, Jove laughs. O gentle Romeo,
  If thou dost love, pronounce it faithfully:

61. *dislike*, displease. 66. *o'er-perch*, fly over and perch beyond. 78. *prorogued*, postponed. *wanting*, lacking. 89. *compliment*, punctiliousness, ceremony.

Or if thou think'st I am too quickly won,
I'll frown and be perverse and say thee nay,
So thou wilt woo; but else, not for the world.
In truth, fair Montague, I am too fond,
And therefore thou mayst think my 'haviour light:
But trust me, gentleman, I'll prove more true   100
Than those that have more cunning to be strange.
I should have been more strange, I must confess,
But that thou overheard'st, ere I was ware,
My true love's passion; therefore pardon me,
And not impute this yielding to light love,
Which the dark night hath so discovered.

ROMEO. Lady, by yonder blessed moon I swear
  That tips with silver all these fruit-tree tops—

JULIET. O, swear not by the moon, the inconstant moon,
  That monthly changes in her circled orb,   110
  Lest that thy love prove likewise variable.

ROMEO. What shall I swear by?

JULIET.   Do not swear at all;
  Or, if thou wilt, swear by thy gracious self,
  Which is the god of my idolatry,
  And I'll believe thee.

ROMEO.   If my heart's dear love—

JULIET. Well, do not swear: although I joy in thee,
  I have no joy of this contract to-night:
  It is too rash, too unadvised, too sudden;
  Too like the lightning, which doth cease to be
  Ere one can say 'It lightens.' Sweet, good night!   120
  This bud of love, by summer's ripening breath,
  May prove a beauteous flower when next we meet.
  Good night, good night! as sweet repose and rest
  Come to thy heart as that within my breast!

ROMEO. O, wilt thou leave me so unsatisfied?

JULIET. What satisfaction canst thou have to-night?

ROMEO. The exchange of thy love's faithful vow for mine.

JULIET. I gave thee mine before thou didst request it:
  And yet I would it were to give again.

ROMEO. Wouldst thou withdraw it? for what purpose, love?   130

JULIET. But to be frank, and give it thee again.
  And yet I wish but for the thing I have:
  My bounty is as boundless as the sea,
  My love as deep; the more I give to thee,

---

98. *fond*, foolish.   101. *strange*, reserved.   106. *discovered*, revealed.   110. *orb*, equivalent to *sphere;* see above, line 17.   131. *frank*, liberal, bounteous.

The more I have, for both are infinite.   (NURSE *calls within*.)
I hear some noise within; dear love, adieu!
Anon, good nurse! Sweet Montague, be true.
Stay but a little; I will come again.   (*Exit, above*.)
ROMEO. O blessed, blessed night! I am afeard,
  Being in night, all this is but a dream,   140
  Too flattering-sweet to be substantial.

(*Re-enter* JULIET, *above*.)
JULIET. Three words, dear Romeo, and good night indeed.
  If that thy bent of love be honourable,
  Thy purpose marriage, send me word to-morrow,
  By one that I'll procure to come to thee,
  Where and what time thou wilt perform the rite;
  And all my fortunes at thy foot I'll lay
  And follow thee my lord throughout the world.
NURSE (*within*). Madam!
JULIET. I come, anon.—But if thou mean'st not well,   150
  I do beseech thee—
NURSE (*within*). Madam!
JULIET.   By and by, I come:—
  To cease thy suit, and leave me to my grief:
  To-morrow will I send.
ROMEO.   So thrive my soul—
JULIET. A thousand times good night!   (*Exit, above*.)
ROMEO. A thousand times the worse, to want thy light.
  Love goes toward love, as schoolboys from their books,
  But love from love, toward school with heavy looks.   (*Retiring*.)

(*Re-enter* JULIET, *above*.)
JULIET. Hist! Romeo, hist! O, for a falconer's voice,
  To lure this tassel-gentle back again!   160
  Bondage is hoarse, and may not speak aloud;
  Else would I tear the cave where Echo lies,
  And make her airy tongue more hoarse than mine,
  With repetition of my Romeo's name.
ROMEO. It is my soul that calls upon my name:
  How silver-sweet sound lovers' tongues by night,
  Like softest music to attending ears!
JULIET. Romeo!
ROMEO.   My dear?
JULIET.   At what o'clock to-morrow
  Shall I send to thee?

143. *bent*, purpose; from the idea of the tension of a bow.   145. *procure*, cause.
151. *By and by*, immediately.   160. *tassel-gentle*, tercel-gentle, the male of the
goshawk.

ROMEO.   At the hour of nine.
JULIET. I will not fail: 'tis twenty years till then.   170
   I have forgot why I did call thee back.
ROMEO. Let me stand here till thou remember it.
JULIET. I shall forget, to have thee still stand there,
   Remembering how I love thy company.
ROMEO. And I'll still stay, to have thee still forget,
   Forgetting any other home but this.
JULIET. 'Tis almost morning; I would have thee gone:
   And yet no further than a wanton's bird;
   Who lets it hop a little from her hand,
   Like a poor prisoner in his twisted gyves,   180
   And with a silk thread plucks it back again,
   So loving-jealous of his liberty.
ROMEO. I would I were thy bird.
JULIET.   Sweet, so would I:
   Yet I should kill thee with much cherishing.
   Good night, good night! parting is such sweet sorrow,
   That I shall say good night till it be morrow.   *(Exit, above.)*
ROMEO. Sleep dwell upon thine eyes, peace in thy breast!
   Would I were sleep and peace, so sweet to rest!
   Hence will I to my ghostly father's cell,
   His help to crave, and my dear hap to tell.   *(Exit.)* 190

SCENE 3: *Friar Laurence's cell.*

(Enter FRIAR LAURENCE, *with a basket.)*
FRIAR LAURENCE. The grey-eyed morn smiles on the frowning night,
   Chequering the eastern clouds with streaks of light,
   And flecked darkness like a drunkard reels
   From forth day's path and Titan's fiery wheels:
   Now, ere the sun advance his burning eye,
   The day to cheer and night's dank dew to dry,
   I must up-fill this osier cage of ours
   With baleful weeds and precious-juiced flowers.
   The earth that's nature's mother is her tomb;
   What is her burying grave that is her womb,   10
   And from her womb children of divers kind
   We sucking on her natural bosom find,
   Many for many virtues excellent,
   None but for some and yet all different.

173. *still,* always. 180. *gyves,* fetters. 189. *ghostly,* spiritual. 190. *dear hap,*
good fortune.
SCENE 3. 3. *flecked,* dappled. 4. *Titan's.* Helios, the sun god, was a descendant
of the race of Titans. 7. *osier cage,* willow basket.

O, mickle is the powerful grace that lies
In herbs, plants, stones, and their true qualities:
For nought so vile that on the earth doth live
But to the earth some special good doth give,
Nor aught so good but strain'd from that fair use
Revolts from true birth, stumbling on abuse: 20
Virtue itself turns vice, being misapplied;
And vice sometimes by action dignified.
Within the infant rind of this small flower
Poison hath residence and medicine power:
For this, being smelt, with that part cheers each part;
Being tasted, slays all senses with the heart.
Two such opposed kings encamp them still
In man as well as herbs, grace and rude will;
And where the worser is predominant,
Full soon the canker death eats up that plant.   30

(*Enter* ROMEO.)
ROMEO. Good morrow, father.
FRIAR LAURENCE.   Benedicite!
What early tongue so sweet saluteth me?
Young son, it argues a distemper'd head
So soon to bid good morrow to thy bed:
Care keeps his watch in every old man's eye,
And where care lodges, sleep will never lie;
But where unbruised youth with unstuff'd brain
Doth couch his limbs, there golden sleep doth reign:
Therefore thy earliness doth me assure
Thou art up-roused by some distemperature;   40
Or if not so, then here I hit it right,
Our Romeo hath not been in bed to-night.
ROMEO. That last is true; the sweeter rest was mine.
FRIAR LAURENCE. God pardon sin! wast thou with Rosaline?
ROMEO. With Rosaline, my ghostly father? no;
I have forgot that name, and that name's woe.
FRIAR LAURENCE. That's my good son: but where hast thou been, then?
ROMEO. I'll tell thee, ere thou ask it me again.
I have been feasting with mine enemy,
Where on a sudden one hath wounded me,   50
That 's by me wounded: both our remedies

15. *mickle*, great. *grace*, beneficent virtue. 16. *qualities*, properties. 30. *canker*, cankerworm. 33. *distemper'd*, ill; a reference to a state of the humors in the body. 34. *morrow*, morning. 37. *unstuff'd*, not overcharged; another reference to the state of the humors.

Within thy help and holy physic lies:
I bear no hatred, blessed man, for, lo,
My intercession likewise steads my foe.
FRIAR LAURENCE. Be plain, good son, and homely in thy drift;
Riddling confession finds but riddling shrift.
ROMEO. Then plainly know my heart's dear love is set
On the fair daughter of rich Capulet:
As mine on hers, so hers is set on mine;
And all combined, save what thou must combine   60
By holy marriage: when and where and how
We met, we woo'd and made exchange of vow,
I'll tell thee as we pass; but this I pray,
That thou consent to marry us to-day.
FRIAR LAURENCE. Holy Saint Francis, what a change is here!
Is Rosaline, whom thou didst love so dear,
So soon forsaken? young men's love then lies
Not truly in their hearts, but in their eyes.
Jesu Maria, what a deal of brine
Hath wash'd thy sallow cheeks for Rosaline!   70
How much salt water thrown away in waste,
To season love, that of it doth not taste!
The sun not yet thy sighs from heaven clears,
Thy old groans ring yet in my ancient ears;
Lo, here upon thy cheek the stain doth sit
Of an old tear that is not wash'd off yet:
If e'er thou wast thyself and these woes thine,
Thou and these woes were all for Rosaline:
And art thou changed? pronounce this sentence then,
Women may fall, when there's no strength in men.   80
ROMEO. Thou chid'st me oft for loving Rosaline.
FRIAR LAURENCE. For doting, not for loving, pupil mine.
ROMEO. And bad'st me bury love.
FRIAR LAURENCE.   Not in a grave,
To lay one in, another out to have.
ROMEO. I pray thee, chide not: she whom I love now
Doth grace for grace and love for love allow;
The other did not so.
FRIAR LAURENCE.   O, she knew well
Thy love did read by rote and could not spell.
But come, young waverer, come, go with me,
In one respect I'll thy assistant be;   90
For this alliance may so happy prove,

52. *physic*, medicine, healing property.   54. *steads*, helps.   88. *did read by rote*, was merely a matter of repeating conventional expressions of love.

To turn your households' rancour to pure love.

ROMEO. O, let us hence; I stand on sudden haste.

FRIAR LAURENCE. Wisely and slow; they stumble that run fast.   (*Exeunt.*)

SCENE 4: *A street.*

(*Enter* BENVOLIO *and* MERCUTIO.)

MERCUTIO. Where the devil should this Romeo be?
    Came he not home to-night?

BENVOLIO. Not to his father's; I spoke with his man.

MERCUTIO. Ah, that same pale hard-hearted wench, that Rosaline,
    Torments him so, that he will sure run mad.

BENVOLIO. Tybalt, the kinsman of old Capulet,
    Hath sent a letter to his father's house.

MERCUTIO. A challenge, on my life.

BENVOLIO. Romeo will answer it.

MERCUTIO. Any man that can write may answer a letter.   10

BENVOLIO. Nay, he will answer the letter's master, how he dares, being
    dared.

MERCUTIO. Alas, poor Romeo! he is already dead; stabbed with a white
    wench's black eye; shot through the ear with a love-song; the very
    pin of his heart cleft with the blind bow-boy's butt-shaft: and is he
    a man to encounter Tybalt?   17

BENVOLIO. Why, what is Tybalt?

MERCUTIO. More than prince of cats, I can tell you. O, he is the coura-
    geous captain of complements. He fights as you sing prick-song,
    keeps time, distance, and proportion; rests me his minim rest, one,
    two, and the third in your bosom: the very butcher of a silk button,
    a duellist, a duellist; a gentleman of the very first house, of the very
    first and second cause: ah, the immortal passado! the punto reverso!
    the hai!   27

BENVOLIO. The what?

MERCUTIO. The pox of such antic, lisping, affecting fantasticoes; these
    new tuners of accents! 'By Jesu, a very good blade! a very tall man!
    a very good whore!' Why, is not this a lamentable thing, grandsire,

93. *stand on,* am in a position calling for.
SCENE 4. 15. *pin,* peg in the center of a target.   16. *butt-shaft,* an unbarbed
arrow.   19. *prince of cats.* The name of the king of cats in *Reynard the Fox* was
Tybalt.   20. *captain of complements,* master of ceremony and outward show.
21. *prick-song,* music written out.   22. *proportion,* rhythm.   23. *minim,* half
measure in music.   24. *butcher of a silk button,* one able to strike a button on
his adversary's person.   26. *first house,* possibly of the best school of fencing.
first and second cause, ready to quarrel for a trifle; probably an allusion to the
supposed code of quarreling.   27. *passado,* forward thrust. *punto reverso,* back-
handed stroke. *hai,* home thrust.   30. *fantasticoes,* coxcombs.   31. *accents,* language. *tall,* fine.

that we should be thus afflicted with these strange flies, these fash-
ion-mongers, these perdona-mi's, who stand so much on the new
form, that they cannot sit at ease on the old bench? O, their bones,
their bones!   37

(*Enter* ROMEO.)

BENVOLIO. Here comes Romeo, here comes Romeo.

MERCUTIO. Without his roe, like a dried herring: O flesh, flesh, how art
thou fishified! Now is he for the numbers that Petrarch flowed in:
Laura to his lady was but a kitchen-wench; marry, she had a better
love to be-rhyme her; Dido a dowdy; Cleopatra a gipsy; Helen and
Hero hildings and harlots; Thisbe a grey eye or so, but not to the
purpose. Signior Romeo, bon jour! there 's a French salutation to
your French slop. You gave us the counterfeit fairly last night.

ROMEO. Good morrow to you both. What counterfeit did I give you?   50

MERCUTIO. The slip, sir, the slip; can you not conceive?

ROMEO. Pardon, good Mercutio, my business was great; and in such a
case as mine a man may strain courtesy.

MERCUTIO. That's as much as to say, such a case as yours constrains a
man to bow in the hams.

ROMEO. Meaning, to court'sy.

MERCUTIO. Thou hast most kindly hit it.

ROMEO. A most courteous exposition.   60

MERCUTIO. Nay, I am the very pink of courtesy.

ROMEO. Pink for flower.

MERCUTIO. Right.

ROMEO. Why, then is my pump well flowered.

MERCUTIO. Well said: follow me this jest now till thou hast worn out
thy pump, that when the single sole of it is worn, the jest may remain after the wearing sole singular.

ROMEO. O single-soled jest, solely singular for the singleness!   70

MERCUTIO. Come between us, good Benvolio; my wits faint.

ROMEO. Switch and spurs, switch and spurs; or I'll cry a match.

35. *flies,* affected persons. *perdona-mi's,* Italian for "pardon me's"; a reference to the affectation of using foreign phrases. 36–37. *form . . . bench.*
Form means both "fashion" and "bench." 37. *bones,* French *bon* with play
on English "bone." 39. *Without his roe,* sometimes explained as a pun on
first syllable of Romeo's name, in which case the last syllables might be taken
as an expression of woe. 41. *Petrarch,* Italian poet of the Renaissance who addressed his sonnets to Laura. 45. *hildings,* good-for-nothings. 48. *slop,* loose
trousers of French fashion. *fairly,* handsomely. 51. *slip.* Counterfeit coins were
called "slips." 56. *case,* mask. 59. *kindly,* naturally. 64. *is my pump well
flowered.* The pump is pinked or perforated in ornamental figures. 69. *single-
soled,* thin; contemptible, with pun on "soul." 70. *singleness,* feebleness. 74.
cry a match, claim a victory.

MERCUTIO. Nay, if thy wits run the wild-goose chase, I have done, for thou hast more of the wild-goose in one of thy wits than, I am sure, I have in my whole five: was I with you there for the goose?

ROMEO. Thou wast never with me for any thing when thou wast not there for the goose.

MERCUTIO. I will bite thee by the ear for that jest.

ROMEO. Nay, good goose, bite not.   82

MERCUTIO. Thy wit is a very bitter sweeting; it is a most sharp sauce.

ROMEO. And is it not well served in to a sweet goose?

MERCUTIO. O, here 's a wit of cheveril, that stretches from an inch narrow to an ell broad!

ROMEO. I stretch it out for that word 'broad;' which added to the goose, proves thee far and wide a broad goose.   91

MERCUTIO. Why, is not this better now than groaning for love? now art thou sociable, now art thou Romeo; now art thou what thou art, by art as well as by nature: for this drivelling love is like a great natural, that runs lolling up and down to hide his bauble in a hole.

BENVOLIO. Stop there, stop there.

MERCUTIO. Thou desirest me to stop in my tale against the hair.   100

BENVOLIO. Thou wouldst else have made thy tale large.

MERCUTIO. O, thou art deceived; I would have made it short: for I was come to the whole depth of my tale; and meant, indeed, to occupy the argument no longer.

ROMEO. Here 's goodly gear!

(*Enter* NURSE *and* PETER.)

MERCUTIO. A sail, a sail!

BENVOLIO. Two, two; a shirt and a smock.

NURSE. Peter!   110

PETER. Anon!

NURSE. My fan, Peter.

MERCUTIO. Good Peter, to hide her face; for her fan 's the fairer face.

NURSE. God ye good morrow, gentlemen.

MERCUTIO. God ye good den, fair gentlewoman.

NURSE. Is it good den?

MERCUTIO. 'Tis no less, I tell you, for the bawdy hand of the dial is now upon the prick of noon.

---

75. *wild-goose chase,* a horse race in which the leading rider might force his competitors to follow him wherever he went.   83. *sweeting,* probably a pun on an apple called the "sweeting."   87. *cheveril,* kid leather.   91. *broad goose,* possibly means that Mercutio is known far and wide as a goose.   96. *natural,* idiot.   100. *against the hair,* against the grain.   107. *gear,* general word meaning "substance" or "stuff."   109. *a shirt . . . smock,* a man and a woman.   119. *prick,* point on the dial of a clock.

NURSE. Out upon you! what a man are you!   120
ROMEO. One, gentlewoman, that God hath made for himself to mar.
NURSE. By my troth, it is well said; 'for himself to mar,' quoth a'?
    Gentlemen, can any of you tell me where I may find the young
    Romeo?
ROMEO. I can tell you; but young Romeo will be older when you have
    found him than he was when you sought him: I am the youngest of
    that name, for fault of a worse.
NURSE. You say well.   130
MERCUTIO. Yea, is the worst well? very well took, i' faith; wisely, wisely.
NURSE. If you be he, sir, I desire some confidence with you.
BENVOLIO. She will indite him to some supper.
MERCUTIO. A bawd, a bawd, a bawd! So ho!
ROMEO. What hast thou found?
MERCUTIO. No hare, sir; unless a hare, sir, in a lenten pie, that is some-
    thing stale and hoar ere it be spent.   (*Sings.*)

> An old hare hoar,   141
> And an old hare hoar,
> Is very good meat in lent:
> But a hare that is hoar
> Is too much for a score,
> When it hoars ere it be spent.

Romeo, will you come to your father's? we'll to dinner, thither.
ROMEO. I will follow you.
MERCUTIO. Farewell, ancient lady; farewell, (*singing*) 'lady, lady, lady.'
                            (*Exeunt* MERCUTIO *and* BENVOLIO.) 151
NURSE. Marry, farewell! I pray you, sir, what saucy merchant was this,
    that was so full of his ropery?
ROMEO. A gentleman, nurse, that loves to hear himself talk, and will
    speak more in a minute than he will stand to in a month.   157
NURSE. An a' speak any thing against me, I'll take him down, an a'
    were lustier than he is, and twenty such Jacks; and if I cannot, I'll
    find those that shall. Scurvy knave! I am none of his flirt-gills; I am
    none of his skains-mates. And thou must stand by too, and suffer
    every knave to use me at his pleasure?
PETER. I saw no man use you at his pleasure; if I had, my weapon

120. *Out upon you*, expression of indignation. 134. *confidence*, the nurse's mistake for "conference." 135. *indite*, Benvolio's malapropism for "invite." 138.
hare, used as a slang word for "courtesan." 144. *hoar*, moldy. 151. *'lady, lady,
lady,'* refrain from the ballad *Chaste Susanna.* 153. *merchant*, fellow. 154.
ropery, the nurse's mistake for "roguery." 160. *Jacks*, used as a term of disparagement. 162. *flirt-gills*, loose women. 163. *skains-mates*, not well understood; sometimes connected with "skein" (of thread) or with "skain," a dagger.

should quickly have been out, I warrant you: I dare draw as soon
as another man, if I see occasion in a good quarrel, and the law on
my side.   169

NURSE. Now, afore God, I am so vexed, that every part about me
quivers. Scurvy knave! Pray you, sir, a word: and as I told you, my
young lady bade me inquire you out; what she bade me say, I will
keep to myself: but first let me tell ye, if ye should lead her into a
fool's paradise, as they say, it were a very gross kind of behaviour, as
they say: for the gentlewoman is young; and, therefore, if you
should deal double with her, truly it were an ill thing to be offered
to any gentlewoman, and very weak dealing.   181

ROMEO. Nurse, commend me to thy lady and mistress. I protest unto
thee—

NURSE. Good heart, and, i' faith, I will tell her as much: Lord, Lord,
she will be a joyful woman.

ROMEO. What wilt thou tell her, nurse? thou dost not mark me.

NURSE. I will tell her, sir, that you do protest; which, as I take it, is a
gentlemanlike offer.

ROMEO. Bid her devise   191
    Some means to come to shrift this afternoon;
    And there she shall at Friar Laurence' cell
    Be shrived and married. Here is for thy pains.

NURSE. No, truly, sir; not a penny.

ROMEO. Go to; I say you shall.

NURSE. This afternoon, sir? well, she shall be there.

ROMEO. And stay, good nurse, behind the abbey wall:
    Within this hour my man shall be with thee,   200
    And bring thee cords made like a tackled stair;
    Which to the high top-gallant of my joy
    Must be my convoy in the secret night.
    Farewell; be trusty, and I'll quit thy pains:
    Farewell; commend me to thy mistress.

NURSE. Now God in heaven bless thee! Hark you, sir.

ROMEO. What say'st thou, my dear nurse?

NURSE. Is your man secret, Did you ne'er hear say, Two may keep
counsel, putting one away?

ROMEO. I warrant thee, my man 's as true as steel.   210

NURSE. Well, sir; my mistress is the sweetest lady—Lord, Lord! when
'twas a little prating thing:—O, there is a nobleman in town, one
Paris, that would fain lay knife aboard; but she, good soul, had as
lief see a toad, a very toad, as see him. I anger her sometimes and

---

183. *protest*, vow. 188. *mark*, attend to. 201. *tackled stair*, rope ladder. 202.
top-gallant, summit. 203. *convoy*, a thing that conducts. 204. *quit*, reward,
requite. 208. *secret*, trustworthy.

tell her that Paris is the properer man; but, I'll warrant you, when
I say so, she looks as pale as any clout in the versal world. Doth not
rosemary and Romeo begin both with a letter?   220

ROMEO. Ay, nurse; what of that? both with an R.

NURSE. Ah, mocker! that 's the dog's name; R is for the—No; I know
it begins with some other letter:—and she hath the prettiest sententious of it, of you and rosemary, that it would do you good to
hear it.

ROMEO. Commend me to thy lady.

NURSE. Ay, a thousand times. (*Exit* ROMEO.) Peter!   230

PETER. Anon!

NURSE. Peter, take my fan, and go before, and apace.   (*Exeunt.*)

SCENE 5: *Capulet's orchard.*

(*Enter* JULIET.)

JULIET. The clock struck nine when I did send the nurse;
   In half an hour she promised to return.
   Perchance she cannot meet him: that 's not so.
   O, she is lame! love's heralds should be thoughts,
   Which ten times faster glide than the sun's beams,
   Driving back shadows over louring hills:
   Therefore do nimble-pinion'd doves draw love,
   And therefore hath the wind-swift Cupid wings.
   Now is the sun upon the highmost hill
   Of this day's journey, and from nine till twelve   10
   Is three long hours, yet she is not come.
   Had she affections and warm youthful blood,
   She would be as swift in motion as a ball;
   My words would bandy her to my sweet love,
   And his to me:
   But old folks, many feign as they were dead;
   Unwieldy, slow, heavy and pale as lead.
   O God, she comes!

(*Enter* NURSE *and* PETER.)
            O honey nurse, what news?

217. *properer,* handsomer. 219. *clout,* rag; a proverbial expression. *versal,*
universal. 220. *a,* the same. 223. *the dog's name.* The letter *R* was thought to
resemble the dog's growl. 226. *sententious.* The nurse probably means "sentences," pithy sayings.
SCENE 5. 7. *love,* Venus, whose chariot was drawn by doves. 14. *bandy,* toss to
and fro. 16. *many,* Johnson: *marry.*

Hast thou met with him? Send thy man away.

NURSE. Peter, stay at the gate.   (*Exit* PETER.)   20

JULIET. Now, good sweet nurse,—O Lord, why look'st thou sad?

Though news be sad, yet tell them merrily;

If good, thou shamest the music of sweet news

By playing it to me with so sour a face.

NURSE. I am a-weary, give me leave awhile:

Fie, how my bones ache! what a jaunce have I had!

JULIET. I would thou hadst my bones, and I thy news.

Nay, come, I pray thee, speak; good, good nurse, speak.

NURSE. Jesu, what haste? can you not stay awhile?

Do you not see that I am out of breath?   30

JULIET. How art thou out of breath, when thou hast breath

To say to me that thou art out of breath?

The excuse that thou dost make in this delay

Is longer than the tale thou dost excuse.

Is thy news good, or bad? answer to that;

Say either, and I'll stay the circumstance:

Let me be satisfied, is 't good or bad?

NURSE. Well, you have made a simple choice; you know not how to
choose a man: Romeo! no, not he; though his face be better than
any man's, yet his leg excels all men's; and for a hand, and a foot,
and a body, though they be not to be talked on, yet they are past
compare: he is not the flower of courtesy, but, I'll warrant him, as
gentle as a lamb. Go thy ways, wench; serve God. What, have you
dined at home?   46

JULIET. No, no: but all this did I know before.

What says he of our marriage? what of that?

NURSE. Lord, how my head aches! what a head have I!

It beats as it would fall in twenty pieces.   50

My back o' t' other side,—O my back, my back!

Beshrew your heart for sending me about,

To catch my death with jaunting up and down!

JULIET. I' faith, I am sorry that thou art not well.

Sweet, sweet, sweet nurse, tell me, what says my love?

NURSE. Your love says, like an honest gentleman, and a courteous,
and a kind, and a handsome, and, I warrant, a virtuous,—Where is
your mother?

JULIET. Where is my mother! why, she is within;   60

Where should she be? How oddly thou repliest!

'Your love says, like an honest gentleman,

Where is your mother?'

---

25. *give me leave*, let me alone. 36. *stay the circumstance*, await details. 52.
Beshrew, common objurgation meaning "ill-luck."

NURSE.   O God's lady dear!
  Are you so hot? marry, come up, I trow;
  Is this the poultice for my aching bones?
  Henceforward do your messages yourself.
JULIET. Here 's such a coil! come, what says Romeo?
NURSE. Have you got leave to go to shrift to-day?
JULIET. I have.
NURSE. Then hie you hence to Friar Laurence' cell;
  There stays a husband to make you a wife: 71
  Now comes the wanton blood up in your cheeks,
  They'll be in scarlet straight at any news.
  Hie you to church; I must another way,
  To fetch a ladder, by the which your love
  Must climb a bird's nest soon when it is dark:
  I am the drudge and toil in your delight,
  But you shall bear the burden soon at night.
  Go; I'll to dinner; hie you to the cell.
JULIET. Hie to high fortune! Honest nurse, farewell.   (*Exeunt.*) 80

SCENE 6: *Friar Laurence's cell.*

(*Enter* FRIAR LAURENCE *and* ROMEO.)
FRIAR LAURENCE. So smile the heavens upon this holy act,
  That after hours with sorrow chide us not!
ROMEO. Amen, amen! but come what sorrow can,
  It cannot countervail the exchange of joy
  That one short minute gives me in her sight:
  Do thou but close our hands with holy words,
  Then love-devouring death do what he dare;
  It is enough I may but call her mine.
FRIAR LAURENCE. These violent delights have violent ends
  And in their triumph die, like fire and powder,   10
  Which as they kiss consume: the sweetest honey
  Is loathsome in his own deliciousness
  And in the taste confounds the appetite:
  Therefore love moderately; long love doth so;
  Too swift arrives as tardy as too slow.

(*Enter* JULIET.)
  Here comes the lady: O, so light a foot
  Will ne'er wear out the everlasting flint:

64. *come up,* expressive of impatience like "go to."   67. *coil,* turmoil, bustle.
SCENE 6. 4. *countervail,* equal.   9. *These violent delights,* etc., express a
premonition of evil.   13. *confounds,* destroys.

A lover may bestride the gossamer
That idles in the wanton summer air,
And yet not fall; so light is vanity.   20
JULIET. Good even to my ghostly confessor.
FRIAR LAURENCE. Romeo shall thank thee, daughter, for us both.
JULIET. As much to him, else is his thanks too much.
ROMEO. Ah, Juliet, if the measure of thy joy
Be heap'd like mine and that thy skill be more
To blazon it, then sweeten with thy breath
This neighbour air, and let rich music's tongue
Unfold the imagined happiness that both
Receive in either by this dear encounter.
JULIET. Conceit, more rich in matter than in words,   30
Brags of his substance, not of ornament:
They are but beggars that can count their worth;
But my true love is grown to such excess
I cannot sum up sum of half my wealth.
FRIAR LAURENCE. Come, come with me, and we will make short work;
For, by your leaves, you shall not stay alone
Till holy church incorporate two in one.   (*Exeunt.*)

ACT III

SCENE 1: *A public place.*

(*Enter* MERCUTIO, BENVOLIO, PAGE, *and* SERVANTS.)
BENVOLIO. I pray thee, good Mercutio, let 's retire:
The day is hot, the Capulets abroad,
And, if we meet, we shall not scape a brawl;
For now, these hot days, is the mad blood stirring.
MERCUTIO. Thou art like one of those fellows that when he enters the
confines of a tavern claps me his sword upon the table and says
'God send me no need of thee!' and by the operation of the second
cup draws it on the drawer, when indeed there is no need.   10
BENVOLIO. Am I like such a fellow?
MERCUTIO. Come, come, thou art as hot a Jack in thy mood as any in
Italy, and as soon moved to be moody, and as soon moody to be
moved.
BENVOLIO. And what to?
MERCUTIO. Nay, an there were two such, we should have none shortly,
for one would kill the other. Thou! why, thou wilt quarrel with a

18. *gossamer,* spider's thread. 26. *blazon,* heraldic term meaning "to describe"
or "to set forth." 28. *Unfold,* make known. 30. *Conceit,* imagination, thought.
ACT III, SCENE 1. 2. *The day is hot.* This offers a little touch of Italian atmosphere. 14. *moody,* angry.

man that hath a hair more, or a hair less, in his beard, than thou hast:
thou wilt quarrel with a man for cracking nuts, having no other
reason but because thou hast hazel eyes: what eye but such an eye
would spy out such a quarrel? Thy head is as full of quarrels as an
egg is full of meat, and yet thy head hath been beaten as addle as
an egg for quarrelling: thou hast quarrelled with a man for coughing in the street, because he hath wakened thy dog that hath lain
asleep in the sun: didst thou not fall out with a tailor for wearing
his new doublet before Easter? with another, for tying his new shoes
with old riband? and yet thou wilt tutor me from quarrelling!   33
BENVOLIO. An I were so apt to quarrel as thou art, any man should
    buy the fee-simple of my life for an hour and a quarter.
MERCUTIO. The fee simple! O simple!
BENVOLIO. By my head, here come the Capulets.
MERCUTIO. By my heel, I care not.

(*Enter* TYBALT *and others.*)
TYBALT. Follow me close, for I will speak to them.   40
    Gentlemen, good den: a word with one of you.
MERCUTIO. And but one word with one of us? couple it with some-
    thing; make it a word and a blow.
TYBALT. You shall find me apt enough to that, sir, an you will give
    me occasion.
MERCUTIO. Could you not take some occasion without giving?
TYBALT. Mercutio, thou consort'st with Romeo,—
MERCUTIO. Consort! what, dost thou make us minstrels? an thou make
    minstrels of us, look to hear nothing but discords: here 's my fiddle-
    stick; here 's that shall make you dance. 'Zounds, consort!   52
BENVOLIO. We talk here in the public haunt of men:
    Either withdraw unto some private place,
    And reason coldly of your grievances,
    Or else depart; here all eyes gaze on us.
MERCUTIO. Men's eyes were made to look, and let them gaze;
    I will not budge for no man's pleasure, I.

(*Enter* ROMEO.)
TYBALT. Well, peace be with you, sir: here comes my man.
MERCUTIO. But I'll be hang'd, sir, if he wear your livery: 60
    Marry, go before to field, he'll be your follower;
    Your worship in that sense may call him 'man.'
TYBALT. Romeo, the hate I bear thee can afford
    No better term than this,—thou art a villain.

47. *consort'st.* To *consort* meant "to accompany" and also "to attend or wait
upon." 52. *'Zounds,* a modified form of the oath, "by God's wounds." 61. *field,*
field of encounter.

ROMEO. Tybalt, the reason that I have to love thee
   Doth much excuse the appertaining rage
   To such a greeting: villain am I none;
   Therefore farewell; I see thou know'st me not.
TYBALT. Boy, this shall not excuse the injuries
   That thou hast done me; therefore turn and draw.   70
ROMEO. I do protest, I never injured thee,
   But love thee better than thou canst devise,
   Till thou shalt know the reason of my love:
   And so, good Capulet,—which name I tender
   As dearly as my own,—be satisfied.
MERCUTIO. O calm, dishonourable, vile submission!
   Alla stoccata carries it away.   (Draws.)
   Tybalt, you rat-catcher, will you walk?
TYBALT. What wouldst thou have with me?   79
MERCUTIO. Good king of cats, nothing but one of your nine lives; that
   I mean to make bold withal, and, as you shall use me hereafter,
   dry-beat the rest of the eight. Will you pluck your sword out of his
   pilcher by the ears? make haste, lest mine be about your ears ere it
   be out.
TYBALT. I am for you.   (Drawing.)
ROMEO. Gentle Mercutio, put thy rapier up.
MERCUTIO. Come, sir, your passado.   (They fight.)
ROMEO. Draw, Benvolio; beat down their weapons.
   Gentlemen, for shame, forbear this outrage!   90
   Tybalt, Mercutio, the prince expressly hath
   Forbidden bandying in Verona streets:
   Hold, Tybalt! good Mercutio!

                            (TYBALT under ROMEO's arm stabs MERCUTIO,
                                      and flies with his followers.)

MERCUTIO.   I am hurt.
   A plague o' both your houses! I am sped.
   Is he gone, and hath nothing?
BENVOLIO.   What, art thou hurt?
MERCUTIO. Ay, ay, a scratch, a scratch; marry, 'tis enough.
   Where is my page? Go, villain, fetch a surgeon.   (Exit PAGE.)
ROMEO. Courage, man; the hurt cannot be much.   98
MERCUTIO. No, 'tis not so deep as a well, nor so wide as a church-
   door; but 'tis enough, 'twill serve: ask for me to-morrow, and you
   shall find me a grave man. I am peppered, I warrant, for this world.

---

77. *Alla stoccata*, Italian, "with the thrust"; i.e., the fencing master wins the
victory.   78. *rat-catcher*, an allusion to Tybalt as king of cats (see II, 4, 19).   81.
make bold, make free with.   83. *dry-beat*, beat soundly.   84. *pilcher*, scabbard.
88. *passado*, forward thrust; used derisively.   94. *sped*, done for.   102. *grave
man*. Mercutio thus makes puns with his last breath.

A plague o' both your houses! 'Zounds, a dog, a rat, a mouse, a cat,
to scratch a man to death! a braggart, a rogue, a villain, that fights
by the book of arithmetic! Why the devil came you between us? I
was hurt under your arm.

ROMEO. I thought all for the best.

MERCUTIO. Help me into some house, Benvolio,   110
  Or I shall faint. A plague o' both your houses!
  They have made worms' meat of me: I have it,
  And soundly too: your houses!   (*Exeunt* MERCUTIO *and* BENVOLIO.)

ROMEO. This gentleman, the prince's near ally,
  My very friend, hath got his mortal hurt
  In my behalf; my reputation stain'd
  With Tybalt's slander,—Tybalt, that an hour
  Hath been my kinsman! O sweet Juliet,
  Thy beauty hath made me effeminate
  And in my temper soften'd valour's steel!   120

(*Re-enter* BENVOLIO.)

BENVOLIO. O Romeo, Romeo, brave Mercutio's dead!
  That gallant spirit hath aspired the clouds,
  Which too untimely here did scorn the earth.

ROMEO. This day's black fate on moe days doth depend;
  This but begins the woe others must end.

BENVOLIO. Here comes the furious Tybalt back again.

ROMEO. Alive, in triumph! and Mercutio slain!
  Away to heaven, respective lenity,
  And fire-eyed fury be my conduct now!

(*Re-enter* TYBALT.)

  Now, Tybalt, take the villain back again,   130
  That late thou gavest me; for Mercutio's soul
  Is but a little way above our heads,
  Staying for thine to keep him company:
  Either thou, or I, or both, must go with him.

TYBALT. Thou, wretched boy, that didst consort him here,
  Shalt with him hence.

ROMEO.   This shall determine that.
                                   (*They fight;* TYBALT *falls.*)

BENVOLIO. Romeo, away, be gone!
  The citizens are up, and Tybalt slain.
  Stand not amazed: the prince will doom thee death,

106. *by the book of arithmetic*, merely by theory. Back of the whole scene lies a
current controversy between the old broadsword style of fencing and the new
French style of rapier fencing.   114. *ally*, kinsman.   115. *very*, true.   124. *moe*,
more.   128. *respective lenity*, considerate gentleness.   129. *conduct*, guide.   139.
doom, adjudge.

If thou art taken: hence, be gone, away!   140
ROMEO. O, I am fortune's fool!
BENVOLIO.   Why dost thou stay?   (*Exit* ROMEO.)

(*Enter* CITIZENS, &c.)
FIRST CITIZEN. Which way ran he that kill'd Mercutio?
   Tybalt, that murderer, which way ran he?
BENVOLIO. There lies that Tybalt.
FIRST CITIZEN.   Up, sir, go with me;
   I charge thee in the prince's name, obey.

(*Enter* PRINCE, *attended;* MONTAGUE, CAPULET, *their*
   WIVES, *and others.*)
PRINCE. Where are the vile beginners of this fray?
BENVOLIO. O noble prince, I can discover all
   The unlucky manage of this fatal brawl:
   There lies the man, slain by young Romeo,
   That slew thy kinsman, brave Mercutio.   150
LADY CAPULET. Tybalt, my cousin! O my brother's child!
   O prince! O cousin! husband! O, the blood is spilt
   Of my dear kinsman! Prince, as thou art true,
   For blood of ours, shed blood of Montague.
   O cousin, cousin!
PRINCE. Benvolio, who began this bloody fray?
BENVOLIO. Tybalt, here slain, whom Romeo's hand did slay;
   Romeo that spoke him fair, bade him bethink
   How nice the quarrel was, and urged withal
   Your high displeasure: all this uttered   160
   With gentle breath, calm look, knees humbly bow'd,
   Could not take truce with the unruly spleen
   Of Tybalt deaf to peace, but that he tilts
   With piercing steel at bold Mercutio's breast,
   Who, all as hot, turns deadly point to point,
   And, with a martial scorn, with one hand beats
   Cold death aside, and with the other sends
   It back to Tybalt, whose dexterity
   Retorts it: Romeo he cries aloud,
   'Hold, friends! friends, part!' and, swifter than his tongue,   170
   His agile arm beats down their fatal points,
   And 'twixt them rushes; underneath whose arm
   An envious thrust from Tybalt hit the life

141. *fortune's fool.* At this crucial moment in the play Romeo again alludes
to destiny. 148. *manage*, management. 158. *fair*, civilly. 159. *nice*, trivial.
162. *take truce*, make peace. *unruly spleen*, ungovernable rage. 163. *tilts*, strikes.
169. *Retorts*, throws back upon his adversary.

Of stout Mercutio, and then Tybalt fled;
But by and by comes back to Romeo,
Who had but newly entertain'd revenge,
And to 't they go like lightning, for, ere I
Could draw to part them, was stout Tybalt slain,
And, as he fell, did Romeo turn and fly.
This is the truth, or let Benvolio die.   180

LADY CAPULET. He is a kinsman to the Montague;
Affection makes him false; he speaks not true:
Some twenty of them fought in this black strife,
And all those twenty could but kill one life.
I beg for justice, which thou, prince, must give;
Romeo slew Tybalt, Romeo must not live.

PRINCE. Romeo slew him, he slew Mercutio;
Who now the price of his dear blood doth owe?

MONTAGUE. Not Romeo, prince, he was Mercutio's friend;
His fault concludes but what the law should end,   190
The life of Tybalt.

PRINCE.   And for that offence
Immediately we do exile him hence:
I have an interest in your hate's proceeding,
My blood for your rude brawls doth lie a-bleeding;
But I'll amerce you with so strong a fine
That you shall all repent the loss of mine:
I will be deaf to pleading and excuses;
Nor tears nor prayers shall purchase out abuses:
Therefore use none: let Romeo hence in haste,
Else, when he 's found, that hour is his last.   200
Bear hence this body and attend our will:
Mercy but murders, pardoning those that kill.   (*Exeunt.*)

SCENE 2: *Capulet's orchard.*

(*Enter* JULIET.)
JULIET. Gallop apace, you fiery-footed steeds,
    Towards Phœbus' lodging: such a waggoner
    As Phæthon would whip you to the west,

---

176. *entertain'd,* harbored thoughts of. 195. *amerce,* punish by fine. 198.
purchase out, redeem, exempt from penalty. *abuses,* misdeeds.
SCENE 2. 3. *Phæthon,* son of Helios, who was allowed to assume the reins of the
sun for a day; not being able to restrain the steeds, he had to be slain by the
thunderbolt of Jupiter in order that the universe might not be destroyed. 6.
runaways' eyes, a famous crux of which there is no satisfactory explanation. The
allusion to Phaethon (l. 3) may here be repeated. *wink,* shut.

And bring in cloudy night immediately.
Spread thy close curtain, love-performing night,
That runaways' eyes may wink, and Romeo
Leap to these arms, untalk'd of and unseen.
Lovers can see to do their amorous rites
By their own beauties; or, if love be blind,
It best agrees with night. Come, civil night,   10
Thou sober-suited matron, all in black,
And learn me how to lose a winning match,
Play'd for a pair of stainless maidenhoods:
Hood my unmann'd blood, bating in my cheeks,
With thy black mantle; till strange love, grown bold,
Think true love acted simple modesty.
Come, night; come, Romeo; come, thou day in night;
For thou wilt lie upon the wings of night
Whiter than new snow on a raven's back.
Come, gentle night, come, loving, black-brow'd night,
Give me my Romeo; and, when he shall die,   21
Take him and cut him out in little stars,
And he will make the face of heaven so fine
That all the world will be in love with night
And pay no worship to the garish sun.
O, I have bought the mansion of a love,
But not possess'd it, and, though I am sold,
Not yet enjoy'd: so tedious is this day
As is the night before some festival
To an impatient child that hath new robes   30
And may not wear them. O, here comes my nurse,
And she brings news; and every tongue that speaks
But Romeo's name speaks heavenly eloquence.

(*Enter* NURSE, *with cords.*)
    Now, nurse, what news? What hast thou there? the cords
    That Romeo bid thee fetch?
NURSE.   Ay, ay, the cords.   (*Throws them down.*)
JULIET. Ay me! what news? why dost thou wring thy hands?
NURSE. Ay, well-a-day; he 's dead, he 's dead, he 's dead!
    We are undone, lady, we are undone!
    Alack the day! he 's gone, he 's killed, he 's dead!
JULIET. Can heaven be so envious?
NURSE.   Romeo can,   40

10. *civil*, well-ordered.   14. *Hood*, cover; term in falconry. The hawk's eyes were covered so that it would not bate or beat the wings. *unmann'd*, another term in falconry meaning "untamed."   38. *undone*, ruined.

Though heaven cannot: O Romeo, Romeo!
Who ever would have thought it? Romeo!
JULIET. What devil art thou, that dost torment me thus?
This torture should be roar'd in dismal hell.
Hath Romeo slain himself? say thou but 'I,'
And that bare vowel 'I' shall poison more
Than the death-darting eye of cockatrice:
I am not I, if there be such an I;
Or those eyes shut, that make thee answer 'I.'
If he be slain, say 'I'; or if not, no: 50
Brief sounds determine of my weal or woe.
NURSE. I saw the wound, I saw it with mine eyes,—
God save the mark!—here on his manly breast:
A piteous corse, a bloody piteous corse;
Pale, pale as ashes, all bedaub'd in blood,
All in gore-blood; I swounded at the sight.
JULIET. O, break, my heart! poor bankrupt, break at once!
To prison, eyes, ne'er look on liberty!
Vile earth, to earth resign; end motion here;
And thou and Romeo press one heavy bier!   60
NURSE. O Tybalt, Tybalt, the best friend I had!
O courteous Tybalt! honest gentleman!
That ever I should live to see thee dead!
JULIET. What storm is this that blows so contrary?
Is Romeo slaughter'd, and is Tybalt dead?
My dear-loved cousin, and my dearer lord?
Then, dreadful trumpet, sound the general doom!
For who is living, if those two are gone?
NURSE. Tybalt is gone, and Romeo banished;
Romeo that kill'd him, he is banished.   70
JULIET. O God! did Romeo's hand shed Tybalt's blood?
NURSE. It did, it did; alas the day, it did!
JULIET. O serpent heart, hid with a flowering face!
Did ever dragon keep so fair a cave?
Beautiful tyrant! fiend angelical!
Dove-feather'd raven! wolvish-ravening lamb!
Despised substance of divinest show!
Just opposite to what thou justly seem'st,
A damned saint, an honourable villain!
O nature, what hadst thou to do in hell,   80

45. *'I,'* ay, yes. 47. *cockatrice*, basilisk, a fabulous serpent which could kill by
its look. 53. *God save the mark*, God forbid; a familiar oath originally intended
to avert ill omen. 56. *gore-blood*, clotted blood. 59. *motion*, power of movement.

When thou didst bower the spirit of a fiend
In mortal paradise of such sweet flesh?
Was ever book containing such vile matter
So fairly bound? O, that deceit should dwell
In such a gorgeous palace!

NURSE.   There 's no trust,
No faith, no honesty in men; all perjured,
All forsworn, all naught, all dissemblers.
Ah, where 's my man? give me some aqua vitæ:
These griefs, these woes, these sorrows make me old.
Shame come to Romeo!

JULIET.   Blister'd be thy tongue   90
For such a wish! he was not born to shame:
Upon his brow shame is ashamed to sit;
For 'tis a throne where honour may be crown'd
Sole monarch of the universal earth.
O, what a beast was I to chide at him!

NURSE. Will you speak well of him that kill'd your cousin?

JULIET. Shall I speak ill of him that is my husband?
Ah, poor my lord, what tongue shall smooth thy name,
When I, thy three-hours wife, have mangled it?
But, wherefore, villain, didst thou kill my cousin?   100
That villain cousin would have kill'd my husband:
Back, foolish tears, back to your native spring;
Your tributary drops belong to woe,
Which you, mistaking, offer up to joy.
My husband lives, that Tybalt would have slain;
And Tybalt 's dead, that would have slain my husband:
All this is comfort; wherefore weep I then?
Some word there was, worser than Tybalt's death,
That murder'd me: I would forget it fain;
But, O, it presses to my memory,   110
Like damned guilty deeds to sinners' minds:
'Tybalt is dead, and Romeo—banished;'
That 'banished,' that one word 'banished,'
Hath slain ten thousand Tybalts. Tybalt's death
Was woe enough, if it had ended there:
Or, if sour woe delights in fellowship
And needly will be rank'd with other griefs,
Why follow'd not, when she said 'Tybalt 's dead,'
Thy father, or thy mother, nay, or both,
Which modern lamentation might have moved?   120

---

81. *bower*, give lodging to.   87. *naught*, worthless.   117. *needly*, of necessity.
120. *modern*, ordinary.

But with a rearward following Tybalt's death,
'Romeo is banished,' to speak that word,
Is father, mother, Tybalt, Romeo, Juliet,
All slain, all dead. 'Romeo is banished!'
There is no end, no limit, measure, bound,
In that word's death; no words can that woe sound.
Where is my father, and my mother, nurse?

NURSE. Weeping and wailing over Tybalt's corse:
Will you go to them? I will bring you thither.

JULIET. Wash they his wounds with tears: mine shall be spent,   130
When theirs are dry, for Romeo's banishment.
Take up those cords: poor ropes, you are beguiled,
Both you and I; for Romeo is exiled:
He made you for a highway to my bed;
But I, a maid, die maiden-widowed.
Come, cords, come, nurse; I'll to my wedding-bed;
And death, not Romeo, take my maidenhead!

NURSE. Hie to your chamber: I'll find Romeo
To comfort you: I wot well where he is.
Hark ye, your Romeo will be here at night: 140
I'll to him; he is hid at Laurence' cell.

JULIET. O, find him! give this ring to my true knight,
And bid him come to take his last farewell.   (*Exeunt.*)

SCENE 3: *Friar Laurence's cell.*

(*Enter* FRIAR LAURENCE.)

FRIAR LAURENCE. Romeo, come forth; come forth, thou fearful man:
Affliction is enamour'd of thy parts,
And thou art wedded to calamity.

(*Enter* ROMEO.)

ROMEO. Father, what news? what is the prince's doom?
What sorrow craves acquaintance at my hand,
That I yet know not?

FRIAR LAURENCE.   Too familiar
Is my dear son with such sour company:
I bring thee tidings of the prince's doom.

ROMEO. What less than dooms-day is the prince's doom?

FRIAR LAURENCE. A gentler judgement vanish'd from his lips,   10
Not body's death, but body's banishment.

121. *rearward,* rear guard.   139. *wot,* know.
SCENE 3.   10. *vanish'd,* issued.

ROMEO. Ha, banishment! be merciful, say 'death;'
For exile hath more terror in his look,
Much more than death: do not say 'banishment.'
FRIAR LAURENCE. Hence from Verona art thou banished:
Be patient, for the world is broad and wide.
ROMEO. There is no world without Verona walls,
But purgatory, torture, hell itself.
Hence-banished is banish'd from the world,
And world's exile is death: then banished,   20
Is death mis-term'd; calling death banishment,
Thou cutt'st my head off with a golden axe,
And smilest upon the stroke that murders me.
FRIAR LAURENCE. O deadly sin! O rude unthankfulness!
Thy fault our law calls death; but the kind prince,
Taking thy part, hath rush'd aside the law,
And turn'd that black word death to banishment:
This is dear mercy, and thou seest it not.
ROMEO. 'Tis torture, and not mercy: heaven is here,
Where Juliet lives; and every cat and dog   30
And little mouse, every unworthy thing,
Live here in heaven and may look on her;
But Romeo may not: more validity,
More honourable state, more courtship lives
In carrion-flies than Romeo: they may seize
On the white wonder of dear Juliet's hand
And steal immortal blessing from her lips,
Who, even in pure and vestal modesty,
Still blush, as thinking their own kisses sin;
But Romeo may not; he is banished: 40
Flies may do this, but I from this must fly:
They are free men, but I am banished.
And say'st thou yet that exile is not death?
Hadst thou no poison mix'd, no sharp-ground knife,
No sudden mean of death, though ne'er so mean,
But 'banished' to kill me?—'banished'?
O friar, the damned use that word in hell;
Howlings attend it: how hast thou the heart,
Being a divine, a ghostly confessor,
A sin-absolver, and my friend profess'd,   50
To mangle me with that word 'banished'?
FRIAR LAURENCE. Thou fond mad man, hear me but speak a word.
ROMEO. O, thou wilt speak again of banishment.

---

26. *rush'd*, thrust (aside). 33. *validity*, value. 34. *courtship*, both courtliness
and wooing. 45. *mean . . . mean*, means . . . base.

FRIAR LAURENCE. I'll give thee armour to keep off that word;
   Adversity's sweet milk, philosophy,
   To comfort thee, though thou art banished.
ROMEO. Yet 'banished'? Hang up philosophy!
   Unless philosophy can make a Juliet,
   Displant a town, reverse a prince's doom,
   It helps not, it prevails not: talk no more.   60
FRIAR LAURENCE. O, then I see that madmen have no ears.
ROMEO. How should they, when that wise men have no eyes?
FRIAR LAURENCE. Let me dispute with thee of thy estate.
ROMEO. Thou canst not speak of that thou dost not feel:
   Wert thou as young as I, Juliet thy love,
   An hour but married, Tybalt murdered,
   Doting like me and like me banished,
   Then mightst thou speak, then mightst thou tear thy hair,
   And fall upon the ground, as I do now,
   Taking the measure of an unmade grave.   (*Knocking within.*) 70
FRIAR LAURENCE. Arise; one knocks; good Romeo, hide thyself.
ROMEO. Not I; unless the breath of heart-sick groans,
   Mist-like, infold me from the search of eyes.   (*Knocking.*)
FRIAR LAURENCE. Hark, how they knock! Who's there? Romeo, arise;
   Thou wilt be taken. Stay awhile! Stand up;   (*Knocking.*)
   Run to my study. By and by! God's will,
   What simpleness is this! I come, I come!   (*Knocking.*)
   Who knocks so hard? whence come you? what's your will?
NURSE (*within*). Let me come in, and you shall know my errand;
   I come from Lady Juliet.
FRIAR LAURENCE.   Welcome, then.   80

(*Enter* NURSE.)
NURSE. O holy friar, O, tell me, holy friar,
   Where is my lady's lord, where's Romeo?
FRIAR LAURENCE. There on the ground, with his own tears made drunk.
NURSE. O, he is even in my mistress' case,
   Just in her case! O woful sympathy!
   Piteous predicament! Even so lies she,
   Blubbering and weeping, weeping and blubbering.
   Stand up, stand up; stand, an you be a man:
   For Juliet's sake, for her sake, rise and stand;
   Why should you fall into so deep an O?   90
ROMEO. Nurse!
NURSE. Ah sir! ah sir! Well, death's the end of all.
ROMEO. Spakest thou of Juliet? how is it with her?

---

63. *dispute,* reason. *estate,* situation.

Doth she not think me an old murderer,
Now I have stain'd the childhood of our joy
With blood removed but little from her own?
Where is she? and how doth she? and what says
My conceal'd lady to our cancell'd love?

NURSE. O, she says nothing, sir, but weeps and weeps;
And now falls on her bed; and then starts up,   100
And Tybalt calls; and then on Romeo cries,
And then down falls again.

ROMEO.   As if that name,
Shot from the deadly level of a gun,
Did murder her; as that name's cursed hand
Murder'd her kinsman. O, tell me, friar, tell me,
In what vile part of this anatomy
Doth my name lodge? tell me that I may sack
The hateful mansion.   (*Drawing his sword.*)

FRIAR LAURENCE.   Hold thy desperate hand:
Art thou a man? thy form cries out thou art:
Thy tears are womanish; thy wild acts denote   110
The unreasonable fury of a beast:
Unseemly woman in a seeming man!
Or ill-beseeming beast in seeming both!
Thou hast amazed me: by my holy order,
I thought thy disposition better temper'd.
Hast thou slain Tybalt? wilt thou slay thyself?
And slay thy lady too that lives in thee,
By doing damned hate upon thyself?
Why rail'st thou on thy birth, the heaven, and earth?
Since birth, and heaven, and earth, all three do meet
In thee at once; which thou at once wouldst lose.   121
Fie, fie, thou shamest thy shape, thy love, thy wit;
Which, like a usurer, abound'st in all,
And usest none in that true use indeed
Which should bedeck thy shape, thy love, thy wit:
Thy noble shape is but a form of wax,
Digressing from the valour of a man;
Thy dear love sworn but hollow perjury,
Killing that love which thou hast vow'd to cherish;
Thy wit, that ornament to shape and love,   130
Mis-shapen in the conduct of them both,
Like powder in a skilless soldier's flask,
Is set a-fire by thine own ignorance,

94. *old* (colloquial), real, actual.   103. *level*, aim.   107. *sack*, destroy.

And thou dismember'd with thine own defence.
What, rouse thee, man! thy Juliet is alive,
For whose dear sake thou wast but lately dead;
There art thou happy: Tybalt would kill thee,
But thou slew'st Tybalt; there art thou happy too:
The law that threaten'd death becomes thy friend
And turns it to exile; there art thou happy: 140
A pack of blessings lights upon thy back;
Happiness courts thee in her best array;
But, like a misbehaved and sullen wench,
Thou pout'st upon thy fortune and thy love:
Take heed, take heed, for such die miserable.
Go, get thee to thy love, as was decreed,
Ascend her chamber, hence and comfort her:
But look thou stay not till the watch be set,
For then thou canst not pass to Mantua;
Where thou shalt live, till we can find a time   150
To blaze your marriage, reconcile your friends,
Beg pardon of the prince, and call thee back
With twenty hundred thousand times more joy
Than thou went'st forth in lamentation.
Go before, nurse: commend me to thy lady;
And bid her hasten all the house to bed,
Which heavy sorrow makes them apt unto:
Romeo is coming.
NURSE. O Lord, I could have stay'd here all the night
To hear good counsel: O, what learning is!   160
My lord, I'll tell my lady you will come.
ROMEO. Do so, and bid my sweet prepare to chide.
NURSE. Here, sir, a ring she bid me give you, sir:
Hie you, make haste, for it grows very late.   (*Exit.*)
ROMEO. How well my comfort is revived by this!
FRIAR LAURENCE. Go hence; good night; and here stands all your state:
Either be gone before the watch be set,
Or by the break of day disguised from hence:
Sojourn in Mantua; I'll find out your man,
And he shall signify from time to time   170
Every good hap to you that chances here:
Give me thy hand; 'tis late: farewell; good night.
ROMEO. But that a joy past joy calls out on me,
It were a grief, so brief to part with thee:
Farewell.   (*Exeunt.*)

151. *blaze*, publish, divulge.   157. *apt*, ready, inclined.   166. *here stands all your
state*, your fortune depends on what follows.

SCENE 4: *A room in Capulet's house.*

(*Enter* CAPULET, LADY CAPULET, *and* PARIS.)

CAPULET. Things have fall'n out, sir, so unluckily,
  That we have had no time to move our daughter:
  Look you, she loved her kinsman Tybalt dearly,
  And so did I:—Well, we were born to die.
  'Tis very late, she'll not come down to-night:
  I promise you, but for your company,
  I would have been a-bed an hour ago.

PARIS. These times of woe afford no time to woo.
  Madam, good night: commend me to your daughter.

LADY CAPULET. I will, and know her mind early to-morrow;
  To-night she is mew'd up to her heaviness.   11

CAPULET. Sir Paris, I will make a desperate tender
  Of my child's love: I think she will be ruled
  In all respects by me; nay, more, I doubt it not.
  Wife, go you to her ere you go to bed;
  Acquaint her here of my son Paris' love;
  And bid her, mark you me, on Wednesday next—
  But, soft! what day is this?

PARIS.   Monday, my lord.

CAPULET. Monday! ha, ha! Well, Wednesday is too soon,
  O' Thursday let it be: o' Thursday, tell her,   20
  She shall be married to this noble earl.
  Will you be ready? do you like this haste?
  We'll keep no great ado,—a friend or two;
  For, hark you, Tybalt being slain so late,
  It may be thought we held him carelessly,
  Being our kinsman, if we revel much:
  Therefore we'll have some half a dozen friends,
  And there an end. But what say you to Thursday?

PARIS. My lord, I would that Thursday were to-morrow.

CAPULET. Well, get you gone: o' Thursday be it, then.   30
  Go you to Juliet ere you go to bed,
  Prepare her, wife, against this wedding-day.
  Farewell, my lord. Light to my chamber, ho!
  Afore me! it is so very very late,
  That we may call it early by and by.
  Good night.   (*Exeunt.*)

SCENE 4. 11. *mew'd,* cooped. 12. *desperate tender,* rash offer. 25. *held,* regarded. 34. *Afore me,* by my life.

SCENE 5: *Capulet's orchard.*

(*Enter* ROMEO *and* JULIET *above, at the window.*)

JULIET. Wilt thou be gone? it is not yet near day:
   It was the nightingale, and not the lark,
   That pierced the fearful hollow of thine ear;
   Nightly she sings on yond pomegranate-tree:
   Believe me, love, it was the nightingale.
ROMEO. It was the lark, the herald of the morn,
   No nightingale: look, love, what envious streaks
   Do lace the severing clouds in yonder east:
   Night's candles are burnt out, and jocund day
   Stands tiptoe on the misty mountain tops.   10
   I must be gone and live, or stay and die.
JULIET. Yond light is not day-light, I know it, I:
   It is some meteor that the sun exhales,
   To be to thee this night a torch-bearer,
   And light thee on thy way to Mantua:
   Therefore stay yet; thou need'st not to be gone.
ROMEO. Let me be ta'en, let me be put to death;
   I am content, so thou wilt have it so.
   I'll say yon grey is not the morning's eye,
   'Tis but the pale reflex of Cynthia's brow;   20
   Nor that is not the lark, whose notes do beat
   The vaulty heaven so high above our heads:
   I have more care to stay than will to go:
   Come, death, and welcome! Juliet wills it so.
   How is 't, my soul? let 's talk; it is not day.
JULIET. It is, it is: hie hence, be gone, away!
   It is the lark that sings so out of tune,
   Straining harsh discords and unpleasing sharps.
   Some say the lark makes sweet division;
   This doth not so, for she divideth us: 30
   Some say the lark and loathed toad change eyes;
   O, now I would they had changed voices too!
   Since arm from arm that voice doth us affray,
   Hunting thee hence with hunt's-up to the day.
   O, now be gone; more light and light it grows.
ROMEO. More light and light; more dark and dark our woes!

SCENE 5. 8. *lace*, stripe. 20. *Cynthia's,* the moon's. 28. *sharps*, high notes. 29. *division*, melody. 31. *change eyes*, an allusion to a popular saying that the toad and the lark had changed eyes, since the lark has ugly eyes and the toad beautiful ones. 34. *hunt's-up*, a song or tune to awaken huntsmen.

(*Enter* NURSE, *to the chamber.*)
NURSE. Madam!
JULIET. Nurse?
NURSE. Your lady mother is coming to your chamber:
   The day is broke; be wary, look about.   (*Exit.*) 40
JULIET. Then, window, let day in, and let life out.
ROMEO. Farewell, farewell! one kiss, and I'll descend.   (*He goeth down.*)
JULIET. Art thou gone so? love, lord, ay, husband, friend!
   I must hear from thee every day in the hour,
   For in a minute there are many days:
   O, by this count I shall be much in years
   Ere I again behold my Romeo!
ROMEO. Farewell!
   I will omit no opportunity
   That may convey my greetings, love, to thee.   50
JULIET. O, think'st thou we shall ever meet again?
ROMEO. I doubt it not; and all these woes shall serve
   For sweet discourses in our time to come.
JULIET. O God, I have an ill-divining soul!
   Methinks I see thee, now thou art below,
   As one dead in the bottom of a tomb:
   Either my eyesight fails, or thou look'st pale.
ROMEO. And trust me, love, in my eye so do you:
   Dry sorrow drinks our blood. Adieu, adieu!   (*Exit.*)
JULIET. O fortune, fortune! all men call thee fickle: 60
   If thou art fickle, what dost thou with him
   That is renown'd for faith? Be fickle, fortune;
   For then, I hope, thou wilt not keep him long,
   But send him back.
LADY CAPULET (*within*). Ho, daughter! are you up?
JULIET. Who is 't that calls? is it my lady mother?
   Is she not down so late, or up so early?
   What unaccustom'd cause procures her hither?

(*Enter* LADY CAPULET.)
LADY CAPULET. Why, how now, Juliet!
JULIET.   Madam, I am not well.   69
LADY CAPULET. Evermore weeping for your cousin's death?
   What, wilt thou wash him from his grave with tears?
   An if thou couldst, thou couldst not make him live;
   Therefore, have done: some grief shows much of love;

---

57. *fails,* errs. 59. *Dry sorrow.* The heat of the body in sorrow and despair was thought to descend into the bowels and dry up the blood. 67. *down,* in bed. 68. *procures,* induces to come.

But much of grief shows still some want of wit.

JULIET. Yet let me weep for such a feeling loss.

LADY CAPULET. So shall you feel the loss, but not the friend
    Which you weep for.

JULIET.   Feeling so the loss,
    I cannot choose but ever weep the friend.

LADY CAPULET. Well, girl, thou weep'st not so much for his death,
    As that the villain lives which slaughter'd him.   80

JULIET. What villain, madam?

LADY CAPULET.   That same villain, Romeo.

JULIET (aside). Villain and he be many miles asunder.—
    God pardon him! I do, with all my heart;
    And yet no man like he doth grieve my heart.

LADY CAPULET. That is, because the traitor murderer lives.

JULIET. Ay, madam, from the reach of these my hands:
    Would none but I might venge my cousin's death!

LADY CAPULET. We will have vengeance for it, fear thou not:
    Then weep no more. I'll send to one in Mantua,
    Where that same banish'd runagate doth live,   90
    Shall give him such an unaccustom'd dram,
    That he shall soon keep Tybalt company:
    And then, I hope, thou wilt be satisfied.

JULIET. Indeed, I never shall be satisfied
    With Romeo, till I behold him—dead—
    Is my poor heart so for a kinsman vex'd:
    Madam, if you could find out but a man
    To bear a poison, I would temper it;
    That Romeo should, upon receipt thereof,
    Soon sleep in quiet. O, how my heart abhors   100
    To hear him named, and cannot come to him,
    To wreak the love I bore my cousin
    Upon his body that hath slaughter'd him!

LADY CAPULET. Find thou the means, and I'll find such a man.
    But now I'll tell thee joyful tidings, girl.

JULIET. And joy comes well in such a needy time:
    What are they, I beseech your ladyship?

LADY CAPULET. Well, well, thou hast a careful father, child;
    One who, to put thee from thy heaviness,
    Hath sorted out a sudden day of joy,   110
    That thou expect'st not nor I look'd not for.

JULIET. Madam, in happy time, what day is that?

---

84. *like*, so much as. 95. *dead*. This word is placed between the clauses so that
it can be understood with either what precedes it or what follows it. 98. *temper*,
used equivocally, meaning "to mix" or "to alloy." 108. *careful*, provident. 112.
in happy time, a vague expression like "by the way."

LADY CAPULET. Marry, my child, early next Thursday morn,
  The gallant, young and noble gentleman,
  The County Paris, at Saint Peter's Church,
  Shall happily make thee there a joyful bride.
JULIET. Now, by Saint Peter's Church and Peter too,
  He shall not make me there a joyful bride.
  I wonder at this haste; that I must wed
  Ere he, that should be husband, comes to woo.   120
  I pray you, tell my lord and father, madam,
  I will not marry yet; and, when I do, I swear,
  It shall be Romeo, whom you know I hate,
  Rather than Paris. These are news indeed!
LADY CAPULET. Here comes your father; tell him so yourself,
  And see how he will take it at your hands.

(*Enter* CAPULET *and* NURSE.)
CAPULET. When the sun sets, the air doth drizzle dew;
  But for the sunset of my brother's son
  It rains downright.
  How now! a conduit, girl? what, still in tears?   130
  Evermore showering? In one little body
  Thou counterfeit'st a bark, a sea, a wind;
  For still thy eyes, which I may call the sea,
  Do ebb and flow with tears; the bark thy body is,
  Sailing in this salt flood; the winds, thy sighs;
  Who, raging with thy tears, and they with them,
  Without a sudden calm, will overset
  Thy tempest-tossed body. How now, wife!
  Have you deliver'd to her our decree?
LADY CAPULET. Ay, sir; but she will none, she gives you thanks.   140
  I would the fool were married to her grave!
CAPULET. Soft! take me with you, take me with you, wife.
  How! will she none? doth she not give us thanks?
  Is she not proud? doth she not count her blest,
  Unworthy as she is, that we have wrought
  So worthy a gentleman to be her bridegroom?
JULIET. Not proud, you have; but thankful, that you have:
  Proud can I never be of what I hate;
  But thankful even for hate, that is meant love.
CAPULET. How now, how now, chop-logic! What is this?
  'Proud' and 'I thank you,' and 'I thank you not;'   151
  And yet 'not proud:' mistress minion, you,

130. *conduit,* water pipe. 140. *will none,* refuses it. 142. *take me with you,* let me understand you. 145. *wrought,* procured. 150. *chop-logic,* a shallow and sophistical arguer. 152. *minion,* favored person.

Thank me no thankings, nor proud me no prouds,
But fettle your fine joints 'gainst Thursday next,
To go with Paris to Saint Peter's Church,
Or I will drag thee on a hurdle thither.
Out, you green-sickness carrion! out, you baggage!
You tallow-face!
LADY CAPULET.   Fie, fie! what, are you mad?
JULIET. Good father, I beseech you on my knees,
Hear me with patience but to speak a word.   160
CAPULET. Hang thee, young baggage! disobedient wretch!
I tell thee what: get thee to church o' Thursday,
Or never after look me in the face:
Speak not, reply not, do not answer me;
My fingers itch. Wife, we scarce thought us blest
That God had lent us but this only child;
But now I see this one is one too much,
And that we have a curse in having her:
Out on her, hilding!
NURSE.   God in heaven bless her!
You are to blame, my lord, to rate her so.   170
CAPULET. And why, my lady wisdom? hold your tongue,
Good prudence; smatter with your gossips, go.
NURSE. I speak no treason.
CAPULET.   O, God ye god-den.
NURSE. May not one speak?
CAPULET.   Peace, you mumbling fool!
Utter your gravity o'er a gossip's bowl;
For here we need it not.
LADY CAPULET.   You are too hot.
CAPULET. God's bread! it makes me mad:
Day, night, hour, tide, time, work, play,
Alone, in company, still my care hath been
To have her match'd: and having now provided   180
A gentleman of noble parentage,
Of fair demesnes, youthful, and nobly train'd,
Stuff'd, as they say, with honourable parts,
Proportion'd as one's thought would wish a man;
And then to have a wretched puling fool,
A whining mammet, in her fortune's tender,
To answer 'I'll not wed; I cannot love,

---

154. *fettle*, make ready. 156. *hurdle*, a conveyance for criminals. 157. *green-sickness*, an anemic ailment of young women; it suggests Juliet's paleness. 170. *rate*, berate, scold. 172. *smatter*, chatter. 175. *gravity*, wisdom; used contemptuously. 177. *God's bread*, an oath by the sacrament. 186. *mammet*, doll. *fortune's tender*, offer of good fortune.

I am too young; I pray you, pardon me.'
But, an you will not wed, I'll pardon you:
Graze where you will, you shall not house with me: 190
Look to 't, think on 't, I do not use to jest.
Thurday is near; lay hand on heart, advise:
An you be mine, I'll give you to my friend;
An you be not, hang, beg, starve, die in the streets,
For, by my soul, I'll ne'er acknowledge thee,
Nor what is mine shall never do thee good:
Trust to 't, bethink you; I'll not be forsworn.   (Exit.)

JULIET. Is there no pity sitting in the clouds,
That sees into the bottom of my grief?
O, sweet my mother, cast me not away!   200
Delay this marriage for a month, a week;
Or, if you do not, make the bridal bed
In that dim monument where Tybalt lies.

LADY CAPULET. Talk not to me, for I'll not speak a word:
Do as thou wilt, for I have done with thee.   (Exit.)

JULIET. O God!—O nurse, how shall this be prevented?
My husband is on earth, my faith in heaven;
How shall that faith return again to earth,
Unless that husband send it me from heaven
By leaving earth? comfort me, counsel me.   210
Alack, alack, that heaven should practise stratagems
Upon so soft a subject as myself!
What say'st thou? hast thou not a word of joy?
Some comfort, nurse.

NURSE.   Faith, here it is.
Romeo is banish'd; and all the world to nothing,
That he dares ne'er come back to challenge you;
Or, if he do, it needs must be by stealth.
Then, since the case so stands as now it doth,
I think it best that you married with the county.
O, he 's a lovely gentleman!   220
Romeo's a dishclout to him: an eagle, madam,
Hath not so green, so quick, so fair an eye
As Paris hath. Beshrew my very heart,
I think you are happy in this second match,
For it excels your first: or if it did not,
Your first is dead; or 'twere as good he were,
As living here and you no use of him.

---

207. *my faith in heaven.* Juliet refers to her marriage vows.   211. *practise,* scheme, contrive. *stratagems,* dreadful deeds.   222. *green.* Green was an admired color for eyes. *quick,* lively.

JULIET. Speakest thou from thy heart?

NURSE.   And from my soul too;
  Or else beshrew them both.

JULIET.   Amen!

NURSE.   What?

JULIET. Well, thou hast comforted me marvellous much.   230
  Go in; and tell my lady I am gone,
  Having displeased my father, to Laurence' cell,
  To make confession and to be absolved.

NURSE. Marry, I will; and this is wisely done.   (*Exit.*)

JULIET. Ancient damnation! O most wicked fiend!
  Is it more sin to wish me thus forsworn,
  Or to dispraise my lord with that same tongue
  Which she hath praised him with above compare
  So many thousand times? Go, counsellor;
  Thou and my bosom henceforth shall be twain.   240
  I'll to the friar, to know his remedy:
  If all else fail, myself have power to die.   (*Exit.*)

ACT IV

SCENE 1: *Friar Laurence's cell.*

(*Enter* FRIAR LAURENCE *and* PARIS.)

FRIAR LAURENCE. On Thursday, sir? the time is very short.

PARIS. My father Capulet will have it so;
  And I am nothing slow to slack his haste.

FRIAR LAURENCE. You say you do not know the lady's mind:
  Uneven is the course, I like it not.

PARIS. Immoderately she weeps for Tybalt's death,
  And therefore have I little talk'd of love;
  For Venus smiles not in a house of tears.
  Now, sir, her father counts it dangerous
  That she doth give her sorrow so much sway,   10
  And in his wisdom hastes our marriage,
  To stop the inundation of her tears;
  Which, too much minded by herself alone
  May be put from her by society:
  Now do you know the reason of this haste

FRIAR LAURENCE (*aside*). I would I knew not why it should be slow'd.
  Look, sir, here comes the lady towards my cell.

ACT IV, SCENE 1.   5. *Uneven,* not straightforward.   13. *minded,* perceived, noticed.

(*Enter* JULIET.)

PARIS. Happily met, my lady and my wife!

JULIET. That may be, sir, when I may be a wife.

PARIS. That may be must be, love, on Thursday next.

JULIET. What must be shall be.

FRIAR LAURENCE.   That 's a certain text.   21

PARIS. Come you to make confession to this father?

JULIET. To answer that, I should confess to you.

PARIS. Do not deny to him that you love me.

JULIET. I will confess to you that I love him.

PARIS. So will ye, I am sure, that you love me.

JULIET. If I do so, it will be of more price,
Being spoke behind your back, than to your face.

PARIS. Poor soul, thy face is much abused with tears.

JULIET. The tears have got small victory by that;   30
For it was bad enough before their spite.

PARIS. Thou wrong'st it, more than tears, with that report.

JULIET. That is no slander, sir, which is a truth;
And what I spake, I spake it to my face.

PARIS. Thy face is mine, and thou hast slander'd it.

JULIET. It may be so, for it is not mine own.
Are you at leisure, holy father, now;
Or shall I come to you at evening mass?

FRIAR LAURENCE. My leisure serves me, pensive daughter, now.
My lord, we must entreat the time alone.   40

PARIS. God shield I should disturb devotion!
Juliet, on Thursday early will I rouse ye:
Till then, adieu; and keep this holy kiss.

JULIET. O, shut the door! and when thou hast done so,   (*Exit.*)
Come weep with me; past hope, past cure, past help!

FRIAR LAURENCE. Ah, Juliet, I already know thy grief;
It strains me past the compass of my wits:
I hear thou must, and nothing may prorogue it,
On Thursday next be married to this county.

JULIET. Tell me not, friar, that thou hear'st of this,   50
Unless thou tell me how I may prevent it:
If, in thy wisdom, thou canst give no help,
Do thou but call my resolution wise,
And with this knife I'll help it presently.
God join'd my heart and Romeo's, thou our hands;
And ere this hand, by thee to Romeo seal'd,
Shall be the label to another deed,
Or my true heart with treacherous revolt

40. *entreat,* ask to have. 41. *shield,* prevent (that). 54. *presently,* at once. 57. *label,* a strip attached to a deed to carry the seal.

Turn to another, this shall slay them both:
Therefore, out of thy long-experienced time,   60
Give me some present counsel, or, behold,
'Twixt my extremes and me this bloody knife
Shall play the umpire, arbitrating that
Which the commission of thy years and art
Could to no issue of true honour bring.
Be not so long to speak; I long to die,
If what thou speak'st speak not of remedy.

FRIAR LAURENCE. Hold, daughter: I do spy a kind of hope,
Which craves as desperate an execution
As that is desperate which we would prevent.   70
If, rather than to marry County Paris,
Thou hast the strength of will to slay thyself,
Then is it likely thou wilt undertake
A thing like death to chide away this shame,
That copest with death himself to scape from it;
And, if thou darest, I'll give thee remedy.

JULIET. O, bid me leap, rather than marry Paris,
From off the battlements of yonder tower;
Or walk in thievish ways; or bid me lurk
Where serpents are; chain me with roaring bears;   80
Or shut me nightly in a charnel-house,
O'er-cover'd quite with dead men's rattling bones,
With reeky shanks and yellow chapless skulls;
Or bid me go into a new-made grave
And hide me with a dead man in his shroud;
Things that, to hear them told, have made me tremble;
And I will do it without fear or doubt,
To live an unstain'd wife to my sweet love.

FRIAR LAURENCE. Hold, then; go home, be merry, give consent
To marry Paris: Wednesday is to-morrow: 90
To-morrow night look that thou lie alone;
Let not thy nurse lie with thee in thy chamber:
Take thou this vial, being then in bed,
And this distilled liquor drink thou off;
When presently through all thy veins shall run
A cold and drowsy humour, for no pulse
Shall keep his native progress, but surcease:
No warmth, no breath, shall testify thou livest;
The roses in thy lips and cheeks shall fade
To paly ashes, thy eyes' windows fall,   100

61. *present*, instant. 62. *extremes*, extreme difficulties. 64. *commission*, author-ity. 75. *copest*, encounterest. 83. *reeky*, malodorous. *chapless*, without the lower jaw. 97. *surcease*, cessation.

Like death, when he shuts up the day of life;
Each part, deprived of supple government,
Shall, stiff and stark and cold, appear like death:
And in this borrow'd likeness of shrunk death
Thou shalt continue two and forty hours,
And then awake as from a pleasant sleep.
Now, when the bridegroom in the morning comes
To rouse thee from thy bed, there art thou dead:
Then, as the manner of our country is,
In thy best robes uncover'd on the bier   110
Thou shalt be borne to that same ancient vault
Where all the kindred of the Capulets lie.
In the mean time, against thou shalt awake,
Shall Romeo by my letters know our drift,
And hither shall he come: and he and I
Will watch thy waking, and that very night
Shall Romeo bear thee hence to Mantua.
And this shall free thee from this present shame;
If no inconstant toy, nor womanish fear,
Abate thy valour in the acting it.   120

JULIET. Give me, give me! O, tell not me of fear!
FRIAR LAURENCE. Hold; get you gone, be strong and prosperous
  In this resolve: I'll send a friar with speed
  To Mantua, with my letters to thy lord.
JULIET. Love give me strength! and strength shall help afford.
  Farewell, dear father!   (*Exeunt.*)

SCENE 2: *Hall in Capulet's house.*

(*Enter* CAPULET, LADY CAPULET, NURSE, *and two* SERVINGMEN.)
CAPULET. So many guests invite as here are writ.   (*Exit* FIRST SERVANT.)
  Sirrah, go hire me twenty cunning cooks.
SECOND SERVANT. You shall have none ill, sir; for I'll try if they can
  lick their fingers.
CAPULET. How canst thou try them so?
SECOND SERVANT. Marry, sir, 'tis an ill cook that cannot lick his own
  fingers: therefore he that cannot lick his fingers goes not with me.
CAPULET. Go, be gone.   (*Exit* SECOND SERVANT.)
  We shall be much unfurnish'd for this time.   10
  What, is my daughter gone to Friar Laurence?
NURSE. Ay, forsooth.
CAPULET. Well, he may chance to do some good on her:
  A peevish self-will'd harlotry it is.

119. *toy,* idle fancy. 120. *Abate,* diminish.
SCENE 2. 14. *peevish,* silly. *harlotry,* hussy.

NURSE. See where she comes from shrift with merry look.

(*Enter* JULIET.)

CAPULET. How now, my headstrong! where have you been gadding?
JULIET. Where I have learn'd me to repent the sin
  Of disobedient opposition
  To you and your behests, and am enjoin'd
  By holy Laurence to fall prostrate here,   20
  And beg your pardon: pardon, I beseech you!
  Henceforward I am ever ruled by you.
CAPULET. Send for the county; go tell him of this:
  I'll have this knot knit up to-morrow morning.
JULIET. I met the youthful lord at Laurence' cell;
  And gave him what becomed love I might,
  Not stepping o'er the bounds of modesty.
CAPULET. Why, I am glad on 't; this is well: stand up:
  This is as 't should be. Let me see the county;
  Ay, marry, go, I say, and fetch him hither.   30
  Now, afore God! this reverend holy friar,
  All our whole city is much bound to him.
JULIET. Nurse, will you go with me into my closet,
  To help me sort such needful ornaments
  As you think fit to furnish me to-morrow?
LADY CAPULET. No, not till Thursday; there is time enough.
CAPULET. Go, nurse, go with her; we'll to church to-morrow.

                  (*Exeunt* JULIET *and* NURSE.)

LADY CAPULET. We shall be short in our provision:
  'Tis now near night.
CAPULET.   Tush, I will stir about,
  And all things shall be well, I warrant thee, wife: 40
  Go thou to Juliet, help to deck up her;
  I'll not to bed to-night; let me alone;
  I'll play the housewife for this once. What, ho!
  They are all forth. Well, I will walk myself
  To County Paris, to prepare him up
  Against to-morrow: my heart is wondrous light,
  Since this same wayward girl is so reclaim'd.   (*Exeunt.*)

SCENE 3: *Juliet's chamber.*

(*Enter* JULIET *and* NURSE.)

JULIET. Ay, those attires are best: but, gentle nurse,
  I pray thee, leave me to myself to-night;

---

26. *becomed*, befitting.   33. *closet*, private room.   35. *furnish*, fit out.

For I have need of many orisons
To move the heavens to smile upon my state,
Which, well thou know'st, is cross and full of sin.

(*Enter* LADY CAPULET.)
LADY CAPULET. What, are you busy, ho? need you my help?
JULIET. No, madam; we have cull'd such necessaries
As are behoveful for our state to-morrow:
So please you, let me now be left alone,
And let the nurse this night sit up with you;   10
For, I am sure, you have your hands full all,
In this so sudden business.
LADY CAPULET.   Good night:
Get thee to bed, and rest; for thou hast need.

(*Exeunt* LADY CAPULET *and* NURSE.)
JULIET. Farewell! God knows when we shall meet again.
I have a faint cold fear thrills through my veins,
That almost freezes up the heat of life:
I'll call them back again to comfort me:
Nurse! What should she do here?
My dismal scene I needs must act alone.
Come, vial.   20
What if this mixture do not work at all?
Shall I be married then to-morrow morning?
No, no: this shall forbid it: lie thou there.

(*Laying down her dagger.*)
What if it be a poison, which the friar
Subtly hath minister'd to have me dead,
Lest in this marriage he should be dishonour'd,
Because he married me before to Romeo?
I fear it is: and yet, methinks, it should not,
For he hath still been tried a holy man.
How if, when I am laid into the tomb,   30
I wake before the time that Romeo
Come to redeem me? there 's a fearful point!
Shall I not, then, be stifled in the vault,
To whose foul mouth no healthsome air breathes in,
And there die strangled ere my Romeo comes?
Or, if I live, is it not very like,
The horrible conceit of death and night,
Together with the terror of the place,—
As in a vault, an ancient receptacle,

SCENE 3. 3. *orisons*, prayers. 5. *cross*, contrary. 8. *behoveful*, needful. 25.
minister'd, administered (something healing or the reverse). 29. *tried*, proved.
After this line, Q_1: *I will not entertain so bad a thought.* 39. *As*, namely.

Where, for these many hundred years, the bones   40
Of all my buried ancestors are pack'd:
Where bloody Tybalt, yet but green in earth,
Lies festering in his shroud; where, as they say,
At some hours in the night spirits resort;—
Alack, alack, is it not like that I,
So early waking, what with loathsome smells,
And shrieks like mandrakes' torn out of the earth,
That living mortals, hearing them, run mad:—
O, if I wake, shall I not be distraught,
Environed with all these hideous fears?   50
And madly play with my forefathers' joints?
And pluck the mangled Tybalt from his shroud?
And, in this rage, with some great kinsman's bone,
As with a club, dash out my desperate brains?
O, look! methinks I see my cousin's ghost
Seeking out Romeo, that did spit his body
Upon a rapier's point: stay, Tybalt, stay!
Romeo, I come! this do I drink to thee.

          (She falls upon her bed, within the curtains.)

SCENE 4: *Hall in Capulet's house.*

(Enter LADY CAPULET *and* NURSE.)
LADY CAPULET. Hold, take these keys, and fetch more spices, nurse.
NURSE. They call for dates and quinces in the pastry.

(Enter CAPULET.)
CAPULET. Come, stir, stir, stir! the second cock hath crow'd,
    The curfew-bell hath rung, 'tis three o'clock:
    Look to the baked meats, good Angelica:
    Spare not for cost.
NURSE.   Go, you cot-quean, go,
    Get you to bed; faith, you'll be sick to-morrow
    For this night's watching.
CAPULET. No, not a whit: what! I have watch'd ere now
    All night for lesser cause, and ne'er been sick.   10
LADY CAPULET. Ay, you have been a mouse-hunt in your time;
    But I will watch you from such watching now.

47. *mandrakes'.* Mandragora or mandrake was a narcotic plant, the root of which
resembled the human form; it was fabled to utter a shriek when torn from the
ground. 50. *fears,* objects of fear. 53. *rage,* madness.
SCENE 4. 2. *pastry,* room in which pastry was made. 4. *curfew-bell,* apparently
rung at other times than at curfew. 5. *baked meats,* pies, pastry. 6. *cot-quean,*
a man who acts the housewife. 8. *watching,* waking. 11. *mouse-hunt,* hunter
of women.

(Exeunt LADY CAPULET *and* NURSE.)

CAPULET. A jealous-hood, a jealous-hood!

(Enter three or four SERVINGMEN, *with spits, logs, and baskets.)*

Now, fellow,

What 's there?

FIRST SERVINGMAN. Things for the cook, sir; but I know not what.

CAPULET. Make haste, make haste.   *(Exit* FIRST SERVINGMAN.)   Sirrah,
    fetch drier logs:

Call Peter, he will show thee where they are.

SECOND SERVINGMAN. I have a head, sir, that will find out logs,

And never trouble Peter for the matter.   *(Exit.)*

CAPULET. Mass, and well said; a merry whoreson, ha!

Thou shalt be logger-head. Good faith, 'tis day: 20

The county will be here with music straight,

For so he said he would: I hear him near.   *(Music within.)*

Nurse! Wife! What, ho! What, nurse, I say!

(Re-enter NURSE.)

Go waken Juliet, go and trim her up;

I'll go and chat with Paris: hie, make haste,

Make haste; the bridegroom he is come already:

Make haste, I say.   *(Exeunt.)*

SCENE 5: *Juliet's chamber.*

(Enter NURSE.)

NURSE. Mistress! what, mistress! Juliet! fast, I warrant her, she:

Why, lamb! why, lady! fie, you slug-a-bed!

Why, love, I say! madam! sweet-heart! why, bride!

What, not a word? you take your pennyworths now;

Sleep for a week; for the next night, I warrant,

The County Paris hath set up his rest,

That you shall rest but little. God forgive me,

Marry, and amen, how sound is she asleep!

I must needs wake her. Madam, madam, madam!

Ay, let the county take you in your bed;   10

He'll fright you up, i' faith. Will it not be?   *(Undraws the curtains.)*

What, dress'd! and in your clothes! and down again!

I must needs wake you: Lady! lady! lady!

Alas, alas! Help, help! my lady 's dead!

13. *jealous-hood,* jealousy. 19. *Mass,* by the Mass. 20. *logger-head,* blockhead.
SCENE 5. 1. *fast,* fast asleep. 4. *pennyworths,* little bits. 6. *set up his rest,* a
phrase from the game of primero meaning to complete your hand and wager
on it; hence, to be resolved.

O, well-a-day, that ever I was born!
Some aqua vitæ, ho! My lord! my lady!

(*Enter* LADY CAPULET.)
LADY CAPULET. What noise is here?
NURSE.   O lamentable day!
LADY CAPULET. What is the matter?
NURSE.   Look, look! O heavy day!
LADY CAPULET. O me, O me! My child, my only life,
  Revive, look up, or I will die with thee!   20
  Help, help! Call help.

(*Enter* CAPULET.)
CAPULET. For shame, bring Juliet forth; her lord is come.
NURSE. She's dead, deceased, she 's dead; alack the day!
LADY CAPULET. Alack the day, she 's dead, she 's dead, she 's dead!
CAPULET. Ha! let me see her: out, alas! she 's cold;
  Her blood is settled, and her joints are stiff;
  Life and these lips have long been separated:
  Death lies on her like an untimely frost
  Upon the sweetest flower of all the field.
NURSE. O lamentable day!
LADY CAPULET.   O woful time!   30
CAPULET. Death, that hath ta'en her hence to make me wail,
  Ties up my tongue, and will not let me speak.

(*Enter* FRIAR LAURENCE *and* PARIS, *with* MUSICIANS.)
FRIAR LAURENCE. Come, is the bride ready to go to church?
CAPULET. Ready to go, but never to return.
  O son! the night before thy wedding-day
  Hath Death lain with thy wife. There she lies,
  Flower as she was, deflowered by him.
  Death is my son-in-law, Death is my heir;
  My daughter he hath wedded: I will die,
  And leave him all; life, living, all is Death's.   40
PARIS. Have I thought long to see this morning's face,
  And doth it give me such a sight as this?
LADY CAPULET. Accursed, unhappy, wretched, hateful day!
  Most miserable hour that e'er time saw
  In lasting labour of his pilgrimage!
  But one, poor one, one poor and loving child,
  But one thing to rejoice and solace in,
  And cruel death hath catch'd it from my sight!

26. *settled*, probably congealed. 41. *thought long*, looked forward to. 43. *unhappy*, fatal.

NURSE. O woe! O woful, woful, woful day!
   Most lamentable day, most woful day,   50
   That ever, ever, I did yet behold!
   O day! O day! O day! O hateful day!
   Never was seen so black a day as this:
   O woful day, O woful day!
PARIS. Beguiled, divorced, wronged, spited, slain!
   Most detestable death, by thee beguiled,
   By cruel cruel thee quite overthrown!
   O love! O life! not life, but love in death!
CAPULET. Despised, distressed, hated, martyr'd, kill'd!
   Uncomfortable time, why camest thou now   60
   To murder, murder our solemnity?
   O child! O child! my soul, and not my child!
   Dead art thou! Alack! my child is dead;
   And with my child my joys are buried.
FRIAR LAURENCE. Peace, ho, for shame! confusion's cure lives not
   In these confusions. Heaven and yourself
   Had part in this fair maid; now heaven hath all,
   And all the better is it for the maid:
   Your part in her you could not keep from death,
   But heaven keeps his part in eternal life.   70
   The most you sought was her promotion;
   For 'twas your heaven she should be advanced:
   And weep ye now, seeing she is advanced
   Above the clouds, as high as heaven itself?
   O, in this love, you love your child so ill,
   That you run mad, seeing that she is well:
   She 's not well married that lives married long;
   But she 's best married that dies married young.
   Dry up your tears, and stick your rosemary
   On this fair corse; and, as the custom is,   80
   In all her best array bear her to church:
   For though fond nature bids us all lament,
   Yet nature's tears are reason's merriment.
CAPULET. All things that we ordained festival,
   Turn from their office to black funeral;
   Our instruments to melancholy bells,
   Our wedding cheer to a sad burial feast,
   Our solemn hymns to sullen dirges change,
   Our bridal flowers serve for a buried corse,

---

61. *solemnity*, festivity. 65. *confusion's*, destruction's. 79. *rosemary*, symbol of immortality and enduring love; therefore used at both funerals and weddings. 83. *Yet . . . merriment.* Nature is here used as the opposite of reason.

And all things change them to the contrary.   90
FRIAR LAURENCE. Sir, go you in; and, madam, go with him;
  And go, Sir Paris; every one prepare
  To follow this fair corse unto her grave:
  The heavens do lour upon you for some ill;
  Move them no more by crossing their high will.

                  (*Exeunt* CAPULET, LADY CAPULET, PARIS, *and* FRIAR.)

FIRST MUSICIAN. Faith, we may put up our pipes, and be gone.
NURSE. Honest good fellows, ah, put up, put up;
  For, well you know, this is a pitiful case.   (*Exit.*)
FIRST MUSICIAN. Ay, by my troth, the case may be amended.   101

(*Enter* PETER.)

PETER. Musicians, O, musicians, 'Heart's ease, Heart's ease:' O, an you
  will have me live, play 'Heart's ease.'
FIRST MUSICIAN. Why 'Heart's ease'?
PETER. O, musicians, because my heart itself plays 'My heart is full of
  woe:' O, play me some merry dump, to comfort me.   108
FIRST MUSICIAN. Not a dump we; 'tis time to play now.
PETER. You will not, then?
FIRST MUSICIAN. No.
PETER. I will then give it you soundly.
FIRST MUSICIAN. What will you give us?
PETER. No money, on my faith, but the gleek; I will give you the
  minstrel.
FIRST MUSICIAN. Then will I give you the serving-creature.
PETER. Then will I lay the serving-creature's dagger on your pate. I
  will carry no crotchets: I'll re you, I'll fa you; do you note me?   121
FIRST MUSICIAN. An you re us and fa us, you note us.
SECOND MUSICIAN. Pray you, put up your dagger, and put out your wit.
PETER. Then have at you with my wit! I will dry-beat you with an iron
  wit, and put up my iron dagger. Answer me like men:
    'When griping grief the heart doth wound,
      And doleful dumps the mind oppress,
    Then music with her silver sound'—   130
  why 'silver sound'? why 'music with her silver sound'?
  What say you, Simon Catling?
FIRST MUSICIAN. Marry, sir, because silver hath a sweet sound.
PETER. Pretty! What say you, Hugh Rebeck?

---

101. *amended*, bettered. 102. *'Heart's ease,'* popular tune, as also *'My heart is
full of woe,'* l. 107. 108. *dump*, mournful tune. 115. *gleek*, jest, gibe. 120.
carry, endure. *crotchets*, meaning both "quarter notes" and "whims." 122. *note*,
set to music; used punningly. 124. *put out*, exert. 128–130. *'When . . . sound.'*
This is a part of a song by Richard Edwards preserved in the *Paradise of Daintie
Devices* (1576). 132. *Catling*. A catling was a small lutestring made of catgut.
135. *Rebeck*. A rebeck was a fiddle with three strings.

SECOND MUSICIAN. I say 'silver sound,' because musicians sound for
   silver.
PETER. Pretty too! What say you, James Soundpost?
THIRD MUSICIAN. Faith, I know not what to say.   140
PETER. O, I cry you mercy; you are the singer: I will say for you. It is
   'music with her silver sound,' because musicians have no gold for
   sounding:
   'Then music with her silver sound
      With speedy help doth lend redress.'   (*Exit.*)
FIRST MUSICIAN. What a pestilent knave is this same!
SECOND MUSICIAN. Hang him, Jack! Come, we'll in here; tarry for the
   mourners, and stay dinner.   (*Exeunt.*)

ACT V

SCENE 1: *Mantua. A street.*

(*Enter* ROMEO.)
ROMEO. If I may trust the flattering truth of sleep,
   My dreams presage some joyful news at hand:
   My bosom's lord sits lightly in his throne;
   And all this day an unaccustom'd spirit
   Lifts me above the ground with cheerful thoughts.
   I dreamt my lady came and found me dead—
   Strange dream, that gives a dead man leave to think!—
   And breathed such life with kisses in my lips,
   That I revived, and was an emperor.
   Ah me! how sweet is love itself possess'd,   10
   When but love's shadows are so rich in joy!

(*Enter* BALTHASAR, *booted.*)
   News from Verona!—How now, Balthasar!
   Dost thou not bring me letters from the friar?
   How doth my lady? Is my father well?
   How fares my Juliet? that I ask again;
   For nothing can be ill, if she be well.
BALTHASAR. Then she is well, and nothing can be ill:
   Her body sleeps in Capels' monument,

---

139. *Soundpost.* A soundpost is the pillar or peg which supports the body of a
stringed instrument. 141. *cry you mercy,* beg your parden. 143. *sounding,*
playing music.
ACT V, SCENE 1. 1. *flattering,* illusive. 2. *presage some joyful news.* The premonition here is ironical. 3. *bosom's lord,* heart. 11. *shadows,* phantoms.

And her immortal part with angels lives.
I saw her laid low in her kindred's vault, 20
And presently took post to tell it you:
O, pardon me for bringing these ill news,
Since you did leave it for my office, sir.
ROMEO. Is it even so? then I defy you, stars!
  Thou know'st my lodging: get me ink and paper,
  And hire post-horses; I will hence to-night.
BALTHASAR. I do beseech you, sir, have patience:
  Your looks are pale and wild, and do import
  Some misadventure.
ROMEO.   Tush, thou art deceived:
  Leave me, and do the thing I bid thee do. 30
  Hast thou no letters to me from the friar?
BALTHASAR. No, my good lord.
ROMEO.   No matter: get thee gone,
  And hire those horses; I'll be with thee straight.

                              (*Exit* BALTHASAR.)

Well, Juliet, I will lie with thee to-night.
Let 's see for means: O mischief, thou art swift
To enter in the thoughts of desperate men!
I do remember an apothecary,—
And hereabouts he dwells,—which late I noted
In tatter'd weeds, with overwhelming brows,
Culling of simples; meagre were his looks, 40
Sharp misery had worn him to the bones:
And in his needy shop a tortoise hung,
An alligator stuff'd, and other skins
Of ill-shaped fishes; and about his shelves
A beggarly account of empty boxes,
Green earthen pots, bladders and musty seeds,
Remnants of packthread and old cakes of roses,
Were thinly scatter'd, to make up a show.
Noting this penury, to myself I said
'An if a man did need a poison now, 50
Whose sale is present death in Mantua,
Here lives a caitiff wretch would sell it him.'
O, this same thought did but forerun my need;
And this same needy man must sell it me.

---

21. *took post*, started with post horses.   24. *then I defy you, stars*. The fatalism
of this utterance is in keeping with the other references to destiny in the play.
39. *weeds*, clothes. *overwhelming*, overhanging.   40. *simples*, medicinal herbs.
45. *beggarly account*, poor array.   47. *cakes of roses*, rose petals caked to be used
as perfume.   52. *caitiff*, poor.

As I remember, this should be the house.
Being holiday, the beggar's shop is shut.
What, ho! apothecary!

(*Enter* APOTHECARY.)
APOTHECARY.   Who calls so loud?
ROMEO. Come hither, man. I see that thou art poor:
    Hold, there is forty ducats: let me have
    A dram of poison, such soon-speeding gear   60
    As will disperse itself through all the veins
    That the life-weary taker may fall dead
    And that the trunk may be discharged of breath
    As violently as hasty powder fired
    Doth hurry from the fatal cannon's womb.
APOTHECARY. Such mortal drugs I have; but Mantua's law
    Is death to any he that utters them.
ROMEO. Art thou so bare and full of wretchedness,
    And fear'st to die? famine is in thy cheeks,
    Need and oppression starveth in thine eyes,   70
    Contempt and beggary hangs upon thy back;
    The world is not thy friend nor the world's law;
    The world affords no law to make thee rich;
    Then be not poor, but break it, and take this.
APOTHECARY. My poverty, but not my will, consents.
ROMEO. I pay thy poverty, and not thy will.
APOTHECARY. Put this in any liquid thing you will,
    And drink it off; and, if you had the strength
    Of twenty men, it would dispatch you straight.
ROMEO. There is thy gold, worse poison to men's souls,
    Doing more murders in this loathsome world,   81
    Than these poor compounds that thou mayst not sell.
    I sell thee poison; thou hast sold me none.
    Farewell: buy food, and get thyself in flesh.
    Come, cordial and not poison, go with me
    To Juliet's grave; for there must I use thee.   (*Exeunt.*)

SCENE 2: *Friar Laurence's cell.*

(*Enter* FRIAR JOHN.)
FRIAR JOHN. Holy Franciscan friar! brother, ho!

---

59. *ducats,* coins, usually gold, of varying value. 63. *trunk,* body. 67. *utters,*
issues, gives out. 80–86. *There . . . thee,* a passage of general reflection but
slightly connected with the action and having no special appropriateness to
Romeo.

(*Enter* FRIAR LAURENCE.)

FRIAR LAURENCE. This same should be the voice of Friar John.
　Welcome from Mantua: what says Romeo?
　Or, if his mind be writ, give me his letter.
FRIAR JOHN. Going to find a bare-foot brother out,
　One of our order, to associate me,
　Here in this city visiting the sick,
　And finding him, the searchers of the town,
　Suspecting that we both were in a house
　Where the infectious pestilence did reign,   10
　Seal'd up the doors, and would not let us forth;
　So that my speed to Mantua there was stay'd.
FRIAR LAURENCE. Who bare my letter, then, to Romeo?
FRIAR JOHN. I could not send it,—here it is again,—
　Nor get a messenger to bring it thee,
　So fearful were they of infection.
FRIAR LAURENCE. Unhappy fortune! by my brotherhood,
　The letter was not nice but full of charge
　Of dear import, and the neglecting it
　May do much danger. Friar John, go hence;   20
　Get me an iron crow, and bring it straight
　Unto my cell.
FRIAR JOHN. Brother, I'll go and bring it thee.   (*Exit.*)
FRIAR LAURENCE. Now must I to the monument alone;
　Within this three hours will fair Juliet wake:
　She will beshrew me much that Romeo
　Hath had no notice of these accidents;
　But I will write again to Mantua,
　And keep her at my cell till Romeo come;   29
　Poor living corse, closed in a dead man's tomb!   (*Exit.*)

SCENE 3: *A churchyard; in it a tomb belonging to the Capulets.*

(*Enter* PARIS, *and his* PAGE *bearing flowers and a torch.*)
PARIS. Give me thy torch, boy: hence, and stand aloof:
　Yet put it out, for I would not be seen.
　Under yond yew-trees lay thee all along,
　Holding thine ear close to the hollow ground;
　So shall no foot upon the churchyard tread,
　Being loose, unfirm, with digging up of graves,

SCENE 2. 4. *mind*, thoughts, message. 6. *associate*, accompany. 8. *searchers*,
officers of the pestilence. 18. *charge*, importance. 21. *iron crow*, crowbar.
SCENE 3. 3. *all along*, at full length.

But thou shalt hear it: whistle then to me,
As signal that thou hear'st something approach.
Give me those flowers. Do as I bid thee, go.
PAGE (*aside*). I am almost afraid to stand alone   10
Here in the churchyard; yet I will adventure.   (*Retires.*)
PARIS. Sweet flower, with flowers thy bridal bed I strew,—
    O woe! thy canopy is dust and stones;—
  Which with sweet water nightly I will dew,
    Or, wanting that, with tears distill'd by moans:
  The obsequies that I for thee will keep
  Nightly shall be to strew thy grave and weep.

                    (*The* PAGE *whistles.*)

The boy gives warning something doth approach.
What cursed foot wanders this way to-night,
To cross my obsequies and true love's rite?   20
What, with a torch! muffle me, night, awhile.   (*Retires.*)

(*Enter* ROMEO *and* BALTHASAR, *with a torch, mattock,* &c.)
ROMEO. Give me that mattock and the wrenching iron.
Hold, take this letter; early in the morning
See thou deliver it to my lord and father.
Give me the light: upon thy life, I charge thee,
Whate'er thou hear'st or seest, stand all aloof,
And do not interrupt me in my course.
Why I descend into this bed of death,
Is partly to behold my lady's face;
But chiefly to take thence from her dead finger   30
A precious ring, a ring that I must use
Ir. de employment: therefore hence, be gone:
But if thou, jealous, dost return to pry
In what I further shall intend to do,
By heaven, I will tear thee joint by joint
And strew this hungry churchyard with thy limbs:
The time and my intents are savage-wild,
More fierce and more inexorable far
Than empty tigers or the roaring sea.
BALTHASAR. I will be gone, sir, and not trouble you.   40
ROMEO. So shalt thou show me friendship. Take thou that:
Live, and be prosperous: and farewell, good fellow.
BALTHASAR (*aside*). For all this same, I'll hide me hereabout:
His looks I fear, and his intents I doubt.   (*Retires.*)
ROMEO. Thou detestable maw, thou womb of death,

16. *obsequies,* dutiful acts performed in memory of the dead.   21. *muffle,* hide.
33. *jealous,* suspicious.   44. *doubt,* suspect.   45–48. *Thou . . . food.* The words
of these lines seem to echo the wrenching of the door.

Gorged with the dearest morsel of the earth,
Thus I enforce thy rotten jaws to open,
And, in despite, I'll cram thee with more food!   *(Opens the tomb.)*
PARIS. This is that banish'd haughty Montague,
    That murder'd my love's cousin, with which grief,   50
    It is supposed, the fair creature died;
    And here is come to do some villainous shame
    To the dead bodies: I will apprehend him.   *(Comes forward.)*
    Stop thy unhallow'd toil, vile Montague!
    Can vengeance be pursued further than death?
    Condemned villain, I do apprehend thee:
    Obey, and go with me; for thou must die.
ROMEO. I must indeed; and therefore came I hither.
    Good gentle youth, tempt not a desperate man;
    Fly hence, and leave me: think upon these gone;   60
    Let them affright thee. I beseech thee, youth,
    Put not another sin upon my head,
    By urging me to fury: O, be gone!
    By heaven, I love thee better than myself;
    For I come hither arm'd against myself:
    Stay not, be gone; live, and hereafter say,
    A madman's mercy bade thee run away.
PARIS. I do defy thy conjurations,
    And apprehend thee for a felon here.   69
ROMEO. Wilt thou provoke me? then have at thee, boy!   *(They fight.)*
PAGE. O Lord, they fight! I will go call the watch.   *(Exit.)*
PARIS. O, I am slain! *(Falls.)* If thou be merciful,
    Open the tomb, lay me with Juliet.   *(Dies.)*
ROMEO. In faith, I will. Let me peruse this face.
    Mercutio's kinsman, noble County Paris!
    What said my man, when my betossed soul
    Did not attend him as we rode? I think
    He told me Paris should have married Juliet:
    Said he not so? or did I dream it so?
    Or am I mad, hearing him talk of Juliet,   80
    To think it was so? O, give me thy hand,
    One writ with me in sour misfortune's book!
    I'll bury thee in a triumphant grave;
    A grave? O, no! a lantern, slaughter'd youth,
    For here lies Juliet, and her beauty makes
    This vault a feasting presence full of light.
    Death, lie thou there, by a dead man interr'd.

---

68. *conjurations*, solemn appeals, which seem perhaps like incantations. **74.**
peruse, scrutinize. **84.** *lantern*, a turret full of windows. **86.** *presence*, presence
chamber.

(Laying PARIS *in the tomb.*)

How oft when men are at the point of death
Have they been merry! which their keepers call
A lightning before death: O, how may I   90
Call this a lightning? O my love! my wife!
Death, that hath suck'd the honey of thy breath,
Hath had no power yet upon thy beauty:
Thou art not conquer'd; beauty's ensign yet
Is crimson in thy lips and in thy cheeks,
And death's pale flag is not advanced there.
Tybalt, liest thou there in thy bloody sheet?
O, what more favour can I do to thee,
Than with that hand that cut thy youth in twain
To sunder his that was thine enemy?   100
Forgive me, cousin! Ah, dear Juliet,
Why art thou yet so fair? shall I believe
That unsubstantial death is amorous,
And that the lean abhorred monster keeps
Thee here in dark to be his paramour?
For fear of that, I still will stay with thee;
And never from this palace of dim night
Depart again: here, here will I remain
With worms that are thy chamber-maids; O, here
Will I set up my everlasting rest,   110
And shake the yoke of inauspicious stars
From this world-wearied flesh. Eyes, look your last!
Arms, take your last embrace! and, lips, O you
The doors of breath, seal with a righteous kiss
A dateless bargain to engrossing death!
Come, bitter conduct, come, unsavoury guide!
Thou desperate pilot, now at once run on
The dashing rocks thy sea-sick weary bark!
Here 's to my love! *(Drinks.)* O true apothecary!
Thy drugs are quick. Thus with a kiss I die.   *(Dies.)* 120

(Enter, at the other end of the churchyard, FRIAR
    LAURENCE, *with a lantern, crow, and spade.*)
FRIAR LAURENCE. Saint Francis be my speed! how oft to-night
    Have my old feet stumbled at graves! Who 's there?
BALTHASAR. Here 's one, a friend, and one that knows you well.

90. *lightning,* a shedding of light; also, a revival of the spirits. 110. *set up my everlasting rest.* See IV, v, 6. The meaning is, "make my final determination," with allusion also to the idea of repose. 115. *dateless,* everlasting. *engrossing,* monopolizing. 121. *speed,* protector and assistant. 122. *stumbled at graves,* a bad omen.

FRIAR LAURENCE. Bliss be upon you! Tell me, good my friend,
 What torch is yond, that vainly lends his light
 To grubs and eyeless skulls? as I discern,
 It burneth in the Capels' monument.
BALTHASAR. It doth so, holy sir; and there 's my master,
 One that you love.
FRIAR LAURENCE.   Who is it?
BALTHASAR.   Romeo.
FRIAR LAURENCE. How long hath he been there?
BALTHASAR.   Full half an hour.   130
FRIAR LAURENCE. Go with me to the vault.
BALTHASAR.   I dare not, sir:
 My master knows not but I am gone hence;
 And fearfully did menace me with death,
 If I did stay to look on his intents.
FRIAR LAURENCE. Stay, then; I'll go alone. Fear comes upon me:
 O, much I fear some ill unlucky thing.
BALTHASAR. As I did sleep under this yew-tree here,
 I dreamt my master and another fought,
 And that my master slew him.
FRIAR LAURENCE.   Romeo!   (*Advances.*)
 Alack, alack, what blood is this, which stains   140
 The stony entrance of this sepulchre?
 What mean these masterless and gory swords
 To lie discolour'd by this place of peace?   (*Enters the tomb.*)
 Romeo! O, pale! Who else? what, Paris too?
 And steep'd in blood? Ah, what an unkind hour
 Is guilty of this lamentable chance!
 The lady stirs.   (*Juliet wakes.*)
JULIET. O comfortable friar! where is my lord?
 I do remember well where I should be,
 And there I am. Where is my Romeo?   (*Noise within.*) 150
FRIAR LAURENCE. I hear some noise. Lady, come from that nest
 Of death, contagion, and unnatural sleep:
 A greater power than we can contradict
 Hath thwarted our intents. Come, come away.
 Thy husband in thy bosom there lies dead;
 And Paris too. Come, I'll dispose of thee
 Among a sisterhood of holy nuns:
 Stay not to question, for the watch is coming;
 Come, go, good Juliet (*Noise again*), I dare no longer stay.
JULIET. Go, get thee hence, for I will not away.   160
         (*Exit* FRIAR LAURENCE.)
 What 's here? a cup, closed in my true love's hand?

Poison, I see, hath been his timeless end:
O churl! drunk all, and left no friendly drop
To help me after? I will kiss thy lips;
Haply some poison yet doth hang on them,
To make me die with a restorative.   (*Kisses him.*)
Thy lips are warm.
FIRST WATCH (*within*). Lead, boy: which way?
JULIET. Yea, noise? then I'll be brief. O happy dagger!
                              (*Snatching* ROMEO's *dagger.*)
This is thy sheath (*Stabs herself*); there rust, and let me die.
                    (*Falls on* ROMEO's *body, and dies.*) 170

(*Enter* WATCH, *with the* PAGE *of* PARIS.)
PAGE. This is the place; there, where the torch doth burn.
FIRST WATCH. The ground is bloody; search about the churchyard:
Go, some of you, whoe'er you find attach.
Pitiful sight! here lies the county slain;
And Juliet bleeding, warm, and newly dead,
Who here hath lain these two days buried.
Go, tell the prince: run to the Capulets:
Raise up the Montagues: some others search:
We see the ground whereon these woes do lie;
But the true ground of all these piteous woes   180
We cannot without circumstance descry.

(*Re-enter some of the* WATCH, *with* BALTHASAR.)
SECOND WATCH. Here's Romeo's man; we found him in the churchyard.
FIRST WATCH. Hold him in safety, till the prince come hither.

(*Re-enter others of the* WATCH, *with* FRIAR LAURENCE.)
THIRD WATCH. Here is a friar, that trembles, sighs, and weeps:
We took this mattock and this spade from him,
As he was coming from this churchyard side.
FIRST WATCH. A great suspicion: stay the friar too.

(*Enter the* PRINCE *and* ATTENDANTS.)
PRINCE. What misadventure is so early up,
That calls our person from our morning's rest?

(*Enter* CAPULET, LADY CAPULET, *and others.*)
CAPULET. What should it be, that they so shriek abroad?
LADY CAPULET. The people in the street cry **Romeo**,   191

162. *timeless*, everlasting or untimely.   165. *Haply*, perhaps.   173. *attach*, arrest.

Some Juliet, and some Paris; and all run,
With open outcry, toward our monument.
PRINCE. What fear is this which startles in our ears?
FIRST WATCH. Sovereign, here lies the County Paris slain;
And Romeo dead; and Juliet, dead before,
Warm and new kill'd.
PRINCE. Search, seek, and know how this foul murder comes.
FIRST WATCH. Here is a friar, and slaughter'd Romeo's man;
With instruments upon them, fit to open 200
These dead men's tombs.
CAPULET. O heavens! O wife, look how our daughter bleeds!
This dagger hath mista'en,—for, lo, his house
Is empty on the back of Montague,—
And it mis-sheathed in my daughter's bosom!
LADY CAPULET. O me! this sight of death is as a bell,
That warns my old age to a sepulchre.

(*Enter* MONTAGUE *and others.*)
PRINCE. Come, Montague; for thou art early up,
To see thy son and heir more early down.
MONTAGUE. Alas, my liege, my wife is dead tonight; 210
Grief of my son's exile hath stopp'd her breath:
What further woe conspires against mine age?
PRINCE. Look, and thou shalt see.
MONTAGUE. O thou untaught! what manners is in this,
To press before thy father to a grave?
PRINCE. Seal up the mouth of outrage for a while,
Till we can clear these ambiguities,
And know their spring, their head, their true descent;
And then will I be general of your woes,
And lead you even to death: meantime forbear, 220
And let mischance be slave to patience.
Bring forth the parties of suspicion.
FRIAR LAURENCE. I am the greatest, able to do least,
Yet most suspected, as the time and place
Doth make against me, of this direful murder:
And here I stand, both to impeach and purge
Myself condemned and myself excused.
PRINCE. Then say at once what thou dost know in this.
FRIAR LAURENCE. I will be brief, for my short date of breath
Is not so long as is a tedious tale. 230
Romeo, there dead, was husband to that Juliet;
And she, there dead, that Romeo's faithful wife:

203. *house,* scabbard.   216. *outrage,* outcry.   226. *purge,* purify, cleanse.

I married them; and their stol'n marriage-day
Was Tybalt's dooms-day, whose untimely death
Banish'd the new-made bridegroom from this city,
For whom, and not for Tybalt, Juliet pined.
You, to remove that siege of grief from her,
Betroth'd and would have married her perforce
To County Paris: then comes she to me,
And, with wild looks, bid me devise some mean   240
To rid her from this second marriage,
Or in my cell there would she kill herself.
Then gave I her, so tutor'd by my art,
A sleeping potion; which so took effect
As I intended, for it wrought on her
The form of death: meantime I writ to Romeo,
That he should hither come as this dire night,
To help to take her from her borrow'd grave,
Being the time the potion's force should cease.
But he which bore my letter, Friar John,   250
Was stay'd by accident, and yesternight
Return'd my letter back. Then all alone
At the prefixed hour of her waking,
Came I to take her from her kindred's vault;
Meaning to keep her closely at my cell,
Till I conveniently could send to Romeo:
But when I came, some minute ere the time
Of her awaking, here untimely lay
The noble Paris and true Romeo dead.
She wakes; and I entreated her come forth,   260
And bear this work of heaven with patience:
But then a noise did scare me from the tomb;
And she, too desperate, would not go with me,
But, as it seems, did violence on herself.
All this I know; and to the marriage
Her nurse is privy: and, if aught in this
Miscarried by my fault, let my old life
Be sacrificed, some hour before his time,
Unto the rigour of severest law.
PRINCE. We still have known thee for a holy man.   270
Where 's Romeo's man? what can he say in this?
BALTHASAR. I brought my master news of Juliet's death;
And then in post he came from Mantua
To this same place, to this same monument.
This letter he early bid me give his father,

247. *as this*, this very. 253. *prefixed*, agreed upon previously. 255. *closely*, secretly. 273. *post*, haste.

And threaten'd me with death, going in the vault,
If I departed not and left him there.
PRINCE. Give me the letter; I will look on it.
Where is the county's page, that raised the watch?
Sirrah, what made your master in this place?   280
PAGE. He came with flowers to strew his lady's grave;
And bid me stand aloof, and so I did:
Anon comes one with light to ope the tomb;
And by and by my master drew on him;
And then I ran away to call the watch.
PRINCE. This letter doth make good the friar's words,
Their course of love, the tidings of her death:
And here he writes that he did buy a poison
Of a poor 'pothecary, and therewithal
Came to this vault to die, and lie with Juliet.   290
Where be these enemies? Capulet! Montague!
See, what a scourge is laid upon your hate,
That heaven finds means to kill your joys with love.
And I for winking at your discords too
Have lost a brace of kinsmen: all are punish'd.
CAPULET. O brother Montague, give me thy hand:
This is my daughter's jointure, for no more
Can I demand.
MONTAGUE.   But I can give thee more:
For I will raise her statue in pure gold;
That while Verona by that name is known,   300
There shall no figure at such rate be set
As that of true and faithful Juliet.
CAPULET. As rich shall Romeo's by his lady's lie;
Poor sacrifices of our enmity!
PRINCE. A glooming peace this morning with it brings;
The sun, for sorrow, will not show his head:
Go hence, to have more talk of these sad things;
Some shall be pardon'd, and some punished:
For never was a story of more woe
Than this of Juliet and her Romeo.   (*Exeunt.*) 310

297. *jointure*, marriage portion.   301. *rate*, value.

Henrik Ibsen

1828–1906

HEDDA GABLER

Translated by Una Ellis-Fermor

CHARACTERS

JÖRGEN TESMAN, *a scholar engaged in
research in the history of civilization*
HEDDA TESMAN, *his wife*
JULIANE TESMAN, *his aunt*
MRS. ELVSTED
BRACK, *a puisne judge*
EJLERT LÖVBORG
BERTE, *the Tesmans' servant*

SCENE: *The action takes place in the Tesmans' villa
on the west side of the town*

ACT I

*A large drawing-room, well furnished, in good taste, and decorated in
dark colors. In the back wall there is a wide doorway with its curtains
pulled back. This opening leads into a smaller room decorated in the
same style as the drawing-room. In the right wall of this outer room is a
folding door that leads into the hall. In the opposite wall, left, is a glass
door also with curtains pulled back. Through its panes can be seen part
of a veranda outside and autumn foliage. In the middle of the stage is
an oval table with a cloth on it and chairs round it. Downstage, against
the right wall are a large, dark porcelain stove, a high-backed armchair,
a padded foot-rest and two stools. Up in the right corner are a corner*

sofa and a little round table. Downstage, left, a little way from the wall, is a sofa. Above the glass door, a piano. On each side of the doorway at the back stands a what-not with terra-cotta and majolica ornaments. Against the back wall of the inner room can be seen a sofa, a table and a chair or two. Over this sofa hangs the portrait of a handsome, elderly man in a general's uniform. Over the table a hanging lamp with a soft, opal glass shade. All round the drawing-room are bouquets of flowers in vases and glasses; others are lying on the tables. The floors in both rooms are covered with thick carpets. Morning light: the sun shines in through the glass doors.

MISS JULIANE TESMAN, *wearing her hat and carrying a parasol, comes in from the hall followed by* BERTE *carrying a bouquet wrapped in paper.* MISS TESMAN *is a comely, sweet-tempered-looking woman of about sixty-five, well but simply dressed in grey outdoor clothes.* BERTE *is a servant getting on in years, with a homely, rather countrified look.*

MISS TESMAN (*stops just inside the door, listens and says softly*). Why, I don't believe they're up yet!

BERTE (*softly, too*). That's what I said, Miss. Think how late the boat came in last night. And on top of that, my goodness! All the things the young mistress *would* unpack before she'd settle down.

MISS TESMAN. Well, well. Let them have their sleep out, of course. But they must have fresh morning air to breathe when they do come out. (*She goes over to the glass door and throws it wide open.*)

BERTE (*standing by the table, not knowing what to do with the bouquet in her hand*). Well, upon my word, there just isn't anywhere left for it. I think I'd better put it here, Miss.   (*She stands it up on the piano.*)

MISS TESMAN. Well now, Berte my dear, you've got a new mistress. Heaven knows it was dreadfully hard for me to part with you!

BERTE (*nearly crying*). What do you think it was for *me*, Miss? I just can't tell you. After all these many years I've been with you two ladies.

MISS TESMAN. We must try to be contented, Berte. There's really nothing else to be done. You know, Jörgen must have you in the house with him. He simply *must*. You have been used to looking after him ever since he was a little boy.

BERTE. Yes, Miss. But I keep thinking of her lying there at home. Poor thing! So helpless and all. And that new girl, too! *She'll* never learn to look after a sick person properly. Never!

MISS TESMAN. Oh, I shall manage to train her. And, you know, I shall take over most of it myself. Berte dear, there's no need for you to worry so much about my poor sister.

BERTE. Yes, but there's another thing, Miss. I'm really afraid I'll never manage to suit the young mistress.

MISS TESMAN. Oh, come now! Just at first, perhaps, there may be one or two things . . .

BERTE. Because, of course, she's a fine lady—and that particular!

MISS TESMAN. You can understand that, can't you, with General Gabler's daughter? Think what she was accustomed to in the General's day. Do you remember her riding along the road with her father? In that long black habit? And feathers in her hat?

BERTE. My, yes! I should think I do. But, upon my word, I never thought it would be a match between her and Mr. Jörgen. Not in those days.

MISS TESMAN. Nor did I. But that reminds me, Berte, while I think of it—you mustn't call Jörgen "Mr." any more. You must say "Doctor."

BERTE. Yes, the young mistress said something about that, too, as soon as they got in last night. Is it true, then, Miss?

MISS TESMAN. Yes, perfectly true. Just think of it, Berte, they made him a doctor abroad! While he was away this time, you know. I didn't know a single word about it, not till he told me down at the pier.

BERTE. Oh, of course, he can be anything—he can. Clever, like he is. But I never thought he'd take up doctoring too.

MISS TESMAN. Oh, it's not *that* kind of a doctor he is. (*With a nod full of meaning.*)   Coming to that, you may soon be able to call him something else—something even grander.

BERTE. You don't say, Miss! What would that be, Miss?

MISS TESMAN (*smiling*). Ah! If only you knew! (*Touched.*)   God bless us! If poor dear Jochum could look up from his grave and see what his little boy has grown up to be! (*Looking about her.*)   Oh, but—I say, Berte! Why *have* you done that? Taken all the covers off the furniture?

BERTE. The mistress said I was to. Says she can't do with covers on the chairs.

MISS TESMAN. Are they going to use this room for every day, then?

BERTE. So it seemed, from what the mistress said. The master—the Doctor— he didn't say anything.

(JÖRGEN TESMAN, *humming to himself, comes into the inner room from the right. He is carrying an empty, unfastened suit-case. He is a youngish-looking man of thirty-three, middle-sized, stoutish, with a round, frank, happy face. His hair and beard are fair; he wears glasses. He is comfortably—almost carelessly—dressed, in an indoor suit.*)

MISS TESMAN. Good morning, good morning, Jörgen!

TESMAN (*in the doorway between the rooms*). Aunt Julle! My dear Aunt Julle! (*Goes up and shakes her hand affectionately.*)   All the way out here so early! Eh?

MISS TESMAN. Well, you can just imagine! I *had* to have a look at you both.

TESMAN. Although you haven't had anything like a proper night's rest!

MISS TESMAN. Oh, that doesn't make a bit of difference to me.

TESMAN. But you did get home from the pier all right? Eh?

MISS TESMAN. Oh yes, quite all right, I'm glad to say. Mr. Brack was so very kind and saw me right to my door.

TESMAN. We *were* so sorry we couldn't give you a lift. But you saw how it was yourself. Hedda had so much luggage that she had to have with her.

MISS TESMAN. Yes, she certainly did have a tremendous lot of luggage.

BERTE *(to* TESMAN). Shall I go in and ask the mistress if there's anything I could help her with?

TESMAN. No, thanks, Berte, you needn't do that. If she wants you for anything, she says she'll ring.

BERTE *(to the right)*. Very well.

TESMAN. Oh, but, here—take this suit-case, will you?

BERTE *(taking it)*. I'll put it up in the attic.   *(Goes out by the hall door.)*

TESMAN. Just think, Aunt Julle, I had that whole suit-case crammed full, just with the stuff I'd copied. You wouldn't believe what I've managed to collect, going through the archives. Curious old things that no one really knows about.

MISS TESMAN. Well, well Jörgen, you certainly haven't wasted your time on your honeymoon.

TESMAN. No, I jolly well haven't! But take your hat off, Aunt Julle. Here, let me unfasten the bow. Eh?

MISS TESMAN *(while he is doing it)*. Bless me! It's just as though you were still at home with us.

TESMAN *(turning and twisting the hat in his hand)*. Why! What a fine, smart hat you've bought yourself!

MISS TESMAN. I got it because of Hedda.

TESMAN. Because of Hedda? Eh?

MISS TESMAN. Yes. So that Hedda shan't be ashamed of me if we go out together.

TESMAN *(patting her cheek)*. *Dear* Aunt Julle! You think of absolutely everything.   *(Puts the hat on a chair by the table.)*   Now, look here; lets sit on the sofa and have a little chat till Hedda comes.

(They sit down. She puts her parasol in the sofa-corner.)

MISS TESMAN *(taking both his hands and looking at him)*. What a blessing it is to have you again, Jörgen, as large as life! My dear! Poor Jochum's own boy!

TESMAN. So it is for me, Aunt Julle, to see *you* again! You who've been my father and my mother.

MISS TESMAN. Yes, I know you'll always have a corner in your heart for your old aunts.

TESMAN. But I suppose there's no improvement in Aunt Rina, eh?

MISS TESMAN. Well, you know, we can't really expect any improvement in her, poor dear. She just lies there, the same as she has all these years. But I hope the good Lord will let me keep her a little longer. For I shan't know what to do with my life otherwise, Jörgen. Especially now, you know, that I haven't got you to look after any more.

TESMAN (*patting her on the back*). Come, come, come!

MISS TESMAN (*with a sudden change*). But just think, Jörgen, you're a married man! And to think it was you who carried off Hedda Gabler! The lovely Hedda Gabler! To think of it! She, who always had so *many* admirers.

TESMAN (*humming a little, with a satisfied smile*). Yes, I expect a certain number of my good friends are going about this town feeling pretty envious. Eh?

MISS TESMAN. And to think that you were able to have such a long honeymoon! Over five months. Nearly six.

TESMAN. Well, for me it's been a kind of research tour as well—with all those old records I had to hunt through. And then, you know, the enormous number of books I had to read.

MISS TESMAN. Yes, that's quite true. (*Dropping her voice a little and speaking confidentially.*)   But look here, Jörgen, haven't you anything . . . anything, well, *special* to tell me?

TESMAN. About the trip?

MISS TESMAN. Yes.

TESMAN. No, I don't think there's anything else, except what I told you in my letters. About my taking my doctorate down there—well, I told you that yesterday.

MISS TESMAN. Oh yes, that kind of thing. Yes. But, I mean, haven't you any . . . well, any hopes . . . er . . . ?

TESMAN. Hopes?

MISS TESMAN. Oh, come, Jörgen! After all, I *am* your old aunt!

TESMAN. Well, yes, of course I have hopes . . .

MISS TESMAN. Ah!

TESMAN. . . . I've the very best hopes of getting a professorship one of these days.

MISS TESMAN. Oh yes, a professorship. Yes.

TESMAN. Or I might say, rather, there's a certainty of my getting it. But, my dear Aunt Julle, you know that yourself perfectly well!

MISS TESMAN (*with a little laugh*). Yes, of course I do. You're quite right. (*Changing her tone.*)   But we were talking about your travels. It must have cost a lot of money, Jörgen?

TESMAN. Ye-es. But, you know, that big fellowship took us a good bit of the way.

MISS TESMAN. But I don't see how you can possibly have made that do for two.

TESMAN. Well, no; one could hardly expect that. Eh?

MISS TESMAN. Especially when it's a lady one's travelling with. For that usually comes more expensive—very much more. I've heard.

TESMAN. Well, yes, of course. It does come rather more expensive. But Hedda had to have that trip, Aunt Julle. She really had to. Nothing else would have done.

MISS TESMAN. No, no. Of course it wouldn't. A honeymoon abroad seems quite a matter of course, nowadays. But tell me now. Have you had a chance yet to have a good look at the house?

TESMAN. You bet I have! I have been wandering round ever since it was light.

MISS TESMAN. And what do you think of it, on the whole?

TESMAN. Splendid! Absolutely splendid! There's only one thing I can't see—what we're going to do with the two empty rooms there between the back sitting-room and Hedda's bedroom.

MISS TESMAN (*with a little laugh*). Oh, my dear Jörgen, there may be a use for them—all in good time.

TESMAN. Yes, you're perfectly right, Aunt Julle! Because, by degrees, as I get a bigger library, well—Eh?

MISS TESMAN. Of course, my dear boy. It was the library I was thinking of.

TESMAN. I'm specially glad for Hedda's sake. She often said, before we were engaged, that she'd never care to live anywhere except in Mrs. Falk's house.

MISS TESMAN. Yes, just fancy! And then its happening like that—the house being for sale! Just as you had started.

TESMAN. Yes, Aunt Julle, the luck certainly was with us. Eh?

MISS TESMAN. But expensive, my dear Jörgen! It will be expensive for you, all this.

TESMAN (*looking at her, a little disheartened*). Yes, I suppose it will, perhaps.

MISS TESMAN. Goodness, yes!

TESMAN. How much do you think? Roughly. Eh?

MISS TESMAN. Oh, I can't possibly tell till all the bills come in.

TESMAN. But fortunately Mr. Brack has arranged the easiest possible terms for me. He wrote and told Hedda so himself.

MISS TESMAN. Well, don't you worry about it, my child. And as for the furniture and carpets, I have given security for them.

TESMAN. Security? My dear Aunt Julle, what kind of security could you give?

MISS TESMAN. I have given a mortgage on the annuity.

TESMAN (*jumping up*). What! On yours and Aunt Rina's annuity?

MISS TESMAN. Yes. I didn't know what else to do, you see.

TESMAN (*standing in front of her*). But, Aunt Julle, have you gone crazy? The annuity! The only thing you and Aunt Rina have to live on!

MISS TESMAN. Now now—don't get so upset about it. The whole thing is just a formality, you know. That's what Mr. Brack said, too. For it was he who so kindly arranged it for me. Just a formality, he said.

TESMAN. Yes, that may be so. But all the same . . .

MISS TESMAN. Because you've got your own salary to rely on now. And— goodness me!—suppose we did have to spend a little too—just at first? Why, it would only be a pleasure for us.

TESMAN. Oh, Aunt Julle, you will never be tired of sacrificing yourself for me.

MISS TESMAN (*getting up and laying her hands on his shoulders*). Have I any other joy in this world but in smoothing the way for you, my dear boy? You who've had neither father nor mother to turn to. And now we've reached our goal, my dear! Things may have looked black now and again. But, thank goodness, you're through that now, Jörgen.

TESMAN. Yes, it's wonderful, really, how everything has worked out.

MISS TESMAN. Yes, and the people who stood in your way, who would have stopped your getting on, you have them at your feet. They have gone down before you, Jörgen—most of all, the person who was most dangerous to you. And there he lies now, on the bed he made for himself, the poor misguided creature.

TESMAN. Have you heard anything of Ejlert? Since I went away, I mean?

MISS TESMAN. No, only that he's supposed to have brought out a new book.

TESMAN. *What?* Ejlert Lövborg? Just recently? Eh?

MISS TESMAN. Yes, so they say. I shouldn't think there can be much in it, would you? Now when *your* new book comes out, that will be quite another story, Jörgen. What is it going to be about?

TESMAN. It's going to be about domestic crafts in Brabant in the Middle Ages.

MISS TESMAN. Well, well! To think you can write about a thing like that!

TESMAN. As a matter of fact, the book may take some time yet. I've got to arrange those enormous collections of material first, you know.

MISS TESMAN. Ah yes. Arranging and collecting—that's what you're so good at. You're not dear Jochum's son for nothing.

TESMAN. I'm looking forward immensely to getting down to it. Especially now that I've got a charming house of my own, my own home to work in.

MISS TESMAN. And first and foremost, my dear, now that you've got the wife your heart was set on.

TESMAN (*giving her a hug*). Why, of course, Aunt Julle! Hedda! Why, that's the loveliest thing of all! (*Looking towards the center doorway.*) I think she's coming. Eh?

(HEDDA *comes in from the left, through the inner room. She is a woman of twenty-nine. Her face and figure show breeding and distinction, her complexion has an even pallor. Her eyes are steel-grey; cold, clear and calm. Her hair is a beautiful light brown, though not noticeably abundant. The loose-fitting morning costume she is wearing is in good style.*)

MISS TESMAN (*going up to* HEDDA). Good morning, Hedda dear! A very good morning to you!

HEDDA (*holding out her hand*). Good morning, my dear Miss Tesman. What an early visit! It was kind of you.

MISS TESMAN (*seeming a little taken aback*). Well, has the bride slept well in her new home?

HEDDA. Oh yes, thank you. Tolerably.

TESMAN. Tolerably! I like that, Hedda! You were sleeping like a log when I got up.

HEDDA. Fortunately. In any case, one has to get used to anything new, Miss Tesman. By degrees. (*Looking to the left.*) Oh! The maid has gone and opened the veranda door! There's a perfect flood of sunlight coming in.

MISS TESMAN (*going towards the door*). Well, we'll shut it, then.

HEDDA. Oh no, don't do that, please. (*To* TESMAN.) Just draw the blinds, my dear, will you? That gives a softer light.

TESMAN (*at the door*). Yes, yes. All right. There you are, Hedda. Now you've got shade *and* fresh air.

HEDDA. Yes, we certainly need fresh air in here. All these precious flowers! But—won't you sit down, Miss Tesman?

MISS TESMAN. No, thank you very much. Now I know everything is going on all right here—thank goodness!—I must see about getting home again. Poor dear, she finds the time very long, lying there.

TESMAN. Give her my love and my best wishes, won't you? And tell her I'll come over and see her later on today.

MISS TESMAN. Yes, yes, I certainly will. But that reminds me, Jörgen. (*Feeling in her bag.*) I nearly forgot it. I've brought something of yours.

TESMAN. What is it, Aunt Julle? Eh?

MISS TESMAN (*bringing out a flat newspaper package and handing it to him*). Look there, my dear boy.

TESMAN (*opening it*). Well, I'm blessed! You've kept them for me, Aunt Julle! That really is sweet of her, Hedda, isn't it? Eh?

HEDDA (*by the what-not on the right*). Yes, my dear. What is it?

TESMAN. My old morning shoes. My slippers—look!

HEDDA. Oh yes. I remember, you often spoke about them while we were away.

TESMAN. Yes, I missed them dreadfully. (*Going up to her.*) Now you shall see them, Hedda.

HEDDA (*going over to the stove*). No, thanks. It really doesn't interest me.

TESMAN (*following her*). Just think, Aunt Rina embroidered them for me in bed, lying ill like that. Oh, you can't imagine how many memories are worked into them!

HEDDA. Not for me, particularly.

MISS TESMAN. Hedda's right about that, Jörgen.

TESMAN. Yes, but I think, now she belongs to the family—

HEDDA (*interrupting*). My dear, we shall never be able to manage with this maid.

MISS TESMAN. Not manage with Berte?

TESMAN. What makes you say that, my dear? Eh?

HEDDA (*pointing*). Look there. She's left her old hat behind her on the chair.

TESMAN (*dropping his slippers on the floor in his dismay*). But, Hedda—

HEDDA. Suppose anyone were to come in and see it?

TESMAN. But—but, Hedda, that is Aunt Julle's hat!

HEDDA. Oh! Is it?

MISS TESMAN (*picking up the hat*). Yes, it's certainly mine. And it isn't old, either, my dear little Hedda.

HEDDA. I really didn't look at it closely, Miss Tesman.

MISS TESMAN (*putting on the hat*). As a matter of fact, it's the first time I've worn it. The very first, it is.

TESMAN. And a beautiful hat it is, too. Really grand!

MISS TESMAN. Oh, it's not all that, my dear Jörgen. (*Looking round her.*) Parasol? Ah, here it is. (*Picking it up.*) For that's mine, too. (*Under her breath.*) Not Berte's.

TESMAN. A new hat and a new parasol! Think of that, Hedda.

HEDDA. Yes, it's very nice. Charming.

TESMAN. Yes, isn't it? Eh? But, Aunt Julle, take a good look at Hedda before you go. See how nice and charming *she* is.

MISS TESMAN. Ah, my dear, there's nothing new in *that*. Hedda has been lovely all her life. (*She nods and goes towards the right.*)

TESMAN (*following her*). Yes, but have you noticed how plump she's grown, and how well she is? How much she's filled out on our travels?

HEDDA (*crossing the room*). Oh, be quiet—!

MISS TESMAN (*who has stopped and turned round*). Filled out?

TESMAN. Of course, you can't see it so well, Aunt Julle, now she has that dress on. But I, who have the opportunity of—

HEDDA (*at the glass door, impatiently*). Oh, you haven't any opportunity!

TESMAN. It must be the mountain air, down there in the Tyrol—

HEDDA (*interrupting curtly*). I am exactly the same as I was when I went away.

TESMAN. Yes, so you keep on saying. But you certainly aren't. Don't you think so too, Aunt Julle?

MISS TESMAN (*gazing at her with clasped hands*). Hedda is lovely—lovely—lovely! (*She goes up to* HEDDA, *takes her head in both hands, and, bending it down, kisses her hair.*) May God bless and take care of our Hedda. For Jörgen's sake.

HEDDA (*freeing herself gently*). Oh—let me go.

MISS TESMAN (*quietly, but with emotion*). I shall come over and see you two every single day.

TESMAN. Yes, do, *please*, Aunt Julle! Eh?

MISS TESMAN. Good-bye. Good-bye.

(*She goes out by the hall door.* TESMAN *goes with her, leaving the door half open. He can be heard repeating his messages to Aunt Rina and thanking her for the shoes. In the meanwhile* HEDDA *crosses the room, raising her arms and clenching her hands, as if in fury. Then she pulls back the curtains from the glass door and stands there looking out. After a moment* TESMAN *comes in again, shutting the door behind him.*)

TESMAN (*picking up the slippers from the floor*). What are you looking at, Hedda?

HEDDA (*calm and controlled again*). I'm just looking at the leaves. They're so yellow, and so withered.

TESMAN (*wrapping up the shoes and putting them on the table*). Well, after all, we're well on in September now.

HEDDA (*disturbed again*). Yes, just think. We're already in—in September.

TESMAN. Don't you think Aunt Julle was rather unlike herself, my dear? A little bit—almost formal? Whatever do you think was the matter? Eh?

HEDDA. I hardly know her, you see. Isn't she like that as a rule?

TESMAN. No, not like she was today.

HEDDA (*moving away from the glass door*). Do you think she was really upset about that business with the hat?

TESMAN. Oh, not much. Perhaps a little, just at the moment.

HEDDA. But what extraordinary manners! To throw her hat down here in the drawing-room. One doesn't do that kind of thing.

TESMAN. Well, you can be sure Aunt Julle won't do it again.

HEDDA. Anyway, I'll make it all right with her.

TESMAN. That's sweet of you, Hedda dear! If you would!

HEDDA. When you go in to see them presently, you might ask her over here for the evening.

TESMAN. Yes, I certainly will. And there's another thing you could do that would please her enormously.

HEDDA. Oh? What?

TESMAN. If you could bring yourself to speak a little more affectionately to her—as if you were one of the family. For my sake, Hedda? Eh?

HEDDA. No, no. You mustn't ask me to do that. I've told you that once already. I'll try to call her "Aunt," and that must be enough.

TESMAN. Oh well, all right. Only it seems to me now that you belong to the family—

HEDDA. Well, I really don't know. . . . (*She goes up towards the center doorway.*)

TESMAN (*after a pause*). Is there anything the matter, Hedda? Eh?

HEDDA. I'm just looking at my old piano. It doesn't go very well with all these other things.

TESMAN. When I get my first salary cheque, we'll see about an exchange.

HEDDA. Oh no, not an exchange. I don't want to get rid of it. We can put it in there, in the back room. And we can have another in its place here. Some time or other, I mean.

TESMAN (*a little subdued*). Yes. We can do that, of course.

HEDDA (*picking up the bouquet from the piano*). These flowers weren't here when we came in last night.

TESMAN. Aunt Julle must have brought them for you.

HEDDA (*looking into the bouquet*). A visiting-card. (*Taking it out and reading it.*) "Will call again later on today." Can you guess who it's from?

TESMAN. No. Who is it? Eh?

HEDDA. It says "Mrs. Elvsted."

TESMAN. Really? The wife of the District Magistrate. Miss Rysing that was.

HEDDA. Yes. Exactly. That girl with the tiresome hair, that she was always showing off. An old flame of yours, I've heard.

TESMAN (*laughing*). Oh, it didn't last long! And it was before I knew you, Hedda. But fancy her being in town.

HEDDA. Odd, that she should call on us. I hardly know her, except that we were at school together.

TESMAN. Yes, I haven't seen her either for—heaven knows how long. I wonder she can bear it up there, in that hole of a place. Eh?

HEDDA (*thinks a moment and says suddenly*). Tell me, isn't it somewhere up there that he lives—er—Ejlert Lövborg?

TESMAN. Yes it is. Up in those parts.

(BERTE *comes in at the hall door.*)

BERTE. She's here again, ma'am. The lady who came and left the flowers an hour ago. (*Pointing.*) The ones you've got in your hand, ma'am.

HEDDA. Oh, is she? Show her in, will you?

(BERTE *opens the door for* MRS. ELVSTED *and goes out herself.* MRS. ELVSTED *is a slender little thing with pretty, soft features. Her eyes are light blue, large, round and slightly prominent, with a startled, questioning expression. Her hair is remarkably fair, almost silver-gilt, and exceptionally thick and wavy. She is a couple of years younger than* HEDDA. *She is wearing a dark calling costume, of a good style but not quite of the latest fashion.*)

HEDDA (*going to meet her in a friendly way*). How are you, my dear Mrs. Elvsted? It's nice to see you once more.

MRS. ELVSTED (*nervous, and trying to control herself*). Yes, it's a very long time since we met.

TESMAN (*giving her his hand*). Or we two either. Eh?

HEDDA. Thank you for your lovely flowers.

MRS. ELVSTED. Oh, please! I would have come here at once, yesterday afternoon. But I heard that you were away.

TESMAN. Have you only just come to town? Eh?

MRS. ELVSTED. I got here about midday yesterday. I was absolutely in despair when I heard that you weren't at home.

HEDDA. In despair? But why?

TESMAN. But my dear, dear Mrs. Rysing—Mrs. Elvsted, I mean—

HEDDA. There isn't anything the matter, is there?

MRS. ELVSTED. Yes, there is. And I don't know a living soul to turn to here in town, except you.

HEDDA (*putting the bouquet down on the table*). Come now, let's sit here on the sofa.

MRS. ELVSTED. No, I feel too worried and restless to sit down.

HEDDA. Oh no, you don't. Come along here.   (*She pulls* MRS. ELVSTED *down onto the sofa and sits beside her.*)

TESMAN. Well now, what is it, Mrs. Elvsted?

HEDDA. Has anything gone wrong up there, at home?

MRS. ELVSTED. Well, it has and it hasn't. Oh, I do so want you not to misunderstand me.

HEDDA. Then the best thing you can do, Mrs. Elvsted, is to tell us all about it.

TESMAN. Because that's what you've come for, isn't it? Eh?

MRS. ELVSTED. Yes, yes, it is, of course. Well, then, I must explain—if you don't know already—that Ejlert Lövborg is in town too.

HEDDA. Lövborg is!

TESMAN. Really? So Ejlert Lövborg's come back again! Fancy that, Hedda!

HEDDA. Quite. I heard all right.

MRS. ELVSTED. He's been here a week now, already. Think of it! A whole week in this dangerous town. And alone! And all the bad company he could get into here!

HEDDA. But, my dear Mrs. Elvsted, why does *he* specially matter to you?

MRS. ELVSTED (*gives her a frightened glance and says quickly*). He used to be the children's tutor.

HEDDA. Your children's?

MRS. ELVSTED. My husband's. I haven't got any.

HEDDA. Your step-children's, then.

MRS. ELVSTED. Yes.

TESMAN (*hesitantly*). Was he . . . er . . . tolerably . . . then . . . I don't quite know how to put it . . . fairly steady in his habits—enough to be given *that* job? Eh?

MRS. ELVSTED. For the last two years there hasn't been a word against him.

TESMAN. Really! Think of that, Hedda!

HEDDA. I heard.

MRS. ELVSTED. Not the least thing, I assure you. Nothing of any kind. But still now, when I know he's here—in this great city—and with plenty of money in his pockets . . . I'm desperately anxious about him now.

TESMAN. But why didn't he stay up there where he was, then? With you and your husband? Eh?

MRS. ELVSTED. Once the book was out he was too restless and excited to stay up there with us.

TESMAN. Oh yes, that reminds me. Aunt Julle said he'd brought out a new book.

MRS. ELVSTED. Yes, a big new book on the history of civilization; a sort of general survey. It's been out a fortnight now. And now that it's gone so well and made such a tremendous stir—

TESMAN. It has, has it? It must be something he had by him from his better days, then.

MRS. ELVSTED. From some time ago, you mean?

TESMAN. Exactly.

MRS. ELVSTED. No, he wrote the whole thing up at our place. Just lately—within the last year.

TESMAN. That's good news, isn't it, Hedda? Just fancy!

MRS. ELVSTED. Yes, indeed. If only it would last.

HEDDA. Have you met him here in town?

MRS. ELVSTED. No, not yet. I had a lot of trouble finding his address. But I got it at last, this morning.

HEDDA (*looking searchingly at her*). You know, it seems a little odd of your husband to . . . er . . .

MRS. ELVSTED (*starting nervously*). Of my husband? What does?

HEDDA. To send you to town on an errand like this. Not to come in and look after his friend himself.

MRS. ELVSTED. Oh, not at all! My husband hasn't time for that. And then there—there was some shopping I had to do.

HEDDA (*with a slight smile*). Ah well, that's a different matter.

MRS. ELVSTED (*getting up quickly, in some distress*). So I do implore you, Mr. Tesman, be good to Ejlert Lövborg if he comes to you! And he's sure to, because you were such good friends in the old days. And besides, you're both working in the same field. On the same subjects, as far as I can make out.

TESMAN. Well anyway, we were at one time.

MRS. ELVSTED. Yes. And that's why I do beseech you—you really will keep a watchful eye on him too, won't you, Mr. Tesman? You do promise me?

TESMAN. Yes, I'll be only too glad to, Mrs. Rysing—

HEDDA. Elvsted.

TESMAN. I really will do what I can for Ejlert. Everything I possibly can. You can be sure of that.

MRS. ELVSTED. Oh, you *are* being kind! (*Clasping his hands.*) Thank you, again and again. (*Frightened.*) Because my husband is so attached to him.

HEDDA (*getting up*). You ought to write to him, my dear. He may not come to see you of his own accord.

TESMAN. Yes, Hedda, that probably would be best. Eh?

HEDDA. And the sooner the better. Now—at once—I think.

MRS. ELVSTED (*beseechingly*). Oh yes? If you *would!*

TESMAN. I'll write this very minute. Have you his address, Mrs.—Elvsted?

MRS. ELVSTED (*taking a small slip of paper out of her pocket and handing it to him*). Here it is.

TESMAN. Good. Good. I'll go in, then. (*Looking round him.*) That reminds me—my slippers? Ah, here they are. (*Picks up the parcel and is just going.*)

HEDDA. Now write really kindly and affectionately. And a good long letter, too.

TESMAN. Yes, I certainly will.

MRS. ELVSTED. But, please, don't say a word about my having asked you to!

TESMAN. Of course not. That goes without saying. Eh? (*He goes through the inner room to the right.*)

HEDDA (*goes up to* MRS. ELVSTED *and says softly*). That's right. Now we've killed two birds with one stone.

MRS. ELVSTED. How do you mean?

HEDDA. Didn't you realize I wanted to get rid of him?

MRS. ELVSTED. Yes, to write his letter.

HEDDA. And also so that I could talk to you alone.

MRS. ELVSTED (*confused*). About this business?

HEDDA. Exactly. About that.

MRS. ELVSTED (*alarmed*). But there isn't anything more, Mrs. Tesman! Nothing at all!

HEDDA. Oh yes there is, now. There's a lot more. That much I do realize. Come over here, and we'll sit and be cosy and friendly together.

(*She pushes* MRS. ELVSTED *into the easy-chair by the stove and sits on one of the stools herself.*)

MRS. ELVSTED (*looking anxiously at her watch*). But my dear Mrs. Tesman, I really meant to go now.

HEDDA. Oh, surely there's no hurry. Now then, suppose you tell me a little about what your home's like.

MRS. ELVSTED. But that's the last thing in the world I wanted to talk about!

HEDDA. Not to me, my dear? After all, we were at school together.

MRS. ELVSTED. Yes, but you were a class above me. How dreadfully frightened of you I was in those days!

HEDDA. Were you frightened of me?

MRS. ELVSTED. Yes. Dreadfully frightened. Because when we met on the stairs you always used to pull my hair.

HEDDA. No, *did* I?

MRS. ELVSTED. Yes, and once you said you would burn it off.

HEDDA. Oh, that was only silly talk, you know.

MRS. ELVSTED. Yes, but I was so stupid in those days. And since then, anyhow, we have drifted such a long, long way part. Our circles were so entirely different.

HEDDA. Well, then, we'll see if we can come together again. Now, look here. When we were at school we used to talk like real close friends and call each other by our Christian names.

MRS. ELVSTED. Oh no, you're making quite a mistake.

HEDDA. I certainly am *not*. I remember it perfectly well. So we are going to tell each other everything, as we did in the old days. (*Moving nearer with her stool.*) There we are! (*Kissing her cheek.*) Now you're to talk to me like a real friend and call me "Hedda."

MRS. ELVSTED (*clasping and patting her hands*). All this goodness and kindness—it's not a bit what I'm used to.

HEDDA. There, there, there! And I'm going to treat *you* like a friend, as I did before, and call you my dear Thora.

MRS. ELVSTED. My name's Thea.

HEDDA. Yes, of course. Of course. I meant Thea. (*Looking sympathetically at her.*) So you're not used to much goodness or kindness, aren't you, Thea? Not in your own home?

MRS. ELVSTED. Ah, if I *had* a home! But I haven't one. Never have had. . . .

HEDDA (*looking at her a moment*). I rather thought it must be something of that sort.

MRS. ELVSTED (*gazing helplessly in front of her*). Yes. Yes. Yes.

HEDDA. I can't quite remember now, but wasn't it as housekeeper that you went up there in the beginning—to the District Magistrate's?

MRS. ELVSTED. Actually it was to have been as governess. But his wife— his late wife—was an invalid and was ill in bed most of the time. So I had to take charge of the house too.

HEDDA. But then, in the end, you became the mistress of the house.

MRS. ELVSTED (*drearily*). Yes, I did.

HEDDA. Let me see. . . . About how long ago is it now?

MRS. ELVSTED. Since I was married?

HEDDA. Yes.

MRS. ELVSTED. It's five years ago now.

HEDDA. Yes, of course. It must be that.

MRS. ELVSTED. Ah! Those five years—or rather the last two or three. Oh, if you could only imagine, Mrs. Tesman—

HEDDA (*giving her a little slap on the hand*). Mrs. Tesman! Come, Thea!

MRS. ELVSTED. Oh yes; I will try! Yes, Hedda, if you had any idea—if you understood—

HEDDA (*casually*). Ejlert Lövborg was up there too for three years or so, I believe?

MRS. ELVSTED (*looking at her doubtfully*). Ejlert Lövborg? Why yes. He was.

HEDDA. Did you know him already? From the old days in town?

MRS. ELVSTED. Hardly at all. Well I mean—by name, of course.

HEDDA. But when you were up there—then, he used to visit you and your husband?

MRS. ELVSTED. Yes, he came over to us every day. You see, he was giving the children lessons. Because, in the long run, I couldn't manage it all myself.

HEDDA. No, I should think not. And your husband? I suppose he is often away from home?

MRS. ELVSTED. Yes. You see, Mrs.—er—you see, Hedda, being District Magistrate he's always having to go out on circuit.

HEDDA (leaning against the arm of the chair). Thea, my poor little Thea. Now you're going to tell me all about it. Just how things are.

MRS. ELVSTED. Very well. You ask me about it, then.

HEDDA. What is your husband really like, Thea? You know what I mean —in everyday life? Is he nice to you?

MRS. ELVSTED (evasively). He's quite sure himself that he does everything for the best.

HEDDA. Only, it seems to me, he must be much too old for you. More than twenty years older, surely?

MRS. ELVSTED (irritably). Yes, there's that too. What with one thing and another, I'm miserable with him. We haven't an idea in common, he and I. Not a thing in the world.

HEDDA. But isn't he fond of you, all the same? I mean, in his own way?

MRS. ELVSTED. Oh, I don't know *what* he feels. I think I'm just useful to him. After all, it doesn't cost much to keep me. I'm cheap.

HEDDA. That's silly of you.

MRS. ELVSTED (shaking her head). It can't be any different. Not with him. He isn't really fond of anyone but himself. And perhaps the children— a little.

HEDDA. And of Ejlert Lövborg, Thea.

MRS. ELVSTED (looking at her). Of Ejlert Lövborg? What makes you think that?

HEDDA. But, my dear—it seems to me, when he sends you all the way into town after him. . . .   (Smiling almost imperceptibly.)   And besides, you said so yourself to my husband.

MRS. ELVSTED (with a nervous start). What? Oh yes, so I did.   (Breaking out, but in a lowered voice.)   No. I might as well tell you now as later. It'll all come out, anyway.

HEDDA. But, my dear Thea—

MRS. ELVSTED. Well, to be quite frank, my husband had no idea I was coming.

HEDDA. *What!* Didn't your husband know about it?

MRS. ELVSTED. No, of course not. And, anyway, he wasn't at home. He was away too. Oh, I couldn't stand it any longer, Hedda! It was simply impossible. I should have been absolutely alone up there in future.

HEDDA. Well? So then?

MRS. ELVSTED. So I packed up some of my things, you see—the ones I needed most. Very quietly, of course. And so I left the place.

HEDDA. Just like that? Nothing more?

MRS. ELVSTED. No . . . And then I took the train straight in to town.

HEDDA. But, my dear, precious child! How did you dare risk it?

MRS. ELVSTED (*getting up and moving across the room*). Well, what on earth could I do?

HEDDA. But what do you think your husband will say when you go back again?

MRS. ELVSTED (*by the table, looking at her*). Back there, to him?

HEDDA. Yes, of course. What then?

MRS. ELVSTED. I'm never going back there to him.

HEDDA (*getting up and going nearer to her*). Then you've left in real earnest, for good and all?

MRS. ELVSTED. Yes. There didn't seem to be anything else for me to do.

HEDDA. And then—your doing it quite openly!

MRS. ELVSTED. Oh, you can't keep that kind of thing secret, in any case.

HEDDA. But, Thea, what do you think people will say about you?

MRS. ELVSTED. Heaven knows, they must say what they like. (*Sitting down on the sofa wearily and sadly.*) I have only done what I *had* to do.

HEDDA (*after a short silence*). What do you mean to do now? What kind of job are you going to get?

MRS. ELVSTED. I don't know yet. I only know that I must live here, where Ejlert Lövborg lives. That is, if I *must* live. . . .

HEDDA (*moves a chair from the table, sits beside her and strokes her hands*). Thea, my dear, how did it happen? This—this friendship between you and Ejlert Lövborg?

MRS. ELVSTED. Oh, it happened by degrees, somehow. I came to have some kind of power over him.

HEDDA. Indeed? And then?

MRS. ELVSTED. He gave up his old habits. Not because I asked him to. I never dared do that. But of course he noticed I didn't like that kind of thing. And so he left off.

HEDDA (*masking an involuntary sneer*). In fact, you've what they call "reclaimed him," you have, little Thea.

MRS. ELVSTED. Yes. At least, he says so himself. And he, for his part, has made me into a real human being! Taught me to think . . . and to understand . . . one thing after another.

HEDDA. Perhaps he gave *you* lessons, too, did he?

MRS. ELVSTED. No, not exactly lessons. . . . But he used to talk to me about such endless numbers of things. And then came the glorious, happy moment when I began to share his work! When he let me help him.

HEDDA. And you did, did you?

MRS. ELVSTED. Yes. When he was writing anything, we always had to work at it together.

HEDDA. I see. Like two good comrades.

MRS ELVSTED (*eagerly*). Comrades! Why, Hedda, that's just what he called it! Oh, I ought to feel so perfectly happy. But I can't, though. Because I really don't know whether it will last.

HEDDA. Aren't you surer of him than that?

MRS. ELVSTED (*drearily*). There's the shadow of a woman standing between Ejlert Lövborg and me.

HEDDA (*looking intently at her*). Who can that be?

MRS. ELVSTED. I don't know. Someone or other from—from his past. Someone he's never really forgotten.

HEDDA. What has he said . . . about it?

MRS. ELVSTED. He only touched on it once—and quite vaguely.

HEDDA. Oh. And what did he say, then?

MRS. ELVSTED. He said that when they parted she wanted to shoot him with a pistol.

HEDDA (*cold and controlled*). How absurd! People don't do that kind of thing here.

MRS. ELVSTED. No. And that's why I thought it must be that red-haired singer that he once—

HEDDA. Yes, that may be.

MRS. ELVSTED. Because I remember people used to talk about her carrying loaded firearms.

HEDDA. Oh well, then, it's obviously she.

MRS. ELVSTED (*wringing her hands*). Yes, but just think, Hedda, now I hear that that singer—she's in town again! Oh, I'm simply desperate!

HEDDA (*glancing towards the inner room*). Sh! Here comes my husband. (*Getting up and whispering.*)   Thea, all this must be between our two selves.

MRS. ELVSTED (*springing up*). Why, yes! For heaven's sake!   (JÖRGEN TESMAN, *with a letter in his hand, comes in from the right through the inner room.*)

TESMAN. There we are! The letter's finished and ready.

HEDDA. That's good. But I think Mrs. Elvsted wants to go now. Wait a minute. I'm going to the garden gate with her.

TESMAN. I say, Hedda, I wonder if Berte could see to this?

HEDDA (*taking the letter*). I'll tell her to.

(BERTE *comes in from the hall.*)

BERTE. Mr. Brack's here and would like to see the master and mistress, please.

HEDDA. Ask Mr. Brack if he will please come in. And—look here—put this letter in the post, will you?

BERTE (*taking the letter*). Certainly, ma'am.

(*She opens the door for* BRACK *and goes out herself. He is a man of forty-*

*five, square but well built and light in his movements. His face is round-
ish, with a fine profile. His hair, still almost black, is short and carefully
waved. His eyes are lively and bright. His eyebrows are thick and so is his
moustache with its clipped ends. He is dressed in a well-cut outdoor suit
—a little too young for his age. He wears an eye-glass, which he now and
then lets fall.)*

BRACK *(bowing, with his hat in his hand).* May one call so early as this?

HEDDA. One certainly may!

TESMAN *(clasping his hand).* You will always be welcome *(Introducing
    him.)*   Mr. Brack, Miss Rysing.

HEDDA. Oh!

BRACK *(bowing).* A great pleasure.

HEDDA *(looking at him and laughing).* It's very nice to have a look at you
    by daylight, Mr. Brack.

BRACK. Any difference, do you think?

HEDDA. Yes; I think a little younger.

BRACK. Thank you—very much.

TESMAN. But what do you say to Hedda? Eh? Doesn't she look well? She's
    positively—

HEDDA. Oh, do leave me out of it, please. What about thanking Mr. Brack
    for all the trouble he has taken?

BRACK. Oh, no, no. It was only a pleasure.

HEDDA. Yes. You're a good friend. But here's Mrs. Elvsted longing to be off.
    Excuse me a moment; I shall be back again directly.

(Mutual good-byes. MRS. ELVSTED *and* HEDDA *go out by the hall door.)*

BRACK. Well now; is your wife fairly satisfied?

TESMAN. Rather! We can't thank you enough. Of course, I gather there
    will have to be a little rearranging. And there's a certain amount
    needed still. We shall have to get a few little things.

BRACK. Is that so? Really?

TESMAN. But you're not to have any trouble over that. Hedda said she
    would see to what was needed herself. But why don't we sit down? Eh?

BRACK. Thanks. Just for a minute.   *(He sits by the table.)*   There's some-
    thing I rather wanted to talk to you about, Tesman.

TESMAN. Is there? Ah, I understand!   *(Sits down.)*   I expect it's the serious
    part of the fun that's coming now. Eh?

BRACK. Oh, there's no great hurry about the financial side. However, I
    could wish we'd managed things a little more economically.

TESMAN. But that wouldn't have done at all! Think of Hedda, my dear
    man. You, who know her so well. I couldn't possibly ask her to live in
    some little suburban house.

BRACK. No. That's just the difficulty.

TESMAN. Besides, luckily it can't be long now before I get my appointment.

BRACK. Well you know, a thing like that can often be a slow business.

TESMAN. Have you heard anything further? Eh?

BRACK. Well, nothing definite— (*Breaking off.*) But that reminds me, there's one piece of news I can tell you.

TESMAN. Oh?

BRACK. Your old friend, Ejlert Lövborg, has come back to town.

TESMAN. I know that already.

BRACK. Do you? How did you come to know?

TESMAN. She told us. The lady who went out with Hedda.

BRACK. Oh, I see. What was her name? I didn't quite catch it.

TESMAN. Mrs. Elvsted.

BRACK. Oh yes; the District Magistrate's wife. Of course, it's up there he's been living.

TESMAN. And just think! I hear, to my great delight, that he's become perfectly steady again.

BRACK. Yes, so I'm assured.

TESMAN. And that he's brought out a new book. Eh?

BRACK. Oh yes.

TESMAN. And it's made quite an impression, too.

BRACK. It's made quite an extraordinary impression.

TESMAN. Well, now! Isn't that good news? He, with his remarkable gifts —I was terribly afraid he'd gone under for good.

BRACK. Yes. That was the general opinion about him.

TESMAN. But I can't imagine what he'll do now? What on earth can he be going to live on? Eh?

(*During the last words,* HEDDA *has come in by the hall door.*)

HEDDA (*to* BRACK, *laughing, with a touch of contempt*). My husband's always worrying about what one's going to live on.

TESMAN. Oh but, my dear, we were talking about poor Ejlert Lövborg.

HEDDA (*looking quickly at him*). Oh, were you? (*Sits in the easy-chair by the stove and asks, with a casual manner.*)   What's wrong with him?

TESMAN. Well, he must have run through that money he inherited long ago. And he can't very well write a new book every year. Eh? So, you see, I really wonder what will become of him.

BRACK. Perhaps I could tell you something about that.

TESMAN. Really?

BRACK. You must remember that he has relatives with a good deal of influence.

TESMAN. Ah, but unfortunately, his relatives have completely washed their hands of him.

BRACK. Once upon a time they called him the hope of the family.

TESMAN. Once upon a time, yes! But he's wrecked all that himself.

HEDDA. Who knows? (*With a slight smile.*)   After all, they've "reclaimed" him up at the Elvsteds' place.

BRACK. And then this book that's come out—

TESMAN. Ah well, let's hope to goodness they'll get something or other for him. I've just written to him. Hedda, my dear, I asked him to come out to us this evening.

BRACK. But, my dear fellow, you're coming to my bachelor party this evening. You promised last night at the pier.

HEDDA. Had you forgotten it, my dear?

TESMAN. Yes, by Jove, I had!

BRACK. In any case, you needn't worry. He isn't likely to come.

TESMAN. Why do you think he won't? Eh?

BRACK (*hesitating a little. Gets up and rests his hands on the back of the chair*). My dear Tesman—and you too, Mrs. Tesman—I can't, in fairness, leave you in ignorance of something that . . . er . . . that—

TESMAN. Something that has to do with Ejlert?

BRACK. That has to do both with you and with him.

TESMAN. But, my dear Brack, tell me what it is!

BRACK. You must be prepared for your appointment not to come so quickly, perhaps, as you wish or expect it to.

TESMAN (*jumping up, uneasily*). Has anything gone wrong? Eh?

BRACK. There may be some competition—perhaps—before the post is filled.

TESMAN. Competition! Fancy that, Hedda!

HEDDA (*leaning further back in the easy-chair*). Well, well, now!

TESMAN. But with whom? Surely, never with—?

BRACK. Yes. Just so. With Ejlert Lövborg.

TESMAN (*clasping his hands*). No, no! That's absolutely unthinkable! It's simply impossible! Eh?

BRACK. Well . . . That's what we may see, all the same.

TESMAN. But look here, Brack, it would be incredibly inconsiderate to me! (*Gesticulating with his arms.*) Because—why, just think!—I'm a married man. We married on our prospects, Hedda and I. Went and got thoroughly in debt, and borrowed money from Aunt Julle too. Why good Lord, the appointment was as good as promised to me! Eh?

BRACK. Steady, old man! No doubt you'll get the job, all right. But it will be contested first.

HEDDA (*motionless in the easy-chair*). Think of that, my dear. It will be almost like a kind of sport.

TESMAN. But, Hedda dearest, how can you take it all so casually?

HEDDA (*as before*). I'm not doing that at all. I'm quite excited about the result.

BRACK. At any rate, Mrs. Tesman, it's as well you should know now how things stand. I mean, before you start making those little purchases I hear you have in mind.

HEDDA. This can't make any difference.

BRACK. Oh, indeed? Then there's no more to be said. Good-bye. (*To*

TESMAN.) When I go for my afternoon stroll, I'll come in and fetch you.

TESMAN. Oh yes. Yes. I really don't know *what* I'm going to do.

HEDDA (*lying back and reaching out her hand*). Good-bye, Mr. Brack. And do come again.

BRACK. Many thanks! Good-bye, good-bye.

TESMAN (*going to the door with him*). Good-bye, my dear Brack. You must excuse me. . . .

(BRACK *goes out by the hall door.*)

TESMAN (*crossing the room*). Well, Hedda, one should never venture into the land of romance. Eh?

HEDDA (*looking at him and smiling*). Do *you* do that?

TESMAN. Why, my dear, it can't be denied. It *was* romantic to go and get married and set up house, simply and solely on our prospects.

HEDDA. You may be right, there.

TESMAN. Well, we have our charming home, anyhow. Think, Hedda, it's the home we both used to dream of—that we fell in love with, I might almost say. Eh?

HEDDA (*getting up slowly and wearily*). It was understood of course, that we should entertain—keep up some sort of establishment.

TESMAN. Goodness, yes! How I used to look forward to it, seeing you as hostess to a chosen circle of friends! Well, well, well. For the present we two must get along by ourselves, Hedda. Just have Aunt Julle out here every now and then. . . . Oh, my, dear, it was to have been so very, very different for you.

HEDDA. Naturally, now I shan't get a man-servant just at first.

TESMAN. No, I'm afraid you can't. There can be no question of keeping a man-servant, you know.

HEDDA. And the saddle-horse that I was going to—

TESMAN (*horrified*). Saddle-horse!

HEDDA. I suppose it's no use even thinking of that now.

TESMAN. Good heavens, no! That goes without saying.

HEDDA (*crossing the room towards the back*). Well, anyhow, I still have one thing to kill time with.

TESMAN (*beaming with pleasure*). Thank heavens for that! But what is it, Hedda? Eh?

HEDDA (*at the center doorway, looking at him with lurking contempt*). My pistols, Jörgen.

TESMAN (*anxiously*). Your pistols!

HEDDA (*with cold eyes*). General Gabler's pistols. (*She goes through the inner room and out to the left.*)

TESMAN (*running to the center doorway and calling after her*). For goodness' sake! Hedda, darling! Don't touch those dangerous things! For my sake, Hedda! Eh?

ACT II

The room at the Tesman's, as in the First Act, except that the piano has been taken away and a graceful little writing-table with a book case put in its place. A smaller table has been put by the sofa on the left; most of the bouquets are gone, but Mrs. Elvsted's stands on the large table in the front of the stage. It is afternoon.

HEDDA, *in an afternoon dress, is alone in the room. She is standing by the open glass door, loading a pistol. The fellow to it lies in an open pistol-case on the writing-table.*

HEDDA (*looking down the garden and calling*). How do you do again, Mr. Brack?

BRACK (*is heard from below, at a little distance*). And you, Mrs. Tesman?

HEDDA (*lifting the pistol and aiming*). I'm going to shoot you, sir!

BRACK (*calling from below*). No, no, no! Don't stand there aiming straight at me.

HEDDA. That comes of using the back way in. (*She shoots*).

BRACK (*nearer*). Are you quite crazy?

HEDDA. Dear me! I didn't hit you, did I?

BRACK (*still outside*). Now stop this nonsense!

HEDDA. Well, come in then.

(BRACK, *dressed as for an informal party, comes in by the glass door. He is carrying a light overcoat on his arm.*)

BRACK. The deuce! Do you still play that game? What are you shooting at?

HEDDA. Oh, I just stand and shoot up into the blue.

BRACK (*taking the pistol gently out of her hand*). If you don't mind, my dear lady. (*Looking at it.*) Ah, this one. I know it well. (*Looking round him.*) Now, where have we got the case? Ah yes, here. (*Puts the pistol away and shuts the case.*) Because we're not going to play that game any more today.

HEDDA. Well, what in heaven's name do you expect me to do with myself?

BRACK. Haven't you had any visitors?

HEDDA (*shutting the glass door*). Not a soul. I suppose everybody we know is still in the country.

BRACK. And isn't Tesman at home either?

HEDDA (*at the writing-table, shutting up the pistol-case in the drawer*). No, the minute he had finished lunch he tore off to his aunts. He didn't expect you so soon.

BRACK. Hm—and I didn't think of that. That was stupid of me.

HEDDA (*turning her head and looking at him*). Why stupid?

BRACK. Because if I had, I should have come here a little—earlier.

HEDDA (*crossing the room*). Well, then you wouldn't have found anyone at all. I was in my room changing after lunch.

BRACK. And there isn't so much as a tiny chink in the door that one could have communicated through?

HEDDA. You've forgotten to arrange anything like that.

BRACK. That was stupid of me, too.

HEDDA. Well, we shall just have to sit down here and wait. My husband won't be home yet awhile.

BRACK. Well, never mind. I'll be patient.

(HEDDA *sits down in the corner of the sofa.* BRACK *lays his coat over the back of the nearest chair and sits down, keeping his hat in his hand. There is a short pause. They look at each other.*)

HEDDA. Well?

BRACK (*in the same tone*). Well?

HEDDA. It was I who asked first.

BRACK (*leaning forward a little*). Come now, let's have a cosy little gossip all to ourselves—Madam Hedda.

HEDDA (*leaning further back on the sofa*). Doesn't it feel like a whole eternity since we last talked to each other? Oh, of course, a word or two last night and this morning—but I don't count that.

BRACK. Not like this, between ourselves? Alone together, you mean?

HEDDA. Yes. More or less that.

BRACK. Here was I, every blessed day, wishing to goodness you were home again.

HEDDA. And there was I, the whole time, wishing exactly the same.

BRACK. You? Really, Madam Hedda! And I, thinking you had thoroughly enjoyed yourself on your travels!

HEDDA. You may be sure I did!

BRACK. But Tesman was always saying so in his letters.

HEDDA. Oh, *he* did all right. Rummaging in libraries is the most entrancing occupation he knows. Sitting and copying out old parchments, or whatever they are.

BRACK (*with a touch of malice*). After all, that is his vocation in life. Partly, at least.

HEDDA. Oh yes, quite; it is. And of course then one can—But as for me! No, my dear sir. I was excruciatingly bored.

BRACK. Do you really mean it? In sober earnest?

HEDDA. Well, you can just imagine it for yourself. To go a whole six months and never meet a soul even remotely connected with our circle. Not a soul to talk to about the things we're interested in.

BRACK. Well, yes. I should feel the lack of that too.

HEDDA. And then, what's the most intolerable thing of all . . .

BRACK. Well?

HEDDA. Everlastingly having to be with . . . with one and the same person. . . .

BRACK (*nodding agreement*). Early and late; I know. At every conceivable moment.

HEDDA. What I said was "everlastingly."

BRACK. Quite. But with our good friend Tesman, I should have thought one would be able . . .

HEDDA. Jörgen Tesman is—a learned man, you must remember.

BRACK. Admittedly.

HEDDA. And learned men are *not* entertaining as travelling companions. Not in the long run, anyhow.

BRACK. Not even a learned man one is in love with?

HEDDA. Oh! Don't use that sentimental word.

BRACK (*slightly taken aback*). Why, what's the matter, Madam Hedda?

HEDDA (*half laughing, half annoyed*). Well, you just try it yourself! Listening to someone talking about the history of civilization, early and late—

BRACK. —Everlastingly—

HEDDA. Yes, exactly! And all this business about domestic crafts in the Middle Ages! That's the most awful part of all.

BRACK (*looking searchingly at her*). But, tell me . . . I don't quite see why, in that case . . . er . . .

HEDDA. Why Jörgen and I ever made a match of it, you mean?

BRACK. Well, let's put it that way; yes.

HEDDA. After all, do you think that's extraordinary?

BRACK. Yes—and no, Madam Hedda.

HEDDA. I had simply danced myself out, my dear sir. My time was up. (*With a little start.*) Ah, no! I'm not going to say that. Nor think it, either.

BRACK. And by Jove, you have no reason to!

HEDDA. Oh, reason! (*Watching him rather carefully.*) And Jörgen Tesman . . . one must admit that he's a thoroughly good creature.

BRACK. Good and reliable. No question.

HEDDA. And I can't see that there's anything actually ridiculous about him. Do you think there is?

BRACK. Ridiculous? No—o. I wouldn't exactly say that.

HEDDA. Quite so. But, anyway, he's an indefatigable researcher. And it's always possible that he may get somewhere in time, after all.

BRACK (*looking at her a little uncertainly*). I thought you believed, like everyone else, that he was going to become a really eminent man.

HEDDA (*with a weary expression*). Yes, so I did. And since he insisted with might and main on being allowed to support me, I don't know why I shouldn't have accepted the offer.

BRACK. No, no. Looking at it from that point of view. . . .

HEDDA. Anyhow, it was more than my other friends and admirers were prepared to do, my dear sir.

BRACK (*laughing*). Well, I can't answer for all the others. But as far as I myself am concerned, you know quite well that I have always preserved —a certain respect for the marriage-tie. In a general way; in the abstract, at least, Madam Hedda.

HEDDA (*jesting*). Ah, but I never had any hopes with regard to you.

BRACK. All I want is to have a pleasant, intimate circle of friends where I can be useful, in one way or another, and can come and go freely like— like a trusted friend.

HEDDA. Of the husband, you mean?

BRACK (*leaning forward*). To be quite frank, preferably of the wife. But of the husband, too, in the second place, of course. I assure you that sort of—shall I call it triangular relationship?—is actually a very pleasant thing for everybody concerned.

HEDDA. Yes. Many a time I longed for a third person on that trip. Driving side by side with just one other person . . . !

BRACK. Fortunately the wedding-journey is over now.

HEDDA (*shaking her head*). The journey will go on for a long time yet. I have only come to a stopping-place on the way.

BRACK. Why, then one jumps out and walks about a little, Madam Hedda.

HEDDA. I never jump out.

BRACK. Don't you really?

HEDDA. No. Because there is always someone at hand who—

BRACK (*laughing*).—Who looks when you leap, you mean?

HEDDA. Precisely.

BRACK. Oh come, you know!

HEDDA (*with a gesture of disagreement*). I don't care for that. I prefer to remain sitting where I am, alone with the other person.

BRACK. But suppose, now, a third person were to get in and join the other two?

HEDDA. Ah well, that's quite a different matter.

BRACK. A trusted and sympathetic friend—

HEDDA. —Someone who could talk entertainingly about all sorts of interesting things—

BRACK. —And nothing learned about him!

HEDDA (*with an audible sigh*). Well, that certainly is a relief.

BRACK (*hearing the hall door open and glancing towards it*). The triangle is complete.

HEDDA (*half aloud*). And so the train goes on.

(JÖRGEN TESMAN, *in a grey outdoor suit and a soft felt hat, comes in from the hall. He has a number of unbound books under his arm and in his pockets.*)

TESMAN (*going up to the table by the corner sofa*). It was pretty hot carrying that load. (*Putting the books down.*)   I'm absolutely streaming, Hedda. Why, there you are, come already, Brack. Eh? Berte didn't say anything about it.

BRACK (*getting up*). I came up through the garden.

HEDDA. What are those books you've brought?

TESMAN (*standing and dipping into them*). They are some new learned publications that I simply had to have.

HEDDA. Learned publications?

BRACK. Ah yes. Learned publications, Mrs. Tesman.

(BRACK *and* HEDDA *exchange an understanding smile.*)

HEDDA. Do you need any more learned publications?

TESMAN. Why, my dear Hedda, one can never have too many of them. One has to keep up with everything that's written and printed.

HEDDA. Yes, of course one does.

TESMAN (*turning over the books*). And look here—I've got hold of Ejlert Lövborg's new book too. (*Holding it out.*)   Perhaps you'd like to have a look at it, Hedda. Eh?

HEDDA. No, thank you very much. Or . . . well perhaps later on.

TESMAN. I dipped into it on the way.

BRACK. Well, what do you think of it—as a learned man?

TESMAN. I think it's remarkable—the balance and judgment it has. He never used to write like this before. (*Gathering the books together.*) Now, I'll take all this in with me. It'll be a treat to cut the pages! And then I must tidy myself up a little, too. (*To* BRACK.)   I say, we don't need to start at once? Eh?

BRACK. Goodness no! There's no hurry for some time yet.

TESMAN. Ah well, I'll take my time, then.   (*Is going out with the books, but stops in the center doorway and turns.*)   Oh, while I think of it, Hedda, Aunt Julle won't be coming out to you this evening.

HEDDA. Won't she? Perhaps it's that business with the hat that's the trouble?

TESMAN. Oh Lord, no! How can you think that of Aunt Julle? No, the thing is Aunt Rina's very ill.

HEDDA. So she always is.

TESMAN. Yes, but today she was particularly bad, poor dear.

HEDDA. Oh, then it's only natural for the other one to stay with her. I must make the best of it.

TESMAN. And you can't imagine, my dear, how glad Aunt Julle was, in spite of that, that you'd got so plump on your holiday.

HEDDA (*half audibly, getting up*). Oh! These everlasting aunts!

TESMAN. Eh?

HEDDA (*going to the glass door*). Nothing.

TESMAN. Oh, all right.

(*He goes through the inner room and out to the right.*)

BRACK. What hat was it you were talking about?

HEDDA. Oh, that was something that happened with Miss Tesman this morning. She had put her hat down there on the chair. (*Looking at him and smiling.*)   And I pretended I thought it was the servant's.

BRACK (*shaking his head*). But my dear Madam Hedda, how could you do that? And to that nice old lady?

HEDDA (*nervously, walking across the room*). Well, you know, that kind of thing comes over me—just like that. And then I can't stop myself. (*Throwing herself down in the easy-chair by the stove.*)   I don't know, myself, how to explain it.

BRACK (*behind the easy-chair*). You're not really happy. That's the trouble.

HEDDA (*looking straight in front of her*). And I don't know why I should be—happy. Perhaps you can tell me, can you?

BRACK. Well, among other things, because you've got the very home you wished for.

HEDDA (*looking up at him and laughing*). Do you believe that fantasy too?

BRACK. Isn't there something in it, though?

HEDDA. Oh yes . . . *Some*thing.

BRACK. Very well?

HEDDA. There's this much in it. Last summer I used Jörgen Tesman to see me home from evening parties.

BRACK. Unfortunately I was going quite another way.

HEDDA. True enough. You certainly were going another way last summer.

BRACK (*laughing*). You ought to be ashamed of yourself, Madam Hedda! Well, but you and Tesman, then?

HEDDA. Why, we came past here one evening. And he, poor creature, was tying himself in knots because he didn't know how to find anything to talk about. And so I felt sorry for the poor, learned man.

BRACK (*smiling doubtfully*). You did, did you? H'm.

HEDDA. Yes. I really did. And so, to help him out of his misery, I just said—quite casually—that I should like to live here, in this villa.

BRACK. No more than that?

HEDDA. Not that evening.

BRACK. But . . . afterwards?

HEDDA. Yes; my thoughtlessness had its consequences, my dear sir.

BRACK. Unfortunately, our thoughtlessness all too often has, Madam Hedda.

HEDDA. Thank you. But, you see, it was through this passion for the villa of the late Mrs. Falk that Jörgen Tesman and I found our way to an understanding. *That* led to our engagement and marriage and wedding trip and everything. Well, well. As one makes one's bed one must lie on it, I was just going to say.

BRACK. This is delightful! And all the time, it seems, you weren't interested in the least?

HEDDA. No. Heaven knows, I wasn't.

BRACK. Well, but now? Now that we have made it more or less comfortable for you?

HEDDA. Oh! I seem to smell lavender and dried roses in all the rooms. But perhaps Aunt Julle brought the smell with her.

BRACK (*laughing*). No, I should think it's more likely the late Mrs. Falk bequeathed it to you!

HEDDA. It reminds one of the departed, all right. Like one's bouquet, the day after a ball. (*Clasping her hands at the back of her neck, leaning back in her chair and looking at him.*) My friend, you can't imagine how horribly bored I'm going to be out here.

BRACK. But won't there be some object or other in life for you to work for, like other people, Madam Hedda?

HEDDA. An object . . . that would have something fascinating about it?

BRACK. Preferably, of course.

HEDDA. Lord knows what kind of an object it could be. I very often wonder— (*Breaking off.*) But that's no use either.

BRACK. It might be. Tell me about it.

HEDDA. Whether I could get my husband to go into politics, I was going to say.

BRACK (*laughing*). Tesman! Oh, come now! Things like politics aren't a bit—they're not at all his line of country.

HEDDA. No, I quite believe you. But suppose I could get him to, all the same?

BRACK. Well, but what satisfaction would you get out of it? When he isn't made that way? Why do you want to make him do it?

HEDDA. Because I'm bored, I tell you. (*After a pause.*) Then you think, do you, it would be absolutely impossible for him to get into the Government?

BRACK. Well you see, my dear Madam Hedda, to do that he'd need to be a fairly rich man in the first place.

HEDDA (*getting up impatiently*). Yes. There we have it. It's this middle-class world that I've got into. (*Crossing the stage.*) It's that that makes life so wretched! So absolutely ludicrous! Because that's what it *is*.

BRACK. I rather fancy the trouble lies somewhere else.

HEDDA. Where?

BRACK. You have never gone through anything that really roused you.

HEDDA. Nothing serious, you mean?

BRACK. Yes, that's one way of putting it, certainly. But now perhaps that may come.

HEDDA (*with a jerk of her head*). Oh, you're thinking of all the bother over that wretched professorship. But that's my husband's affair entirely. I'm not wasting so much as a thought on it.

BRACK. No, no. That wasn't what I was thinking of either. But suppose now there comes what, in rather solemn language, is called a serious claim on you, one full of responsibility? (*Smiling.*)   A new claim, little Madam Hedda.

HEDDA (*angrily*). Be quiet! You'll never see anything of the kind.

BRACK (*gently*). We'll talk about it in a year's time—at most.

HEDDA (*shortly*). I have no gift for that kind of thing, Mr. Brack. Not for things that make claims on me!

BRACK. Why shouldn't you have a gift, like most other women, for the calling that—?

HEDDA (*over by the glass door*). Oh, be quiet, I tell you! It often seems to me that I've only got a gift for one thing in the world.

BRACK (*going nearer*). And what is that, if I may ask?

HEDDA (*stands looking out*). For boring myself to death. Now you know. (*Turning and looking towards the inner room with a laugh.*)   Ah, just so! Here is our professor.

BRACK (*quietly, and with a warning*). Now then, Madam Hedda!

(JÖRGEN TESMAN, *dressed for the party, carrying his gloves and hat, comes through the inner room from the right.*)

TESMAN. Hedda, Ejlert Lövborg hasn't sent to say he isn't coming? Eh?

HEDDA. No.

TESMAN. Ah, you'll see, then. We shall have him along in a little while.

BRACK. Do you really think he'll come?

TESMAN. Yes, I'm almost sure he will. Because that's only a vague rumor, you know—what you told us this morning.

BRACK. Is it?

TESMAN. Yes. At least, Aunt Julle said she didn't for one moment believe he'd stand in my way again. Just think of it!

BRACK. Oh well, then, everything's quite all right.

TESMAN (*putting his hat, with his gloves in it, on a chair to the right*). Yes, but I really must wait as long as possible for him, if you don't mind.

BRACK. We've plenty of time for that. No one will turn up at my place before seven, or half past.

TESMAN. Oh well, we can keep Hedda company till then. And see what happens.

HEDDA (*putting BRACK's overcoat and hat over on the corner sofa*). And if the worst comes to the worst, Mr. Lövborg can stay here with me.

BRACK (*trying to take his things himself*). Please let me, Mrs. Tesman! What do you mean by "the worst"?

HEDDA. If he won't go with you and my husband.

TESMAN (*looking at her dubiously*). But, Hedda dear, do you think that would quite do, for him to stay here with you? Eh? Remember, Aunt Julle can't come.

HEDDA. No, but Mrs. Elvsted's coming. So the three of us will have tea together.

TESMAN. Oh, that'll be all right, then.

BRACK (*smiling*). And perhaps that might be the wisest plan for him, too.

HEDDA. Why?

BRACK. Good gracious, my dear lady, you've often enough said hard things about my little bachelor parties. They weren't suitable for any but men of the strongest principles.

HEDDA. But surely Mr. Lövborg is a man of strong enough principles now? A converted sinner—

(BERTE *appears at the hall door.*)

BERTE. There's a gentleman, ma'am, who'd like to see you.

HEDDA. Yes, show him in.

TESMAN (*quietly*). I'm sure it's he. Just fancy!

(EJLERT LÖVBORG *comes in from the hall. He is slight and thin, the same age as* TESMAN *but looking older and played out. His hair and beard are dark brown, his face is long and pale but with two patches of color on the cheek-bones. He is dressed in a well-cut black suit, quite new, and is carrying dark gloves and a top-hat. He remains standing near the door and bows abruptly. He seems a little embarrassed.*)

TESMAN (*crossing to him and shaking his hand*). Well, my dear Ejlert, so at last we meet once more!

EJLERT LÖVBORG (*speaking with lowered voice*). Thank you for your letter, Jörgen. (*Approaching* HEDDA.) May I shake hands with you too, Mrs. Tesman?

HEDDA (*taking his hand*). I am glad to see you, Mr. Lövborg. (*With a gesture.*) I don't know whether you two—

LÖVBORG (*with a slight bow*). Mr. Brack, I think.

BRACK (*returning it*). Of course we do. Some years ago—

TESMAN (*to* LÖVBORG, *with his hands on his shoulders*). And now you're to make yourself absolutely at home, Ejlert. Musn't he, Hedda? For you're going to settle down in town again, I hear. Eh?

LÖVBORG. I am.

TESMAN. Well, that's only natural. Oh, look here, I've got hold of your new book. But I really haven't had the time to read it yet.

LÖVBORG. You may as well save yourself the trouble.

TESMAN. Why may I?

LÖVBORG. Because there isn't much in it.

TESMAN. Well! Fancy your saying that!

BRACK. But it's very highly spoken of, I hear.

LÖVBORG. That's exactly what I wanted. So I wrote a book that everybody could agree with.

BRACK. Very wise.

TESMAN. Yes, but my dear Ejlert—

LÖVBORG. Because now I'm going to try and build myself up a position again. To begin over again.

TESMAN (*a little embarrassed*). I see; that's what it is? Eh?

LÖVBORG (*smiling puts down his hat and takes a packet wrapped in paper out of his pocket*). But when this one comes out, Jörgen Tesman, you must read it. For this is my first real book—the first I have put myself into.

TESMAN. Really? And what kind of book is that?

LÖVBORG. It's the continuation.

TESMAN. Continuation? Of what?

LÖVBORG. Of the book.

TESMAN. Of the new one?

LÖVBORG. Of course.

TESMAN. But my dear Ejlert, that one comes down to our own times!

LÖVBORG. It does. And this one deals with the future.

TESMAN. With the future? But, good gracious, we don't know anything about that.

LÖVBORG. No. But there are one or two things to be said about it, all the same. (*Opening the package.*) Here, you see—

TESMAN. But that's not your handwriting?

LÖVBORG. I dictated it. (*Turning over the pages.*) It's divided into two sections. The first is about the factors that will control civilization in the future. And the second part, here (*turning over the later pages*), this is about the probable direction civilization will take.

TESMAN. Amazing! It would never occur to me to write about a thing like that.

HEDDA (*drumming on the panes of the glass door*). Hm. No . . . it wouldn't.

LÖVBORG (*puts the MS. into the envelope and lays the packet on the table*). I brought it with me because I thought of reading you a little of it this evening.

TESMAN. My dear fellow, that was very good of you. But, this evening . . . ? (*He looks across at* BRACK.)   I don't quite know how it's to be managed.

LÖVBORG. Well, another time then. There's no hurry.

BRACK. I'll explain, Mr Lövborg. There's a little affair at my place tonight. Chiefly for Tesman, you know—

LÖVBORG (*looking for his hat*). Ah, then I won't keep you—

BRACK. No, look here; won't you give me the pleasure of joining us?

LÖVBORG (*shortly and decidedly*). No, I can't do that. Thank you very much.

BRACK. Oh, nonsense! Please do. We shall be a small, select circle. And, believe me, we shall have quite a "gay" time, as Mad—Mrs. Tesman puts it.

LÖVBORG. I don't doubt it. But all the same—

BRACK. So you could take your manuscript along and read it to Tesman there, at my place. I've got plenty of rooms.

TESMAN. Yes, what about it, Ejlert? You could do that! Eh?

HEDDA (*intervening*). But, my dear, if Mr Lövborg really doesn't want to! I'm sure he would much rather stay here and have supper with me.

LÖVBORG (*looking at her*). With you, Mrs. Tesman?

HEDDA. And with Mrs. Elvsted.

LÖVBORG. Oh. (*Casually.*) I met her for a moment this morning.

HEDDA. Did you? Yes, she's coming out. So it's almost imperative for you to stay, Mr. Lövborg. Otherwise she'll have no one to see her home.

LÖVBORG. That's true. Well, thank you very much, Mrs. Tesman; then I'll stay here.

HEDDA. I'll just have a word with the maid.

(*She goes to the hall door and rings.* BERTE *comes in.* HEDDA *talks to her in an undertone and points to the inner room.* BERTE *nods and goes out again.*)

TESMAN (*at the same time, to* EJLERT LÖVBORG). Look here, Ejlert, is it this new material—about the future—that your going to lecture on?

LÖVBORG. Yes.

TESMAN. Because I heard at the book-shop that you are going to give a course of lectures here in the autumn.

LÖVBORG. I am. You musn't think hardly of me for it, Tesman.

TESMAN. Good gracious, no! But—

LÖVBORG. I can quite understand that it must be rather annoying for you.

TESMAN (*dispiritedly*). Oh, I can't expect you to . . . for my sake . . .

LÖVBORG. But I'm waiting till you've got your appointment.

TESMAN. Waiting? Yes, but—but aren't you going to try for it, then? Eh?

LÖVBORG. No. I only want a *succès d'estime*.

TESMAN. But, good Lord! Aunt Julle was right after all, then! Of course that was it, I knew! Hedda! Think of it, my dear! Ejlert Lövborg isn't going to stand in our way at all!

HEDDA (*shortly*). Our way? Please leave me out of it.

(*She goes up towards the inner room where* BERTE *is putting a tray with decanters and glasses on the table.* HEDDA *nods approvingly and comes down again.* BERTE *goes out.*)

TESMAN (*at the same time*). But what about you, Judge? What do you say to this? Eh?

BRACK. Why, I should say that honor and a *succès d'estime* . . . they can be very pleasant things—

TESMAN. They certainly can. But all the same—

HEDDA (*looking at* TESMAN *with a cold smile*). You look to me as though you'd been thunderstruck.

TESMAN. Well, something like that . . . I almost feel . . .

BRACK. As a matter of fact, a thunderstorm has just passed over us, Mrs. Tesman.

HEDDA (*with a gesture towards the inner room*). Wouldn't you men like to go in and have a glass of cold punch?

BRACK (*looking at his watch*). By way of stirrup-cup? That wouldn't be a bad idea.

TESMAN. Good, Hedda! Excellent! I feel so light-hearted now, that—

HEDDA. Won't you too, Mr. Lövborg?

LÖVBORG (*with a gesture of refusal*). No, thank you very much. Not for me.

BRACK. But, good Lord! Cold punch isn't poison, so far as I know.

LÖVBORG. Not for everybody, perhaps!

HEDDA. I'll entertain Mr. Lövborg in the meantime.

TESMAN. That's right, Hedda dear. You do that.

(*He and BRACK go into the inner room and sit down. During what follows they drink punch, smoke cigarettes and carry on a lively conversation. EJLERT LÖVBORG remains standing by the stove. HEDDA goes to the writing-table.*)

HEDDA (*raising her voice a little*). I'll show you some photographs, if you like. My husband and I made a trip through the Tyrol on our way home.

(*She brings an album and puts it on the table by the sofa, sitting down herself in the farthest corner. EJLERT LÖVBORG goes nearer, stands and looks at her. Then he takes a chair and sits down on her left with his back to the inner-room.*)

HEDDA (*opening the album*). Do you see this mountain range, Mr. Lövborg? It's the Ortler Group. My husband has written it underneath. Here it is: "The Ortler Group at Meran."

LÖVBORG (*who has been looking intently at her, speaking softly and slowly*). Hedda—Gabler.

HEDDA (*glancing quickly at him*). Hush, now!

LÖVBORG (*repeating softly*). Hedda Gabler.

HEDDA (*looking at the album*). Yes, that was my name once upon a time. In the days—when we two knew one another.

LÖVBORG. And in the future—for the whole of my life—then, I must break myself of the habit of saying Hedda Gabler?

HEDDA (*going on turning over the pages*). Yes, you must. And I think you'd better practice it in good time. The sooner the better, I should say.

LÖVBORG (*with resentment in his voice*). Hedda Gabler married? And married to—Jörgen Tesman.

HEDDA. Yes. That's what happened.

LÖVBORG. Oh, Hedda, Hedda, how could you throw yourself away like that?

HEDDA (*looking sharply at him*). Now! None of that, please.

LÖVBORG. None of what?

(TESMAN *comes in and goes towards the sofa.*)

HEDDA (*hearing him coming, and speaking indifferently*). And this one, Mr. Lövborg, is from the Vale of Ampezzo. Just look at the mountain peaks there. (*Looking affectionately up at* TESMAN.) What is it these queer peaks are called, my dear?

TESMAN. Let me see. Oh, those are the Dolomites.

HEDDA. Oh, of course! Those are the Dolomites, Mr. Lövborg.

TESMAN. Hedda, dear, I just wanted to ask if we shouldn't bring you a little punch? For you, at any rate. Eh?

HEDDA. Well, yes; thank you. And a few cakes, perhaps.

TESMAN. No cigarettes?

HEDDA. No, thanks.

TESMAN. Right.

(*He goes into the inner room and out to the right.* BRACK *stays sitting in the inner room, with an eye on* HEDDA *and* LÖVBORG *from time to time.*)

LÖVBORG (*in a low voice, as before*). Answer me, now, Hedda my dear. How could you go and do this?

HEDDA (*apparently intent on the album*). If you go on saying "dear" to me, I won't talk to you.

LÖVBORG. Mayn't I even do it when we are alone?

HEDDA. No. You can think it if you like. But you mustn't say it.

LÖVBORG. Ah, I understand. It offends . . . your love for Jörgen Tesman.

HEDDA (*glancing at him and smiling*). Love? That's good!

LÖVBORG. Isn't it love, then?

HEDDA. There isn't going to be any kind of disloyalty, anyhow. I won't have that sort of thing.

LÖVBORG. Hedda, answer me just one thing—

HEDDA. Hush!

(TESMAN, *with a tray, comes from the inner room.*)

TESMAN. Look at the good things we've got here. (*He puts the tray on the table.*)

HEDDA. Why are you bringing it yourself?

TESMAN (*filling the glasses*). Why, because I think it's so jolly waiting on you, Hedda.

HEDDA. Oh, but you've filled both glasses now. And Mr. Lövborg won't have any.

TESMAN. No, but Mrs. Elvsted will be here soon.

HEDDA. Oh, of course; Mrs. Elvsted—

TESMAN. Had you forgotten her? Eh?

HEDDA. We've got so absorbed in this. (*Showing him a picture.*) Do you remember that little village?

TESMAN. Ah, that's the one below the Brenner Pass! It was there we stayed the night—

HEDDA. —And met all those jolly tourists.

TESMAN. That's it. It was there. Just think, if we could have had *you* with us, Ejlert! Well, well!

(*He goes in again and sits down with* BRACK.)

LÖVBORG. Answer me just this one thing, Hedda.

HEDDA. Well?

LÖVBORG. Was there no love in your feeling for me either? Not a touch—not a flicker of love in that either?

HEDDA. I wonder if there actually was? To me it seems as if we were two good comrades. Two real, close friends. (*Smiling.*) You, especially, were absolutely frank.

LÖVBORG. It was you who wanted that.

HEDDA. When I look back at it, there really was something fine, something enthralling. There was a kind of courage about it, about this hidden intimacy, this comradeship that not a living soul so much as guessed at.

LÖVBORG. Yes, there was, Hedda! Wasn't there? When I came up to see your father in the afternoons. . . . And the General used to sit right over by the windows reading the papers, with his back to us . . .

HEDDA. And we used to sit on the corner sofa.

LÖVBORG. Always with the same illustrated paper in front of us.

HEDDA. Yes, for the lack of an album.

LÖVBORG. Yes, Hedda; and when I used to confess to you! Told you things about myself that no one else knew in those days. Sat there and owned up to going about whole days and nights blind drunk. Days and nights on end. Oh, Hedda, what sort of power in you was it—that forced me to confess things like that?

HEDDA. Do you think it was some power in me?

LÖVBORG. Yes, how else can I account for it? And all these—these questions you used to put to me . . . indirectly.

HEDDA. And that you understood so perfectly well.

LÖVBORG. To think you could sit and ask questions like that! Quite frankly.

HEDDA. Indirectly, mind you.

LÖVBORG. Yes, but frankly, all the same. Cross-question me about . . . about all that kind of thing.

HEDDA. And to think you could answer, Mr. Lövborg.

LÖVBORG. Yes, that's just what I can't understand, looking back. But tell me now, Hedda, wasn't it love that was at the bottom of that relationship? Wasn't it, on your side, as though you wanted to purify and absolve me, when I made you my confessor? Wasn't it that?

HEDDA. No, not quite.

LÖVBORG. What made you do it, then?

HEDDA. Do you find it so impossible to understand, that a young girl, when there's an opportunity . . . in secret . . .

LÖVBORG. Well?

HEDDA. That one should want to have a glimpse of a world that . . .

LÖVBORG. That . . . ?

HEDDA. That one isn't allowed to know about?

LÖVBORG. So that was it, then?

HEDDA. That . . . that as well, I rather think.

LÖVBORG. The bond of our common hunger for life. But why couldn't that have gone on, in any case?

HEDDA. That was your own fault.

LÖVBORG. It was you who broke it off.

HEDDA. Yes, when there was imminent danger of our relationship becoming serious. You ought to be ashamed of yourself, Ejlert Lövborg. How could you take advantage of—your unsuspecting comrade!

LÖVBORG (*clenching his hands*). Oh, why didn't you make a job of it! Why didn't you shoot me down when you threatened to!

HEDDA. Yes . . . I'm as terrified of scandal as all that.

LÖVBORG. Yes, Hedda; you are a coward at bottom.

HEDDA. An awful coward. (*Changing her tone.*) But it was lucky for you. And now you have consoled yourself so delightfully up at the Elvsteds'.

LÖVBORG. I know what Thea has told you.

HEDDA. And you have told her something about us two?

LÖVBORG. Not a word. She's too stupid to understand a thing like that.

HEDDA. Stupid?

LÖVBORG. She is stupid about that sort of thing.

HEDDA. And I'm a coward. (*She leans nearer to him, without meeting his eyes, and says more softly*). But now *I* will confess something to *you*.

LÖVBORG (*eagerly*). Well?

HEDDA. That, my not daring to shoot you down—

LÖVBORG. Yes?

HEDDA. That wasn't my worst piece of cowardice . . . that night.

LÖVBORG (*looks at her a moment, understands and whispers passionately*). Ah, Hedda! Hedda Gabler! Now I see a glimpse of the hidden foundation of our comradeship. You and I! Then it *was* your passion for life—

HEDDA (*quietly, with a sharp, angry glance*). Take care! Don't assume anything like that.

(*It has begun to get dark. The hall door is opened from outside by* BERTE.)

HEDDA (*shutting the album with a snap and calling out with a smile*). There you are at last, Thea darling! Come along in!

(*MRS ELVSTED comes in from the hall, dressed for the evening. The door is closed behind her.*)

HEDDA (*on the sofa, stretching her arms towards her*). My precious Thea—you can't think how I've been longing for you to come!

(MRS. ELVSTED, *in the meanwhile, exchanges slight greetings with the men in the inner room and then comes across to the table holding her hand out to* HEDDA. EJLERT LÖVBORG *has got up. He and* MRS. ELVSTED *greet each other with a silent nod.*)

MRS. ELVSTED. Oughtn't I to go in and say a word or two to your husband?

HEDDA. Not a bit of it! Let them be. They're going out directly.

MRS. ELVSTED. Are they going out?

HEDDA. Yes, they're going to make a night of it.

MRS. ELVSTED (*quickly, to* LÖVBORG). You're not, are you?

LÖVBORG. No.

HEDDA. Mr. Lövborg—is staying here with us.

MRS. ELVSTED (*takes a chair and is going to sit beside him*). Oh, it *is* nice to be here!

HEDDA. No, no, Thea my child! Not there. You're coming over here, right beside me. I want to be in the middle.

MRS. ELVSTED. All right; just as you like. (*She goes round the table and sits on the sofa on* HEDDA'S *right.* LÖVBORG *sits down on his chair again.*)

LÖVBORG (*to* HEDDA, *after a little pause*). Isn't she lovely, just to look at?

HEDDA (*stroking her hair lightly*). Only to look at?

LÖVBORG. Yes. Because *we* two—she and I—we really *are* comrades. We trust each other absolutely. That's how it is we can sit and talk to each other quite frankly.

HEDDA. Nothing indirect about it, Mr. Lövborg?

LÖVBORG. Oh well . . .

MRS. ELVSTED (*softly, leaning close to* HEDDA). Oh, Hedda, I am so happy! Just think, he says I have inspired him, too!

HEDDA (*looking at her with a smile*). He says that, does he?

LÖVBORG. And then she has the courage that leads to action, Mrs. Tesman.

MRS. ELVSTED. Good gracious! *Me?* Courage?

LÖVBORG. Immense—when her comrade is concerned.

HEDDA. Ah, courage. Yes. If one only had that.

LÖVBORG. What do you mean?

HEDDA. Then perhaps one could even *live* at last. (*Changing her tone suddenly.*) But now, Thea, my dear, you must have a nice glass of cold punch.

MRS. ELVSTED. No, thank you. I never drink anything like that.

HEDDA. Well you, then, Mr. Lövborg.

LÖVBORG. Thank you, I don't either.

MRS. ELVSTED. No, he doesn't either.

HEDDA (*looking at him steadily*). But suppose I want you to?

LÖVBORG. That wouldn't alter it.

HEDDA (*laughing*). So I, poor thing, have no power over you at all?

LÖVBORG. Not where that's concerned.

HEDDA. But, joking apart, I think you ought to, all the same. For your own sake.

MRS. ELVSTED. Oh, but, Hedda!

LÖVBORG. How do you mean?

HEDDA. Or, rather, on account of other people.

LÖVBORG. Really?

HEDDA. Otherwise people might easily get the idea that you didn't feel absolutely secure. Not really sure of yourself.

MRS. ELVSTED (*softly*). Oh *no*, Hedda!

LÖVBORG. People may think what they like, for the present.

MRS. ELVSTED (*happily*). Exactly!

HEDDA. I saw it so plainly with Judge Brack just this minute.

LÖVBORG. What did you see?

HEDDA. That contemptuous smile of his when you were afraid to go in there with them.

LÖVBORG. Afraid! Naturally I preferred to stay here and talk to you.

MRS. ELVSTED. That was quite understandable, Hedda!

HEDDA. But Judge Brack couldn't be expected to guess that. And I noticed too that he smiled and glanced at my husband when you were afraid to go to this harmless little party with them either.

LÖVBORG. Afraid! Did you say I was afraid?

HEDDA. I don't. But that's how Judge Brack understood it.

LÖVBORG. Let him, then.

HEDDA. So you're not going with them?

LÖVBORG. I am staying here with you and Thea.

MRS. ELVSTED. Why, yes, Hedda; of course.

HEDDA (*smiling and nodding approvingly at* LÖVBORG). There! Quite immovable. A man of unshaken principles, always. You know, that's what a man should be. (*Turning to* MRS. ELVSTED *and patting her.*) Now, wasn't that what I said, when you came in here this morning in such a state of distraction—

LÖVBORG (*with surprise*). Distraction?

MRS. ELVSTED (*in terror*). Hedda! Oh, Hedda!

HEDDA. Now you see for yourself! There's not the slightest need for you to go about in this deadly anxiety— (*Breaking off.*) There! Now we can all three be cheerful.

LÖVBORG (*who has made a startled gesture*). What on earth is all this, Mrs. Tesman?

MRS. ELVSTED. Oh heavens, heavens, Hedda! What are you saying? What are you doing?

HEDDA. Keep quiet. That detestable Judge Brack has got his eye on you.

LÖVBORG. So it was deadly anxiety . . . on my behalf.

MRS. ELVSTED (*softly and in misery*). Oh, Hedda! How *could* you!

LÖVBORG (*looking intently at her for a moment, his face haggard*). So *that* was my comrade's absolute faith in me.

MRS. ELVSTED (*beseeching*). Oh, my dear, my dear—you must listen to me before—

LÖVBORG (*takes one of the filled glasses, lifts it and says softly in a strained voice*). Your health, Thea! (*He empties his glass, puts it down and takes the other.*)

MRS. ELVSTED (*softly*). Oh, Hedda, Hedda! Did you *want* this to happen?

HEDDA. Want it? Are you crazy?

LÖVBORG. And a health to you too, Mrs. Tesman. Thank you for the truth. Here's to it. (*He drains his glass and is about to fill it again.*)

HEDDA (*pinching her arm*). They can hear what you're saying.

MRS. ELVSTED (*with a faint cry*). Oh!

LÖVBORG (*to* BRACK). You were so kind as to ask me to join you.

BRACK. Oh, are you coming, after all?

LÖVBORG. Yes, thank you very much.

BRACK. I'm delighted.

LÖVBORG (*putting his parcel in his pocket and speaking to* TESMAN). Because I should like to show you one or two things before I hand it in.

TESMAN. Fancy! That will be jolly. But, Hedda dear, how are you going to get Mrs. Elvsted home, eh?

HEDDA. We'll manage that somehow.

LÖVBORG (*looking toward the women*). Mrs. Elvsted? I'll come back again and fetch her, of course. (*Coming nearer.*) Round about ten o'clock, Mrs. Tesman? Will that do?

HEDDA. Certainly. That will do beautifully.

TESMAN. Oh well, everything's all right, then. But you mustn't expect *me* as early as that, Hedda.

HEDDA. My dear, stay—as long as ever you like.

MRS. ELVSTED (*in suppressed anxiety*). I shall wait here, then, Mr. Lövborg, till you come.

LÖVBORG (*with his hat in his hand*). All right, Mrs. Elvsted.

BRACK. And so the procession starts, gentlemen. I hope we shall have a gay time, as a certain charming lady puts it.

HEDDA. Ah, if only that charming lady could be there, invisible—

BRACK. Why invisible?

HEDDA. So as to hear a little of your gaiety—uncensored, Mr. Brack.

BRACK (*laughing*). I shouldn't advise the charming lady to try!

HEDDA (*laying a hand on his arm*). Now, then. No more for the moment. Remember you're going to a party.

MRS. ELVSTED. No, no, no!

HEDDA. Hush! They're looking at you.

LÖVBORG (*putting down his glass*). Now, Thea, my dear, tell the truth!

MRS. ELVSTED. Yes!

LÖVBORG. Did your husband know that you had followed me?

MRS. ELVSTED (*wringing her hands*). Oh, Hedda! You hear what he's asking me?

LÖVBORG. Was it an understanding between you and him, that you should come to town and spy on me? Perhaps it was he himself who made you do it? Ah yes, no doubt he wanted me in the office again! Or did he miss me at the card-table?

MRS. ELVSTED (*softly, with a moan*). Oh, Ejlert, Ejlert!

LÖVBORG (*seizing a glass and about to fill it*). A health to the old District Magistrate, too!

HEDDA (*checking him*). No more now. Remember, you're going out to read your book to my husband.

LÖVBORG (*calmly, putting down the glass*). It was stupid of me, Thea, all this. To take it like that, I mean. And don't be angry with me; dear old friend. You shall see, you and the others, that even if I came to grief once, yet . . . Now I'm on my feet again. Thanks to your help, Thea!

MRS. ELVSTED (*radiant with joy*). Thank heaven!

(BRACK, *in the meantime, has looked at his watch. He and* TESMAN *get up and come into the drawing-room.*)

BRACK (*getting his hat and overcoat*). Well, Mrs. Tesman, our time's up now.

HEDDA. I expect it is.

LÖVBORG (*getting up*). Mine too, Mr. Brack.

MRS. ELVSTED (*softly, and imploring*). Oh, Ejlert, don't!

TESMAN (*laughing, too*). Oh, Hedda, you're simply priceless! Just think!

BRACK. Well, good-bye, good-bye, ladies.

LÖVBORG (*taking leave with a bow*). About ten o'clock, then.

(BRACK, LÖVBORG *and* TESMAN *go out by the hall door. At the same time* BERTE *comes in from the inner room with a lighted lamp, which she puts on the drawing-room table. She goes out again the same way.*)

MRS. ELVSTED (*who has got up and is wandering restlessly about the room*). Hedda, Hedda, where is all this going to end?

HEDDA. Ten o'clock—then he will come. I can see him. With vineleaves[1] in his hair. Flushed and confident.

MRS ELVSTED. Yes, if only it would be like that.

HEDDA. And then, you see, then he'll have got control of himself again. Then he will be a free man for the rest of his days.

MRS. ELVSTED. Heavens, yes. If only he would come like that. As you see him.

HEDDA. He'll come like that—"so and no otherwise." (*Getting up and going nearer.*) Go on doubting him as long as you like. I believe in him. And now we'll try . . .

[1] *Lövborg* means "leaf-castle."

MRS. ELVSTED. There's something behind all this, Hedda.

HEDDA. True; there is. I want, for once in my life, to have power over a human being's fate.

MRS. ELVSTED. But haven't you got that?

HEDDA. I have not. And never have had.

MRS. ELVSTED. Not over your husband's?

HEDDA. That *would* be worth having, wouldn't it? Ah, if you could only realize how poor I am. And here are you, offered such riches! (*Throwing her arms passionately round her.*)   I think I shall burn your hair off, after all.

MRS. ELVSTED. Let go! Let go! I'm frightened of you, Hedda!

BERTE (*in the doorway between the rooms*). Tea's laid in the dining-room, ma'am.

HEDDA. Good. We're coming.

MRS. ELVSTED. No, no, no! I'd rather go home alone. At once!

HEDDA. Nonsense! You must have tea first, you little goose. And then, at ten o'clock, Ejlert Lövborg will come—with vineleaves in his hair.

(*She pulls* MRS. ELVSTED, *almost by force, toward the doorway.*)

ACT III

The room at the Tesmans'. The curtains across the middle door-way are closed and so are those in front of the glass door. The lamp, with its shade on, is burning, turned half-down, on the table. The door of the stove is open and there has been a fire in it, which is now nearly out.

MRS. ELVSTED, *wrapped up in a large shawl with her feet on a footstool, is close to the stove, lying sunk in the easy-chair.* HEDDA *is lying asleep on the sofa with her clothes on and a rug over her.*

After a pause, MRS. ELVSTED *sits up quickly in her chair and listens intently. Then she sinks back wearily again, crying softly.*

MRS. ELVSTED. Not yet! Oh, heavens, heavens! Not yet!   (BERTE *comes stealing in cautiously by the hall door. She has a letter in her hand.*)

MRS. ELVSTED (*turning and whispering eagerly*). Well? Has anyone come?

BERTE. Yes. A girl's just been with this letter.

MRS. ELVSTED (*quickly, holding out her hand*). A letter! Give it to me!

BERTE. No, ma'am, it's for the Doctor.

MRS. ELVSTED. Oh.

BERTE. It was Miss Tesman's maid who came with it. I'll put it here on the table.

MRS. ELVSTED. Yes, do.

BERTE (*putting down the letter*). I think I'd better put the lamp out. It's smoking.

MRS. ELVSTED. Yes, put it out. It'll very soon be light now.

BERTE (*putting it out*). It's quite light, ma'am.

MRS. ELVSTED. Why, it's broad daylight! And still not back!

BERTE. Lord bless you, ma'am, I thought this was how it would be.

MRS. ELVSTED. You thought so?

BERTE. Yes. When I saw that a certain person had come back to town again, well . . . And when he went off with them . . . One's heard enough about that gentleman before today.

MRS. ELVSTED. Don't speak so loud. You'll wake Mrs. Tesman.

BERTE (*looking towards the sofa and sighing*). Gracious, yes; let her sleep, poor thing. Shall I put a bit more on the fire?

MRS. ELVSTED. No, thank you; not for me.

BERTE. Very good.   (*She goes out quietly by the hall door.*)

HEDDA (*waking as the door shuts and looking up*). What's that?

MRS. ELVSTED. It was only the maid.

HEDDA (*looking round her*). In here? Oh yes, I remember now. (*She sits up on the sofa, stretches and rubs her eyes.*)   What's the time, Thea?

MRS. ELVSTED (*looking at her watch*). It's past seven.

HEDDA. What time did my husband come back?

MRS. ELVSTED. He isn't back.

HEDDA. He hasn't come home yet?

MRS. ELVSTED (*getting up*). No one's come back at all.

HEDDA. And we sat here and kept ourselves awake, waiting up for them till nearly four o'clock!

MRS. ELVSTED (*wringing her hands*). And *how* I waited for him!

HEDDA (*yawning and speaking with her hand in front of her mouth*). Ah, well, we might have saved ourselves that trouble.

MRS. ELVSTED. Did you get a little sleep afterwards?

HEDDA. Oh yes. I slept quite well, I think. Didn't you?

MRS. ELVSTED. Not a wink! I couldn't, Hedda! It was absolutely impossible.

HEDDA (*getting up and going across to her*). There, there, there! There's nothing to worry about. I can see perfectly well what's happened.

MRS. ELVSTED. Why, what do you think then? Tell me! Please!

HEDDA. Well, of course they kept things up frightfully late at the Judge's.

MRS. ELVSTED. Heavens, yes. They must have done. But, all the same—

HEDDA. And then, you see, my husband didn't like to come home and disturb us by ringing in the middle of the night. (*Laughing.*) Perhaps he didn't much care to show himself either—not straight after making a gay night of it.

MRS. ELVSTED. But, Hedda dear, where would he have gone?

HEDDA. He's gone up to his aunts', of course, and slept there. They keep his old room ready.

MRS. ELVSTED. No, he can't be with them. Because a letter came for him a little while ago from Miss Tesman. There it is.

HEDDA. Really? (*Looking at the address.*) Yes. That's certainly from

Aunt Julle; it's her handwriting. Well, then, he's stayed on at the Judge's place. And Ejlert Lövborg, he's sitting reading to him—with vineleaves in his hair.

MRS. ELVSTED. Oh, Hedda, you're just saying things you don't believe yourself.

HEDDA. You really are a little goose, Thea.

MRS. ELVSTED. Well, I suppose I am—worse luck.

HEDDA. And you look simply tired to death.

MRS. ELVSTED. Yes, I am tired to death.

HEDDA. Well then, you're going to do as I tell you. You're going into my room and you're going to lie down on the bed for a little while.

MRS. ELVSTED. Oh no. I shan't sleep, anyway.

HEDDA. Yes, you *are* to.

MRS. ELVSTED. Yes, but surely your husband must be home soon. And then I must find out at once . . .

HEDDA. I'll let you know all right when he comes.

MRS. ELVSTED. Well; you promise me, Hedda?

HEDDA. Yes, you can be sure I will. You just go in and go to sleep in the meantime.

MRS. ELVSTED. Thank you. I'll try to, then. (*She goes out through the inner room.*)

(HEDDA *goes over to the glass door and pulls back the curtains. Broad daylight pours into the room. She takes a small hand-mirror from the writing-table, looks at herself in it and tidies her hair. Then she crosses to the hall door and presses the bell. After a moment* BERTE *comes to the door.*)

BERTE. Is there anything you want, ma'am?

HEDDA. Yes, will you make up the fire? I'm simply freezing here.

BERTE. Bless us! I'll have it warm in no time.

(*She rakes the remains of the fire together and puts some wood on.*)

BERTE (*stopping to listen*). There was a ring at the front door, ma'am.

HEDDA. You go and answer it, then. I'll see to the fire myself.

BERTE. It'll soon burn up.   (*She goes out by the hall door.*)

(HEDDA *kneels on the footstool and puts some more wood into the stove. After a short pause,* JÖRGEN TESMAN *comes in from the hall. He looks tired and rather grave. He steals towards the middle doorway on tiptoe and is about to slip through the curtains.*)

HEDDA (*at the stove, without looking up*). Good morning.

TESMAN (*turning*). Hedda! (*Coming towards her.*) But what on earth! You up as early as this? Eh?

HEDDA. Yes, I got up very early today.

TESMAN. And I was so certain you were lying asleep still! Just fancy, Hedda!

HEDDA. Don't speak so loudly. Mrs. Elvsted is lying down in my room.

TESMAN. Did Mrs. Elvsted stay the night here?

HEDDA. Of course. Nobody came to fetch her.

TESMAN. That's true; nobody did.

HEDDA (*shutting the door of the stove and getting up*). Well, did you have a good time at the Judge's?

TESMAN. Have you been worrying about me, eh?

HEDDA. No, that would never occur to me. I was just asking whether you had a good time.

TESMAN. Not bad. It was rather jolly for once. Mostly at the beginning, as far as I was concerned. Because then Ejlert read me some of his book. We got there more than an hour too soon. Just fancy! And Brack had so much to see to. But then Ejlert read to me.

HEDDA (*sitting down on the right-hand side of the table*). Well now, tell me about it.

TESMAN (*sitting down on a footstool by the stove*). My goodness, Hedda! You can't think what a book that's going to be! I should think it's one of the most remarkable things that's ever been written. Just think!

HEDDA. No doubt. That doesn't interest me.

TESMAN. I must admit one thing, Hedda. When he had read it, a perfectly detestable feeling came over me.

HEDDA. Detestable?

TESMAN. There I was *envying* Ejlert for having been able to write a thing like that! Just think, Hedda!

HEDDA. Yes, yes. I am.

TESMAN. And then to know that he, with the gifts he has . . . Yes he's quite irreclaimable. What a tragedy!

HEDDA. You mean, I suppose, that he has more spirit than other people.

TESMAN. Oh no. The point is—there's no moderation in him.

HEDDA. And what happened, then, in the end?

TESMAN. Well, I really think the best way to describe it is an orgy, Hedda.

HEDDA. Did he have vineleaves in his hair?

TESMAN. Vineleaves? No, I didn't notice any. But he made a long, wandering speech in honor of the woman who had inspired him in his work. Well, that was how he put it.

HEDDA. Did he say who she was?

TESMAN. No, he didn't do that. But I can't imagine it could be anybody but Mrs. Elvsted. You watch!

HEDDA. Oh, well. . . . Where did you part from him, then?

TESMAN. On the way back. We broke up—the last of us—at the same time. And Brack came along with us to get a breath of fresh air. And so, you see, we agreed to see Ejlert home. Because, to tell the truth, he'd had far more than he could carry.

HEDDA. I can quite imagine that.

TESMAN. But here's the extraordinary part of it, Hedda. Or rather, the sad part of it, I ought to say. I—I'm almost ashamed to tell you, for Ejlert's sake.

HEDDA. Oh, go on! So—?

TESMAN. Well, as we were on the way back, you see, I happened to be a little behind the others. Only for a minute or two. You see?

HEDDA. Yes, yes. But what then?

TESMAN. And then, as I was hurrying to catch them up, what do you think I found by the roadside. Eh?

HEDDA. No, how could I know?

TESMAN. Don't say anything about it to anyone, Hedda. You understand. Promise me, for Ejlert's sake. (*Taking a paper parcel out of his coat pocket.*)   Just think! I found this.

HEDDA. Isn't that the parcel he had with him yesterday?

TESMAN. It is. It's the whole of that precious, irreplaceable manuscript of his. And that's what he'd gone and lost, without noticing it. Just think, Hedda! Such a sad—

HEDDA. But why didn't you give the packet back to him at once, then?

TESMAN. Well, I didn't dare to. Not in the state he was in.

HEDDA. Didn't you tell any of the others you'd found it, either?

TESMAN. Certainly not. I didn't want to do that for Ejlert's sake, you know.

HEDDA. Then there's no one who knows you've got Ejlert Lövborg's manuscript?

TESMAN. No. And no one must find out, either.

HEDDA. What did you talk to him about afterwards, then?

TESMAN. I didn't get a chance to talk to him again, you see. Because when we got into the streets, he and two or three others got away from us. Just think!

HEDDA. Oh? They must have seen him home, then.

TESMAN. Yes, it looks as if they had. And Brack went off, too.

HEDDA. And where ever have you been since?

TESMAN. Well, I and some of the others went on home with one of the gay lads and had morning coffee at his place. Or night coffee, it would be better to call it. Eh? But as soon as I've had a moment's rest—and when I think Ejlert's slept it off, poor fellow—I must go over to him with this.

HEDDA (*holding out her hand for the package*). No, don't give it up! Not directly, I mean. Let me read it first.

TESMAN. Oh, Hedda, my dear, I couldn't do that. I really couldn't.

HEDDA. You couldn't?

TESMAN. No. You can just imagine how frantic he will be when he wakes up and misses the manuscript. Because he's got no copy of it, you realize! He said so himself.

HEDDA (*looking searchingly at him*). Can't a thing like that be written again, then? Re-written?

TESMAN. No, I don't think that would ever work. It's a matter of inspiration, you know.

HEDDA. Yes, of course. I suppose that's it (*Casually.*) Oh, by the way, there's a letter for you here.

TESMAN. Really?

HEDDA (*passing it to him*). It came early this morning.

TESMAN. Why, it's from Aunt Julle! (*He puts down the paper package on the other footstool, opens the letter, runs through it and jumps up.*) Oh, Hedda! She says poor Aunt Rina's dying.

HEDDA. Well, that was to be expected.

TESMAN. And that if I want to see her again I must be quick. I'll run across there at once.

HEDDA (*checking a smile*). Run?

TESMAN. Oh, Hedda dear, if only you could bring yourself to come along, too! Just think!

HEDDA (*getting up and dismissing the matter wearily*). No, no. Don't ask me to do things like that. I don't want to think of illness or death. You mustn't ask me to have anything to do with ugly things.

TESMAN. Oh well, then. (*Bustling about.*) My hat? My overcoat? Oh yes; in the hall. Oh, I do so hope I'm not going to be too late, Hedda! Eh?

(BERTE *comes to the hall door.*)

BERTE. Judge Brack's outside, asking can he come in?

TESMAN. At this moment! No, I really can't see him now.

HEDDA. But I can. (*To* BERTE.) Ask the Judge to come in. (BERTE *goes out.*)

HEDDA (*quickly, in a whisper*). The parcel! (*She snatches it from the stool.*)

TESMAN. Yes, give it to me!

HEDDA. No, no. I'll keep it for you till you get back.

(*She crosses to the writing-table and puts it in the bookcase.* TESMAN *is in such a hurry that he cannot get his gloves on.* BRACK *comes in from the hall.*)

HEDDA (*nodding to him*). Well, you are an early bird.

BRACK. Yes, don't you think so? (*To* TESMAN.) Are you going out, too?

TESMAN. Yes, I simply must go and see the Aunts. Just think, the invalid one, she's dying, poor thing.

BRACK. Dear, dear! Is she? Then you certainly mustn't let me keep you. At such a serious moment—

TESMAN. Yes, I really must be off. Good-bye, good-bye! (*He hurries out through the hall door.*)

HEDDA (*coming nearer to* BRACK). It seems to have been rather more than "gay" at your place last night, Mr. Brack.

BRACK. So much so that I haven't had my clothes off, Madam Hedda.

HEDDA. Not you either?

BRACK. No, as you see. Well, what has Tesman been telling you about the night's adventures?

HEDDA. Oh, just a dull story. That they'd gone and had coffee somewhere.

BRACK. I know all about that coffee-party. Ejlert Lövborg wasn't with them, I think?

HEDDA. No, they'd seen him home before that.

BRACK. Tesman, too?

HEDDA. No; but some of the others, he said.

BRACK (*smiling*). Jörgen Tesman really is a simple soul, Madam Hedda.

HEDDA. Heaven knows he is. Is there something behind this, then?

BRACK. Yes, It's no good denying . . .

HEDDA. Well, then let's sit down, my friend. Then you can tell your story.

(*She sits down on the left of the table, with* BRACK *at the long side, near her.*)

HEDDA. Well, now?

BRACK. I had good reasons for keeping track of my guests last night—or rather, of some of my guests.

HEDDA. And I suppose Ejlert Lövborg was one of them.

BRACK. I must admit he was.

HEDDA. Now you are making me really curious.

BRACK. Do you know where he and a few others spent the rest of the night, Madam Hedda?

HEDDA. If it's the sort of thing that can be told, tell me.

BRACK. Oh yes, it can be told all right. Well, they fetched up at an extremely lively party.

HEDDA. Of the "gay" kind?

BRACK. Of the very gayest.

HEDDA. Go on, please. I want to hear some more.

BRACK. Lövborg had had an invitation beforehand as well. I knew all about that. But he'd refused to go then, because he's turned over a new leaf now—as you know.

HEDDA. Up at the Elvsteds'. Yes. But he went, then, all the same?

BRACK. Yes. You see, Madam Hedda, unfortunately the inspiration took him at my place last night.

HEDDA. Yes, I gather he found inspiration there.

BRACK. Pretty violent inspiration. Anyway, he changed his mind, I imagine. For we men are unfortunately not always so firm in our principles as we ought to be.

HEDDA. How do you know all this?

BRACK. From the police themselves.

HEDDA (*gazing in front of her*). So that's how it was? Then he had no vine-leaves in his hair.

BRACK. Vineleaves, Madam Hedda?

HEDDA (*changing her tone*). But tell me, now. What's your real reason for following up Ejlert Lövborg's movements like this?

BRACK. Well, it obviously can't be a matter of complete indifference to me, if it comes out at the trial that he had come straight from my place.

HEDDA. Will there be a trial too, then?

BRACK. Of course. However, that might pass. . . . But, as a friend of the house, I felt bound to give you and Tesman a full account of his night's exploits.

HEDDA. And why, Mr. Brack?

BRACK. Well, because I have a shrewd misgiving that he means to use you as a kind of screen.

HEDDA. Why, how can you imagine such a thing?

BRACK. Good Lord, we're not blind, Madam Hedda! You watch. This Mrs. Elvsted, she won't be leaving town again in a hurry.

HEDDA. Well, even supposing there is something between them, there must be plenty of other places where they can meet.

BRACK. No other home. Every decent house will be closed again to Ejlert Lövborg from now onwards.

HEDDA. And so ought mine to be, you mean?

BRACK. Yes. I admit it would be extremely unpleasant to me if this man were on a firm footing here. If he were to force his way in, superfluous and an intruder, into—

HEDDA. Into the triangle?

BRACK. Precisely. It would simply amount to my finding myself without a home.

HEDDA (*looking at him with a smile*). Ah yes. The only cock in the yard. That's your idea.

BRACK (*nodding slowly and dropping his voice*). Yes, that is my idea. And I'll fight for that idea with all the means at my command.

HEDDA (*her smile dying away*). You are really a dangerous person, when it comes to the point.

BRACK. Do you think so?

HEDDA. Yes, I am beginning to think so now. I'm heartily thankful you've no hold or power over me—and I hope you never will.

BRACK (*laughing equivocally*). Well, well, Madam Hedda. You may be right there. Who knows what I mightn't prove capable of in that case?

HEDDA. Now look here, Mr. Brack. That sounds almost as though you were threatening me.

BRACK (*getting up*). Oh, far from it! The triangle, you see, is best formed and maintained by free consent.

HEDDA. That's what I think, too.

BRACK. Yes. Well, now I've said what I wanted to and I must see about getting home again. Good-bye, Madam Hedda. (*He goes toward the glass door.*)

HEDDA (*getting up*). Are you going through the garden?

BRACK. Yes, it's shorter for me.

HEDDA. Yes, and what's more, it's a back way.

BRACK. Quite true. I have nothing against back ways. They can be quite attractive at times.

HEDDA. When someone's practicing shooting, do you mean?

BRACK (*at the door, laughing to her*). Oh, I don't think people shoot their farmyard cocks.

HEDDA (*laughing, too*). No, not when one has only the one.

(*They nod good-bye to each other, laughing. He goes out. She shuts the door after him.*

HEDDA *stands a moment, serious now, and looks out. Then she goes across and peeps in through the curtains over the middle doorway and then goes to the writing-table, takes the packet out of the bookcase and is just going to look through it when* BERTE's *voice is heard, speaking loudly, in the hall.* HEDDA *turns and listens, then quickly locks the package in the drawer and puts the key on the inkstand.*

EJLERT LÖVBORG, *with his overcoat on and his hat in his hand, flings open the hall door. He looks disturbed and excited.*)

LÖVBORG (*speaking towards the hall*). And I tell you I must go in and I will. There now!

(*He shuts the door, turns, sees* HEDDA, *controls himself at once and bows.*)

HEDDA (*at the writing-table*). Well, Mr. Lövborg, it's rather late to come and fetch Thea.

LÖVBORG. Or rather early to come and call on you. I apologize.

HEDDA. How do you know that she is still with me?

LÖVBORG. They said at her lodgings that she had been out all night.

HEDDA (*going to the center table*). Did you notice anything about the people, when they said that?

LÖVBORG (*looking at her inquiringly*). Notice anything about them?

HEDDA. I mean, did it look as if they were drawing their own conclusions?

LÖVBORG (*understanding suddenly*). Oh yes, of course; that's true. I am dragging her down with me. Actually, though, I didn't notice anything. Tesman isn't up yet?

HEDDA. No, I don't think so.

LÖVBORG. When did he get home?

HEDDA. Pretty late.

LÖVBORG. Did he tell you anything?

HEDDA. Yes, I gathered that things had been very merry at Judge Brack's.

LÖVBORG. Nothing more?

HEDDA. No, I don't think so. But anyhow, I was so terribly sleepy—

(MRS. ELVSTED *comes in through the curtains in the middle doorway.*)

MRS. ELVSTED (*going towards him*). Oh, Ejlert! At last!

LÖVBORG. Yes, at last. And too late.

MRS. ELVSTED (*looking anxiously at him*). What is too late?

LÖVBORG. Everything's too late now. It's all up with me.

MRS. ELVSTED. No, no! Don't say that!

LÖVBORG. You'll say so yourself when you hear.

MRS. ELVSTED. I won't hear anything.

HEDDA. Perhaps you'd rather talk to her alone? If so, I'll go.

LÖVBORG. No, you stay too, please. I beg you to.

MRS. ELVSTED. Yes, but I won't hear anything, I tell you.

LÖVBORG. It's not last night's escapades I want to talk about.

MRS. ELVSTED. What is it, then?

LÖVBORG. Just this: our ways must part now.

MRS. ELVSTED. Part?

HEDDA (*involuntarily*). I knew it!

LÖVBORG. Because I don't need you any more, Thea.

MRS. ELVSTED. And you can stand here and say that? Not need me any more! I can still help you, can't I, as I did before? Surely we are going on working together?

LÖVBORG. I don't propose to work in future.

MRS. ELVSTED (*in despair*). What shall I do with my life, then?

LÖVBORG. You must try to go on living as though you had never known me.

MRS. ELVSTED. But I *can't* do that!

LÖVBORG. Try to, Thea. You must go home again—

MRS. ELVSTED (*protesting fiercely*). Never in this life! Where you are, there will I be too. I won't let myself be driven away like this. I will stay here and be with you when the book comes out.

HEDDA (*half audibly, in suspense*). Ah, the book, of course!

LÖVBORG (*looking at her*). My book and Thea's. For that is what it is.

MRS. ELVSTED. Yes, that's what I feel it is. And that's why I have the right to be with you when it comes out. I want to see respect and honor showered on you again. And the joy—I want to share the joy with you.

LÖVBORG. Thea, our book will never come out.

HEDDA. Ah!

MRS. ELVSTED. Never come out!

LÖVBORG. *Can't* ever come out.

MRS. ELVSTED (*in agonized foreboding*). Ejlert, what have you done with the manuscript?

HEDDA (*looking intently at him*). Yes, the manuscript?

MRS. ELVSTED. Where is it?

LÖVBORG. You'd better not ask me, Thea.

MRS. ELVSTED. But I want to know. I've a right to know, at once.

LÖVBORG. The manuscript . . . oh well, then . . . I have torn the manuscript into a thousand pieces.

MRS. ELVSTED (*shrieking*). Oh no, no!

HEDDA (*involuntarily*). But that's not—!

LÖVBORG (*looking at her*). Not true, you think?

HEDDA (*controlling herself*). I suppose it is, of course. If you say so yourself. . . . But it sounded so fantastic.

LÖVBORG. True, all the same.

MRS. ELVSTED (*wringing her hands*). Oh, heavens, heavens, Hedda! Torn his own work to pieces!

LÖVBORG. I have torn my own life to pieces. So I might as well tear up my life's work, too.

MRS. ELVSTED. And you did it last night, then?

LÖVBORG. Yes, I tell you. Into a thousand pieces. And scattered them out in the fjord. Far out. There at least there is clean sea water. Let them drift in it. Drift with the wind and the tides. And, after a time, they will sink. Deeper and deeper. As I shall, Thea.

MRS. ELVSTED. Do you know, Ejlert, this, what you have done to the book— all my life, it will seem to me as if you had killed a little child.

LÖVBORG. You are right. It is like murdering a child.

MRS. ELVSTED. But how could you? After all, I had a share in the child, too.

HEDDA (*scarcely audible*). Ah, the child. . . .

MRS. ELVSTED (*with a gasp*). It's all over, then. Well, well. I'll go now, Hedda.

HEDDA. But you're not going to leave town?

MRS. ELVSTED. Oh, I don't know myself what I'm going to do. Everything is dark ahead of me now.

(*She goes out by the hall door.*)

HEDDA (*standing and waiting for a moment*). So you are not going to see her home, Mr. Lövborg?

LÖVBORG. I? Through the streets? Suppose people were to see her walking with me?

HEDDA. Of course, I don't know what else happened to you last night. But is it something so absolutely irreparable?

LÖVBORG. It won't stop at last night only. I know that well enough. But, the point is, I don't *want* to live that kind of life. I don't want to start again, any more, now. It is the courage to live, and to challenge life, that she has broken in me.

HEDDA (*looking straight before her*). That pretty little fool has played her part in a human being's fate. (*Looking at him.*) Still, how could you treat her so callously, all the same?

LÖVBORG. Oh, don't say it was callous!

HEDDA. To go and destroy what has filled her soul all this long, long time! You don't call that callous?

LÖVBORG. I can tell you the truth, Hedda.

HEDDA. The truth?

LÖVBORG. Promise me first, give me your word, that Thea shall never know what I tell you.

HEDDA. You have my word for it.

LÖVBORG. Good. Then I will tell you that that was not the truth—the story I told you just now.

HEDDA. About the manuscript?

LÖVBORG. Yes. I didn't tear it to pieces. Nor throw it into the fjord, either.

HEDDA. Well, but—where is it, then?

LÖVBORG. I have destroyed it just the same. Utterly and completely, Hedda.

HEDDA. I don't understand all this.

LÖVBORG. Thea said that what I had done was as good as child-murder to her.

HEDDA. Yes. That's what she said.

LÖVBORG. But that—killing his child—is not the worst thing a father can do to it.

HEDDA. *That's* not the worst?

LÖVBORG. No. It was that worst thing that I wanted to save Thea from hearing.

HEDDA. And what is that worst thing, then?

LÖVBORG. Suppose now, Hedda, that a man, along towards morning, say, after a wild, riotous night, came home to his child's mother and said: Look here. I have been here and there, in such-and-such places. And I took the child with me. In such-and-such places. And I lost the child. Lost it completely. The devil knows what hands it's fallen into, who's got it in his clutches.

HEDDA. Oh but, when all's said and done, this—well, this was only a book.

LÖVBORG. Thea's whole soul was in that book.

HEDDA. Yes, I understand that.

LÖVBORG. And so you understand also that there is no future before us, her and me.

HEDDA. And what are you going to do, then?

LÖVBORG. Nothing. Only make an end of the whole business. The sooner the better.

HEDDA (*a step nearer*). Ejlert Lövborg, listen to me. Could you not see to it that—that it is done beautifully?

LÖVBORG. Beautifully? (*Smiling.*) With vineleaves in the hair, as you used to imagine once upon a time—

HEDDA. Ah, not vineleaves. I don't believe in that any more. But beautifully, nevertheless. For once. Good-bye. You must go now, and not come here again.

LÖVBORG. Good-bye, Madam. Remember me to Jörgen Tesman. (*About to go.*)

HEDDA. Wait a minute. You shall have a souvenir to take with you.

(*She goes to the writing-table and opens the drawer and the pistol-case. She comes back to* LÖVBORG *again with one of the pistols.*)

LÖVBORG (*looking at her*). Is *that* the souvenir?

HEDDA (*nodding slowly*). Do you recognize it? It was aimed at you once.

LÖVBORG. You should have used it then.

HEDDA. There it is. Use it yourself now.

LÖVBORG (*putting the pistol in his breast pocket*). Thanks.

HEDDA. And beautifully, Ejlert Lövborg. Promise me that.

LÖVBORG. Good-bye, Hedda Gabler. (*He goes out by the hall door.*)

(HEDDA *listens a moment at the door. Then she goes across to the writing-table and takes out the manuscript in its package. She glances inside the wrapper, pulls some of the sheets half out and looks at them. Then she goes across and sits down in the easy-chair by the stove with the packet in her lap. After a moment, she opens the stove-door and then the packet.*)

HEDDA (*throwing some of the leaves into the fire and whispering to herself*). Now I am burning your child, Thea. You, with your curly hair. (*Throwing a few more leaves into the stove.*) Your child and Ejlert Lövborg's. (*Throwing in the rest.*) I'm burning it—burning your child.

ACT IV

The same rooms at the Tesmans' house. Evening. The drawing-room is in darkness. The inner room is lighted by the hanging lamp over the table. The curtains are drawn across the glass door.

HEDDA, *dressed in black, is walking to and fro in the dark room. Then she goes into the inner room and away to the left side. A few chords on the piano are heard. Then she comes back again and into the drawing-room.*

BERTE *comes in from the right through the inner room with a lighted lamp, which she puts on the table in front of the corner sofa in the drawing-room. Her eyes are red with crying and she has black ribbons in her cap. She goes quietly and discreetly out to the right.* HEDDA *goes across to the glass door, draws the curtain aside a little and looks out into the darkness.*

Soon after, MISS TESMAN *comes in from the hall door, dressed in mourning, with a hat and veil. Hedda goes towards her and holds out her hand.*

MISS TESMAN. Yes, Hedda, here I am dressed in mourning. Because now my poor sister's trials are over at last.

HEDDA. I have heard already, as you see. My husband sent a note out to me.

MISS TESMAN. Yes, he promised he would. But I thought all the same, that to Hedda—here, in the house of the living—I ought myself to bring the news of her death.

HEDDA. It was very kind of you.

MISS TESMAN. Ah, Rina should not have died at such a moment. Hedda's home ought not to be sad just now.

HEDDA (*changing the subject*). She died very peacefully, didn't she, Miss Tesman?

MISS TESMAN. Ah, it was such a beautiful, peaceful release! And then she had the unspeakable happiness of seeing Jörgen once more, so that she was really able to say good-bye to him. Perhaps he hasn't come back yet?

HEDDA. No. He wrote that I mustn't expect him just yet. But do sit down.

MISS TESMAN. No, thank you, my dear, precious Hedda. I should like to, but I have so little time. She must be prepared and made ready as well as I can. She shall go into her grave looking beautiful.

HEDDA. Can't I help you with anything?

MISS TESMAN. Oh, don't think of that! Hedda Tesman mustn't do that kind of thing. Nor dwell on the thought, either. Not at such a time. Certainly not.

HEDDA. Ah, thoughts . . . they are not so easily mastered.

MISS TESMAN (*going on*). Well, bless us. That's how things go in this world. At home we shall be sewing for Rina. And there will be sewing to be done here too, I think, soon. But that will be a different kind, thank God!

(JÖRGEN TESMAN *comes in by the hall door.*)

HEDDA. Ah, it's a good thing you're back at last.

TESMAN. Are you here, Aunt Julle? With Hedda? Fancy!

MISS TESMAN. I was just going again, dear boy. Well, did you see to all those things you promised to do?

TESMAN. No, I'm really afraid I've forgotten half of them, you know. I must run in and see you again tomorrow. My head is so muddled today. I can't keep my ideas together.

MISS TESMAN. But, my dear Jörgen. You mustn't take it like this.

TESMAN. No? How, then . . . do you think?

MISS TESMAN. You must be glad in your grief. Glad of what has happened. As I am.

TESMAN. Oh yes, yes. You are thinking of Aunt Rina, of course.

HEDDA. It will be lonely for you now, Miss Tesman.

MISS TESMAN. Just at first, yes. But that won't last very long, I hope. Dear Rina's little room won't stand empty, I know.

TESMAN. Really? Who do you want to take it? Eh?

MISS TESMAN. Oh, there is always some poor sick person or other who needs care and attention, unfortunately.

HEDDA. Do you really want to take a burden like that on you again?

MISS TESMAN. Burden! God forgive you, my child. It has never been a burden to me.

HEDDA. But if a strange person is going to come, why—

MISS TESMAN. Oh, one soon makes friends with sick folk. And I sadly need someone to live for—I, too. Well, thank God there may be things here, too, of one sort and another, that an old aunt can lend a hand with.

HEDDA. Oh, don't bother about things here—

TESMAN. Just think how happy we three could be together, if—

HEDDA. If—?

TESMAN (*uneasily*). Oh, nothing. It'll all come right. Let's hope so. Eh?

MISS TESMAN. Well, well. You two have plenty to talk to each other about, I expect. (*Smiling.*) And perhaps Hedda has something to tell you too, Jörgen. Good-bye. Now I must go home to Rina. (*Turning at the door.*) Dear, dear, how strange it is to think of it! Now Rina is with me and with our dear Jochum, too.

TESMAN. Yes, to think of it, Aunt Julle! Eh?

(MISS TESMAN *goes out by the hall door.*)

HEDDA (*her eyes, cold and searching, following* TESMAN). I almost think the death has affected you more than it has her.

TESMAN. Oh, it's not only Aunt Rina's death. It's Ejlert; I'm so worried about him.

HEDDA (*quickly*). Has anything fresh happened to him?

TESMAN. I meant to have run over to him this afternoon and told him that his manuscript was in safe keeping.

HEDDA. Well, didn't you find him, then?

TESMAN. No, he wasn't at home. But afterwards I met Mrs. Elvsted, and she told me he had been here early this morning.

HEDDA. Yes, directly you'd gone.

TESMAN. And he seems to have said that he had torn up the manuscript. Eh?

HEDDA. Yes, he insisted he had.

TESMAN. But, good heavens, he must have been absolutely off his head! And so, of course, you didn't dare give it back to him, Hedda?

HEDDA. No, he didn't take it.

TESMAN. But you told him, all right, that we had it?

HEDDA. No. (*Quickly.*) Did you tell Mrs. Elvsted we had?

TESMAN. No, I didn't quite like to do that. But you ought to have told him yourself. Suppose he goes off in despair and does himself some injury? Let me have the manuscript, Hedda. I will dash over to him with it at once. Where is the parcel?

HEDDA (*cold and immovable, leaning against the easy-chair*). I haven't got it any longer.

TESMAN. You haven't got it. What on earth do you mean by that?

HEDDA. I have burnt it. Every scrap of it.

TESMAN (*with a start of terror*). Burnt it! Burnt Ejlert Lövborg's manuscript!

HEDDA. Don't scream like that. The maid might hear you.

TESMAN. Burnt! But, good God! No, no, no! This is simply impossible!

HEDDA. Well, it's true, all the same.

TESMAN. But do you realize what you have done, Hedda? It's against the law, to treat lost property like that! Think of it! You just ask Judge Brack and he'll tell you.

HEDDA. I shouldn't advise you to talk about it either to the Judge or to anyone else.

TESMAN. But how could you go and do anything so unheard of? How could such an idea come into your head? How could it come over you? Tell me that. Eh?

HEDDA (*suppressing a scarcely perceptible smile*). I did it for your sake, Jörgen.

TESMAN. For my sake!

HEDDA. When you came home in the morning and told me that he'd been reading to you—

TESMAN. Yes, yes, what about it?

HEDDA. You admitted then that you envied him his work.

TESMAN. Good heavens, I didn't mean it literally!

HEDDA. All the same, I couldn't bear the thought of someone else throwing you into the shade.

TESMAN (*in an outburst of mingled doubt and joy*). Hedda! Is it true what you're saying? Yes, but . . . but . . . I've never known you show your affection in this sort of way before.

HEDDA. Oh well, you'd better know, then, that—just at present— (*Breaking off, violently.*) No, you can go and ask Aunt Julle. She'll tell you all about it.

TESMAN. Ah, I rather think I understand, Hedda! (*Clasping his hands together.*) Good heavens! Good heavens! Can it be possible? Eh?

HEDDA. Don't shout so. The maid might hear you.

TESMAN (*laughing, beside himself with joy*). The maid! No, you really are priceless, Hedda! "The maid"! Why, it's only Berte! I'll go out and tell Berte myself.

HEDDA (*clenching her hands in desperation*). Oh, it'll be the death of me. It'll be the death of me, all this!

TESMAN. What will, Hedda? Eh?

HEDDA (*cold and controlled*). All this grotesque nonsense, Jörgen.

TESMAN. Nonsense! That I'm so delighted? But, all the same . . . perhaps I had better not say anything to Berte.

HEDDA. Oh yes, why not that, too?

TESMAN. No, no, not yet. But Aunt Julle must certainly know about it. And then, too, that you are beginning to call me Jörgen! Think of it! Oh, Aunt Julle *will* be so glad! So glad!

HEDDA. When she hears that I have burnt Ejlert Lövborg's manuscript, for your sake?

TESMAN. No, that reminds me. That business with the manuscript—no one must get to know about that, of course. But that you feel like this towards me, Hedda, Aunt Julle must certainly hear that! Still, my dear, I should like to know myself whether this kind of thing is usual with young wives. Eh?

HEDDA. You'd better ask Aunt Julle about that, too, I think.

TESMAN. Yes, I certainly will some time. (*Looking worried and dubious again.*) But . . . but that manuscript. Oh heavens, it's dreadful to think of poor Ejlert, all the same!

(MRS. ELVSTED, *dressed as on her first visit, with her hat and out-door clothes, comes in by the hall door.*)

MRS. ELVSTED (*greeting them quickly and speaking in agitation*). Oh, Hedda, dear, I hope you won't mind my coming again?

HEDDA. What's the matter, Thea?

TESMAN. Is it something to do with Ejlert Lövborg again? Eh?

MRS. ELVSTED. Yes, I'm terribly afraid some accident has happened to him.

HEDDA (*seizing her by the arm*). Ah—do you think so?

TESMAN. Bless me, whatever makes you think that, Mrs. Elvsted?

MRS. ELVSTED. Why, because I heard them talking about him at the boarding-house, just as I came in. Oh, there are the most incredible rumors about him in town today!

TESMAN. Yes, do you know, I heard that too. Yet I could swear that he went straight home to bed. Just fancy!

HEDDA. Well, what did they say at the boarding-house?

MRS. ELVSTED. I didn't gather anything definite. Either they didn't know very much or . . . They stopped talking when they saw me. And as for asking—I didn't dare do that.

TESMAN (*walking about restlessly*). We'll hope—we'll hope you misunderstood them, Mrs. Elvsted.

MRS. ELVSTED. No, no, I am certain it was he they were talking about. And, as I heard it, they said something about the hospital, or—

TESMAN. The hospital!

HEDDA. No! That can't be true.

MRS. ELVSTED. Oh, I was so dreadfully frightened about him. So I went to his lodgings and asked for him there.

HEDDA. Could you bring yourself to do that, Thea?

MRS. ELVSTED. Yes, what else was I to do? I didn't feel as if I could bear the uncertainty any longer.

TESMAN. But you didn't find him either, did you? Eh?

MRS. ELVSTED. No. And the people didn't know anything about him. They said he hadn't been home since yesterday afternoon.

TESMAN. Yesterday! Fancy their saying that!

MRS. ELVSTED. Oh, I think there's only one explanation—something dreadful must have happened to him!

TESMAN. Hedda, my dear, suppose I were to go in and make some inquiries?

HEDDA. No. Don't mix yourself up in this business.

(BRACK, *with his hat in his hand, comes in by the hall door, which* BERTE *opens and shuts after him. He looks grave and bows silently.*)

TESMAN. Oh, it's you, my dear Judge? Eh?

BRACK. Yes, it was imperative for me to see you this evening.

TESMAN. I can see that you have had Aunt Julle's news.

BRACK. Yes, I have heard that, too.

TESMAN. Isn't it sad? Eh?

BRACK. Well, my dear Tesman, it depends how you look at it.

TESMAN (*looking doubtfully at him*). Has anything else happened?

BRACK. Yes, something else.

HEDDA (*in suspense*). Anything sad, Mr. Brack?

BRACK. That, too, depends on how you look at it, Mrs. Tesman.

MRS. ELVSTED (*breaking out, involuntarily*). Oh, it's something about Ejlert Lövborg!

BRACK (*glancing at her*). What makes you think that, Madam? Do you happen to know anything already?

MRS. ELVSTED (*confused*). No, no; not at all! But—

TESMAN. But, good heavens, man, tell us!

BRACK (*shrugging his shoulders*). Well, I'm sorry to say Ejlert Lövborg has been taken to the hospital. As a matter of fact, he's dying.

MRS. ELVSTED (*crying out*). My God! My God!

TESMAN. In hospital? And dying?

HEDDA (*involuntarily*). So quickly, then!

MRS. ELVSTED (*wailing*). And we parted in anger, Hedda!

HEDDA (*whispering*). Come now, Thea! *Thea!*

MRS. ELVSTED (*without taking any notice*). I must go to him! I must see him alive!

BRACK. It won't be any use, my dear lady. Nobody's allowed to see him.

MRS. ELVSTED. Well, at least tell me what's happened to him. What is the matter?

TESMAN. Why, surely he never did it himself! Eh?

HEDDA. I'm sure he *did*.

TESMAN. Hedda, how can you?

BRACK (*with his eyes fixed steadily on her*). Unfortunately, you have guessed quite right, Mrs. Tesman.

MRS. ELVSTED. Oh, how terrible!

TESMAN. So he did it himself! Think of it!

HEDDA. Shot himself!

BRACK. Rightly guessed again, Mrs. Tesman.

MRS. ELVSTED (*trying to control herself*). When did it happen, Mr. Brack?

BRACK. This afternoon. Between three and four.

TESMAN. But, dear, dear—where did he do it, then? Eh?

BRACK (*a little uncertainly*). Where? Why, I suppose at his lodgings.

MRS. ELVSTED. No, that can't be right. Because I was there between six and seven.

BRACK. Well, somewhere else, then. I don't exactly know; I only know that he was found. . . . He had shot himself in the chest.

MRS. ELVSTED. Oh, how dreadful to think of! That he should end like this.

HEDDA (*to* BRACK). Was it in the chest?

BRACK. Yes, as I said.

HEDDA. Not in the temple, then?

BRACK. In the chest, Mrs. Tesman.

HEDDA. Yes, well . . . the chest is a good place, too.

BRACK. How do you mean, Mrs. Tesman?

HEDDA (*evasively*). Oh, nothing—nothing.

TESMAN. And the wound is dangerous, you say? Eh?

BRACK. The wound is absolutely fatal. Most likely it's all over already.

MRS. ELVSTED. Yes, yes, I feel sure it is. It is all over! All over! Oh, Hedda!

TESMAN. But tell me, how did you find out all this?

BRACK (*shortly*). From one of the police. Whom I had occasion to speak to.

HEDDA (*in a ringing voice*). Something done, at last!

TESMAN (*horrified*). Good heavens! What are you saying Hedda?

HEDDA. That there is an element of beauty in this.

BRACK. Hm. Mrs. Tesman—

TESMAN. Of beauty! Fancy that!

MRS. ELVSTED. Oh, Hedda, how can you talk of beauty in a thing like that!

HEDDA. Ejlert Lövborg has balanced his account with himself. He has had the courage to do . . . what had to be done.

MRS. ELVSTED. No, don't ever believe that it happened in that way. What he has done was done in a moment of madness.

TESMAN. Done in despair.

HEDDA. It was not. Of that I am certain.

MRS. ELVSTED. Yes, it was. In a moment of madness. Just as when he tore up our manuscript.

BRACK (*in surprise*). Manuscript? The book, do you mean? Has he torn that up?

MRS. ELVSTED. Yes, he did it last night.

TESMAN (*whispering softly*). Oh, Hedda, we shall never get clear of this business.

BRACK. Hm. That was odd.

TESMAN (*walking about the room*). Fancy Ejlert going out of the world like that! And not even leaving behind him the book that would have made his name immortal.

MRS. ELVSTED. Oh, if only it could be put together again!

TESMAN. Yes, just think if it could! I don't know what I wouldn't give—

MRS. ELVSTED. Perhaps it can, Mr. Tesman.

TESMAN. What do you mean?

MRS. ELVSTED (*looking in her handbag*). Look here. I have kept the loose notes that he used for dictating from.

HEDDA (*a step nearer*). Ah!

TESMAN. You've kept them, Mrs. Elvsted! Eh?

MRS. ELVSTED. Yes, I have them here. I took them with me when I came away, and here they've been, lying in my handbag.

TESMAN. Just let me see them!

MRS. ELVSTED (*passes him a stack of small sheets*). But they're in such a muddle. All mixed up together.

TESMAN. Fancy, if we could get it straight, though! Perhaps if we help each other—

MRS. ELVSTED. Oh yes! Let's try, at any rate!

TESMAN. It *shall* be done! It *must!* I will give my life to this.

HEDDA. You, Jörgen? Your life?

TESMAN. Yes. Or, rather, all my spare time. My own stuff must wait for the present. You understand, Hedda? Eh? It's something I owe to Ejlert's memory.

HEDDA. Perhaps it is.

TESMAN. And so, my dear Mrs. Elvsted, we will pull ourselves together. Heaven knows, it's no use brooding over what's done. Eh? We must try to make our minds as calm as possible, and—

MRS. ELVSTED. Yes, yes, Mr. Tesman. I will do the best I can.

TESMAN. Well, come along. We must look over the notes at once. Where shall we sit? Here? No, in here in the back room. Excuse me, my dear Judge. Now come with me, Mrs. Elvsted.

MRS. ELVSTED. Dear God! If only it could be done!

(TESMAN *and* MRS. ELVSTED *go into the inner room. She takes off her hat and overcoat. They both sit down at the table under the hanging lamp and become absorbed in concentrated examination of the papers.* HEDDA *goes across to the stove and sits in the easy-chair. Shortly afterwards* BRACK *goes across to her.)*

HEDDA *(half-aloud)*. Ah, Mr. Brack, what a feeling of release it gives one, this business with Ejlert Lövborg.

BRACK. Release, Madam Hedda? Well, it certainly is a release for him—

HEDDA. I mean for me. A feeling of release, in knowing that there really can be such a thing in the world as free and fearless action. Something irradiated with spontaneous beauty.

BRACK *(smiling)*. Hm. My dear Madam Hedda—

HEDDA. Oh yes. I know what you are going to say. Because you're a professional man too, in your way, like . . . Oh well!

BRACK *(looking steadily at her)*. Ejlert Lövborg meant more to you than you are perhaps willing to admit to yourself. Or am I wrong there?

HEDDA. I don't answer that kind of question. I only know that Ejlert Lövborg had the courage to live life in his own way. And now—this great deed, with all its beauty? That he had the strength and will to break away from the feast of life . . . and so early.

BRACK. I am very sorry, Madam Hedda, but I must deprive you of your pretty illusion.

HEDDA. Illusion?

BRACK. Which you would have been deprived of soon, in any case.

HEDDA. And what is it?

BRACK. He did not shoot himself intentionally.

HEDDA. Not intentionally?

BRACK. No. This affair of Ejlert Lövborg did not happen quite as I described it.

HEDDA *(in suspense)*. Have you been keeping something back? What is it?

BRACK. For poor Mrs. Elvsted's sake I did make one or two slight modifications.

HEDDA. What were they?

BRACK. In the first place, he is actually dead already.

HEDDA. In hospital?

BRACK. Yes, and without regaining consciousness.

HEDDA. What else did you keep back?

BRACK. The fact that the thing didn't happen at his lodgings.

HEDDA. Well, that doesn't really make much difference.

BRACK. It does, rather. For I must tell you Ejlert Lövborg was found shot in—in Mademoiselle Diana's boudoir.

HEDDA *(half gets up, but sinks back again)*. That's impossible, Mr. Brack. He can't have been *there* again today!

BRACK. He was there this afternoon. He came to demand something that, he said, they had taken away from him. Talked wildly about a child that had been lost—

HEDDA. Ah! So that was why . . .

BRACK. I thought perhaps it might have been his manuscript. But I gather that he destroyed that himself. So it must have been his wallet.

HEDDA. It must have been. And it was there, then, that he was found?

BRACK. Yes, there. With a discharged pistol that had gone off in his breast-pocket. The shot had wounded him fatally.

HEDDA. In the chest—yes.

BRACK. No. It hit him in the stomach.

HEDDA (*looking up at him with an expression of disgust*). That too! The ridiculous and the sordid lies like a curse on everything I so much as touch.

BRACK. There is something more, Madam Hedda. Something that can also be classed as "sordid."

HEDDA. What is that?

BRACK. The pistol that he had on him—

HEDDA (*breathless*). Well! What about it?

BRACK. He must have stolen it.

HEDDA (*jumping up*). Stolen! That's not true! That he did not!

BRACK. No other explanation is possible. He *must* have stolen it. . . . Hush!

(TESMAN *and* MRS. ELVSTED *have got up from the table in the inner room and come into the drawing-room.*)

TESMAN (*with papers in both hands*). Look here, Hedda, it's hardly possible for me to see in there under the hanging lamp. Just think!

HEDDA. Yes. I am.

TESMAN. I wonder if you would mind our sitting at your writing-table for a little while. Eh?

HEDDA. I don't mind. (*Quickly.*) Wait a minute! Let me tidy it up first.

TESMAN. Oh, you needn't do that, Hedda. There's plenty of room.

HEDDA. No, no. Just let me tidy it, I tell you. I'll take all this in and put it on the piano for the time being. There!

(*She has pulled out something covered with music paper from under the bookshelf, puts some more sheets on it and carries it all in to the left in the inner room.* TESMAN *puts the loose papers on the writing-table and moves the lamp there from the corner table. He and* MRS. ELVSTED *sit down and settle to work again.* HEDDA *comes back.*)

HEDDA (*behind* MRS. ELVSTED's *chair, ruffling her hair gently*). Well, my precious Thea, how is Ejlert Lövborg's memorial getting on?

MRS. ELVSTED (*looking up dispiritedly*). Oh dear! It looks as if it's going to be terribly difficult to straighten out.

TESMAN. It *must* be done. There is nothing else for it. And this—getting another man's papers in order—it's just the job for me.

(HEDDA *goes over to the stove and sits on one of the footstools.* BRACK *stands over her, leaning against the easy-chair.*)

HEDDA (*whispers*). What was it you said about the pistol?

BRACK (*softly*). That he must have stolen it.

HEDDA. Why, precisely, stolen?

BRACK. Because any other explanation ought to be impossible, Madam Hedda.

HEDDA. Really?

BRACK (*glancing at her*). Of course, Ejlert Lövborg was here this morning. Wasn't he?

HEDDA. Yes.

BRACK. Were you alone with him?

HEDDA. Yes, for a time.

BRACK. Didn't you go out of the room while he was here?

HEDDA. No.

BRACK. Think it over. Were you never out of it for a moment?

HEDDA. Well, perhaps just for a moment—out in the hall.

BRACK. And where was your pistol-case in the meantime?

HEDDA. I kept that in . . . I had it locked in . . .

BRACK. Well, Madam Hedda?

HEDDA. The case was there on the writing-table.

BRACK. Have you looked since to see whether both pistols are there?

HEDDA. No.

BRACK. Well, there's no need. I saw the pistol Lövborg had on him. And I knew it again at once, from yesterday. And from longer ago too.

HEDDA. Have you got it?

BRACK. No, the police have it.

HEDDA. What will the police do with the pistol?

BRACK. See if they can trace the owner.

HEDDA. Do you think they can find out?

BRACK (*bending over her and whispering*). No, Hedda Gabler. Not so long as I keep silence.

HEDDA (*looking askance at him*). And if you do *not* keep silence—what then?

BRACK (*shrugging his shoulders*). There is always the other way out: the pistol was stolen.

HEDDA (*firmly*). Rather death!

BRACK (*smiling*). That is the kind of thing one *says*. One doesn't *do* it.

HEDDA (*without answering*). And suppose, now, the pistol isn't stolen. And the owner is discovered. Then what happens?

BRACK. Well, Hedda, what happens then is a scandal.

HEDDA. Scandal!

BRACK. Scandal. Yes! The thing you have such a deadly fear of. Of course you will have to appear in court. Both you and Mademoiselle Diana.

She will have to explain how the thing happened. Whether it was accident or homicide. . . . Did he try to pull the pistol out of his pocket to threaten her? And is that how it went off? Or did she snatch the pistol out of his hand, shoot him and put it back in his pocket again? She's quite equal to that. She's a hefty young woman, that same Mademoiselle Diana.

HEDDA. But all these repulsive details don't concern me.

BRACK. No. But you will have to answer the question: Why did you give Ejlert Lövborg the pistol? And what conclusions will people draw from the fact that you did give it him?

HEDDA (*dropping her head*). That's true. I didn't think of that.

BRACK. Well, fortunately there is no danger, so long as I say nothing.

HEDDA (*looking up at him*). So I am in your power, Mr. Brack. From now on, you have a hold over me.

BRACK (*whispering softly*). My dearest Hedda, believe me I shall not abuse the position.

HEDDA. In your power, all the same. At the mercy of your will and demands. And so a slave! A slave!   (*Getting up impatiently.*) No! That thought I cannot tolerate. Never!

BRACK (*looking at her half mockingly*). And yet one usually manages to tolerate the inevitable.

HEDDA (*returning his look*). Yes, possibly. (*She goes across to the writing-table.*)

HEDDA (*suppressing an involuntary smile and imitating* TESMAN's *intonation*). Well, is it getting on all right, Jörgen? Eh?

TESMAN. The Lord only knows, my dear. In any case, there's months of work here.

HEDDA (*as before*). Well, fancy that! (*Letting her hands stray gently through* MRS. ELVSTED's *hair.*) Doesn't it feel strange to you, Thea? Here you are sitting with Jörgen Tesman just as you once sat with Ejlert Lövborg.

MRS. ELVSTED. Well, if only I could inspire your husband too—

HEDDA. Oh, that will come all right—in time.

TESMAN. Yes, do you know, Hedda, I really think I am beginning to feel something of the kind. But you go back and sit down with Judge Brack again.

HEDDA. Is there nothing here I can help you two with?

TESMAN. Not a thing in the world. (*Turning his head.*) Would you be so kind as to keep Hedda company for the time being, Judge Brack?

BRACK (*with a glance at* HEDDA). It will give me the very greatest pleasure.

HEDDA. Thanks. But I'm tired tonight. I will lie down for a little while on the sofa in there.

TESMAN. Yes do, my dear. Eh?

(HEDDA *goes into the inner room and draws the curtains after her. There is a short pause. Suddenly she is heard playing a wild dance tune on the piano.*)

MRS. ELVSTED (*jumping up from her chair*). Oh! What is that?

TESMAN (*running to the doorway*). But, Hedda, my dearest—don't play dance music this evening. Think of Aunt Rina! And of Ejlert, too!

HEDDA (*putting out her head between the hangings*). And of Aunt Julle. And of all the rest of them. I will be quiet in future. (*She pulls the curtains to again after her.*)

TESMAN (*at the writing-table*). It upsets her to see us at this sad task, of course. I tell you what, Mrs. Elvsted. You shall move into Aunt Julle's and I'll come over in the evenings. And then we can sit and work there. Eh?

MRS. ELVSTED. Yes, perhaps that would be the best plan—

HEDDA (*in the inner room*). I can hear perfectly well what you are saying. But how am I going to get through the evenings out here?

TESMAN (*turning over the papers*). Oh, I'm sure Judge Brack will be kind enough to come out and see you.

BRACK (*in the easy-chair, calling gaily*). Willingly! Every single evening, Mrs. Tesman. We shall have a very pleasant time together here, you and I.

HEDDA (*clearly and distinctly*). Yes, that is what you are looking forward to, isn't it, Mr. Brack? You, as the only cock in the yard.

(*A shot is heard within.* TESMAN, MRS. ELVSTED, *and* BRACK *jump up.*)

TESMAN. Ah! Now she's playing with the pistols again.

(*He pulls the curtains aside and runs in. So does* MRS. ELVSTED. HEDDA *is lying lifeless, stretched out on the sofa. Confusion and cries.* BERTE *comes in distractedly from the right.*)

TESMAN (*shrieking to* BRACK). Shot herself! Shot herself in the temple! Think of it!

BRACK (*half-collapsed in the easy-chair*). But, merciful God! One doesn't *do* that kind of thing!

J. M. Synge

1871–1909

THE PLAYBOY OF THE WESTERN WORLD[1]

CHARACTERS

PEGEEN MIKE FLAHERTY

MICHAEL JAMES FLAHERTY

CHRISTY MAHON

SHAWN KEOGH

WIDOW QUIN

OLD MAHON

PHILLY CULLEN

JIMMY FARRELL

SUSAN BRADY

NELLY

HONOR BLAKE

SARA TANSEY

TOWN CRIER

Other GIRLS *and* MEN

ACT I

(Country public-house or shebeen,[2] very rough and untidy. There is a sort of counter on the right with shelves, holding many bottles and jugs,

---

[1] PLAYBOY, suggests in the Irish idiom either a trickster or one who is proficient at games; *Western World,* western Ireland.   [2] SHEBEEN, a tavern.

184

just seen above it. Empty barrels stand near the counter. At back, a little to left of counter, there is a door into the open air, then, more to the left, there is a settle with shelves above it, with more jugs, and a table beneath a window. At the left there is a large open fireplace, with turf fire, and a small door into inner room. PEGEEN, *a wild-looking but fine girl, of about twenty, is writing at table. She is dressed in the usual peasant dress.*)

PEGEEN (*slowly as she writes*). Six yards of stuff for to make a yellow gown. A pair of lace boots with lengthy heels on them and brassy eyes. A hat is suited[3] for a wedding-day. A fine-tooth comb. To be sent with three barrels of porter in Jimmy Farrell's creel cart on the evening of the coming Fair to Mister Michael James Flaherty. With the best compliments of this season. Margaret Flaherty.

SHAWN KEOGH (*a fat and fair young man comes in as she signs, looks round awkwardly, when he sees she is alone*). Where's himself?

PEGEEN (*without looking at him*). He's coming. (*She directs letter.*) To Mister Sheamus Mulroy, Wine and Spirit Dealer, Castlebar.

SHAWN (*uneasily*). I didn't see him on the road.

PEGEEN. How would you see him (*licks stamp and puts it on letter*) and it dark night this half-hour gone by?

SHAWN (*turning towards door again*). I stood a while outside wondering would I have a right to pass on or to walk in and see you, Pegeen Mike (*comes to fire*), and I could hear the cows breathing and sighing in the stillness of the air, and not a step moving any place from this gate to the bridge.

PEGEEN (*putting letter in envelope*). It's above at the crossroads he is, meeting Philly Cullen and a couple more are going along with him to Kate Cassidy's wake.

SHAWN (*looking at her blankly*). And he's going that length in the dark night.

PEGEEN (*impatiently*). He is surely, and leaving me lonesome on the scruff of the hill. (*She gets up and puts envelope on dresser, then winds clock.*) Isn't it long the nights are now, Shawn Keogh, to be leaving a poor girl with her own self counting the hours to the dawn of day?

SHAWN (*with awkward humour*). If it is, when we're wedded in a short while you'll have no call to complain, for I've little will to be walking off to wakes or weddings in the darkness of the night.

PEGEEN (*with rather scornful good-humour*). You're making mighty certain Shaneen, that I'll wed you now.

SHAWN. Aren't we after making a good bargain, the way we're only waiting these days on Father Reilly's dispensation from the bishops, or the Court of Rome.

PEGEEN (*looking at him teasingly, washing up at dresser*). It's a wonder,

[3] IS SUITED, appropriate.

Shaneen, the Holy Father'd be taking notice of the likes of you; for if I was him I wouldn't bother with this place where you'll meet none but Red Linahan, has a squint in his eye, and Patcheen is lame in his heel, or the mad Mulrannies were driven from California and they lost in their wits. We're a queer lot these times to go troubling the Holy Father on his sacred seat.

SHAWN (*scandalized*). If we are, we're as good this place as another, maybe, and as good these times as we were for ever.

PEGEEN (*with scorn*). As good, is it? Where now will you meet the like of Daneen Sullivan knocked the eye from a peeler;[4] or Marcus Quin, God rest him, got six months for maiming ewes, and he a great warrant to tell stories of holy Ireland till he'd have the old women shedding down tears about their feet. Where will you find the like of them, I'm saying?

SHAWN (*timidly*). If you don't, it's a good job, maybe; for (*with peculiar emphasis on the words*) Father Reilly has small conceit to have[5] that kind walking around and talking to the girls.

PEGEEN (*impatiently throwing water from basin out of the door*). Stop tormenting me with Father Reilly (*imitating his voice*) when I'm asking only what way I'll pass these twelve hours of dark, and not take my death with the fear. (*Looking out of door.*)

SHAWN (*timidly*). Would I fetch you the Widow Quin, maybe?

PEGEEN. Is it the like of that murderer? You'll not, surely.

SHAWN (*going to her, soothingly*). Then I'm thinking himself will stop along with you when he sees you taking on; for it'll be a long night-time with great darkness, and I'm after feeling a kind of fellow above in the furzy ditch, groaning wicked like a maddening dog, the way it's good cause you have, maybe, to be fearing now.

PEGEEN (*turning on him sharply*). What's that? Is it a man you seen?

SHAWN (*retreating*). I couldn't see him at all; but I heard him groaning out, and breaking his heart. It should have been a young man from his words speaking.

PEGEEN (*going after him*). And you never went near to see was he hurted or what ailed him at all?

SHAWN. I did not, Pegeen Mike. It was a dark, lonesome place to be hearing the like of him.

PEGEEN. Well, you're a daring fellow, and if they find his corpse stretched above in the dews of dawn, what'll you say then to the peelers, or the Justice of the Peace?

SHAWN (*thunderstruck*). I wasn't thinking of that. For the love of God, Pegeen Mike, don't let on I was speaking of him. Don't tell your father and the men is coming above; for if they heard that story they'd have great blabbing this night at the wake.

PEGEEN. I'll maybe tell them, and I'll maybe not.

---

4 PEELER, policeman.　5 SMALL CONCEIT TO HAVE, little sympathy for.

SHAWN. They are coming at the door. Will you whisht,[6] I'm saying?

PEGEEN. Whisht yourself.

(She goes behind counter. MICHAEL JAMES, *fat jovial publican, comes in followed by* PHILLY CULLEN, *who is thin and mistrusting, and* JIMMY FARRELL, *who is fat and amorous, about forty-five.)*

MEN *(together)*. God bless you! The blessing of God on this place!

PEGEEN. God bless you kindly.

MICHAEL *(to men, who go to the counter)*. Sit down now, and take your rest. *(Crosses to* SHAWN *at the fire.)* And how is it you are, Shawn Keogh? Are you coming over the sands to Kate Cassidy's wake?

SHAWN. I am not, Michael James. I'm going home the short cut to my bed.

PEGEEN *(speaking across the counter)*. He's right, too, and have you no shame, Michael James, to be quitting off for the whole night, and leaving myself lonesome in the shop?

MICHAEL *(good-humouredly)*. Isn't it the same whether I go for the whole night or a part only? and I'm thinking it's a queer daughter you are if you'd have me crossing backward through the Stooks of the Dead Women,[7] with a drop taken.

PEGEEN. If I am a queer daughter, it's a queer father'd be leaving me lonesome these twelve hours of dark, and I piling the turf with the dogs barking, and the calves mooing, and my own teeth rattling with the fear.

JIMMY *(flatteringly)*. What is there to hurt you, and you a fine, hardy girl would knock the head of any two men in the place?

PEGEEN *(working herself up)*. Isn't there the harvest boys with their tongues red for drink, and the ten tinkers is camped in the east glen, and the thousand militia—bad cess[8] to them!—walking idle through the land. There's lots surely to hurt me, and I won't stop alone in it, let himself do what he will.

MICHAEL. If you're that afeard, let Shawn Keogh stop along with you. It's the will of God, I'm thinking, himself should be seeing to you now.

(They all turn on SHAWN.)*

SHAWN *(in horrified confusion)*. I would and welcome, Michael James, but I'm afeard of Father Reilly; and what at all would the Holy Father and the Cardinals of Rome be saying if they heard I did the like of that?

MICHAEL *(with contempt)*. God help you! Can't you sit in by the hearth with the light lit and herself beyond in the room? You'll do that surely, for I've heard tell there's a queer fellow above, going mad or getting his death, maybe, in the gripe[9] of the ditch, so she'd be safer this night with a person here.

6 WHISHT, hush.   7 STOOKS OF THE DEAD WOMAN, a place.   8 CESS, luck.   9 GRIPE, gutter.

SHAWN (*with plaintive despair*). I'm afeard of Father Reilly, I'm saying. Let you not be tempting me, and we near married itself.

PHILLY (*with cold contempt*). Lock him in the west room. He'll stay then and have no sin to be telling to the priest.

MICHAEL (*to* SHAWN, *getting between him and the door*). Go up now.

SHAWN (*at the top of his voice*). Don't stop me, Michael James. Let me out of the door, I'm saying, for the love of the Almighty God. Let me out. (*Trying to dodge past him.*) Let me out of it, and may God grant you His indulgence in the hour of need.

MICHAEL (*loudly*). Stop your noising, and sit down by the hearth.

(*Gives him a push and goes to counter laughing.*)

SHAWN (*turning back, wringing his hands*). Oh, Father Reilly, and the saints of God, where will I hide myself today? Oh, St. Joseph and St. Patrick and St. Brigid and St. James, have mercy on me now! (SHAWN *turns round, sees door clear, and makes a rush for it.*)

MICHAEL (*catching him by the coat-tail*). You'd be going, is it?

SHAWN (*screaming*). Leave me go, Michael James, leave me go, you old Pagan, leave me go, or I'll get the curse of the priests on you, and of the scarlet-coated bishops of the Courts of Rome. (*With a sudden movement he pulls himself out of his coat, and disappears out of the door, leaving his coat in* MICHAEL's *hands.*)

MICHAEL (*turning round, and holding up coat*). Well, there's the coat of a Christian man. Oh, there's sainted glory this day in the lonesome west; and by the will of God I've got you a decent man, Pegeen, you'll have no call to be spying after if you've a score of young girls, maybe, weeding in your fields.

PEGEEN (*taking up the defence of her property*). What right have you to be making game of a poor fellow for minding the priest, when it's your own the fault is, not paying a penny pot-boy to stand along with me and give me courage in the doing of my work? (*She snaps the coat away from him, and goes behind counter with it.*)

MICHAEL (*taken aback*). Where would I get a pot-boy? Would you have me send the bellman screaming in the streets of Castlebar?

SHAWN (*opening the door a chink and putting in his head, in a small voice*). Michael James!

MICHAEL (*imitating him*). What ails you?

SHAWN.' The queer dying fellow's beyond looking over the ditch. He's come up, I'm thinking, stealing your hens. (*Looks over his shoulder.*) God help me, he's following me now (*he runs into room*), and if he's heard what I said, he'll be having my life, and I going home lonesome in the darkness of the night.

(*For a perceptible moment they watch the door with curiosity. Someone coughs outside. Then* CHRISTY MAHON, *a slight young man, comes in very tired and frightened and dirty.*)

CHRISTY (*in a small voice*). God save all here!

MEN. God save you kindly!

CHRISTY (*going to the counter*). I'd trouble you for a glass of porter, woman of the house.

(*He puts down coin.*)

PEGEEN (*serving him*). You're one of the tinkers, young fellow, is beyond camped in the glen?

CHRISTY. I am not; but I'm destroyed walking.

MICHAEL (*patronizingly*). Let you come up then to the fire. You're looking famished with the cold.

CHRISTY. God reward you. (*He takes up his glass and goes a little way across to the left, then stops and looks about him.*) Is it often the polis[10] do be coming into this place, master of the house?

MICHAEL. If you'd come in better hours, you'd have seen "Licensed for the Sale of Beer and Spirits, to be Consumed on the Premises," written in white letters above the door, and what would the polis want spying on me, and not a decent house within four miles, the way every living Christian is a bona fide, saving one widow alone?

CHRISTY (*with relief*). It's a safe house, so. (*He goes over to the fire, sighing and moaning. Then he sits down, putting his glass beside him, and begins gnawing a turnip, too miserable to feel the others staring at him with curiosity.*)

MICHAEL (*going after him*). Is it yourself is fearing the polis? You're wanting,[11] maybe?

CHRISTY. There's many wanting.

MICHAEL. Many, surely, with the broken harvest and the ended wars. (*He picks up some stockings, etc., that are near the fire, and carries them away furtively.*) It should be larceny, I'm thinking?

CHRISTY (*dolefully*). I had it in my mind it was a different word and a bigger.

PEGEEN. There's a queer lad. Were you never slapped in school, young fellow, that you don't know the name of your deed?

CHRISTY (*bashfully*). I'm slow at learning, a middling scholar only.

MICHAEL. If you're a dunce itself, you'd have a right to know that larceny's robbing and stealing. Is it for the like of that you're wanting?

CHRISTY (*with a flash of family pride*). And I the son of a strong farmer (*with a sudden qualm*), God rest his soul, could have bought up the whole of your old house a while since, from the butt of his tail-pocket, and not have missed the weight of it gone.

MICHAEL (*impressed*). If it's not stealing, it's maybe something big.

CHRISTY (*flattered*). Aye; it's maybe something big.

JIMMY. He's a wicked-looking young fellow. Maybe he followed after a young woman on a lonesome night.

CHRISTY (*shocked*). Oh, the saints forbid, mister; I was all times a decent lad.

PHILLY (*turning on* JIMMY). You're a silly man, Jimmy Farrell. He said his father was a farmer a while since, and there's himself now in a poor state. Maybe the land was grabbed from him, and he did what any decent man would do.

MICHAEL (*to* CHRISTY, *mysteriously*). Was it bailiffs?

CHRISTY. The divil a one.

MICHAEL. Agents?

CHRISTY. The divil a one.

MICHAEL. Landlords?

CHRISTY (*peevishly*). Ah, not at all, I'm saying. You'd see the like of them stories on any little paper of a Munster town. But I'm not calling to mind any person, gentle, simple, judge or jury, did the like of me.

(*They all draw nearer with delighted curiosity.*)

PHILLY. Well, that lad's a puzzle-the-world.

JIMMY. He'd beat Dan Davies' circus, or the holy missioners making sermons on the villainy of man. Try him again, Philly.

PHILLY. Did you strike golden guineas out of solder, young fellow, or shilling coins itself?

CHRISTY. I did not, mister, not sixpence nor a farthing coin.

JIMMY. Did you marry three wives maybe? I'm told there's a sprinkling have done that among the holy Luthers of the preaching north.

CHRISTY (*shyly*). I never married with one, let alone with a couple or three.

PHILLY. Maybe he went fighting for the Boers, the like of the man beyond, was judged to be hanged, quartered, and drawn. Were you off east, young fellow, fighting bloody wars for Kruger and the freedom of the Boers?

CHRISTY. I never left my own parish till Tuesday was a week.

PEGEEN (*coming from counter*). He's done nothing, so. (*To* CHRISTY.) If you didn't commit murder or a bad, nasty thing; or false coining, or robbery, or butchery, or the like of them, there isn't anything that would be worth your troubling for to run from now. You did nothing at all.

CHRISTY (*his feelings hurt*). That's an unkindly thing to be saying to a poor orphaned traveller, has a prison behind him, and hanging before, and hell's gap gaping below.

PEGEEN (*with a sign to the men to be quiet*). You're only saying it. You did nothing at all. A soft lad the like of you wouldn't slit the windpipe of a screeching sow.

CHRISTY (*offended*). You're not speaking the truth.

PEGEEN (*in mock rage*). Not speaking the truth, is it? Would you have me knock the head of you with the butt of the broom?

CHRISTY (*twisting round on her with a sharp cry of horror*). Don't strike me. I killed my poor father, Tuesday was a week, for doing the like of that.

PEGEEN (*with blank amazement*). Is it killed your father?

CHRISTY (*subsiding*). With the help of God I did, surely, and that the Holy Immaculate Mother may intercede for his soul.

PHILLY (*retreating with* JIMMY). There's a daring fellow.

JIMMY. Oh, glory be to God!

MICHAEL (*with great respect*). That was a hanging crime, mister honey. You should have had good reason for doing the like of that.

CHRISTY (*in a very reasonable tone*). He was a dirty man, God forgive him, and he getting old and crusty, the way I couldn't put up with him at all.

PEGEEN. And you shot him dead?

CHRISTY (*shaking his head*). I never used weapons. I've no licence, and I'm a law-fearing man.

MICHAEL. It was with a hilted knife maybe? I'm told, in the big world, it's bloody knives they use.

CHRISTY (*loudly, scandalized*). Do you take me for a slaughter-boy?

PEGEEN. You never hanged him, the way Jimmy Farrell hanged his dog from the licence, and had it screeching and wriggling three hours at the butt of a string, and himself swearing it was a dead dog, and the peelers swearing it had life?

CHRISTY. I did not, then. I just riz the loy[12] and let fall the edge of it on the ridge of his skull, and he went down at my feet like an empty sack, and never let a grunt or groan from him at all.

MICHAEL (*making a sign to* PEGEEN *to fill* CHRISTY's *glass*). And what way weren't you hanged, mister? Did you bury him then?

CHRISTY (*considering*). Aye. I buried him then. Wasn't I digging spuds in the field?

MICHAEL. And the peelers never followed after you the eleven days that you're out?

CHRISTY (*shaking his head*). Never a one of them, and I walking forward facing hog, dog, or divil on the highway of the road.

PHILLY (*nodding wisely*). It's only with a common weekday kind of a murderer them lads would be trusting their carcase, and that man should be a great terror when his temper's roused.

MICHAEL. He should then. (*To* CHRISTY.) And where was it, mister honey, that you did the deed?

CHRISTY (*looking at him with suspicion*). Oh, a distant place, master of the house, a windy corner of high, distant hills.

PHILLY (*nodding with approval*). He's a close man, and he's right, surely.

---

12 RIZ THE LOY, raised the spade.

PEGEEN. That'd be a lad with a sense of Solomon to have for a pot-boy, Michael James, if it's the truth you're seeking one at all.

PHILLY. The peelers is fearing him, and if you'd that lad in the house there isn't one of them would come smelling around if the dogs itself were lapping poteen from the dung-pit of the yard.

JIMMY. Bravery's a treasure in a lonesome place, and a lad would[13] kill his father, I'm thinking, would face a foxy divil with a pitchpike on the flags of hell.

PEGEEN. It's the truth they're saying, and if I'd that lad in the house, I wouldn't be fearing the looséd kharki[14] cut-throats, or the walking dead.

CHRISTY (*swelling with surprise and triumph*). Well, glory be to God!

MICHAEL (*with deference*). Would you think well to stop here and be pot-boy, mister honey, if we gave you good wages, and didn't destroy you with the weight of work.

SHAWN (*coming forward uneasily*). That'd be a queer kind to bring into a decent, quiet household with the like of Pegeen Mike.

PEGEEN (*very sharply*). Will you whisht? Who's speaking to you?

SHAWN (*retreating*). A bloody-handed murderer the like of . . .

PEGEEN (*snapping at him*). Whisht, I am saying; we'll take no fooling from your like at all.   (*To* CHRISTY *with a honeyed voice.*)   And you, young fellow, you'd have a right to stop, I'm thinking, for we'd do our all and utmost to content your needs.

CHRISTY (*overcome with wonder*). And I'd be safe this place from the searching law?

MICHAEL. You would, surely. If they're not fearing you, itself, the peelers in this place is decent, drouthy poor fellows, wouldn't touch a cur dog and not give warning in the dead of night.

PEGEEN (*very kindly and persuasively*). Let you stop a short while anyhow. Aren't you destroyed walking with your feet in bleeding blisters, and your whole skin needing washing like a Wicklow sheep.

CHRISTY (*looking round with satisfaction*). It's a nice room, and if it's not humbugging me you are, I'm thinking that I'll surely stay.

JIMMY (*jumps up*). Now, by the grace of God, herself will be safe this night, with a man killed his father holding danger from the door, and let you come on, Michael James, or they'll have the best stuff drunk at the wake.

MICHAEL (*going to the door with men*). And begging your pardon, mister, what name will we call you, for we'd like to know?

CHRISTY. Christopher Mahon.

MICHAEL. Well, God bless you, Christy, and a good rest till we meet again when the sun'll be rising to the noon of day.

CHRISTY. God bless you all.

MEN. God bless you.

---

13 WOULD, who would.   14 LOOSÉD KHARKI, British soldiers in khaki uniforms.

(*They go out, except* SHAWN, *who lingers at the door.*)

SHAWN (*to* PEGEEN). Are you wanting me to stop along with you and keep you from harm?

PEGEEN (*gruffly*). Didn't you say you were fearing Father Reilly?

SHAWN. There'd be no harm staying now, I'm thinking, and himself in it too.

PEGEEN. You wouldn't stay when there was need for you, and let you step off nimble this time when there's none.

SHAWN. Didn't I say it was Father Reilly . . .

PEGEEN. Go on, then, to Father Reilly (*in a jeering tone*), and let him put you in the holy brotherhoods, and leave that lad to me.

SHAWN. If I meet the Widow Quin . . .

PEGEEN. Go on, I'm saying, and don't be waking this place with your noise. (*She hustles him out and bolts door.*)   That lad would wear the spirits from the saints of peace.   (*Bustles about, then takes off her apron and pins it up in the window as a blind,* CHRISTY *watching her timidly. Then she comes to him and speaks with bland good-humour.*)   Let you stretch out now by the fire, young fellow. You should be destroyed travelling.

CHRISTY (*shyly again, drawing off his boots*). I'm tired surely, walking wild eleven days, and waking fearful in the night. (*He holds up one of his feet, feeling his blisters, and looking at them with compassion.*)

PEGEEN (*standing beside him, watching him with delight*). You should have had great people in your family, I'm thinking, with the little, small feet you have, and you with a kind of a quality name, the like of what you'd find on the great powers and potentates of France and Spain.

CHRISTY (*with pride*). We were great, surely, with wide and windy acres of rich Munster land.

PEGEEN. Wasn't I telling you, and you a fine, handsome young fellow with a noble brow?

CHRISTY (*with a flash of delighted surprise*). Is it me?

PEGEEN. Aye. Did you never hear that from the young girls where you come from in the west or south?

CHRISTY (*with venom*). I did not, then. Oh, they're bloody liars in the naked parish where I grew a man.

PEGEEN. If they are itself, you've heard it these days, I'm thinking, and you walking the world telling out your story to young girls or old.

CHRISTY. I've told my story no place till this night, Pegeen Mike, and it's foolish I was here, maybe, to be talking free; but you're decent people, I'm thinking, and yourself a kindly woman, the way I wasn't fearing you at all.

PEGEEN (*filling a sack with straw*). You've said the like of that, maybe, in every cot and cabin where you've met a young girl on your way.

CHRISTY (*going over to her, gradually raising his voice*). I've said it nowhere all this night, I'm telling you; for I've seen none the like of you the eleven long days I am walking the world, looking over a low ditch or a high ditch on my north or south, into stony, scattered fields, or scribes[15] of bog, where you'd see young, limber girls, and fine, prancing women making laughter with the men.

PEGEEN. If you weren't destroyed travelling, you'd have as much talk and streeleen,[16] I'm thinking, as Owen Roe O'Sullivan or the poets of the Dingle Bay; and I've heard all times it's the poets are your like—fine, fiery fellows with great rages when their temper's roused.

CHRISTY (*drawing a little nearer to her*). You've a power of rings, God bless you, and would there be any offence if I was asking are you single now?

PEGEEN. What would I want wedding so young?

CHRISTY (*with relief*). We're alike, so.

PEGEEN (*she puts sack on settle and beats it up*). I never killed my father. I'd be afeard to do that, except I was the like of yourself with blind rages tearing me within, for I'm thinking you should have had great tussling when the end was come.

CHRISTY (*expanding with delight at the first confidential talk he has ever had with a woman*). We had not then. It was a hard woman was come over the hill; and if he was always a crusty kind when he'd a hard woman setting him on, not the divil himself or his four fathers could put up with him at all.

PEGEEN (*with curiosity*). And isn't it a great wonder that one wasn't fearing you?

CHRISTY (*very confidentially*). Up to the day I killed my father, there wasn't a person in Ireland knew the kind I was, and I there drinking, waking, eating, sleeping, a quiet, simple poor fellow with no man giving me heed.

PEGEEN (*getting a quilt out of cupboard and putting it on the sack*). It was the girls were giving you heed, maybe, and I'm thinking it's most conceit you'd have to be gaming with their like.

CHRISTY (*shaking his head, with simplicity*). Not the girls itself, and I won't tell you a lie. There wasn't anyone heeding me in that place saving only the dumb beasts of the field. (*He sits down at fire.*)

PEGEEN (*with disappointment*). And I thinking you should have been living the like of a king of Norway or the eastern world. (*She comes and sits beside him after placing bread and mug of milk on the table.*)

CHRISTY (*laughing piteously*). The like of a king, is it? And I after toiling, moiling, digging, dodging from the dawn till dusk; with never a sight of joy or sport saving only when I'd be abroad in the dark night poaching rabbits on hills, for I was a divil to poach, God forgive me (*very naïvely*), and I near got six months for going with a dung fork and stabbing a fish.

---

15 SCRIBES, patches.   16 STREELEEN, chatter.

PEGEEN. And it's that you'd call sport, is it, to be abroad in the darkness with yourself alone?

CHRISTY. I did, God help me, and there I'd be as happy as the sunshine of St. Martin's Day, watching the light passing the north or the patches of fog, till I'd hear a rabbit starting to screech and I'd go running in the furze. Then, when I'd my full share, I'd come walking down where you'd see the ducks and geese stretched sleeping on the highway of the road, and before I'd pass the dunghill, I'd hear himself snoring out—a loud, lonesome snore he'd be making all times, the while he was sleeping; and he a man'd be raging all times, the while he was waking, like a gaudy officer you'd hear cursing and damning and swearing oaths.

PEGEEN. Providence and Mercy, spare us all!

CHRISTY. It's that you'd say surely if you seen him and he after drinking for weeks, rising up in the red dawn, or before it maybe, and going out into the yard as naked as an ash-tree in the moon of May, and shy-ing clods against the visage of the stars till he'd put the fear of death into the banbhs[17] and the screeching sows.

PEGEEN. I'd be well-nigh afeard of that lad myself, I'm thinking. And there was no one in it but the two of you alone?

CHRISTY. The divil a one, though he'd sons and daughters walking all great states and territories of the world, and not a one of them, to this day, but would say their seven curses on him, and they rousing up to let a cough or sneeze, maybe, in the deadness of the night.

PEGEEN (nodding her head). Well, you should have been a queer lot. I never cursed my father the like of that, though I'm twenty and more years of age.

CHRISTY. Then you'd have cursed mine, I'm telling you, and he a man never gave peace to any, saving when he'd get two months or three, or be locked in the asylums for battering peelers or assaulting men (with depression), the way it was a bitter life he led me till I did up a Tuesday and halve his skull.

PEGEEN (putting her hand on his shoulder). Well, you'll have peace in this place, Christy Mahon, and none to trouble you, and it's near time a fine lad like you should have your good share of the earth.

CHRISTY. It's time surely, and I a seemly fellow with great strength in me and bravery of . . . (Someone knocks.)

CHRISTY (clinging to PEGEEN). Oh, glory! it's late for knocking, and this last while I'm in terror of the peelers, and the walking dead. (Knock-ing again.)

PEGEEN. Who's there?

VOICE (outside). Me.

PEGEEN. Who's me?

VOICE. The Widow Quin.

---

[17] BANBHS, suckling pigs.

PEGEEN (*jumping up and giving him the bread and milk*). Go on now with your supper, and let on to be sleepy, for if she found you were such a warrant to talk, she'd be stringing gabble till the dawn of day.

(*He takes bread and sits shyly with his back to the door.*)

PEGEEN (*opening the door, with temper*). What ails you, or what is it you're wanting at this hour of the night?

WIDOW QUIN (*coming in a step and peering at* CHRISTY). I'm after meeting Shawn Keogh and Father Reilly below, who told me of your curiosity man, and they fearing by this time he was maybe roaring, romping on your hands with drink.

PEGEEN (*pointing to* CHRISTY). Look now is he roaring, and he stretched out drowsy with his supper and his mug of milk. Walk down and tell that to Father Reilly and to Shaneen Keogh.

WIDOW QUIN (*coming forward*). I'll not see them again, for I've their word to lead that lad forward for to lodge with me.

PEGEEN (*in blank amazement*). This night is it?

WIDOW QUIN (*going over*). This night. "It isn't fitting," says the priesteen, "to have his likeness lodging with an orphaned girl." (*To* CHRISTY.) God save you, mister!

CHRISTY (*shyly*). God save you kindly!

WIDOW QUIN (*looking at him with half-amused curiosity*). Well, aren't you a little smiling fellow? It should have been great and bitter torments did rouse your spirits to a deed of blood.

CHRISTY (*doubtfully*). It should, maybe.

WIDOW QUIN. It's more than "maybe" I'm saying, and it'd soften my heart to see you sitting so simple with your cup and cake, and you fitter to be saying your catechism than slaying your da.

PEGEEN (*at counter, washing glasses*). There's talking when any'd see he's fit to be holding his head high with the wonders of the world. Walk on from this, for I'll not have him tormented, and he destroyed travelling since Tuesday was a week.

WIDOW QUIN (*peaceably*). We'll be walking surely when his supper's done, and you'll find we're great company, young fellow, when it's of the like of you and me you'd hear the penny poets singing in an August Fair.

CHRISTY (*innocently*). Did you kill your father?

PEGEEN (*contemptuously*). She did not. She hit himself with a worn pick, and the rusted poison did corrode his blood the way he never overed it, and died after. That was a sneaky kind of murder did win small glory with the boys itself. (*She crosses to* CHRISTY's *left*.)

WIDOW QUIN (*with good humour*). If it didn't, maybe all knows a widow woman has buried her children and destroyed her man is a wiser comrade for a young lad than a girl, the like of you, who'd go helter-skeltering after any man would let you a wink upon the road.

PEGEEN (*breaking out into a wild rage*). And you'll say that, Widow Quin, and you gasping with the rage you had racing the hill beyond to look upon his face.

WIDOW QUIN (*laughing derisively*). Me, is it? Well, Father Reilly has cuteness to divide you now. (*She pulls* CHRISTY *up*.) There's great temptation in a man did slay his da, and we'd best be going, young fellow; so rise up and come with me.

PEGEEN (*seizing his arm*). He'll not stir. He's pot-boy in this place, and I'll . not have him stolen off and kidnapped while himself's abroad.

WIDOW QUIN. It'd be a crazy pot-boy'd lodge him in the shebeen where he works by day, so you'd have a right to come on, young fellow, till you see my little houseen, a perch off on the rising hill.

PEGEEN. Wait till morning, Christy Mahon. Wait till you lay eyes on her leaky thatch is growing more pasture for her buck goat than her square of fields, and she without a tramp itself to keep in order her place at all.

WIDOW QUIN. When you see me contriving in my little gardens, Christy Mahon, you'll swear the Lord God formed me to be living lone, and that there isn't my match in Mayo for thatching, or mowing, or shearing a sheep.

PEGEEN (*with noisy scorn*). It's true the Lord God formed you to contrive indeed. Doesn't the world know you reared a black ram at your own breast, so that the Lord Bishop of Connaught felt the elements of a Christian, and he eating it after in a kidney stew? Doesn't the world know you've been seen shaving the foxy skipper from France for a threepennybit and a sop of grass tobacco would wring the liver from a mountain goat you'd meet leaping the hills?

WIDOW QUIN (*with amusement*). Do you hear her now, young fellow? Do you hear the way she'll be rating at your own self when a week is by?

PEGEEN (*to* CHRISTY). Don't heed her. Tell her to go on into her pigsty and not plague us here.

WIDOW QUIN. I'm going; but he'll come with me.

PEGEEN (*shaking him*). Are you dumb, young fellow?

CHRISTY (*timidly to* WIDOW QUIN). God increase you; but I'm pot-boy in this place, and it's here I liefer stay.

PEGEEN (*triumphantly*). Now you have heard him, and go on from this.

WIDOW QUIN (*looking round the room*). It's lonesome this hour crossing the hill, and if he won't come along with me, I'd have a right maybe to stop this night with yourselves. Let me stretch out on the settle, Pegeen Mike; and himself can lie by the hearth.

PEGEEN (*short and fiercely*). Faith, I won't. Quit off or I will send you now.

WIDOW QUIN (*gathering her shawl up*). Well, it's a terror to be aged a score. (*To* CHRISTY.) God bless you now, young fellow, and let you be wary, or there's right torment will await you here if you go romancing with her like, and she waiting only, as they bade me say, on a sheepskin parchment to be wed with Shawn Keogh of Killakeen.

CHRISTY (*going to* PEGEEN *as she bolts door*). What's that she's after saying?

PEGEEN. Lies and blather, you've no call to mind. Well, isn't Shawn Keogh an impudent fellow to send up spying on me? Wait till I lay hands on him. Let him wait, I'm saying.

CHRISTY. And you're not wedding him at all?

PEGEEN. I wouldn't wed him if a bishop came walking for to join us here.

CHRISTY. That God in glory may be thanked for that.

PEGEEN. There's your bed now. I've put a quilt upon you I'm after quilting a while since with my own two hands, and you'd best stretch out now for your sleep, and may God give you a good rest till I call you in the morning when the cocks will crow.

CHRISTY (*as she goes to inner room*). May God and Mary and St. Patrick bless you and reward you for your kindly talk. (*She shuts the door behind her. He settles his bed slowly, feeling the quilt with immense satisfaction.*) Well, it's a clean bed and soft with it, and it's great luck and company I've won me in the end of time—two fine women fighting for the likes of me—till I'm thinking this night wasn't I a foolish fellow not to kill my father in the years gone by.

ACT II

(*Scene as before. Brilliant morning light.* CHRISTY, *looking bright and cheerful, is cleaning a girl's boots.*)

CHRISTY (*to himself, counting jugs on dresser*). Half a hundred beyond. Ten there. A score that's above. Eighty jugs. Six cups and a broken one. Two plates. A power of glasses. Bottles, a schoolmaster'd be hard set to count, and enough in them, I'm thinking, to drunken all the wealth and wisdom of the county Clare. (*He puts down the boot carefully.*) There's her boots now, nice and decent for her evening use, and isn't it grand brushes she has? (*He puts them down and goes by degrees to the looking-glass.*) Well, this'd be a fine place to be my whole life talking out with swearing Christians, in place of my old dogs and cat; and I stalking around, smoking my pipe and drinking my fill, and never a day's work but drawing a cork an odd time, or wiping a glass, or rinsing out a shiny tumbler for a decent man. (*He takes the looking-glass from the wall and puts it on the back of a chair; then sits down in front of it and begins washing his face.*) Didn't I know rightly, I was handsome, though it was the divil's own mirror we had beyond, would twist a squint across an angel's brow; and I'll be growing fine from this day, the way I'll have a soft lovely skin on me and won't be the like of the clumsy young fellows do be ploughing all times in the earth and dung. (*He starts.*) Is she coming again? (*He looks out.*)

Stranger girls. God help me, where'll I hide myself away and my long neck naked to the world? (*He looks out.*) I'd best go to the room maybe till I'm dressed again.

(*He gathers up his coat and the looking-glass, and runs into the inner room. The door is pushed open, and* SUSAN BRADY *looks in, and knocks on door.*)

SUSAN. There's nobody in it.   (*Knocks again.*)

NELLY (*pushing her in and following her, with* HONOR BLAKE *and* SARA TANSEY). It'd be early for them both to be out walking the hill.

SUSAN. I'm thinking Shawn Keogh was making game of us, and there's no such man in it at all.

HONOR (*pointing to straw and quilt*). Look at that. He's been sleeping there in the night. Well, it'll be a hard case if he's gone off now, the way we'll never set our eyes on a man killed his father, and we after rising early and destroying ourselves running fast on the hill.

NELLY. Are you thinking them's his boots?

SARA (*taking them up*). If they are, there should be his father's track on them. Did you never read in the papers the way murdered men do bleed and drip?

SUSAN. Is that blood there, Sara Tansey?

SARA (*smelling it*). That's bog water, I'm thinking; but it's his own they are, surely, for I never seen the like of them for whitey mud, and red mud, and turf on them, and the fine sands of the sea. That man's been walking, I'm telling you. (*She goes down right, putting on one of his boots.*)

SUSAN (*going to window*). Maybe he's stolen off to Belmullet with the boots of Michael James, and you'd have a right so to follow after him, Sara Tansey, and you the one yoked the ass cart and drove ten miles to set your eyes on the man bit the yellow lady's nostril on the northern shore. (*She looks out.*)

SARA (*running to window, with one boot on*). Don't be talking, and we fooled today. (*Putting on the other boot.*) There's a pair do fit me well and I'll be keeping them for walking to the priest, when you'd be ashamed this place, going up winter and summer with nothing worth while to confess at all.

HONOR (*who has been listening at door*). Whisht! there's someone inside the room.   (*She pushes door a chink open.*)   It's a man.

(SARA *kicks off boots and puts them where they were. They all stand in a line looking through chink.*)

SARA. I'll call him. Mister! Mister! (*He puts in his head.*) Is Pegeen within?

CHRISTY (*coming in as meek as a mouse, with the looking-glass held behind his back*). She's above on the cnuceen,[18] seeking the nanny goats, the way she'd have a sup of goats' milk for to colour my tea.

SARA. And asking your pardon, is it you's the man killed his father?

CHRISTY (*sidling towards the nail where the glass was hanging*). I am, God help me!

SARA (*taking eggs she has brought*). Then my thousand welcomes to you, and I've run up with a brace of duck's eggs for your food to-day. Pegeen's ducks is no use, but these are the real rich sort. Hold out your hand and you'll see it's no lie I'm telling you.

CHRISTY (*coming forward shyly, and holding out his left hand*). They're a great and weighty size.

SUSAN. And I run up with a pat of butter, for it'd be a poor thing to have you eating your spuds dry, and you after running a great way since you did destroy your da.

CHRISTY. Thank you kindly.

HONOR. And I brought you a little cut of a cake, for you should have a thin stomach on you, and you that length walking the world.

NELLY. And I brought you a little laying pullet—boiled and all she is— was crushed at the fall of night by the curate's car. Feel the fat of that breast, mister.

CHRISTY. It's bursting, surely. (*He feels it with back of his hand, in which he holds the presents.*)

SARA. Will you pinch it? Is your right hand too sacred for to use at all? (*She slips round behind him.*) It's a glass he has. Well, I never seen to this day a man with a looking-glass held to his back. Them that kills their fathers is a vain lot surely.

(GIRLS *giggle*.)

CHRISTY (*smiling innocently and piling presents on glass*). I'm very thankful to you all to-day. . . .

WIDOW QUIN (*coming in quickly, at door*). Sara Tansey, Susan Brady, Honor Blake! What in glory has you here at this hour of day?

GIRLS (*giggling*). That's the man killed his father.

WIDOW QUIN (*coming to them*). I know well it's the man; and I'm after putting him down in the sports below for racing, leaping, pitching, and the Lord knows what.

SARA (*exuberantly*). That's right, Widow Quin. I'll bet my dowry that he'll lick the world.

WIDOW QUIN. If you will, you'd have a right to have him fresh and nourished in place of nursing a feast. (*Taking presents.*) Are you fasting or fed, young fellow?

CHRISTY. Fasting, if you please.

WIDOW QUIN (*loudly*). Well, you're the lot. Stir up now and give him his

18 CNUCEEN, hill.

breakfast. (*To* CHRISTY.) Come here to me (*she puts him on bench beside her while the girls make tea and get his breakfast*), and let you tell us your story before Pegeen will come, in place of grinning your ears off like the moon of May.

CHRISTY (*beginning to be pleased*). It's a long story; you'd be destroyed listening.

WIDOW QUIN. Don't be letting on to be shy, a fine, gamey, treacherous lad the like of you. Was it in your house beyond you cracked his skull?

CHRISTY (*shy but flattered*). It was not. We were digging spuds in his cold, sloping, stony, divil's patch of a field.

WIDOW QUIN. And you went asking money of him, or making talk of getting a wife would drive him from his farm?

CHRISTY I did not, then; but there I was digging and digging, and "You squinting idiot," says he, "let you walk down now and tell the priest you'll wed the Widow Casey in a score of days."

WIDOW QUIN. And what kind was she?

CHRISTY (*with horror*). A walking terror from beyond the hills, and she two score and five years, and two hundred-weights and five pounds in the weighing scales, with a limping leg on her, and a blinded eye, and she a woman of noted misbehaviour with the old and young.

GIRLS (*clustering round him, serving him*). Glory be.

WIDOW QUIN. And what did he want driving you to wed with her? (*She takes a bit of the chicken.*)

CHRISTY (*eating with growing satisfaction*). He was letting on I was wanting a protector from the harshness of the world, and he without a thought the whole while but how he'd have her hut to live in and her gold to drink.

WIDOW QUIN. There's maybe worse than a dry hearth and a widow woman and your glass at night. So you hit him then?

CHRISTY (*getting almost excited*). I did not. "I won't wed her," says I, "when all know she did suckle me for six weeks when I came into the world, and she a hag this day with a tongue on her has the crows and seabirds scattered, the way they wouldn't cast a shadow on her garden with the dread of her curse."

WIDOW QUIN (*teasingly*). That one should be right company.

SARA (*eagerly*). Don't mind her. Did you kill him then?

CHRISTY. "She's too good for the like of you," says he, "and go on now or I'll flatten you out like a crawling beast has passed under a dray." "You will not if I can help it," says I. "Go on," says he, "or I'll have the divil making garters of your limbs tonight." "You will not if I can help it," says I. (*He sits up brandishing his mug.*)

SARA. You were right surely.

CHRISTY (*impressively*). With that the sun came out between the cloud and the hill, and it shining green in my face. "God have mercy on your soul," says he, lifting a scythe. "Or on your own," said I, raising the loy.

SUSAN. That's a grand story.

HONOR. He tells it lovely.

CHRISTY (*flattered and confident, waving bone*). He gave a drive with the scythe, and I gave a lep to the east. Then I turned around with my back to the north, and I hit a blow on the ridge of his skull, laid him stretched out, and he split to the knob of his gullet. (*He raises the chicken bone to his Adam's apple.*)

GIRLS (*together*). Well, you're a marvel! Oh, God bless you! You're the lad, surely!

SUSAN. I'm thinking the Lord God sent him this road to make a second husband to the Widow Quin, and she with a great yearning to be wedded, though all dread her here. Lift him on her knee, Sara Tansey.

WIDOW QUIN. Don't tease him.

SARA (*going over to dresser and counter very quickly, and getting two glasses and porter*). You're heroes, surely, and let you drink a supeen with your arms linked like the outlandish lovers in the sailor's song. (*She links their arms and gives them the glasses.*) There now. Drink a health to the wonders of the western world, the pirates, preachers, poteen-makers, with the jobbing jockies;[19] parching peelers, and the juries fill their stomachs selling judgments of the English law. (*Brandishing the bottle.*)

WIDOW QUIN. That's a right toast, Sara Tansey. Now, Christy.

(*They drink with their arms linked, he drinking with his left hand, she with her right. As they are drinking, PEGEEN MIKE comes in with a milkcan and stands aghast. They all spring away from CHRISTY. He goes down left. WIDOW QUIN remains seated.*)

PEGEEN (*angrily, to SARA*). What is it you're wanting?

SARA (*twisting her apron*). An ounce of tobacco.

PEGEEN. Have you tuppence?

SARA. I've forgotten my purse.

PEGEEN. Then you'd best be getting it and not be fooling us here. (*To the WIDOW QUIN, with more elaborate scorn.*) And what is it you're wanting, Widow Quin?

WIDOW QUIN (*insolently*). A penn'orth of starch.

PEGEEN (*breaking out*). And you without a white shift or a shirt in your whole family since the drying of the flood. I've no starch for the like of you, and let you walk on now to Killamuck.

WIDOW QUIN (*turning to CHRISTY, as she goes out with the GIRLS*). Well, you're mighty huffy this day, Pegeen Mike, and you, young fellow, let you not forget the sports and racing when the noon is by. (*They go out.*)

PEGEEN (*imperiously*). Fling out that rubbish and put them cups away.

19 JOBBING JOCKIES, robbing peddlers.

(CHRISTY *tidies away in great haste.*) Shove in the bench by the wall. (*He does so.*) And hang that glass on the nail. What disturbed it at all?

CHRISTY (*very meekly*). I was making myself decent only, and this a fine country for young lovely girls.

PEGEEN (*sharply*). Whisht your talking of girls. (*Goes to counter on right.*)

CHRISTY. Wouldn't any wish to be decent in a place . . .

PEGEEN. Whisht, I'm saying.

CHRISTY (*looks at her face for a moment with great misgivings, then as a last effort takes up a loy, and goes towards her, with feigned assurance*). It was with a loy the like of that I killed my father.

PEGEEN (*still sharply*). You've told me that story six times since the dawn of day.

CHRISTY (*reproachfully*). It's a queer thing you wouldn't care to be hearing it and them girls after walking four miles to be listening to me now.

PEGEEN (*turning round astonished*). Four miles?

CHRISTY (*apologetically*). Didn't himself say there were only bona fides living in the place?

PEGEEN. It's bona fides by the road they are, but that lot came over the river lepping the stones. It's not three perches[20] when you go like that, and I was down this morning looking on the papers the post-boy does have in his bag. (*With meaning and emphasis.*) For there was great news this day, Christopher Mahon. (*She goes into room on left.*)

CHRISTY (*suspiciously*). Is it news of my murder?

PEGEEN (*inside*). Murder, indeed.

CHRISTY (*loudly*). A murdered da?

PEGEEN (*coming in again and crossing right*). There was not, but a story filled half a page of the hanging of a man. Ah, that should be a fearful end, young fellow, and it worst of all for a man destroyed his da; for the like of him would get small mercies, and when it's dead he is they'd put him in a narrow grave, with cheap sacking wrapping him round, and pour down quicklime on his head, the way you'd see a woman pouring any frish-frash[21] from a cup.

CHRISTY (*very miserably*). Oh, God help me. Are you thinking I'm safe? You were saying at the fall of night I was shut of jeopardy and I here with yourselves.

PEGEEN (*severely*). You'll be shut of jeopardy no place if you go talking with a pack of wild girls the like of them do be walking abroad with the peelers, talking whispers at the fall of night.

CHRISTY (*with terror*). And you're thinking they'd tell?

PEGEEN (*with mock sympathy*). Who knows, God help you?

CHRISTY (*loudly*). What joy would they have to bring hanging to the likes of me?

PEGEEN. It's queer joys they have, and who knows the thing they'd do, if

20 THREE PERCHES, about sixteen feet.   21 FRISH-FRASH, dregs.

it'd make the green stones cry itself to think of you swaying and swig-
gling at the butt of a rope, and you with a fine, stout neck, God bless
you! the way you'd be a half an hour, in great anguish, getting your
death.

CHRISTY (*getting his boots and putting them on*). If there's that terror of
them, it'd be best, maybe, I went on wandering like Esau or Cain and
Abel on the sides of Neifin or the Erris plain.

PEGEEN (*beginning to play with him*). It would, maybe, for I've heard the
Circuit Judges this place is a heartless crew.

CHRISTY (*bitterly*). It's more than Judges this place is a heartless crew.
(*Looking up at her.*) And isn't it a poor thing to be starting again,
and I a lonesome fellow will be looking out on women and girls the
way the needy fallen spirits do be looking on the Lord?

PEGEEN. What call have you to be that lonesome when there's poor girls
walking Mayo in their thousands now?

CHRISTY (*grimly*). It's well you know what call I have. It's well you
know it's a lonesome thing to be passing small towns with the lights
shining sideways when the night is down, or going in strange places with
a dog noising before you and a dog noising behind, or drawn to the
cities where you'd hear a voice kissing and talking deep love in every
shadow of the ditch, and you passing on with an empty, hungry stomach
failing from your heart.

PEGEEN. I'm thinking you're an odd man, Christy Mahon. The oddest walking fellow I ever set my eyes on to this hour today.

CHRISTY. What would any be but odd men and they living lonesome in the
world?

PEGEEN. I'm not odd, and I'm my whole life with my father only.

CHRISTY (*with infinite admiration*). How would a lovely, handsome woman
the like of you be lonesome when all men should be thronging around
to hear the sweetness of your voice, and the little infant children should
be pestering your steps, I'm thinking, and you walking the roads.

PEGEEN. I'm hard set to know what way a coaxing fellow the like of yourself should be lonesome either.

CHRISTY. Coaxing.

PEGEEN. Would you have me think a man never talked with the girls would
have the words you've spoken today? It's only letting on you are to be
lonesome, the way you'd get around me now.

CHRISTY. I wish to God I was letting on; but I was lonesome all times, and
born lonesome, I'm thinking, as the moon of dawn. (*Going to door.*)

PEGEEN (*puzzled by his talk*). Well, it's a story I'm not understanding at all
why you'd be worse than another, Christy Mahon, and you a fine lad
with the great savagery to destroy your da.

CHRISTY. It's little I'm understanding myself, saving only that my heart's
scalded this day, and I going off stretching out the earth between us, the
way I'll not be waking near you another dawn of the year till the two

of us do arise to hope or judgment with the saints of God, and now I'd best be going with my wattle[22] in my hand, for hanging is a poor thing (*turning to go*), and it's little welcome only is left me in this house today.

PEGEEN (*sharply*). Christy. (*He turns round.*) Come here to me. (*He goes towards her.*) Lay down that switch and throw some sods on the fire. You're pot-boy in this place, and I'll not have you mitch[23] off from us now.

CHRISTY. You were saying I'd be hanged if I stay.

PEGEEN (*quite kindly at last*). I'm after going down and reading the fearful crimes of Ireland for two weeks or three, and there wasn't a word of your murder. (*Getting up and going over to the counter.*) They've likely not found the body. You're safe so with ourselves.

CHRISTY (*astonished, slowly*). It's making game of me you were (*following her with fearful joy*), and I can stay so, working at your side, and I not lonesome from this mortal day.

PEGEEN. What's to hinder you staying, except the widow woman or the young girls would inveigle you off?

CHRISTY (*with rapture*). And I'll have your words from this day filling my ears, and that look is come upon you meeting my two eyes, and I watching you loafing around in the warm sun, or rinsing your ankles when the night is come.

PEGEEN (*kindly, but a little embarrassed*). I'm thinking you'll be a loyal young lad to have working around, and if you vexed me a while since with your leaguing with the girls, I wouldn't give a thraneen for a lad hadn't a mighty spirit in him and a gamey heart.

(SHAWN KEOGH *runs in carrying a cleeve*[24] *on his back, followed by the* WIDOW QUIN.)

SHAWN (*to* PEGEEN). I was passing below, and I seen your mountainy sheep eating cabbages in Jimmy's field. Run up or they'll be bursting, surely.

PEGEEN. Oh, God mend them!

(*She puts a shawl over her head and runs out.*)

CHRISTY (*looking from one to the other. Still in high spirits*). I'd best go to her aid maybe. I'm handy with ewes.

WIDOW QUIN (*closing the door*). She can do that much, and there is Shaneen has long speeches for to tell you now. (*She sits down with an amused smile.*)

SHAWN (*taking something from his pocket and offering it to* CHRISTY). Do you see that, mister?

CHRISTY (*looking at it*). The half of a ticket to the Western States!

SHAWN (*trembling with anxiety*). I'll give it to you and my new hat

22 WATTLE, switch. 23 MITCH, steal. 24 CLEEVE, basket.

(*pulling it out of hamper*); and my breeches with the double seat (*pulling it out*); and my new coat is woven from the blackest shearings for three miles around (*giving him the coat*); I'll give you the whole of them, and my blessing, and the blessing of Father Reilly itself, maybe, if you'll quit from this and leave us in the peace we had till last night at the fall of dark.

CHRISTY (*with a new arrogance*). And for what is it you're wanting to get shut of me?

SHAWN (*looking to the* WIDOW *for help*). I'm a poor scholar with middling faculties to coin a lie, so I'll tell you the truth, Christy Mahon. I'm wedding with Pegeen beyond, and I don't think well of having a clever, fearless man the like of you dwelling in her house.

CHRISTY (*almost pugnaciously*). And you'd be using bribery for to banish me?

SHAWN (*in an imploring voice*). Let you not take it badly, mister honey; isn't beyond the best place for you, where you'll have golden chains and shiny coats and you riding upon hunters with the ladies of the land. (*He makes an eager sign to the* WIDOW QUIN *to come to help him.*)

WIDOW QUIN (*coming over*). It's true for him, and you'd best quit off and not have that poor girl setting her mind on you, for there's Shaneen thinks she wouldn't suit you, though all is saying that she'll wed you now.

(CHRISTY *beams with delight.*)

SHAWN (*in terrified earnest*). She wouldn't suit you, and she with the divil's own temper the way you'd be strangling one another in a score of days. (*He makes the movement of strangling with his hands.*) It's the like of me only that she's fit for; a quiet simple fellow wouldn't raise a hand upon her if she scratched itself.

WIDOW QUIN (*putting* SHAWN'S *hat on* CHRISTY). Fit them clothes on you anyhow, young fellow, and he'd maybe loan them to you for the sports. (*Pushing him towards inner door.*) Fit them on and you can give your answer when you have them tried.

CHRISTY (*beaming, delighted with the clothes*). I will then. I'd like herself to see me in them tweeds and hat. (*He goes into room and shuts the door.*)

SHAWN (*in great anxiety*). He'd like herself to see them. He'll not leave us, Widow Quin. He's a score of divils in him the way it's well-nigh certain he will wed Pegeen.

WIDOW QUIN (*jeeringly*). It's true all girls are fond of courage and do hate the like of you.

SHAWN (*walking about in desperation*). Oh, Widow Quin, what'll I be doing now? I'd inform again him, but he'd burst from Kilmainham[25]

---

25 KILMAINHAM, a prison.

and he'd be sure and certain to destroy me. If I wasn't so God-fearing, I'd near have courage to come behind him and run a pike into his side. Oh, it's a hard case to be an orphan and not to have your father that you're used to, and you'd easy kill and make yourself a hero in the sight of all. (*Coming up to her.*) Oh, Widow Quin, will you find me some contrivance when I've promised you a ewe?

WIDOW QUIN. A ewe's a small thing, but what would you give me if I did wed him and did save you so?

SHAWN (*with astonishment*). You?

WIDOW QUIN. Aye. Would you give me the red cow you have and the mountainy ram, and the right of way across your rye path, and a load of dung at Michaelmas, and turbary upon the western hill?

SHAWN (*radiant with hope*). I would, surely, and I'd give you the wedding-ring I have, and the loan of a new suit, the way you'd have him decent on the wedding-day. I'd give you two kids for your dinner, and a gallon of poteen, and I'd call the piper on the long car to your wedding from Crossmolina or from Ballina. I'd give you . . .

WIDOW QUIN. That'll do, so, and let you whisht, for he's coming now again.

(CHRISTY *comes in very natty in the new clothes.* WIDOW QUIN *goes to him admiringly.*)

WIDOW QUIN. If you seen yourself now, I'm thinking you'd be too proud to speak to at all, and it'd be a pity surely to have your like sailing from Mayo to the western world.

CHRISTY (*as proud as a peacock*). I'm not going. If this is a poor place itself, I'll make myself contented to be lodging here.

(WIDOW QUIN *makes a sign to* SHAWN *to leave them.*)

SHAWN. Well, I'm going measuring the racecourse while the tide is low, so I'll leave you the garments and my blessing for the sports today. God bless you! (*He wriggles out.*)

WIDOW QUIN (*admiring* CHRISTY). Well, you're mighty spruce, young fellow. Sit down now while you're quiet till you talk with me.

CHRISTY (*swaggering*). I'm going abroad on the hillside for to seek Pegeen.

WIDOW QUIN. You'll have time and plenty for to seek Pegeen, and you heard me saying at the fall of night the two of us should be great company.

CHRISTY. From this out I'll have no want of company when all sorts is bringing me their food and clothing (*he swaggers to the door, tightening his belt*), the way they'd set their eyes upon a gallant orphan cleft his father with one blow to the breeches belt. (*He opens door, then staggers back.*) Saints of glory! Holy angels from the throne of light!

WIDOW QUIN (*going over*). What ails you?

CHRISTY. It's the walking spirit of my murdered da!

WIDOW QUIN (*looking out*). Is it that tramper?

CHRISTY (*wildly*). Where'll I hide my poor body from that ghost of hell?

(*The door is pushed open, and* OLD MAHON *appears on threshold.* CHRISTY *darts in behind door.*)

WIDOW QUIN (*in great amusement*). God save you, my poor man.

MAHON (*gruffly*). Did you see a young lad passing this way in the early morning or the fall of night?

WIDOW QUIN. You're a queer kind to walk in not saluting at all.

MAHON. Did you see the young lad?

WIDOW QUIN (*stiffly*). What kind was he?

MAHON. An ugly young streeler[26] with a murderous gob[27] on him, and a little switch in his hand. I met a tramper seen him coming this way at the fall of night.

WIDOW QUIN. There's harvest hundreds do be passing these days for the Sligo boat. For what is it you're wanting him, my poor man?

MAHON. I want to destroy him for breaking the head on me with the clout of a loy. (*He takes off a big hat, and shows his head in a mass of bandages and plaster, with some pride.*)   It was he did that, and amn't I a great wonder to think I've traced him ten days with that rent in my crown?

WIDOW QUIN (*taking his head in both hands and examining it with extreme delight*). That was a great blow. And who hit you? A robber maybe?

MAHON. It was my own son hit me, and he the divil a robber, or anything else, but a dirty, stuttering lout.

WIDOW QUIN (*letting go his skull and wiping her hands in her apron*). You'd best be wary of a mortified scalp, I think they call it, lepping around with that wound in the splendour of the sun. It was a bad blow, surely, and you should have vexed him fearful to make him strike that gash in his da.

MAHON. Is it me?

WIDOW QUIN (*amusing herself*). Aye. And isn't it a great shame when the old and hardened do torment the young?

MAHON (*raging*). Torment him, is it? And I after holding out with the patience of a martyred saint till there's nothing but destruction on, and I'm driven out in my old age with none to aid me.

WIDOW QUIN (*greatly amused*). It's a sacred wonder the way that wickedness will spoil a man.

MAHON. My wickedness, is it? Amn't I after saying it is himself has me destroyed, and he a lier on walls, a talker of folly, a man you'd see stretched the half of the day in the brown ferns with his belly to the sun.

WIDOW QUIN. Not working at all?

---

26 STREELER, vagrant.   27 GOB, face.

MAHON. The divil a work, or if he did itself, you'd see him raising up a haystack like the stalk of a rush, or driving our last cow till he broke her leg at the hip, and when he wasn't at that he'd be fooling over little birds he had—finches and felts—or making mugs at his own self in the bit of a glass we had hung on the wall.

WIDOW QUIN (*looking at* CHRISTY). What way was he so foolish? It was running wild after the girls maybe?

MAHON (*with a shout of derision*). Running wild, is it? If he seen a red petticoat coming swinging over the hill, he'd be off to hide in the sticks, and you'd see him shooting out his sheep's eyes between the little twigs and the leaves, and his two ears rising like a hare looking out through a gap. Girls, indeed!

WIDOW QUIN. It was drink maybe?

MAHON. And he a poor fellow would get drunk on the smell of a pint. He'd a queer rotten stomach, I'm telling you, and when I gave him three pulls from my pipe a while since, he was taken with contortions till I had to send him in the ass-cart to the females' nurse.

WIDOW QUIN (*clasping her hands*). Well, I never, till this day, heard tell of a man the like of that!

MAHON. I'd take a mighty oath you didn't, surely, and wasn't he the laughing joke of every female woman where four baronies meet, the way the girls would stop their weeding if they seen him coming the road to let a roar at him, and call him the looney of Mahon's.

WIDOW QUIN. I'd give the world and all to see the like of him. What kind was he?

MAHON. A small, low fellow.

WIDOW QUIN. And dark?

MAHON. Dark and dirty.

WIDOW QUIN (*considering*). I'm thinking I seen him.

MAHON (*eagerly*). An ugly young blackguard.

WIDOW QUIN. A hideous, fearful villain, and the spit of you.

MAHON. What way is he fled?

WIDOW QUIN. Gone over the hills to catch a coasting steamer to the north or south.

MAHON. Could I pull up on him now?

WIDOW QUIN. If you'll cross the sands below where the tide is out, you'll be in it as soon as himself, for he had to go round ten miles by the top of the bay. (*She points to the door.*) Strike down by the head beyond and then follow on the roadway to the north and east.

(MAHON *goes abruptly.*)

WIDOW QUIN (*shouting after him*). Let you give him a good vengeance when you come up with him, but don't put yourself in the power of the law, for it'd be a poor thing to see a judge in his black cap reading out his sentence on a civil warrior the like of you. (*She swings the door to and looks at* CHRISTY, *who is cowering in terror, for a moment, then she bursts into a laugh.*) Well, you're the walking Playboy of the Western World, and that's the poor man you had divided to his breeches belt.

CHRISTY (*looking out; then, to her*). What'll Pegeen say when she hears that story? What'll she be saying to me now?

WIDOW QUIN. She'll knock the head of you, I'm thinking, and drive you from the door. God help her to be taking you for a wonder, and you a little schemer making up a story you destroyed your da.

CHRISTY (*turning to the door, nearly speechless with rage, half to himself*). To be letting on he was dead, and coming back to his life, and following after me like an old weasel tracing a rat, and coming in here laying desolation between my own self and the fine women of Ireland, and he a kind of carcase that you'd fling upon the sea. . . .

WIDOW QUIN (*more soberly*). There's talking for a man's one only son.

CHRISTY (*breaking out*). His one son, is it? May I meet him with one tooth and it aching, and one eye to be seeing seven and seventy divils in the twists of the road, and one old timber leg on him to limp into the scalding grave. (*Looking out.*) There he is now crossing the strands, and that the Lord God would send a high wave to wash him from the world.

WIDOW QUIN (*scandalized*). Have you no shame? (*Putting her hand on his shoulder and turning him round.*) What ails you? Near crying, is it?

CHRISTY (*in despair and grief*). Amn't I after seeing the love-light of the star of knowledge shining from her brow, and hearing words would put you thinking on the holy Brigid speaking to the infant saints, and now she'll be turning again, and speaking hard words to me, like an old woman with a spavindy[28] ass she'd have, urging on a hill.

WIDOW QUIN. There's poetry talk for a girl you'd see itching and scratching, and she with a stale stink of poteen on her from selling in the shop.

CHRISTY (*impatiently*). It's her like is fitted to be handling merchandise in the heavens above, and what'll I be doing now, I ask you, and I a kind of wonder was jilted by the heavens when a day was by.

(*There is a distant noise of* GIRLS' *voices.* WIDOW QUIN *looks from window and comes to him, hurriedly.*)

WIDOW QUIN. You'll be doing like myself, I'm thinking, when I did destroy my man, for I'm above many's the day, odd times in great spirits, abroad in the sunshine, darning a stocking or stitching a shift; and odd times again looking out on the schooners, hookers, trawlers is sailing the sea, and I thinking on the gallant hairy fellows are drifting beyond, and myself long years living alone.

CHRISTY (*interested*). You're like me, so.

28 SPAVINDY, lame.

WIDOW QUIN. I am your like, and it's for that I'm taking a fancy to you, and I with my little houseen above where there'd be myself to tend you, and none to ask were you a murderer or what at all.

CHRISTY. And what would I be doing if I left Pegeen?

WIDOW QUIN. I've nice jobs you could be doing—gathering shells to make a white-wash for our hut within, building up a little goose-house, or stretching a new skin on an old curagh[29] I have, and if my hut is far from all sides, it's there you'll meet the wisest old men, I tell you, at the corner of my wheel, and it's there yourself and me will have great times whispering and hugging. . . .

VOICES (outside, calling far away). Christy! Christy Mahon! Christy!

CHRISTY. Is it Pegeen Mike?

WIDOW QUIN. It's the young girls, I'm thinking, coming to bring you to the sports below, and what is it you'll have me to tell them now?

CHRISTY. Aid me for to win Pegeen. It's herself only that I'm seeking now. (WIDOW QUIN gets up and goes to window.) Aid me for to win her, and I'll be asking God to stretch a hand to you in the hour of death, and lead you short cuts through the Meadows of Ease, and up the floor of Heaven to the Footstool of the Virgin's Son.

WIDOW QUIN. There's praying!

VOICES (nearer). Christy! Christy Mahon!

CHRISTY (with agitation). They're coming. Will you swear to aid and save me, for the love of Christ?

WIDOW QUIN (looks at him for a moment). If I aid you, will you swear to give me a right of way I want, and a mountainy ram, and a load of dung at Michaelmas, the time that you'll be master here?

CHRISTY. I will, by the elements and stars of night.

WIDOW QUIN. Then we'll not say a word of the old fellow, the way Pegeen won't know your story till the end of time.

CHRISTY. And if he chances to return again?

WIDOW QUIN. We'll swear he's a maniac and not your da. I could take an oath I seen him raving on the sands today.

(GIRLS run in.)

SUSAN. Come on to the sports below. Pegeen says you're to come.

SARA TANSEY. The lepping's beginning, and we've a jockey's suit to fit upon you for the mule race on the sands below.

HONOR. Come on, will you?

CHRISTY. I will then if Pegeen's beyond.

SARA. She's in the boreen[30] making game of Shaneen Keogh.

CHRISTY. Then I'll be going to her now. (He runs out, followed by the GIRLS.)

WIDOW QUIN. Well, if the worst comes in the end of all, it'll be great game

[29] CURAGH, boat.   [30] BOREEN, lane.

to see there's none to pity him but a widow woman, the like of me, has buried her children and destroyed her man.   (*She goes out.*)

ACT III

(*Scene as before. Later in the day.* JIMMY *comes in, slightly drunk.*)

JIMMY (*calls*). Pegeen!   (*Crosses to inner door.*)   Pegeen Mike!   (*Comes back again into the room.*)   Pegeen!   (PHILLY *comes in in the same state. To* PHILLY.)   Did you see herself?

PHILLY. I did not; but I sent Shawn Keogh with the ass-cart for to bear him home.   (*Trying cupboards, which are locked.*)   Well, isn't he a nasty man to get into such staggers at a morning wake; and isn't herself the divil's daughter for locking, and she so fussy after that young gaffer, you might take your death with drouth and none to heed you?

JIMMY. It's little wonder she'd be fussy, and he after bringing bankrupt ruin on the roulette man, and the trick-o'-the-loop man, and breaking the nose of the cockshot-man, and winning all in the sports below, racing, lepping, dancing, and the Lord knows what! He's right luck, I'm telling you.

PHILLY. If he has, he'll be rightly hobbled yet, and he not able to say ten words without making a brag of the way he killed his father, and the great blow he hit with the loy.

JIMMY. A man can't hang by his own informing, and his father should be rotten by now.

(OLD MAHON *passes window slowly.*)

PHILLY. Supposing a man's digging spuds in that field with a long spade, and supposing he flings up the two halves of that skull, what'll be said then in the papers and the courts of law?

JIMMY. They'd say it was an old Dane, maybe, was drowned in the flood. (OLD MAHON *comes in and sits down near door listening.*)   Did you never hear tell of the skulls they have in the city of Dublin, ranged out like blue jugs in a cabin of Connaught?

PHILLY. And you believe that?

JIMMY (*pugnaciously*). Didn't a lad see them and he after coming from harvesting in the Liverpool boat? "They have them there," says he, "making a show of the great people there was one time walking the world. White skulls and black skulls and yellow skulls, and some with full teeth, and some haven't only but one."

PHILLY. It was no lie, maybe, for when I was a young lad there was a graveyard beyond the house with the remnants of a man who had thighs as long as your arm. He was a horrid man, I'm telling you, and there was many a fine Sunday I'd put him together for fun, and he with shiny bones, you wouldn't meet the like of these days in the cities of the world.

MAHON (*getting up*). You wouldn't, is it? Lay your eyes on that skull, and tell me where and when there was another the like of it, is splintered only from the blow of a loy.

PHILLY. Glory be to God! And who hit you at all?

MAHON (*triumphantly*). It was my own son hit me. Would you believe that?

JIMMY. Well, there's wonders hidden in the heart of man!

PHILLY (*suspiciously*). And what way was it done?

MAHON (*wandering about the room*). I'm after walking hundreds and long scores of miles, winning clean beds and the fill of my belly four times in the day, and I doing nothing but telling stories of that naked truth. (*He comes to them a little aggressively.*)   Give me a supeen and I'll tell you now.

(WIDOW QUIN *comes in and stands aghast behind him. He is facing* JIMMY *and* PHILLY, *who are on the left.*)

JIMMY. Ask herself beyond. She's the stuff hidden in her shawl.

WIDOW QUIN (*coming to* MAHON *quickly*). You here, is it? You didn't go far at all?

MAHON. I seen the coasting steamer passing, and I got a drouth upon me and a cramping leg, so I said, "The divil go along with him," and turned again. (*Looking under her shawl.*) And let you give me a supeen, for I'm destroyed travelling since Tuesday was a week.

WIDOW QUIN (*getting a glass, in a cajoling tone*). Sit down then by the fire and take your ease for a space. You've a right to be destroyed indeed, with your walking, and fighting, and facing the sun. (*Giving him poteen from a stone jar she has brought in.*)   There now is a drink for you, and may it be to your happiness and length of life.

MAHON (*taking glass greedily, and sitting down by fire*). God increase you!

WIDOW QUIN (*taking men to the right stealthily*). Do you know what? That man's raving from his wound today, for I met him a while since telling a rambling tale of a tinker had him destroyed. Then he heard of Christy's deed, and he up and says it was his son had cracked his skull. Oh, isn't madness a fright, for he'll go killing someone yet, and he thinking it's the man has struck him so?

JIMMY (*entirely convinced*). It's a fright surely. I knew a party was kicked in the head by a red mare, and he went killing horses a great while, till he eat the insides of a clock and died after.

PHILLY (*with suspicion*). Did he see Christy?

WIDOW QUIN. He didn't. (*With a warning gesture.*) Let you not be putting him in mind of him, or you'll be likely summoned if there's murder done. (*Looking round at* MAHON.) Whisht! He's listening. Wait now till you hear me taking him easy and unravelling all. (*She goes to* MAHON.) And what way are you feeling, mister? Are you in contentment now?

MAHON (*slightly emotional from his drink*). I'm poorly only, for it's a hard story the way I'm left today, when it was I did tend him from his hour of birth, and he a dunce never reached his second book, the way he'd come from school, many's the day, with his legs lamed under him, and he blackened with his beatings like a tinker's ass. It's a hard story, I'm saying, the way some do have their next and nighest raising up a hand of murder on them, and some is lonesome getting their death with lamentation in the dead of night.

WIDOW QUIN (*not knowing what to say*). To hear you talking so quiet, who'd know you were the same fellow we seen pass today?

MAHON. I'm the same surely. The wrack and ruin of three-score years; and it's a terror to live that length, I tell you, and to have your sons going to the dogs against you, and you wore out scolding them, and skelping[31] them, and God knows what.

PHILLY (*to* JIMMY). He's not raving. (*To* WIDOW QUIN.) Will you ask him what kind was his son?

WIDOW QUIN (*to* MAHON, *with a peculiar look*). Was your son that hit you a lad of one year and a score maybe, a great hand at racing and lepping and licking the world?

MAHON (*turning on her with a roar of rage*). Didn't you hear me say he was the fool of men, the way from this out he'll know the orphan's lot, with old and young making game of him, and they swearing, raging, kicking at him like a mangy cur.

(*A great burst of cheering outside, some way off.*)

MAHON (*putting his hands to his ears*). What in the name of God do they want roaring below?

WIDOW QUIN (*with the shade of a smile*). They're cheering a young lad, the champion Playboy of the Western World.

(*More cheering.*)

MAHON (*going to window*). It'd split my heart to hear them, and I with pulses in my brain-pan for a week gone by. Is it racing they are?

JIMMY (*looking from door*). It is, then. They are mounting him for the mule race will be run upon the sands. That's the playboy on the winkered mule.

MAHON (*puzzled*). That lad, is it? If you said it was a fool he was, I'd have laid a mighty oath he was the likeness of my wandering son. (*Uneasily, putting his hand to his head.*) Faith, I'm thinking I'll go walking for to view the race.

WIDOW QUIN (*stopping him, sharply*). You will not. You'd best take the

---

31 SKELPING, whipping.

road to Belmullet, and not be dilly-dallying in this place where there isn't a spot you could sleep.

PHILLY (*coming forward*). Don't mind her. Mount there on the bench and you'll have a view of the whole. They're hurrying before the tide will rise, and it'd be near over if you went down the pathway through the crags below.

MAHON (*mounts on bench*, WIDOW QUIN *beside him*). That's a right view again the edge of the sea. They're coming now from the point. He's leading. Who is he at all?

WIDOW QUIN. He's the champion of the world, I tell you, and there isn't a hap'orth[32] isn't falling lucky to his hands today.

PHILLY (*looking out, interested in the race*). Look at that. They're pressing him now.

JIMMY. He'll win it yet.

PHILLY. Take your time, Jimmy Farrell. It's too soon to say.

WIDOW QUIN (*shouting*). Watch him taking the gate. There's riding.

JIMMY (*cheering*). More power to the young lad!

MAHON. He's passing the third.

JIMMY. He'll lick them yet.

WIDOW QUIN. He'd lick them if he was running races with a score itself.

MAHON. Look at the mule he has, kicking the stars.

WIDOW QUIN. There was a lep! (*Catching hold of* MAHON *in her excitement*.) He's fallen? He's mounted again! Faith, he's passing them all!

JIMMY. Look at him skelping her!

PHILLY. And the mountain girls hooshing him on!

JIMMY. It's the last turn! The post's cleared for them now!

MAHON. Look at the narrow place. He'll be into the bogs! (*With a yell.*) Good rider! He's through it again!

JIMMY. He neck and neck!

PHILLY. Good boy to him! Flames, but he's in! (*Great cheering, in which all join.*)

MAHON (*with hesitation*). What's that? They're raising him up. They're coming this way. (*With a roar of rage and astonishment.*) It's Christy, by the stars of God! I'd know his way of spitting and he astride the moon. (*He jumps down and makes a run for the door, but* WIDOW QUIN *catches him and pulls him back.*)

WIDOW QUIN. Stay quiet, will you? That's not your son. (*To* JIMMY.) Stop him, or you'll get a month for the abetting of manslaughter and be fined as well.

JIMMY. I'll hold him.

MAHON (*struggling*). Let me out! Let me out, the lot of you, till I have my vengeance on his head today.

WIDOW QUIN (*shaking him, vehemently*). That's not your son. That's a

32 HAP'ORTH, halfpennyworth.

man is going to make a marriage with the daughter of this house, a place with fine trade, with a licence, and with poteen too.

MAHON (*amazed*). That man marrying a decent and a moneyed girl! Is it mad yous are? Is it in a crazy-house for females that I'm landed now?

WIDOW QUIN. It's mad yourself is with the blow upon your head. That lad is the wonder of the western world.

MAHON. I seen it's my son.

WIDOW QUIN. You seen that you're mad. (*Cheering outside.*) Do you hear them cheering him in the zig-zags of the road? Aren't you after saying that your son's a fool, and how would they be cheering a true idiot born?

MAHON (*getting distressed*). It's maybe out of reason that that man's himself. (*Cheering again.*) There's none surely will go cheering him. Oh, I'm raving with a madness that would fright the world. (*He sits down with his hand to his head.*) There was one time I seen ten scarlet divils letting on they'd cork my spirit in a gallon can; and one time I seen rats as big as badgers sucking the lifeblood from the butt of my lug;[33] but I never till this day confused that dribbling idiot with a likely man. I'm destroyed surely.

WIDOW QUIN. And who'd wonder when it's your brain-pan that is gaping now?

MAHON. Then the blight of the sacred drouth upon myself and him, for I never went mad to this day, and I not three weeks with the Limerick girls drinking myself silly and parlatic[34] from the dusk to dawn. (*To* WIDOW QUIN, *suddenly.*) Is my visage astray?

WIDOW QUIN. It is, then. You're a sniggering maniac, a child could see.

MAHON (*getting up more cheerfully*). Then I'd best be going to the union[35] beyond, and there'll be a welcome before me, I tell you (*with great pride*), and I a terrible and fearful case, the way that there I was one time, screeching in a straightened waistcoat, with seven doctors writing out my sayings in a printed book. Would you believe that?

WIDOW QUIN. If you're a wonder itself, you'd best be hasty, for them lads caught a maniac one time and pelted the poor creature till he ran out, raving and foaming, and was drowned in the sea.

MAHON (*with philosophy*). It's true mankind is the divil when your head's astray. Let me out now and I'll slip down the boreen, and not see them so.

WIDOW QUIN (*showing him out*). That's it. Run to the right, and not a one will see. (*He runs off.*)

PHILLY (*wisely*). You're at some gaming, Widow Quin; but I'll walk after him and give him his dinner and a time to rest, and I'll see then if he's raving or as sane as you.

WIDOW QUIN (*annoyed*). If you go near that lad, let you be wary of your

---

[33] LUG, ear lobe. [34] PARLATIC, paralytic. [35] UNION, workhouse for the poor.

head, I'm saying. Didn't you hear him telling he was crazed at times?

PHILLY. I heard him telling a power; and I'm thinking we'll have right sport before night will fall. (*He goes out.*)

JIMMY. Well, Philly's a conceited and foolish man. How could that madman have his senses and his brain-pan slit? I'll go after them and see him turn on Philly now.

(*He goes;* WIDOW QUIN *hides poteen behind counter. Then hubbub outside.*)

VOICES. There you are! Good jumper! Grand lepper! Darlint boy! He's the racer! Bear him on, will you!

(CHRISTY *comes in, in jockey's dress, with* PEGEEN MIKE, SARA, *and other* GIRLS *and* MEN.)

PEGEEN (*to crowd*). Go on now and don't destroy him and he drenching with sweat. Go along, I'm saying, and have your tug-of-warring till he's dried his skin.

CROWD. Here's his prizes! A bagpipes! A fiddle was played by a poet in the years gone by! A flat and three-thorned blackthorn would lick the scholars out of Dublin town!

CHRISTY (*taking prizes from the* MEN). Thank you kindly, the lot of you. But you'd say it was little only I did this day if you'd seen me a while since striking my one single blow.

TOWN CRIER (*outside ringing a bell*). Take notice, last event of this day! Tug-of-warring on the green below! Come on, the lot of you! Great achievements for all Mayo men!

PEGEEN. Go on and leave him for to rest and dry. Go on, I tell you, for he'll do no more.

(*She hustles crowd out;* WIDOW QUIN *following them.*)

MEN (*going*). Come on, then. Good luck for the while!

PEGEEN (*radiantly, wiping his face with her shawl*). Well, you're the lad, and you'll have great times from this out when you could win that wealth of prizes, and you sweating in the heat of noon!

CHRISTY (*looking at her with delight*). I'll have great times if I win the crowning prize I'm seeking now, and that's your promise that you'll wed me in a fortnight, when our banns is called.

PEGEEN (*backing away from him*). You've right daring to go ask me that, when all knows you'll be starting to some girl in your own townland, when your father's rotten in four months, or five.

CHRISTY (*indignantly*). Starting from you, is it? (*He follows her.*) I will not, then, and when the airs is warming, in four months or five, it's then yourself and me should be pacing Neifin in the dews of night, the times sweet smells do be rising, and you'd see a little, shiny new moon, maybe, sinking on the hills.

PEGEEN (*looking at him playfully*). And it's that kind of a poacher's love you'd make, Christy Mahon, on the sides of Neifin, when the night is down?

CHRISTY. It's little you'll think if my love's a poacher's, or an earl's itself, when you'll feel my two hands stretched around you, and I squeezing kisses on your puckered lips, till I'd feel a kind of pity for the Lord God is all ages sitting lonesome in His golden chair.

PEGEEN. That'll be right fun, Christy Mahon, and any girl would walk her heart out before she'd meet a young man was your like for eloquence, or talk at all.

CHRISTY (*encouraged*). Let you wait, to hear me talking, till we're astray in Erris, when Good Friday's by, drinking a sup from a well, and making mighty kisses with our wetted mouths, or gaming in a gap of sunshine, with yourself stretched back unto your necklace, in the flowers of the earth.

PEGEEN (*in a low voice, moved by his tone*). I'd be nice so, is it?

CHRISTY (*with rapture*). If the mitred bishops seen you that time, they'd be the like of the holy prophets, I'm thinking, do be straining the bars of Paradise to lay eyes on the Lady Helen of Troy, and she abroad, pacing back and forward, with a nosegay in her golden shawl.

PEGEEN (*with real tenderness*). And what is it I have, Christy Mahon, to make me fitting entertainment for the like of you, that has such poet's talking, and such bravery of heart.

CHRISTY (*in a low voice*). Isn't there the light of seven heavens in your heart alone, the way you'll be an angel's lamp to me from this out, and I abroad in the darkness, spearing salmons in the Owen or the Carrowmore?

PEGEEN. If I was your wife I'd be along with you those nights, Christy Mahon, the way you'd see I was a great hand at coaxing bailiffs, or coining funny nicknames for the stars of night.

CHRISTY. You, is it? Taking your death in the hailstones, or in the fogs of dawn.

PEGEEN. Yourself and me would shelter easy in a narrow bush (*with a qualm of dread*); but we're only talking, maybe, for this would be a poor, thatched place to hold a fine lad is the like of you.

CHRISTY (*putting his arm round her*). If I wasn't a good Christian, it's on my naked knees I'd be saying my prayers and paters to every jack-straw you have roofing your head, and every stony pebble is paving the laneway to your door.

PEGEEN (*radiantly*). If that's the truth I'll be burning candles from this out to the miracles of God that have brought you from the south to-day, and I with my gowns bought ready, the way that I can wed you, and not wait at all.

CHRISTY. It's miracles, and that's the truth. Me there toiling a long while, and walking a long while, not knowing at all I was drawing all times nearer to this holy day.

PEGEEN. And myself, a girl, was tempted often to go sailing the seas till I'd marry a Jew-man, with ten kegs of gold, and I not knowing at all there was the like of you drawing nearer, like the stars of God.

CHRISTY. And to think I'm long years hearing women talking that talk, to all bloody fools, and this the first time I've heard the like of your voice talking sweetly for my own delight.

PEGEEN. And to think it's me is talking sweetly, Christy Mahon, and I the fright of seven townlands for my biting tongue. Well, the heart's a wonder; and, I'm thinking, there won't be our like in Mayo, for gallant lovers, from this hour today. (*Drunken singing is heard outside.*) There's my father coming from the wake, and when he's had his sleep we'll tell him, for he's peaceful then.   (*They separate.*)

MICHAEL (*singing outside*).

> The jailer and the turnkey
> They quickly ran us down,
> And brought us back as prisoners
> Once more to Cavan town.

(*He comes in supported by* SHAWN.)

> There we lay bewailing
> All in a prison bound. . . .

(*He sees* CHRISTY. *Goes and shakes him drunkenly by the hand, while* PEGEEN *and* SHAWN *talk on the left.*)

MICHAEL (*to* CHRISTY). The blessing of God and the holy angels on your head, young fellow. I hear tell you're after winning all in the sports below; and wasn't it a shame I didn't bear you along with me to Kate Cassidy's wake, a fine, stout lad, the like of you, for you'd never see the match of it for flows of drink, the way when we sunk her bones at noonday in her narrow grave, there were five men, aye, and six men, stretched out retching speechless on the holy stones.

CHRISTY (*uneasily, watching* PEGEEN). Is that the truth?

MICHAEL. It is, then; and aren't you a louty schemer to go burying your poor father unbeknownst when you'd a right to throw him on the crupper of a Kerry mule and drive him westwards, like holy Joseph in the days gone by, the way we could have given him a decent burial, and not have him rotting beyond, and not a Christian drinking a smart drop to the glory of his soul?

CHRISTY (*gruffly*). It's well enough he's lying, for the likes of him.

MICHAEL (*slapping him on the back*). Well, aren't you a hardened slayer? It'll be a poor thing for the household man where you go sniffing for a female wife; and (*pointing to* SHAWN) look beyond at that shy and decent Christian I have chosen for my daughter's hand, and I after getting the gilded dispensation this day for to wed them now.

CHRISTY. And you'll be wedding them this day, is it?

MICHAEL (*drawing himself up*). Aye. Are you thinking, if I'm drunk itself, I'd leave my daughter living single with a little frisky rascal is the like of you?

PEGEEN (*breaking away from* SHAWN). Is it the truth the dispensation's come?

MICHAEL (*triumphantly*). Father Reilly's after reading it in gallous Latin, and "It's come in the nick of time," says he; "so I'll wed them in a hurry, dreading that young gaffer who'd capsize the stars."

PEGEEN (*fiercely*). He's missed his nick of time, for it's that lad, Christy Mahon, that I'm wedding now.

MICHAEL (*loudly, with horror*). You'd be making him a son to me, and he wet and crusted with his father's blood?

PEGEEN. Aye. Wouldn't it be a bitter thing for a girl to go marrying the like of Shaneen, and he a middling kind of a scarecrow, with no savagery or fine words in him at all?

MICHAEL (*gasping and sinking on a chair*). Oh, aren't you a heathen daughter to go shaking the fat of my heart, and I swamped and drownded with the weight of drink? Would you have them turning on me the way that I'd be roaring to the dawn of day with the wind upon my heart? Have you not a word to aid me, Shaneen? Are you not jealous at all?

SHAWN (*in great misery*). I'd be afeard to be jealous of a man did slay his da.

PEGEEN. Well, it'd be a poor thing to go marrying your like. I'm seeing there's a world of peril for an orphan girl, and isn't it a great blessing I didn't wed you before himself came walking from the west or south?

SHAWN. It's a queer story you'd go picking a dirty tramp up from the highways of the world.

PEGEEN (*playfully*). And you think you're a likely beau to go straying along with the shiny Sundays of the opening year, when it's sooner on a bullock's liver you'd put a poor girl thinking than on the lily or the rose?

SHAWN. And have you no mind of my weight of passion, and the holy dispensation, and the drift of heifers I'm giving, and the golden ring?

PEGEEN. I'm thinking you're too fine for the like of me, Shawn Keogh of Killakeen, and let you go off till you'd find a radiant lady with droves of bullocks on the plains of Meath, and herself bedizened in the diamond jewelleries of Pharaoh's ma. That'd be your match, Shaneen. So God save you now!   (*She retreats behind* CHRISTY.)

SHAWN. Won't you hear me telling you . . . ?

CHRISTY (*with ferocity*). Take yourself from this, young fellow, or I'll maybe add a murder to my deeds today.

MICHAEL (*springing up with a shriek*). Murder, is it? Is it mad yous are? Would you go making murder in this place, and it piled with poteen for our drink to-night? Go on to the foreshore if it's fighting you want, where the rising tide will wash all traces from the memory of man. (*Pushing* SHAWN *towards* CHRISTY.)

SHAWN (*shaking himself free, and getting behind* MICHAEL). I'll not fight him, Michael James. I'd liefer live a bachelor, simmering in passions to the end of time, than face a lepping savage the like of him has descended from the Lord knows where. Strike him yourself, Michael James, or you'll ·lose my drift of heifers and my blue bull from Sneem.

MICHAEL. Is it me fight him, when it's father-slaying he's bred to now? (*Pushing* SHAWN.)   Go on, you fool, and fight him now.

SHAWN (*coming forward a little*). Will I strike him with my hand?

MICHAEL. Take the loy is on your western side.

SHAWN. I'd be afeard of the gallows if I struck with that.

CHRISTY (*taking up the loy*). Then I'll make you face the gallows or quit off from this.   (SHAWN *flies out the door.*)

CHRISTY. Well, fine weather be after him (*going to* MICHAEL, *coaxingly*), and I'm thinking you wouldn't wish to have that quaking blackguard in your house at all. Let you give us your blessing and hear her swear her faith to me, for I'm mounted on the spring-tide of the stars of luck, the way it'll be good for any to have me in the house.

PEGEEN (*at the other side of* MICHAEL). Bless us now, for I swear to God I'll wed him, and I'll not renege.

MICHAEL (*standing up in the center, holding on to both of them*). It's the will of God, I'm thinking, that all should win an easy or a cruel end, and it's the will of God that all should rear up lengthy families for the nurture of the earth. What's a single man, I ask you, eating a bit in one house and drinking a sup in another, and he with no place of his own, like an old braying jackass strayed upon the rocks? (*To* CHRISTY.)   It's many would be in dread to bring your like into their house for to end them, maybe, with a sudden end; but I'm a decent man of Ireland, and I liefer face the grave untimely and I seeing a score of grandsons growing up little gallant swearers by the name of God, than go peopling my bedside with puny weeds the like of what you'd breed, I'm thinking, out of Shaneen Keogh. (*He joins their hands.*)   A daring fellow is the jewel of the world, and a man did split his father's middle with a single clout should have the bravery of ten, so may God and Mary and St. Patrick bless you, and increase you from this mortal day.

CHRISTY *and* PEGEEN. Amen, O Lord!

(*Hubbub outside.* OLD MAHON *rushes in, followed by all the crowd, and* WIDOW QUIN. *He makes a rush at* CHRISTY, *knocks him down, and begins to beat him.*)

PEGEEN (*dragging back his arm*). Stop that, will you? Who are you at all?

MAHON. His father, God forgive me!

PEGEEN (*drawing back*). Is it rose from the dead?

MAHON. Do you think I look so easy quenched with the tap of a loy?

(*Beats* CHRISTY *again.*)

PEGEEN (*glaring at* CHRISTY). And it's lies you told, letting on you had him slitted, and you nothing at all.

CHRISTY (*catching* MAHON's *stick*). He's not my father. He's a raving maniac would scare the world. (*Pointing to* WIDOW QUIN.)   Herself knows it is true.

CROWD. You're fooling Pegeen! The Widow Quin seen him this day, and you likely knew! You're a liar!

CHRISTY (*dumbfounded*). It's himself was a liar, lying stretched out with an open head on him, letting on he was dead.

MAHON. Weren't you off racing the hills before I got my breath with the start I had seeing you turn on me at all?

PEGEEN. And to think of the coaxing glory we had given him, and he after doing nothing but hitting a soft blow and chasing northward in a sweat of fear. Quit off from this.

CHRISTY (*piteously*). You've seen my doings this day, and let you save me from the old man; for why would you be in such a scorch of haste to spur me to destruction now?

PEGEEN. It's there your treachery is spurring me, till I'm hard set to think you're the one I'm after lacing in my heart-strings half an hour gone by. (*To* MAHON.)   Take him on from this, for I think bad the world should see me raging for a Munster liar, and the fool of men.

MAHON. Rise up now to retribution, and come on with me.

CROWD (*jeeringly*). There's the playboy! There's the lad thought he'd rule the roost in Mayo! Slate him now, mister.

CHRISTY (*getting up in shy terror*). What is it drives you to torment me here, when I'd asked the thunders of the might of God to blast me if I ever did hurt to any saving only that one single blow.

MAHON (*loudly*). If you didn't, you're a poor good-for-nothing, and isn't it by the like of you the sins of the whole world are committed?

CHRISTY (*raising his hands*). In the name of the Almighty God . . .

MAHON. Leave troubling the Lord God. Would you have Him sending down drouths, and fevers, and the old hen and the cholera morbus?

CHRISTY (*to* WIDOW QUIN). Will you come between us and protect me now?

WIDOW QUIN. I've tried a lot, God help me, and my share is done.

CHRISTY (*looking round in desperation*). And I must go back into my torment, is it, or run off like a vagabond straying through the unions with the dust of August making mudstains in the gullet of my throat; or the winds of March blowing on me till I'd take an oath I felt them making whistles of my ribs within?

SARA. Ask Pegeen to aid you. Her like does often change.

CHRISTY. I will not, then, for there's torment in the splendor of her like, and she a girl any moon of midnight would take pride to meet, facing southwards on the heaths of Keel. But what did I want crawling forward to scorch my understandings at her flaming brow?

PEGEEN (*to* MAHON, *vehemently, fearing she will break into tears*). Take him on from this or I'll set the young lads to destroy him here.

MAHON (*going to him, shaking his stick*). Come on now if you wouldn't have the company to see you skelped.

PEGEEN (*half-laughing, through her tears*). That's it, now the world will see him pandied,[36] and he an ugly liar was playing off the hero, and the fright of men.

CHRISTY (*to* MAHON, *very sharply*). Leave me go!

CROWD. That's it. Now, Christy. If them two set fighting, it will lick the world.

MAHON (*making a grab at* CHRISTY). Come here to me.

CHRISTY (*more threatening*). Leave me go, I'm saying.

MAHON. I will, maybe, when your legs is limping, and your back is blue.

CROWD. Keep it up, the two of you. I'll back the old one. Now the playboy.

CHRISTY (*in low and intense voice*). Shut your yelling, for if you're after making a mighty man of me this day by the power of a lie, you're setting me now to think if it's a poor thing to be lonesome it's worse, maybe, go mixing with the fools of earth.

(MAHON *makes a movement towards him.*)

CHRISTY (*almost shouting*). Keep off . . . lest I do show a blow unto the lot of you would set the guardian angels winking in the clouds above. (*He swings round with a sudden rapid movement and picks up a loy.*)

CROWD (*half-frightened, half-amused*). He's going mad! Mind yourselves! Run from the idiot!

CHRISTY. If I am an idiot, I'm after hearing my voice this day saying words would raise the top-knot on a poet in a merchant's town. I've won your racing, and your lepping, and . . .

MAHON. Shut your gullet and come on with me.

CHRISTY. I'm going, but I'll stretch you first.

(*He runs at* OLD MAHON *with the loy, chases him out of the door, followed by crowd and* WIDOW QUIN. *There is a great noise outside, then a yell, and dead silence for a moment.* CHRISTY *comes in, half-dazed, and goes to fire.*)

WIDOW QUIN (*coming in hurriedly, and going to him*). They're turning again you. Come on, or you'll be hanged, indeed.

CHRISTY. I'm thinking, from this out, Pegeen'll be giving me praises, the same as in the hours gone by.

[36] PANDIED, beaten.

WIDOW QUIN (*impatiently*). Come by the back door. I'd think bad to have you stifled on the gallows tree.

CHRISTY (*indignantly*). I will not, then. What good'd be my lifetime if I left Pegeen?

WIDOW QUIN. Come on, and you'll be no worse than you were last night; and you with a double murder this time to be telling to the girls.

CHRISTY. I'll not leave Pegeen Mike.

WIDOW QUIN (*impatiently*). Isn't there the match of her in every parish public, from Binghamstown unto the plain of Meath? Come on, I tell you, and I'll find you finer sweethearts at each waning moon.

CHRISTY. It's Pegeen I'm seeking only, and what'd I care if you brought me a drift of chosen females, standing in their shifts itself, maybe, from this place to the eastern world?

SARA (*runs in, pulling off one of her petticoats*). They're going to hang him. (*Holding out petticoat and shawl.*) Fit these upon him, and let him run off to the east.

WIDOW QUIN. He's raving now; but we'll fit them on him, and I'll take him to the ferry to the Achill boat.

CHRISTY (*struggling feebly*). Leave me go, will you? when I'm thinking of my luck today, for she will wed me surely, and I a proven hero in the end of all.

(*They try to fasten petticoat round him.*)

WIDOW QUIN. Take his left hand, and we'll pull him now. Come on, young fellow.

CHRISTY (*suddenly starting up*). You'll be taking me from her? You're jealous, is it, of her wedding me? Go on from this. (*He snatches up a stool, and threatens them with it.*)

WIDOW QUIN (*going*). It's in the madhouse they should put him, not in jail, at all. We'll go by the back door to call the doctor, and we'll save him so.

(*She goes out, with* SARA, *through inner room.* MEN *crowd in the doorway.* CHRISTY *sits down again by the fire.*)

MICHAEL (*in a terrified whisper*). Is the old lad killed surely?

PHILLY. I'm after feeling the last gasps quitting his heart. (*They peer in at* CHRISTY.)

MICHAEL (*with a rope*). Look at the way he is. Twist a hangman's knot on it, and slip it over his head, while he's not minding at all.

PHILLY. Let you take it, Shaneen. You're the soberest of all that's here.

SHAWN. Is it me to go near him, and he the wickedest and the worst with me? Let you take it, Pegeen Mike.

PEGEEN. Come on, so. (*She goes forward with the others, and they drop the double hitch over his head.*)

CHRISTY. What ails you?

SHAWN (*triumphantly, as they pull the rope tight on his arms*). Come on to the peelers, till they stretch you now.

CHRISTY. Me!

MICHAEL. If we took pity on you the Lord God would, maybe, bring us ruin from the law today, so you'd best come easy, for hanging is an easy and a speedy end.

CHRISTY. I'll not stir. (*To* PEGEEN.)   And what is it you'll say to me, and I after doing it this time in the face of all?

PEGEEN. I'll say, a strange man is a marvel, with his mighty talk; but what's a squabble in your backyard, and the blow of a loy, have taught me that there's a great gap between a gallous story and a dirty deed. (*To* MEN.)   Take him on from this, or the lot of us will be likely put on trial for his deed to-day.

CHRISTY (*with horror in his voice*). And it's yourself will send me off, to have a horny-fingered hangman hitching his bloody slipknots at the butt of my ear.

MEN (*pulling rope*). Come on, will you?

(*He is pulled down on the floor.*)

CHRISTY (*twisting his legs round the table*). Cut the rope, Pegeen, and I'll quit the lot of you, and live from this out, like the madmen of Keel, eating muck and green weeds on the faces of the cliffs.

PEGEEN. And leave us to hang, is it, for a saucy liar, the like of you? (*To* MEN.)   Take him on, out from this.

SHAWN. Pull a twist on his neck, and squeeze him so.

PHILLY. Twist yourself. Sure he cannot hurt you, if you keep your distance from his teeth alone.

SHAWN. I'm afeard of him. (*To* PEGEEN.)   Lift a lighted sod, will you, and scorch his leg.

PEGEEN (*blowing the fire with a bellows*). Leave go now, young fellow, or I'll scorch your shins.

CHRISTY. You're blowing for to torture me. (*His voice rising and growing stronger.*)   That's your kind, is it? Then let the lot of you be wary, for, if I've to face the gallows, I'll have a gay march down, I tell you, and shed the blood of some of you before I die.

SHAWN (*in terror*). Keep a good hold, Philly. Be wary, for the love of God. For I'm thinking he would liefest wreak his pains on me.

CHRISTY (*almost gaily*). If I do lay my hands on you, it's the way you'll be at the fall of night, hanging as a scarecrow for the fowls of hell. Ah, you'll have a gallous jaunt, I'm saying, coaching out through Limbo with my father's ghost.

SHAWN (*to* PEGEEN). Make haste, will you? Oh, isn't he a holy terror, and isn't it true for Father Reilly, that all drink's a curse that has the lot of you so shaky and uncertain now?

CHRISTY. If I can wring a neck among you, I'll have a royal judgment look-ing on the trembling jury in the courts of law. And won't there be crying out in Mayo the day I'm stretched upon the rope, with ladies in their silks and satins snivelling in their lacy kerchiefs, and they rhyming songs and ballads on the terror of my fate?   (*He squirms round on the floor and bites* SHAWN's *leg.*)

SHAWN (*shrieking*). My leg's bit on me. He's the like of a mad dog, I'm thinking, the way that I will surely die.

CHRISTY (*delighted with himself*). You will, then, the way you can shake out hell's flags of welcome for my coming in two weeks or three, for I'm thinking Satan hasn't many have killed their da in Kerry, and in Mayo too.

(OLD MAHON *comes in behind on all fours and looks on unnoticed.*)

MEN (*to* PEGEEN). Bring the sod, will you?

PEGEEN (*coming over*). God help him so.   (*Burns his leg.*)

CHRISTY (*kicking and screaming*). Oh, glory be to God!   (*He kicks loose from the table, and they all drag him towards the door.*)

JIMMY (*seeing* OLD MAHON). Will you look what's come in?

(*They all drop* CHRISTY *and run left.*)

CHRISTY (*scrambling on his knees face to face with* OLD MAHON). Are you coming to be killed a third time, or what ails you now?

MAHON. For what is it they have you tied?

CHRISTY. They're taking me to the peelers to have me hanged for slaying you.

MICHAEL (*apologetically*). It is the will of God that all should guard their little cabins from the treachery of law, and what would my daughter be doing if I was ruined or was hanged itself?

MAHON (*grimly, loosening* CHRISTY). It's little I care if you put a bag on her back, and went picking cockles till the hour of death; but my son and myself will be going our own way, and we'll have great times from this out telling stories of the villainy of Mayo, and the fools is here. (*To* CHRISTY, *who is freed.*)   Come on now.

CHRISTY. Go with you, is it? I will then, like a gallant captain with his heathen slave. Go on now and I'll see you from this day stewing my oat-meal and washing my spuds, for I'm master of all fights from now. (*Pushing* MAHON.)   Go on, I'm saying.

MAHON. Is it me?

CHRISTY. Not a word out of you. Go on from this.

MAHON (*walking out and looking back at* CHRISTY *over his shoulder*). Glory be to God!   (*With a broad smile.*)   I am crazy again.   (*Goes.*)

CHRISTY. Ten thousand blessings upon all that's here, for you've turned me a likely gaffer in the end of all, the way I'll go romancing through a romping lifetime from this hour to the dawning of the judgment day. *(He goes out.)*

MICHAEL. By the will of God, we'll have peace now for our drinks. Will you draw the porter, Pegeen?

SHAWN *(going up to her)*. It's a miracle Father Reilly can wed us in the end of all, and we'll have none to trouble us when his vicious bite is healed.

PEGEEN *(hitting him a box on the ear)*. Quit my sight. *(Putting her shawl over her head and breaking out into wild lamentations.)* Oh, my grief, I've lost him surely. I've lost the only Playboy of the Western World.

Tennessee Williams

b. 1914

THE GLASS MENAGERIE

The Author's Production Notes

Being a "memory play," *The Glass Menagerie* can be presented with unusual freedom of convention. Because of its considerably delicate or tenuous material, atmospheric touches and subtleties of direction play a particularly important part. Expressionism and all other unconventional techniques in drama have only one valid aim, and that is a closer approach to truth. When a play employs unconventional techniques, it is not, or certainly shouldn't be, trying to escape its responsibility of dealing with reality, or interpreting experience, but is actually or should be attempting to find a closer approach, a more penetrating and vivid expression of things as they are. The straight realistic play with its genuine frigidaire and authentic ice-cubes, its characters that speak exactly as its audience speaks, corresponds to the academic landscape and has the same virtue of a photographic likeness. Everyone should know nowadays the unimportance of the photographic in art: that truth, life, or reality is an organic thing which the poetic imagination can represent or suggest, in essence, only through transformation, through changing into other forms than those which were merely present in appearance.

These remarks are not meant as a preface only to this particular play. They have to do with a conception of a new, plastic theatre which must take the place of the exhausted theatre of realistic conventions if the theatre is to resume vitality as a part of our culture.

THE SCREEN DEVICE

There is *only one important difference between the original and acting version of the play* and that is the *omission* in the latter of the device which I tentatively included in my *original* script. This device was the use of a screen on which were projected magic-lantern slides bearing images or titles. I do not regret the omission of this device from the present Broadway production. The extraordinary power of Miss Taylor's performance made it suitable to have the utmost simplicity in the physical production. But I think it may be interesting to some readers to see how this device was conceived. So I am putting it into the published manuscript. These images and legends, projected from behind, were cast on a section of wall between the front-room and dining-room areas, which should be indistinguishable from the rest when not in use.

The purpose of this will probably be apparent. It is to give accent to certain values in each scene. Each scene contains a particular point (or several) which is structurally the most important. In an episodic play, such as this, the basic structure or narrative line may be obscured from the audience; the effect may seem fragmentary rather than architectural. This may not be the fault of the play so much as a lack of attention in the audience. The legend or image upon the screen will strengthen the effect of what is merely allusion in the writing and allow the primary point to be made more simply and lightly than if the entire responsibility were on the spoken lines. Aside from this structural value, I think the screen will have a definite emotional appeal, less definable but just as important. An imaginative producer or director may invent many other uses for this device than those indicated in the present script. In fact the possibilities of the device seem much larger to me than the instance of this play can possibly utilize.

THE MUSIC

Another extra-literary accent in this play is provided by the use of music. A single recurring tune, "The Glass Menagerie," is used to give emotional emphasis to suitable passages. This tune is like circus music, not when you are on the grounds or in the immediate vicinity of the parade, but when you are at some distance and very likely thinking of something else. It seems under those circumstances to continue almost interminably and it weaves in and out of your preoccupied consciousness; then it is the lightest, most delicate music in the world and perhaps the saddest. It expresses the surface vivacity of life with the underlying strain of immutable and inexpressible sorrow. When you look at a piece of delicately spun glass you think of two things: how beautiful it is and how easily it can be broken. Both of those ideas should be woven into the recurring tune, which dips in and out of the play as if it were carried on a wind that changes. It serves as a thread of connection and allusion between the narrator with his separate point in time and space and the subject of his story. Between each episode it returns as reference to the emotion, nostalgia, which is the first condition of the play. It is primarily

LAURA's music and therefore comes out most clearly when the play focuses upon her and the lovely fragility of glass which is her image.

THE LIGHTING

The lighting in the play is not realistic. In keeping with the atmosphere of memory, the stage is dim. Shafts of light are focused on selected areas or actors, sometimes in contradistinction to what is the apparent center. For instance, in the quarrel scene between TOM and AMANDA, in which LAURA has no active part, the clearest pool of light is on her figure. This is also true of the supper scene, when her silent figure on the sofa should remain the visual center. The light upon LAURA should be distinct from the others, having a peculiar pristine clarity such as light used in early religious portraits of female saints or madonnas. A certain correspondence to light in religious paintings, such as El Greco's, where the figures are radiant in atmosphere that is relatively dusky, could be effectively used throughout the play. [It will also permit a more effective use of the screen.] A free, imaginative use of light can be of enormous value in giving a mobile, plastic quality to plays of a more or less static nature.

T. W.

CHARACTERS

AMANDA WINGFIELD, *the mother. A little woman of great but confused vitality clinging frantically to another time and place. Her characterization must be carefully created, not copied from type. She is not paranoiac, but her life is paranoia. There is much to admire in Amanda, and as much to love and pity as there is to laugh at. Certainly she has endurance and a kind of heroism, and though her foolishness makes her unwittingly cruel at times, there is tenderness in her slight person.*

LAURA WINGFIELD, *her daughter. Amanda, having failed to establish contact with reality, continues to live vitally in her illusions, but Laura's situation is even graver. A childhood illness has left her crippled, one leg slightly shorter than the other, and held in a brace. This defect need not be more than suggested on the stage. Stemming from this, Laura's separation increases till she is like a piece of her own glass collection, too exquisitely fragile to move from the shelf.*

TOM WINGFIELD, *her son and the narrator of the play. A poet with a job in a warehouse. His nature is not remorseless, but to escape from a trap he has to act without pity.*

JIM O'CONNOR, *the gentleman caller. A nice ordinary, young man.*

SCENE: *An alley in St. Louis.*

PART I: *Preparation for a Gentleman Caller.*

PART II: *The Gentleman calls.*

TIME: *Now and the Past.*

SCENE 1

(The Wingfield apartment is in the rear of the building, one of those vast hive-like conglomerations of cellular living-units that flower as warty growths of overcrowded urban centers of lower middle-class population and are symptomatic of the impulse of this largest and fundamentally enslaved section of American society to avoid fluidity and differentiation and to exist and function as one interfused mass of automatism.

The apartment faces an alley and is entered by a fire-escape, a structure whose name is a touch of accidental poetic truth, for all of these huge buildings are always burning with the slow and implacable fires of human desperation. The fire-escape is included in the set—that is, the landing of it and steps descending from it.

231

The scene is memory and is therefore nonrealistic. Memory takes a lot of poetic license. It omits some details; others are exaggerated, according to the emotional value of the articles it touches, for memory is seated predominantly in the heart. The interior is therefore rather dim and poetic.

At the rise of the curtain, the audience is faced with the dark, grim rear wall of the Wingfield tenement. This building, which runs parallel to the footlights, is flanked on both sides by dark, narrow alleys which run into murky canyons of tangled clotheslines, garbage cans and the sinister latticework of neighboring fire-escapes. It is up and down these side alleys that exterior entrances and exits are made, during the play. At the end of TOM'S *opening commentary, the dark tenement wall slowly reveals [by means of a transparency] the interior of the ground floor Wingfield apartment.*

Downstage is the living room, which also serves as a sleeping room for LAURA, *the sofa unfolding to make her bed. Upstage, center, and divided by a wide arch or second proscenium with transparent faded portieres [or second curtain], is the dining room. In an old-fashioned what-not in the living room are seen scores of transparent glass animals. A blown-up photograph of the father hangs on the wall of the living room, facing the audience, to the left of the archway. It is the face of a very handsome young man in a doughboy's First World War cap. He is gallantly smiling, ineluctably smiling, as if to say, "I will be smiling forever."*

The audience hears and sees the opening scene in the dining room through both the transparent fourth wall of the building and the transparent gauze portieres of the dining-room arch. It is during this revealing scene that the fourth wall slowly ascends, out of sight. This transparent exterior wall is not brought down again until the very end of the play, during TOM'S *final speech.*

The narrator is an undisguised convention of the play. He takes whatever license with dramatic convention as is convenient to his purposes.

TOM *enters dressed as a merchant sailor from alley, stage left, and strolls across the front of the stage to the fire-escape. There he stops and lights a cigarette. He addresses the audience.)*

TOM. Yes, I have tricks in my pocket, I have things up my sleeve. But I am the opposite of a stage magician. He gives you illusion that has the appearance of truth. I give you truth in the pleasant disguise of illusion. To begin with, I turn back time. I reverse it to that quaint period, the thirties, when the huge middle class of America was matriculating in a school for the blind. Their eyes had failed them, or they had failed their eyes, and so they were having their fingers pressed forcibly down on the fiery Braille alphabet of a dissolving economy. In Spain there was revolution. Here there was only shouting and confusion. In Spain there was Guernica. Here there were disturbances of labor, sometimes pretty violent, in otherwise peaceful cities such as Chicago, Cleveland, Saint Louis . . . . This is the social background of the play.

(*Music*)

The play is memory. Being a memory play, it is dimly lighted, it is sentimental, it is not realistic. In memory everything seems to happen to music. That explains the fiddle in the wings. I am the narrator of the play, and also a character in it. The other characters are my mother, Amanda, my sister, Laura, and a gentleman caller who appears in the final scenes. He is the most realistic character in the play, being an emissary from a world of reality that we were somehow set apart from. But since I have a poet's weakness for symbols, I am using this character also as a symbol; he is the long delayed but always expected something that we live for. There is a fifth character in the play who doesn't appear except in this larger-than-life-size photograph over the mantel. This is our father who left us a long time ago. He was a telephone man who fell in love with long distances; he gave up his job with the telephone company and skipped the light fantastic out of town . . . . The last we heard of him was a picture post-card from Mazatlan, on the Pacific coast of Mexico, containing a message of two words—"Hello— Good-bye!" and no address. I think the rest of the play will explain itself. . . .

(AMANDA's *voice becomes audible through the portieres.*)

(LEGEND ON SCREEN: *"Où sont les neiges."*)

(*He divides the portieres and enters the upstage area.*)

(AMANDA *and* LAURA *are seated at a drop-leaf table. Eating is indicated by gestures without food or utensils.* AMANDA *faces the audience.* TOM *and* LAURA *are seated in profile.*)

(*The interior has lit up softly and through the scrim we see* AMANDA *and* LAURA *seated at the table in the upstage area.*)

AMANDA (*calling*). Tom?
TOM. Yes, Mother.
AMANDA. We can't say grace until you come to the table!
TOM. Coming, Mother. (*He bows slightly and withdraws, reappearing a few moments later in his place at the table.*)
AMANDA (*to her son*). Honey, don't *push* with your *fingers.* If you have to push with something, the thing to push with is a crust of bread. And chew—chew! Animals have sections in their stomachs which enable them to digest food without mastication, but human beings are supposed to chew their food before they swallow it down. Eat food leisurely, son, and really enjoy it. A well-cooked meal has lots of delicate flavors that

have to be held in the mouth for appreciation. So chew your food and give your salivary glands a chance to function!

TOM (*deliberately lays his imaginary fork down and pushes his chair back from the table*). I haven't enjoyed one bite of this dinner because of your constant directions on how to eat it. It's you that make me rush through meals with your hawk-like attention to every bite I take. Sickening—spoils my appetite—all this discussion of—animals' secretion—salivary glands—mastication!

AMANDA (*lightly*). Temperament like a Metropolitan star! (*He rises and crosses downstage.*)   You're not excused from the table.

TOM. I'm getting a cigarette.

AMANDA. You smoke too much.

LAURA (*rises*). I'll bring in the blanc mange.

(*He remains standing with his cigarette by the portieres during the following.*)

AMANDA (*rising*). No, sister, no, sister—you be the lady this time and I'll be the darky.

LAURA. I'm already up.

AMANDA. Resume your seat, little sister—I want you to stay fresh and pretty—for gentlemen callers!

LAURA. I'm not expecting any gentlemen callers.

AMANDA (*crossing out to kitchenette. Airily*). Sometimes they come when they are least expected! Why, I remember one Sunday afternoon in Blue Mountain—   (*Enters kitchenette.*)

TOM. I know what's coming!

LAURA. Yes. But let her tell it.

TOM. Again?

LAURA. She loves to tell it.

(AMANDA *returns with bowl of dessert.*)

AMANDA. One Sunday afternoon in Blue Mountain—your mother received —*seventeen!*—gentlemen callers! Why, sometimes there weren't chairs enough to accommodate them all. We had to send the nigger over to bring in folding chairs from the parish house.

TOM (*remaining at portieres*). How did you entertain those gentlemen callers?

AMANDA. I understood the art of conversation!

TOM. I bet you could talk.

AMANDA. Girls in those days *knew* how to talk, I can tell you.

TOM. Yes?

(IMAGE: AMANDA *as a girl on a porch, greeting callers.*)

AMANDA. They knew how to entertain their gentlemen callers. It wasn't enough for a girl to be possessed of a pretty face and a graceful figure—

although I wasn't slighted in either respect. She also needed to have a nimble wit and a tongue to meet all occasions.

TOM. What did you talk about?

AMANDA. Things of importance going on in the world! Never anything coarse or common or vulgar. (*She addresses* TOM *as though he were seated in the vacant chair at the table though he remains by portieres. He plays this scene as though he held the book.*) My callers were gentlemen—all! Among my callers were some of the most prominent young planters of the Mississippi Delta—planters and sons of planters!

(TOM *motions for music and a spot of light on* AMANDA. *Her eyes lift, her face glows, her voice becomes rich and elegiac.*)

(SCREEN LEGEND: "*Où sont les neiges.*")

There was young Champ Laughlin who later became vice-president of the Delta Planters Bank. Hadley Stevenson who was drowned in Moon Lake and left his widow one hundred and fifty thousand in Government bonds. There were the Cutrere brothers, Wesley and Bates. Bates was one of my bright particular beaux! He got in a quarrel with that wild Wainwright boy. They shot it out on the floor of Moon Lake Casino. Bates was shot through the stomach. Died in the ambulance on his way to Memphis. His widow was well-provided for, came into eight or ten thousand acres, that's all. She married him on the rebound—never loved her—carried my picture on him the night he died! And there was that boy that every girl in the Delta had set her cap for! That beautiful, brilliant young Fitzhugh boy from Greene County!

TOM. What did he leave his widow?

AMANDA. He never married! Gracious, you talk as though all of my old admirers had turned up their toes to the daisies!

TOM. Isn't this the first you've mentioned that still survives?

AMANDA. That Fitzhugh boy went North and made a fortune—came to be known as the Wolf of Wall Street! He had the Midas touch, whatever he touched turned to gold! And I could have been Mrs. Duncan J. Fitzhugh, mind you! But—I picked your *father*!

LAURA (*rising*). Mother, let me clear the table.

AMANDA. No, dear, you go in front and study your typewriter chart. Or practice your shorthand a little. Stay fresh and pretty.—It's almost time for our gentlemen callers to start arriving. (*She flounces girlishly toward the kitchenette.*) How many do you suppose we're going to entertain this afternoon?

(TOM *throws down the paper and jumps up with a groan.*)

LAURA (*alone in the dining room*). I don't believe we're going to receive any, Mother.

AMANDA (*reappearing, airily*). What? No one—not one? You must be joking! (LAURA *nervously echoes her laugh. She slips in a fugitive manner through the half-open portieres and draws them gently behind her. A shaft of very clear light is thrown on her face against the faded tapestry of the curtains.* MUSIC: *"The Glass Menagerie" under faintly. Lightly.*) Not one gentleman caller? It can't be true! There must be a flood, there must have been a tornado!

LAURA. It isn't a flood, it's not a tornado, Mother. I'm just not popular like you were in Blue Mountain. . . . (TOM *utters another groan.* LAURA *glances at him with a faint, apologetic smile. Her voice catching a little.*) Mother's afraid I'm going to be an old maid.

(*The scene dims out with "Glass Menagerie" music*)

SCENE 2

(*"Laura, Haven't You Ever Liked Some Boy?"*)

(*On the dark stage the screen is lighted with the image of blue roses.*)

(*Gradually* LAURA'S *figure becomes apparent and the screen goes out. The music subsides.*)

(LAURA *is seated in the delicate ivory chair at the small claw-foot table. She wears a dress of soft violet material for a kimono—her hair tied back from her forehead with a ribbon. She is washing and polishing her collection of glass.*)

(AMANDA *appears on the fire-escape steps. At the sound of her ascent,* LAURA *catches her breath, thrusts the bowl of ornaments away and seats herself stiffly before the diagram of the typewriter keyboard as though it held her spellbound. Something has happened to* AMANDA. *It is written in her face as she climbs to the landing: a look that is grim and hopeless and a little absurd. She has on one of those cheap or imitation velvety-looking cloth coats with imitation fur collar. Her hat is five or six years old, one of those dreadful cloche hats that were worn in the late twenties and she is clasping an enormous black patent-leather pocketbook with nickel clasps and initials. This is her full-dress outfit, the one she usually wears to the D.A.R. Before entering she looks through the door. She purses her lips, opens her eyes very wide, rolls them upward and shakes her head. Then she slowly lets herself in the door. Seeing her mother's expression* LAURA *touches her lips with a nervous gesture.*)

LAURA. Hello, Mother, I was— (*She makes a nervous gesture toward the chart on the wall.* AMANDA *leans against the shut door and stares at* LAURA *with a martyred look.*)

AMANDA. Deception? Deception? (*She slowly removes her hat and gloves, continuing the sweet suffering stare. She lets the hat and gloves fall on the floor—a bit acting.*)

LAURA (*shakily*). How was the D.A.R. meeting? (AMANDA *slowly opens her purse and removes a dainty white handkerchief which she shakes out delicately and delicately touches to her lips and nostrils.*) Didn't you go to the D.A.R. meeting, Mother?

AMANDA (*Faintly, almost inaudibly*).—No.—No. (*Then more forcibly.*) I did not have the strength—to go to the D.A.R. In fact, I did not have the courage! I wanted to find a hole in the ground and hide myself in it forever! (*She crosses slowly to the wall and removes the diagram of the typewriter keyboard. She holds it in front of her for a second, staring at it sweetly and sorrowfully—then bites her lip and tears it in two pieces.*)

LAURA (*faintly*). Why did you do that, Mother? (AMANDA *repeats the same procedure with the chart of the Gregg Alphabet.*) Why are you—

AMANDA. Why? Why? How old are you, Laura?

LAURA. Mother, you know my age.

AMANDA. I thought that you were an adult; it seems that I was mistaken.

(*She crosses slowly to the sofa and sinks down and stares at* LAURA.)

LAURA. Please don't stare at me, Mother.

(AMANDA *closes her eyes and lowers her head. Count ten.*)

AMANDA. What are we going to do, what is going to become of us, what is the future?

(*Count ten.*)

LAURA. Has something happened, Mother? (AMANDA *draws a long breath and takes out the handkerchief again. Dabbing process.*) Mother, has—something happened?

AMANDA. I'll be all right in a minute, I'm just bewildered— (*Count five.*) —by life. . . .

LAURA. Mother, I wish that you would tell me what's happened!

AMANDA. As you know, I was supposed to be inducted into my office at the D.A.R. this afternoon. (IMAGE: *a swarm of typewriters.*) But I stopped off at Rubicam's business college to speak to your teachers about your having a cold and asked them what progress they thought you were making down there.

LAURA. Oh. . . .

AMANDA. I went to the typing instructor and introduced myself as your mother. She didn't know who you were. Wingfield, she said. We don't have any such student enrolled at the school! I assured her she did, that you had been going to classes since early in January. "I wonder," she said, "if you could be talking about that terribly shy little girl who dropped out of school after only a few days' attendance?" "No," I said, "Laura, my daughter, has been going to school every day for the past six weeks!" "Excuse me," she said. She took the attendance book out and there was your name, unmistakably printed, and all the dates you were absent until they decided that you had dropped out of school. I still said, "No, there must have been some mistake! There must have been some mix-up in the records!" And she said, "No—I remember her perfectly now. Her hands shook so that she couldn't hit the right keys! The first time we gave a speed-test, she broke down completely—was sick at the stomach and almost had to be carried into the wash-room! After that morning she never showed up any more. We phoned the house but never got any answer—while I was working at Famous and Barr, I suppose, demonstrating those—Oh!" I felt so weak I could barely keep on my feet! I had to sit down while they got me a glass of water! Fifty dollars' tuition, all of our plans—my hopes and ambitions for you—just gone up the spout, just gone up the spout like that. (LAURA *draws a long breath and gets awkwardly to her feet. She crosses to the victrola and winds it up.*)   What are you doing?

LAURA. Oh!   (*She releases the handle and returns to her seat.*)

AMANDA. Laura, where have you been going when you've gone out pretending that you were going to business college?

LAURA. I've just been going out walking.

AMANDA. That's not true.

LAURA. It is. I just went walking.

AMANDA. Walking? Walking? In winter? Deliberately courting pneumonia in that light coat? Where did you walk to, Laura?

LAURA. All sorts of places—mostly in the park.

AMANDA. Even after you'd started catching that cold?

LAURA. It was the lesser of two evils, Mother.   (IMAGE: *winter scene in park.*)   I couldn't go back up. I—threw up—on the floor!

AMANDA. From half past seven till after five every day you mean to tell me you walked around in the park, because you wanted to make me think that you were still going to Rubicam's Business College?

LAURA. It wasn't as bad as it sounds. I went inside places to get warmed up.

AMANDA. Inside where?

LAURA. I went in the art museum and the bird-houses at the Zoo. I visited the penguins every day! Sometimes I did without lunch and went to the movies. Lately I've been spending most of my afternoons in the Jewel-box, that big glass house where they raise the tropical flowers.

AMANDA. You did all this to deceive me, just for deception?   (LAURA *looks down.*)   Why?

LAURA. Mother, when you're disappointed, you get that awful suffering look on your face, like the picture of Jesus' mother in the museum!

AMANDA. Hush!

LAURA. I couldn't face it.

(*Pause. A whisper of strings.*)

(LEGEND: "*The crust of humility.*")

AMANDA (*hopelessly fingering the huge pocketbook*). So what are we going to do the rest of our lives? Stay home and watch the parades go by? Amuse ourselves with the glass menagerie, darling? Eternally play those worn-out phonograph records your father left as a painful reminder of him? We won't have a business career—we've given that up because it gave us nervous indigestion! (*Laughs wearily.*) What is there left but dependency all our lives? I know so well what becomes of unmarried women who aren't prepared to occupy a position. I've seen such pitiful cases in the South—barely tolerated spinsters living upon the grudging patronage of sister's husband or brother's wife!—stuck away in some little mousetrap of a room—encouraged by one in-law to visit another—little birdlike women without any nest—eating the crust of humility all their life! Is that the future that we've mapped out for ourselves? I swear it's the only alternative I can think of! It isn't a very pleasant alternative, is it? Of course—some girls do *marry.* (LAURA *twists her hands nervously.*) Haven't you ever liked some boy?

LAURA. Yes. I liked one once. (*Rises.*)   I came across his picture a while ago.

AMANDA (*with some interest*). He gave you his picture?

LAURA. No, it's in the year-book.

AMANDA (*disappointed*). Oh—a high-school boy.

(SCREEN IMAGE: JIM *as high-school hero bearing a silver cup.*)

LAURA. Yes. His name was Jim. (LAURA *lifts the heavy annual from the claw-foot table.*)   Here he is in *The Pirates of Penzance.*

AMANDA (*absently*). The what?

LAURA. The operetta the senior class put on. He had a wonderful voice and we sat across the aisle from each other Mondays, Wednesdays and Fridays in the Aud. Here he is with the silver cup for debating! See his grin?

AMANDA (*absently*). He must have had a jolly disposition.

LAURA. He used to call me—Blue Roses.

(IMAGE: *Blue Roses.*)

AMANDA. Why did he call you such a name as that?

LAURA. When I had that attack of pleurosis—he asked me what was the matter when I came back. I said pleurosis—he thought that I said Blue Roses! So that's what he always called me after that. Whenever he saw me, he'd holler, "Hello, Blue Roses!" I didn't care for the girl that he

went out with. Emily Meisenbach. Emily was the best-dressed girl at
Soldan. She never struck me, though, as being sincere . . . It says in the
Personal Section—they're engaged. That's—six years ago! They must be
married by now.

AMANDA. Girls that aren't cut out for business careers usually wind up
married to some nice man. (*Gets up with a spark of revival.*) Sister,
that's what you'll do!

(LAURA *utters a startled, doubtful laugh. She reaches quickly for a piece of
glass.*)

LAURA. But, Mother—
AMANDA. Yes? (*Crossing to photograph.*)
LAURA (*in a tone of frightened apology*). I'm—crippled!

(IMAGE: *Screen.*)

AMANDA. Nonsense! Laura, I've told you never, never to use that word.
Why, you're not crippled, you just have a little defect—hardly noticeable,
even! When people have some slight disadvantage like that, they culti-
vate other things to make up for it—develop charm—and vivacity—and—
charm! That's all you have to do! (*She turns again to the photograph.*)
One thing your father had *plenty of*—was *charm!*

(TOM *motions to the fiddle in the wings.*)

(*The scene fades out with music.*)

SCENE 3

(LEGEND ON SCREEN: *"After the fiasco—"*)

(TOM *speaks from the fire-escape landing.*)

TOM. After the fiasco at Rubicam's Business College, the idea of getting a
gentleman caller for Laura began to play a more and more important
part in Mother's calculations. It became an obsession. Like some arche-
type of the universal unconscious, the image of the gentleman caller
haunted our small apartment. . . .

(IMAGE: *Young man at door with flowers.*)

An evening at home rarely passed without some allusion to this image,
this spectre, this hope. . . . Even when he wasn't mentioned, his presence hung in Mother's preoccupied look and in my sister's frightened,
apologetic manner—hung like a sentence passed upon the Wingfields!
Mother was a woman of action as well as words. She began to take
logical steps in the planned direction. Late that winter and in the early
spring—realizing that extra money would be needed to properly feather
the nest and plume the bird—she conducted a vigorous campaign on the

telephone, roping in subscribers to one of those magazines for matrons called *The Homemaker's Companion,* the type of journal that features the serialized sublimations of ladies of letters who think in terms of delicate cup-like breasts, slim, tapering waists, rich, creamy thighs, eyes like wood-smoke in autumn, fingers that soothe and caress like strains of music, bodies as powerful as Etruscan sculpture.

(SCREEN IMAGE: *Glamor Magazine cover.*)

(AMANDA *enters with phone on long extension cord. She is spotted in the dim stage.*)

AMANDA. Ida Scott? This is Amanda Wingfield! We *missed* you at the D.A.R. last Monday! I said to myself: She's probably suffering with that sinus condition! How is that sinus condition? Horrors! Heaven have mercy!—You're a Christian martyr, yes, that's what you are, a Christian martyr! Well, I just now happened to notice that your subscription to the *Companion's* about to expire! Yes, it expires with the next issue, honey!—just when that wonderful new serial by Bessie Mae Hopper is getting off to such an exciting start. Oh, honey, it's something that you can't miss! You remember how *Gone With the Wind* took everybody by storm? You simply couldn't go out if you hadn't read it. All everybody *talked* was Scarlett O'Hara. Well, this is a book that critics already compare to *Gone With the Wind.* It's the *Gone With the Wind* of the post-World War generation!—What?—Burning?—Oh, honey, don't let them burn, go take a look in the oven and I'll hold the wire! Heavens—I think she's hung up!

(*Dim out.*)

(LEGEND ON SCREEN: *"You think I'm in love with Continental Shoemakers?"*)

(*Before the stage is lighted, the violent voices of* TOM *and* AMANDA *are heard. They are quarreling behind the portieres. In front of them stands* LAURA *with clenched hands and panicky expression. A clear pool of light on her figure throughout this scene.*)

TOM. What in Christ's name am I—
AMANDA (*shrilly*). Don't you use that—
TOM. Supposed to do!
AMANDA. Expression! Not in my—
TOM. Ohhh!
AMANDA. Presence! Have you gone out of your senses?
TOM. I have, that's true, *driven* out!
AMANDA. What is the matter with you, you—big—big—idiot!
TOM. Look!—I've got *no thing,* no single thing—
AMANDA. Lower your voice!

TOM. In my life here that I can call my own! Everything **is**—

AMANDA. Stop that shouting!

TOM. Yesterday you confiscated my books! You had the **nerve to**—

AMANDA. I took that horrible novel back to the library—yes! That **hideous** book by that insane Mr. Lawrence. (TOM *laughs wildly*.) I cannot con- trol the output of diseased minds or people who cater to them— (TOM *laughs still more wildly*.) But I won't allow such filth brought into my house! No, no, no, no, no!

TOM. House, house! Who pays rent on it, who makes a slave of himself to—

AMANDA (*fairly screeching*). Don't you DARE to—

TOM. No, no *I* musn't say things! *I've* got to just—

AMANDA. Let me tell you—

TOM. I don't want to hear any more! (*He tears the portieres open. The upstage area is lit with a turgid smoky red glow.*)

(AMANDA's *hair is in metal curlers and she wears a very old bathrobe, much too large for her slight figure, a relic of the faithless Mr. Wing- field.*)

(*An upright typewriter and a wild disarray of manuscripts are on the drop- leaf table. The quarrel was probably precipitated by* AMANDA's *interrup- tion of his creative labor. A chair lying overthrown on the floor.*)

(*Their gesticulating shadows are cast on the ceiling by the fiery glow.*)

AMANDA. You *will* hear more, you—

TOM. No, I won't hear more, I'm going out!

AMANDA. You come right back in—

TOM. Out, out, out! Because I'm—

AMANDA. Come back here, Tom Wingfield! I'm not through talking to you!

TOM. Oh, go—

LAURA (*desperately*).—Tom!

AMANDA. You're going to listen, and no more insolence from you! I'm at the end of my patience! (*He comes back toward her.*)

TOM. What do you think I'm at? Aren't I supposed to have any patience to reach the end of, Mother? I know, I know. It seems unimportant to you, what I'm *doing*—what I *want* to do—having a little *difference* between them! You don't think that—

AMANDA. I think you've been doing things that you're ashamed of. That's why you act like this. I don't believe that you go every night to the movies. Nobody goes to the movies night after night. Nobody in their right minds goes to the movies as often as you pretend to. People don't go to the movies at nearly midnight, and movies don't let out at two A.M. Come in stumbling. Muttering to yourself like a maniac! You get three hours' sleep and then go to work. Oh, I can picture the way you're doing down there. Moping, doping, because you're in no condition.

TOM (*wildly*). No, I'm in no condition!

AMANDA. What right have you got to jeopardize your job? Jeopardize the security of us all? How do you think we'd manage if you were—

TOM. Listen! You think I'm crazy *about* the *warehouse*? (*He bends fiercely toward her slight figure.*)   You think I'm in love with the Continental Shoemakers? You think I want to spend fifty-five *years* down there in that—*celotex interior!* with—*fluorescent—tubes!* Look! I'd rather somebody picked up a crowbar and battered out my brains—than go back mornings! I *go!* Every time you come in yelling that God damn *"Rise and Shine!"* *"Rise and Shine!"* I say to myself, "How *lucky dead* people are! But I get up. I *go!* For sixty-five dollars a month I give up all that I dream of doing and being *ever!* And you say self—*self's* all I ever think of. Why, listen, if self is what I thought of, Mother, I'd be where he is—*gone!*   (*Pointing to father's picture.*)   As far as the system of transportation reaches!   (*He starts past her. She grabs his arm.*)   Don't grab at me, Mother!

AMANDA. Where are you going?

TOM. I'm going to the *movies!*

AMANDA. I don't believe that lie!

TOM (*crouching toward her, overtowering her tiny figure. She backs away, gasping*). I'm going to opium dens! Yes, opium dens, dens of vice and criminals' hang-outs, Mother. I've joined the Hogan gang, I'm a hired assassin, I carry a tommy-gun in a violin case! I run a string of cat-houses in the Valley! They call me Killer, Killer Wingfield, I'm leading a double-life, a simple, honest warehouse worker by day, by night a dynamic *czar* of the *underworld, Mother.* I go to gambling casinos, I spin away fortunes on the roulette table! I wear a patch over one eye and a false mustache, sometimes I put on green whiskers. On those occasions they call me—*El Diablo!* Oh, I could tell you things to make you sleepless! My enemies plan to dynamite this place. They're going to blow us all sky-high some night! I'll be glad, very happy, and so will you! You'll go up, up on a broomstick, over Blue Mountain with seventeen gentlemen callers! You ugly—babbling old—*witch.* . . .   (*He goes through a series of violent, clumsy movements, seizing his overcoat, lunging to the door, pulling it fiercely open. The women watch him, aghast. His arm catches in the sleeve of the coat as he struggles to pull it on. For a moment he is pinioned by the bulky garment. With an outraged groan he tears the coat off again, splitting the shoulder of it, and hurls it across the room. It strikes against the shelf of* LAURA's *glass collection, there is a tinkle of shattering glass.* LAURA *cries out as if wounded.*)

(MUSIC. LEGEND: *"The glass menagerie."*)

LAURA (*shrilly*). *My glass!*—menagerie. . . .   (*She covers her face and turns away.*)

(*But* AMANDA *is still stunned and stupefied by the "ugly witch" so that she barely notices this occurrence. Now she recovers her speech.*)

AMANDA (*in an awful voice*). I won't speak to you—until you apologize! (*She crosses through portieres and draws them together behind her.* TOM *is left with* LAURA. LAURA *clings weakly to the mantel with her face averted.* TOM *stares at her stupidly for a moment. Then he crosses to shelf. Drops awkwardly on his knees to collect the fallen glass, glancing at* LAURA *as if he would speak but couldn't.*)

(*"The Glass Menagerie" steals in as the scene dims out.*)

SCENE 4

(*The interior is dark. Faint light in the alley. A deep-voiced bell in a church is tolling the hour of five as the scene commences.*

TOM *appears at the top of the alley. After each solemn boom of the bell in the tower, he shakes a little noise-maker or rattle as if to express the tiny spasm of man in contrast to the sustained power and dignity of the Almighty. This and the unsteadiness of his advance make it evident that he has been drinking.*

As he climbs the few steps to the fire-escape landing light steals up inside. LAURA *appears in night-dress, observing* TOM'S *empty bed in the front room.* TOM *fishes in his pockets for door-key, removing a motley assortment of articles in the search, including a perfect shower of movie-ticket stubs and an empty bottle. At last he finds the key, but just as he is about to insert it, it slips from his fingers. He strikes a match and crouches below the door.*)

TOM (*bitterly*). One crack—and it falls through!

(LAURA *opens the door.*)

LAURA. Tom! Tom, what are you doing?
TOM. Looking for a door-key.
LAURA. Where have you been all this time?
TOM. I have been to the movies.
LAURA. All this time at the movies?
TOM. There was a very long program. There was a Garbo picture and a Mickey Mouse and a travelogue and a newsreel and a preview of coming attractions. And there was an organ solo and a collection for the milk-fund—simultaneously—which ended up in a terrible fight between a fat lady and an usher!
LAURA (*innocently*). Did you have to stay through everything?

TOM. Of course! And, oh, I forgot! There was a big stage show! The head-liner on this stage show was Malvolio the Magician. He performed wonderful tricks, many of them, such as pouring water back and forth between pitchers. First it turned to wine and then it turned to beer and then it turned to whiskey. I know it was whiskey it finally turned into because he needed somebody to come up out of the audience to help him, and I came up—both shows! It was Kentucky Straight Bourbon. A very generous fellow, he gave souvenirs. (*He pulls from his back pocket a shimmering rainbow-colored scarf.*) He gave me this. This is his magic scarf. You can have it, Laura. You wave it over a canary cage and you get a bowl of gold-fish. You wave it over the gold-fish bowl and they fly away canaries. . . . But the wonderfullest trick of all was the coffin trick. We nailed him into a coffin and he got out of the coffin without removing one nail. (*He has come inside.*) There is a trick that would come in handy for me—get me out of this 2 by 4 situation! (*Flops onto bed and starts removing shoes.*)

LAURA. Tom—Shhh!

TOM. What're you shushing me for?

LAURA. You'll wake up Mother.

TOM. Goody, goody! Pay 'er back for all those "Rise an' Shines." (*Lies down, groaning.*) You know it don't take much intelligence to get your-self into a nailed-up coffin, Laura. But who in hell ever got himself out of one without removing one nail?

(*As if in answer, the father's grinning photograph lights up.*)

(*Scene dims out.*)

(*Immediately following: The church bell is heard striking six. At the sixth stroke the alarm clock goes off in* AMANDA's *room, and after a few moments we hear her calling: "Rise and Shine! Rise and Shine! Laura, go tell your brother to rise and shine!"*)

TOM (*sitting up slowly*). I'll rise—but I won't shine.

(*The light increases.*)

AMANDA. Laura, tell your brother his coffee is ready.

(LAURA *slips into front room.*)

LAURA. Tom!—It's nearly seven. Don't make Mother nervous. (*He stares at her stupidly. Beseechingly.*) Tom, speak to Mother this morning. Make up with her, apologize, speak to her!

TOM. She won't to me. It's her that started not speaking.

LAURA. If you just say you're sorry she'll start speaking.

TOM. Her not speaking—is that such a tragedy?

LAURA. Please—please!

AMANDA (*calling from kitchenette*). Laura, are you going to do what I asked you to do, or do I have to get dressed and go out myself?

LAURA. Going, going—soon as I get on my coat! (*She pulls on a shapeless felt hat with nervous, jerky movement, pleadingly glancing at* TOM. *Rushes awkwardly for coat. The coat is one of* AMANDA'S, *inaccurately made-over, the sleeves too short for* LAURA.) Butter and what else?

AMANDA (*entering upstage*). Just butter. Tell them to charge it.

LAURA. Mother, they make such faces when I do that.

AMANDA. Sticks and stones can break our bones, but the expression on Mr. Garfinkel's face won't harm us! Tell your brother his coffee is getting cold.

LAURA (*at door*). Do what I asked you, will you, will you, Tom?

(*He looks sullenly away.*)

AMANDA. Laura, go now or just don't go at all!

LAURA (*rushing out*). Going—going! (*A second later she cries out.* TOM *springs up and crosses to door.* AMANDA *rushes anxiously in.* TOM *opens the door.*)

TOM. Laura?

LAURA. I'm all right. I slipped, but I'm all right.

AMANDA (*peering anxiously after her*). If anyone breaks a leg on those fire-escape steps, the landlord ought to be sued for every cent he possesses! (*She shuts door. Remembers she isn't speaking and returns to other room.*)

(*As* TOM *enters listlessly for his coffee, she turns her back to him and stands rigidly facing the window on the gloomy gray vault of the area-way. Its light on her face with its aged but childish features is cruelly sharp, satirical as a Daumier print.*)

(MUSIC UNDER: "*Ave Maria.*")

(TOM *glances sheepishly but sullenly at her averted figure and slumps at the table. The coffee is scalding hot; he sips it and gasps and spits it back in the cup. At his gasp,* AMANDA *catches her breath and half turns. Then catches herself and turns back to window.*)

(TOM *blows on his coffee, glancing sidewise at his mother. She clears her throat.* TOM *clears his. He starts to rise. Sinks back down again, scratches his head, clears his throat again.* AMANDA *coughs.* TOM *raises his cup in both hands to blow on it, his eyes staring over the rim of it at his mother for several moments. Then he slowly sets the cup down and awkwardly and hesitantly rises from the chair.*)

TOM (*hoarsely*). Mother. I—I apologize, Mother. (AMANDA *draws a quick shuddering breath. Her face works grotesquely. She breaks into child-*

like tears.)   I'm sorry for what I said, for everything that I said, I didn't mean it.

AMANDA (*sobbingly*). My devotion has made me a witch and so I make myself hateful to my children!

TOM. No, you *don't*.

AMANDA. I worry so much, don't sleep, it makes me nervous!

TOM (*gently*). I understand that.

AMANDA. I've had to put up a solitary battle all these years. But you're my right-hand bower! Don't fall down, don't fail!

TOM (*gently*). I try, Mother.

AMANDA (*with great enthusiasm*). Try and you will SUCCEED! (*The notion makes her breathless.*)   Why, you—you're just *full* of natural endowments! Both of my children—they're *unusual* children! Don't you think I know it? I'm so—*proud!* Happy and—feel I've—so much to be thankful for but—Promise me one thing, Son!

TOM. What, Mother?

AMANDA. Promise, son, you'll—never be a drunkard!

TOM (*turns to her grinning*). I will never be a drunkard, Mother.

AMANDA. That's what frightened me so, that you'd be drinking! Eat a bowl of Purina!

TOM. Just coffee, Mother.

AMANDA. Shredded wheat biscuit?

TOM. No. No, Mother, just coffee.

AMANDA. You can't put in a day's work on an empty stomach. You've got ten minutes—don't gulp! Drinking too-hot liquids makes cancer of the stomach. . . . Put cream in.

TOM. No, thank you.

AMANDA. To cool it.

TOM. No! No, thank you, I want it black.

AMANDA. I know, but it's not good for you. We have to do all that we can to build ourselves up. In these trying times we live in, all that we have to cling to is—each other. . . . That's why it's so important to—Tom, I—I sent out your sister so I could discuss something with you. If you hadn't spoken I would have spoken to you. (*Sits down.*)

TOM (*gently*). What is it, Mother, that you want to discuss?

AMANDA. *Laura!*

(TOM *puts his cup down slowly.*)

(LEGEND ON SCREEN: "*Laura.*")

(MUSIC: "*The Glass Menagerie.*")

TOM—Oh.—Laura . . .

AMANDA (*touching his sleeve*). You know how Laura is. So quiet but—still water runs deep! She notices things and I think she—broods about them. (TOM *looks up.*)   A few days ago I came in and she was crying.

TOM. What about?

AMANDA. You.

TOM. Me?

AMANDA. She has an idea that you're not happy here.

TOM. What gave her that idea?

AMANDA. What gives her any idea? However, you do act strangely. I—I'm not criticizing, understand *that!* I know your ambitions do not lie in the warehouse, that like everybody in the whole wide world—you've had to—make sacrifices, but—Tom—Tom—life's not easy, it calls for—Spartan endurance! There's so many things in my heart that I cannot describe to you! I've never told you but I—*loved* your father. . . .

TOM (*gently*). I know that, Mother.

AMANDA. And you—when I see you taking after his ways! Staying out late—and—well, you *had* been drinking the night you were in that—terrifying condition! Laura says that you hate the apartment and that you go out nights to get away from it! Is that true, Tom?

TOM. No. You say there's so much in your heart that you can't describe to me. That's true of me, too. There's so much in my heart that I can't describe to *you!* So let's respect each other's—

AMANDA. But, why—*why,* Tom—are you always so *restless?* Where do you *go* to, nights?

TOM. I—go to the movies.

AMANDA. Why do you go to the movies so much, Tom?

TOM. I go to the movies because—I like adventure. Adventure is something I don't have much of at work, so I go to the movies.

AMANDA. But, Tom, you go to the movies *entirely* too *much!*

TOM. I like a lot of adventure.

(AMANDA *looks baffled, then hurt. As the familiar inquisition resumes he becomes hard and impatient again.* AMANDA *slips back into her querulous attitude toward him.*)

(IMAGE ON SCREEN: *Sailing vessel with jolly roger.*)

AMANDA. Most young men find adventure in their careers.

TOM. Then most young men are not employed in a warehouse.

AMANDA. The world is full of young men employed in warehouses and offices and factories.

TOM. Do all of them find adventure in their careers?

AMANDA. They do or they do without it! Not everybody has a craze for adventure.

TOM. Man is by instinct a lover, a hunter, a fighter, and none of those instincts are given much play at the warehouse!

AMANDA. Man is by instinct! Don't quote instinct to me! Instinct is something that people have got away from! It belongs to animals! Christian adults don't want it!

TOM. What do Christian adults want, then, Mother?

AMANDA. Superior things! Things of the mind and the spirit! Only animals have to satisfy instincts! Surely your aims are somewhat higher than theirs! Than monkeys—pigs—

TOM. I reckon they're not.

AMANDA. You're joking. However, that isn't what I wanted to discuss.

TOM (*rising*). I haven't much time.

AMANDA (*pushing his shoulders*). Sit down.

TOM. You want me to punch in red at the warehouse, Mother?

AMANDA. You have five minutes. I want to talk about Laura.

(LEGEND: *"Plans and provisions."*)

TOM. All right! What about Laura?

AMANDA. We have to be making some plans and provisions for her. She's older than you, two years, and nothing has happened. She just drifts along doing nothing. It frightens me terribly how she just drifts along.

TOM. I guess she's the type that people call home girls.

AMANDA. There's no such type, and if there is, it's a pity! That is unless the home is hers, with a husband!

TOM. What?

AMANDA. Oh, I can see the handwriting on the wall as plain as I see the nose in front of my face! It's terrifying! More and more you remind me of your father! He was out all hours without explanation!—Then *left!* *Good-bye!* And me with the bag to hold. I saw that letter you got from the Merchant Marine. I know what you're dreaming of. I'm not standing here blindfolded. Very well, then. Then *do* it! But not till there's somebody to take your place.

TOM. What do you mean?

AMANDA. I mean that as soon as Laura has got somebody to take care of her, married, a home of her own, independent—why, then you'll be free to go wherever you please, on land, on sea, whichever way the wind blows you! But until that time you've got to look out for your sister. I don't say me because I'm old and don't matter! I say for your sister because she's young and dependent. I put her in business college—a dismal failure! Frightened her so it made her sick at the stomach. I took her over to the Young People's League at the church. Another fiasco. She spoke to nobody, nobody spoke to her. Now all she does is fool with those pieces of glass and play those worn-out records. What kind of a life is that for a girl to lead?

TOM. What can I do about it?

AMANDA. Overcome selfishness! Self, self, self is all that you ever think of!

(TOM *springs up and crosses to get his coat. It is ugly and bulky. He pulls on a cap with earmuffs.*) Where is your muffler? Put your wool muffler on! (*He snatches it angrily from the closet and tosses it around his neck and pulls both ends tight.*) Tom! I haven't said what I had in mind to ask you.

TOM. I'm too late to—

AMANDA (*catching his arm—very importunately. Then shyly*). Down at the warehouse, aren't there some—nice young men?

TOM. No!

AMANDA. There *must* be—*some* . . .

TOM. Mother—

(*Gesture*)

AMANDA. Find out one that's clean-living—doesn't drink and—ask him out for sister!

TOM. What?

AMANDA. For *sister!* To *meet!* Get *acquainted!*

TOM (*stamping to door*). Oh, my go-osh!

AMANDA. Will you? (*He opens door. Imploringly.*) Will you? (*He starts down.*) Will you? *Will* you, dear?

TOM (*calling back*). Yes!

(AMANDA *closes the door hesitantly and with a troubled but faintly hopeful expression.*)

(SCREEN IMAGE: *Glamor Magazine Cover.*)

(*Spot* AMANDA *at phone.*)

AMANDA. Ella Cartwright? This is Amanda Wingfield! How are you, honey? How is that kidney condition?

(*Count five.*)

Horrors!

(*Count five.*)

You're a Christian martyr, yes, honey, that's what you are, a Christian martyr! Well, I just now happened to notice in my little red book that your subscription to the *Companion* has just run out! I knew that you wouldn't want to miss out on the wonderful serial starting in this new issue. It's by Bessie Mae Hopper; the first thing she's written since *Honeymoon for Three.* Wasn't that a strange and interesting story? Well, this one is even lovelier, I believe. It has a sophisticated, society background. It's all about the horsey set on Long Island!

(Fade out.)

SCENE 5

(LEGEND ON SCREEN: *"Annunciation." Fade with music.*)
(*It is early dusk of a spring evening. Supper has just been finished in the
Wingfield apartment.* AMANDA *and* LAURA *in light-colored dresses are
removing dishes from the table, in the upstage area, which is shadowy,
their movements formalized almost as a dance or ritual, their moving
forms as pale and silent as moths.*
TOM, *in white shirt and trousers, rises from the table and crosses toward
the fire-escape.*)
AMANDA (*as he passes her*). Son, will you do me a favor?
TOM. What?
AMANDA. Comb your hair! You look so pretty when your hair is combed!
(TOM *slouches on sofa with evening paper. Enormous caption "Franco
Triumphs."*)   There is only one respect in which I would like you to
emulate your father.
TOM. What respect is that?
AMANDA. The care he always took of his appearance. He never allowed
himself to look untidy.   (*He throws down the paper and crosses to fire-
escape.*)   Where are you going?
TOM. I'm going out to smoke.
AMANDA. You smoke too much. A pack a day at fifteen cents a pack. How
much would that amount to in a month? Thirty times fifteen is how
much, Tom? Figure it out and you will be astounded at what you could
save. Enough to give you a night-school course in accounting at Washington U! Just think what a wonderful thing that would be for you,
Son!

(TOM *is unmoved by the thought.*)

TOM. I'd rather smoke.   (*He steps out on landing, letting the screen door
slam.*)
AMANDA (*sharply*). I know! That's the tragedy of it. . . .   (*Alone, she turns
to look at her husband's picture.*)

(DANCE MUSIC: *"All the World Is Waiting for the Sunrise!"*)

TOM (*to the audience*). Across the alley from us was the Paradise Dance
Hall. On evenings in spring the windows and doors were open and the
music came outdoors. Sometimes the lights were turned out except for
a large glass sphere that hung from the ceiling. It would turn slowly
about and filter the dusk with delicate rainbow colors. Then the orchestra played a waltz or a tango, something that had a slow and sensuous rhythm. Couples would come outside, to the relative privacy of the

alley. You could see them kissing behind ash-pits and telephone poles. This was the compensation for lives that passed like mine, without any change or adventure. Adventure and change were imminent in this year. They were waiting around the corner for all these kids. Suspended in the mist over Berchtesgaden, caught in the folds of Chamberlain's umbrella—. In Spain there was Guernica! But here there was only hot swing music and liquor, dance halls, bars, and movies, and sex that hung in the gloom like a chandelier and flooded the world with brief, deceptive rainbows. . . . All the world was waiting for bombardments!

(AMANDA *turns from the picture and comes outside.*)

AMANDA (*sighing*). A fire-escape landing's a poor excuse for a porch. (*She spreads a newspaper on a step and sits down, gracefully and demurely as if she were settling into a swing on a Mississippi veranda.*) What are you looking at?

TOM. The moon.

AMANDA. Is there a moon this evening?

TOM. It's rising over Garfinkel's Delicatessen.

AMANDA. So it is! A little silver slipper of a moon. Have you made a wish on it yet?

TOM. Um-hum.

AMANDA. What did you wish for?

TOM. That's a secret.

AMANDA. A secret, huh? Well, I won't tell mine either. I will be just as mysterious as you.

TOM. I bet I can guess what yours is.

AMANDA. Is my head so transparent?

TOM. You're not a sphinx.

AMANDA. No, I don't have secrets. I'll tell you what I wished for on the moon. Success and happiness for my precious children! I wish for that whenever there's a moon, and when there isn't a moon, I wish for it, too.

TOM. I thought perhaps you wished for a gentleman caller.

AMANDA. Why do you say that?

TOM. Don't you remember asking me to fetch one?

AMANDA. I remember suggesting that it would be nice for your sister if you brought home some nice young man from the warehouse. I think that I've made that suggestion more than once.

TOM. Yes, you have made it repeatedly.

AMANDA. Well?

TOM. We are going to have one.

AMANDA. *What?*

TOM. A gentleman caller!

(*The annunciation is celebrated with music.*)

(AMANDA *rises.*)

(IMAGE ON SCREEN: *Caller with bouquet.*)

AMANDA. You mean you have asked some nice young man to come over?
TOM. Yep. I've asked him to dinner.
AMANDA. You really did?
TOM. I did!
AMANDA. You did, and did he—*accept?*
TOM. He did!
AMANDA. Well, well—well, well! That's—lovely!
TOM. I thought that you would be pleased.
AMANDA. It's definite, then?
TOM. Very definite.
AMANDA. Soon?
TOM. Very soon.
AMANDA. For heaven's sake, stop putting on and tell me some things, will you?
TOM. What things do you want me to tell you?
AMANDA. *Naturally* I would like to know when he's *coming!*
TOM. He's coming tomorrow.
AMANDA. *Tomorrow?*
TOM. Yep. Tomorrow.
AMANDA. But, Tom!
TOM. Yes, Mother?
AMANDA. Tomorrow gives me no time!
TOM. Time for what?
AMANDA. Preparations! Why didn't you phone me at once, as soon as you asked him, the minute that he accepted? Then, don't you see, I could have been getting ready!
TOM. You don't have to make any fuss.
AMANDA. Oh, Tom, Tom, Tom, of course I have to make a fuss! I want things nice, not sloppy! Not thrown together. I'll certainly have to do some fast thinking, won't I?
TOM. I don't see why you have to think at all.
AMANDA. You just don't know. We can't have a gentleman caller in a pigsty! All my wedding silver has to be polished, the monogrammed table linen ought to be laundered! The windows have to be washed and fresh curtains put up. And how about clothes? We have to *wear* something, don't we?
TOM. Mother, this boy is no one to make a fuss over!
AMANDA. Do you realize he's the first young man we've introduced to your sister? It's terrible, dreadful, disgraceful that poor little sister has never received a single gentleman caller! Tom, come inside! (*She opens the screen door.*)
TOM. What for?

AMANDA. I want to ask you some things.

TOM. If you're going to make such a fuss, I'll call it off, I'll tell him not to come!

AMANDA. You certainly won't do anything of the kind. Nothing offends people worse than broken engagements. It simply means I'll have to work like a Turk! We won't be brilliant, but we will pass inspection. Come on inside.   (TOM *follows, groaning.*)   Sit down.

TOM. Any particular place you would like me to sit?

AMANDA. Thank heavens I've got that new sofa! I'm also making payments on a floor lamp I'll have sent out! And put the chintz covers on, they'll brighten things up! Of course I'd hoped to have these walls repapered. . . . What is the young man's name?

TOM. His name is O'Connor.

AMANDA. That, of course, means fish—tomorrow is Friday! I'll have that salmon loaf—with Durkee's dressing! What does he do? He works at the warehouse?

TOM. Of course! How else would I—

AMANDA. Tom, he—doesn't drink?

TOM. Why do you ask me that?

AMANDA. Your father *did!*

TOM. Don't get started on that!

AMANDA. He *does* drink, then?

TOM. Not that I know of!

AMANDA. Make sure, be certain! The last thing I want for my daughter's a boy who drinks!

TOM. Aren't you being a little bit premature? Mr. O'Connor has not yet appeared on the scene!

AMANDA. But will tomorrow. To meet your sister, and what do I know about his character? Nothing! Old maids are better off than wives of drunkards!

TOM. Oh, my God!

AMANDA. Be still!

TOM (*leaning forward to whisper*). Lots of fellows meet girls whom they don't marry!

AMANDA. Oh, talk sensibly, Tom—and don't be sarcastic!   (*She has gotten a hairbrush.*)

TOM. What are you doing?

AMANDA. I'm brushing that cow-lick down! What is this young man's position at the warehouse?

TOM (*submitting grimly to the brush and the interrogation*). This young man's position is that of a shipping clerk, Mother.

AMANDA. Sounds to me like a fairly responsible job, the sort of a job *you* would be in if you just had more *get-up*. What is his salary? Have you any idea?

TOM. I would judge it to be approximately eighty-five dollars a month.

AMANDA. Well—not princely, but—

TOM. Twenty more than I make.

AMANDA. Yes, how well I know! But for a family man, eighty-five dollars a month is not much more than you can just get by on. . . .

TOM. Yes, but Mr. O'Connor is not a family man.

AMANDA. He might be, mightn't he? Some time in the future?

TOM. I see. Plans and provisions.

AMANDA. You are the only young man that I know of who ignores the fact that the future becomes the present, the present the past, and the past turns into everlasting regret if you don't plan for it!

TOM. I will think that over and see what I can make of it.

AMANDA. Don't be supercilious with your mother! Tell me some more about this—what do you call him?

TOM. James D. O'Connor. The D. is for Delaney.

AMANDA. Irish on *both* sides! *Gracious!* And doesn't drink?

TOM. Shall I call him up and ask him right this minute?

AMANDA. The only way to find out about those things is to make discreet inquiries at the proper moment. When I was a girl in Blue Mountain and it was suspected that a young man drank, the girl whose attentions he had been receiving, if any girl *was,* would sometimes speak to the minister of his church, or rather her father would if her father was living, and sort of feel him out on the young man's character. That is the way such things are discreetly handled to keep a young woman from making a tragic mistake!

TOM. Then how did you happen to make a tragic mistake?

AMANDA. That innocent look of your father's had everyone fooled! He *smiled*—the world was *enchanted!* No girl can do worse than put herself at the mercy of a handsome appearance! I hope that Mr. O'Connor is not too good-looking.

TOM. No, he's not too good-looking. He's covered with freckles and hasn't too much of a nose.

AMANDA. He's not right-down homely, though?

TOM. Not right-down homely. Just medium homely, I'd say.

AMANDA. Character's what to look for in a man.

TOM. That's what I've always said, Mother.

AMANDA. You've never said anything of the kind and I suspect you would never give it a thought.

TOM. Don't be so suspicious of me.

AMANDA. At least I hope he's the type that's up and coming.

TOM. I think he really goes in for self-improvement.

AMANDA. What reason have you to think so?

TOM. He goes to night school.

AMANDA (*beaming*). Splendid! What does he do, I mean study?

TOM. Radio engineering and public speaking!

AMANDA. Then he has visions of being advanced in the world! Any young man who studies public speaking is aiming to have an executive job some day! And radio engineering? A thing for the future! Both of these facts are very illuminating. Those are the sort of things that a mother should know concerning any young man who comes to call on her daughter. Seriously or—not.

TOM. One little warning. He doesn't know about Laura. I didn't let on that we had dark ulterior motives. I just said, why don't you come and have dinner with us? He said okay and that was the whole conversation.

AMANDA. I bet it was! You're eloquent as an oyster. However, he'll know about Laura when he gets here. When he sees how lovely and sweet and pretty she is, he'll thank his lucky stars he was asked to dinner.

TOM. Mother, you mustn't expect too much of Laura.

AMANDA. What do you mean?

TOM. Laura seems all those things to you and me because she's ours and we love her. We don't even notice she's crippled any more.

AMANDA. Don't say crippled! You know that I never allow that word to be used!

TOM. But face facts, Mother. She is and—that's not all—

AMANDA. What do you mean "not all"?

TOM. Laura is very different from other girls.

AMANDA. I think the difference is all to her advantage.

TOM. Not quite all—in the eyes of others—strangers—she's terribly shy and lives in a world of her own and those things make her seem a little peculiar to people outside the house.

AMANDA. Don't say peculiar.

TOM. Face the facts. She is.

(*The dance-hall music changes to a tango that has a minor and somewhat ominous tone.*)

AMANDA. In what way is she peculiar—may I ask?

TOM (*gently*). She lives in a world of her own—a world of—little glass ornaments, Mother. . . . (*Gets up.* AMANDA *remains holding brush, looking at him, troubled.*) She plays old phonograph records and— that's about all— (*He glances at himself in the mirror and crosses to door.*)

AMANDA (*sharply*). Where are you going?

TOM. I'm going to the movies. (*Out screen door.*)

AMANDA. Not to the movies, every night to the movies! (*Follows quickly to screen door.*) I don't believe you always go to the movies! (*He is gone.* AMANDA *looks worriedly after him for a moment. Then vitality and optimism return and she turns from the door. Crossing to portieres.*) Laura! Laura! (LAURA *answers from kitchenette.*)

LAURA. Yes, Mother.

AMANDA. Let those dishes go and come in front! (LAURA *appears with dish towel. Gaily.*)   Laura, come here and make a wish on the moon!

(SCREEN IMAGE: *Moon.*)

LAURA (*entering*). Moon—moon?

AMANDA. A little silver slipper of a moon. Look over your left shoulder, Laura, and make a wish!   (LAURA *looks faintly puzzled as if called out of sleep.* AMANDA *seizes her shoulders and turns her at an angle by the door.*)   Now! Now, darling, *wish!*

LAURA. What shall I wish for, Mother?

AMANDA (*her voice trembling and her eyes suddenly filling with tears*). Happiness! Good Fortune!

(*The violin rises and the stage dims out.*)

SCENE 6

(IMAGE: *High school hero.*)

TOM. And so the following evening I brought Jim home to dinner. I had known Jim slightly in high school. In high school Jim was a hero. He had tremendous Irish good nature and vitality with the scrubbed and polished look of white chinaware. He seemed to move in a continual spotlight. He was a star in basketball, captain of the debating club, president of the senior class and the glee club and he sang the male lead in the annual light operas. He was always running or bounding, never just walking. He seemed always at the point of defeating the law of gravity. He was shooting with such velocity through his adolescence that you would logically expect him to arrive at nothing short of the White House by the time he was thirty. But Jim apparently ran into more interference after his graduation from Soldan. His speed had definitely slowed. Six years after he left high school he was holding a job that wasn't much better than mine.

(IMAGE: *Clerk.*)

He was the only one at the warehouse with whom I was on friendly terms. I was valuable to him as someone who could remember his former glory, who had seen him win basketball games and the silver cup in debating. He knew of my secret practice of retiring to a cabinet of the wash-room to work on poems when business was slack in the warehouse. He called me Shakespeare. And while the other boys in the warehouse regarded me with suspicious hostility, Jim took a humorous attitude toward me. Gradually his attitude affected the others, their hostility wore off and they also began to smile at me as people smile at an oddly fashioned dog who trots across their path at some distance. I knew that Jim and Laura had known each other at Soldan, and I had

heard Laura speak admiringly of his voice. I didn't know if Jim remembered her or not. In high school Laura had been as unobtrusive as Jim
had been astonishing. If he did remember Laura, it was not as my sister,
for when I asked him to dinner, he grinned and said, "You know,
Shakespeare, I never thought of you as having folks!" He was about to
discover that I did. . . .

(LIGHT UPSTAGE.)

(LEGEND ON SCREEN: *"The accent of a coming foot."*)

(*Friday evening. It is about five o'clock of a late spring evening which
comes "scattering poems in the sky."*)

(*A delicate lemony light is in the Wingfield apartment.*)

(AMANDA *has worked like a Turk in preparation for the gentleman caller.
The results are astonishing. The new floor lamp with its rose-silk shade
is in place, a colored paper lantern conceals the broken light fixture in
the ceiling, new billowing white curtains are at the windows, chintz
covers are on chairs and sofa, a pair of new sofa pillows make their
initial appearance.*)

(*Open boxes and tissue paper are scattered on the floor.*)

(LAURA *stands in the middle with lifted arms while* AMANDA *crouches
before her, adjusting the hem of the new dress, devout and ritualistic.
The dress is colored and designed by memory. The arrangement of*
LAURA's *hair is changed; it is softer and more becoming. A fragile, unearthly prettiness has come out in* LAURA: *she is like a piece of translu-
cent glass touched by light, given a momentary radiance, not actual,
not lasting.*)

AMANDA (*impatiently*). Why are you trembling?
LAURA. Mother, you've made me so nervous!
AMANDA. How have I made you nervous?
LAURA. By all this fuss! You make it seem so important!
AMANDA. I don't understand you, Laura. You couldn't be satisfied with
  just sitting home, and yet whenever I try to arrange something for you,
  you seem to resist it. (*She gets up.*) Now take a look at yourself. No,
  wait! Wait just a moment—I have an idea!
LAURA. What is it now?

(AMANDA *produces two powder puffs which she wraps in handkerchiefs
and stuffs in* LAURA's *bosom.*)

LAURA. Mother, what are you doing?
AMANDA. They call them "Gay Deceivers"!
LAURA. I won't wear them!

AMANDA. You will!

LAURA. Why should I?

AMANDA. Because, to be painfully honest, your chest is flat.

LAURA. You make it seem like we were setting a trap.

AMANDA. All pretty girls are a trap, a pretty trap, and men expect them to be.

(LEGEND: *"A pretty trap."*)

Now look at yourself, young lady. This is the prettiest you will ever be! I've got to fix myself now! You're going to be surprised by your mother's appearance! (*She crosses through portieres, humming gaily.*)

(LAURA *moves slowly to the long mirror and stares solemnly at herself.*)

(*A wind blows the white curtains inward in a slow, graceful motion and with a faint, sorrowful sighing.*)

AMANDA (*off stage*). It isn't dark enough yet. (LAURA *turns slowly before the mirror with a troubled look.*)

(LEGEND ON SCREEN: *"This is my sister: celebrate her with strings!"* Music.)

AMANDA (*laughing, off*). I'm going to show you something. I'm going to make a spectacular appearance!

LAURA. What is it, Mother?

AMANDA. Possess your soul in patience—you will see! Something I've resurrected from that old trunk! Styles haven't changed so terribly much after all. . . . (*She parts the portieres.*) Now just look at your mother! (*She wears a girlish frock of yellowed voile with a blue silk sash. She carries a bunch of jonquils—the legend of her youth is nearly revived. Feverishly.*) This is the dress in which I led the cotillion. Won the cakewalk twice at Sunset Hill, wore one spring to the Governor's ball in Jackson! See how I sashayed around the ballroom, Laura? (*She raises her skirt and does a mincing step around the room.*) I wore it on Sundays for my gentlemen callers! I had it on the day I met your father —I had malaria fever all that spring. The change of climate from East Tennessee to the Delta—weakened resistance—I had a little temperature all the time—not enough to be serious—just enough to make me restless and giddy!—Invitations poured in—parties all over the Delta!—"Stay in bed," said Mother, "you have fever!"—but I just wouldn't.—I took quinine but kept on going, going!—Evenings, dances!—Afternoons, long, long rides! Picnics—lovely!—So lovely, that country in May.—All lacy with dogwood, literally flooded with jonquils!—That was the spring I had the craze for jonquils. Jonquils became an absolute obsession. Mother said, "Honey, there's no more room for jonquils." And still I kept on bringing in more jonquils. Whenever, wherever I saw them, I'd say, "Stop! Stop! I see jonquils!" I made the young men help me gather the jonquils! It was a joke, Amanda and her jonquils! Finally there were

no more vases to hold them, every available space was filled with jonquils. No vases to hold them? All right, I'll hold them myself! And then
I— (*She stops in front of the picture. Music.*) met your father!
Malaria fever and jonquils and then—this—boy. . . . (*She switches on
the rose-colored lamp.*) I hope they get here before it starts to rain.
(*She crosses upstage and places the jonquils in bowl on table.*)   I gave
your brother a little extra change so he and Mr. O'Connor could take
the service car home.
LAURA (*with altered look*). What did you say his name was?
AMANDA. O'Connor.
LAURA. What is his first name?
AMANDA. I don't remember. Oh, yes, I do. It was—Jim!

(LAURA *sways slightly and catches hold of a chair.*)

(LEGEND ON SCREEN: *"Not Jim!"*)

LAURA (*faintly*). Not—Jim!
AMANDA. Yes, that was it, it was Jim! I've never known a Jim that wasn't
nice!

(MUSIC: *Ominous.*)

LAURA. Are you sure his name is Jim O'Connor?
AMANDA. Yes. Why?
LAURA. Is he the one that Tom used to know in high school?
AMANDA. He didn't say so. I think he just got to know him at the ware-
house.
LAURA. There was a Jim O'Connor we both knew in high school—   (*Then,
with effort.*)   If that is the one that Tom is bringing to dinner—you'll
have to excuse me, I won't come to the table.
AMANDA. What sort of nonsense is this?
LAURA. You asked me once if I'd ever liked a boy. Don't you remember
I showed you this boy's picture?
AMANDA. You mean the boy you showed me in the year book?
LAURA. Yes, that boy.
AMANDA. Laura, Laura, were you in love with that boy?
LAURA. I don't know, Mother. All I know is I couldn't sit at the table if
it was him!
AMANDA. It won't be him! It isn't the least bit likely. But whether it is or
not, you will come to the table. You will not be excused.
LAURA. I'll have to be, Mother.
AMANDA. I don't intend to humor your silliness, Laura. I've had too much
from you and your brother, both! So just sit down and compose yourself
till they come. Tom has forgotten his key so you'll have to let them in,
when they arrive.
LAURA (*panicky*). Oh, Mother—*you* answer the door!

AMANDA (*lightly*). I'll be in the kitchen—busy!

LAURA. Oh, Mother, please answer the door, don't make me do it!

AMANDA (*crossing into kitchenette*). I've got to fix the dressing for the salmon. Fuss, fuss—silliness!—over a gentleman caller!

(*Door swings shut.* LAURA *is left alone.*)

(LEGEND: *"Terror!"*)

(*She utters a low moan and turns off the lamp—sits stiffly on the edge of the sofa, knotting her fingers together.*)

(LEGEND ON SCREEN: *"The opening of a door!"*)

(TOM *and* JIM *appear on the fire-escape steps and climb to landing. Hearing their approach,* LAURA *rises with a panicky gesture. She retreats to the portieres.*)

(*The doorbell.* LAURA *catches her breath and touches her throat. Low drums.*)

AMANDA (*calling*). Laura, sweetheart! The door!

(LAURA *stares at it without moving.*)

JIM. I think we just beat the rain.

TOM. Uh-huh.   (*He rings again, nervously.* JIM *whistles and fishes for a cigarette.*)

AMANDA (*very, very gaily*). Laura, that is your brother and Mr. O'Connor! Will you let them in, darling?

(LAURA *crosses toward kitchenette door.*)

LAURA (*breathlessly*). Mother—you go to the door!

(AMANDA *steps out of kitchenette and stares furiously at* LAURA. *She points imperiously at the door.*)

LAURA. Please, please!

AMANDA (*in a fierce whisper*). What is the matter with you, you silly thing?

LAURA (*desperately*). Please, you answer it, *please!*

AMANDA. I told you I wasn't going to humor you, Laura. Why have you chosen this moment to lose your mind?

LAURA. Please, please, please, you go!

AMANDA. You'll have to go to the door because I can't!

LAURA (*despairingly*). I can't either!

AMANDA. Why?

LAURA. I'm *sick!*

AMANDA. I'm sick, too—of your nonsense! Why can't you and your brother be normal people? Fantastic whims and behavior!   (TOM *gives a long ring.*)   Preposterous goings on! Can you give me one reason—   (*Calls out lyrically.*)   Coming! Just one second!—why you should be afraid to open a door? Now you answer it, Laura!

LAURA. Oh, oh, oh . . .   (*She returns through the portieres. Darts to the victrola and winds it frantically and turns it on.*)

AMANDA. Laura Wingfield, you march right to that door!

LAURA. Yes—yes, Mother!

(*A faraway, scratchy rendition of "Dardanella" softens the air and gives her strength to move through it. She slips to the door and draws it cautiously open.*)

(TOM *enters with the caller,* JIM O'CONNOR.)

TOM. Laura, this is Jim. Jim, this is my sister, Laura.

JIM (*stepping inside*). I didn't know that Shakespeare had a sister!

LAURA (*retreating stiff and trembling from the door*). How—how do you do?

JIM (*heartily extending his hand*). Okay!

(LAURA *touches it hesitantly with hers.*)

JIM. Your hand's *cold,* Laura!

LAURA. Yes, well—I've been playing the victrola. . . .

JIM. Must have been playing classical music on it! You ought to play a little hot swing music to warm you up!

LAURA. Excuse me—I haven't finished playing the victrola. . . .   (*She turns awkwardly and hurries into the front room. She pauses a second by the victrola. Then catches her breath and darts through the portieres like a frightened deer.*)

JIM (*grinning*). What was the matter?

TOM. Oh—with Laura? Laura is—terribly shy.

JIM. Shy, huh? It's unusual to meet a shy girl nowadays. I don't believe you ever mentioned you had a sister.

TOM. Well, now you know. I have one. Here is the *Post Dispatch.* You want a piece of it?

JIM. Uh-huh.

TOM. What piece? The comics?

JIM. Sports!   (*Glances at it.*)   Ole Dizzy Dean is on his bad behavior.

TOM (*disinterest*).   Yeah?   (*Lights cigarette and crosses back to fire-escape door.*)

JIM. Where are *you* going?

TOM. I'm going out on the terrace.

JIM (*goes after him*). You know, Shakespeare—I'm going to sell you a bill of goods!

TOM. What goods?

JIM. A course I'm taking.

TOM. Huh?

JIM. In public speaking! You and me, we're not the warehouse type.

TOM. Thanks—that's good news. But what has public speaking got to do with it?

JIM. It fits you for—executive positions!

TOM. Awww.

JIM. I tell you it's done a helluva lot for me.

(IMAGE: *Executive at desk.*)

TOM. In what respect?

JIM. In every! Ask yourself what is the difference between you an' me and men in the office down front? Brains?—No!—Ability?—No! Then what? Just one little thing—

TOM. What is that one little thing?

JIM. Primarily it amounts to—social poise! Being able to square up to people and hold your own on any social level!

AMANDA (*off stage*). Tom?

TOM. Yes, Mother?

AMANDA. Is that you and Mr. O'Connor?

TOM. Yes, Mother.

AMANDA. Well, you just make yourselves comfortable in there.

TOM. Yes, Mother.

AMANDA. Ask Mr. O'Connor if he would like to wash his hands.

JIM. Aw, no—no—thank you—I took care of that at the warehouse. Tom—

TOM. Yes?

JIM. Mr. Mendoza was speaking to me about you.

TOM. Favorably?

JIM. What do you think?

TOM. Well—

JIM. You're going to be out of a job if you don't wake up.

TOM. I am waking up—

JIM. You show no signs.

TOM. The signs are interior.

(IMAGE ON SCREEN: *The sailing vessel with Jolly Roger again.*)

TOM. I'm planning to change. (*He leans over the rail speaking with quiet exhilaration. The incandescent marquees and signs of the first-run movie houses light his face from across the alley. He looks like a voyager.*)   I'm right at the point of committing myself to a future that doesn't include the warehouse and Mr. Mendoza or even a night-school course in public speaking.

JIM. What are you gassing about?

TOM. I'm tired of the movies.

JIM. Movies!

TOM. Yes, movies! Look at them—   (*A wave toward the marvels of Grand*

Avenue.)   All of those glamorous people—having adventures—hogging it all, gobbling the whole thing up! You know what happens? People go to the *movies* instead of *moving!* Hollywood characters are supposed to have all the adventures for everybody in America, while everybody in America sits in a dark room and watches them have them! Yes, until there's a war. That's when adventure becomes available to the masses! *Everyone's* dish, not only Gable's! Then the people in the dark room come out of the dark room to have some adventures themselves—Goody, goody!—It's our turn now, to go to the South Sea Islands—to make a safari —to be exotic, far-off!—But I'm not patient. I don't want to wait till then. I'm tired of the *movies* and I am *about* to *move!*

JIM (*incredulously*). Move?

TOM. Yes.

JIM. When?

TOM. Soon!

JIM. Where? Where?

(*Theme three music seems to answer the question, while Tom thinks it over. He searches among his pockets.*)

TOM. I'm starting to boil inside. I know I seem dreamy, but inside—well, I'm boiling!—Whenever I pick up a shoe, I shudder a little thinking how short life is and what I am doing!—Whatever that means, I know it doesn't mean shoes—except as something to wear on a traveler's feet! (*Finds paper.*)   Look—

JIM. What?

TOM. I'm a member.

JIM (*reading*). The Union of Merchant Seamen.

TOM. I paid my dues this month, instead of the light bill.

JIM. You will regret it when they turn the lights off.

TOM. I won't be here.

JIM. How about your mother?

TOM. I'm like my father. The bastard son of a bastard! See how he grins? And he's been absent going on sixteen years!

JIM. You're just talking, you drip. How does your mother feel about it?

TOM. Shhh!—Here comes Mother! Mother is not acquainted with my plans!

AMANDA (*enters portieres*). Where are you all?

TOM. On the terrace, Mother.

(*They start inside. She advances to them.* TOM *is distinctly shocked at her appearance. Even* JIM *blinks a little. He is making his first contact with girlish Southern vivacity and in spite of the night-school course in public speaking is somewhat thrown off the beam by the unexpected outlay of social charm.*)

(*Certain responses are attempted by* JIM *but are swept aside by* AMANDA'S *gay laughter and chatter.* TOM *is embarrassed but after the first shock* JIM *reacts very warmly. Grins and chuckles, is altogether won over.)*

(IMAGE: AMANDA *as a girl.*)

AMANDA *(coyly smiling, shaking her girlish ringlets).* Well, well, well, so this is Mr. O'Connor. Introductions entirely unnecessary. I've heard so much about you from my boy. I finally said to him, Tom—good gracious! —why don't you bring this paragon to supper? I'd like to meet this nice young man at the warehouse!—Instead of just hearing you sing his praises so much! I don't know why my son is so stand-offish—that's not Southern behavior! Let's sit down and—I think we could stand a little more air in here! Tom, leave the door open. I felt a nice fresh breeze a moment ago. Where has it gone to? Mmm, so warm already! And not quite summer, even. We're going to burn up when summer really gets started. However, we're having—we're having a very light supper. I think light things are better fo' this time of year. The same as light clothes are. Light clothes an' light food are what warm weather calls fo'. You know our blood gets so thick during th' winter—it takes a while fo' us to *adjust* ou'selves!—when the season changes . . . . It's come so quick this year. I wasn't prepared. All of a sudden—heavens! Already summer!—I ran to the trunk an' pulled out this light dress—Terribly old! Historical almost! But feels so good—so good an' co-ol, y' know. . .

TOM. Mother—

AMANDA. Yes, honey?

TOM. How about—supper?

AMANDA. Honey, you go ask Sister if supper is ready! You know that Sister is in full charge of supper! Tell her you hungry boys are waiting for it. *(To Jim.)* Have you met Laura?

JIM. She—

AMANDA. Let you in? Oh, good, you've met already! It's rare for a girl as sweet an' pretty as Laura to be domestic! But Laura is, thank heavens, not only pretty but also very domestic. I'm not at all. I never was a bit. I never could make a thing but angel-food cake. Well, in the South we had so many servants. Gone, gone, gone. All vestige of gracious living! Gone completely! I wasn't prepared for what the future brought me. All of my gentlemen callers were sons of planters and so of course I assumed that I would be married to one and raise my family on a large piece of land with plenty of servants. But man proposes—and woman accepts the proposal!—To vary that old, old saying a little bit—I married no planter! I married a man who worked for the telephone company!— That gallantly smiling gentleman over there! *(Points to the picture.)* A telephone man who—fell in love with long distance!—Now he travels and I don't even know where!—But what am I going on for about my— tribulations? Tell me yours—I hope you don't have any! Tom?

TOM (*returning*). Yes, Mother?

AMANDA. Is supper nearly ready?

TOM. It looks to me like supper is on the table.

AMANDA. Let me look— (*She rises prettily and looks through portieres.*) Oh, lovely!—But where is Sister?

TOM. Laura is not feeling well and she says that she thinks she'd better not come to the table.

AMANDA. What?—Nonsense!—Laura? Oh, Laura!

LAURA (*off stage, faintly*). Yes, Mother.

AMANDA. You really must come to the table. We won't be seated until you come to the table! Come in, Mr. O'Connor. You sit over there, and I'll— Laura? Laura Wingfield! You're keeping us waiting, honey! We can't say grace until you come to the table!

(*The back door is pushed weakly open and* LAURA *comes in. She is obviously quite faint, her lips trembling, her eyes wide and staring. She moves unsteadily toward the table.*)

(LEGEND: "*Terror!*")

(*Outside a summer storm is coming abruptly. The white curtains billow inward at the windows and there is a sorrowful murmur and deep blue dusk.*)

(LAURA *suddenly stumbles—she catches at a chair with a faint moan.*)

TOM. Laura!

AMANDA. Laura!

(*There is a clap of thunder.*)

(LEGEND: "*Ah!*")

(*Despairingly.*)   Why, Laura, you *are* sick, darling! Tom, help your sister into the living room, dear! Sit in the living room, Laura—rest on the sofa. Well! (*To the gentleman caller.*)   Standing over the hot stove made her ill!—I told her that it was just too warm this evening, but— (TOM *comes back in.* LAURA *is on the sofa.*)   Is Laura all right now?

TOM. Yes.

AMANDA. What *is* that? Rain? A nice cool rain has come up. (*She gives the gentleman caller a frightened look.*)   I think we may—have grace— now . . . . (TOM *looks at her stupidly.*)   Tom, honey—you say grace!

TOM. Oh . . . . "For these and all thy mercies—" (*They bow their heads,* AMANDA *stealing a nervous glance at* JIM. *In the living room* LAURA, *stretched on the sofa, clenches her hand to her lips, to hold back a shuddering sob.*)   God's Holy Name be praised—

(*The scene dims out.*)

SCENE 7

A SOUVENIR.

(Half an hour later. Dinner is just being finished in the upstage area which is concealed by the drawn portieres.

As the curtain rises LAURA is still huddled upon the sofa, her feet drawn under her, her head resting on a pale blue pillow, her eyes wide and mysteriously watchful. The new floor lamp with its shade of rose-colored silk gives a soft, becoming light to her face, bringing out the fragile, unearthly prettiness which usually escapes attention. There is a steady murmur of rain, but it is slackening and stops soon after the scene begins; the air outside becomes pale and luminous as the moon breaks out.

A moment after the curtain rises, the lights in both rooms flicker and go out.)

JIM. Hey, there, Mr. Light Bulb!

(AMANDA *laughs nervously.*)

(LEGEND: *"Suspension of a public service."*)

AMANDA. Where was Moses when the lights went out? IIa-ha. Do you know the answer to that one, Mr. O'Connor?

JIM. No, Ma'am, what's the answer?

AMANDA. In the dark!   (JIM *laughs appreciatively.*)   Everybody sit still. I'll light the candles. Isn't it lucky we have them on the table? Where's a match? Which of you gentlemen can provide a match?

JIM. Here.

AMANDA. Thank you, sir.

JIM. Not at all, Ma'am!

AMANDA. I guess the fuse has burnt out. Mr. O'Connor, can you tell a burnt-out fuse? I know I can't and Tom is a total loss when it comes to mechanics. (SOUND: *Getting up: voices recede a little to kitchenette.*)   Oh, be careful you don't bump into something. We don't want our gentleman caller to break his neck. Now wouldn't that be a fine howdy-do?

JIM. Ha-ha! Where is the fuse-box?

AMANDA. Right here next to the stove. Can you see anything?

JIM. Just a minute.

AMANDA. Isn't electricity a mysterious thing? Wasn't it Benjamin Franklin who tied a key to a kite? We live in such a mysterious universe, don't we? Some people say that science clears up all the mysteries for us. In my opinion it only creates more! Have you found it yet?

JIM. No, Ma'am. All these fuses look okay to me.

AMANDA. Tom!

TOM. Yes, Mother?

AMANDA. That light bill I gave you several days ago. The one I told you we got the notices about?

(LEGEND: *"Ha!"*)

TOM. Oh.—Yeah.

AMANDA. Didn't! I might have known it!

JIM. Shakespeare probably wrote a poem on that light bill, Mrs. Wingfield.

AMANDA. I might have known better than to trust him with it! There's such a high price for negligence in this world!

JIM. Maybe the poem will win a ten-dollar prize.

AMANDA. We'll just have to spend the remainder of the evening in the nineteenth century, before Mr. Edison made the Mazda lamp!

JIM. Candlelight is my favorite kind of light.

AMANDA. That shows you're romantic! But that's no excuse for Tom. Well, we got through dinner. Very considerate of them to let us get through dinner before they plunged us into everlasting darkness, wasn't it, Mr. O'Connor?

JIM. Ha-ha!

AMANDA. Tom, as a penalty for your carelessness you can help me with the dishes.

JIM. Let me give you a hand.

AMANDA. Indeed you will not!

JIM. I ought to be good for something.

AMANDA. Good for something? (*Her tone is rhapsodic.*) *You?* Why, Mr. O'Connor, nobody, *nobody's* given me this much entertainment in years—as you have!

JIM. Aw, now, Mrs. Wingfield!

AMANDA. I'm not exaggerating, not one bit! But Sister is all by her lonesome. You go keep her company in the parlor! I'll give you this lovely old candelabrum that used to be on the altar at the church of the Heavenly Rest. It was melted a little out of shape when the church burnt down. Lightning struck it one spring. Gypsy Jones was holding a revival at the time and he intimated that the church was destroyed because the Episcopalians gave card parties.

JIM. Ha-ha.

AMANDA. And how about you coaxing Sister to drink a little wine? I think it would be good for her! Can you carry both at once?

JIM. Sure. I'm Superman!

AMANDA. Now, Thomas, get into this apron!

(*The door of kitchenette swings closed on* AMANDA'S *gay laughter; the flickering light approaches the portieres.*)

(LAURA *sits up nervously as he enters. Her speech at first is low and breathless from the almost intolerable strain of being alone with a stranger.*)

(THE LEGEND: *"I don't suppose you remember me at all!"*)

(*In her first speeches in this scene, before* JIM's *warmth overcomes her paralyzing shyness,* LAURA's *voice is thin and breathless as though she has just run up a steep flight of stairs.*)

(JIM's *attitude is gently humorous. In playing this scene it should be stressed that while the incident is apparently unimportant, it is to* LAURA *the climax of her secret life.*)

JIM. Hello, there, Laura.

LAURA (*faintly*). Hello.   (*She clears her throat.*)

JIM. How are you feeling now? Better?

LAURA. Yes. Yes, thank you.

JIM. This is for you. A little dandelion wine.   (*He extends it toward her with extravagant gallantry.*)

LAURA. Thank you.

JIM. Drink it—but don't get drunk!   (*He laughs heartily.* LAURA *takes the glass uncertainly; laughs shyly.*)   Where shall I set the candles?

LAURA. Oh—oh, anywhere . . .

JIM. How about here on the floor? Any objections?

LAURA. No.

JIM. I'll spread a newspaper under to catch the drippings. I like to sit on the floor. Mind if I do?

LAURA. Oh, no.

JIM. Give me a pillow?

LAURA. What?

JIM. A pillow!

LAURA. Oh . . .   (*Hands him one quickly.*)

JIM. How about you? Don't you like to sit on the floor?

LAURA. Oh—yes.

JIM. Why don't you, then?

LAURA. I—will.

JIM. Take a pillow!   (LAURA *does. Sits on the other side of the candelabrum.* JIM *crosses his legs and smiles engagingly at her.*)   I can't hardly see you sitting way over there.

LAURA. I can—see you.

JIM. I know, but that's not fair, I'm in the limelight.   (LAURA *moves her pillow closer.*)   Good! Now I can see you! Comfortable?

LAURA. Yes.

JIM. So am I. Comfortable as a cow! Will you have some gum?

LAURA. No, thank you.

JIM. I think that I will indulge, with your permission.   (*Musingly un-*

wraps it and holds it up.) Think of the fortune made by the guy that invented the first piece of chewing gum. Amazing, huh? The Wrigley Building is one of the sights of Chicago.—I saw it summer before last when I went up to the Century of Progress. Did you take in the Century of Progress?

LAURA. No, I didn't.

JIM. Well, it was quite a wonderful exposition. What impressed me most was the Hall of Science. Gives you an idea of what the future will be in America, even more wonderful than the present time is! (*Pause. Smiling at her.*) Your brother tells me you're shy. Is that right, Laura?

LAURA. I—don't know.

JIM. I judge you to be an old-fashioned type of girl. Well, I think that's a pretty good type to be. Hope you don't think I'm being too personal—do you?

LAURA (*hastily, out of embarrassment*). I believe I *will* take a piece of gum, if you—don't mind. (*Clearing her throat.*) Mr. O'Connor, have you—kept up with your singing?

JIM. Singing? Me?

LAURA. Yes. I remember what a beautiful voice you had.

JIM. When did you hear me sing?

(VOICE OFF STAGE IN THE PAUSE.)

VOICE (*off stage*).

> O blow, ye winds, heigh-ho,
> A-roving I will go!
> I'm off to my love
> With a boxing glove—
> Ten thousand miles away!

JIM. You say you've heard me sing?

LAURA. Oh, yes! Yes, very often . . . I don't suppose—you remember me—at all?

JIM (*smiling doubtfully*). You know I have an idea I've seen you before. I had that idea soon as you opened the door. It seemed almost like I was about to remember your name. But the name that I started to call you—wasn't a name! And so I stopped myself before I said it.

LAURA. Wasn't it—Blue Roses?

JIM (*springs up, grinning*). Blue Roses!—My gosh, yes—Blue Roses! That's what I had on my tongue when you opened the door! Isn't it funny what tricks your memory plays! I didn't connect you with high school somehow or other. But that's where it was; it was high school. I didn't even know you were Shakespeare's sister! Gosh, I'm sorry.

LAURA. I didn't expect you to. You—barely knew me!

JIM. But we did have a speaking acquaintance, huh?

LAURA. Yes, we—spoke to each other.

JIM. When did you recognize me?

LAURA. Oh, right away!

JIM. Soon as I came in the door?

LAURA. When I heard your name I thought it was probably you. I knew that Tom used to know you a little in high school. So when you came in the door—Well, then I was—sure.

JIM. Why didn't you *say* something, then?

LAURA (*breathlessly*). I didn't know what to say, I was—too surprised!

JIM. For goodness' sakes! You know, this sure is funny!

LAURA. Yes! Yes, isn't it, though . . .

JIM. Didn't we have a class in something together!

LAURA. Yes, we did.

JIM. What class was that?

LAURA. It was—singing—Chorus!

JIM. Aw!

LAURA. Mondays, Wednesdays and Fridays.

JIM. Now I remember—you always came in late.

LAURA. Yes, it was so hard for me, getting upstairs. I had that brace on my leg—it clumped so loud!

JIM. I never heard any clumping.

LAURA (*wincing at the recollection*). To me it sounded like—thunder!

JIM. Well, well, I never even noticed.

LAURA. And everybody was seated before I came in. I had to walk in front of all those people. My seat was in the back row. I had to go clumping all the way up the aisle with everyone watching!

JIM. You shouldn't have been self-conscious.

LAURA. I know, but I was. It was always such a relief when the singing started.

JIM. Aw, yes, I've placed you now! I used to call you Blue Roses. How was it that I got started calling you that?

LAURA. I was out of school a little while with pleurosis. When I came back you asked me what was the matter. I said I had pleurosis—you thought I said Blue Roses. That's what you always called me after that!

JIM. I hope you didn't mind.

LAURA. Oh, no—I liked it. You see, I wasn't acquainted with many—people. . . .

JIM. As I remember you sort of stuck by yourself.

LAURA. I—I—never have had much luck at—making friends.

JIM. I don't see why you wouldn't.

LAURA. Well, I—started out badly.

JIM. You mean being—

LAURA. Yes, it sort of—stood between me—

JIM. You shouldn't have let it!

LAURA. I know, but it did, and—

JIM. You were shy with people!

LAURA. I tried not to be but never could—

JIM. Overcome it?

LAURA. No, I—I never could!

JIM. I guess being shy is something you have to work out of kind of gradually.

LAURA (*sorrowfully*). Yes—I guess it—

JIM. Takes time!

LAURA. Yes—

JIM. People are not so dreadful when you know them. That's what you have to remember! And everybody has problems, not just you, but practically everybody has got some problems. You think of yourself as having the only problems, as being the only one who is disappointed. But just look around you and you will see lots of people as disappointed as you are. For instance, I hoped when I was going to high school that I would be further along at this time, six years later, than I am now— You remember that wonderful write-up I had in *The Torch?*

LAURA. Yes! (*She rises and crosses to table.*)

JIM. It said I was bound to succeed in anything I went into! (LAURA *returns with the annual.*) Holy Jeez! *The Torch!* (*He accepts it reverently. They smile across it with mutual wonder.* LAURA *crouches beside him and they begin to turn through it.* LAURA's *shyness is dissolving in his warmth.*)

LAURA. Here you are in *The Pirates of Penzance!*

JIM (*wistfully*). I sang the baritone lead in that operetta.

LAURA (*raptly*). So—*beautifully!*

JIM (*protesting*). Aw—

LAURA. Yes, yes—beautifully—beautifully!

JIM. You heard me?

LAURA. All three times!

JIM. No!

LAURA. Yes!

JIM. All three performances?

LAURA (*looking down*). Yes.

JIM. Why?

LAURA. I—wanted to ask you to—autograph my program.

JIM. Why didn't you ask me to?

LAURA. You were always surrounded by your own friends so much that I never had a chance to.

JIM. You should have just—

LAURA. Well, I—thought you might think I was—

JIM. Thought I might think you was—what?

LAURA. Oh—

JIM (*with reflective relish*). I was beleaguered by females in those days.

LAURA. You were terribly popular!

JIM. Yeah—

LAURA. You had such a—friendly way—

JIM. I was spoiled in high school.

LAURA. Everybody—liked you!

JIM. Including you?

LAURA. I—yes, I—I did, too— (*She gently closes the book in her lap.*)

JIM. Well, well, well!—Give me that program, Laura. (*She hands it to him. He signs it with a flourish.*)   There you are—better late than never!

LAURA. Oh, I—what a—surprise!

JIM. My signature isn't worth very much right now. But some day—maybe—it will increase in value! Being disappointed is one thing and being discouraged is something else. I am disappointed but I am not discouraged. I'm twenty-three years old. How old are you?

LAURA. I'll be twenty-four in June.

JIM. That's not old age!

LAURA. No, but—

JIM. You finished high school?

LAURA (*with difficulty*). I didn't go back.

JIM. You mean you dropped out?

LAURA. I made bad grades in my final examinations. (*She rises and replaces the book and the program. Her voice strained.*)   How is—Emily Meisenbach getting along?

JIM. Oh, that kraut-head!

LAURA. Why do you call her that?

JIM. That's what she was.

LAURA. You're not still—going with her?

JIM. I never see her.

LAURA. It said in the Personal Section that you were—engaged!

JIM. I know, but I wasn't impressed by that—propaganda!

LAURA. It wasn't—the truth?

JIM. Only in Emily's optimistic opinion!

LAURA. Oh—

(LEGEND: *"What have you done since high school?"*)

(JIM *lights a cigarette and leans indolently back on his elbows smiling at* LAURA *with a warmth and charm which lights her inwardly with altar candles. She remains by the table and turns in her hands a piece of glass to cover her tumult.*)

JIM (*after several reflective puffs on a cigarette*). What have you done since high school? (*She seems not to hear him.*) Huh? (LAURA *looks up.*)   I said what have you done since high school, Laura?

LAURA. Nothing much.

JIM. You must have been doing something these six long years.

LAURA. Yes.

JIM. Well, then, such as what?

LAURA. I took a business course at business college—

JIM. How did that work out?

LAURA. Well, not very—well—I had to drop out, it gave me—indigestion—

(JIM *laughs gently.*)

JIM. What are you doing now?

LAURA. I don't do anything—much. Oh, please don't think I sit around doing nothing! My glass collection takes up a good deal of time. Glass is something you have to take good care of.

JIM. What did you say—about glass?

LAURA. Collection I said—I have one— (*She clears her throat and turns away again, acutely shy.*)

JIM (*abruptly*). You know what I judge to be the trouble with you? Inferiority complex! Know what that is? That's what they call it when someone low-rates himself! I understand it because I had it, too. Although my case was not so aggravated as yours seems to be. I had it until I took up public speaking, developed my voice, and learned that I had an aptitude for science. Before that time I never thought of myself as being outstanding in any way whatsoever! Now I've never made a regular study of it, but I have a friend who says I can analyze people better than doctors that make a profession of it. I don't claim that to be necessarily true, but I can sure guess a person's psychology, Laura! (*takes out his gum*) Excuse me, Laura. I always take it out when the flavor is gone. I'll use this scrap of paper to wrap it in. I know how it is to get it stuck on a shoe. Yep—that's what I judge to be your principal trouble. A lack of confidence in yourself as a person. You don't have the proper amount of faith in yourself. I'm basing that fact on a number of your remarks and also on certain observations I've made. For instance that clumping you thought was so awful in high school. You said that you even dreaded to walk into class. You see what you did? You dropped out of school, you gave up an education because of a clump, which as far as I know was practically non-existent! A little physical defect is what you have. Hardly noticeable even! Magnified thousands of times by imagination! You know what my strong advice to you is? Think of yourself as *superior* in some way!

LAURA. In what way would I think?

JIM. Why, man alive, Laura! Just look about you a little. What do you see? A world full of common people! All of 'em born and all of 'em going to die! Which of them has one-tenth of your good points! Or mine! Or anyone else's, as far as that goes—Gosh! Everybody excels in some one thing. Some in many! (*Unconsciously glances at himself in the mirror.*) All you've got to do is discover in *what!* Take me, for instance. (*He adjusts his tie at the mirror.*) My interest happens to lie in electrodynamics. I'm taking a course in radio engineering at night school,

Laura, on top of a fairly responsible job at the warehouse. I'm taking that course and studying public speaking.

LAURA. Ohhhh.

JIM. Because I believe in the future of television! (*Turning back to her.*) I wish to be ready to go up right along with it. Therefore I'm planning to get in on the ground floor. In fact I've already made the right connections and all that remains is for the industry itself to get under way! Full steam— (*His eyes are starry.*) *Knowledge—Zzzzzp! Money— Zzzzzzp!—Power!* That's the cycle democracy is built on! (*His attitude is convincingly dynamic.* LAURA *stares at him, even her shyness eclipsed in her absolute wonder. He suddenly grins.*) I guess you think I think a lot of myself!

LAURA. No—o-o-o, I—

JIM. Now how about you? Isn't there something you take more interest in than anything else?

LAURA. Well, I do—as I said—have my—glass collection— (*A peal of girlish laughter from the kitchen.*)

JIM. I'm not right sure I know what you're talking about. What kind of glass is it?

LAURA. Little articles of it, they're ornaments mostly! Most of them are little animals made out of glass, the tiniest little animals in the world. Mother calls them a glass menagerie! Here's an example of one, if you'd like to see it! This one is one of the oldest. It's nearly thirteen. (MUSIC: "*The Glass Menagerie.*") (*He stretches out his hand.*) Oh, be careful— if you breathe, it breaks!

JIM. I'd better not take it. I'm pretty clumsy with things.

LAURA. Go on, I trust you with him! (*Places it in his palm.*) There now— you're holding him gently! Hold him over the light, he loves the light! You see how the light shines through him?

JIM. It sure does shine!

LAURA. I shouldn't be partial, but he is my favorite one.

JIM. What kind of a thing is this one supposed to be?

LAURA. Haven't you noticed the single horn on his forehead?

JIM. A unicorn, huh?

LAURA. Mmm-hmmm!

JIM. Unicorns, aren't they extinct in the modern world?

LAURA. I know!

JIM. Poor little fellow, he must feel sort of lonesome.

LAURA (*smiling*). Well, if he does he doesn't complain about it. He stays on a shelf with some horses that don't have horns and all of them seem to get along nicely together.

JIM. How do you know?

LAURA (*lightly*). I haven't heard any arguments among them!

JIM (*grinning*). No arguments, huh? Well, that's a pretty good sign! Where shall I set him?

LAURA. Put him on the table. They all like a change of scenery once in a while!

JIM (*stretching*). Well, well, well, well—Look how big my shadow is when I stretch!

LAURA. Oh, oh, yes—it stretches across the ceiling!

JIM (*crossing to door*). I think it's stopped raining. (*Opens fire-escape door.*)   Where does the music come from?

LAURA. From the Paradise Dance Hall across the alley.

JIM. How about cutting the rug a little, Miss Wingfield?

LAURA. Oh, I—

JIM. Or is your program filled up? Let me have a look at it. (*Grasps imaginary card.*) Why, every dance is taken! I'll just have to scratch some out. (WALTZ MUSIC: "*La Golondrina.*") Ahhh, a waltz! (*He executes some sweeping turns by himself then holds his arms toward* LAURA.)

LAURA (*breathlessly*). I—can't dance!

JIM. There you go, that inferiority stuff.

LAURA. I've never danced in my life!

JIM. Come on, try!

LAURA. Oh, but I'd step on you!

JIM. I'm not made of glass.

LAURA. How—how—how do we start?

JIM. Just leave it to me. You hold your arms out a little.

LAURA. Like this?

JIM. A little bit higher. Right. Now don't tighten up, that's the main thing about it—relax.

LAURA (*laughing breathlessly*). It's hard not to.

JIM. Okay.

LAURA. I'm afraid you can't budge me.

JIM. What do you bet I can't?   (*He swings her into motion.*)

LAURA. Goodness, yes, you can!

JIM. Let yourself go, now, Laura, just let yourself go.

LAURA. I'm—

JIM. Come on!

LAURA. Trying!

JIM. Not so stiff—Easy does it!

LAURA. I know but I'm—

JIM. Loosen th' backbone! There now, that's a lot better.

LAURA. Am I?

JIM. Lots, lots better!   (*He moves her about the room in a clumsy waltz.*)

LAURA. Oh, my!

JIM. Ha-ha!

LAURA. Oh, my goodness!

JIM. Ha-ha-ha!   (*They suddenly bump into the table.* JIM *stops.*)   What did we hit on?

LAURA. Table.

JIM. Did something fall off it? I think—

LAURA. Yes.

JIM. I hope that it wasn't the little glass horse with the horn!

LAURA. Yes.

JIM. Aw, aw, aw. Is it broken?

LAURA. Now it is just like all the other horses.

JIM. It's lost it's—

LAURA. Horn! It doesn't matter. Maybe it's a blessing in disguise.

JIM. You'll never forgive me. I bet that that was your favorite piece of glass.

LAURA. I don't have favorites much. It's no tragedy, Freckles. Glass breaks so easily. No matter how careful you are. The traffic jars the shelves and things fall off them.

JIM. Still I'm awfully sorry that I was the cause.

LAURA (*smiling*). I'll just imagine he had an operation. The horn was removed to make him feel less—freakish! (*They both laugh.*) Now he will feel more at home with the other horses, the ones that don't have horns. . . .

JIM. Ha-ha, that's very funny! (*Suddenly serious.*) I'm glad to see that you have a sense of humor. You know—you're—well—very different! Surprisingly different from anyone else I know! (*His voice becomes soft and hesitant with a genuine feeling.*) Do you mind me telling you that? (LAURA *is abashed beyond speech.*) I mean it in a nice way . . . . (LAURA *nods shyly, looking away.*) You make me feel sort of—I don't know how to put it! I'm usually pretty good at expressing things, but— This is something that I don't know how to say! (LAURA *touches her throat and clears it—turns the broken unicorn in her hands.*) (*Even softer.*) Has anyone ever told you that you were pretty? (*Pause: music.*) (LAURA *looks up slowly, with wonder, and shakes her head.*) Well, you are! In a very different way from anyone else. And all the nicer because of the difference, too. (*His voice becomes low and husky.* LAURA *turns away, nearly faint with the novelty of her emotions.*) I wish that you were my sister. I'd teach you to have some confidence in yourself. The different people are not like other people, but being different is nothing to be ashamed of. Because other people are not such wonderful people. They're one hundred times one thousand. You're one times one! They walk all over the earth. You just stay here. They're common as—weeds, but—you—well, you're *Blue Roses!*

(IMAGE ON SCREEN: *Blue Roses.*)

(*Music changes.*)

LAURA. But blue is wrong for—roses . . .

JIM. It's right for you!—You're—pretty!

LAURA. In what respect am I pretty?

Jim. In all respects—believe me! Your eyes—your hair—are pretty! Your hands are pretty! (*He catches hold of her hand.*) You think I'm making this up because I'm invited to dinner and have to be nice. Oh, I could do that! I could put on an act for you, Laura, and say lots of things without being very sincere. But this time I am. I'm talking to you sincerely. I happened to notice you had this inferiority complex that keeps you from feeling comfortable with people. Somebody needs to build your confidence up and make you proud instead of shy and turning away and—blushing—Somebody—ought to—Ought to—*kiss* you, Laura! (*His hand slips slowly up her arm to her shoulder.*) (*Music swells tumultuously.*) (*He suddenly turns her about and kisses her on the lips.*) (*When he releases her,* Laura *sinks on the sofa with a bright, dazed look.*) (Jim *backs away and fishes in his pocket for a cigarette.*)

(Legend on screen: *"Souvenir."*)

Stumble-john! (*He lights the cigarette, avoiding her look.*) (*There is a peal of girlish laughter from* Amanda *in the kitchen.*) (Laura *slowly raises and opens her hand. It still contains the little broken glass animal. She looks at it with a tender, bewildered expression.*) Stumble-john! I shouldn't have done that—That was way off the beam. You don't smoke, do you? (*She looks up, smiling, not hearing the question.*) (*He sits beside her a little gingerly. She looks at him speechlessly—waiting.*) (*He coughs decorously and moves a little farther aside as he considers the situation and senses her feelings, dimly, with perturbation.*) (*Gently.*) Would you—care for a—mint? (*She doesn't seem to hear him but her look grows brighter even.*) Peppermint—Life-Saver? My pocket's a regular drug store—wherever I go . . . . (*He pops a mint in his mouth. Then gulps and decides to make a clean breast of it. He speaks slowly and gingerly.*) Laura, you know, if I had a sister like you, I'd do the same thing as Tom. I'd bring out fellows and—introduce her to them. The right type of boys of a type to—appreciate her. Only—well—he made a mistake about me. Maybe I've got no call to be saying this. That may not have been the idea in having me over. But what if it was? There's nothing wrong about that. The only trouble is that in my case—I'm not in a situation to—do the right thing. I can't take down your number and say I'll phone. I can't call up next week and—ask for a date. I thought I had better explain the situation in case you—misunderstood it and—hurt your feelings. . . . (*Pause.*) (*Slowly, very slowly,* Laura's *look changes, her eyes returning slowly from his to the ornament in her palm.*) (Amanda *utters another gay laugh in the kitchen.*)

Laura (*faintly*). You—won't—call again?

Jim. No, Laura, I can't. (*He rises from the sofa.*) As I was just explaining, I've—got strings on me. Laura, I've—been going steady! I go out all the time with a girl named Betty. She's a home-girl like you, and Catholic, and Irish, and in a great many ways we—get along fine. I met her last summer on a moonlight boat trip up the river to Alton, on the *Majestic*. Well—right away from the start it was—love!

(LEGEND: *Love!*)

(LAURA *sways slightly forward and grips the arm of the sofa. He fails to notice, now enrapt in his own comfortable being.*)   Being in love has made a new man of me!   (*Leaning stiffly forward, clutching the arm of the sofa,* LAURA *struggles visibly with her storm. But* JIM *is oblivious, she is a long way off.*)   The power of love is really pretty tremendous! Love is something that—changes the whole world, Laura!   (*The storm abates a little and* LAURA *leans back. He notices her again.*)   It happened that Betty's aunt took sick, she got a wire and had to go to Centralia. So Tom—when he asked me to dinner—I naturally just accepted the invitation, not knowing that you—that he—that I—   (*He stops awkwardly.*)   Huh—I'm a stumble-john!   (*He flops back on the sofa.*)   (*The holy candles in the altar of* LAURA'S *face have been snuffed out. There is a look of almost infinite desolation.*)   (JIM *glances at her uneasily.*)   I wish that you would—say something.   (*She bites her lip which was trembling and then bravely smiles. She opens her hand again on the broken glass ornament. Then she gently takes his hand and raises it level with her own. She carefully places the unicorn in the palm of his hand, then pushes his fingers closed upon it.*)   What are you—doing that for? You want me to have him?—Laura?   (*She nods.*)   What for?

LAURA. A—souvenir . . . .

(*She rises unsteadily and crouches beside the victrola to wind it up.*)

(LEGEND ON SCREEN: *"Things have a way of turning out so badly!"*)

(OR IMAGE: *"Gentleman caller waving good-bye!—gaily."*)

(*At this moment* AMANDA *rushes brightly back in the front room. She bears a pitcher of fruit punch in an old-fashioned cut-glass pitcher and a plate of macaroons. The plate has a gold border and poppies painted on it.*)

AMANDA. Well, well, well! Isn't the air delightful after the shower? I've made you children a little liquid refreshment.   (*Turns gaily to the gentleman caller.*)   Jim, do you know that song about lemonade?

> "Lemonade, lemonade
> Made in the shade and stirred with a spade—
> Good enough for any old maid!"

JIM (*uneasily*). Ha-ha! No—I never heard it.
AMANDA. Why Laura! You look so serious!

JIM. We were having a serious conversation.

AMANDA. Good! Now you're better acquainted!

JIM (*uncertainly*). Ha-ha! Yes.

AMANDA. You modern young people are much more serious-minded than my generation. I was so gay as a girl!

JIM. You haven't changed, Mrs. Wingfield.

AMANDA. Tonight I'm rejuvenated! The gaiety of the occasion, Mr. O'Connor! (*She tosses her head with a peal of laughter. Spills lemonade.*) Oooo! I'm baptizing myself!

JIM. Here—let me—

AMANDA (*setting the pitcher down*). There now. I discovered we had some maraschino cherries. I dumped them in, juice and all!

JIM. You shouldn't have gone to that trouble, Mrs. Wingfield.

AMANDA. Trouble, trouble? Why, it was loads of fun! Didn't you hear me cutting up in the kitchen? I bet your ears were burning! I told Tom how outdone with him I was for keeping you to himself so long a time! He should have brought you over much, much sooner! Well, now that you've found your way, I want you to be a very frequent caller! Not just occasional but all the time. Oh, we're going to have a lot of gay times together! I see them coming! Mmmm, just breathe that air! So fresh, and the moon's so pretty! I'll skip back out—I know where my place is when young folks are having a—serious conversation!

JIM. Oh, don't go out, Mrs. Wingfield. The fact of the matter is I've got to be going.

AMANDA. Going, now? You're joking! Why, it's only the shank of the evening, Mr. O'Connor!

JIM. Well, you know how it is.

AMANDA. You mean you're a young workingman and have to keep workingmen's hours. We'll let you off early tonight. But only on the condition that next time you stay later. What's the best night for you? Isn't Saturday night the best night for you workingmen?

JIM. I have a couple of time-clocks to punch, Mrs. Wingfield. One at morning, another one at night!

AMANDA. My, but you *are* ambitious! You work at night, too?

JIM. No, Ma'am, not work but—Betty! (*He crosses deliberately to pick up his hat. The band at the Paradise Dance Hall goes into a tender waltz.*)

AMANDA. Betty? Betty? Who's—Betty! (*There is an ominous cracking sound in the sky.*)

JIM. Oh, just a girl. The girl I go steady with! (*He smiles charmingly. The sky falls.*)

(LEGEND: *"The sky falls."*)

AMANDA (*a long-drawn exhalation*). Ohhhh . . . Is it a serious romance, Mr. O'Connor?

JIM. We're going to be married the second Sunday in June.

AMANDA. Ohhhh—how nice! Tom didn't mention that you were engaged to be married.

JIM. The cat's not out of the bag at the warehouse yet. You know how they are. They call you Romeo and stuff like that. (*He stops at the oval mirror to put on his hat. He carefully shapes the brim and the crown to give a discreetly dashing effect.*) It's been a wonderful evening, Mrs. Wingfield. I guess this is what they mean by Southern hospitality.

AMANDA. It really wasn't anything at all.

JIM. I hope it don't seem like I'm rushing off. But I promised Betty I'd pick her up at the Wabash depot, an' by the time I get my jalopy down there her train'll be in. Some women are pretty upset if you keep 'em waiting.

AMANDA. Yes, I know—The tyranny of women! (*Extends her hand.*) Good-bye, Mr. O'Connor. I wish you luck—and happiness—and success! All three of them, and so does Laura!—Don't you, Laura?

LAURA. Yes!

JIM (*taking her hand*). Good-bye, Laura. I'm certainly going to treasure that souvenir. And don't you forget the good advice I gave you. (*Raises his voice to a cheery shout.*) So long, Shakespeare! Thanks again, ladies—Good night!

(*He grins and ducks jauntily out.*)

(*Still bravely grimacing,* AMANDA *closes the door on the gentleman caller. Then she turns back to the room with a puzzled expression. She and* LAURA *don't dare to face each other.* LAURA *crouches beside the victrola to wind it.*)

AMANDA (*faintly*). Things have a way of turning out so badly. I don't believe that I would play the victrola. Well, well—well—Our gentleman caller was engaged to be married! Tom!

TOM (*from back*). Yes, Mother?

AMANDA. Come in here a minute. I want to tell you something awfully funny.

TOM (*enters with .nacaroon and a glass of lemonade*). Has the gentleman caller gotten away already?

AMANDA. The gentleman caller has made an early departure. What a wonderful joke you played on us!

TOM. How do you mean?

AMANDA. You didn't mention that he was engaged to be married.

TOM. Jim? Engaged?

AMANDA. That's what he just informed us.

TOM. I'll be jiggered! I didn't know about that.

AMANDA. That seems very peculiar.

TOM. What's peculiar about it?

AMANDA. Didn't you call him your best friend down at the warehouse?

TOM. He is, but how did I know?

AMANDA. It seems extremely peculiar that you wouldn't know your best friend was going to be married!

TOM. The warehouse is where I work, not where I know things about people!

AMANDA. You don't know things anywhere! You live in a dream; you manufacture illusions! (*He crosses to door.*)   Where are you going?

TOM. I'm going to the movies.

AMANDA. That's right, now that you've had us make such fools of ourselves. The effort, the preparations, all the expense! The new floor lamp, the rug, the clothes for Laura! All for what? To entertain some other girl's fiancé! Go to the movies, go! Don't think about us, a mother deserted, an unmarried sister who's crippled and has no job! Don't let anything interfere with your selfish pleasure! Just go, go, go—to the movies!

TOM. All right, I will! The more you shout about my selfishness to me the quicker I'll go, and I won't go to the movies!

AMANDA. Go, then! Then go to the moon—you selfish dreamer!

(TOM *smashes his glass on the floor. He plunges out on the fire-escape, slamming the door.* LAURA *screams—cut by door.*)

(*Dance-hall music up.* TOM *goes to the rail and grips it desperately, lifting his face in the chill white moonlight penetrating the narrow abyss of the alley.*)

(LEGEND ON SCREEN: "*And so good-bye . . .*")

(TOM'S *closing speech is timed with the interior pantomime. The interior scene is played as though viewed through soundproof glass.* AMANDA *appears to be making a comforting speech to* LAURA *who is huddled upon the sofa. Now that we cannot hear the mother's speech, her silliness is gone and she has dignity and tragic beauty.* LAURA'S *dark hair hides her face until at the end of the speech she lifts it to smile at her mother.* AMANDA'S *gestures are slow and graceful, almost dancelike, as she comforts the daughter. At the end of her speech she glances a moment at the father's picture—then withdraws through the portieres. At the close of* TOM'S *speech,* LAURA *blows out the candles, ending the play.*)

TOM. I didn't go to the moon, I went much further—for time is the longest distance between two places—Not long after that I was fired for writing a poem on the lid of a shoe-box. I left Saint Louis. I descended the steps of this fire-escape for a last time and followed, from then on, in my father's footsteps, attempting to find in motion what was lost in space— I traveled around a great deal. The cities swept about me like dead leaves, leaves that were brightly colored but torn away from the branches. I would have stopped, but I was pursued by something. It always came upon me unawares, taking me altogether by surprise. Perhaps it was a familiar bit of music. Perhaps it was only a piece of transparent glass—

Perhaps I am walking along a street at night, in some strange city, before I have found companions. I pass the lighted window of a shop where perfume is sold. The window is filled with pieces of colored glass, tiny transparent bottles in delicate colors, like bits of a shattered rainbow. Then all at once my sister touches my shoulder. I turn around and look into her eyes . . . . Oh, Laura, Laura, I tried to leave you behind me, but I am more faithful than I intended to be! I reach for a cigarette, I cross the street, I run into the movies or a bar, I buy a drink, I speak to the nearest stranger—anything that can blow your candles out! (LAURA *bends over the candles.*) —for nowadays the world is lit by lightning! Blow out your candles, Laura—and so good-bye. . . .

(She blows the candles out.)

(The scene dissolves.)

POETIC EXPERIENCE

public poems
and
private visions

CONTENTS

English Lyrical Ballads

> *The Twa Corbies* 295
> *Edward* 296
> *Sir Patrick Spens* 297

Christopher Marlowe

> *The Passionate Shepherd to His Love* 300

Sir Walter Raleigh

> *The Nymph's Reply to the Shepherd* 301

Edmund Spenser

> from *Amoretti*
>> *XXXI. Ah! why hath Nature to so hard a heart*
>> 302
>> *LXXIX. Men call you fair, and you do credit*
>> *it* 302

William Shakespeare: Cycle of Conflict

> SONNETS
>> *I. From fairest creatures we desire increase*
>> 304
>> *II. When forty winters shall besiege thy brow*
>> 305
>> *XII. When I do count the clock that tells the*
>> *time* 305
>> *XVIII. Shall I compare thee to a summer's day?*
>> 306
>> *XIX. Devouring Time, blunt thou the lion's*
>> *paws* 306
>> *XXIX. When, in disgrace with fortune and men's*
>> *eyes* 307
>> *XXX. When to the sessions of sweet silent*
>> *thought* 307
>> *XXXV. No more be grieved at that which thou*
>> *hast done* 308
>> *XLII. That thou hast her, it is not all my grief*
>> 308
>> *LV. Not marble, nor the gilded monuments*
>> 309
>> *LXV. Since brass, nor stone, nor earth, nor*
>> *boundless sea* 309

LXVIII. *Thus is his cheek the map of days outworn* 310

LXXIII. *That time of year thou mayst in me behold* 310

LXXXVI. *Was it the proud full sail of his great verse* 310

XCIV. *They that have power to hurt and will do none* 311

XCV. *How sweet and lovely dost thou make the shame* 312

CVI. *When in the chronicle of wasted time* 312

CXVI. *Let me not to the marriage of true minds* 313

CXXVII. *In the old age black was not counted fair* 313

CXXIX. *The expense of spirit in a waste of shame* 314

CXXX. *My mistress' eyes are nothing like the sun* 314

CXXXVIII. *When my love swears that she is made of truth* 315

CXLIV. *Two loves I have of comfort and despair* 315

CXLVI. *Poor soul, the centre of my sinful earth* 316

CXLVII. *My love is as a fever, longing still* 316

CLII. *In loving thee thou know'st I am forsworn* 317

John Donne: From Eros to Agape

Community 318
Song (Go and catch a falling star) 319
The Apparition 320
A Valediction: Of Weeping 320
The Flea 321
The Sun Rising 322
A Valediction: Forbidding Mourning 323
The Ecstasy 324
The Canonization 327
HOLY SONNETS
VII. *At the round earth's imagined corners, blow* 328
X. *Death be not proud, though some have called thee* 329

287

XIII. *What if this present were the world's last night?* 329

XIV. *Batter my heart, three-personed God; for You* 330

Ben Jonson

Come, My Celia 331
Still to Be Neat 331

Robert Herrick

Delight in Disorder 333
Upon Julia's Clothes 333
Corinna's Going A-Maying 334

Andrew Marvell

To His Coy Mistress 336

John Milton

On His Having Arrived at the Age of Twenty-Three 338
On His Blindness 338

Alexander Pope

from *An Essay on Man*
from *Epistle I. Of the Nature and State of Man, With Respect to the Universe* 340
from *Epistle II. Of the Nature and State of Man with Respect to Himself, as an Individual* 345

Thomas Gray

Elegy Written in a Country Churchyard 346

Robert Burns

To a Mouse 350
Auld Lang Syne 351

William Blake: Innocence and Experience

To Spring 353
To Autumn 353
The Blossom 354
Ah! Sun-flower 354
The Sick Rose 355
The Lamb 355
The Tyger 356

The Fly   357
Song (My silks and fine array)   357
The Divine Image   358
from *Songs of Innocence*
    The Chimney Sweeper   359
from *Songs of Experience*
    The Chimney Sweeper   360
The Garden of Love   360
I Asked a Thief to Steal Me a Peach   360
London   361
The Clod and the Pebble   362
A Poison Tree   362
Mad Song   363
Are Not the Joys of Morning Sweeter   363
O Lapwing, Thou Fliest Around the Heath
    364
Thou Hast a Lap Full of Seed   364
Preface to Milton   364

William Wordsworth

Composed upon Westminster Bridge   366
The World Is Too Much with Us   366

Samuel Taylor Coleridge

Kubla Khan   368

George Noel Gordon, Lord Byron

She Walks in Beauty   370
When a Man Hath No Freedom   370

Percy Bysshe Shelley

Ode to the West Wind   372
Ozymandias   375

John Keats

To Autumn   376
Ode on a Grecian Urn   377

Alfred, Lord Tennyson

Ulysses   379
The Eagle: A Fragment   381

Robert Browning

Porphyria's Lover   382
My Last Duchess   383

      Meeting at Night   385

Matthew Arnold

    Dover Beach   386

Walt Whitman

    Out of the Cradle Endlessly Rocking   388
    When I Heard the Learn'd Astronomer   393

Emily Dickinson: Aesthetics of Estrangement

    613: *They shut me up in Prose*   394
    501: *This World is not Conclusion*   394
  1400: *What mystery pervades a well!*   395
  1068: *Further in Summer than the Birds*   396
  1593: *There came a Wind like a Bugle*   396
   519: *'Twas warm – at first – like Us*   397
   547: *I've seen a Dying Eye*   397
   465: *I heard a Fly buzz – when I died*   398
   712: *Because I could not stop for Death*   398
   670: *One need not be a Chamber – to be Haunted*   399
   258: *There's a certain Slant of light*   400
   280: *I felt a Funeral, in my Brain*   400
   341: *After great pain, a formal feeling comes*   401
   822: *This Consciousness that is aware*   401
   508: *I'm ceded – I've stopped being Theirs*   402
   326: *I cannot dance upon my Toes*   402
   675: *Essential Oils – are wrung*   403
  1129: *Tell all the Truth but tell it slant*   403
  1071: *Perception of an object costs*   404
   290: *Of Bronze – and Blaze*   404
   451: *The Outer – from the Inner*   405
   328: *A Bird came down the Walk*   405
  1261: *A word dropped careless on a Page*   406
  1651: *A Word made Flesh is seldom*   406

Gerard Manley Hopkins

    God's Grandeur   407
    Pied Beauty   407
    Spring and Fall   408

Thomas Hardy

    Channel Firing   409
    The Convergence of the Twain   410

A. E. Housman

    Terence, This Is Stupid Stuff   412

Rupert Brooke
>   *Heaven*   415

Wilfred Owen
>   *Dulce et Decorum Est*   417

William Butler Yeats: The Dominion of the Imagination
>   *Down by the Salley Gardens*   418
>   *Adam's Curse*   418
>   *The Fascination of What's Difficult*   420
>   *A Dialogue of Self and Soul*   420
>   *Crazy Jane Talks with the Bishop*   422
>   *The Lake Isle of Innisfree*   423
>   *The Wild Old Wicked Man*   423
>   *Why Should Not Old Men Be Mad?*   425
>   *The Song of Wandering Aengus*   426
>   *Sailing to Byzantium*   426
>   *Easter, 1916*   428
>   *The Second Coming*   430
>   *Leda and the Swan*   431
>   *Lapis Lazuli*   432

Robert Frost
>   *Birches*   434
>   *Once by the Pacific*   435

T. S. Eliot
>   *The Love Song of J. Alfred Prufrock*   437
>   *Journey of the Magi*   441

William Carlos Williams
>   *The Yachts*   443
>   *Spring and All*   444
>   *The Red Wheelbarrow*   445

Ezra Pound
>   *In a Station of the Metro*   446
>   *The River-Merchant's Wife: A Letter*   446
>   *Ancient Music*   447

H. D. (Hilda Doolittle)
>   *Hymn*   448

Claude McKay
>   *America*   449

Edna St. Vincent Millay

    Spring   450
    Siege   450

E. E. Cummings

    anyone lived in a pretty how town   452
    if i have made, my lady, intricate   453

Wallace Stevens

    Thirteen Ways of Looking at a Blackbird   454
    Sunday Morning   456

W. H. Auden

    O Where Are You Going   460
    Mundus et Infans   460

Theodore Roethke

    The Waking   463
    My Papa's Waltz   463

Kenneth Patchen

    O When I Take My Love Out Walking   465

Robert E. Hayden

    The Diver   466

Dylan Thomas

    The Force That through the Green Fuse Drives the Flower   468
    Do Not Go Gentle into That Good Night   469

Gwendolyn Brooks

    from *The Children of the Poor*
        #4: First fight. Then fiddle. Ply the slipping string   470

Lawrence Ferlinghetti

    The Pennycandystore   471

Alan Dugan

    Tribute to Kafka for Someone Taken   472

James Dickey

    The Performance   473

Leonard E. Nathan

      Fall's Girl   475

Lucien Stryk

      The Cannery   476
      The Pit   476

Gary Snyder

      from *Myths & Texts (Hunting)*
          #8 *"this poem is for deer"*   478

LeRoi Jones

      An Agony. As Now.   480

English Lyrical Ballads

THE TWA CORBIES

As I was walking all alane,
I heard twa corbies making a mane;
The tane unto the t'other say,
"Where sall we gang and dine-to-day?"

"In behint yon auld fail dyke,   5
I wot there lies a new slain knight;
And naebody kens that he lies there,
But his hawk, his hound, and lady fair.

"His hound is to the hunting gane,
His hawk to fetch the wild-fowl hame,   10
His lady's ta'en another mate,
So we may mak' our dinner sweet.

"Ye'll sit on his white hause-bane,
And I'll pike out his bonny blue e'en;
Wi' ae lock o' his gowden hair   15
We'll theek our nest when it grows bare.

"Mony a ane for him makes mane,
But nane sall ken where he is gane;
O'er his white banes, when they are bare,
The wind sall blaw for evermair."   20

TWA CORBIES. two crows. 1. *alane*, alone. 2. *mane*, moan, plaint. 3. *tane*, the, the one. 4. *sall we gang*, shall we go. 5. *auld fail dyke*, old turf wall. 7. *kens*, knows. 13. *hause-bane*, neck-bone. 14. *e'en*, eye. 15. *wi'ae*, with a. 16. *theek*, thatch.

EDWARD

"Why dois your brand sae drap wi bluid,
    Edward, Edward,
Why dois your brand sae drap wi bluid,
    And why sae sad gang yee O?"
"O I hae killed my hauke sae guid,   5
    Mither, mither,
O I hae killed my hauke sae guid,
    And I had nae mair bot hee O."

"Your haukis bluid was nevir sae reid,
    Edward, Edward,   10
Your haukis bluid was nevir sae reid,
    My deir son I tell thee O."
"O I hae killed my reid-roan steid,
    Mither, mither,
O I hae killed my reid-roan steid,   15
    That erst was sae fair and frie O."

"Your steid was auld, and ye hae gat mair,
    Edward, Edward,
Your steid was auld, and ye hae gat mair,
    Sum other dule ye drie O."
"O I hae killed my fadir deir,   20
    Mither, mither,
O I hae killed my fadir deir,
    Alas, and wae is mee O!"

"And whatten penance wul ye drie for that,   25
    Edward, Edward?
And whatten penance will ye drie for that?
    My deir son, now tell me O."
"Ile set my feit in yonder boat,
    Mither, mither,   30
Ile set my feit in yonder boat,
    And Ile fare ovir the sea O."

"And what wul ye doe wi your towirs and your ha,
    Edward, Edward?
And what wul ye doe wi your towirs and your ha,   35
    That were sae fair to see O?"
"Ile let thame stand tul they doun fa,

Mither, mither,
Ile let thame stand tul they doun fa,
  For here nevir mair maun I bee O."   40

"And what wul ye leive to your bairns and your wife,
     Edward, Edward?
And what wul ye leive to your bairns and your wife,
  Whan ye gang ovir the sea O?"
"The warldis room, late them beg thrae life,   45
     Mither, mither,
The warldis room, late them beg thrae life,
  For thame nevir mair wul I see O."

"And what wul ye leive to your ain mither deir,
     Edward, Edward?   50
And what wul ye leive to your ain mither deir?
  My deir son, now tell me O."
"The curse of hell frae me sall ye beir,
     Mither, mither,
The curse of hell frae me sall ye beir,   55
  Sic counseils ye gave to me O."

SIR PATRICK SPENS

The king sits in Dunfermline toune
  Drinking the blude-red wine:
"O whar will I get guid sailor,
  To sail this schip of mine?"

Up and spak an eldern knicht,   5
  Sat at the kings richt kne:
"Sir Patrick Spens is the best sailor
  That sails upon the se."

EDWARD. 4. *gang*, go. 5. *hauke*, hawk. *guid*, good. 16. *erst*, once. 20. *dule*, sorrow. 25. *drie*, suffer. 33. *towirs*, towers. *ha*, hall. 37. *fa*, fall. 40. *maun*, might. 41. *bairns*, children. 45. *warldis*, world's. *thrae*, through. 53. *frae*, from. *beir*, bear. 56. *sic*, such.

The king has written a braid letter,
   And signed it wi his hand,
And sent it to Sir Patrick Spens,
   Was walking on the sand.   10

The first line that Sir Patrick red,
   A loud lauch lauched he;
The next line that Sir Patrick red,
   The teir blinded his ee.   15

"O wha is this has don this deid,
   This ill deid don to me,
To send me out this time o' the yeir,
   To sail upon the se!   20

"Mak hast, mak haste, my mirry men all
   Our guid schip sails the morne":
"O say na sae, my master deir,
   For I feir a deadlie storme.

"Late late yestreen I saw the new moone,   25
   Wi the auld moone in hir arme,
And I feir, I feir, my deir master,
   That we will cum to harme."

O our Scots nobles wer richt laith
   To weet their cork-heild schoone;   30
Bot lang owre a' the play wer playd,
   Thair hats they swam aboone.

O lang, lang may their ladies sit,
   Wi thair fans into their hand,
Or eir they se Sir Patrick Spens   35
   Cum sailing to the land.

O lang, lang may the ladies stand,
   Wi thair gold kems in their hair,
Waiting for thair ain deir lords,
   For they'll se thame na mair.   40

Haf owre, haf owre to Aberdour,
  It's fiftie fadom deip,
And thair lies guid Sir Patrick Spens,
  Wi the Scots lords at his feit.

Sir patrick spens. 9. *braid letter*, letter written on a long sheet. 16. *ee*, eye.
23. *na*, not. 25-26. a bad omen. 29. *laith*, loath. 30. *cork-heild schoone*, cork-
heeled shoes. 31. *Bot . . . played*, but long before the play was played. 32.
they, the hats. *aboone*, above. 35. *eir*, before. 39. *ain*, own. 41. *owre*, way.

Christopher Marlowe

1564–1593

THE PASSIONATE SHEPHERD TO HIS LOVE

Come live with me and be my Love,
And we will all the pleasures prove
That hills and valleys, dales and fields,
Woods or steepy mountain yields.

And we will sit upon the rocks,   5
Seeing the shepherds feed their flocks
By shallow rivers, to whose falls
Melodious birds sing madrigals.

And I will make thee beds of roses
And a thousand fragrant posies;   10
A cap of flowers, and a kirtle
Embroidered all with leaves of myrtle;

A gown made of the finest wool
Which from our pretty lambs we pull;
Fair-linéd slippers for the cold,   15
With buckles of the purest gold;

A belt of straw and ivy buds
With coral clasps and amber studs—
And if these pleasures may thee move,
Come live with me and be my Love.   20

The shepherd swains shall dance and sing
For thy delight each May morning—
If these delights thy mind may move,
Then live with me and be my Love.

THE PASSIONATE SHEPHERD TO HIS LOVE.   11. *kirtle,* gown.

Sir Walter Raleigh

1552?–1618

THE NYMPH'S REPLY TO THE SHEPHERD

If all the world and love were young,
And truth in every shepherd's tongue,
These pretty pleasures might me move,
To live with thee and be thy love.

But time drives flocks from field to fold,   5
When rivers rage, and rocks grow cold;
And Philomel becometh dumb;
The rest complains of cares to come.

The flowers do fade, and wanton fields
To wayward Winter reckoning yields;   10
A honey tongue, a heart of gall,
Is fancy's spring, but sorrow's fall.

Thy gowns, thy shoes, thy bed of roses,
Thy cap, thy kirtle, and thy posies,
Soon break, soon wither, soon forgotten,   15
In folly ripe, in reason rotten.

Thy belt of straw and ivy buds,
Thy coral clasps and amber studs,
All these in me no means can move,
To come to thee and be thy love.   20

But could youth last, and love still breed,
Had joys no date, nor age no need,
Then these delights my mind might move,
To live with thee and be thy love.

THE NYMPH'S REPLY TO THE SHEPHERD. 7. *Philomel.* Philomel was raped by her brother-in-law who cut out her tongue so that she could not reveal his crime. The gods transformed her into a nightingale to save her from further harm.

Edmund Spenser

1552–1599

from AMORETTI

XXXI

Ah! why hath Nature to so hard a heart
Given so goodly gifts of beauty's grace!
Whose pride depraves each other better part,
And all those precious ornaments deface.
Sith to all other beasts of bloody race   5
A dreadful countenance she given hath
That with their terror all the rest may chase,
And warn to shun the danger of their wrath.
But my proud one doth work the greater scath,
Through sweet allurement of her lovely hue;   10
That she the better may in bloody bath
Of such poor thralls her cruel hands imbrue.
   But, did she know how ill these two accord,
   Such cruelty she would have soon abhorred.

LXXIX

Men call you fair, and you do credit it,
For that yourself ye daily such do see:
But the true fair, that is the gentle wit,
And virtuous mind, is much more praised of me:
For all the rest, however fair it be,   5
Shall turn to nought and lose that glorious hue;
But only that is permanent and free
From frail corruption, that doth flesh ensue.
That is true beauty: that doth argue you
To be divine, and born of heavenly seed;   10

Derived from that fair Spirit, from whom all true
And perfect beauty did at first proceed:
    He only fair, and what he fair hath made;
    All other fair, like flowers, untimely fade.

---

xxxi. 8. *danger*. In addition to its common meaning, the word suggested to an Elizabethan reader the disdain and scornfulness of a proud lover.

William Shakespeare

1564–1616

cycle of conflict

SONNETS

I

From fairest creatures we desire increase,
That thereby beauty's rose might never die,
But as the riper should by time decease,
His tender heir might bear his memory:
But thou, contracted to thine own bright eyes,   5
Feed'st thy light's flame with self-substantial fuel,
Making a famine where abundance lies,
Thyself thy foe, to thy sweet self too cruel.
Thou that art now the world's fresh ornament
And only herald to the gaudy spring,   10
Within thine own bud buriest thy content
And, tender churl, makest waste in niggarding.
  Pity the world, or else this glutton be,
    To eat the world's due, by the grave and thee.

Sonnets edited and annotated by Hardin Craig. I. 5. *contracted,* engaged, es-
poused. 6. *self-substantial,* fuel of the substance of the flame itself (Dowden).
11. *thy content,* that which is contained in you; potential fatherhood (Pooler).
12. *makest . . . niggarding,* squander your substance by being miserly. The
Sonnets are replete with such instances of oxymoron. 14. *by . . . thee,* by death
and by your wilfully remaining childless.

II

When forty winters shall besiege thy brow,
And dig deep trenches in thy beauty's field,
Thy youth's proud livery, so gazed on now,
Will be a tatter'd weed, of small worth held:
Then being ask'd where all thy beauty lies,   5
Where all the treasure of thy lusty days,
To say, within thine own deep-sunken eyes,
Were an all-eating shame and thriftless praise.
How much more praise deserved thy beauty's use,
If thou couldst answer 'This fair child of mine   10
Shall sum my count and make my old excuse,'
Proving his beauty by succession thine!
   This were to be new made when thou art old,
   And see thy blood warm when thou feel'st it cold.

XII

When I do count the clock that tells the time,
And see the brave day sunk in hideous night;
When I behold the violet past prime,
And sable curls all silver'd o'er with white;
When lofty trees I see barren of leaves   5
Which erst from heat did canopy the herd,
And summer's green all girded up in sheaves
Borne on the bier with white and bristly beard,
Then of thy beauty do I question make,
That thou among the wastes of time must go,   10
Since sweets and beauties do themselves forsake
And die as fast as they see others grow;
   And nothing 'gainst Time's scythe can make defence
   Save breed, to brave him when he takes thee hence.

II. 4. *tatter'd weed*, worn-out garment. 8. *an all-eating . . . praise.* The phrases
may be parallel: the shame of gluttony and the praise of extravagance, since you
devour the world's due and are an unthrift of your beauty (Pooler). 9. *deserved*,
would deserve (subjunctive). *use*, investment.

XII. 6. *erst*, formerly. 11. *sweets . . . forsake*, sweetness and beauty forsake
sweet and beautiful things. 14. *Save . . . him*, except children whose youth
nay set the scythe of Time at defiance.

XVIII

Shall I compare thee to a summer's day?
Thou art more lovely and more temperate:
Rough winds do shake the darling buds of May,
And summer's lease hath all too short a date:
Sometime too hot the eye of heaven shines,　　　　　5
And often is his gold complexion dimm'd;
And every fair from fair sometime declines,
By chance or nature's changing course untrimm'd;
But thy eternal summer shall not fade
Nor lose possession of that fair thou owest;　　　　　10
Nor shall Death brag thou wander'st in his shade,
When in eternal lines to time thou growest:
　　So long as men can breathe or eyes can see,
　　So long lives this and this gives life to thee.

XIX

Devouring Time, blunt thou the lion's paws,
And make the earth devour her own sweet brood;
Pluck the keen teeth from the fierce tiger's jaws,
And burn the long-lived phœnix in her blood;
Make glad and sorry seasons as thou fleets,　　　　　5
And do whate'er thou wilt, swift-footed Time,
To the wide world and all her fading sweets;
But I forbid thee one most heinous crime:
O, carve not with thy hours my love's fair brow,
Nor draw no lines there with thine antique pen;　　　　　10
Him in thy course untainted do allow
For beauty's pattern to succeeding men.
　　Yet, do thy worst, old Time: despite thy wrong,
　　My love shall in my verse ever live young.

XVIII. This and the following sonnet develop the theme of the immortalizing power of poetry. 7. *every . . . declines.* Cf. XII, 11. 8. *untrimm'd,* stripped of ornaments. 12. *to . . . growest.* To grow to time is to be incorporated or become one with it and so to live while time lasts (Pooler).

XIX. 5. *fleets,* fleetest. 11. *untainted,* a metaphor from tilting; a taint was a hit (Pooler).

XXIX

When, in disgrace with fortune and men's eyes,
I all alone beweep my outcast state
And trouble deaf heaven with my bootless cries
And look upon myself and curse my fate,
Wishing me like to one more rich in hope,   5
Featured like him, like him with friends possess'd,
Desiring this man's art and that man's scope,
With what I most enjoy contented least;
Yet in these thoughts myself almost despising,
Haply I think on thee, and then my state,   10
Like to the lark at break of day arising
From sullen earth, sings hymns at heaven's gate;
    For thy sweet love remember'd such wealth brings
    That then I scorn to change my state with kings.

XXX

When to the sessions of sweet silent thought
I summon up remembrance of things past,
I sigh the lack of many a thing I sought,
And with old woes new wail my dear time's waste:
Then can I drown an eye, unused to flow,   5
For precious friends hid in death's dateless night,
And weep afresh love's long since cancell'd woe,
And moan the expense of many a vanish'd sight:
Then can I grieve at grievances foregone,
And heavily from woe to woe tell o'er   10
The sad account of fore-bemoaned moan,
Which I new pay as if not paid before.
    But if the while I think on thee, dear friend,
    All losses are restored and sorrows end.

xxix. 6. *Featured*, situated (Onions); more likely, formed; i.e., envying their good looks, their beauty of face. *like him, like him*, not a repetition but, as Pooler points out, "like a second man, like a third." 7. *scope*, probably implies both "range of powers" and "opportunity."

xxx. 1–2. *sessions . . . summon.* The metaphor is that of a court of law. Unlike many of the sonnets this one does not sustain the figure. 4. *new wail*, lament anew. 8. *expense*, that which is spent. 9. *foregone*, past.

XXXV

No more be grieved at that which thou hast done:
Roses have thorns, and silver fountains mud;
Clouds and eclipses stain both moon and sun,
And loathsome canker lives in sweetest bud.
All men make faults, and even I in this,   5
Authorizing thy trespass with compare,
Myself corrupting, salving thy amiss,
Excusing thy sins more than thy sins are;
For to thy sensual fault I bring in sense—
Thy adverse party is thy advocate—   10
And 'gainst myself a lawful plea commence:
Such civil war is in my love and hate
   That I an accessary needs must be
   To that sweet thief which sourly robs from me.

XLII

That thou hast her, it is not all my grief,
And yet it may be said I loved her dearly;
That she hath thee, is of my wailing chief,
A loss in love that touches me more nearly.
Loving offenders, thus I will excuse ye: 5
Thou dost love her, because thou know'st I love her;
And for my sake even so doth she abuse me,
Suffering my friend for my sake to approve her.
If I lose thee, my loss is my love's gain,
And losing her, my friend hath found that loss;   10
Both find each other, and I lose both twain,
And both for my sake lay on me this cross:
   But here's the joy; my friend and I are one;
   Sweet flattery! then she loves but me alone.

---

xxxv. 3. *stain*, grow dim, be obscured, soiled (Pooler). *both moon and sun*. Fleay thought this a reference to Elizabeth (i.e., Cynthia, the moon goddess) and Southampton, with whom he assumed Shakespeare to be out of favor. 6. *Authorizing*, sanctioning, justifying. 7. *salving*, parallel in construction with *Authorizing*, *corrupting*, and *Excusing*. *amiss*, misdeed. 8. *Excusing . . . are*, making the excuse more than proportioned to the offense (Steevens). 9. *sensual*, pertaining to the flesh. *sense*, pertaining to the rational faculty; i.e., I reason away your offenses. 14. *sourly*, cruelly.

xlii. 3. *is . . . chief*, is chief cause of my lamentation. 8. *approve*, try, test. 9. *my love's*, hers whom I love. 14. *flattery*, gratifying deception (Onions).

LV

Not marble, nor the gilded monuments
Of princes, shall outlive this powerful rhyme;
But you shall shine more bright in these contents
Than unswept stone besmear'd with sluttish time.
When wasteful war shall statues overturn,   5
And broils root out the work of masonry,
Nor Mars his sword nor war's quick fire shall burn
The living record of your memory.
'Gainst death and all-oblivious enmity
Shall you pace forth; your praise shall still find room   10
Even in the eyes of all posterity
That wear this world out to the ending doom.
　So, till the judgment that yourself arise,
　You live in this, and dwell in lovers' eyes.

LXV

Since brass, nor stone, nor earth, nor boundless sea,
But sad mortality o'er-sways their power,
How with this rage shall beauty hold a plea,
Whose action is no stronger than a flower?
O, how shall summer's honey breath hold out   5
Against the wreckful siege of battering days,
When rocks impregnable are not so stout,
Nor gates of steel so strong, but Time decays?
O fearful meditation! where, alack,
Shall Time's best jewel from Time's chest lie hid?   10
Or what strong hand can hold his swift foot back?
Or who his spoil of beauty can forbid?
　O, none, unless this miracle have might,
　That in black ink my love may still shine bright.

LV. 3. *these contents*, i.e., the contents of my poems written in praise of you.
4. *unswept stone*, parallel with *contents;* i.e., *in* is to be supplied from the
preceding line (Pooler). 9. *all-oblivious*, causing to be forgotten. 12. *wear . . .
out*, i.e., outlast (**Pooler**). 13. *till . . . arise*, till the decree of the judgment day
that you arise from **the** dead (Beeching).

LXV. 1–2. *Since . . . power*, an elliptical clause: Since there is neither brass,
etc., but that sad mortality o'ersways, etc. The ellipsis shows the closeness of the
idea to the preceding sonnet. 4. *action*, case (for permanence); legal figure. 10.
Time's chest. The chest of Time is the repository into which he is poetically
supposed to throw those things which he designs to be forgotten (Steevens). 12.
spoil, act of spoiling; possibly, spoils, booty.

LXVIII

Thus is his cheek the map of days outworn,
When beauty lived and died as flowers do now,
Before these bastard signs of fair were born,
Or durst inhabit on a living brow;
Before the golden tresses of the dead,   5
The right of sepulchres, were shorn away,
To live a second life on second head;
Ere beauty's dead fleece made another gay:
In him those holy antique hours are seen,
Without all ornament, itself and true,   10
Making no summer of another's green,
Robbing no old to dress his beauty new;
    And him as for a map doth Nature store,
    To show false Art what beauty was of yore.

LXXIII

That time of year thou mayst in me behold
When yellow leaves, or none, or few, do hang
Upon those boughs which shake against the cold,
Bare ruin'd choirs, where late the sweet birds sang.
In me thou see'st the twilight of such day   5
As after sunset fadeth in the west,
Which by and by black night doth take away,
Death's second self, that seals up all in rest.
In me thou see'st the glowing of such fire
That on the ashes of his youth doth lie,   10
As the death-bed whereon it must expire
Consumed with that which it was nourish'd by.
    This thou perceivest, which makes thy love more strong,
    To love that well which thou must leave ere long.

LXXXVI

Was it the proud full sail of his great verse,
Bound for the prize of all too precious you,
That did my ripe thoughts in my brain inhearse,
Making their tomb the womb wherein they grew?
Was it his spirit, by spirits taught to write   5
Above a mortal pitch, that struck me dead?
No, neither he, nor his compeers by night

Giving him aid, my verse astonished.
He, nor that affable familiar ghost
Which nightly gulls him with intelligence,   10
As victors of my silence cannot boast;
I was not sick of any fear from thence:
　　But when your countenance fill'd up his line,
　　Then lack'd I matter; that enfeebled mine.

XCIV

They that have power to hurt and will do none,
That do not do the thing they most do show,
Who, moving others, are themselves as stone,
Unmoved, cold, and to temptation slow,
They rightly do inherit heaven's graces   5
And husband nature's riches from expense;
They are the lords and owners of their faces,
Others but stewards of their excellence.
The summer's flower is to the summer sweet,
Though to itself it only live and die,   10
But if that flower with base infection meet,
The basest weed outbraves his dignity:
　　For sweetest things turn sourest by their deeds;
　　Lilies that fester smell far worse than weeds.

LXVIII. This sonnet contrasts the real beauty of youth with artificial beauty.
The subject of the sonnet is the epitome of natural beauty. 1. *map*, picture,
image. 3. *bastard . . . fair*, i.e., cosmetics. 10. *itself*. Malone conjectured *himself*, thinking the antecedent to be *him* (l. 9). Pooler refers the pronoun to *holy
antique hours*, singular in idea, since the phrase means "the beauty of the past";
itself is equivalent to "unadulterated."

LXXIII. Alden calls this sonnet the finest example in the Shakespearean mode.
Note the three figures of decay—autumn, sunset, and expiring fire—each occupy-
ing a quatrain; also the noble couplet of personal application. 4. *choirs*, that
part of cathedrals where the service is said; in apposition with *boughs* (l. 3).
This image was probably suggested to Shakespeare by our desolated monasteries.
The resemblance between the vaulting of a Gothic aisle and an avenue of trees
whose upper branches meet and form an arch overhead is too striking not to be
acknowledged. When the roof of the one is shattered, and the boughs of the
other leafless, the comparison becomes yet more solemn and picturesque
(Steevens). 12. *that*, i.e., the ashes of what was formerly the fuel.

LXXXVI. This sonnet is devoted to generous praise of his rival. Some critics
have seen in it an indication that Chapman was the rival poet. 1. *proud
full sail*. F. J. Furnivall saw in this an allusion to Chapman's hexameters in his
translation of Homer. 7. *compeers by night*, spirits visiting and aiding the poet
in his dreams. 8. *astonished*, struck dumb.

XCIV. 6. *expense*, waste, expenditure. 7. *They . . . faces*, they are completely
masters of themselves.

XCV

How sweet and lovely dost thou make the shame
Which, like a canker in the fragrant rose,
Doth spot the beauty of thy budding name!
O, in what sweets dost thou thy sins enclose!
That tongue that tells the story of thy days,   5
Making lascivious comments on thy sport,
Cannot dispraise but in a kind of praise;
Naming thy name blesses an ill report.
O, what a mansion have those vices got
Which for their habitation chose out thee,   10
Where beauty's veil doth cover every blot,
And all things turn to fair that eyes can see!
    Take heed, dear heart, of this large privilege;
    The hardest knife ill-used doth lose his edge.

CVI

When in the chronicle of wasted time
I see descriptions of the fairest wights,
And beauty making beautiful old rhyme
In praise of ladies dead and lovely knights,
Then, in the blazon of sweet beauty's best,   5
Of hand, of foot, of lip, of eye, of brow,
I see their antique pen would have express'd
Even such a beauty as you master now.
So all their praises are but prophecies
Of this our time, all you prefiguring;   10
And, for they look'd but with divining eyes,
They had not skill enough your worth to sing:
    For we, which now behold these present days,
    Have eyes to wonder, but lack tongues to praise.

xcv. 2. *canker*, worm that destroys buds and leaves. The figure is frequent in the early works of Shakespeare; cf. xxxv, 4.

cvi. 1. *wasted*, past. 2. *wights*, persons. 5. *blazon*, heraldic metaphor, meaning here "glorification." 7. *antique*, accented on the first syllable. 8. *master*, possess, control. 11. *And, for*, and because.

CXVI

Let me not to the marriage of true minds
Admit impediments. Love is not love
Which alters when it alteration finds,
Or bends with the remover to remove:
O, no! it is an ever-fixed mark   5
That looks on tempests and is never shaken;
It is the star to every wandering bark,
Whose worth's unknown, although his height be taken.
Love 's not Time's fool, though rosy lips and cheeks
Within his bending sickle's compass come;   10
Love alters not with his brief hours and weeks,
But bears it out even to the edge of doom.
   If this be error and upon me proved,
   I never writ, nor no man ever loved.

CXXVII

In the old age black was not counted fair,
Or if it were, it bore not beauty's name;
But now is black beauty's successive heir,
And beauty slander'd with a bastard shame:
For since each hand hath put on nature's power,   5
Fairing the foul with art's false borrow'd face,
Sweet beauty hath no name, no holy bower,
But is profaned, if not lives in disgrace.
Therefore my mistress' brows are raven black,
Her eyes so suited, and they mourners seem   10
At such who, not born fair, no beauty lack,
Slandering creation with a false esteem:
   Yet so they mourn, becoming of their woe,
   That every tongue says beauty should look so.

CXVI. 4. *Or . . . remove,* or inclines to inconstancy at the demand of the inconstant. 8. *Whose . . . taken.* The star has an influence over and above the determination of its altitude (for purposes of navigation). 9. *fool,* plaything. 11. *his,* i.e., Time's. 12. *But . . . doom,* endures or holds out to the very day of judgment.

CXXVII. 1. *In . . . fair.* Black was traditionally associated with ugliness. 3. *successive heir,* lawful successor. 9. *brows.* Many editors retain the Q reading *eyes,* i.e., eyebrows. 10. *suited,* clad. 12. *Slandering . . . esteem,* dishonoring nature by a false reputation for beauty. 13. *becoming of,* gracing.

CXXIX

The expense of spirit in a waste of shame
Is lust in action; and till action, lust
Is perjured, murderous, bloody, full of blame,
Savage, extreme, rude, cruel, not to trust,
Enjoy'd no sooner but despised straight,   5
Past reason hunted, and no sooner had
Past reason hated, as a swallow'd bait
On purpose laid to make the taker mad;
Mad in pursuit and in possession so;
Had, having, and in quest to have, extreme;   10
A bliss in proof, and proved, a very woe;
Before, a joy proposed; behind, a dream.
   All this the world well knows; yet none knows well
   To shun the heaven that leads men to this hell.

CXXX

My mistress' eyes are nothing like the sun;
Coral is far more red than her lips' red;
If snow be white, why then her breasts are dun;
If hairs be wires, black wires grow on her head.
I have seen roses damask'd, red and white,   5
But no such roses see I in her cheeks;
And in some perfumes is there more delight
Than in the breath that from my mistress reeks.
I love to hear her speak, yet well I know
That music hath a far more pleasing sound;   10
I grant I never saw a goddess go;
My mistress, when she walks, treads on the ground:
   And yet, by heaven, I think my love as rare
   As any she belied with false compare.

CXXIX. This famous sonnet, loosely connected with those that precede and follow it, deals with the ravages of lust; cf. CXLVI, note. 1. *expense*, expenditure, waste.

CXXX. 5. *damask'd*, like a pattern in damask cloth; woven with a pattern of satin on one side.

CXXXVIII

When my love swears that she is made of truth
I do believe her, though I know she lies,
That she might think me some untutor'd youth,
Unlearned in the world's false subtleties.
Thus vainly thinking that she thinks me young,   5
Although she knows my days are past the best,
Simply I credit her false-speaking tongue:
On both sides thus is simple truth suppress'd.
But wherefore says she not she is unjust?
And wherefore say not I that I am old?   10
O, love's best habit is in seeming trust,
And age in love loves not to have years told:
    Therefore I lie with her and she with me,
    And in our faults by lies we flatter'd be.

CXLIV

Two loves I have of comfort and despair,
Which like two spirits do suggest me still:
The better angel is a man right fair,
The worser spirit a woman colour'd ill.
To win me soon to hell, my female evil   5
Tempteth my better angel from my side,
And would corrupt my saint to be a devil,
Wooing his purity with her foul pride.
And whether that my angel be turn'd fiend
Suspect I may, yet not directly tell;   10
But being both from me, both to each friend,
I guess one angel in another's hell:
    Yet this shall I ne'er know, but live in doubt,
    Till my bad angel fire my good one out.

CXXXVIII. This sonnet is I. in *The Passionate Pilgrim*. 2. *believe her*, i.e., pretend to believe her. 11. *habit*, deportment, with play on the idea of habiliment, that which is put on.

CXLIV. The second sonnet in *The Passionate Pilgrim*. It depicts the conflict in the poet's mind between his affection for his friend and his mistress. 2. *suggest*, tempt (Malone); prompt (to good or evil). 8. *foul*, wicked. 11. *from me*, away from me. The poet suspects they are together. 14. *fire . . . out*, drive out with fire; an expression still in common use.

CXLVI

Poor soul, the centre of my sinful earth,
[Thrall to] these rebel powers that thee array,
Why dost thou pine within and suffer dearth,
Painting thy outward walls so costly gay?
Why so large cost, having so short a lease,   5
Dost thou upon thy fading mansion spend?
Shall worms, inheritors of this excess,
Eat up thy charge? is this thy body's end?
Then, soul, live thou upon thy servant's loss,
And let that pine to aggravate thy store;   10
Buy terms divine in selling hours of dross;
Within be fed, without be rich no more:
   So shalt thou feed on Death, that feeds on men,
   And Death once dead, there's no more dying then.

CXLVII

My love is as a fever, longing still
For that which longer nurseth the disease,
Feeding on that which doth preserve the ill,
The uncertain sickly appetite to please.
My reason, the physician to my love,   5
Angry that his prescriptions are not kept,
Hath left me, and I desperate now approve
Desire is death, which physic did except.
Past cure I am, now reason is past care,
And frantic-mad with evermore unrest;   10
My thoughts and my discourse as madmen's are,
At random from the truth vainly express'd;
   For I have sworn thee fair and thought thee bright,
   Who art as black as hell, as dark as night.

CXLVI. A profound sonnet, not connected with the preceding, which says it is folly to adorn and feed the body instead of the mind. The body will die, but the soul will conquer death. Tucker Brooke places this sonnet and CXXIX at the end of the "Dark Lady" sequence, regarding them as moral reflections following on her dismissal. 1. *sinful earth*, the body. 2. [*Thrall to*], anonymous conjecture; Q, Globe, *et al.*, leave blank. 8. *thy charge*, that on which thou hast expended so much. 10. *aggravate*, increase. 11. *Buy terms divine*, purchase long periods of divine salvation.

CXLVII. This sonnet is associated in theme with CXLIV—his hopeless love for an unworthy mistress. 7–8. *I . . . except*, I, being in despair, now recognize that desire to be fatal, which took exception to the teaching of physic (Stopes). 9. *cure . . . care*, an adaptation of the proverb, things past cure are past care.

CLII

In loving thee thou know'st I am forsworn,
But thou art twice forsworn, to me love swearing,
In act thy bed-vow broke and new faith torn
In vowing new hate after new love bearing.
But why of two oaths' breach do I accuse thee,   5
When I break twenty? I am perjured most;
For all my vows are oaths but to misuse thee
And all my honest faith in thee is lost,
For I have sworn deep oaths of thy deep kindness,
Oaths of thy love, thy truth, thy constancy,   10
And, to enlighten thee, gave eyes to blindness,
Or made them swear against the thing they see;
   For I have sworn thee fair; more perjured I,
   To swear against the truth so foul a lie!

CLII.   9. *kindness*, affection, tenderness.   11. *to enlighten thee*, in order to invest thee with brightness; she was a dark lady.

John Donne

1572–1631

from eros to agape

COMMUNITY

Good we must love, and must hate ill,
For ill is ill, and good good still,
   But there are things indifferent,
Which we may neither hate, nor love,
But one, and then another prove,
   As we shall find our fancy bent. 5

If then at first wise Nature had
Made women either good or bad,
   Then some we might hate, and some choose;
But since she did them so create,
That we may neither love, nor hate, 10
   Only this rests: All, all may use.

If they were good it would be seen,
Good is as visible as green,
   And to all eyes itself betrays;
If they were bad, they could not last, 15
Bad doth itself, and others, waste;
   So, they deserve nor blame, nor praise.

But they are ours as fruits are ours,
He that but tastes, he that devours,
   And he that leaves all, doth as well; 20
Changed loves are but changed sorts of meat,
And when he hath the kernel eat,
   Who doth not fling away the shell?

SONG

Go and catch a falling star,
   Get with child a mandrake root,
Tell me where all past years are,
   Or who cleft the Devil's foot,
Teach me to hear mermaids singing,   5
   Or to keep off envy's stinging,
       And find
       What wind
Serves to advance an honest mind.

If thou be'st born to strange sights,   10
   Things invisible to see,
Ride ten thousand days and nights,
   Till age snow white hairs on thee,
Thou, when thou return'st, wilt tell me
   All strange wonders that befell thee,   15
       And swear
       Nowhere
Lives a woman true, and fair.

If thou findst one, let me know,
   Such a pilgrimage were sweet.   20
Yet do not; I would not go,
   Though at next door we might meet;
Though she were true, when you met her,
   And last, till you write your letter,
       Yet she   25
       Will be
False, ere I come, to two, or three.

COMMUNITY. 5. *prove,* approve. 12. *this rests,* this notion remains. 14. *green,* a condensation of natural imagery which follows. 20–21. *tastes, devours, leaves,* suggests the philosophies of moderation, sensualism, asceticism.

SONG. 2. *mandrake root,* a forked root shaped like the human figure. Invested with demonic mysticism, it was believed to screech when plucked from the ground, thereby driving the picker insane. 4. *Devil's foot,* repetition of the forked image, emphasizing the radical (root: *radix*), demonic nature of the human psyche. 5. *mermaids singing,* the sirens of the *Odyssey,* whose supernatural song hypnotically lured sailors onto treacherous rocks.

THE APPARITION

When by thy scorn, O murd'ress, I am dead,
    And that thou thinkst thee free
From all solicitation from me,
Then shall my ghost come to thy bed,
And thee, fained vestal, in worse arms shall see;   5
Then thy sick taper will begin to wink,
And he, whose thou art then, being tired before,
Will, if thou stir, or pinch to wake him, think
    Thou call'st for more,
And in false sleep will from thee shrink,   10
And then, poor aspen wretch, neglected thou
Bathed in a cold quicksilver sweat wilt lie,
    A verier ghost than I;
What I will say, I will not tell thee now,
Lest that preserve thee; and since my love is spent,   15
I had rather thou shouldst painfully repent,
Than by my threat'nings rest still innocent.

A VALEDICTION: OF WEEPING

    Let me pour forth
My tears before thy face, whilst I stay here,
For thy face coins them, and thy stamp they bear,
And by this mintage they are something worth,
    For thus they be   5
    Pregnant of thee;
Fruits of much grief they are, emblems of more,
When a tear falls, that thou falls which it bore,
So thou and I are nothing then, when on a diverse shore.

    On a round ball   10
A workman that hath copies by, can lay
An Europe, Afric, and an Asia,
And quickly make that, which was nothing, *All;*

THE APPARITION. 5. *fained*, a complicated pun on "feigned." 11. *aspen*, quaking aspen tree which has leaves of tremulous quality and silver cast. 12. *quicksilver*, mercury: silver color; messenger god of Roman myth who was sometimes characterized as cunning and diabolical; base metal in alchemistic experiments.

So doth each tear
Which thee doth wear,   15
A globe, yea world, by that impression grow,
Till thy tears mixed with mine do overflow
This world, by waters sent from thee, my heaven dissolved so.

O more than Moon,
Draw not up seas to drown me in thy sphere,   20
Weep me not dead, in thine arms, but forbear
To teach the sea what it may do too soon;
Let not the wind
Example find
To do me more harm than it purposeth;   25
Since thou and I sigh one another's breath,
Whoe'er sighs most is cruellest, and hastes the other's death.

THE FLEA

Mark but this flea, and mark in this
How little that which thou deny'st me is;
It sucked me first, and now sucks thee,
And in this flea our two bloods mingled be;
Thou know'st that this cannot be said   5
A sin, nor shame, nor loss of maidenhead,
Yet this enjoys before it woo,
And pampered swells with one blood made of two,
And this, alas, is more than we would do.

Oh stay, three lives in one flea spare,   10
Where we almost, yea more than married are.
This flea is you and I, and this
Our marriage bed, and marriage temple is;
Though parents grudge, and you, we're met
And cloistered in these living walls of jet.   15
Though use make you apt to kill me,
Let not to that, self-murder added be,
And sacrilege, three sins in killing three.

A VALEDICTION: OF WEEPING. 2. *tears*. Tears, along with sighs, were thought to slightly shorten one's life. 10. *round ball*, symbol of perfection ironically reminiscent of the teardrop. 15. *wear*, suggests simultaneously bearing an image and wasting. 18. *dissolved*, see l. 2, note. 19. *moon*, symbol of mutability, inconstancy.

Cruel and sudden, hast thou since
Purpled thy nail in blood of innocence?   20
Wherein could this flea guilty be,
Except in that drop which it sucked from thee?
Yet thou triumph'st, and say'st that thou
Find'st not thyself, nor me, the weaker now;
   'Tis true; then learn how false, fears be;   25
   Just so much honor, when thou yield'st to me,
   Will waste, as this flea's death took life from thee.

THE SUN RISING

    Busy old fool, unruly sun,
     Why dost thou thus,
Through windows, and through curtains, call on us?
Must to thy motions lovers' seasons run?
      Saucy pedantic wretch, go chide   5
      Late schoolboys, and sour prentices,
   Go tell court-huntsmen that the King will ride,
   Call country ants to harvest offices;
Love, all alike, no season knows, nor clime,
Nor hours, days, months, which are the rags of time.   10

    Thy beams, so reverend and strong
     Why shouldst thou think?
I could eclipse and cloud them with a wink,
But that I would not lose her sight so long:
      If her eyes have not blinded thine,   15
      Look, and tomorrow late, tell me
   Whether both the Indias of spice and mine
   Be where thou leftst them, or lie here with me.
Ask for those kings whom thou saw'st yesterday,
And thou shalt hear, All here in one bed lay.   20

    She's all states, and all princes I,
     Nothing else is.
Princes do but play us; compared to this,
All honor's mimic, all wealth alchemy.

THE FLEA. 8. *And . . . two.* Lovers' blood was thought to mingle during intercourse. Consequently, the flea takes on the aspects of the womb. 10. *three lives,* suggestive of the Trinity. 20. *Purpled,* color of royalty and crucifixion. *nail,* pun. *blood of innocence,* Christian sacrifice.

Thou, sun, art half as happy as we,   25
    In that the world's contracted thus;
Thine age asks ease, and since thy duties be
    To warm the world, that's done in warming us.
Shine here to us, and thou art everywhere;
This bed thy center is, these walls thy sphere.   30

A VALEDICTION: FORBIDDING MOURNING

As virtuous men pass mildly away,
    And whisper to their souls to go,
Whilst some of their sad friends do say,
    "The breath goes now," and some say, "No,"

So let us melt, and make no noise,   5
    No tear-floods, nor sigh-tempests move;
'Twere profanation of our joys
    To tell the laity our love.

Moving of the earth brings harms and fears,
    Men reckon what it did and meant;   10
But trepidation of the spheres,
    Though greater far, is innocent.

Dull sublunary lovers' love
    (Whose soul is sense) cannot admit
Absence, because it doth remove   15
    Those things which elemented it.

But we, by a love so much refined
    That our selves know not what it is,
Inter-assured of the mind,
    Care less, eyes, lips, and hands to miss.   20

Our two souls therefore, which are one,
    Though I must go, endure not yet
A breach, but an expansion,
    Like gold to airy thinness beat.

THE SUN RISING. 17. *Whether . . . mine,* East Indies, famous for spices; West
Indies, famous for metals.

If they be two, they are two so   25
   As stiff twin compasses are two:
Thy soul, the fixed foot, makes no show
   To move, but doth, if the other do;

And though it in the center sit,
   Yet when the other far doth roam,   30
It leans, and hearkens after it,
   And grows erect, as that comes home.

Such wilt thou be to me, who must,
   Like the other foot, obliquely run;
Thy firmness makes my circle just,   35
   And makes me end where I begun.

THE ECSTASY

Where, like a pillow on a bed,
   A pregnant bank swelled up, to rest
The violet's reclining head,
   Sat we two, one another's best.

Our hands were firmly cemented   5
   With a fast balm, which thence did spring;
Our eye-beams twisted, and did thread
   Our eyes, upon one double string;

So to intergraft our hands, as yet
   Was all the means to make us one,   10
And pictures in our eyes to get
   Was all our propagation.

As, 'twixt two equal armies, Fate
   Suspends uncertain victory,

A VALEDICTION: FORBIDDING MOURNING. 1. *virtuous men*, those whose spiritual harmony was of such perfection that they could easily pass from the physical world into the spiritual without violence. 6. *tear-floods . . . sigh-tempest*. Tears and sighs were thought to shorten one's life. 13. *sublunary*. Within the Ptolemaic universe, Adam's sin corrupted all matter beneath the moon thereby admitting change, inconstancy, and death into the world. 35. *circle*, symbol of perfection.

Our souls (which to advance their state   15
   Were gone out) hung 'twixt her and me.

And whilst our souls negotiate there,
   We like sepulchral statues lay;
All day, the same our postures were,
   And we said nothing, all the day.   20

If any, so by love refined
   That he souls' language understood,
And by good love were grown all mind,
   Within convenient distance stood,

He (though he knew not which soul spake,   25
   Because both meant, both spake the same)
Might thence a new concoction take,
   And part far purer than he came.

This Ecstasy doth unperplex,
   We said, and tell us what we love;   30
We see by this it was not sex;
   We see we saw not what did move:

But as all several souls contain
   Mixture of things, they know not what,
Love these mixed souls doth mix again,   35
   And makes both one, each this and that.

A single violet transplant,
   The strength, the color, and the size,
(All which before was poor, and scant)
   Redoubles still, and multiplies.   40

When love, with one another so
   Interinanimates two souls,
That abler soul, which thence doth flow,
   Defects of loneliness controls.

We then, who are this new soul, know   45
   Of what we are composed, and made,
For the atomies of which we grow
   Are souls, whom no change can invade.

But oh, alas, so long, so far
   Our bodies why do we forbear   50

They're ours, though they're not we, we are
 The intelligences, they the sphere.

We owe them thanks because they thus
 Did us to us at first convey,
Yielded their forces, sense, to us,   55
 Nor are dross to us, but allay.

On man heaven's influence works not so,
 But that it first imprints the air;
So soul into the soul may flow,
 Though it to body first repair.   60

As our blood labors to beget
 Spirits as like souls as it can,
Because such fingers need to knit
 That subtle knot which makes us man:

So must pure lovers' souls descend   65
 To affections, and to faculties,
Which sense may reach and apprehend,
 Else a great Prince in prison lies.

To our bodies turn we then, that so
 Weak men on love revealed may look;   70
Love's mysteries in souls do grow,
 But yet the body is his book.

And if some lover, such as we,
 Have heard this dialogue of one,
Let him still mark us, he shall see   75
 Small change, when we're to bodies gone.

THE ECSTASY. 3. *violets*, symbol of faithfulness. *head*, phallic image. 4. *best*, the words "best" and "rest" when "intergrafted" propagate a third entity, "breast." 6. *balm*, perspiration. 7. *eye-beams*. Light beams were believed to emanate from the eye. 52. *sphere*. Just as the spheres were governed by supernatural "intelligences," so the bodies of men were governed by their spirits. 56. *dross* and *allay*, suggests the process of metal refinement; see l. 21. 58. *air*. Astrologists believed heaven's influence from the stars was transmitted to man by the air. 62. *spirits*, blood-produced vapors which "knitted" body and soul. 72. *book*, suggests the Bible with reference to the mysteries and the passion. 74. *dialogue of one*. "Dialogue" is derived from the Greek (*di:* twice; *logos:* word), which literally says "two words of one," reinforcing the theme of spiritual union and heightening its paradoxical nature.

THE CANONIZATION

For God's sake, hold your tongue, and let me love,
  Or chide my palsy, or my gout,
My five gray hairs, or ruined fortune flout,
  With wealth your state, your mind with arts improve,
    Take you a course, get you a place,   5
    Observe his honor, or his grace,
Or the King's real, or his stamped face
  Contemplate; what you will, approve,
  So you will let me love.

Alas, alas, who's injured by my love?   10
  What merchant's ships have my sighs drowned?
Who says my tears have overflowed his ground?
  When did my colds a forward spring remove?
    When did the heats which my veins fill
    Add one more to the plaguy bill?   15
Soldiers find wars, and lawyers find out still
  Litigious men, which quarrels move,
  Though she and I do love.

Call us what you will, we are made such by love;
  Call her one, me another fly,   20
We're tapers too, and at our own cost die,
  And we in us find the eagle and the dove.
    The phoenix riddle hath more wit
    By us; we two being one, are it.
So, to one neutral thing both sexes fit.   25
  We die and rise the same, and prove
  Mysterious by this love.

We can die by it, if not live by love,
  And if unfit for tombs and hearse
Our legend be, it will be fit for verse;   30
  And if no piece of chronicle we prove,
    We'll build in sonnets pretty rooms;
    As well a well-wrought urn becomes
The greatest ashes, as half-acre tombs,
  And by these hymns, all shall approve   35
  Us *canonized* for Love.

And thus invoke us: "You, whom reverend love
  Made one another's hermitage;

You, to whom love was peace, that now is rage;
  Who did the whole world's soul extract, and drove   40
    Into the glasses of your eyes
    (So made such mirrors, and such spies,
That they did all to you epitomize)
    Countries, towns, courts: beg from above
    A pattern of your love!"   45

HOLY SONNETS

VII

At the round earth's imagined corners, blow
Your trumpets, angels, and arise, arise
From death, you numberless infinities
Of souls, and to your scattered bodies go,
All whom the flood did, and fire shall o'erthrow,   5
All whom war, dearth, age, agues, tyrannies,
Despair, law, chance, hath slain, and you whose eyes
Shall behold God and never taste death's woe.
But let them sleep, Lord, and me mourn a space,
For if above all these my sins abound,   10
'Tis late to ask abundance of Thy grace
When we are there; here on this lowly ground,
Teach me how to repent; for that's as good
As if Thou hadst sealed my pardon with Thy blood.

THE CANONIZATION. Note progression in tone from ironic flippancy to sincere reverence. 1. *For God's sake,* should be read literally as well as figuratively. 7. *stamped face,* coined. 8. *approve,* try. 11–15. *What . . . bill?* These images are based upon the belief that each man was thought to be a replica of the universe. 11–12. *sighs, tears,* thought to shorten life. 15. *plaguy bill,* death list of plague victims. 20. *fly,* suggests short life span and open promiscuity. 21. *tapers.* Candles are self-consuming. *die,* colloquial synonym for sexual intercourse which was believed to shorten one's life through the rage and fire of passion. 22. *eagle,* suggests strength, loyalty, and masculine virtues. *dove,* suggests peace, meekness, and feminine virtues. 23. *phoenix,* a hermaphroditic bird of mythology that procreated itself by rising from the ashes of its own funeral pyre every six hundred years; symbol of immortality. *phoenix riddle,* appears in the Oedipus myth: "What has four legs in the morning, two legs at noon, and three at evening?" Oedipus' answer was man—he crawls in infancy, stands upright in maturity, and walks with a crutch during old age. *wit,* meaning. 25. *thing,* mankind; see *phoenix riddle,* l. 23. 30. *legend,* inscription on tomb; degree of historical interpretation that approaches mythology; saints' lives. 45. *love.* Note where the word love appears in this poem.

X

Death be not proud, though some have called thee
Mighty and dreadful, for thou art not so;
For those whom thou think'st thou dost overthrow
Die not, poor death, nor yet canst thou kill me.
From rest and sleep, which but thy pictures be,   5
Much pleasure; then from thee much more must flow,
And soonest our best men with thee do go,
Rest of their bones, and soul's delivery.
Thou art slave to fate, chance, kings, and desperate men,
And dost with poison, war, and sickness dwell;   10
And poppy or charms can make us sleep as well,
And better than thy stroke; why swell'st thou then?
One short sleep past, we wake eternally,
And death shall be no more; death, thou shalt die.

XIII

What if this present were the world's last night?
Mark in my heart, O soul, where thou dost dwell,
The picture of Christ crucified, and tell
Whether that countenance can thee affright,
Tears in His eyes quench the amazing light,   5
Blood fills His frowns, which from His pierced head fell.
And can that tongue adjudge thee unto hell,
Which prayed forgiveness for His foe's fierce spite?
No, no; but as in my idolatry
I said to all my profane mistresses,   10
Beauty, of pity, foulness only is
A sign of rigor: so I say to thee,
To wicked spirits are horrid shapes assigned,
This beauteous form assures a piteous mind.

HOLY SONNET VII. 1. *corners*. The earth was at one time believed to be square; Rev. 7:1, "I saw four angels standing on the four corners of the earth, that no wind should blow . . . ." 8. *death's woe*. Luke 9:27, "There are some of them that stand here, who shall in no wise taste of death."

HOLY SONNET X. 11. *poppy*, flower from which opium is derived.

HOLY SONNET XIII. 14. *beauteous form*, based on a platonic notion that the state of the soul is incarnated in the body; a beauteous form reflected the harmony of the soul.

XIV

Batter my heart, three-personed God; for You
As yet but knock, breathe, shine, and seek to mend;
That I may rise and stand, o'erthrow me, and bend
Your force, to break, blow, burn, and make me new.
I, like an usurped town, to another due,   5
Labor to admit You, but Oh, to no end!
Reason, Your viceroy in me, me should defend,
But is captived, and proves weak or untrue.
Yet dearly I love You, and would be loved fain,
But am betrothed unto Your enemy: 10
Divorce me, untie or break that knot again,
Take me to You, imprison me, for I,
Except You enthrall me, never shall be free,
Nor ever chaste, except You ravish me.

HOLY SONNET XIV. 1. *three-personed,* trinity.

Ben Jonson

1572–1637

COME, MY CELIA

Come, my Celia, let us prove,
While we can, the sports of love;
Time will not be ours forever;
He at length our good will sever.
Spend not then his gifts in vain. 5
Suns that set may rise again;
But if once we lose this light,
'Tis with us perpetual night.
Why should we defer our joys?
Fame and rumor are but toys. 10
Cannot we delude the eyes
Of a few poor household spies,
Or his easier ears beguile,
So removéd by our wile?
'Tis no sin love's fruit to steal; 15
But the sweet thefts to reveal,
To be taken, to be seen,
These have crimes accounted been.

STILL TO BE NEAT

Still to be neat, still to be dressed,
As you were going to a feast;
Still to be powdered, still perfumed;

COME, MY CELIA.   1. *prove*, try.

Lady, it is to be presumed,
Though art's hid causes are not found,   5
All is not sweet, all is not sound.

Give me a look, give me a face
That makes simplicity a grace;
Robes loosely flowing, hair as free;
Such sweet neglect more taketh me   10
Then all th' adulteries of art.
They strike mine eyes, but not my heart.

Robert Herrick

DELIGHT IN DISORDER

A sweet disorder in the dress
Kindles in clothes a wantonness.
A lawn about the shoulders thrown
Into a fine distraction;
An erring lace, which here and there   5
Enthrals the crimson stomacher;
A cuff neglectful, and thereby
Ribbands to flow confusedly;
A winning wave, deserving note,
In the tempestuous petticoat;   10
A careless shoestring, in whose tie
I see a wild civility;—
Do more bewitch me, than when art
Is too precise in every part.

UPON JULIA'S CLOTHES

Whenas in silks my Julia goes,
Then, then, methinks, how sweetly flows
The liquefaction of her clothes.

Next, when I cast mine eyes, and see
That brave vibration, each way free,   5
Oh, how that glittering taketh me!

CORINNA'S GOING A-MAYING

Get up, get up for shame, the blooming morn
Upon her wings presents the god unshorn.
　See how Aurora throws her fair
　Fresh-quilted colors through the air:
　Get up, sweet slug-a-bed, and see　　　　　　　　5
　The dew bespangling herb and tree.
Each flower has wept and bowéd toward the east
Above an hour since: yet you not dressed;
　Nay! not so much as out of bed?
　When all the birds have matins said　　　　　　10
　And sung their thankful hymns, 't is s'n,
　Nay, profanation, to keep in,
Whenas a thousand virgins on this day
Spring, sooner than the lark, to fetch in May.

Rise, and put on your foliage, and be seen　　　　15
To come forth, like the springtime, fiesh and green,
　And sweet as Flora. Take no care
　For jewels for your gown or hair·
　Fear not; the leaves will strew
　Gems in abundance upon you:　　　　　　　　20
Besides, the childhood of the day has kept,
Against you come, some orient pearls unwept;
　Come and receive them while the light
　Hangs on the dew-locks of the night:
　And Titan on the eastern hill　　　　　　　　25
　Retires himself, or else stands still
Till you come forth. Wash, dress, be brief in praying:
Few beads are best when once we go a-Maying.

Come, my Corinna, come; and, coming mark
How each field turns a street, each street a park　30
　Made green and trimmed with trees; see how
　Devotion gives each house a bough
　Or branch: each porch, each door ere this
　An ark, a tabernacle is,
Made up of white-thorn, neatly interwove;　　　35
As if here were those cooler shades of love.
　Can such delights be in the street
　And open fields and we not see 't?
　Come, we'll abroad; and let's obey
　The proclamation made for May:　　　　　　　40

And sin no more, as we have done, by staying;
But, my Corinna, come, let's go a-Maying.

There's not a budding boy or girl this day
But is got up, and gone to bring in May.
 A deal of youth, ere this, is come   45
 Back, and with white-thorn laden home.
 Some have dispatched their cakes and cream
 Before that we have left to dream:
And some have wept, and wooed, and plighted troth,
And chose their priest, ere we can cast off sloth: 50
 Many a green-gown has been given;
 Many a kiss, both odd and even:
 Many a glance too has been sent
 From out the eye, love's firmament;
Many a jest told of the keys betraying   55
This night, and locks picked, yet we're not a-Maying.

Come, let us go while we are in our prime;
And take the harmless folly of the time.
 We shall grow old apace, and die
 Before we know our liberty.   60
 Our life is short, and our days run
 As fast away as does the sun;
And, as a vapor or a drop of rain,
Once lost, can ne'er be found again,
 So when or you or I are made   65
 A fable, song, or fleeting shade,
 All love, all liking, all delight
 Lies drowned with us in endless night.
Then while time serves, and we are but decaying,
Come, my Corinna, come let's go a-Maying.   70

CORINNA'S GOING A-MAYING. 3. *Aurora*, Roman goddess of dawn. 17. *Flora*, Roman goddess of flowers. 25. *Titan*, in Greek mythology, a race of giants overthrown by the Olympian gods. 28. *beads*, praying beads. 34. *ark, a tabernacle.* The ark was a sacred chest of Hebrew ceremony, containing the Ten Commandments. The tabernacle is a box on the Christian altar containing the Holy Eucharist.

Andrew Marvell

1621–1678

TO HIS COY MISTRESS

Had we but world enough, and time,
This coyness, lady, were no crime.
We would sit down, and think which way
To walk, and pass our long love's day.
Thou by the Indian Ganges' side   5
Shouldst rubies find: I by the tide
Of Humber would complain. I would
Love you ten years before the flood,
And you should, if you please, refuse
Till the conversion of the Jews;   10
My vegetable love should grow
Vaster than empires and more slow;
An hundred years should go to praise
Thine eyes, and on thy forehead gaze;
Two hundred to adore each breast,   15
But thirty thousand to the rest;
An age at least to every part,
And the last age should show your heart.
For, lady, you deserve this state;
Nor would I love at lower rate.   20

But at my back I always hear
Time's wingéd chariot hurrying near;
And yonder all before us lie
Deserts of vast eternity.
Thy beauty shall no more be found,   25
Nor in thy marble vault shall sound
My echoing song; then worms shall try

That long preserved virginity;
And your quaint honor turn to dust,
And into ashes all my lust: 30
The grave's a fine and private place,
But none, I think, do there embrace.

Now therefore, while the youthful hue
Sits on thy skin like morning dew,
And while thy willing soul transpires   35
At every pore with instant fires,
Now let us sport us while we may,
And now, like amorous birds of prey,
Rather at once our time devour
Than languish in his slow-chapped power,   40
Let us roll all our strength and all
Our sweetness up into one ball,
And tear our pleasures with rough strife
Thorough the iron gates of life:
Thus, though we cannot make our sun   45
Stand still, yet we will make him run.

To HIS COY MISTRESS. Note the syllogistic structure. 5. *Ganges'*, river in
northern India. 7. *Humber*, the place in eastern England where the current
of the rivers Ouse and Trent collide with the ocean tide. 8. *flood*, the great
flood of Genesis. 10. *conversion*. According to Scripture, the world will end
when all Jews are converted to Christianity. 11. *vegetable*, suggests rapid
organic growth. 29. *quaint*, proud. 40. *slow-chapped*, slowly crushing.

John Milton

1608–1674

ON HIS HAVING ARRIVED AT THE AGE OF TWENTY-THREE

How soon hath Time, the subtle thief of youth,
Stolen on his wing my three and twentieth year!
My hasting days fly on with full career,
But my late spring no bud or blossom shew'th.
Perhaps my semblance might deceive the truth   5
That I to manhood am arrived so near;
And inward ripeness doth much less appear,
That some more timely-happy spirits endu'th.
Yet be it less or more, or soon or slow,
It shall be still in strictest measure even   10
To that same lot, however mean or high,
Toward which Time leads me, and the will of Heaven;
All is, if I have grace to use it so,
As ever in my great Task-Master's eye.

ON HIS BLINDNESS

When I consider how my light is spent
Ere half my days in this dark world and wide,
And that one talent which is death to hide
Lodged with me useless, though my soul more bent

On his having arrived at the age of twenty-three.   8. *timely-happy spirits,* people whose spiritual growth is comparable with their physical growth.

To serve therewith my Maker, and present   5
My true account, lest He returning chide;
"Doth God exact day-labor, light denied?"
I fondly ask. But Patience, to prevent
That murmur, soon replies, "God doth not need
Either man's work or his own gifts. Who best   10
Bear his mild yoke, they serve him best. His state
Is kingly: thousands at his bidding speed,
And post o'er land and ocean without rest;
They also serve who only stand and wait."

Alexander Pope

1688–1744

from AN ESSAY ON MAN

To Henry St. John, Lord Bolingbroke

From Epistle I. Of the Nature and State of Man,
With Respect to the Universe

Awake, my St. John! leave all meaner things
To low ambition, and the pride of kings.
Let us (since life can little more supply
Than just to look about us and to die)
Expatiate free o'er all this scene of man;   5
A mighty maze! but not without a plan;
A wild, where weeds and flowers promiscuous shoot,
Or garden, tempting with forbidden fruit.
Together let us beat this ample field,
Try what the open, what the covert yield;   10
The latent tracts, the giddy heights, explore
Of all who blindly creep, or sightless soar;
Eye Nature's walks, shoot folly as it flies,
And catch the manners living as they rise;
Laugh where we must, be candid where we can;   15
But vindicate the ways of God to man.

1. Say first, of God above, or man below,
What can we reason, but from what we know?
Of man, what see we but his station here,
From which to reason, or to which refer?   20
Through worlds unnumbered though the God be known,
'Tis ours to trace him only in our own.
He, who through vast immensity can pierce,
See worlds on worlds compose one universe,

Observe how system into system runs,   25
What other planets circle other suns,
What varied Being peoples every star,
May tell why Heaven has made us as we are.
But of this frame the bearings, and the ties,
The strong connections, nice dependencies,   30
Gradations just, has thy pervading soul
Looked through? or can a part contain the whole?
   Is the great chain, that draws all to agree,
And drawn supports, upheld by God, or thee?

   2. Presumptuous man! the reason wouldst thou find,   35
Why formed so weak, so little, and so blind?
First, if thou canst, the harder reason guess,
Why formed no weaker, blinder, and no less!
Ask of thy mother earth, why oaks are made
Taller or stronger than the weeds they shade?   40
Or ask of yonder argent fields above,
Why Jove's satellites are less than Jove?
   Of systems possible, if 'tis confessed
That Wisdom Infinite must form the best,
Where all must full or not coherent be,   45
And all that rises, rise in due degree;
Then, in the scale of reasoning life, 'tis plain,
There must be, somewhere, such a rank as man:
And all the question (wrangle e'er so long)
Is only this, if God has placed him wrong?   50
   Respecting man, whatever wrong we call,
May, must be right, as relative to all.
In human works, though labored on with pain,
A thousand movements scarce one purpose gain;
In God's, one single can its end produce;   55
Yet serves to second too some other use.
So man, who here seems principal alone,
Perhaps acts second to some sphere unknown,
Touches some wheel, or verges to some goal;
'Tis but a part we see, and not a whole.   60
   When the proud steed shall know why man restrains
His fiery course, or drives him o'er the plains;
When the dull ox, why now he breaks the clod,
Is now a victim, and now Egypt's god:
Then shall man's pride and dullness comprehend   65
His actions', passions', being's use and end;
Why doing, suffering, checked, impelled; and why
This hour a slave, the next a deity.

Then say not man's imperfect, Heaven in fault;
Say rather, man's as perfect as he ought: 70
His knowledge measured to his state and place,
His time a moment, and a point his space.
If to be perfect in a certain sphere,
What matter, soon or late, or here or there?
The blest today is as completely so,   75
As who began a thousand years ago.

   3. Heaven from all creatures hides the book of Fate,
All but the page prescribed, their present state:
From brutes what men, from men what spirits know:
Or who could suffer Being here below?   80
The lamb thy riot dooms to bleed today,
Had he thy reason, would he skip and play?
Pleased to the last, he crops the flowery food,
And licks the hand just raised to shed his blood.
O blindness to the future! kindly given,   85
That each may fill the circle marked by Heaven:
Who sees with equal eye, as God of all,
A hero perish, or a sparrow fall,
Atoms or systems into ruin hurled,
And now a bubble burst, and now a world.   90
   Hope humbly then; with trembling pinions soar;
Wait the great teacher Death, and God adore!
What future bliss, he gives not thee to know,
But gives that hope to be thy blessing now.
Hope springs eternal in the human breast: 95
Man never is, but always to be blest:
The soul, uneasy and confined from home,
Rests and expatiates in a life to come.
   Lo! the poor Indian, whose untutored mind
Sees God in clouds, or hears him in the wind;   100
His soul proud Science never taught to stray
Far as the solar walk, or milky way;
Yet simple Nature to his hope has given,
Behind the cloud-topped hill, an humbler heaven;
Some safer world in depth of woods embraced,   105
Some happier island in the watery waste,
Where slaves once more their native land behold,
No fiends torment, no Christians thirst for gold!
To be, contents his natural desire,
He asks no angel's wing, no seraph's fire;   110
But thinks, admitted to that equal sky,
His faithful dog shall bear him company.

4. Go, wiser thou! and, in thy scale of sense,
Weigh thy opinion against Providence;
Call imperfection what thou fancy'st such,   115
Say, here he gives too little, there too much;
Destroy all creatures for thy sport or gust,
Yet cry, if man's unhappy, God's unjust;
If man alone engross not Heaven's high care,
Alone made perfect here, immortal there: 120
Snatch from his hand the balance and the rod,
Rejudge his justice, be the God of God!
In pride, in reasoning pride, our error lies;
All quit their sphere, and rush into the skies.
Pride still is aiming at the blest abodes,   125
Men would be angels, angels would be gods.
Aspiring to be gods, if angels fell,
Aspiring to be angels, men rebel:
And who but wishes to invert the laws
Of order, sins against the Eternal Cause.   130

• • •

6. What would this man? Now upward will he soar,
And little less than angel, would be more;
Now looking downwards, just as grieved appears   175
To want the strength of bulls, the fur of bears.
Made for his use all creatures if he call,
Say what their use, had he the powers of all?
Nature to these, without profusion, kind,
The proper organs, proper powers assigned;   180
Each seeming want compénsated of course,
Here with degrees of swiftness, there of force;
All in exact proportion to the state;
Nothing to add, and nothing to abate.
Each beast, each insect, happy in its own;   185
Is Heaven unkind to man, and man alone?
Shall he alone, whom rational we call,
Be pleased with nothing, if not blessed with all?
   The bliss of man (could pride that blessing find)
Is not to act or think beyond mankind;   190
No powers of body or of soul to share,
But what his nature and his state can bear.
Why has not man a microscopic eye?
For this plain reason, man is not a fly.
Say what the use, were finer optics given,   195
To inspect a mite, not comprehend the heaven?

Or touch, if tremblingly alive all o'er,
To smart and agonize at every pore?
Or quick effluvia darting through the brain,
Die of a rose in aromatic pain?   200
If nature thundered in his opening ears,
And stunned him with the music of the spheres,
How would he wish that Heaven had left him still
The whispering zephyr, and the purling rill?
Who finds not Providence all good and wise,   205
Alike in what it gives, and what denies?

● ● ●

9. What if the foot, ordained the dust to tread,
Or hand, to toil, aspired to be the head?   260
What if the head, the eye, or ear repined
To serve mere engines to the ruling Mind?
Just as absurd for any part to claim
To be another, in this general frame:
Just as absurd, to mourn the tasks or pains,   265
The great directing MIND of ALL ordains.
    All are but parts of one stupendous whole,
Whose body Nature is, and God the soul;
That, changed through all, and yet in all the same,
Great in the earth, as in the ethereal frame,   270
Warms in the sun, refreshes in the breeze,
Glows in the stars, and blossoms in the trees,
Lives through all life, extends through all extent,
Spreads undivided, operates unspent,
Breathes in our soul, informs our mortal part,   275
As full, as perfect, in a hair as heart;
As full, as perfect, in vile man that mourns,
As the rapt seraph that adores and burns;
To him no high, no low, no great, no small;
He fills, he bounds, connects, and equals all.   280

    10. Cease then, nor ORDER imperfection name:
Our proper bliss depends on what we blame.
Know thy own point: this kind, this due degree
Of blindness, weakness, Heaven bestows on thee.
Submit—In this, or any other sphere,   285
Secure to be as blest as thou canst bear:
Safe in the hand of one disposing Power,
Or in the natal, or the mortal hour.
All Nature is but art, unknown to thee;
All chance, direction, which thou canst not see;   290

All discord, harmony not understood;
All partial evil, universal good:
And, spite of pride, in erring reason's spite,
One truth is clear: *Whatever is, is right.*

From Epistle II. Of the Nature and State of Man
    With Respect to Himself, as an Individual

  1. Know then thyself, presume not God to scan;
The proper study of mankind is Man.
Placed on this isthmus of a middle state,
A being darkly wise, and rudely great:
With too much knowledge for the skeptic side,   5
With too much weakness for the Stoic's pride,
He hangs between; in doubt to act, or rest,
In doubt to deem himself a god, or beast;
In doubt his mind or body to prefer,
Born but to die, and reasoning but to err;   10
Alike in ignorance, his reason such,
Whether he thinks too little, or too much:
Chaos of thought and passion, all confused;
Still by himself abused, or disabused;
Created half to rise, and half to fall;   15
Great lord of all things, yet a prey to all;
Sole judge of truth, in endless error hurled:
The glory, jest, and riddle of the world!

From AN ESSAY ON MAN. *Epistle I.*   1. *St. John,* Henry St. John, Viscount
Bolingbroke, patron and advisor to Pope. 5. *Expatiate,* wander. 41. *argent
fields,* silvery heavens. 42. *Jove,* patriarchal god of Roman mythology. 73.
sphere, area of activity or endeavor.

Thomas Gray

1716–1771

ELEGY WRITTEN IN A COUNTRY CHURCHYARD

The curfew tolls the knell of parting day,
   The lowing herd wind slowly o'er the lea,
The plowman homeward plods his weary way,
   And leaves the world to darkness and to me.

Now fades the glimmering landscape on the sight,   5
   And all the air a solemn stillness holds,
Save where the beetle wheels his droning flight,
   And drowsy tinklings lull the distant folds;

Save that from yonder ivy-mantled tower
   The moping owl does to the moon complain   10
Of such as, wandering near her secret bower,
   Molest her ancient solitary reign.

Beneath those rugged elms, that yew-tree's shade,
   Where heaves the turf in many a moldering heap,
Each in his narrow cell forever laid,   15
   The rude forefathers of the hamlet sleep.

The breezy call of incense-breathing Morn,
   The swallow twittering from the straw-built shed,
The cock's shrill clarion, or the echoing horn,
   No more shall rouse them from their lowly bed.   20

For them no more the blazing hearth shall burn,
   Or busy housewife ply her evening care;
No children run to lisp their sire's return,
   Or climb his knees the envied kiss to share.

Oft did the harvest to their sickle yield,   25
   Their furrow oft the stubborn glebe has broke;
How jocund did they drive their team afield!
   How bowed the woods beneath their sturdy stroke!

Let not Ambition mock their useful toil,
   Their homely joys, and destiny obscure;   30
Nor Grandeur hear, with a disdainful smile,
   The short and simple annals of the poor.

The boast of heraldry, the pomp of power,
   And all that beauty, all that wealth e'er gave,
Awaits alike the inevitable hour: 35
   The paths of glory lead but to the grave.

Nor you, ye proud, impute to these the fault,
   If Memory o'er their tomb no trophies raise,
Where through the long-drawn aisle and fretted vault
   The pealing anthem swells the note of praise.   40

Can storied urn or animated bust
   Back to its mansion call the fleeting breath?
Can Honor's voice provoke the silent dust,
   Or Flattery soothe the dull cold ear of Death?

Perhaps in this neglected spot is laid   45
   Some heart once pregnant with celestial fire;
Hands that the rod of empire might have swayed,
   Or waked to ecstasy the living lyre.

But Knowledge to their eyes her ample page
   Rich with the spoils of time did ne'er unroll;   50
Chill Penury repressed their noble rage,
   And froze the genial current of the soul.

Full many a gem of purest ray serene
   The dark unfathomed caves of ocean bear;
Full many a flower is born to blush unseen,   55
   And waste its sweetness on the desert air.

Some village Hampden that with dauntless breast
   The little tyrant of his fields withstood;
Some mute inglorious Milton here may rest,
   Some Cromwell guiltless of his country's blood.   60

The applause of listening senates to command,
   The threats of pain and ruin to despise,
To scatter plenty o'er a smiling land,
   And read their history in a nation's eyes,

Their lot forbade; nor circumscribed alone   65
    Their growing virtues, but their crimes confined;
Forbade to wade through slaughter to a throne,
    And shut the gates of mercy on mankind,

The struggling pangs of conscious truth to hide,
    To quench the blushes of ingenuous shame,   70
Or heap the shrine of Luxury and Pride
    With incense kindled at the Muse's flame.

Far from the madding crowd's ignoble strife,
    Their sober wishes never learned to stray;
Along the cool sequestered vale of life   75
    They kept the noiseless tenor of their way.

Yet ev'n bones from insult to protect
    Some frail memorial still erected nigh,
With uncouth rimes and shapeless sculpture decked,
    Implores the passing tribute of a sigh.   80

Their name, their years, spelt by the unlettered Muse,
    The place of fame and elegy supply;
And many a holy text around she strews,
    That teach the rustic moralist to die.

For who, to dumb Forgetfulness a prey,   85
    This pleasing anxious being e'er resigned,
Left the warm precincts of the cheerful day,
    Nor cast one longing, lingering look behind?

On some fond breast the parting soul relies,
    Some pious drops the closing eye requires;   90
Ev'n from the tomb the voice of Nature cries,
    Ev'n in our ashes live their wonted fires.

For thee, who mindful of the unhonored dead
    Dost in these lines their artless tale relate;
If chance, by lonely Contemplation led,   95
    Some kindred spirit shall inquire thy fate,

Haply some hoary-headed swain may say,
    "Oft have we seen him at the peep of dawn
Brushing with hasty steps the dews away
    To meet the sun upon the upland lawn.   100

"There at the foot of yonder nodding beech,
   That wreathes its old fantastic roots so high,
His listless length at noontide would he stretch,
   And pore upon the brook that babbles by.

"Hard by yon wood, now smiling as in scorn,   105
   Muttering his wayward fancies he would rove,
Now drooping, woeful wan, like one forlorn,
   Or crazed with care, or crossed in hopeless love.

"One morn I missed him on the customed hill,
   Along the heath, and near his favorite tree;   110
Another came; nor yet beside the rill,
   Nor up the lawn, nor at the wood was he;

"The next with dirges due in sad array
   Slow through the church-way path we saw him borne.
Approach and read (for thou canst read) the lay,   115
   Graved on the stone beneath yon aged thorn."

THE EPITAPH

Here rests his head upon the lap of Earth
   A youth to Fortune and to Fame unknown.
Fair Science frowned not on his humble birth,
   And Melancholy marked him for her own.   120

Large was his bounty, and his soul sincere,
   Heaven did a recompense as largely send;
He gave to Misery all he had, a tear,
   He gained from Heaven ('twas all he wished) a friend.

No farther seek his merits to disclose,   125
   Or draw his frailties from their dread abode,
(There they alike in trembling hope repose),
   The bosom of his Father and his God.

ELEGY WRITTEN IN A COUNTRY CHURCHYARD. 19. *echoing horn*, huntsman's horns. 26. *glebe*, sod. 33. *heraldry*, the system of signifying emblems of nobility. 41. *storied*, inscribed with pictures. *animated*, lifelike. 57. *Hampden*, John Hampden (1594–1643), a patriot who opposed unjust taxes. 59. *Milton*, John Milton (1608–1674), English poet. 60. *Cromwell*, Oliver Cromwell (1599–1658), Lord Protector of England.

Robert Burns

1759–1796

TO A MOUSE

On Turning up Her Nest with the Plow, November 1785

Wee, sleekit, cowrin, tim'rous beastie,
O, what a panic's in thy breastie!
Thou need na start awa sae hasty
   Wi' bickering brattle!
I wad be laith to rin an' chase thee,   5
   Wi' murdering pattle!

I'm truly sorry man's dominion
Has broken Nature's social union,
An' justifies that ill opinion
   Which makes thee startle   10
At me, thy poor, earth-born companion
   An' fellow-mortal!

I doubt na, whyles, but thou may thieve;
What then? poor beastie, thou maun live:
A daimen icker in a thrave   15
   'S a sma' request;
I'll get a blessin wi' the lave,
   An' never miss 't!

Thy wee-bit housie, too, in ruin!
Its silly wa's the win's are strewin!   20
An' naething, now, to big a new ane,
   O' foggage green!
An' bleak December's win's ensuin,
   Baith snell an' keen!

Thou saw the fields laid bare an' waste,   25
An' weary winter comin' fast,
An' cozie here, beneath the blast,
    Thou thought to dwell,
Till, crash! the cruel coulter passed
    Out through thy cell.   30

That wee bit heap o' leaves an' stibble,
Has cost thee monie a weary nibble!
Now thou's turned out, for a' thy trouble,
    But house or hald,
To thole the winter's sleety dribble,   35
    An' cranreuch cauld!

But Mousie, thou art no thy lane,
In proving foresight may be vain:
The best-laid schemes o' mice an' men
    Gang aft agley,   40
An' lea'e us naught but grief an' pain,
    For promised joy!

Still thou art blest, compared wi' me!
The present only toucheth thee:
But och! I backward cast my e'e,   45
    On prospects drear!
An' forward, though I canna see,
    I guess an' fear!

AULD LANG SYNE

Should auld acquaintance be forgot,
    And never brought to min'?
Should auld acquaintance be forgot,
    And auld lang syne?

To a mouse. 4. *bickering brattle*, reckless scamper. 6. *pattle*, an instrument used to clean a plowshare. 15. *daimen . . . thrave*, occasional ear in a shock. 17. *lave*, remainder. 20. *silly*, feeble. 21. *big*, build. 22. *foggage*, moss. 24. *snell*, sharp, bitter. 29. *coulter*, plowshare. 34. *But*, without. *hald*, abode. 35. *thole*, endure. 36. *cranreuch*, hoarfrost. 37. *no thy lane*, not alone. 40. *Gang aft agley*, often go awry.

CHORUS

For auld lang syne, my dear,   5
   For auld lang syne,
We'll tak a cup o' kindness yet
   For auld lang syne.

And surely ye'll be your pint-stowp,
   And surely I'll be mine!   10
And we'll tak a cup o' kindness yet
   For auld lang syne.

We twa hae run about the braes,
   And pu'd the gowans fine;
But we've wandered monie a weary fit   15
   Sin' auld lang syne.

We twa hae paidled i' the burn,
   From mornin' sun till dine;
But seas between us braid hae roared
   Sin' auld lang syne.   20

And there's a hand, my trusty fiere,
   And gie's a hand o' thine;
And we'll tak a right guid-willie waught
   For auld lang syne.

AULD LANG SYNE: old long since, *i.e., days long ago.* 9. *And . . . pint-stowp,* you will buy your pint. 13. *braes,* hillsides. 14. *gowans,* daisies. 15. *fit,* foot. 17. *paidled,* paddled. *burn,* brook. 19. *braid,* broad, wide. 21. *fiere,* friend. 23. *right . . . waught,* hearty good-will drink.

William Blake

1757–1827

innocence and experience

TO SPRING

O thou with dewy locks, who lookest down
Thro' the clear windows of the morning, turn
Thine angel eyes upon our western isle,
Which in full choir hails thy approach, O Spring!

The hills tell each other, and the list'ning   5
Vallies hear; all our longing eyes are turned
Up to thy bright pavillions: issue forth,
And let thy holy feet visit our clime.

Come o'er the eastern hills, and let our winds
Kiss thy perfumed garments; let us taste   10
Thy morn and evening breath; scatter thy pearls
Upon our love-sick land that mourns for thee.

O deck her forth with thy fair fingers; pour
Thy soft kisses on her bosom; and put
Thy golden crown upon her languish'd head,   15
Whose modest tresses were bound up for thee!

TO AUTUMN

O Autumn, laden with fruit, and stained
With the blood of the grape, pass not, but sit
Beneath my shady roof; there thou may'st rest,
And tune thy jolly voice to my fresh pipe;
And all the daughters of the year shall dance!   5
Sing now the lusty song of fruits and flowers.

"The narrow bud opens her beauties to
The sun, and love runs in her thrilling veins;
Blossoms hang round the brows of morning, and
Flourish down the bright cheek of modest eve,   10
Till clust'ring Summer breaks forth into singing,
And feather'd clouds strew flowers round her head.

"The spirits of the air live on the smells
Of fruit; and joy, with pinions light, roves round
The gardens, or sits singing in the trees."   15
Thus sang the jolly Autumn as he sat;
Then rose, girded himself, and o'er the bleak
Hills fled from our sight; but left his golden load.

THE BLOSSOM

Merry, Merry Sparrow!
Under leaves so green
A happy Blossom
Sees you swift as arrow
Seek your cradle narrow   5
Near my Bosom.

Pretty, Pretty Robin!
Under leaves so green
A happy Blossom
Hears you sobbing, sobbing,   10
Pretty, Pretty Robin,
Near my Bosom.

AH! SUN-FLOWER

Ah, Sun-flower! weary of time,
Who countest the steps of the Sun,
Seeking after that sweet golden clime
Where the traveller's journey is done:

Where the Youth pined away with desire,   5
And the pale Virgin shrouded in snow
Arise from their graves, and aspire
Where my Sun-flower wishes to go.

THE SICK ROSE

O Rose, thou art sick!
The invisible worm
That flies in the night,
In the howling storm,

Has found out thy bed   5
Of crimson joy,
And his dark secret love
Does thy life destroy.

THE LAMB

   Little Lamb, who made thee?
   Dost thou know who made thee?
Gave thee life, & bid thee feed
By the stream & o'er the mead;
Gave thee clothing of delight,   5
Softest clothing, wooly, bright;
Gave thee such a tender voice,
Making all the vales rejoice?
   Little Lamb, who made thee?
   Dost thou know who made thee?   10

   Little Lamb, I'll tell thee,
   Little Lamb, I'll tell thee:
He is called by thy name,
For he calls himself a Lamb.
He is meek, & he is mild;   15
He became a little child.
I a child, & thou a lamb,
We are called by his name.
   Little Lamb, God bless thee!
   Little Lamb, God bless thee!   20

THE LAMB. 4. *mead*, meadow. 13. *He . . . name*, Christ, in this instance
recognized as the symbol of slaughtered innocence.

THE TYGER

Tyger! Tyger! burning bright
In the forests of the night,
What immortal hand or eye
Could frame thy fearful symmetry?

In what distant deeps or skies   5
Burnt the fire of thine eyes?
On what wings dare he aspire?
What the hand dare seize the fire?

And what shoulder, & what art,
Could twist the sinews of thy heart?   10
And when thy heart began to beat,
What dread hand? & what dread feet?

What the hammer? what the chain?
In what furnace was thy brain?
What the anvil? what dread grasp   15
Dare its deadly terrors clasp?

When the stars threw down their spears,
And water'd heaven with their tears,
Did he smile his work to see?
Did he who made the Lamb make thee?   20

Tyger! Tyger! burning bright
In the forests of the night,
What immortal hand or eye,
Dare frame thy fearful symmetry?

THE TYGER. Blake wrote this poem as a work antithetical in theme to "The Lamb" in *Songs of Innocence*. Whereas the image of the lamb expresses passive innocence, the tiger suggests energy of an inexplicable source; the realization of energy. 1. *Tyger*, the poet's original spelling of the word, retained partly because the title of the poem was incorporated in an illustration. 3–4. *What . . . symmetry?* Note recurrent pattern of rhetorical questions. 8. *What the . . . fire.* Prometheus stole fire from the gods for man. 17–18. *When . . . tears.* These lines recall the lament of Urizen (a Satanic figure in Blake's cosmology) from *The Four Zoas:*

I called the stars around my feet in the night of councils dark;
The stars threw down their spears & fled naked away.
We fell.

The stars are thereby linked with negative and restraining forces in the universe which frustrate and corrupt the creative energies.

THE FLY

Little Fly,
Thy summer's play
My thoughtless hand
Has brush'd away.

Am not I   5
A fly like thee?
Or art not thou
A man like me?

For I dance,
And drink, & sing,   10
Till some blind hand
Shall brush my wing.

If thought is life
And strength & breath,
And the want   15
Of thought is death;

Then am I
A happy fly,
If I live
Or if I die.   20

SONG

My silks and fine array,
  My smiles and languish'd air,
By love are driv'n away;
  And mournful lean Despair
Brings me yew to deck my grave: 5
Such end true lovers have.

His face is fair as heav'n,
  When springing buds unfold;

THE FLY. This poem typifies Blake's propensity for ironic intention on the
part of the speaker, which brings up the question of whether or not the speaker
actually feels linked to the fly.

O why to him was't giv'n,
   Whose heart is wintry cold?   10
His breast is love's all worship'd tomb,
Where all love's pilgrims come.

Bring me an axe and spade,
   Bring me a winding sheet;
When I my grave have made,   15
   Let winds and tempests beat:
Then down I'll lie, as cold as clay.
True love doth pass away!

THE DIVINE IMAGE

To Mercy, Pity, Peace, and Love
All pray in their distress;
And to these virtues of delight
Return their thankfulness.

For Mercy, Pity, Peace, and Love   5
Is God, our father dear,
And Mercy, Pity, Peace, and Love
Is Man, his child and care.

For Mercy has a human heart,
Pity a human face,   10
And Love, the human form divine,
And Peace, the human dress.

Then every man, of every clime,
That prays in his distress,
Prays to the human form divine,   15
Love, Mercy, Pity, Peace.

And all must love the human form,
In heathen, turk, or jew;
Where Mercy, Love, & Pity dwell
There God is dwelling too.   20

SONG: MY SILKS AND FINE ARRAY.   5. *yew.* The yew tree is commonly associated with graveyards.   14. *winding sheet,* shroud.

THE CHIMNEY SWEEPER

When my mother died I was very young,
And my father sold me while yet my tongue
Could scarcely cry " 'weep! 'weep! 'weep! 'weep!"
So your chimney I sweep, & in soot I sleep.

There's little Tom Dacre, who cried when his head,   5
That curl'd like a lamb's back, was shav'd: so I said
"Hush, Tom! never mind it, for when your head's bare
You know that the soot cannot spoil your white hair."

And so he was quiet, & that very night,
As Tom was a-sleeping, he had such a sight!   10
That thousands of sweepers, Dick, Joe, Ned, & Jack,
Were all of them lock'd up in coffins of black.

And by came an Angel who had a bright key,
And he open'd the coffins & set them all free;
Then down a green plain leaping, laughing, they run,   15
And wash in a river, and shine in the Sun.

Then naked & white, all their bags left behind,
They rise upon clouds and sport in the wind;
And the Angel told Tom, if he'd be a good boy,
He'd have God for his father, & never want joy.   20

And so Tom awoke; and we rose in the dark,
And got with our bags & our brushes to work.
Tho' the morning was cold, Tom was happy & warm;
So if all do their duty they need not fear harm.

THE CHIMNEY SWEEPER: from *Songs of Innocence*. In Blake's cosmology the chimney sweeper is one of the images symbolizing human oppression. Children were important to this profession because their size facilitated working in the narrow quarters of chimney ducts. In 1788 the English Parliament passed a law prohibiting the employment of boys until they were eight years old, but the law was ignored. 2. *sold me*. Boys were sold to the sweeps for a period of about seven years for two to eight guineas. 6. *shav'd*. The boys' heads were shaved to protect them from catching fire. 21. *dark*. Boys went to work at five in the summer and seven in the winter.

THE CHIMNEY SWEEPER

A little black thing among the snow,
Crying ' 'weep! 'weep!' in notes of woe!
"Where are thy father & mother? say?"
"They are both gone up to the church to pray.

"Because I was happy upon the heath,   5
And smil'd among the winter's snow,
They clothed me in the clothes of death,
And taught me to sing the notes of woe.

"And because I am happy & dance & sing,
They think they have done me no injury,   10
And are gone to praise God & his Priest & King,
Who make up a heaven of our misery."

THE GARDEN OF LOVE

I went to the Garden of Love,
And saw what I never had seen:
A Chapel was built in the midst,
Where I used to play on the green.

And the gates of this Chapel were shut,   5
And "Thou shalt not" writ over the door;
So I turn'd to the Garden of Love
That so many sweet flowers bore;

And I saw it was filled with graves,
And tomb-stones where flowers should be;   10
And Priests in black gowns were walking their rounds,
And binding with briars my joys & desires.

I ASKED A THIEF TO STEAL ME A PEACH

I asked a thief to steal me a peach:
He turned up his eyes.
I ask'd a lithe lady to lie her down:
Holy & meek she cries—

THE CHIMNEY SWEEPER: from *Songs of Experience*. 9. *And because . . . sing.*
One such festive occasion was May Day when the chimney sweeps put on wigs
and performed for alms.

As soon as I went   5
An angel came.
He wink'd at the thief
And smil'd at the dame.

And without one word said
Had a peach from the tree   10
And still as a maid
Enjoy'd the lady.

LONDON

I wander thro' each charter'd street,
Near where the charter'd Thames does flow,
And mark in every face I meet
Marks of weakness, marks of woe.

In every cry of every Man,   5
In every Infant's cry of fear,
In every voice, in every ban,
The mind-forg'd manacles I hear.

How the Chimney-sweeper's cry
Every black'ning Church appalls;   10
And the hapless Soldier's sigh
Runs in blood down Palace walls.

But most thro' midnight streets I hear
How the youthful Harlot's curse
Blasts the new born Infant's tear,   15
And blights with plagues the Marriage hearse.

THE GARDEN OF LOVE: deals with the repression of natural freedom. See "Ah!
Sunflower" as a variant on the idea of natural vegetable growth linked to human
psychological repression.

LONDON. 1. *charter'd street*, streets mapped and marked according city charter
or governmental agreement; also rented out. 3. *mark*, to notice closely; note
turn in meaning of the word in the following line. 7. *ban*, the term implies
two meanings: 1) wedding banns, or the publication of wedding announcements,
and 2) a prohibitive decree. 15. *Infant's tear*. The term carries a meaning
beyond natural fact since newborn babies do not cry tears. One reading suggests
inflammation of the eyelids, even blindness, caused by syphilitic birth. 16.
Marriage hearse, ironic modification of the term referring to the carriage used
in marriage ceremony.

THE CLOD AND THE PEBBLE

"Love seeketh not Itself to please,
Nor for itself hath any care,
But for another gives its ease,
And builds a Heaven in Hell's despair."

So sung a little Clod of Clay   5
Trodden with the cattle's feet,
But a Pebble of the brook
Warbled out these metres meet:

"Love seeketh only Self to please,
To bind another to Its delight,   10
Joys in another's loss of ease,
And builds a Hell in Heaven's despite."

A POISON TREE

I was angry with my friend:
I told my wrath, my wrath did end.
I was angry with my foe:
1 told it not, my wrath did grow.

And I water'd it in fears,   5
Night & morning with my tears;
And I sunned it with smiles,
And with soft deceitful wiles.

And it grew both day and night,
Till it bore an apple bright;   10
And my foe beheld it shine,
And he knew that it was mine,

And into my garden stole
When the night had veil'd the pole:
In the morning glad I see   15
My foe outstretch'd beneath the tree.

MAD SONG

The wild winds weep,
  And the night is a-cold;
Come hither, Sleep,
  And my griefs unfold:
But lo! the morning peeps   5
  Over the eastern steeps,
And the rustling birds of dawn
The earth do scorn.

Lo! to the vault
  Of paved heaven,   10
With sorrow fraught
  My notes are driven:
They strike the ear of night,
  Make weep the eyes of day;
They make mad the roaring winds,   15
  And with tempests play.

Like a fiend in a cloud,
  With howling woe,
After night I do croud,
  And with night will go;   20
I turn my back to the east,
From whence comforts have increas'd;
For light doth seize my brain
With frantic pain.

ARE NOT THE JOYS OF MORNING SWEETER

Are not the joys of morning sweeter
Than the joys of night?
And are the vig'rous joys of youth
Ashamed of the light?

Let age & sickness silent rob   5
The vineyards in the night;
But those who burn with vig'rous youth
Pluck fruits before the light.

ARE NOT THE JOYS OF MORNING SWEETER. 1–4. *Are . . . light,* the feeling of madness may be better appreciated in "Mad Song" by comparing the joy in light, health, and youth in this lyric.

O LAPWING, THOU FLIEST AROUND THE HEATH

O lapwing, thou fliest around the heath,
Nor seest the net that is spread beneath.
Why dost thou not fly among the corn fields?
They cannot spread nets where a harvest yields.

THOU HAST A LAP FULL OF SEED

Thou hast a lap full of seed,
And this is a fine country.
Why dost thou not cast thy seed
And live in it merrily?

Shall I cast it on the sand   5
And turn it into fruitful land?
For on no other ground
Can I sow my seed
Without tearing up
Some stinking weed.   10

PREFACE TO MILTON

And did those feet in ancient time
Walk upon England's mountains green?
And was the holy Lamb of God
On England's pleasant pastures seen?

And did the Countenance Divine   5
Shine forth upon our clouded hills?
And was Jerusalem builded here
Among these dark Satanic Mills?

Bring me my Bow of burning gold:
Bring me my Arrows of desire:
Bring me my Spear: O clouds unfold!   10
Bring me my Chariot of fire.

I will not cease from Mental Fight,
Nor shall my Sword sleep in my hand
Till we have built Jerusalem   15
In England's green & pleasant Land.

PREFACE TO MILTON. 1. *And . . . time,* this poem begins a longer work in which
Blake explains himself as an incarnation of the spirit of John Milton, author
of *Paradise Lost,* but the "feet" may have an even more "ancient" reference
since it was believed that once Christ had wandered England. 7. *Jerusalem.*
The new Jerusalem will appear as the Bride of Christ the Lamb and will
mark the end of this world and the beginning of the new. 8. *Satanic Mills.*
Wickedness for Blake was manifested through the rational, the mechanical;
mills suggest the Industrial Revolution which was concurrent with the rational-
ism of the eighteenth century.

William Wordsworth

1770–1850

COMPOSED UPON WESTMINSTER BRIDGE

Earth has not anything to show more fair:
Dull would he be of soul who could pass by
A sight so touching in its majesty:
This City now doth like a garment wear
The beauty of the morning; silent, bare,   5
Ships, towers, domes, theaters, and temples lie
Open unto the fields, and to the sky;
All bright and glittering in the smokeless air.
Never did sun more beautifully steep
In his first splendor valley, rock, or hill;   10
Ne'er saw I, never felt, a calm so deep!
The river glideth at his own sweet will:
Dear God! the very houses seem asleep;
And all that mighty heart is lying still!

THE WORLD IS TOO MUCH WITH US

The world is too much with us; late and soon,
Getting and spending, we lay waste our powers:
Little we see in Nature that is ours;
We have given our hearts away, a sordid boon!
The sea that bares her bosom to the moon;   5
The winds that will be howling at all hours,
And are up-gathered now like sleeping flowers;
For this, for everything, we are out of tune;

It moves us not.—Great God! I'd rather be
A Pagan suckled in a creed outworn;   10
So might I, standing on this pleasant lea,
Have glimpses that would make me less forlorn;
Have sight of Proteus rising from the sea;
Or hear old Triton blow his wreathéd horn.

THE WORLD IS TOO MUCH WITH US.   13–14. *Proteus*, sea god who could assume
many shapes; *Triton*, a sea god.

Samuel Taylor Coleridge

1772–1834

KUBLA KHAN

In Xanadu did Kubla Khan
A stately pleasure-dome decree:
Where Alph, the sacred river, ran
Through caverns measureless to man
  Down to a sunless sea.   5
So twice five miles of fertile ground
With walls and towers were girdled round:
And here were gardens bright with sinuous rills,
Where blossomed many an incense-bearing tree;
And here were forests ancient as the hills,   10
Enfolding sunny spots of greenery.
But oh! that deep romantic chasm which slanted
Down the green hill athwart a cedarn cover!
A savage place! as holy and enchanted
As e'er beneath a waning moon was haunted   15
By woman wailing for her demon-lover!
And from this chasm, with ceaseless turmoil seething,
As if this earth in fast thick pants were breathing,
A mighty fountain momently was forced;
Amid whose swift half-intermitted burst   20
Huge fragments vaulted like rebounding hail,
Or chaffy grain beneath the thresher's flail:
And 'mid these dancing rocks at once and ever
It flung up momently the sacred river.
Five miles meandering with a mazy motion   25
Through wood and dale the sacred river ran,
Then reached the caverns measureless to man,
And sank in tumult to a lifeless ocean:
And 'mid this tumult Kubla heard from far
Ancestral voices prophesying war!   30

The shadow of the dome of pleasure
Floated midway on the waves;
Where was heard the mingled measure
From the fountain and the caves.
It was a miracle of rare device,   35
A sunny pleasure-dome with caves of ice!
   A damsel with a dulcimer
   In a vision once I saw:
   It was an Abyssinian maid,
   And on her dulcimer she played,   40
   Singing of Mount Abora.
   Could I revive within me,
   Her symphony and song,
   To such a deep delight 'twould win me,
That with music loud and long,   45
I would build that dome in air,
That sunny dome! those caves of ice!
And all who heard should see them there,
And all should cry, Beware! Beware!
His flashing eyes, his floating hair!   50
Weave a circle round him thrice,
And close your eyes with holy dread,
For he on honey-dew hath fed,
And drunk the milk of Paradise.

KUBLA KHAN.   Thirteenth-century Mongolian emperor noted for the grandeur of his court and the ferociousness of his ancestors.

George Noel Gordon, Lord Byron

1788–1824

SHE WALKS IN BEAUTY

She walks in beauty, like the night
  Of cloudless climes and starry skies;
And all that's best of dark and bright
  Meet in her aspect and her eyes:
Thus mellowed to that tender light   5
  Which heaven to gaudy day denies.

One shade the more, one ray the less,
  Had half impaired the nameless grace
Which waves in every raven tress,
  Or softly lightens o'er her face;   10
Where thoughts serenely sweet express
  How pure, how dear their dwelling-place.

And on that cheek, and o'er that brow,
  So soft, so calm, yet eloquent,
The smiles that win, the tints that glow,   15
  But tell of days in goodness spent,
A mind at peace with all below,
  A heart whose love is innocent!

WHEN A MAN HATH NO FREEDOM

When a man hath no freedom to fight for at home,
  Let him combat for that of his neighbors;
  Let him think of the glories of Greece and of Rome,
  And get knocked on the head for his labors.

To do good to mankind is the chivalrous plan,   5
    And is always as nobly requited;
Then battle for freedom wherever you can,
    And, if not shot or hanged, you'll get knighted.

WHEN A MAN HATH NO FREEDOM.   Byron died in Greece, April 19, 1824, preparing to fight for Greek independence from the Turks.

Percy Bysshe Shelley

1792–1822

ODE TO THE WEST WIND

1

O wild West Wind, thou breath of Autumn's being,
Thou, from whose unseen presence the leaves dead
Are driven, like ghosts from an enchanter fleeing,

Yellow, and black, and pale, and hectic red,
Pestilence-stricken multitudes: O thou,   5
Who chariotest to their dark wintry bed

The wingéd seeds, where they lie cold and low,
Each like a corpse within its grave, until
Thine azure sister of the Spring shall blow

Her clarion o'er the dreaming earth, and fill   10
(Driving sweet buds like flocks to feed in air)
With living hues and odors plain and hill:

Wild Spirit, which art moving everywhere;
Destroyer and preserver; hear, oh, hear!

2

Thou on whose stream, mid the steep sky's commotion,   15
Loose clouds like earth's decaying leaves are shed,
Shook from the tangled boughs of Heaven and Ocean,

Angels of rain and lightning: there are spread
On the blue surface of thine aëry surge,
Like the bright hair uplifted from the head   20

Of some fierce Maenad, even from the dim verge
Of the horizon to the zenith's height,
The locks of the approaching storm. Thou dirge

Of the dying year, to which this closing night
Will be the dome of a vast sepulcher,   25
Vaulted with all thy congregated might

Of vapors, from whose solid atmosphere
Black rain, and fire, and hail will burst: oh, hear!

3

Thou who didst waken from his summer dreams
The blue Mediterranean, where he lay,   30
Lulled by the coil of his crystalline streams,

Beside a pumice isle in Baiae's bay,
And saw in sleep old palaces and towers
Quivering within the wave's intenser day,

All overgrown with azure moss and flowers   35
So sweet, the sense faints picturing them! Thou
For whose path the Atlantic's level powers

Cleave themselves into chasms, while far below
The sea-blooms and the oozy woods which wear
The sapless foliage of the ocean, know   40

Thy voice, and suddenly grow gray with fear,
And tremble and despoil themselves: oh, hear!

4

If I were a dead leaf thou mightest bear,
If I were a swift cloud to fly with thee;
A wave to pant beneath thy power, and share   45

The impulse of thy strength, only less free
Than thou, O uncontrollable! If even
I were as in my boyhood, and could be

The comrade of thy wanderings over Heaven,
As then, when to outstrip thy skyey speed   50
Scarce seemed a vision; I would ne'er have striven

As thus with thee in prayer in my sore need.
Oh, lift me as a wave, a leaf, a cloud!
I fall upon the thorns of life! I bleed!

A heavy weight of hours has chained and bowed   55
One too like thee: tameless, and swift, and proud.

5

Make me thy lyre, even as the forest is:
What if my leaves are falling like its own!
The tumult of thy mighty harmonies

Will take from both a deep, autumnal tone,   60
Sweet though in sadness. Be thou, Spirit fierce,
My spirit! Be thou me, impetuous one!

Drive my dead thoughts over the universe
Like withered leaves to quicken a new birth!
And, by the incantation of this verse,   65

Scatter, as from an unextinguished hearth
Ashes and sparks, my words among mankind!
Be through my lips to unawakened earth

The trumpet of a prophecy! O Wind,
If Winter comes, can Spring be far behind?   70

ODE TO THE WEST WIND. 9. *sister of the Spring*, south wind. 10. *clarion*, an instrument of the trumpet family that produces a shrill note. 21. *Maenad*, ancient Greek priestess who presided over the orgiastic rites of Bacchus, god of wine and nature. The ceremony consisted of frenetic dances. 32. *pumice*, light porous volcanic substance. *Baiae*, near the bay of Naples where Roman emperors erected palaces. 39–42. *sea-blooms . . . hear*: "The vegetation at the bottom of the sea, of rivers, and of lakes, sympathizes with that of the land in the change of seasons, and is consequently influenced by the winds which announce it." [SHELLEY'S NOTE.] 57. *lyre*. When the wind blows through the Aeolian lyre it makes music.

OZYMANDIAS

I met a traveler from an antique land
Who said: "Two vast and trunkless legs of stone
Stand in the desert. Near them, on the sand,
Half sunk, a shattered visage lies, whose frown,
And wrinkled lip, and sneer of cold command,   5
Tell that its sculptor well those passions read
Which yet survive, stamped on these lifeless things,
The hand that mocked them, and the heart that fed:
And on the pedestal these words appear:
'My name is Ozymandias, king of kings: 10
Look on my works, ye Mighty, and despair!'
Nothing beside remains. Round the decay
Of that colossal wreck, boundless and bare
The lone and level sands stretch far away."

John Keats

1795–1821

TO AUTUMN

Season of mists and mellow fruitfulness,
  Close bosom-friend of the maturing sun;
Conspiring with him how to load and bless
  With fruit the vines that round the thatch-eaves run;
To bend with apples the mossed cottage trees,   5
  And fill all fruit with ripeness to the core;
    To swell the gourd, and plump the hazel shells
With a sweet kernel; to set budding more,
  And still more, later flowers for the bees,
    Until they think warm days will never cease,   10
    For Summer has o'er-brimmed their clammy cells.

Who hath not seen thee oft amid thy store?
  Sometimes whoever seeks abroad may find
Thee sitting careless on a granary floor,
  Thy hair soft-lifted by the winnowing wind;   15
Or on a half-reaped furrow sound asleep,
  Drowsed with the fume of poppies, while thy hook
    Spares the next swath and all its twinéd flowers:
And sometime like a gleaner thou dost keep
  Steady thy laden head across a brook;   20
  Or by a cider-press, with patient look,
    Thou watchest the last oozings, hours by hours.

Where are the songs of Spring? Ay, where are they?
  Think not of them, thou hast thy music too—
While barréd clouds bloom the soft-dying day,   25
  And touch the stubble-plains with rosy hue;
Then in a wailful choir the small gnats mourn

Among the river sallows, borne aloft
   Or sinking as the light wind lives or dies;
And full-grown lambs loud bleat from hilly bourn;   30
    Hedge-crickets sing; and now with treble soft
   The redbreast whistles from a garden-croft,
      And gathering swallows twitter in the skies.

ODE ON A GRECIAN URN

Thou still unravished bride of quietness,
   Thou foster-child of Silence and slow Time,
Sylvan historian, who canst thus express
   A flowery tale more sweetly than our rime:
What leaf-fringed legend haunts about thy shape   5
   Of deities or mortals, or of both,
     In Tempe or the dales of Arcady?
   What men or gods are these? What maidens loth?
What mad pursuit? What struggle to escape?
     What pipes and timbrels? What wild ecstasy?   10

Heard melodies are sweet, but those unheard
   Are sweeter; therefore, ye soft pipes, play on;
Not to the sensual ear, but, more endeared,
   Pipe to the spirit ditties of no tone:
Fair youth, beneath the trees, thou canst not leave   15
   Thy song, nor ever can those trees be bare;
     Bold Lover, never, never canst thou kiss,
Though winning near the goal—yet, do not grieve;
     She cannot fade, though thou hast not thy bliss,
   Forever wilt thou love, and she be fair!   20

Ah, happy, happy boughs! that cannot shed
   Your leaves, nor ever bid the Spring adieu;
And, happy melodist, unwearièd,
   Forever piping songs forever new.
More happy love! more happy, happy love!   25

To AUTUMN. 15. *winnowing*, separating chaff from grain. 28. *sallows*, willows. 30. *bourn*, domain. 31. *Hedge-crickets*, grasshoppers. 32. *croft*, enclosure.

Forever warm and still to be enjoyed,
　　Forever panting, and forever young;
All breathing human passion far above,
　　That leaves a heart high-sorrowful and cloyed,
　　　A burning forehead, and a parching tongue.　　　30

Who are these coming to the sacrifice?
　　To what green altar, O mysterious priest,
Lead'st thou that heifer lowing at the skies,
　　And all her silken flanks with garlands dressed?
What little town by river or seashore,　　　35
　　Or mountain-built with peaceful citadel,
　　　Is emptied of this folk, this pious morn?
And, little town, thy streets forevermore
　　Will silent be; and not a soul to tell
　　　Why thou art desolate, can e'er return.　　　40

O Attic shape! Fair attitude! with brede
　　Of marble men and maidens overwrought,
With forest branches and the trodden weed;
　　Thou, silent form! dost tease us out of thought
As doth eternity: Cold Pastoral!　　　45
　　When old age shall this generation waste,
　　　Thou shalt remain, in midst of other woe
Than ours, a friend to man, to whom thou say'st,
　　"Beauty is truth, truth beauty,—that is all
　　　Ye know on earth, and all ye need to know."　　　50

ODE ON A GRECIAN URN. 3. *Sylvan*, pastoral, originating from woodland. 7.
Tempe, valley in Greece representing rural beauty. *Arcady*, Arcadia, an ancient
Greek state representing the same pastoral idea. 41. *Attic*, Athenian.

Alfred, Lord Tennyson

1809–1892

ULYSSES

It little profits that an idle king,
By this still hearth, among these barren crags,
Matched with an aged wife, I mete and dole
Unequal laws unto a savage race,
That hoard, and sleep, and feed, and know not me.   5
I cannot rest from travel; I will drink
Life to the lees. All times I have enjoyed
Greatly, have suffered greatly, both with those
That loved me, and alone; on shore, and when
Through scudding drifts the rainy Hyades   10
Vexed the dim sea. I am become a name;
For always roaming with a hungry heart
Much have I seen and known—cities of men
And manners, climates, councils, governments,
Myself not least, but honored of them all—   15
And drunk delight of battle with my peers,
Far on the ringing plains of windy Troy.
I am a part of all that I have met;
Yet all experience is an arch wherethrough
Gleams that untraveled world whose margin fades   20
Forever and forever when I move.
How dull it is to pause, to make an end,
To rust unburnished, not to shine in use!
As though to breathe were life! Life piled on life
Were all too little, and of one to me   25
Little remains; but every hour is saved
From that eternal silence, something more,
A bringer of new things; and vile it were
For some three suns to store and hoard myself,

And this gray spirit yearning in desire   30
To follow knowledge like a sinking star,
Beyond the utmost bound of human thought.
    This is my son, mine own Telemachus,
To whom I leave the scepter and the isle—
Well-loved of me, discerning to fulfill   35
This labor, by slow prudence to make mild
A rugged people, and through soft degrees
Subdue them to the useful and the good.
Most blameless is he, centered in the sphere
Of common duties, decent not to fail   40
In offices of tenderness, and pay
Meet adoration to my household gods,
When I am gone. He works his work, I mine.
    There lies the port; the vessel puffs her sail;
There gloom the dark, broad seas. My mariners,   45
Souls that have toiled, and wrought, and thought with me—
That ever with a frolic welcome took
The thunder and the sunshine, and opposed
Free hearts, free foreheads—you and I are old;
Old age hath yet his honor and his toil.   50
Death closes all; but something ere the end,
Some work of noble note, may yet be done,
Not unbecoming men that strove with gods.
The lights begin to twinkle from the rocks;
The long day wanes; the slow moon climbs; the deep   55
Moans round with many voices. Come, my friends.
'Tis not too late to seek a newer world.
Push off, and sitting well in order smite
The sounding furrows; for my purpose holds
To sail beyond the sunset, and the baths   60
Of all the western stars, until I die.
It may be that the gulfs will wash us down;
It may be we shall touch the Happy Isles,
And see the great Achilles, whom we knew.
Though much is taken, much abides; and though   65
We are not now that strength which in old days
Moved earth and heaven, that which we are, we are—
One equal temper of heroic hearts,
Made weak by time and fate, but strong in will
To strive, to seek, to find, and not to yield.   70

ULYSSES.   2. *crags*, the barren island of Ithaca.   3. *wife*, Penelope.   10. *Hyades*, cluster of five stars announcing rain.   63. *Happy Isles*, Elysium, the place where the virtuous, such as Achilles, went after death.

THE EAGLE: A FRAGMENT

He clasps the crag with crooked hands;
Close to the sun in lonely lands,
Ringed with the azure world, he stands.

The wrinkled sea beneath him crawls;
He watches from his mountain walls,   5
And like a thunderbolt he falls.

Robert Browning

1812–1889

PORPHYRIA'S LOVER

The rain set early in tonight,
    The sullen wind was soon awake,
It tore the elm-tops down for spite,
    And did its worst to vex the lake:
    I listened with heart fit to break.   5
When glided in Porphyria; straight
    She shut the cold out and the storm,
And kneeled and made the cheerless grate
    Blaze up, and all the cottage warm;
    Which done, she rose, and from her form   10
Withdrew the dripping cloak and shawl,
    And laid her soiled gloves by, untied
Her hat and let the damp hair fall,
    And, last, she sat down by my side
    And called me. When no voice replied,   15
She put my arm about her waist,
    And made her smooth white shoulder bare,
And all her yellow hair displaced,
    And, stooping, made my cheek lie there,
    And spread, o'er all, her yellow hair,   20
Murmuring how she loved me—she
    Too weak, for all her heart's endeavor,
To set its struggling passion free
    From pride, and vainer ties dissever,
    And give herself to me forever.   25
But passion sometimes would prevail,
    Nor could tonight's gay feast restrain
A sudden thought of one so pale
    For love of her, and all in vain:

So, she was come through wind and rain.   30
Be sure I looked up at her eyes
       Happy and proud; at last I knew
Porphyria worshiped me: surprise
       Made my heart swell, and still it grew
       While I debated what to do.   35
That moment she was mine, mine, fair,
       Perfectly pure and good: I found
A thing to do, and all her hair
       In one long yellow string I wound
       Three times her little throat around,   40
And strangled her. No pain felt she;
       I am quite sure she felt no pain.
As a shut bud that holds a bee,
       I warily oped her lids: again
       Laughed the blue eyes without a stain.   45
And I untightened next the tress
       About her neck; her cheek once more
Blushed bright beneath my burning kiss:
       I propped her head up as before,
       Only, this time my shoulder bore   50
Her head, which droops upon it still:
       The smiling rosy little head,
So glad it has its utmost will,
       That all it scorned at once is fled,
       And I, its love, am gained instead!   55
Porphyria's love: she guessed not how
       Her darling one wish would be heard.
And thus we sit together now,
       And all night long we have not stirred,
       And yet God has not said a word!   60

MY LAST DUCHESS

Ferrara

That's my last Duchess painted on the wall,
Looking as if she were alive. I call
That piece a wonder, now; Frà Pandolf's hands
Worked busily a day, and there she stands.
Will 't please you sit and look at her? I said   5
"Frà Pandolf" by design, for never read
Strangers like you that pictured countenance,

The depth and passion of its earnest glance,
But to myself they turned (since none puts by
The curtain I have drawn for you, but I)   10
And seemed as they would ask me, if they durst,
How such a glance came there; so, not the first
Are you to turn and ask thus. Sir, 'twas not
Her husband's presence only, called that spot
Of joy into the Duchess' cheek; perhaps   15
Frà Pandolf chanced to say, "Her mantle laps
Over my lady's wrist too much," or "Paint
Must never hope to reproduce the faint
Half-flush that dies along her throat." Such stuff
Was courtesy, she thought, and cause enough   20
For calling up that spot of joy. She had
A heart—how shall I say?—too soon made glad,
Too easily impressed; she liked whate'er
She looked on, and her looks went everywhere.
Sir, 'twas all one! My favor at her breast,   25
The dropping of the daylight in the West,
The bough of cherries some officious fool
Broke in the orchard for her, the white mule
She rode with round the terrace—all and each
Would draw from her alike the approving speech,   30
Or blush, at least. She thanked men—good! but thanked
Somehow—I know not how—as if she ranked
My gift of a nine-hundred-years-old name
With anybody's gift. Who'd stoop to blame
This sort of trifling? Even had you skill   35
In speech—which I have not—to make your will
Quite clear to such an one, and say, "Just this
Or that in you disgusts me; here you miss,
Or there exceed the mark"—and if she let
Herself be lessoned so, nor plainly set   40
Her wits to yours, forsooth, and made excuse—
E'en then would be some stooping; and I choose
Never to stoop. Oh, sir, she smiled, no doubt,
Whene'er I passed her; but who passed without
Much the same smile? This grew; I gave commands;   45
Then all smiles stopped together. There she stands
As if alive. Will 't please you rise? We'll meet
The company below, then. I repeat,
The Count your master's known munificence
Is ample warrant that no just pretense   50
Of mine for dowry will be disallowed;
Though his fair daughter's self, as I avowed

At starting, is my object. Nay, we'll go
Together down, sir. Notice Neptune, though,
Taming a sea-horse, thought a rarity,   55
Which Claus of Innsbruck cast in bronze for me!

MEETING AT NIGHT

The gray sea and the long black land;
And the yellow half-moon large and low;
And the startled little waves that leap
In fiery ringlets from their sleep,
As I gain the cove with pushing prow,   5
And quench its speed i' the slushy sand.

Then a mile of warm sea-scented beach;
Three fields to cross till a farm appears;
A tap at the pane, the quick sharp scratch
And blue spurt of a lighted match,   10
And a voice less loud, through its joys and fears,
Than the two hearts beating each to each!

MY LAST DUCHESS, spoken by the Duke of Ferrara as he negotiates his next
marriage. 3. *Frà Pandolf*, an imaginary artist, as Claus of Innsbruck in l. 56.

Matthew Arnold

1822–1888

DOVER BEACH

The sea is calm tonight,
The tide is full, the moon lies fair
Upon the straits;—on the French coast the light
Gleams and is gone; the cliffs of England stand,
Glimmering and vast, out in the tranquil bay.   5
Come to the window, sweet is the night-air!

Only, from the long line of spray
Where the sea meets the moon-blanched land,
Listen! you hear the grating roar
Of pebbles which the waves draw back, and fling,   10
At their return, up the high strand,
Begin, and cease, and then again begin,
With tremulous cadence slow, and bring
The eternal note of sadness in.

Sophocles long ago   15
Heard it on the Aegean, and it brought
Into his mind the turbid ebb and flow
Of human misery; we
Find also in the sound a thought,
Hearing it by this distant northern sea.   20

The Sea of Faith
Was once, too, at the full, and round earth's shore
Lay like the folds of a bright girdle furled.
But now I only hear
Its melancholy, long, withdrawing roar,   25
Retreating, to the breath
Of the night-wind, down the vast edges drear
And naked shingles of the world.

Ah, love, let us be true
To one another! for the world, which seems   30
To lie before us like a land of dreams,
So various, so beautiful, so new,
Hath really neither joy, nor love, nor light,
Nor certitude, nor peace, nor help for pain;
And we are here as on a darkling plain   35
Swept with confused alarms of struggle and flight,
Where ignorant armies clash by night.

Walt Whitman

1819–1892

OUT OF THE CRADLE ENDLESSLY ROCKING

Out of the cradle endlessly rocking,
Out of the mockingbird's throat, the musical shuttle,
Out of the Ninth-month midnight,
Over the sterile sands and the fields beyond, where the child leaving
   his bed wandered alone, bareheaded, barefoot,
Down from the showered halo, 5
Up from the mystic play of shadows twining and twisting as if they
   were alive,
Out from the patches of briers and blackberries,
From the memories of the bird that chanted to me,
From your memories sad brother, from the fitful risings and fallings
   I heard,
From under that yellow half-moon late-risen and swollen as if with
   tears, 10
From those beginning notes of yearning and love there in the mist,
From the thousand responses of my heart never to cease,
From the myriad thence-aroused words,
From the word stronger and more delicious than any,
From such as now they start the scene revisiting, 15
As a flock, twittering, rising, or overhead passing,
Borne hither, ere all eludes me, hurriedly,
A man, yet by these tears a little boy again,
Throwing myself on the sand, confronting the waves,
I, chanter of pains and joys, uniter of here and hereafter, 20
Taking all hints to use them, but swiftly leaping beyond them,
A reminiscence sing.

Once Paumanok,
When the lilac scent was in the air and Fifth-month grass was
   growing,

Up this seashore in some briers,   25
Two feathered guests from Alabama, two together,
And their nest, and four light-green eggs spotted with brown,
And every day the he-bird to and fro near at hand,
And every day the she-bird crouched on her nest, silent, with bright
    eyes,
And every day I, a curious boy, never too close, never disturbing
    them,   30
Cautiously peering, absorbing, translating.

Shine! shine! shine!
Pour down your warmth, great sun!
While we bask, we two together.
Two together!   35
Winds blow south, or winds blow north,
Day come white, or night come black,
Home, or rivers and mountains from home,
Singing all time, minding no time,
While we two keep together.   40

Till of a sudden,
Maybe killed, unknown to her mate,
One forenoon the she-bird crouched not on the nest,
Nor returned that afternoon, nor the next,
Nor ever appeared, again.   45
And thenceforward all summer in the sound of the sea,
And at night under the full of the moon in calmer weather,
Over the hoarse surging of the sea,
Or flitting from brier to brier by day,
I saw, I heard at intervals the remaining one, the he-bird,   50
The solitary guest from Alabama.

Blow! blow! blow!
Blow up sea winds along Paumanok's shore;
I wait and I wait till you blow my mate to me.

Yes, when the stars glistened,   55
All night long on the prong of a moss-scalloped stake,
Down almost amid the slapping waves,
Sat the lone singer wonderful causing tears.

He called on his mate,
He poured forth the meanings which I of all men know.   60

Yes my brother I know,
The rest might not, but I have treasured every note,
For more than once dimly down to the beach gliding,
Silent, avoiding the moonbeams, blending myself with the shadows,
Recalling now the obscure shapes, the echoes, the sounds and sights
    after their sorts,   65
The white arms out in the breakers tirelessly tossing,
I, with bare feet, a child, the wind wafting my hair,
Listened long and long.
Listened to keep, to sing, now translating the notes,
Following you my brother.   70

Soothe! soothe! soothe!
Close on its wave soothes the wave behind,
And again another behind embracing and lapping, every one close,
But my love soothes not me, not me.
Low hangs the moon, it rose late,   '75
It is lagging—O I think it is heavy with love, with love.

O madly the sea pushes upon the land,
With love, with love.

O night! do I not see my love fluttering out among the breakers?
What is that little black thing I see there in the white?   80

Loud! loud! loud!
Loud I call to you, my love!
High and clear I shoot my voice over the waves,
Surely you must know who is here, is here,
You must know who I am, my love.   85

Low-hanging moon!
What is that dusky spot in your brown yellow?
O it is the shape, the shape of my mate!
O moon do not keep her from me any longer.

Land! land! O land!   90
Whichever way I turn, O I think you could give me my mate back
*   again if you only would,*
For I am almost sure I see her dimly whichever way I look.

O rising stars!
Perhaps the one I want so much will rise, will rise with some of you.

O throat! O trembling throat!   95
Sound clearer through the atmosphere!
Pierce the woods, the earth,
Somewhere listening to catch you must be the one I want.

Shake out carols.
Solitary here, the night's carols!   100
Carols of lonesome love! death's carols!
Carols under that lagging, yellow, waning moon!
O under the moon where she droops almost down into the sea!
O reckless despairing carols.

But soft! sink low!   105
Soft! let me just murmur,
And do you wait a moment you husky-noised sea,
For somewhere I believe I heard my mate responding to me,
So faint, I must be still, be still to listen,
But not altogether still, for then she might not come immediately to
   me.   110

Hither my love!
Here I am! here!
With this just-sustained note I announce myself to you,
This gentle call is for you my love, for you.

Do not be decoyed elsewhere,   115
That is the whistle of the wind, it is not my voice,
That is the fluttering, the fluttering of the spray,
Those are the shadows of leaves.

O darkness! O in vain!
O I am very sick and sorrowful.   120

O brown halo in the sky near the moon, drooping upon the sea!
O troubled reflection in the sea!
O throat! O throbbing heart!
And I singing uselessly, uselessly all the night.

O past! O happy life! O songs of joy!   125
In the air, in the woods, over fields,
Loved! loved! loved! loved! loved!
But my mate no more, no more with me!
We two together no more.

The aria sinking,   130
All else continuing, the stars shining,
The winds blowing, the notes of the bird continuous echoing,
With angry moans the fierce old mother incessantly moaning,
On the sands of Paumanok's shore gray and rustling,
The yellow half-moon enlarged, sagging down, drooping, the face of
    the sea almost touching,   135
The boy ecstatic, with his bare feet the waves, with his hair the
    atmosphere dallying,
The love in the heart long pent, now loose, now at last tumultuously
    bursting,
The aria's meaning, the ears, the soul, swiftly depositing,
The strange tears down the cheeks coursing,
The colloquy there, the trio, each uttering,   140
The undertone, the savage old mother incessantly crying,
To the boy's soul's questions sullenly timing, some drowned secret
    hissing,
To the outsetting bard.

Demon or bird! (said the boy's soul).
Is it indeed toward your mate you sing? or is it really to me?   145
For I, that was a child, my tongue's use sleeping, now I have heard
    you,
Now in a moment I know what I am for, I awake,
And already a thousand singers, a thousand songs, clearer, louder
    and more sorrowful than yours,
A thousand warbling echoes have started to life within me, never to
    die.

O you singer solitary, singing by yourself, projecting me,   150
O solitary me listening, never more shall I cease perpetuating you,
Never more shall I escape, never more the reverberations,
Never more the cries of unsatisfied love be absent from me,
Never again leave me to be the peaceful child I was before what
    there in the night,
By the sea under the yellow and sagging moon,   155
The messenger there aroused, the fire, the sweet hell within,
The unknown want, the destiny of me.

O give me the clue! (it lurks in the night here somewhere),
O if I am to have so much, let me have more!
A word then (for I will conquer it),   160
The word final, superior to all,
Subtle, sent up—what is it?—I listen;

Are you whispering it, and have been all the time, you sea waves?
Is that it from your liquid rims and wet sands?

Whereto answering, the sea,   165
Delaying not, hurrying not,
Whispered me through the night, and very plainly before daybreak,
Lisped to me the low and delicious word death,
And again death, death, death, death,
Hissing melodious, neither like the bird nor like my aroused child's
    heart,   170
But edging near as privately for me rustling at my feet,
Creeping thence steadily up to my ears and laving me soft all over,
Death, death, death, death, death.

Which I do not forget,
But fuse the song of my dusky demon and brother,   175
That he sang to me in the moonlight on Paumanok's gray beach,
With the thousand responsive songs at random,
My own songs awaked from that hour,
And with them the key, the word up from the waves,
The word of the sweetest song and all songs,   180
That strong and delicious word which, creeping to my feet,
(Or like some old crone rocking the cradle, swathed in sweet
    garments, bending aside),
The sea whispered me.

WHEN I HEARD THE LEARN'D ASTRONOMER

When I heard the learn'd astronomer,
When the proofs, the figures, were ranged in columns before me,
When I was shown the charts and diagrams, to add, divide, and
    measure them,
When I sitting heard the astronomer where he lectured with much
    applause in the lecture-room,
How soon unaccountable I became tired and sick,   5
Till rising and gliding out I wander'd off by myself,
In the mystical moist night-air, and from time to time,
Look'd up in perfect silence at the stars.

OUT OF THE CRADLE ENDLESSLY ROCKING. 3. *Nine-month midnight*, September;
epithet suggesting Whitman's Quaker background, the native practice of measuring time, and the human period of gestation. 23. *Paumanok*, Indian name
for Long Island, New York. 130. *Aria*, operatic air, generally for solo voice.

Emily Dickinson

1830–1886

aesthetics of estrangement

613

They shut me up in Prose—
As when a little Girl
They put me in the Closet—
Because they liked me "still"—

Still! Could themself have peeped—   5
And seen my Brain—go round—
They might as wise have lodged a Bird
For Treason—in the Pound—

Himself has but to will
And easy as a Star   10
Abolish his Captivity—
And laugh—No more have I—

501

This World is not Conclusion.
A Species stands beyond—
Invisible, as Music—
But positive, as Sound—
It beckons, and it baffles—   5
Philosophy—don't know—
And through a Riddle, at the last—
Sagacity, must go—
To guess it, puzzles scholars—

To gain it, Men have borne   10
Contempt of Generations
And Crucifixion, shown—
Faith slips—and laughs, and rallies—
Blushes, if any see—
Plucks at a twig of Evidence—   15
And asks a Vane, the way—
Much Gesture, from the Pulpit—
Strong Hallelujahs roll—
Narcotics cannot still the Tooth
That nibbles at the soul—   20

1400

What mystery pervades a well!
That water lives so far—
A neighbor from another world
Residing in a jar

Whose limit none have ever seen,   5
But just his lid of glass—
Like looking every time you please
In an abyss's face!

The grass does not appear afraid,
I often wonder he   10
Can stand so close and look so bold
At what is awe to me.

Related somehow they may be,
The sedge stands next the sea—
Where he is floorless   15
And does no timidity betray

But nature is a stranger yet;
That ones that cite her most
Have never passed her haunted house,
Nor simplified her ghost.   20

THIS WORLD IS NOT CONCLUSION. 16. *Vane*, weathervane, fickle instrument sensi-tive to external pressures.

To pity those that know her not
Is helped by the regret
That those who know her, know her less
The nearer her they get.

1068

Further in Summer than the Birds
Pathetic from the Grass
A minor Nation celebrates
Its unobtrusive Mass.

No Ordinance be seen   5
So gradual the Grace
A pensive Custom it becomes
Enlarging Loneliness.

Antiquest felt at Noon
When August burning low   10
Arise this spectral Canticle
Repose to typify

Remit as yet no Grace
No Furrow on the Glow
Yet a Druidic Difference   15
Enhances Nature now

1593

There came a Wind like a Bugle—
It quivered through the Grass
And a Green Chill upon the Heat
So ominous did pass
We barred the Windows and the Doors   5
As from an Emerald Ghost—
The Doom's electric Moccasin

WHAT MYSTERY PERVADES A WELL. 18. *That . . . most*, romantic nature poets
and philosophers in the Wordsworth, Whitman tradition.

FURTHER THAN THE BIRDS. 3. *Nation*, crickets. Miss Dickinson entitled this poem,
"My Cricket." See Charles Anderson, *Emily Dickinson's Poetry: Stairway of Surprise* (New York: Holt, Rinehart & Winston, Inc., 1960), p. 169. 5. *Ordinance*,
an established church ritual, especially the communion. 6. *gradual*, in addition
to meaning moderate and regular, suggests the part of the mass between epistle
and gospel in which appropriate songs are sung. 10. *August*, in addition to the
month, it suggests solemn reverence. 11. *Canticle*, hymn. 15. *Druidic*, ancient
Celtic priests who presided over pagan rites dedicated to nature.

That very instant passed—
On a strange Mob of panting Trees
And Fences fled away   10
And Rivers where the Houses ran
Those looked that lived—that Day—
The Bell within the steeple wild
The flying tidings told—
How much can come   15
And much can go,
And yet abide the World!

519

'Twas warm—at first—like Us—
Until there crept upon
A Chill—like frost upon a Glass—
Till all the scene—be gone.

The Forehead copied Stone—   5
The Fingers grew too cold
To ache—and like a Skater's Brook—
The busy eyes—congealed—

It straightened—that was all—
It crowded Cold to Cold—   10
It multiplied indifference—
As Pride were all it could—

And even when with Cords—
'Twas lowered, like a Weight—
It made no Signal, nor demurred,   15
But dropped like Adamant.

547

I've seen a Dying Eye
Run round and round a Room—
In search of Something—as it seemed—
Then Cloudier become—
And then—obscure with Fog—   5
And then—be soldered down
Without disclosing what it be
'Twere blessed to have seen—

465

I heard a Fly buzz—when I died—
The Stillness in the Room
Was like the Stillness in the Air—
Between the Heaves of Storm—

The Eyes around—had wrung them dry—   5
And Breaths were gathering firm
For that last Onset—when the King
Be witnessed—in the Room—

I willed my Keepsakes—Signed away
What portion of me be   10
Assignable—and then it was
There interposed a Fly—

With Blue—uncertain stumbling Buzz—
Between the light—and me—
And then the Windows failed—and then   15
I could not see to see—

712

Because I could not stop for Death—
He kindly stopped for me—
The Carriage held but just Ourselves—
And Immortality.

We slowly drove—He knew no haste   5
And I had put away
My labor and my leisure too,
For His Civility—

We passed the School, where Children strove
At Recess—in the Ring—   10
We passed the Fields of Gazing Grain—
We passed the Setting Sun—

I HEARD A 'FLY BUZZ WHEN I DIED. 7. *King*. Miss Dickinson's religious contemporaries believed God's presence could be sensed in the room at the moment of
death.

Or rather—He passed Us—
The Dews drew quivering and Chill—
For only Gossamer, my Gown—   15
My Tippet—only Tulle—

We paused before a House that seemed
A Swelling of the Ground—
The Roof was scarcely visible—
The Cornice—in the Ground—   20

Since then—'tis Centuries—and yet
Feels shorter than the Day
I first surmised the Horses' Heads
Were toward Eternity—

670

One need not be a Chamber—to be Haunted—
One need not be a House—
The Brain has Corridors—surpassing
Material Place—

Far safer, of a Midnight Meeting   5
External Ghost
Than its interior Confronting—
The Cooler Host.

Far safer, through an Abbey gallop,
The Stones a'chase—   10
Than Unarmed, one's a'self encounter—
In lonesome Place—

Ourself behind ourself, concealed—
Should startle most—
Assassin hid in our Apartment   15
Be Horror's least.

The Body—borrows a Revolver—
He bolts the Door—
O'erlooking a superior spectre—
Or More—   20

258

There's a certain Slant of light,
Winter Afternoons—
That oppresses, like the Heft
Of Cathedral Tunes—

Heavenly Hurt, it gives us—   5
We can find no scar,
But internal difference,
Where the Meanings, are—

None may teach it—Any—
'Tis the Seal Despair—   10
An imperial affliction
Sent us of the Air—

When it comes, the Landscape listens—
Shadows—hold their breath—
When it goes, 'tis like the Distance   15
On the look of Death—

280

I felt a Funeral, in my Brain,
And Mourners to and fro
Kept treading—treading—till it seemed
That Sense was breaking through—

And when they all were seated,   5
A Service, like a Drum—
Kept beating—beating—till I thought
My Mind was going numb—

And then I heard them lift a Box
And creak across my Soul   10
With those same Boots of Lead, again,
Then Space—began to toll,

As all the Heavens were a Bell—
And Being, but an Ear,
And I, and Silence, some strange Race   15
Wrecked, solitary, here—

And then a Plank in Reason, broke,
And I dropped down, and down—
And hit a World, at every plunge,
And Finished knowing—then—   20

341

After great pain, a formal feeling comes—
The Nerves sit ceremonious, like Tombs—
The stiff Heart questions was it He, that bore.
And Yesterday, or Centuries before?

The Feet, mechanical, go round—   5
Of Ground, or Air, or Ought—
A Wooden way
Regardless grown,
A Quartz contentment, like a stone—

This is the Hour of Lead—   10
Remembered, if outlived,
As Freezing persons, recollect the Snow—
First—Chill—then Stupor—then the letting go—

822

This Consciousness that is aware
Of Neighbors and the Sun
Will be the one aware of Death
And that itself alone

Is traversing the interval   5
Experience between
And most profound experiment
Appointed unto Men—

How adequate unto itself
Its properties shall be   10
Itself unto itself and none
Shall make discovery.

AFTER GREAT PAIN, A FORMAL FEELING COMES.   9. *Quartz*, a type of metamorphic
rock (sandstone) formed under great pressure.

Adventure most unto itself
The Soul condemned to be—
Attended by a single Hound   15
Its own identity.

508

I'm ceded—I've stopped being Theirs—
The name They dropped upon my face
With water, in the country church
Is finished using, now—
And They can put it with my Dolls,   5
My childhood, and the string of spools,
I've finished threading—too—

Baptized, before, without the choice,
But this time, consciously, of Grace—
Unto supremest name—   10
Called to my Full—The Crescent dropped—
Existence's whole Arc, filled up,
With one small Diadem.

My second Rank—too small the first—
Crowned—Crowing—on my Father's breast—   15
A half unconscious Queen—
But this time—Adequate—Erect,
With Will to choose, or to reject,
And I choose, just a Crown—

326

I cannot dance upon my Toes—
No Man instructed me—
But oftentimes, among my mind,
A Glee possesseth me,

That had 1 Ballet knowledge—   5
Would put itself abroad
In Pirouette to blanch a Troupe—
Or lay a Prima, mad,

And though I had no Gown of Gauze—
No Ringlet, to my Hair,   10

Nor hopped to Audiences—like Birds,
One Claw upon the Air,

Nor tossed my shape in Eider Balls,
Nor rolled on wheels of snow
Till I was out of sight, in sound,   15
The House encore me so—

Nor any know I know the Art
I mention—easy—Here—
Nor any Placard boast me—
It's full as Opera—   20

675

Essential Oils—are wrung—
The Attar from the Rose
Be not expressed by Suns—alone—
It is the gift of Screws—

The General Rose—decay—   5
But this—in Lady's Drawer
Make Summer—When the Lady lie
In Spiceless Sepulchre.

1129

Tell all the Truth but tell it slant—
Success in Circuit lies
Too bright for our infirm Delight
The Truth's superb surprise
As Lightning to the Children eased   5
With explanation kind

I CANNOT DANCE UPON MY TOES. Miss Dickinson included this poem in her fifth
letter to Thomas W. Higginson, a critic who urged her to compose more conventional verse. See Charles Anderson, *Stairway of Surprise*, pp. 23–24. 20.
Opera, means literally "work," "labor."

ESSENTIAL OILS—ARE WRUNG. 6. *Lady's Drawer*. After she died Miss Dickinson's
poems were found in a drawer.

The Truth must dazzle gradually
Or every man be blind—

1071

Perception of an object costs
Precise the Object's loss—
Perception in itself a Gain
Replying to its Price—

The Object Absolute—is nought—   5
Perception sets it fair
And then upbraids a Perfectness
That situates so far—

290

Of Bronze—and Blaze—
The North—Tonight—
So adequate—it forms—
So preconcerted with itself—
So distant—to alarms—   5
An Unconcern so sovereign
To Universe, or me—
Infects my simple spirit
With Taints of Majesty—
Till I take vaster attitudes—   10
And strut upon my stem—
Disdaining Men, and Oxygen,
For Arrogance of them—

My Splendors, are Menagerie—
But their Competeless Show   15
Will entertain the Centuries
When I, am long ago,
An Island in dishonored Grass—
Whom none but Beetles—know.

TELL ALL THE TRUTH BUT TELL IT SLANT. 2. *Circuit,* suggestive of a complete (electrical) pattern or system.

OF BRONZE—AND BLAZE. 2. *North.* The *aurora borealis* inspired this poem.

451

The Outer—from the Inner
Derives its Magnitude—
'Tis Duke, or Dwarf, according
As is the Central Mood—

The fine—unvarying Axis   5
That regulates the Wheel—
Though Spokes—spin—more conspicuous
And fling a dust—the while.

The Inner—paints the Outer—
The Brush without the Hand—   10
Its Picture publishes—precise—
As is the inner Brand—

On fine—Arterial Canvas—
A Cheek—perchance a Brow—
The Star's whole Secret—in the Lake—   15
Eyes were not meant to know.

328

A Bird came down the Walk—
He did not know I saw—
He bit an Angleworm in halves
And ate the fellow, raw,

And then he drank a Dew   5
From a convenient Grass—
And then hopped sidewise to the Wall
To let a Beetle pass—

He glanced with rapid eyes
That hurried all around—   10
They looked like frightened Beads, I thought—
He stirred his Velvet Head

Like one in danger, Cautious,
I offered him a Crumb
And he unrolled his feathers   15
And rowed him softer home—

Than Oars divide the Ocean,
Too silver for a seam—
Or Butterflies, off Banks of Noon
Leap, plashless as they swim.   20

1261

A Word dropped careless on a Page
May stimulate an eye
When folded in perpetual seam
The Wrinkled Maker lie

Infection in the sentence breeds   5
We may inhale Despair
At distances of Centuries
From the Malaria—

1651

A Word made Flesh is seldom
And tremblingly partook
Nor then perhaps reported
But have I not mistook
Each one of us has tasted   5
With ecstasies of stealth
The very food debated
To our specific strength—

A Word that breathes distinctly
Has not the power to die   10
Cohesive as the Spirit
It may expire if He—
"Made Flesh and dwelt among us"
Could condescension be
Like this consent of Language   15
This loved Philology.

A WORD MADE FLESH IS SELDOM. 13. *Made . . . us,* see John 1:14, "And the word
was made flesh, and dwelt among us (and we beheld his glory, the glory as of the
only begotten of the Father) full of grace and truth."

Gerard Manley Hopkins

1844–1889

GOD'S GRANDEUR

The world is charged with the grandeur of God.
  It will flame out, like shining from shook foil;
  It gathers to a greatness, like the ooze of oil
Crushed. Why do men then now not reck his rod?
Generations have trod, have trod, have trod;   5
  And all is seared with trade; bleared, smeared with toil;
  And wears man's smudge and shares man's smell: the soil
Is bare now, nor can foot feel, being shod.

And for all this, nature is never spent;
  There lives the dearest freshness deep down things;   10
And though the last lights off the black West went,
  Oh, morning, at the brown brink eastward, springs—
Because the Holy Ghost over the bent
  World broods with warm breast and with ah! bright wings.

PIED BEAUTY

Glory be to God for dappled things—
  For skies of couple-color as a brinded cow;
    For rose-moles all in stipple upon trout that swim;
Fresh-firecoal chestnut-falls; finches' wings;
    Landscape plotted and pieced—fold, fallow, and plow;   5
    And all trades, their gear and tackle and trim.

All things counter, original, spare, strange;
  Whatever is fickle, freckled (who knows how?)
    With swift, slow; sweet, sour; adazzle, dim;
He fathers-forth whose beauty is past change: 10
      Praise him.

SPRING AND FALL

To A Young Child

Márgarét, are you gríeving
Over Goldengrove unleaving?
Leáves, líke the things of man, you
With your fresh thoughts care for, can you?
Ah! ás the heart grows older   5
It will come to such sights colder
By and by, nor spare a sigh
Though worlds of wanwood leafmeal lie;
And yet you wíll weep and know why.
Now no matter, child, the name: 10
Sórrow's springs áre the same,
Nor mouth had, no nor mind, expressed
What heart heard of, ghost guessed:
It ís the blight man was born for,
It is Margaret you mourn for.   15

SPRING AND FALL. 2. *unleaving,* the trees of the grove losing their leaves. 8.
wanwood, dark wood. *leafmeal,* suggests minor progression of time, as in piece-
meal or inchmeal.

Thomas Hardy

CHANNEL FIRING

That night your great guns, unawares,
Shook all our coffins as we lay,
And broke the chancel window-squares,
We thought it was the Judgment-day

And sat upright. While drearisome   5
Arose the howl of wakened hounds:
The mouse let fall the altar-crumb,
The worms drew back into the mounds,

The glebe cow drooled. Till God called, "No;
It's gunnery practice out at sea   10
Just as before you went below;
The world is as it used to be:

"All nations striving strong to make
Red war yet redder. Mad as hatters
They do no more for Christés sake   15
Than you who are helpless in such matters.

"That this is not the judgment-hour
For some of them's a blessed thing,
For if it were they'd have to scour
Hell's floor for so much threatening. . . .   20
"Ha, ha! It will be warmer when
I blow the trumpet (if indeed
I ever do; for you are men,
And rest eternal sorely need)."

So down we lay again. "I wonder,   25
Will the world ever saner be,"

Said one, "than when He sent us under
In our indifferent century!"

And many a skeleton shook his head.
"Instead of preaching forty year,"   30
My neighbor Parson Thirdly said,
"I wish I had stuck to pipes and beer."

Again the guns disturbed the hour,
Roaring their readiness to avenge,
As far inland as Stourton Tower,   35
And Camelot, and starlit Stonehenge.

THE CONVERGENCE OF THE TWAIN

(Lines on the Loss of the "Titanic")

1

In a solitude of the sea
Deep from human vanity
And the Pride of Life that planned her, stilly couches she.

2

Steel chambers, late the pyres
Of her salamandrine fires,   5
Cold currents thrid, and turn to rhythmic tidal lyres.

3

Over the mirrors meant
To glass the opulent
The sea-worm crawls—grotesque, slimed, dumb, indifferent.

4

Jewels in joy designed   10
To ravish the sensuous mind
Lie lightless, all their sparkles bleared and black and blind.

CHANNEL FIRING: gunnery practice in the English Channel before World War I.
9. *glebe,* field. 15. *Christe's,* older form of "Christ." 35. *Stourton Tower,* a
tower presumably near the river Stour in Dorset or in the town of Stour Head,
England. 36. *Camelot,* legendary kingdom of King Arthur. *Stonehenge,* prehistoric circle of stones, site of ancient rituals.

5

    Dim moon-eyed fishes near
    Gaze at the gilded gear
And query: "What does this vaingloriousness down here?". . .   15

6

    Well: while was fashioning
    This creature of cleaving wing
The Immanent Will that stirs and urges everything

7

    Prepared a sinister mate
    For her—so gaily great—   20
A Shape of Ice, for the time far and dissociate.

8

    And as the smart ship grew
    In stature, grace, and hue,
In shadowy silent distance grew the Iceberg too.

9

    Alien they seemed to be;   25
    No mortal eye could see
The intimate welding of their later history,

10

    Or sign that they were bent
    By paths coincident
On being anon twin halves of one august event,   30

11

    Till the Spinner of the Years
    Said "Now!" And each one hears,
And consummation comes, and jars two hemispheres.

THE CONVERGENCE OF THE TWAIN. The Titanic, a product of prewar optimism and assurance, was a luxury liner of grandiose dimensions and hailed as "unsinkable." On its maiden voyage, the Titanic grazed an iceberg and sank, April 15, 1912. 5. *salamandrine*, reference to the mythical salamander, a lizard which was supposed to be able to live in fire, or which was itself the spirit of fire. 6. *thrid*, thread.

A. E. Housman

1859–1936

TERENCE, THIS IS STUPID STUFF

"Terence, this is stupid stuff:
You eat your victuals fast enough;
There can't be much amiss, 'tis clear,
To see the rate you drink your beer.
But oh, good Lord, the verse you make,   5
It gives a chap the bellyache.
The cow, the old cow, she is dead;
It sleeps well, the hornéd head:
We poor lads, 'tis our turn now
To hear such tunes as killed the cow.   10
Pretty friendship 'tis to rhyme
Your friends to death before their time
Moping melancholy mad:
Come, pipe a tune to dance to, lad."

Why, if 'tis dancing you would be,   15
There's brisker pipes than poetry.
Say, for what were hopyards meant,
Or why was Burton built on Trent?
Oh many a peer of England brews
Livelier liquor than the Muse,   20
And malt does more than Milton can
To justify God's ways to man.
Ale, man, ale's the stuff to drink
For fellows whom it hurts to think:
Look into the pewter pot   25
To see the world as the world's not.
And faith, 'tis pleasant till 'tis past:
The mischief is that 'twill not last.

Oh I have been to Ludlow fair
And left my necktie God knows where,   30
And carried halfway home, or near,
Pints and quarts of Ludlow beer:
Then the world seemed none so bad,
And I myself a sterling lad;
And down in lovely muck I've lain,   35
Happy till I woke again.
Then I saw the morning sky.
Heigho, the tale was all a lie;
The world, it was the old world yet,
I was I, my things were wet,   40
And nothing now remained to do
But begin the game anew.

Therefore, since the world has still
Much good, but much less good than ill,
And while the sun and moon endure   45
Luck's a chance, but trouble's sure,
I'd face it as a wise man would,
And train for ill and not for good.
'Tis true the stuff I bring for sale
Is not so brisk a brew as ale: 50
Out of a stem that scored the hand
I wrung it in a weary land.
But take it: if the smack is sour,
The better for the embittered hour;
It should do good to heart and head   55
When your soul is in my soul's stead;
And I will friend you, if I may,
In the dark and cloudy day.

There was a king reigned in the East:
There, when kings will sit to feast,   60
They get their fill before they think
With poisoned meat and poisoned drink.
He gathered all that springs to birth
From the many-venomed earth;
First a little, thence to more,   65
He sampled all her killing store;
And easy, smiling, seasoned sound,
Sate the king when healths went round.
They put arsenic in his meat
And stared aghast to watch him eat;   70

They poured strychnine in his cup
And shook to see him drink it up:
They shook, they stared as white's their shirt.
Them it was their poison hurt.
—I tell the tale that I heard told.   75
Mithridates, he died old.

TERENCE, THIS IS STUPID STUFF.   18. *Burton*, English town famous for its breweries.
19. *peer*, beer barons or brewery magnates elevated to the peerage.   20. *Muse*,
patron goddess of artistic inspiration.   21. *Milton*. One of John Milton's purposes in his epic poem *Paradise Lost* was to "justify the ways of God to men"
(Book I, l. 26).   25. *pewter pot*, drinking mug.   29. *Ludlow*, a market town in
Shropshire.   76. *Mithridates*, King of Pontus who allegedly immunized himself
against poison by consuming small doses daily; see Pliny's *Natural History*.

Rupert Brooke

1887–1915

HEAVEN

Fish (fly-replete, in depth of June,
Dawdling away their wat'ry noon)
Ponder deep wisdom, dark or clear,
Each secret fishy hope or fear.
Fish say, they have their Stream and Pond;   5
But is there anything Beyond?
This life cannot be All, they swear,
For how unpleasant, if it were!
One may not doubt that, somehow, Good
Shall come of Water and of Mud;   10
And, sure, the reverent eye must see
A Purpose in Liquidity.
We darkly know, by Faith we cry,
The future is not Wholly Dry.
Mud unto mud!—Death eddies near—   15
Not here the appointed End, not here!
But somewhere, beyond Space and Time,
Is wetter water, slimier slime!
And there (they trust) there swimmeth One
Who swam ere rivers were begun,   20
Immense, of fishy form and mind,
Squamous, omnipotent, and kind;
And under that Almighty Fin,
The littlest fish may enter in.
Oh! never fly conceals a hook,   25
Fish say, in the Eternal Brook,
But more than mundane weeds are there,
And mud, celestially fair;
Fat caterpillars drift around,
And Paradisal grubs are found;   30

Unfading moths, immortal flies,
And the worm that never dies.
And in that Heaven of all their wish,
There shall be no more land, say fish.

Wilfred Owen

1893–1918

DULCE ET DECORUM EST

Bent double, like old beggars under sacks,
Knock-kneed, coughing like hags, we cursed through sludge,
Till on the haunting flares we turned our backs,
And towards our distant rest began to trudge.
Men marched asleep. Many had lost their boots,   5
But limped on, blood-shod. All went lame, all blind;
Drunk with fatigue; deaf even to the hoots
Of gas-shells dropping softly behind.

Gas! GAS! Quick, boys—An ecstasy of fumbling,
Fitting the clumsy helmets just in time,   10
But someone still was yelling out and stumbling
And floundering like a man in fire or lime.—
Dim through the misty panes and thick green light,
As under a green sea, I saw him drowning.

In all my dreams before my helpless sight   15
He plunges at me, guttering, choking, drowning.

If in some smothering dreams, you too could pace
Behind the wagon that we flung him in,
And watch the white eyes writhing in his face,
His hanging face, like a devil's sick of sin;   20
If you could hear, at every jolt, the blood
Come gargling from the froth-corrupted lungs,
Bitten as the cud
Of vile, incurable sores on innocent tongues,—
My friend, you would not tell with such high zest   25
To children ardent for some desperate glory,
The old Lie: *Dulce et decorum est*
Pro patria mori.

DULCE ET DECORUM EST. 27–28. *Dulce . . . mori*, quotation from Horace, "Sweet and becoming it is to die for one's country."

William Butler Yeats

1865–1939

the dominion of the imagination

DOWN BY THE SALLEY GARDENS

Down by the salley gardens my love and I did meet;
She passed the salley gardens with little snow-white feet.
She bid me take love easy, as the leaves grow on the tree;
But I, being young and foolish, with her would not agree.

In a field by the river my love and I did stand,   5
And on my leaning shoulder she laid her snow-white hand.
She bid me take life easy, as the grass grows on the weirs;
But I was young and foolish, and now am full of tears.

ADAM'S CURSE

We sat together at one summer's end,
That beautiful mild woman, your close friend,
And you and I, and talked of poetry.
I said: "A line will take us hours maybe;
Yet if it does not seem a moment's thought,   5
Our stitching and unstitching has been naught.

DOWN BY THE SALLEY GARDENS: a paraphrase version of a popular folk song,
"Down by My Sally's Gardens." 1. *salley*, sallow, willowy. The willow tree is
a classic symbol of sadness. 7. *weirs*, backwaters produced by an obstruction
of river or stream.

Better go down upon your marrow-bones
And scrub a kitchen pavement, or break stones
Like an old pauper, in all kinds of weather;
For to articulate sweet sounds together   10
Is to work harder than all these, and yet
Be thought an idler by the noisy set
Of bankers, schoolmasters, and clergymen
The martyrs call the world."

               And thereupon   15
That beautiful mild woman for whose sake
There's many a one shall find out all heartache
On finding that her voice is sweet and low
Replied: "To be born woman is to know—
Although they do not talk of it at school—   20
That we must labour to be beautiful."

I said: "It's certain there is no fine thing
Since Adam's fall but needs much labouring.
There have been lovers who thought love should be
So much compounded of high courtesy   25
That they would sigh and quote with learned looks
Precedents out of beautiful old books;
Yet now it seems an idle trade enough."

We sat grown quiet at the name of love;
We saw the last embers of daylight die,   30
And in the trembling blue-green of the sky
A moon, worn as if it had been a shell
Washed by time's waters as they rose and fell
About the stars and broke in days and years.

I had a thought for no one's but your ears: 35
That you were beautiful, and that I strove
To love you in the old high way of love;
That it had all seemed happy, and yet we'd grown
As weary-hearted as that hollow moon.

ADAM'S CURSE. After Adam and Eve's sin, God imposed pain and labor upon
mankind (see Genesis 3:16–19). 25. *high courtesy*, courtly tradition of the
middle ages, highly ritualized ceremony of sexual assignation. 32. *moon*. In
this instance Yeats' use of the moon image has the classical meaning of
mutability, change, and imperfection.

THE FASCINATION OF WHAT'S DIFFICULT

The fascination of what's difficult
Has dried the sap out of my veins, and rent
Spontaneous joy and natural content
Out of my heart. There's something ails our colt
That must, as if it had not holy blood   5
Nor on Olympus leaped from cloud to cloud,
Shiver under the lash, strain, sweat and jolt
As though it dragged road-metal. My curse on plays
That have to be set up in fifty ways,
On the day's war with every knave and dolt,   10
Theatre business, management of men.
I swear before the dawn comes round again
I'll find the stable and pull out the bolt.

A DIALOGUE OF SELF AND SOUL

I

My Soul. I summon to the winding ancient stair;
Set all your mind upon the steep ascent,
Upon the broken, crumbling battlement,
Upon the breathless starlit air,
Upon the star that marks the hidden pole;   5
Fix every wandering thought upon
That quarter where all thought is done:
Who can distinguish darkness from the soul?

My Self. The consecrated blade upon my knees
Is Sato's ancient blade, still as it was,   10
Still razor-keen, still like a looking-glass
Unspotted by the centuries;
That flowering, silken old embroidery, torn
From some court-lady's dress and round
The wooden scabbard bound and wound,   15
Can, tattered, still protect, faded adorn.

THE FASCINATION OF WHAT'S DIFFICULT: written when Yeats was director-manager of the Abbey Theatre. "Subject. To complain of the fascination of what's difficult. It spoils spontaneity and pleasure, and wastes time. Repeat the line ending difficult three times and rhyme on bolt, exalt, colt, jolt" (Yeats' diary for September 1909). 4. *colt*, Pegasus, creature of Greek mythology; a winged horse, symbol of poetic inspiration, whose haunt was Mount Olympus, home of the gods.

My Soul. Why should the imagination of a man
   Long past his prime remember things that are
   Emblematical of love and war?
   Think of ancestral night that can,   20
   If but imagination scorn the earth
   And intellect its wandering
   To this and that and t'other thing,
   Deliver from the crime of death and birth.

My Self. Montashigi, third of his family, fashioned it   25
   Five hundred years ago, about it lie
   Flowers from I know not what embroidery—
   Heart's purple—and all these I set
   For emblems of the day against the tower
   Emblematical of the night,   30
   And claim as by a soldier's right
   A charter to commit the crime once more.

My Soul. Such fullness in that quarter overflows
   And falls into the basin of the mind
   That man is stricken deaf and dumb and blind,   35
   For intellect no longer knows
   Is from the *Ought,* or *Knower* from the *Known*—
   That is to say, ascends to Heaven;
   Only the dead can be forgiven;
But when I think of that my tongue's a stone.   40

II

My Self. A living man is blind and drinks his drop.
   What matter if the ditches are impure?
   What matter if I live it all once more?
   Endure that toil of growing up;
   The ignominy of boyhood; the distress   45
   Of boyhood changing into man;
   The unfinished man and his pain
   Brought face to face with his own clumsiness;

   The finished man among his enemies?—
   How in the name of Heaven can he escape   50
   That defiling and disfigured shape
   The mirror of malicious eyes
   Casts upon his eyes until at last
   He thinks that shape must be his shape?
   And what's the good of an escape   55
   If honor find him in the wintry blast?

I am content to live it all again
And yet again, if it be life to pitch
Into the frog-spawn of a blind man's ditch,
A blind man battering blind men;   60
Or into that most fecund ditch of all,
The folly that man does
Or must suffer, if he woos
A proud woman not kindred of his soul.

I am content to follow to its source,   65
Every event in action or in thought;
Measure the lot; forgive myself the lot!
When such as I cast out remorse
So great a sweetness flows into the breast
We must laugh and we must sing,   70
We are blest by everything,
Everything we look upon is blest.

CRAZY JANE TALKS WITH THE BISHOP

I met the Bishop on the road
And much said he and I.
"Those breasts are flat and fallen now,
Those veins must soon be dry;
Live in a heavenly mansion,   5
Not in some foul sty."

"Fair and foul are near of kin,
And fair needs foul," I cried.
"My friends are gone, but that's a truth
Nor grave nor bed denied,   10
Learned in bodily lowliness
And in the heart's pride.

"A woman can be proud and stiff
When on love intent;
But Love has pitched his mansion in   15
The place of excrement;
For nothing can be sole or whole
That has not been rent."

A DIALOGUE OF SELF AND SOUL. 1. *stair*, opposed to the life of the "Self"—action, passion—the tower stair suggests an elevated withdrawal from the active life. 10. *Sato's*, Junza Sato; both he and Yeats were members of a secret society. When he gave Yeats the sword he told him it was the symbol of life and the embroideried sheath the symbol of beauty.

THE LAKE ISLE OF INNISFREE

I will arise and go now, and go to Innisfree,
And a small cabin build there, of clay and wattles made;
Nine bean rows will I have there, a hive for the honey bee,
And live alone in the bee-loud glade.

And I shall have some peace there, for peace comes dropping slow,   5
Dropping from the veils of the morning to where the cricket sings;
There midnight's all a glimmer, and noon a purple glow,
And evening full of the linnet's wings.

I will arise and go now, for always night and day
I hear lake water lapping with low sounds by the shore;   10
While I stand on the roadway, or on the pavements gray,
I hear it in the deep heart's core.

THE WILD OLD WICKED MAN

"Because I am mad about women
I am mad about the hills,"
Said that wild old wicked man
Who travels where God wills.
"Not to die on the straw at home,   5
Those hands to close these eyes,
That is all I ask, my dear,
From the old man in the skies.
            Daybreak and a candle-end.

"Kind are all your words, my dear,   10
Do not the rest withhold.
Who can know the year, my dear,
When an old man's blood grows cold?
I have what no young man can have
Because he loves too much.   15

THE LAKE ISLE OF INNISFREE: island in Lough Gill, County Sligo. Under the influence of Thoreau's *Walden*, Yeats had always desired "to live some day in a cottage on a little island call Innisfree." 2. *wattles*, reinforcing made from weaving twigs and branches into natural fabric. 7. *noon . . . glow*. According to Yeats, this image should suggest the reflection of heather on the water under noon light. 8. *linnet's wings*. The linnet in Yeats suggests magnanimity and constancy of mind.

Words I have that can pierce the heart,
But what can he do but touch?"
    Daybreak and a candle-end.

Then said she to that wild old man,
His stout stick under his hand,   20
"Love to give or to withhold
Is not at my command.
I gave it all to an older man:
That old man in the skies.
Hands that are busy with His beads   25
Can never close those eyes."
    Daybreak and a candle-end.

"Go your ways, O go your ways,
I choose another mark,
Girls down on the seashore   30
Who understand the dark;
Bawdy talk for the fishermen;
A dance for the fisher-lads;
When dark hangs upon the water
They turn down their beds.   35
    Daybreak and a candle-end.

"A young man in the dark am I,
But a wild old man in the light,
That can make a cat laugh, or
Can touch by mother wit   40
Things hid in their marrow-bones
From time long passed away,
Hid from all those warty lads
That by their bodies lay.
    Daybreak and a candle-end.   45

"All men live in suffering,
I know as few can know,
Whether they take the upper road
Or stay content on the low,
Rower bent in his row-boat   50
Or weaver bent at his loom,
Horseman erect upon horseback
Or child hid in the womb.
    Daybreak and a candle-end.

"That some stream of lightning   55
From the old man in the skies
Can burn out that suffering
No right-taught man denies.
But a coarse old man am I,
I choose the second-best,   60
I forget it all awhile
Upon a woman's breast."
           Daybreak and a candle-end.

WHY SHOULD NOT OLD MEN BE MAD?

Why should not old men be mad?
Some have known a likely lad
That had a sound fly-fisher's wrist
Turn to a drunken journalist;
A girl that knew all Dante once   5
Live to bear children to a dunce;
A Helen of social welfare dream,
Climb on a wagonette to scream.
Some think it a matter of course that chance
Should starve good men and bad advance,   10
That if their neighbours figured plain,
As though upon a lighted screen,
No single story would they find
Of an unbroken happy mind,
A finish worthy of the start.   15
Young men know nothing of this sort,
Observant old men know it well;
And when they know what old books tell,
And that no better can be had,
Know why an old man should be mad.   20

THE WILD OLD WICKED MAN. 25. *beads,* praying beads, rosary. 39. *cat,* suggestive of the old man's demonism. "In Ireland one hears much of demon cats" (*Irish Fairy and Folk Tales,* ed. W. B. Yeats).

WHY SHOULD NOT OLD MEN BE MAD? 3. *fly-fisher's wrist.* The fisherman image suggested to Yeats the idea of search or seeking, probing depths. 5. *Dante,* Dante Alighieri (1265–1321), a poet whose *Divine Comedy* best represents the medieval imagination and the medieval concept of hell. 7. *Helen,* Maud Gonne, Irish actress and revolutionary, compared to Helen of Troy.

THE SONG OF WANDERING AENGUS

I went out to the hazel wood,
Because a fire was in my head,
And cut and peeled a hazel wand,
And hooked a berry to a thread;
And when white moths were on the wing,   5
And moth-like stars were flickering out,
I dropped the berry in a stream
And caught a little silver trout.

When I had laid it on the floor,
I went to blow the fire a-flame,   10
But something rustled on the floor,
And some one called me by my name:
It had become a glimmering girl
With apple blossom in her hair
Who called me by my name and ran   15
And faded through the brightening air.

Though I am old w'th wandering
Through hollow lands and hilly lands,
I will find out where she has gone,
And kiss her lips and take her hands;   20
And walk among long dappled grass,
And pluck till time and times are done
The silver apples of the moon,
The golden apples of the sun.

SAILING TO BYZANTIUM

I

That is no country for old men. The young
In one another's arms, birds in the trees
(Those dying generations) at their song,
The salmon-falls, the mackerel-crowded seas,
Fish, flesh, or fowl, commend all summer long   5

THE SONG OF WANDERING AENGUS. Aengus was a type of Irish Bacchus, the god
of youth and beauty, the ancient Celtic "master of love." In this poem, contrary
to tradition, Aengus, the immortal youth, ages. 1. *hazel*, suggests the supernatural. 23. *silver*, imperfection. 24. *golden*, perfection, immortality.

Whatever is begotten, born, and dies.
Caught in that sensual music, all neglect
Monuments of unaging intellect.

II

An aged man is but a paltry thing,
A tattered coat upon a stick, unless   10
Soul clap its hands and sing, and louder sing
For every tatter in its mortal dress;
Nor is there singing school but studying
Monuments of its own magnificence;
And therefore I have sailed the seas and come   15
To the holy city of Byzantium.

III

O sages, standing in God's holy fire
As in the gold mosaic of a wall,
Come from the holy fire, perne in a gyre,
And be the singing-masters of my soul.   20
Consume my heart away—sick with desire
And fastened to a dying animal
It knows not what it is—and gather me
Into the artifice of eternity.

IV

Once out of nature I shall never take   25
My bodily form from any natural thing,
But such a form as Grecian goldsmiths make
Of hammered gold and gold enamelling
To keep a drowsy emperor awake;
Or set upon a golden bough to sing   30
To lords and ladies of Byzantium
Of what is past, or passing, or to come.

SAILING TO BYZANTIUM. Byzantium, now Istanbul, once center of Eastern Christian civilization, represented to Yeats a spiritual center of antiquity. "I think that in early Byzantium, maybe never before or since in recorded history, religious, aesthetic and practical life were one, that architect and artificers . . . spoke to the multitude and the few alike." The artists were "absorbed in their subject-matter" toward "the vision of a whole people" (*A Vision*, p. 279 ff.). 19. *perne in a gyre*, i.e., spin in spiral motion. "Perne" is a bobbin or spool on which something is wound. 26. *natural*, the sensual, biological world which the speaker rejects in favor of immortal artifice (art). 27. *form*. Yeats wrote, "I have read somewhere that in the Emperor's palace at Byzantium was a tree made of gold and silver, and artificial birds that sang." Hans Christian Andersen's *Emperor's Nightingale* is a possible source. 30. *golden bough*, suggests the golden bough of the *Aeneid* which enabled Aeneas to enter Hades and to learn of the past and future.

EASTER, 1916

I have met them at close of day
Coming with vivid faces
From counter or desk among grey
Eighteenth-century houses.
I have passed with a nod of the head   5
Or polite meaningless words,
Or have lingered awhile and said
Polite meaningless words,
And thought before I had done
Of a mocking tale or a gibe   10
To please a companion
Around the fire at the club,
Being certain that they and I
But lived where motley is worn:
All changed, changed utterly: 15
A terrible beauty is born.

That woman's days were spent
In ignorant good will,
Her nights in argument
Until her voice grew shrill.   20
What voice more sweet than hers
When, young and beautiful,
She rode to harriers?
This man had kept a school
And rode our wingèd horse;   25
This other his helper and friend
Was coming into his force;
He might have won fame in the end,
So sensitive his nature seemed,
So daring and sweet his thought.   30
The other man I had dreamed
A drunken, vainglorious lout.
He had done most bitter wrong
To some who are near my heart,
Yet I number him in the song;   35
He, too, had resigned his part
In the casual comedy;
He, too, has been changed in his turn,

Transformed utterly:
A terrible beauty is born.   40

Hearts with one purpose alone
Through summer and winter seem
Enchanted to a stone
To trouble the living stream.
The horse that comes from the road,   45
The rider, the birds that range
From cloud to tumbling cloud,
Minute by minute they change;
A shadow of cloud on the stream
Changes minute by minute;   50
A horse-hoof slides on the brim,
And a horse plashes within it;
The long-legged moor-hens dive,
And hens to moor-cocks call;
Minute by minute they live: 55
The stone's in the midst of all.

Too long a sacrifice
Can make a stone of the heart.
O when may it suffice?
That is Heaven's part, our part   60
To mutter name upon name,
As a mother names her child
When sleep at last has come
On limbs that had run wild.
Was it but nightfall?   65
No, no, not night but death;
Was it needless death after all?
For England may keep faith
For all that is done and said.
We know their dream; enough   70
To know they dreamed and are dead;
And what if excess of love
Bewildered them till they died?
I write it out in a verse—
MacDonagh and MacBride   75
And Connolly and Pearse
Now and in time to be,
Wherever green is worn,

Are changed, changed utterly:
A terrible beauty is born.   80

THE SECOND COMING

Turning and turning in the widening gyre
The falcon cannot hear the falconer;
Things fall apart: the center cannot hold;
Mere anarchy is loosed upon the world,
The blood-dimmed tide is loosed, and everywhere   5
The ceremony of innocence is drowned;
The best lack all conviction, while the worst
Are full of passionate intensity.

Surely some revelation is at hand;
Surely the Second Coming is at hand.   10
The Second Coming! Hardly are those words out
When a vast image out of *Spiritus Mundi*
Troubles my sight: somewhere in sands of the desert
A shape with lion body and the head of a man,
A gaze blank and pitiless as the sun,   15
Is moving its slow thighs, while all about it
Reel shadows of the indignant desert birds.
The darkness drops again; but now I know
That twenty centuries of stony sleep

EASTER, 1916: occasioned by an uprising of Irish revolutionaries in Dublin on
April 24, 1916, Easter Sunday, against British authority. This rebellion became
the inspiration for future revolutionary movements against British rule. 14.
motley, patched colors, signifying the costume of a fool; note variation of this
line (l. 78). 17. *That woman's*, Constance Gore-Booth, an aristocratic friend
who later became an embittered revolutionary. She represents the beautiful
woman turned harsh. 24. *This man*, Patrick Pearse, poet and scholar who
fought to restore the Gaelic language in Ireland. 25. *wingèd horse*, Pegasus,
creature of Greek mythology, symbol of poetic inspiration. 26. *friend*, Thomas
MacDonagh, poet. 32. *lout*, Major John MacBride, who, to Yeats' chagrin,
married Maud Gonne. 68. *England . . . faith*. The Easter Rebellion was partly
caused by England's failure to recognize the Irish Home Rule Act of 1912. 76.
Connolly, James Connolly, one of the insurrectionist leaders. 78. *green*, national color of Ireland.

Were vexed to nightmare by a rocking cradle,   20
And what rough beast, its hour come round at last,
Slouches towards Bethlehem to be born?

LEDA AND THE SWAN

A sudden blow: the great wings beating still
Above the staggering girl, her thighs caressed
By the dark webs, her nape caught in his bill,
He holds her helpless breast upon his breast.

How can those terrified vague fingers push   5
The feathered glory from her loosening thighs?
And how can body, laid in that white rush,
But feel the strange heart beating where it lies?

A shudder in the loins engenders there
The broken wall, the burning roof and tower   10
And Agamemnon dead.
                    Being so caught up,
So mastered by the brute blood of the air,
Did she put on his knowledge with his power
Before the indifferent beak could let her drop?   15

THE SECOND COMING: a Christian term signaling the millennium. Yeats has adopted this term to indicate that period occurring roughly every two thousand years when a new civilization arises out of the debris of a previous one. 1. *gyre,* a spinning movement, spiral, illustrating the cycles of history, symbolized here by the falcon's flight; pronounced with a hard *g,* as in "girl." 4. *mere,* archaic meaning intended: absolute, sheer, unqualified; see Edward A. Bloom, et al., eds., *Order of Poetry: An Introduction* (New York: Odyssey Press, 1961), p. 46. 4–8. Source for these lines presumably Aeschylus, *Libation Bearers,* ll. 61–70. 12. *Spiritus Mundi,* world spirit, roughly on the principle of Jungian collective unconscious.

LEDA AND THE SWAN. Zeus, in the form of a swan, raped Leda, Queen of Sparta, resulting in the birth of Helen and Clytemnestra, an act in Yeats' cosmology indicative of the energies or forces that promoted the rise of Greek civilization. "I imagine the annunciation that founded Greece as made to Leda, remembering that they showed in a Spartan temple, strung up to the roof as a holy relic, an unhatched egg of hers; and that from one of her eggs came Love and from the other War" (*A Vision,* p. 268). 11. *Agamemnon,* king of Mycenae and commander of the Greeks during the Trojan campaign. A transitional figure, his death at the hands of his wife Clytemnestra marks the end of an empire.

LAPIS LAZULI

(For Harry Clifton)

I have heard that hysterical women say
They are sick of the palette and fiddle-bow,
Of poets that are always gay,
For everybody knows or else should know
That if nothing drastic is done   5
Aeroplane and Zeppelin will come out,
Pitch like King Billy bomb-balls in
Until the town lie beaten flat.

All perform their tragic play,
There struts Hamlet, there is Lear,   10
That's Ophelia, that Cordelia;
Yet they, should the last scene be there,
The great stage curtain about to drop,
If worthy their prominent part in the play,
Do not break up their lines to weep.   15
They know that Hamlet and Lear are gay;
Gaiety transfiguring all that dread.
All men have aimed at, found and lost;
Black out; Heaven blazing into the head:
Tragedy wrought to its uttermost.   20
Though Hamlet rambles and Lear rages,
And all the drop-scenes drop at once
Upon a hundred thousand stages,
It cannot grow by an inch or an ounce.

On their own feet they came, or on shipboard,   25
Camel-back, horse-back, ass-back, mule-back,
Old civilisations put to the sword.
Then they and their wisdom went to rack:
No handiwork of Callimachus,
Who handled marble as if it were bronze,   30
Made draperies that seemed to rise
When sea-wind swept the corner, stands;
His long lamp-chimney shaped like the stem
Of a slender palm, stood but a day;
All things fall and are built again,   35
And those that build them again are gay.

Two Chinamen, behind them a third,
Are carved in lapis lazuli,
Over them flies a long-legged bird,
A symbol of longevity;   40
The third, doubtless a serving-man,
Carries a musical instrument.

Every discoloration of the stone,
Every accidental crack or dent,
Seems a water-course or an avalanche,   45
Or lofty slope where it still snows
Though doubtless plum or cherry-branch
Sweetens the little half-way house
Those Chinamen climb towards, and I
Delight to imagine them seated there;   50
There, on the mountain and the sky,
On all the tragic scene they stare.
One asks for mournful melodies;
Accomplished fingers begin to play.
Their eyes mid many wrinkles, their eyes,   55
Their ancient, glittering eyes, are gay.

LAPIS LAZULI: semiprecious, opaque stone, azure blue in color, the material of an
oriental carving in Yeats' possession. He remarked in a letter to Dorothy
Wellesley in 1935 that the asceticism of the East pre-empts tragic awareness; it is
up to the West to "raise the heroic cry." 7. *King Billy*, reference to a ballad
depicting the Battle of the Boyne (1690) between King William III and James II:

> *King James he pitched his tents between the line for to retire,*
> *But King William threw his bomb balls and set them all afire.*

29. *Callimachus,* Greek sculptor (fifth century B.C.) who pioneered a realistic
technique of sculpture. 39. *bird,* stork.

Robert Frost

1874–1963

BIRCHES

When I see birches bend to left and right
Across the lines of straighter darker trees,
I like to think some boy's been swinging them.
But swinging doesn't bend them down to stay.
Ice storms do that. Often you must have seen them   5
Loaded with ice a sunny winter morning
After a rain. They click upon themselves
As the breeze rises, and turn many-colored
As the stir cracks and crazes their enamel.
Soon the sun's warmth makes them shed crystal shells   10
Shattering and avalanching on the snow crust—
Such heaps of broken glass to sweep away
You'd think the inner dome of heaven had fallen.
They are dragged to the withered bracken by the load,
And they seem not to break; though once they are bowed   15
So low for long, they never right themselves:
You may see their trunks arching in the woods
Years afterwards, trailing their leaves on the ground
Like girls on hands and knees that throw their hair
Before them over their heads to dry in the sun.   20
But I was going to say when Truth broke in
With all her matter-of-fact about the ice storm
I should prefer to have some boy bend them
As he went out and in to fetch the cows—
Some boy too far from town to learn baseball,   25
Whose only play was what he found himself,
Summer or winter, and could play alone.
One by one he subdued his father's trees
By riding them down over and over again
Until he took the stiffness out of them.   30

And not one but hung limp, not one was left
For him to conquer. He learned all there was
To learn about not launching out too soon
And so not carrying the tree away
Clear to the ground. He always kept his poise   35
To the top branches, climbing carefully
With the same pains you use to fill a cup
Up to the brim, and even above the brim.
Then he flung outward, feet first, with a swish,
Kicking his way down through the air to the ground.   40
So was I once myself a swinger of birches,
And so I dream of going back to be.
It's when I'm weary of considerations,
And life is too much like a pathless wood
Where your face burns and tickles with the cobwebs   45
Broken across it, and one eye is weeping
From a twig's having lashed across it open.
I'd like to get away from earth awhile
And then come back to it and begin over.
May no fate willfully misunderstand me   50
And half grant what I wish and snatch me away
Not to return. Earth's the right place for love:
I don't know where it's likely to go better.
I'd like to go by climbing a birch tree,
And climb black branches up a snow-white trunk   55
Toward heaven, till the tree could bear no more,
But dipped its top and set me down again.
That would be good both going and coming back.
One could do worse than be a swinger of birches.

ONCE BY THE PACIFIC

The shattered water made a misty din.
Great waves looked over others coming in,
And thought of doing something to the shore
That water never did to land before.

The clouds were low and hairy in the skies,   5
Like locks blown forward in the gleam of eyes.
You could not tell, and yet it looked as if
The shore was lucky in being backed by cliff,

The cliff in being backed by continent;
It looked as if a night of dark intent   10
Was coming, and not only a night, an age.
Someone had better be prepared for rage.

There would be more than ocean water broken
Before God's last *Put out the Light* was spoken.

T. S. Eliot

1888–1965

THE LOVE SONG OF J. ALFRED PRUFROCK

S'io credesse che mia risposta fosse
A persona che mai tornasse al mondo,
Questa fiamma staria senza piu scosse.
Ma perciocche giammai di questo fondo
Non torno vivo alcun, s'i'odo il vero,
Senza tema d'infamia ti rispondo.

Let us go then, you and I,
When the evening is spread out against the sky
Like a patient etherised upon a table;
Let us go, through certain half-deserted streets,
The muttering retreats   5
Of restless nights in one-night cheap hotels
And sawdust restaurants with oyster-shells:
Streets that follow like a tedious argument
Of insidious intent
To lead you to an overwhelming question .   10
Oh, do not ask, "What is it?"
Let us go and make our visit.

In the room the women come and go
Talking of Michelangelo.

The yellow fog that rubs its back upon the window-panes,   15
The yellow smoke that rubs its muzzle on the window-panes
Licked its tongue into the corners of the evening,

Lingered upon the pools that stand in drains,
Let fall upon its back the soot that falls from chimneys,
Slipped by the terrace, made a sudden leap,   20
And seeing that it was a soft October night,
Curled once about the house, and fell asleep.

And indeed there will be time
For the yellow smoke that slides along the street,
Rubbing its back upon the window-panes;   25
There will be time, there will be time
To prepare a face to meet the faces that you meet;
There will be time to murder and create,
And time for all the works and days of hands
That lift and drop a question on your plate;   30
Time for you and time for me,
And time yet for a hundred indecisions,
And for a hundred visions and revisions,
Before the taking of a toast and tea.

In the room the women come and go   35
Talking of Michelangelo.

And indeed there will be time
To wonder, "Do I dare?" and, "Do I dare?"
Time to turn back and descend the stair,
With a bald spot in the middle of my hair—   40
[They will say: "How his hair is growing thin!"]
My morning coat, my collar mounting firmly to the chin,
My necktie rich and modest, but asserted by a simple pin—
[They will say: "But how his arms and legs are thin!"]
Do I dare   45
Disturb the universe?
In a minute there is time
For decisions and revisions which a minute will reverse.

For I have known them all already, known them all:—
Have known the evenings, mornings, afternoons,   50
I have measured out my life with coffee spoons;
I know the voices dying with a dying fall
Beneath the music from a farther room.
  So how should I presume?

And I have known the eyes already, known them all—   55
The eyes that fix you in a formulated phrase,
And when I am formulated, sprawling on a pin,
When I am pinned and wriggling on the wall,
Then how should I begin
To spit out all the butt-ends of my days and ways?   60
   And how should I presume?

And I have known the arms already, known them all—
Arms that are braceleted and white and bare
[But in the lamplight, downed with light brown hair!]
Is it perfume from a dress   65
That makes me so digress?
Arms that lie along a table, or wrap about a shawl.
   And should I then presume?
   And how should I begin?

      ● ● ●

Shall I say, I have gone at dusk through narrow streets   70
And watched the smoke that rises from the pipes
Of lonely men in shirt-sleeves, leaning out of windows? . . .

I should have been a pair of ragged claws
Scuttling across the floors of silent seas.

      ● ● ●

And the afternoon, the evening, sleeps so peacefully!   75
Smoothed by long fingers,
Asleep . . . tired . . . or it malingers,
Stretched on the floor, here beside you and me.
Should I, after tea and cakes and ices,
Have the strength to force the moment to its crisis?   80
But though I have wept and fasted, wept and prayed,
Though I have seen my head [grown slightly bald] brought in upon
   a platter,
I am no prophet—and here's no great matter;
I have seen the moment of my greatness flicker,
And I have seen the eternal Footman hold my coat, and snicker,   85
And in short, I was afraid.

And would it have been worth it, after all,
After the cups, the marmalade, the tea,
Among the porcelain, among some talk of you and me,
Would it have been worth while,   90

To have bitten off the matter with a smile,
To have squeezed the universe into a ball
To roll it toward some overwhelming question,
To say: "I am Lazarus, come from the dead,
Come back to tell you all, I shall tell you all"—   95
If one, settling a pillow by her head,
   Should say: "That is not what I meant at all.
   That is not it, at all."

And would it have been worth it, after all,
Would it have been worth while,   100
After the sunsets and the dooryards and the sprinkled streets,
After the novels, after the teacups, after the skirts that trail along the
   floor—
And this, and so much more?—
It is impossible to say just what I mean!
But as if a magic lantern threw the nerves in patterns on a screen: 105
Would it have been worth while
If one, settling a pillow or throwing off a shawl,
And turning toward the window, should say:
   "That is not it at all,
   That is not what I meant, at all."   110

• • •

No! I am not Prince Hamlet, nor was meant to be;
Am an attendant lord, one that will do
To swell a progress, start a scene or two,
Advise the prince; no doubt, an easy tool,
Deferential, glad to be of use,   115
Politic, cautious, and meticulous;
Full of high sentence, but a bit obtuse;
At times, indeed, almost ridiculous—
Almost, at times, the Fool.

I grow old . . . I grow old . . .   120
I shall wear the bottoms of my trousers rolled.

Shall I part my hair behind? Do I dare to eat a peach?
I shall wear white flannel trousers, and walk upon the beach.
I have heard the mermaids singing, each to each.

I do not think that they will sing to me.   125

I have seen them riding seaward on the waves
Combing the white hair of the waves blown back
When the wind blows the water white and black.

We have lingered in the chambers of the sea
By sea-girls wreathed with seaweed red and brown   130
Till human voices wake us, and we drown.

JOURNEY OF THE MAGI

"A cold coming we had of it,
Just the worst time of the year
For a journey, and such a long journey:
The ways deep and the weather sharp,
The very dead of winter."   5
And the camels galled, sore-footed, refractory,
Lying down in the melting snow.
There were times we regretted
The summer palaces on slopes, the terraces,
And the silken girls bringing sherbet.   10
Then the camel men cursing and grumbling
And running away, and wanting their liquor and women,
And the night-fires going out, and the lack of shelters,
And the cities hostile and the towns unfriendly
And the villages dirty and charging high prices: 15
A hard time we had of it.

THE LOVE SONG OF J. ALFRED PRUFROCK: a dramatic monologue spoken by a middle-aged man considering his own spiritual destitution, but not without a sense of pride. Prufrock's confession is as open as the speaker's, Guido da Montefeltro, in Dante's twenty-seventh canto of the *Inferno* with which Eliot prefaces the poem: "If I thought my answer were to one who could ever return to the world, this flame would shake no more [*i.e.*, I would no longer speak to you]; but since, if I hear true, no living person ever returned from this abyss, without fear of shame I answer you." In both cases, Guido and Prufrock confess openly without fear of betrayal or shame. 29. *works and days*. Hesiod, a Greek poet of the eighth century B.C., wrote *Works and Days*, a poem about useful agricultural labor which contrasts with Prufrock's intended meaning. 52. *I . . . fall*, ironic reference to Shakespeare's *Twelfth Night* (I, i, 4): "That strain again! It had a dying fall." 73. *claws*, refers to the sideways movement of crabs. 82. *head*. Salome requested John the Baptist's head on a platter; see Mark 6:17–28. 113. *progress*, in Elizabethan drama, the movement of a royal or noble person across the stage. 117. *sentence*, archaic meaning: sententious, opinionated.

At the end we preferred to travel all night,
Sleeping in snatches,
With the voices singing in our ears, saying
That this was all folly.   20

Then at dawn we came down to a temperate valley,
Wet, below the snow line, smelling of vegetation;
With a running stream and a water-mill beating the darkness,
And three trees on the low sky,
And an old white horse galloped away in the meadow.   25
Then we came to a tavern with vine-leaves over the lintel,
Six hands at an open door dicing for pieces of silver,
And feet kicking the empty wine-skins.
But there was no information, and so we continued
And arrived at evening, not a moment too soon   30
Finding the place; it was (you may say) satisfactory.

All this was a long time ago, I remember,
And I would do it again, but set down
This set down
This: were we led all that way for   35
Birth or Death? There was a Birth, certainly,
We had evidence and no doubt. I had seen birth and death,
But had thought they were different; this Birth was
Hard and bitter agony for us, like Death, our death.
We returned to our places, these Kingdoms,   40
But no longer at ease here, in the old dispensation,
With an alien people clutching their gods.
I should be glad of another death.

JOURNEY OF THE MAGI.   The speaker, one of the three wise men, reminisces about
the journey to Jerusalem, Christ's nativity. The recollection shifts in space and
time.

William Carlos Williams

1883–1963

THE YACHTS

contend in a sea which the land partly encloses
shielding them from the too heavy blows
of an ungoverned ocean which when it chooses

tortures the biggest hulls, the best man knows
to pit against its beatings, and sinks them pitilessly.   5
Mothlike in mists, scintillant in the minute

brilliance of cloudless days, with broad bellying sails
they glide to the wind tossing green water
from their sharp prows while over them the crew crawls

ant-like, solicitously grooming them, releasing,   10
making fast as they turn, lean far over and having
caught the wind again, side by side, head for the mark.

In a well guarded arena of open water surrounded by
lesser and greater craft which, sycophant, lumbering
and flittering follow them, they appear youthful, rare   15

as the light of a happy eye, live with the grace
of all that in the mind is fleckless, free and
naturally to be desired. Now the sea which holds them

is moody, lapping their glossy sides, as if feeling
for some slightest flaw but fails completely.   20
Today no race. Then the wind comes again. The yachts

move, jockeying for a start, the signal is set and they

are off. Now the waves strike at them but they are too
well made, they slip through, though they take in canvas.

Arms with hands grasping seek to clutch at the prows.   25
Bodies thrown recklessly in the way are cut aside.
It is a sea of faces about them in agony, in despair

until the horror of the race dawns staggering the mind,
the whole sea become an entanglement of watery bodies
lost to the world bearing what they cannot hold. Broken,   30

beaten, desolate, reaching from the dead to be taken up
they cry out, failing, failing! their cries rising
in waves still as the skillful yachts pass over.

SPRING AND ALL

By the road to the contagious hospital
under the surge of the blue
mottled clouds driven from the
northeast—a cold wind. Beyond, the
waste of broad, muddy fields   5
brown with dried weeds, standing and fallen

patches of standing water
the scattering of tall trees

All along the road the reddish
purplish, forked, upstanding, twiggy   10
stuff of bushes and small trees
with dead, brown leaves under them
leafless vines—

Lifeless in appearance, sluggish
dazed spring approaches—   15

They enter the new world naked,
cold, uncertain of all
save that they enter. All about them
the cold, familiar wind—

Now the grass, tomorrow   20
the stiff curl of wildcarrot leaf

One by one objects are defined—
It quickens: clarity, outline of leaf
But now the stark dignity of
entrance—Still, the profound change   25
has come upon them: rooted they
grip down and begin to awaken

THE RED WHEELBARROW

so much depends
upon

a red wheel
barrow

glazed with rain   5
water

beside the white
chickens

Ezra Pound

b. 1885

IN A STATION OF THE METRO

The apparition of these faces in the crowd;
Petals on a wet, black bough.

THE RIVER-MERCHANT'S WIFE: A LETTER

While my hair was still cut straight across my forehead
Played I about the front gate, pulling flowers.
You came by on bamboo stilts, playing horse,
You walked about my seat, playing with blue plums.
And we went on living in the village of Chokan: 5
Two small people, without dislike or suspicion.

At fourteen I married My Lord you.
I never laughed, being bashful.
Lowering my head, I looked at the wall.
Called to, a thousand times, I never looked back.   10

At fifteen I stopped scowling,
I desired my dust to be mingled with yours
Forever and forever and forever.
Why should I climb the look out?

At sixteen you departed,   15
You went into far Ku-to-yen, by the river of swirling eddies,
And you have been gone five months.
The monkeys make sorrowful noise overhead.

You dragged your feet when you went out.
By the gate now, the moss is grown, the different mosses,   20
Too deep to clear them away!
The leaves fall early this autumn, in wind.
The paired butterflies are already yellow with August
Over the grass in the West garden;
They hurt me. I grow older.   25
If you are coming down through the narrows of the river Kiang,
Please let me know beforehand,
And I will come out to meet you
            As far as Cho-fu-Sa.

ANCIENT MUSIC

            Winter is icummen in,
            Lhude sing Goddamm,
            Raineth drop and staineth slop,
            And how the wind doth ramm!
                    Sing: Goddamm.   5
            Skiddeth bus and sloppeth us,
            An ague hath my ham.
            Freezeth river, turneth liver,
                    Damn you, sing: Goddamm.
            Goddamm, Goddamm, 'tis why I am, Goddamm,   10
                    So 'gainst the winter's balm.
            Sing goddamm, damm, sing Goddamm.
            Sing goddamm, sing goddamm, DAMM.

THE RIVER-MERCHANT'S WIFE: A LETTER: Pound's translation of a Chinese poem by
Rihaku (Li Po), eighth century.

ANCIENT MUSIC: Adapted from the medieval lyric, "The Cuckoo Song":
            Sumer is icumen in,
                Lhude sing cuccu!
            Groweth sed and bloweth med [meadow]
                And springeth the wude [wood] nu.
                    Sing cuccu!
            Awe bleteth after lomb,
                Lhouth after calve cu,
            Bulluc sterteth [leaps], bucke verteth [breaks wind];
                Murie sing cuccu!
                    Cuccu, cuccu.
                Wel singes thu cuccu,
                Ne swik [cease] thu naver nu.
            Sing cuccu nu! Sing cuccu!
            Sing cuccu! Sing cuccu nu!

H. D. (Hilda Doolittle)

1886–1961

HYMN

Of unguent in a jar,
We may ensample myrrh;

So were His fragrance stored,
Sealed up, compact, secure,

In flawless alabaster,   5
But for the spear;

This is the wound of grace,
This is the nesting place

Of the white dove,
This is the wound of love;   10

The spear opened for us
The rose of purple fire,

The rose of iciest breath,
White rose of death;

The spear opened for us   15
The narrow way

Into the dust,
To the eternal day.

Claude McKay

1890–1948

AMERICA

Although she feeds me bread of bitterness,
And sinks into my throat her tiger's tooth,
Stealing my breath of life, I will confess
I love this cultured hell that tests my youth!
Her vigor flows like tides into my blood,   5
Giving me strength erect against her hate.
Her bigness sweeps my being like a flood.
Yet as a rebel fronts a king in state,
I stand within her walls with not a shred
Of terror, malice, not a word of jeer.   10
Darkly I gaze into the days ahead,
And see her might and granite wonders there,
Beneath the touch of Time's unerring hand,
Like priceless treasures sinking in the sand.

Edna St. Vincent Millay

1892–1950

SPRING

To what purpose, April, do you return again?
Beauty is not enough.
You can no longer quiet me with the redness
Of little leaves opening stickily.
I know what I know.   5
The sun is hot on my neck as I observe
The spikes of the crocus.
The smell of the earth is good.
It is apparent that there is no death.
But what does that signify?   10
Not only underground are the brains of men
Eaten by maggots.
Life in itself
Is nothing,
An empty cup, a flight of uncarpeted stairs.   15
It is not enough that yearly, down this hill,
April
Comes like an idiot, babbling and strewing flowers.

SIEGE

This I do, being mad:
Gather baubles about me,
Sit in a circle of toys, and all the time
Death beating the door in.

White jade and an orange pitcher,   5
Hindu idol, Chinese god,—
Maybe next year, when I'm richer—
Carved beads and a lotus pod . . . .

And all this time
Death beating the door in.   10

E. E. Cummings

1894–1962

ANYONE LIVED IN A PRETTY HOW TOWN

anyone lived in a pretty how town
(with up so floating many bells down)
spring summer autumn winter
he sang his didn't he danced his did.

Women and men (both little and small)   5
cared for anyone not at all
they sowed their isn't they reaped their same
sun moon stars rain

children guessed (but only a few
and down they forgot as up they grew   10
autumn winter spring summer)
that noone loved him more by more

when by now and tree by leaf
she laughed his joy she cried his grief
bird by snow and stir by still   15
anyone's any was all to her

someones married their everyones
laughed their cryings and did their dance
(sleep wake hope and then) they
said their nevers they slept their dream   20

stars rain sun moon
(and only the snow can begin to explain
how children are apt to forget to remember
with up so floating many bells down)

one day anyone died i guess   25
(and noone stooped to kiss his face)
busy folk buried them side by side
little by little and was by was

all by all and deep by deep
and more by more they dream their sleep   30
noone and anyone earth by april
wish by spirit and if by yes.

Women and men (both dong and ding)
summer autumn winter spring
reaped their sowing and went their came   35
sun moon stars rain

IF I HAVE MADE, MY LADY, INTRICATE

if i have made, my lady, intricate
imperfect various things chiefly which wrong
your eyes (frailer than most deep dreams are frail)
songs less firm than your body's whitest song
upon my mind—if i have failed to snare   5
the glance too shy—if through my singing slips
the very skillful strangeness of your smile
the keen primeval silence of your hair

—let the world say "his most wise music stole
nothing from death"—

                    you only will create   10
(who are so perfectly alive) my shame:
lady through whose profound and fragile lips
the sweet small clumsy feet of April came

into the ragged meadow of my soul.

Wallace Stevens

1879–1955

THIRTEEN WAYS OF LOOKING AT A BLACKBIRD

I

Among twenty snowy mountains,
The only moving thing
Was the eye of the blackbird.

II

I was of three minds,
Like a tree   5
In which there are three blackbirds.

III

The blackbird whirled in the autumn winds.
It was a small part of the pantomime.

IV

A man and a woman
Are one.   10
A man and a woman and a blackbird
Are one.

V

I do not know which to prefer,
The beauty of inflections
Or the beauty of innuendoes,   15
The blackbird whistling
Or just after.

VI

Icicles filled the long window
With barbaric glass.
The shadow of the blackbird   20
Crossed it, to and fro.
The mood
Traced in the shadow
An indecipherable cause.

VII

O thin men of Haddam,   25
Why do you imagine golden birds?
Do you not see how the blackbird
Walks around the feet
Of the women about you?

VIII

I know noble accents   30
And lucid, inescapable rhythms;
But I know, too,
That the blackbird is involved
In what I know.

IX

When the blackbird flew out of sight,   35
It marked the edge
Of one of many circles.

X

At the sight of blackbirds
Flying in a green light,
Even the bawds of euphony   40
Would cry out sharply.

XI

He rode over Connecticut
In a glass coach.
Once, a fear pierced him,
In that he mistook   45
The shadow of his equipage
For blackbirds.

XII

The river is moving.
The blackbird must be flying.

XIII

It was evening all afternoon.   50
It was snowing
And it was going to snow.
The blackbird sat
In the cedar-limbs.

SUNDAY MORNING

I

Complacencies of the peignoir, and late
Coffee and oranges in a sunny chair,
And the green freedom of a cockatoo
Upon a rug mingle to dissipate
The holy hush of ancient sacrifice.   5
She dreams a little, and she feels the dark
Encroachment of that old catastrophe,
As a calm darkens among water lights.
The pungent oranges and bright, green wings
Seem things in some procession of the dead,   10
Winding across wide water, without sound.
The day is like wide water, without sound,
Stilled for the passing of her dreaming feet
Over the seas, to silent Palestine,
Dominion of the blood and sepulcher.   15

II

Why should she give her bounty to the dead?
What is divinity if it can come
Only in silent shadows and in dreams?
Shall she not find in comforts of the sun,
In pungent fruit and bright, green wings, or else   20
In any balm or beauty of the earth,
Things to be cherished like the thought of heaven?
Divinity must live within herself:
Passions of rain, or moods in falling snow;

Grievings in loneliness, or unsubdued   25
Elations when the forest blooms; gusty
Emotions on wet roads on autumn nights;
All pleasures and all pains, remembering
The bough of summer and the winter branch.
These are the measures destined for her soul.   30

III

Jove in the clouds had his inhuman birth.
No mother suckled him, no sweet land gave
Large-mannered motions to his mythy mind.
He moved among us, as a muttering king,
Magnificent, would move among his hinds,   35
Until our blood, commingling, virginal,
With heaven, brought such requital to desire
The very hinds discerned it, in a star.
Shall our blood fail? Or shall it come to be
The blood of paradise? And shall the earth   40
Seem all of paradise that we shall know?
The sky will be much friendlier then than now,
A part of labor and a part of pain,
And next in glory to enduring love,
Not this dividing and indifferent blue.   45

IV

She says, "I am content when wakened birds,
Before they fly, test the reality
Of misty fields, by their sweet questionings;
But when the birds are gone, and their warm fields
Return no more, where, then, is paradise?"   50
There is not any haunt of prophecy,
Nor any old chimera of the grave,
Neither the golden underground, nor isle
Melodious, where spirits gat them home,
Nor visionary south, nor cloudy palm   55
Remote on heaven's hill, that has endured
As April's green endures; or will endure
Like her remembrance of awakened birds,
Or her desire for June and evening, tipped
By the consummation of the swallow's wings.   60

V

She says, "But in contentment I still feel
The need of some imperishable bliss."

Death is the mother of beauty; hence from her,
Alone, shall come fulfillment to our dreams
And our desires. Although she strews the leaves   65
Of sure obliteration on our paths,
The path sick sorrow took, the many paths
Where triumph rang its brassy phrase, or love
Whispered a little out of tenderness,
She makes the willow shiver in the sun   70
For maidens who were wont to sit and gaze
Upon the grass, relinquished to their feet.
She causes boys to pile new plums and pears
On disregarded plate. The maidens taste
And stray impassioned in the littering leaves.   75

VI

Is there no change of death in paradise?
Does ripe fruit never fall? Or do the boughs
Hang always heavy in that perfect sky,
Unchanging, yet so like our perishing earth,
With rivers like our own that seek for seas   80
They never find, the same receding shores
That never touch with inarticulate pang?
Why set the pear upon those riverbanks
Or spice the shores with odors of the plum?
Alas, that they should wear our colors there,   85
The silken weavings of our afternoons,
And pick the strings of our insipid lutes!
Death is the mother of beauty, mystical,
Within whose burning bosom we devise
Our earthly mothers waiting, sleeplessly.   90

VII

Supple and turbulent, a ring of men
Shall chant in orgy on a summer morn
Their boisterous devotion to the sun,
Not as a god, but as a god might be,
Naked among them, like a savage source.   95
Their chant shall be a chant of paradise,
Out of their blood, returning to the sky;
And in their chant shall enter, voice by voice,
The windy lake wherein their lord delights,
The trees, like seraphim, and echoing hills,   100
That choir among themselves long afterward.

They shall know well the heavenly fellowship
Of men that perish and of summer morn.
And whence they came and whither they shall go
The dew upon their feet shall manifest.   105

VIII

She hears, upon that water without sound,
A voice that cries, "The tomb in Palestine
Is not the porch of spirits lingering.
It is the grave of Jesus, where he lay."
We live in an old chaos of the sun,   110
Or old dependency of day and night,
Or island solitude, unsponsored, free,
Of that wide water, inescapable.
Deer walk upon our mountains, and the quail
Whistle about us their spontaneous cries;   115
Sweet berries ripen in the wilderness;
And, in the isolation of the sky,
At evening, casual flocks of pigeons make
Ambiguous undulations as they sink,
Downward to darkness, on extended wings.   120

SUNDAY MORNING. 1. *peignoir*, luxurious housecoat (French). 52. *chimera*, a monster bred of fantasy. 53. *golden underground . . . isle/Melodius*, ancient Greek concepts of afterlife, the underworld havens of departed souls and resting place of victorious warriors.

W. H. Auden

b. 1907

O WHERE ARE YOU GOING

"O where are you going?" said reader to rider,
"That valley is fatal when furnaces burn,
Yonder's the midden whose odours will madden,
That gap is the grave where the tall return."

"O do you imagine," said fearer to farer,   5
"That dusk will delay on your path to the pass,
Your diligent looking discover the lacking
Your footsteps feel from granite to grass?"

"O what was that bird," said horror to hearer,
"Did you see that shape in the twisted trees?   10
Behind you swiftly the figure comes softly,
The spot on your skin is a shocking disease."

"Out of this house"—said rider to reader,
"Yours never will"—said farer to fearer,
"They're looking for you"—said hearer to horror,   15
As he left them there, as he left them there.

MUNDUS ET INFANS

(For Albert and Angelyn Stevens)

Kicking his mother until she let go of his soul
Has given him a healthy appetite: clearly, her rôle
  In the New Order must be
To supply and deliver his raw materials free;

Should there be any shortage,   5
She will be held responsible; she also promises
To show him all such attentions as befit his age.
    Having dictated peace,

With one fist clenched behind his head, heel drawn up to thigh
The cocky little ogre dozes off, ready,   10
    Though, to take on the rest
Of the world at the drop of a hat or the mildest
    Nudge of the impossible,
Resolved, cost what it may, to seize supreme power and
Sworn to resist tyranny to the death with all   15
    Forces at his command.

A pantheist not a solipsist, he co-operates
With a universe of large and noisy feeling-states
    Without troubling to place
Them anywhere special, for, to his eyes, Funnyface   20
    Or Elephant as yet
Mean nothing. His distinction between Me and Us
Is a matter of taste; his seasons are Dry and Wet;
    He thinks as his mouth does.

Still, his loud iniquity is still what only the   25
Greatest of saints become—someone who does not lie:
    He because he cannot
Stop the vivid present to think, they by having got
    Past reflection into
A passionate obedience in time. We have our Boy-   30
Meets-Girl era of mirrors and muddle to work through,
    Without rest, without joy.

Therefore we love him because his judgments are so
Frankly subjective that his abuse carries no
    Personal sting. We should   35
Never dare offer our helplessness as a good
    Bargain, without at least
Promising to overcome a misfortune we blame
History or Banks or the Weather for: but this beast
    Dares to exist without shame.   40

Let him praise our Creator with the top of his voice,
Then, and the motions of his bowels; let us rejoice
    That he lets us hope, for
He may never become a fashionable or
    Important personage: 45

However bad he may be, he has not yet gone mad;
Whoever we are now, we were no worse at his age;
   So of course we ought to be glad

When he bawls the house down. Has he not a perfect right
To remind us at every moment how we quite   50
   Rightly expect each other
To go upstairs or for a walk, if we must cry over
   Spilt milk, such as our wish
That, since apparently we shall never be above
Either or both, we had never learned to distinguish   55
   Between hunger and love?

MUNDUS ET INFANS: the world and the child.   17. *pantheist*, one who sees God
in all things. *solipsist*, one who believes that knowledge is restricted to the experience of the self.

Theodore Roethke

1908–1963

THE WAKING

I wake to sleep, and take my waking slow.
I feel my fate in what I cannot fear.
I learn by going where I have to go.

We think by feeling. What is there to know?
I hear my being dance from ear to ear   5
I wake to sleep, and take my waking slow.

Of those so close beside me, which are you?
God bless the Ground! I shall walk softly there,
And learn by going where I have to go.

Light takes the Tree; but who can tell us how?   10
The lowly worm climbs up a winding stair;
I wake to sleep, and take my waking slow.

Great Nature has another thing to do
To you and me; so take the lively air,
And, lovely, learn by going where to go.   15

This shaking keeps me steady. I should know.
What falls away is always. And is near.
I wake to sleep, and take my waking slow.
I learn by going where I have to go.

MY PAPA'S WALTZ

The whisky on your breath
Could make a small boy dizzy;

But I hung on like death:
Such waltzing was not easy.

We romped until the pans   5
Slid from the kitchen shelf;
My mother's countenance
Could not unfrown itself.

The hand that held my wrist
Was battered on one knuckle;   10
At every step you missed
My right ear scraped a buckle.

You beat time on my head
With a palm caked hard by dirt,
Then waltzed me off to bed   15
Still clinging to your shirt.

Kenneth Patchen

b. 1911

O WHEN I TAKE MY LOVE OUT WALKING

O when I take my love out walking
In the soft frosted stillness of this summer morn

Then are the mysteries all around us
O what can I say!
    the ever-known, the ever-new   5
    like her they seem
O lully, lullay
    only **this** moment is real
Here at the edge of the world
    and the throne. The rest's a lie   10
    which shadows scheme.

Now gentle flowers are awash on the sleeping hill
And as I bend to kiss her opened lips
O then do the wonders and the sparklings seem
A shabby tinsel show for my dear queen.   15

Robert E. Hayden

b. 1913

THE DIVER

Sank through easeful
azure. Flower
creatures flashed and
shimmered there—
lost images   5
fadingly remembered.
Swiftly descended
into canyon of cold
nightgreen emptiness.
Freefalling, weightless   10
as in dreams of
wingless flight,
plunged through infra-
space and came to
the dead ship,   15
carcass that swarmed with
voracious life.
Angelfish, their
lively blue and
yellow prised from   20
darkness by the
flashlight's beam,
thronged her portholes.
Moss of bryozoans
blurred, obscured her   25
metal. Snappers,
gold groupers explored her,
fearless of bubbling
manfish. I entered

the wreck, awed by her silence,   30
feeling more keenly
the iron cold.
With flashlight probing
fogs of water
saw the sad slow   35
dance of gilded
chairs, the ectoplasmic
swirl of garments,
drowned instruments
of buoyancy,   40
drunken shoes. Then
livid gesturings,
eldritch hide and
seek of laughing
faces. I yearned to   45
find those hidden
ones, to fling aside
the mask and call to them,
yield to rapturous
whisperings, have   50
done with self and
every dinning
vain complexity.
Yet in languid
frenzy strove, as   55
one freezing fights off
sleep desiring sleep;
strove against the
cancelling arms that
suddenly surrounded   60
me, fled the numbing
kisses that I craved.
Reflex of life-wish?
Respirator's brittle
belling? Swam from   65
the ship somehow;
somehow began the
measured rise.

Dylan Thomas

1914–1953

THE FORCE THAT THROUGH THE GREEN FUSE DRIVES THE FLOWER

The force that through the green fuse drives the flower
Drives my green age; that blasts the roots of trees
Is my destroyer.
And I am dumb to tell the crooked rose
My youth is bent by the same wintry fever.   5

The force that drives the water through the rocks
Drives my red blood; that dries the mouthing streams
Turns mine to wax.
And I am dumb to mouth unto my veins
How at the mountain spring the same mouth sucks.   10

The hand that whirls the water in the pool
Stirs the quicksand; that ropes the blowing wind
Hauls my shroud sail.
And I am dumb to tell the hanging man
How of my clay is made the hangman's lime.   15

The lips of time leech to the fountain head;
Love drips and gathers, but the fallen blood
Shall calm her sores.
And I am dumb to tell a weather's wind
How time has ticked a heaven round the stars.   20

And I am dumb to tell the lover's tomb
How at my sheet goes the same crooked worm.

DO NOT GO GENTLE INTO THAT GOOD NIGHT

Do not go gentle into that good night,
Old age should burn and rave at close of day;
Rage, rage against the dying of the light.

Though wise men at their end know dark is right,
Because their words had forked no lightning they   5
Do not go gentle into that good night.

Good men, the last wave by, crying how bright
Their frail deeds might have danced in a green bay,
Rage, rage against the dying of the light.

Wild men who caught and sang the sun in flight,   10
And learn, too late, they grieved it on its way,
Do not go gentle into that good night.

Grave men, near death, who see with blinding sight
Blind eyes could blaze like meteors and be gay,
Rage, rage against the dying of the light.   15

And you, my father, there on the sad height,
Curse, bless, me now with your fierce tears, I pray.
Do not go gentle into that good night.
Rage, rage against the dying of the light.

Gwendolyn Brooks

b. 1917

from THE CHILDREN OF THE POOR

#4

First fight. Then fiddle. Ply the slipping string
With feathery sorcery; muzzle the note
With hurting love; the music that they wrote
Bewitch, bewilder. Qualify to sing
Threadwise. Devise no salt, no hempen thing   5
For the dear instrument to bear. Devote
The bow to silks and honey. Be remote
A while from malice and from murdering.
But first to arms, to armor. Carry hate
In front of you and harmony behind.   10
Be deaf to music and to beauty blind.
Win war. Rise bloody, maybe not too late
For having first to civilize a space
Wherein to play your violin with grace.

Lawrence Ferlinghetti

b. 1919

THE PENNYCANDYSTORE

The pennycandystore beyond the El
is where I first
        fell in love
            with unreality
Jellybeans glowed in the semi-gloom   5
of that september afternoon
A cat upon the counter moved among
              the licorice sticks
      and tootsie rolls
   and Oh Boy Gum   10

Outside the leaves were falling as they died

A wind had blown away the sun

A girl ran in
Her hair was rainy
Her breasts were breathless in the little room   15

Outside the leaves were falling
        and they cried
           Too soon! too soon!

THE PENNYCANDYSTORE. 1. *El,* an abbreviation for elevated transit systems.

Alan Dugan

b. 1923

TRIBUTE TO KAFKA FOR SOMEONE TAKEN

The party is going strong.
The doorbell rings. It's
for someone named me.
I'm coming. I take
a last drink, a last   5
puff on a cigarette,
a last kiss at a girl,
and step into the hall,
                            bang,

shutting out the laughter. "Is   10
your name you?" "Yes."
"Well come along then."
"See here. See here. See here."

TRIBUTE TO KAFKA FOR SOMEONE TAKEN: a reference to Franz Kafka's (1883–1924)
The Trial whose hero faces an unknown sentence by mysterious accusers.

James Dickey

b. 1923

THE PERFORMANCE

The last time I saw Donald Armstrong
He was staggering oddly off into the sun,
Going down, of the Philippine Islands.
I let my shovel fall, and put that hand
Above my eyes, and moved some way to one side   5
That his body might pass through the sun,

And I saw how well he was not
Standing there on his hands,
On his spindle shanked forearms balanced,
Unbalanced, with his big feet looming and waving   10
In the great, untrustworthy air
He flew in each night, when it darkened.

Dust fanned in scraped puffs from the earth
Between his arms, and blood turned his face inside out,
To demonstrate its suppleness   15
Of veins, as he perfected his role.
Next day, he toppled his head off
On an island beach to the south,

And the enemy's two-handed sword
Did not fall from anyone's hands   20
At that miraculous sight,
As the head rolled over upon
Its wide-eyed face, and fell
Into the inadequate grave

He had dug for himself, under pressure.   25
Yet I put my flat hand to my eyebrows

Months later, to see him again
In the sun, when I learned how he died,
And imagined him, there,
Come, judged, before his small captors,   30

Doing all his lean tricks to amaze them—
The back somersault, the kip-up—
And at last, the stand on his hands,
Perfect, with his feet together,
His head down, evenly breathing,   35
As the sun poured up from the sea

And the headsman broke down
In a blaze of tears, in that light
Of the thin, long human frame
Upside down in its own strange joy,   40
And, if some other one had not told him,
Would have cut off the feet

Instead of the head,
And if Armstrong had not presently risen
In kingly, round-shouldered attendance,   45
And then knelt down in himself
Beside his hacked, glittering grave, having done
All things in this life that he could.

THE PERFORMANCE: the setting of the poem is the Philippine Islands during the Second World War. 19. *sword*, Japanese samurai sword.

Leonard E. Nathan

b. 1924

FALL'S GIRL

Against the wind, she took the field—long hair,
A golden squall of little wings; her breast,
A white billow where her skirt's high crest
Broke like a wavetop on the pitching air
That laid her long brown rushing legs half bare   5
To the wind's fondling, as beautifully distressed,
She clapped her stretched arms down and vainly pressed
Choppy silks to thighs. Beyond her, where
A blowzy hectic row of sycamore
Cast a thousand leaves each plunge and toss   10
Of an ill wind, all things else might drift
To common desolation; that is their loss;
Her errand was (it seemed) to find one door
And, in her own sweet time, betray her gift.

Lucien Stryk

b. 1925

THE CANNERY

In summer this town is full of rebels
Come up from Tennessee to shell the peas.

And wetbacks roam the supermarts, making
A Tijuana of the drab main street.

The Swedes and Poles who work at Wurlitzer,   5
And can't stand music, are all dug in:

Doors are bolted, their pretty children warned,
Where they wait for the autumnal peace.

At night the cannery's like a train,
A runaway, cans flung up like clinkers.   10

Sometimes on an evening hot as Southland
When even fear won't keep the windows down,

One hears the drawl of Tennessee, the quick
Laugh of Mexico in the empty streets.

THE PIT

Twenty years. I still remember
The sun-blown stench, and the pit
At least two hundred yards from
The cove we'd anchored guns in.

They were blasting at the mountains,   5
The beach was nearly ours.

The smell kept leaking back.
I thought of garbage cans
Behind chopsuey restaurants
Of home, strangely appealing on   10
A summer's night, meaning another
Kind of life. Which made the difference.

When the three of us, youngest in
The crew, were handed poles and told
To get the deadmen underground   15
Or join them, we saw it a sullen
Sort of lark. And lashed to trees,
The snipers had us dancing.

Ducks for those vultures in the boughs,
Poles poking through the powder-   20
Bitten grass, we zigzagged
Toward the pit as into
The arse of death, the wittiest
Of us said but did not laugh.

At last we reached it, half full   25
Of sand and crawling. We clamped
Nose, mouth, wrenched netted helmets
To the chin, yet poles probed forward
Surgically, touching for spots
The maggots had not jelled.   30

Somehow we got the deadmen under,
Along with empty lobster tins,
Bottles, gear and ammo. Somehow
We plugged the pit and slipped back
To the guns. Then for days   35
We had to helmet bathe downwind.

I stuck my pole, clean end high,
Behind the foxhole, a kind of
Towelpeg and a something more.
I'd stare it out through jungle haze,   40
And wonder. Ask anyone who
Saw it: nobody won that war.

Gary Snyder

b. 1930

from MYTHS & TEXTS (HUNTING)

#8 "this poem is for deer"

"I dance on all the mountains
On five mountains, I have a dancing place
When they shoot at me I run
To my five mountains"

Missed a last shot   5
At the Buck, in twilight
So we came back sliding
On dry needles through cold pines.
Scared out a cottontail
Whipped up the winchester   10
Shot off its head.
The white body rolls and twitches
In the dark ravine
As we run down the hill to the car.

           deer foot down scree   15
Picasso's fawn, Issa's fawn,
Deer on the autumn mountain
Howling like a wise man
Stiff springy jumps down the snowfields
Head held back, forefeet out,   20
Balls tight in a tough hair sack
Keeping the human soul from care
           on the autumn mountain
Standing in late sun, ear-flick
Tail-flick, gold mist of flies   25
Whirling from nostril to eyes.

Home by night
                drunken eye
Still picks out Taurus
Low, and growing high: 30
                four-point buck
Dancing in the headlights
                on the lonely road
A mile past the mill-pond,
With the car stopped, shot   35
That wild silly blinded creature down.

Pull out the hot guts
                with hard bare hands
While night-frost chills the tongue
                and eye   40
The cold horn-bones.
The hunter's belt
                just below the sky
Warm blood in the car trunk.
Deer-smell,   45
                the limp tongue.
Deer don't want to die for me.
                I'll drink sea-water
Sleep on beach pebbles in the rain
Until the deer come down to die   50
                in pity for my pain.

Le Roi Jones

b. 1934

AN AGONY. AS NOW.

I am inside someone
who hates me. I look
out from his eyes. Smell
what fouled tunes come in
to his breath. Love his   5
wretched women.

Slits in the metal, for sun. Where
my eyes sit turning, at the cool air
the glance of light, or hard flesh
rubbed against me, a woman, a man,   10
without shadow, or voice, or meaning.

This is the enclosure (flesh,
where innocence is a weapon. An
abstraction. Touch. (Not mine.
Or yours, if you are the soul I had   15
and abandoned when I was blind and had
my enemies carry me as a dead man
(if he is beautiful, or pitied.

It can be pain. (As now, as all his
flesh hurts me.) It can be that. Or   20
pain. As when she ran from me into
that forest.
           Or pain, the mind
silver spiraled whirled against the
sun, higher than even old men thought   25
God would be. Or pain. And the other. The
yes. (Inside his books, his fingers. They

are withered yellow flowers and were never
beautiful.) The yes. You will, lost soul, say
'beauty.' Beauty, practiced, as the tree. The   30
slow river. A white sun in its wet sentences.

Or, the cold men in their gale. Ecstasy. Flesh
or soul. The yes. (Their robes blown. Their bowls
empty. They chant at my heels, not at yours.) Flesh
or soul, as corrupt. Where the answer moves too quickly.   35
Where the God is a self, after all.)

Cold air blown through narrow blind eyes. Flesh,
white hot metal. Glows as the day with its sun.
It is a human love, I live inside. A bony skeleton
you recognize as words or simple feeling.   40

But it has no feeling. As the metal, is hot, it is not,
given to love.

It burns the thing
inside it. And that thing
screams.   45

NARRATIVE EXPERIENCE
the private voice

CONTENTS

James Joyce
      ARABY   485

Graham Greene
      THE BASEMENT ROOM   490

Nathaniel Hawthorne
      MY KINSMAN, MAJOR MOLINEUX   510

Ralph Ellison
      FLYING HOME   525

Ernest Hemingway
      SOLDIER'S HOME   541

James Baldwin
      SONNY'S BLUES   547

Mary McCarthy
      "CRUEL AND BARBAROUS TREATMENT"   573

William Faulkner
      DRY SEPTEMBER   583

John Cheever
      TORCH SONG   593

Anton Chekhov
      GOOSEBERRIES   606

Flannery O'Connor
      A GOOD MAN IS HARD TO FIND   615

Leo Tolstoy
      THE DEATH OF IVAN ILYCH   628

Alternate Contents   **673**

Index of Authors and Titles   **676**

Index of First Lines of Poems   **679**

James Joyce

1882–1941

ARABY

North Richmond Street, being blind, was a quiet street except at the hour when the Christian Brothers' School set the boys free. An uninhabited house of two storeys stood at the blind end, detached from its neighbours in a square ground. The other houses of the street, conscious of decent lives within them, gazed at one another with brown imperturbable faces.

The former tenant of our house, a priest, had died in the back drawing-room. Air, musty from having been long enclosed, hung in all the rooms, and the waste room behind the kitchen was littered with old useless papers. Among these I found a few paper-covered books, the pages of which were curled and damp: *The Abbot,* by Walter Scott, *The Devout Communicant* and *The Memoirs of Vidocq.* I liked the last best because its leaves were yellow. The wild garden behind the house contained a central apple-tree and a few straggling bushes under one of which I found the late tenant's rusty bicycle-pump. He had been a very charitable priest; in his will he had left all his money to institutions and the furniture of his house to his sister.

When the short days of winter came dusk fell before we had well eaten our dinners. When we met in the street the houses had grown sombre. The space of sky above us was the colour of ever-changing violet and towards it the lamps of the street lifted their feeble lanterns. The cold air stung us and we played till our bodies glowed. Our shouts echoed in the silent street. The career of our play brought us through the dark muddy lanes behind the houses where we ran the gantlet of the rough tribes from the cottages, to the back doors of the dark dripping gardens where odours arose from the ashpits, to the dark odorous stables where a coachman smoothed and combed the horse or shook music from the buckled harness. When we returned to the street light from the kitchen windows had filled the areas. If my uncle was seen turning the corner we hid in the shadow until we had seen him safely housed. Or if Mangan's sister came out on

the doorstep to call her brother in to his tea we watched her from our
shadow peer up and down the street. We waited to see whether she would
remain or go in and, if she remained, we left our shadow and walked up
to Mangan's steps resignedly. She was waiting for us, her figure defined by
the light from the half-opened door. Her brother always teased her before
he obeyed and I stood by the railings looking at her. Her dress swung as
she moved her body and the soft rope of her hair tossed from side to side.

Every morning I lay on the floor in the front parlour watching her door.
The blind was pulled down to within an inch of the sash so that I could
not be seen. When she came out on the doorstep my heart leaped. I ran
to the hall, seized my books and followed her. I kept her brown figure
always in my eye and, when we came near the point at which our ways
diverged, I quickened my pace and passed her. This happened morning
after morning. I had never spoken to her, except for a few casual words,
and yet her name was like a summons to all my foolish blood.

Her image accompanied me even in places the most hostile to romance.
On Saturday evenings when my aunt went marketing I had to go to carry
some of the parcels. We walked through the flaring streets, jostled by
drunken men and bargaining women, amid the curses of labourers, the
shrill litanies of shop-boys who stood on guard by the barrels of pigs'
cheeks, the nasal chanting of street-singers, who sang a *come-all-you* about
O'Donovan Rossa, or a ballad about the troubles in our native land. These
noises converged in a single sensation of life for me: I imagined that I
bore my chalice safely through a throng of foes. Her name sprang to my
lips at moments in strange prayers and praises which I myself did not
understand. My eyes were often full of tears (I could not tell why) and
at times a flood from my heart seemed to pour itself out into my bosom.
I thought little of the future. I did not know whether I would ever speak
to her or not or, if I spoke to her, how I could tell her of my confused
adoration. But my body was like a harp and her words and gestures were
like fingers running upon the wires.

One evening I went into the back drawing-room in which the priest had
died. It was a dark rainy evening and there was no sound in the house.
Through one of the broken panes I heard the rain impinge upon the
earth, the fine incessant needles of water playing in the sodden beds. Some
distant lamp or lighted window gleamed below me. I was thankful that I
could see so little. All my senses seemed to desire to veil themselves and,
feeling that I was about to slip from them, I pressed the palms of my
hands together until they trembled, murmuring: *O love! O love!* many
times.

At last she spoke to me. When she addressed the first words to me I was
so confused that I did not know what to answer. She asked me was I going
to *Araby*. I forget whether I answered yes or no. It would be a splendid
bazaar, she said; she would love to go.

—And why can't you? I asked.

While she spoke she turned a silver bracelet round and round her wrist. She could not go, she said, because there would be a retreat that week in her convent. Her brother and two other boys were fighting for their caps and I was alone at the railings. She held one of the spikes, bowing her head towards me. The light from the lamp opposite our door caught the white curve of her neck, lit up her hair that rested there and, falling, lit up the hand upon the railing. It fell over one side of her dress and caught the white border of a petticoat, just visible as she stood at ease.

—It's well for you, she said.

—If I go, I said, I will bring you something.

What innumerable follies laid waste my waking and sleeping thoughts after that evening! I wished to annihilate the tedious intervening days. I chafed against the work of school. At night in my bedroom and by day in the classroom her image came between me and the page I strove to read. The syllables of the word *Araby* were called to me through the silence in which my soul luxuriated and cast an Eastern enchantment over me. I asked for leave to go to the bazaar on Saturday night. My aunt was surprised and hoped it was not some Freemason affair. I answered few questions in class. I watched my master's face pass from amiability to sternness; he hoped I was not beginning to idle. I could not call my wandering thoughts together. I had hardly any patience with the serious work of life which, now that it stood between me and my desire, seemed to me child's play, ugly monotonous child's play.

On Saturday morning I reminded my uncle that I wished to go to the bazaar in the evening. He was fussing at the hall-stand, looking for the hat-brush, and answered me curtly:

—Yes, boy, I know.

As he was in the hall I could not go into the front parlour and lie at the window. I left the house in bad humour and walked slowly towards the school. The air was pitilessly raw and already my heart misgave me.

When I came home to dinner my uncle had not yet been home. Still it was early. I sat staring at the clock for some time and, when its ticking began to irritate me, I left the room. I mounted the staircase and gained the upper part of the house. The high cold empty gloomy rooms liberated me and I went from room to room singing. From the front window I saw my companions playing below in the street. Their cries reached me weakened and indistinct and, leaning my forehead against the cool glass, I looked over at the dark house where she lived. I may have stood there for an hour, seeing nothing but the brown-clad figure cast by my imagination, touched discreetly by the lamplight at the curved neck, at the hand upon the railings and at the border below the dress

When I came downstairs again I found Mrs. Mercer sitting at the fire. She was an old garrulous woman, a pawnbroker's widow, who collected used stamps for some pious purpose. I had to endure the gossip of the tea-table. The meal was prolonged beyond an hour and still my uncle did not come. Mrs. Mercer stood up to go: she was sorry she couldn't wait any longer, but it was after eight o'clock and she did not like to be out late, as the night air was bad for her. When she had gone I began to walk up and down the room, clenching my fists. My aunt said:

—I'm afraid you may put off your bazaar for this night of Our Lord.

At nine o'clock I heard my uncle's latchkey in the halldoor. I heard him talking to himself and heard the hallstand rocking when it had received the weight of his overcoat. I could interpret these signs. When he was midway through his dinner I asked him to give me the money to go to the bazaar. He had forgotten.

—The people are in bed and after their first sleep now, he said.

I did not smile. My aunt said to him energetically:

—Can't you give him the money and let him go? You've kept him late enough as it is.

My uncle said he was very sorry he had forgotten. He said he believed in the old saying: *All work and no play makes Jack a dull boy*. He asked me where I was going and, when I had told him a second time he asked me did I know *The Arab's Farewell to his Steed*. When I left the kitchen he was about to recite the opening lines of the piece to my aunt.

I held a florin tightly in my hand as I strode down Buckingham Street towards the station. The sight of the streets thronged with buyers and glaring with gas recalled to me the purpose of my journey. I took my seat in a third-class carriage of a deserted train. After an intolerable delay the train moved out of the station slowly. It crept onward among ruinous houses and over the twinkling river. At Westland Row Station a crowd of people pressed to the carriage doors; but the porters moved them back, saying that it was a special train for the bazaar. I remained alone in the bare carriage. In a few minutes the train drew up beside an improvised wooden platform. I passed out on to the road and saw by the lighted dial of a clock that it was ten minutes to ten. In front of me was a large building which displayed the magical name.

I could not find any sixpenny entrance and, fearing that the bazaar would be closed, I passed in quickly through a turnstile, handing a shilling to a weary-looking man. I found myself in a big hall girdled at half its height by a gallery. Nearly all the stalls were closed and the greater part of the hall was in darkness. I recognized a silence like that which pervades a church after a service. I walked into the centre of the bazaar timidly. A few people were gathered about the stalls which were still open. Before a curtain, over which the words *Café Chantant* were written in coloured lamps, two men were counting money on a salver. I listened to the fall of the coins.

Remembering with difficulty why I had come I went over to one of the stalls and examined porcelain vases and flowered tea-sets. At the door of the stall a young lady was talking and laughing with two young gentlemen. I remarked their English accents and listened vaguely to their conversation.

—O, I never said such a thing!

—O, but you did!

—O, but I didn't!

—Didn't she say that?

—Yes. I heard her.

—O, there's a . . . fib!

Observing me the young lady came over and asked me did I wish to buy anything. The tone of her voice was not encouraging; she seemed to have spoken to me out of a sense of duty. I looked humbly at the great jars that stood like eastern guards at either side of the dark entrance to the stall and murmured:

—No, thank you.

The young lady changed the position of one of the vases and went back to the two young men. They began to talk of the same subject. Once or twice the young lady glanced at me over her shoulder.

I lingered before her stall, though I knew my stay was useless, to make my interest in her wares seem the more real. Then I turned away slowly and walked down the middle of the bazaar. I allowed the two pennies to fall against the sixpence in my pocket. I heard a voice call from one end of the gallery that the light was out. The upper part of the hall was now completely dark.

Gazing up into the darkness I saw myself as a creature driven and derided by vanity; and my eyes burned with anguish and anger.

Graham Greene

b. 1904

THE BASEMENT ROOM

1

When the front door had shut them out and the butler Baines had turned back into the dark heavy hall, Philip began to live. He stood in front of the nursery door, listening until he heard the engine of the taxi die out along the street. His parents were gone for a fortnight's holiday; he was "between nurses," one dismissed and the other not arrived; he was alone in the great Belgravia house with Baines and Mrs. Baines.

He could go anywhere, even through the green baize door to the pantry or down the stairs to the basement living-room. He felt a stranger in his home because he could go into any room and all the rooms were empty.

You could only guess who had once occupied them: the rack of pipes in the smoking-room beside the elephant tusks, the carved wood tobacco jar; in the bedroom the pink hangings and pale perfumes and the three-quarter finished jars of cream which Mrs. Baines had not yet cleared away; the high glaze on the never-opened piano in the drawing-room, the china clock, the silly little tables and the silver: but here Mrs. Baines was already busy, pulling down the curtains, covering the chairs in dust-sheets.

"Be off out of here, Master Philip," and she looked at him with her hateful peevish eyes, while she moved round, getting everything in order, meticulous and loveless and doing her duty.

Philip Lane went downstairs and pushed at the baize door; he looked into the pantry, but Baines was not there, then he set foot for the first time on the stairs to the basement. Again he had the sense: this is life. All his seven nursery years vibrated with the strange, the new experience. His crowded busy brain was like a city which feels the earth tremble at a distant earthquake shock. He was apprehensive, but he was happier than he had ever been. Everything was more important than before.

Baines was reading a newspaper in his shirt-sleeves. He said: "Come in,

Phil, and make yourself at home. Wait a moment and I'll do the honours,"
and going to a white cleaned cupboard he brought out a bottle of ginger-
beer and half a Dundee cake. "Half-past eleven in the morning," Baines
said. "It's opening time, my boy," and he cut the cake and poured out the
ginger-beer. He was more genial than Philip had ever known him, more
at his ease, a man in his own home.

"Shall I call Mrs. Baines?" Philip asked, and he was glad when Baines
said no. She was busy. She liked to be busy, so why interfere with her
pleasure?

"A spot of drink at half-past eleven," Baines said, pouring himself out
a glass of ginger-beer, "gives an appetite for chop and does no man any
harm."

"A chop?" Philip asked.

"Old Coasters," Baines said, "call all food chop."

"But it's not a chop?"

"Well, it might be, you know, cooked with palm oil. And then some
paw-paw to follow."

Philip looked out of the basement window at the dry stone yard, the
ash-can and the legs going up and down beyond the railings.

"Was it hot there?"

"Ah, you never felt such heat. Not a nice heat, mind, like you get in the
park on a day like this. Wet," Baines said, "corruption." He cut himself a
slice of cake. "Smelling of rot," Baines said, rolling his eyes round the
small basement room, from clean cupboard to clean cupboard, the sense
of bareness, of nowhere to hide a man's secrets. With an air of regret for
something lost he took a long draught of ginger-beer.

"Why did father live out there?"

"It was his job," Baines said, "same as this is mine now. And it was
mine then too. It was a man's job. You wouldn't believe it now, but I've
had forty niggers under me, doing what I told them to."

"Why did you leave?"

"I married Mrs. Baines."

Philip took the slice of Dundee cake in his hand and munched it round
the room. He felt very old, independent and judicial; he was aware that
Baines was talking to him as man to man. He never called him Master
Philip as Mrs. Baines did, who was servile when she was not authoritative.

Baines had seen the world; he had seen beyond the railings, beyond the
tired legs of typists, the Pimlico parade to and from Victoria. He sat there
over his ginger pop with the resigned dignity of an exile; Baines didn't
complain; he had chosen his fate; and if his fate was Mrs. Baines he had
only himself to blame.

But today, because the house was almost empty and Mrs. Baines was
upstairs and there was nothing to do, he allowed himself a little acidity.

"I'd go back tomorrow if I had the chance."

"Did you ever shoot a nigger?"

"I never had any call to shoot," Baines said. "Of course I carried a gun. But you didn't need to treat them bad. That just made them stupid. Why," Baines said, bowing his thin grey hair with embarrassment over the ginger pop, "I loved some of those damned niggers. I couldn't help loving them. There they'd be, laughing, holding hands; they liked to touch each other; it made them feel fine to know the other fellow was round.

"It didn't mean anything we could understand; two of them would go about all day without loosing hold, grown men; but it wasn't love; it didn't mean anything we could understand."

"Eating between meals," Mrs. Baines said. "What would your mother say, Master Philip?"

She came down the steep stairs to the basement, her hands full of pots of cream and salve, tubes of grease and paste. "You oughtn't to encourage him, Baines," she said, sitting down in a wicker armchair and screwing up her small ill-humoured eyes at the Coty lipstick, Pond's cream, the Leichner rouge and Cyclax powder and Elizabeth Arden astringent.

She threw them one by one into the wastepaper basket. She saved only the cold cream. "Telling the boy stories," she said. "Go along to the nursery, Master Philip, while I get lunch."

Philip climbed the stairs to the baize door. He heard Mrs. Baines's voice like the voice in a nightmare when the small Price light has guttered in the saucer and the curtains move; it was sharp and shrill and full of malice, louder than people ought to speak, exposed.

"Sick to death of your ways, Baines, spoiling the boy. Time you did some work about the house," but he couldn't hear what Baines said in reply. He pushed open the baize door, came up like a small earth animal in his grey flannel shorts into a wash of sunlight on a parquet floor, the gleam of mirrors dusted and polished and beautified by Mrs. Baines.

Something broke downstairs, and Philip sadly mounted the stairs to the nursery. He pitied Baines; it occurred to him how happily they could live together in the empty house if Mrs. Baines were called away. He didn't want to play with his Meccano sets; he wouldn't take out his train or his soldiers; he sat at the table with his chin on his hands: this is life; and suddenly he felt responsible for Baines, as if he were the master of the house and Baines an ageing servant who deserved to be cared for. There was not much one could do; he decided at least to be good.

He was not surprised when Mrs. Baines was agreeable at lunch; he was used to her changes. Now it was "another helping of meat, Master Philip," or "Master Philip, a little more of this nice pudding." It was a pudding he liked, Queen's pudding with a perfect meringue, but he wouldn't eat a second helping lest she might count that a victory. She was the kind of woman who thought that any injustice could be counterbalanced by something good to eat.

She was sour, but she liked making sweet things; one never had to complain of a lack of jam or plums; she ate well herself and added soft sugar to the meringue and the strawberry jam. The half light through the basement window set the motes moving above her pale hair like dust as she sifted the sugar, and Baines crouched over his plate saying nothing.

Again Philip felt responsibility. Baines had looked forward to this, and Baines was disappointed: everything was being spoilt. The sensation of disappointment was one which Philip could share; knowing nothing of love or jealousy or passion, he could understand better than anyone this grief, something hoped for not happening, something promised not fulfilled, something exciting turning dull. "Baines," he said, "will you take me for a walk this afternoon?"

"No," Mrs. Baines said, "no. That he won't. Not with all the silver to clean."

"There's a fortnight to do it in," Baines said.

"Work first, pleasure afterwards." Mrs. Baines helped herself to some more meringue.

Baines suddenly put down his spoon and fork and pushed his plate away. "Blast," he said.

"Temper," Mrs. Baines said softly, "temper. Don't you go breaking any more things, Baines, and I won't have you swearing in front of the boy. Master Philip, if you've finished you can get down." She skinned the rest of the meringue off the pudding.

"I want to go for a walk," Philip said.

"You'll go and have a rest."

"I will go for a walk."

"Master Philip," Mrs. Baines said. She got up from the table, leaving her meringue unfinished, and came towards him, thin, menacing, dusty in the basement room. "Master Philip, you do as you're told." She took him by the arm and squeezed it gently; she watched him with a joyless passionate glitter and above her head the feet of the typists trudged back to the Victoria offices after the lunch interval.

"Why shouldn't I go for a walk?" But he weakened; he was scared and ashamed of being scared. This was life; a strange passion he couldn't understand moving in the basement room. He saw a small pile of broken glass swept into a corner by the wastepaper basket. He looked to Baines for help and only intercepted hate; the sad hopeless hate of something behind bars.

"Why shouldn't I?" he repeated.

"Master Philip," Mrs. Baines said, "you've got to do as you're told. You mustn't think just because your father's away there's nobody here to—"

"You wouldn't dare," Philip cried, and was startled by Baines's low interjection, "There's nothing she wouldn't dare."

"I hate you," Philip said to Mrs. Baines. He pulled away from her and ran to the door, but she was there before him; she was old, but she was quick.

"Master Philip," she said, "you'll say you're sorry." She stood in front of the door quivering with excitement. "What would your father do if he heard you say that?"

She put a hand out to seize him, dry and white with constant soda, the nails cut to the quick, but he backed away and put the table between them, and suddenly to his surprise she smiled; she became again as servile as she had been arrogant. "Get along with you, Master Philip," she said with glee. "I see I'm going to have my hands full till your father and mother come back."

She left the door unguarded and when he passed her she slapped him playfully. "I've got too much to do today to trouble about you. I haven't covered half the chairs," and suddenly even the upper part of the house became unbearable to him as he thought of Mrs. Baines moving round shrouding the sofas, laying out the dust-sheets.

So he wouldn't go upstairs to get his cap but walked straight out across the shining hall into the street, and again, as he looked this way and looked that way, it was life he was in the middle of.

2

It was the pink sugar cakes in the window on a paper doily, the ham, the slab of mauve sausage, the wasps driving like small torpedoes across the pane that caught Philip's attention. His feet were tired by pavements; he had been afraid to cross the road, had simply walked first in one direction, then in the other. He was nearly home now; the square was at the end of the street; this was a shabby outpost of Pimlico, and he smudged the pane with his nose, looking for sweets, and saw between the cakes and ham a different Baines. He hardly recognized the bulbous eyes, the bald forehead. It was a happy, bold and buccaneering Baines, even though it was, when you looked closer, a desperate Baines.

Philip had never seen the girl. He remembered Baines had a niece and he thought that this might be her. She was thin and drawn, and she wore a white mackintosh; she meant nothing to Philip; she belonged to a world about which he knew nothing at all. He couldn't make up stories about her, as he could make them up about withered Sir Hubert Reed, the Permanent Secretary, about Mrs. Wince-Dudley, who came up once a year from Penstanley in Suffolk with a green umbrella and an enormous black handbag, as he could make them up about the upper servants in all the houses where he went to tea and games. She just didn't belong; he thought of mermaids and Undine; but she didn't belong there either, nor to the adventures of Emil, nor to the Bastables. She sat there looking at an iced pink cake in the detachment and mystery of the completely dis-inherited, looking at the half-used pots of powder which Baines had set out on the marble-topped table between them.

Baines was urging, hoping, entreating, commanding, and the girl looked at the tea and the china pots and cried. Baines passed his handkerchief across the table, but she wouldn't wipe her eyes; she screwed it in her palm and let the tears run down, wouldn't do anything, wouldn't speak, would only put up a silent despairing resistance to what she dreaded and wanted and refused to listen to at any price. The two brains battled over the tea-cups loving each other, and there came to Philip outside, beyond the ham and wasps and dusty Pimlico pane, a confused indication of the struggle.

He was inquisitive and he didn't understand and he wanted to know. He went and stood in the doorway to see better, he was less sheltered than he had ever been; other people's lives for the first time touched and pressed and moulded. He would never escape that scene. In a week he had forgotten it, but it conditioned his career, the long austerity of his life; when he was dying he said, "Who is she?"

Baines had won; he was cocky and the girl was happy. She wiped her face, she opened a pot of powder, and their fingers touched across the table. It occurred to Philip that it would be amusing to imitate Mrs. Baines's voice and call "Baines" to him from the door.

It shrivelled them; you couldn't describe it in any other way; it made them smaller, they weren't happy any more and they weren't bold. Baines was the first to recover and trace the voice, but that didn't make things as they were. The sawdust was spilled out of the afternoon; nothing you did could mend it, and Philip was scared. "I didn't mean . . ." He wanted to say that he loved Baines, that he had only wanted to laugh at Mrs. Baines. But he had discovered that you couldn't laugh at Mrs. Baines. She wasn't Sir Hubert Reed, who used steel nibs and carried a pen-wiper in his pocket; she wasn't Mrs. Wince-Dudley; she was darkness when the night-light went out in a draught; she was the frozen blocks of earth he had seen one winter in a graveyard when someone said, "They need an electric drill"; she was the flowers gone bad and smelling in the little closet room at Penstanley. There was nothing to laugh about. You had to endure her when she was there and forget about her quickly when she was away, suppress the thought of her, ram it down deep.

Baines said, "It's only Phil," beckoned him in and gave him the pink iced cake the girl hadn't eaten, but the afternoon was broken, the cake was like dry bread in the throat. The girl left them at once; she even forgot to take the powder; like a small icicle in her white mackintosh she stood in the doorway with her back to them, then melted into the afternoon.

"Who is she?" Philip asked. "Is she your niece?"

"Oh, yes," Baines said, "that's who she is; she's my niece," and poured the last drops of water on to the coarse black leaves in the teapot.

"May as well have another cup," Baines said.

"The cup that cheers," he said hopelessly, watching the bitter black fluid drain out of the spout.

"Have a glass of ginger pop, Phil?"

"I'm sorry. I'm sorry, Baines."

"It's not your fault, Phil. Why, I could believe it wasn't you at all, but her. She creeps in everywhere." He fished two leaves out of his cup and laid them on the back of his hand, a thin soft flake and a hard stalk. He beat them with his hand: "Today," and the stalk detached itself, "tomorrow, Wednesday, Thursday, Friday, Saturday, Sunday," but the flake wouldn't come, stayed where it was, drying under his blows, with a resistance you wouldn't believe it to possess. "The tough one wins," Baines said.

He got up and paid the bill and out they went into the street. Baines said, "I don't ask you to say what isn't true. But you needn't mention to Mrs. Baines you met us here."

"Of course not," Philip said, and catching something of Sir Hubert Reed's manner, "I understand, Baines." But he didn't understand a thing: he was caught up in other people's darkness.

"It was stupid," Baines said. "So near home, but I hadn't time to think, you see. I'd got to see her."

"Of course, Baines."

"I haven't time to spare," Baines said. "I'm not young. I've got to see that she's all right."

"Of course you have, Baines."

"Mrs. Baines will get it out of you if she can."

"You can trust me, Baines," Philip said in a dry important Reed voice; and then, "Look out. She's at the window watching." And there indeed she was, looking up at them, between the lace curtains, from the basement room, speculating. "Need we go in, Baines?" Philip asked, cold lying heavy on his stomach like too much pudding; he clutched Baines's arm.

"Careful," Baines said softly, "careful."

"But need we go in, Baines? It's early. Take me for a walk in the park." "Better not."

"But I'm frightened, Baines."

"You haven't any cause," Baines said. "Nothing's going to hurt you. You just run along upstairs to the nursery. I'll go down by the area and talk to Mrs. Baines." But even he stood hesitating at the top of the stone steps, pretending not to see her where she watched between the curtains. "In at the front door, Phil, and up the stairs."

Philip didn't linger in the hall; he ran, slithering on the parquet Mrs. Baines had polished, to the stairs. Through the drawing-room doorway on the first floor he saw the draped chairs; even the china clock on the mantel was covered like a canary's cage; as he passed it, it chimed the hour, muffled and secret under the duster. On the nursery table he found his supper laid out: a glass of milk and a piece of bread and butter, a sweet biscuit and a little cold Queen's pudding without the meringue. He had no appetite; he strained his ears for Mrs. Baines's coming, for the sound of voices, but the basement held its secrets; the green baize door shut off that world. He drank the milk and ate the biscuit, but he didn't touch the rest, and presently he could hear the soft precise footfalls of Mrs. Baines on the stairs: she was a good servant, she walked softly; she was a determined woman, she walked precisely.

But she wasn't angry when she came in; she was ingratiating as she opened the night nursery door—"Did you have a good walk, Master Philip?"—pulled down the blinds, laid out his pyjamas, came back to clear his supper. "I'm glad Baines found you. Your mother wouldn't have liked your being out alone." She examined the tray. "Not much appetite, have you, Master Philip? Why don't you try a little of this nice pudding? I'll bring you up some more jam for it."

"No, no, thank you, Mrs. Baines," Philip said.

"You ought to eat more," Mrs. Baines said. She sniffed round the room like a dog. "You didn't take any pots out of the wastepaper basket in the kitchen, did you, Master Philip?"

"No," Philip said.

"Of course you wouldn't. I just wanted to make sure." She patted his shoulder and her fingers flashed to his lapel; she picked off a tiny crumb of pink sugar. "Oh, Master Philip," she said, "that's why you haven't any appetite. You've been buying sweet cakes. That's not what your pocket money's for."

"But I didn't," Philip said. "I didn't."

She tasted the sugar with the tip of her tongue.

"Don't tell lies to me, Master Philip. I won't stand for it any more than your father would."

"I didn't, I didn't," Philip said. "They gave it me. I mean Baines," but she had pounced on the word "they." She had got what she wanted; there was no doubt about that, even when you didn't know what it was she wanted. Philip was angry and miserable and disappointed because he hadn't kept Baines's secret. Baines oughtn't to have trusted him; grown-up people should keep their own secrets, and yet here was Mrs. Baines immediately entrusting him with another.

"Let me tickle your palm and see if you can keep a secret." But he put his hand behind him; he wouldn't be touched. "It's a secret between us, Master Philip, that I know all about them. I suppose she was having tea with him," she speculated.

"Why shouldn't she?" he said, the responsibility for Baines weighing on his spirit, the idea that he had got to keep her secret when he hadn't kept Baines's making him miserable with the unfairness of life. "She was nice."

"She was nice, was she?" Mrs. Baines said in a bitter voice he wasn't used to.

"And she's his niece."

"So that's what he said," Mrs. Baines struck softly back at him like the clock under the duster. She tried to be jocular. "The old scoundrel. Don't you tell him I know, Master Philip." She stood very still between the table and the door, thinking very hard, planning something. "Promise you won't tell. I'll give you that Meccano set, Master Philip. . . ."

He turned his back on her; he wouldn't promise, but he wouldn't tell. He would have nothing to do with their secrets, the responsibilities they were determined to lay on him. He was only anxious to forget. He had received already a larger dose of life than he had bargained for, and he was scared. "A 2A Meccano set, Master Philip." He never opened his Meccano set again, never built anything, never created anything, died, the old dilettante, sixty years later, nothing to show rather than preserve the memory of Mrs. Baines's malicious voice saying good night, her soft determined footfalls on the stairs to the basement, going down, going down.

3

The sun poured in between the curtains and Baines was beating a tattoo on the water-can. "Glory, glory," Baines said. He sat down on the end of the bed and said, "I beg to announce that Mrs. Baines has been called away. Her mother's dying. She won't be back till tomorrow."

"Why did you wake me up so early?" Philip said. He watched Baines with uneasiness; he wasn't going to be drawn in; he'd learnt his lesson. It wasn't right for a man of Baines's age to be so merry. It made a grown person human in the same way that you were human. For if a grown-up could behave so childishly, you were liable too to find yourself in their world. It was enough that it came at you in dreams: the witch at the corner, the man with a knife. So "It's very early," he complained, even though he loved Baines, even though he couldn't help being glad that Baines was happy. He was divided by the fear and the attraction of life.

"I want to make this a long day," Baines said. "This is the best time." He pulled the curtains back. "It's a bit misty. The cat's been out all night. There she is, sniffing round the area. They haven't taken in any milk at 59. Emma's shaking out the mats at 63." He said, "This was what I used to think about on the Coast: somebody shaking mats and the cat coming home. I can see it today," Baines said, "just as if I was still in Africa. Most days you don't notice what you've got. It's a good life if you don't weaken." He put a penny on the washstand. "When you've dressed, Phil, run and get a *Mail* from the barrow at the corner. I'll be cooking the sausages."

"Sausages?"

"Sausages," Baines said. "We're going to celebrate today. A fair bust." He celebrated at breakfast, reckless, cracking jokes, unaccountably merry and nervous. It was going to be a long, long day, he kept on coming back to that: for years he had waited for a long day, he had sweated in the damp Coast heat, changed shirts, gone down with fever, lain between the blankets and sweated, all in the hope of this long day, that cat sniffing round the area, a bit of mist, the mats beaten at 63. He propped the *Mail* in front of the coffee-pot and read pieces aloud. He said, "Cora Down's been married for the fourth time." He was amused, but it wasn't his idea of a long day. His long day was the Park, watching the riders in the Row, seeing Sir Arthur Stillwater pass beyond the rails ("He dined with us once in Bo; up from Freetown; he was governor there"), lunch at the Corner House for Philip's sake (he'd have preferred himself a glass of stout and some oysters at the York bar), the Zoo, the long bus ride home in the last summer light: the leaves in the Green Park were beginning to turn and the motors nuzzled out of Berkeley Street with the low sun gently glowing on their wind-screens. Baines envied no one, not Cora Down, or Sir Arthur Stillwater, or Lord Sandale, who came out on to the steps of the Army and Navy and then went back again because he hadn't got anything to do and might as well look at another paper. "I said don't let me see you touch that black again." Baines had led a man's life; everyone on top of the bus pricked their ears when he told Philip all about it.

"Would you have shot him?" Philip asked, and Baines put his head back and tilted his dark respectable man-servant's hat to a better angle as the bus swerved round the artillery memorial.

"I wouldn't have thought twice about it. I'd have shot to kill," he boasted, and the bowed figure went by, the steel helmet, the heavy cloak, the down-turned rifle and the folded hands.

"Have you got the revolver?"

"Of course I've got it," Baines said. "Don't I need it with all the burglaries there've been?" This was the Baines whom Philip loved: not Baines singing and carefree, but Baines responsible, Baines behind barriers, living his man's life.

All the buses streamed out from Victoria like a convoy of aeroplanes to bring Baines home with honour. "Forty blacks under me," and there waiting near the area steps was the proper conventional reward, love at lighting-up time.

"It's your niece," Philip said, recognizing the white mackintosh, but not the happy sleepy face. She frightened him like an unlucky number; he nearly told Baines what Mrs. Baines had said; but he didn't want to bother, he wanted to leave things alone.

"Why, so it is," Baines said. "I shouldn't wonder if she was going to have a bite of supper with us." But he said they'd play a game, pretend they didn't know her, slip down the area steps, "and here," Baines said, "we are," lay the table, put out the cold sausages, a bottle of beer, a bottle of ginger pop, a flagon of harvest burgundy. "Everyone his own drink," Baines said. "Run upstairs, Phil, and see if there's been a post."

Philip didn't like the empty house at dusk before the lights went on. He hurried. He wanted to be back with Baines. The hall lay there in quiet and shadow prepared to show him something he didn't want to see. Some letters rustled down, and someone knocked. "Open in the name of the Republic." The tumbrils rolled, the head bobbed in the bloody basket.

Knock, knock, and the postman's footsteps going away. Philip gathered the letters. The slit in the door was like the grating in a jeweller's window. He remembered the policeman he had seen peer through. He had said to his nurse, "What's he doing?" and when she said, "He's seeing if everything's all right," his brain immediately filled with images of all that might be wrong. He ran to the baize door and the stairs. The girl was already there and Baines was kissing her. She leant breathless against the dresser.

"This is Emmy, Phil."

"There's a letter for you, Baines."

"Emmy," Baines said, "it's from her." But he wouldn't open it. "You bet she's coming back."

"We'll have supper, anyway," Emmy said. "She can't harm that."

"You don't know her," Baines said, "Nothing's safe. Damn it," he said, "I was a man once," and he opened the letter.

"Can I start?" Philip asked, but Baines didn't hear; he presented in his stillness and attention an example of the importance grown-up people attached to the written word: you had to write your thanks, not wait and speak them, as if letters couldn't lie. But Philip knew better than that, sprawling his thanks across a page to Aunt Alice who had given him a doll he was too old for. Letters could lie all right, but they made the lie permanent: they lay as evidence against you; they made you meaner than the spoken word.

"She's not coming back till tomorrow night," Baines said. He opened the bottles, he pulled up the chairs, he kissed Emmy again against the dresser.

"You oughtn't to," Emmy said, "with the boy here."

"He's got to learn," Baines said, "like the rest of us," and he helped Philip to three sausages. He only took one himself; he said he wasn't hungry; but when Emmy said she wasn't hungry either he stood over her and made her eat. He was timid and rough with her; he made her drink the harvest burgundy because he said she needed building up; he wouldn't take no for an answer, but when he touched her his hands were light and clumsy too, as if he were afraid to damage something delicate and didn't know how to handle anything so light.

"This is better than milk and biscuits, eh?"

"Yes," Philip said, but he was scared, scared for Baines as much as for himself. He couldn't help wondering at every bite, at every draught of the ginger pop, what Mrs. Baines would say if she ever learnt of this meal; he couldn't imagine it, there was a depth of bitterness and rage in Mrs. Baines you couldn't sound. He said, "She won't be coming back tonight?" but you could tell by the way they immediately understood him that she wasn't really away at all; she was there in the basement with them, driving them to longer drinks and louder talk, biding her time for the right cutting word. Baines wasn't really happy; he was only watching happiness from close to instead of from far away.

"No " he said, "she'll not be back till late tomorrow." He couldn't keep his eyes off happiness; he'd played around as much as other men, he kept on reverting to the Coast as if to excuse himself for his innocence; he wouldn't have been so innocent if he'd lived his life in London, so innocent when it came to tenderness. "If it was you, Emmy," he said, looking at the white dresser, the scrubbed chairs, "this'd be like a home." Already the room was not quite so harsh; there was a little dust in corners, the silver needed a final polish, the morning's paper lay untidily on a chair. "You'd better go to bed, Phil; it's been a long day."

They didn't leave him to find his own way up through the dark shrouded house; they went with him, turning on lights, touching each other's fingers on the switches; floor after floor they drove the night back; they spoke softly among the covered chairs; they watched him undress, they didn't make him wash or clean his teeth, they saw him into bed and lit his night-light and left his door ajar. He could hear their voices on the stairs, friendly, like the guests he heard at dinner-parties when they moved down to the hall, saying good night. They belonged; wherever they were they made a home. He heard a door open and a clock strike, he heard their voices for a long while, so that he felt they were not far away and he was safe. The voices didn't dwindle, they simply went out, and he could be sure that they were still somewhere not far from him, silent together in one of the many empty rooms, growing sleepy together as he grew sleepy after the long day.

He just had time to sigh faintly with satisfaction, because this too perhaps had been life, before he slept and the inevitable terrors of sleep came round him: a man with a tricolor hat beat at the door on His Majesty's service, a bleeding head lay on the kitchen table in a basket, and the Siberian wolves crept closer. He was bound hand and foot and couldn't move; they leapt round him breathing heavily; he opened his eyes and Mrs. Baines was there, her grey untidy hair in threads over his face, her black hat askew. A loose hairpin fell on the pillow and one musty thread brushed his mouth. "Where are they?" she whispered. "Where are they?"

4

Philip watched her in terror. Mrs. Baines was out of breath as if she had been searching all the empty rooms, looking under loose covers.

With her untidy grey hair and her black dress buttoned to her throat, her gloves of black cotton, she was so like the witches of his dreams that he didn't dare to speak. There was a stale smell in her breath.

"She's here," Mrs. Baines said; "you can't deny she's here." Her face was simultaneously marked with cruelty and misery; she wanted to "do things" to people, but she suffered all the time. It would have done her good to scream, but she daren't do that: it would warn them. She came ingratiatingly back to the bed where Philip lay rigid on his back and whispered, "I haven't forgotten the Meccano set. You shall have it tomorrow, Master Philip. We've got secrets together, haven't we? Just tell me where they are."

He couldn't speak. Fear held him as firmly as any nightmare. She said, "Tell Mrs. Baines, Master Philip. You love your Mrs. Baines, don't you?" That was too much; he couldn't speak, but he could move his mouth in terrified denial, wince away from her dusty image.

She whispered, coming closer to him, "Such deceit. I'll tell your father. I'll settle with you myself when I've found them. You'll smart; I'll see you smart." Then immediately she was still, listening. A board had creaked on the floor below, and a moment later, while she stooped listening above his bed, there came the whispers of two people who were happy and sleepy together after a long day. The night-light stood beside the mirror and Mrs. Baines could see bitterly there her own reflection, misery and cruelty wavering in the glass, age and dust and nothing to hope for. She sobbed without tears, a dry, breathless sound; but her cruelty was a kind of pride which kept her going; it was her best quality, she would have been merely pitiable without it. She went out of the door on tiptoe, feeling her way across the landing, going so softly down the stairs that no one behind a shut door could hear her. Then there was complete silence again; Philip could move; he raised his knees; he sat up in bed; he wanted to die. It wasn't fair, the walls were down again between his world and theirs; but this time it was something worse than merriment that the grown people made him share; a passion moved in the house he recognized but could not understand.

It wasn't fair, but he owed Baines everything: the Zoo, the ginger pop, the bus ride home. Even the supper called on his loyalty. But he was frightened; he was touching something he touched in dreams: the bleeding head, the wolves, the knock, knock, knock. Life fell on him with savagery: you couldn't blame him if he never faced it again in sixty years. He got out of bed, carefully from habit put on his bedroom slippers, and tiptoed to the door: it wasn't quite dark on the landing below because the curtains had been taken down for the cleaners and the light from the street came in through the tall windows. Mrs. Baines had her hand on the glass door-knob; she was very carefully turning it; he screamed, "Baines, Baines."

Mrs. Baines turned and saw him cowering in his pyjamas by the banisters; he was helpless, more helpless even than Baines, and cruelty grew at the sight of him and drove her up the stairs. The nightmare was on him again and he couldn't move; he hadn't any more courage left for ever; he'd spent it all, had been allowed no time to let it grow, no years of gradual hardening; he couldn't even scream.

But the first cry had brought Baines out of the best spare bedroom and he moved quicker than Mrs. Baines. She hadn't reached the top of the stairs before he'd caught her round the waist. She drove her black cotton gloves at his face and he bit her hand. He hadn't time to think, he fought her savagely like a stranger, but she fought back with knowledgeable hate. She was going to teach them all and it didn't really matter whom she began with; they had all deceived her; but the old image in the glass was by her side, telling her she must be dignified, she wasn't young enough to yield her dignity; she could beat his face, but she mustn't bite; she could push, but she mustn't kick.

Age and dust and nothing to hope for were her handicaps. She went over the banisters in a flurry of black clothes and fell into the hall; she lay before the front door like a sack of coals which should have gone down the area into the basement. Philip saw; Emmy saw; she sat down suddenly in the doorway of the best spare bedroom with her eyes open as if she were too tired to stand any longer. Baines went slowly down into the hall.

It wasn't hard for Philip to escape; they'd forgotten him completely; he went down the back, the servants' stairs because Mrs. Baines was in the hall; he didn't understand what she was doing lying there; like the startling pictures in a book no one had read to him, the things he didn't understand terrified him. The whole house had been turned over to the grown-up world; he wasn't safe in the night nursery; their passions had flooded it. The only thing he could do was to get away, by the back stair, and up through the area, and never come back. You didn't think of the cold, of the need of food and sleep; for an hour it would seem quite possible to escape from people for ever.

He was wearing pyjamas and bedroom slippers when he came up into the square, but there was no one to see him. It was that hour of the evening in a residential district when everyone is at the theatre or at home. He climbed over the iron railings into the little garden: the plane-trees spread their large pale palms between him and the sky. It might have been an illimitable forest into which he had escaped. He crouched behind a trunk and the wolves retreated; it seemed to him between the little iron seat and the tree-trunk that no one would ever find him again. A kind of embittered happiness and self-pity made him cry; he was lost; there wouldn't be any more secrets to keep; he surrendered responsibility once and for all. Let grown-up people keep to their world and he would keep to his, safe in the small garden between the plane-trees. "In the lost childhood of Judas Christ was betrayed"; you could almost see the small unformed face hardening into the deep dilettante selfishness of age.

Presently the door of 48 opened and Baines looked this way and that; then he signalled with his hand and Emmy came; it was as if they were only just in time for a train, they hadn't a chance of saying good-bye; she went quickly by, like a face at a window swept past the platform, pale and unhappy and not wanting to go. Baines went in again and shut the door; the light was lit in the basement, and a policeman walked round the square, looking into the areas. You could tell how many families were at home by the lights behind the first-floor curtains.

Philip explored the garden: it didn't take long: a twenty-yard square of bushes and plane-trees, two iron seats and a gravel path, a padlocked gate at either end, a scuffle of old leaves. But he couldn't stay: something stirred in the bushes and two illuminated eyes peered out at him like a Siberian wolf, and he thought how terrible it would be if Mrs. Baines found him there. He'd have no time to climb the railings; she'd seize him from behind.

He left the square at the unfashionable end and was immediately among the fish-and-chip shops, the little stationers selling Bagatelle, among the accommodation addresses and the dingy hotels with open doors. There were few people about because the pubs were open, but a blowzy woman carrying a parcel called out to him across the street and the commissionaire outside a cinema would have stopped him if he hadn't crossed the road. He went deeper: you could go farther and lose yourself more completely here than among the plane-trees. On the fringe of the square he was in danger of being stopped and taken back: it was obvious where he belonged: but as he went deeper he lost the marks of his origin. It was a warm night: any child in those free-living parts might be expected to play truant from bed. He found a kind of camaraderie even among grown-up people; he might have been a neighbour's child as he went quickly by, but they weren't going to tell on him, they'd been young once themselves. He picked up a protective coating of dust from the pavements, of smuts from the trains which passed along the backs in a spray of fire. Once he was caught in a knot of children running away from something or somebody, laughing as they ran; he was whirled with them round a turning and abandoned, with a sticky fruit-drop in his hand.

He couldn't have been more lost; but he hadn't the stamina to keep on. At first he feared that someone would stop him; after an hour he hoped that someone would. He couldn't find his way back, and in any case he was afraid of arriving home alone; he was afraid of Mrs. Baines, more afraid than he had ever been. Baines was his friend, but something had happened which gave Mrs. Baines all the power. He began to loiter on purpose to be noticed, but no one noticed him. Families were having a last breather on the door-steps, the refuse bins had been put out and bits of cabbage stalks soiled his slippers. The air was full of voices, but he was cut off; these people were strangers and would always now be strangers; they were marked by Mrs. Baines and he shied away from them into a deep class-consciousness. He had been afraid of policemen, but now he wanted one to take him home; even Mrs. Baines could do nothing against a policeman. He sidled past a constable who was directing traffic, but he was too busy to pay any attention. Philip sat down against a wall and cried.

It hadn't occurred to him that that was the easiest way, that all you had to do was to surrender, to show you were beaten and accept kindness. . . . It was lavished on him at once by two women and a pawnbroker. Another policeman appeared, a young man with a sharp incredulous face. He looked as if he noted everything he saw in pocketbooks and drew conclusions. A woman offered to see Philip home, but he didn't trust her: she wasn't a match for Mrs. Baines immobile in the hall. He wouldn't give his address; he said he was afraid to go home. He had his way; he got his protection. "I'll take him to the station," the policeman said, and holding him awkwardly by the hand (he wasn't married; he had his career to make) he led him round the corner, up the stone stairs into the little bare overheated room where Justice waited.

5

Justice waited behind a wooden counter on a high stool; it wore a heavy moustache; it was kindly and had six children ("three of them nippers like yourself"); it wasn't really interested in Philip, but it pretended to be, it wrote the address down and sent a constable to fetch a glass of milk. But the young constable was interested; he had a nose for things.

"Your home's on the telephone, I suppose," Justice said. "We'll ring them up and say you are safe. They'll fetch you very soon. What's your name, sonny?"

"Philip."

"Your other name."

"I haven't got another name." He didn't want to be fetched; he wanted to be taken home by someone who would impress even Mrs. Baines. The constable watched him, watched the way he drank the milk, watched him when he winced away from questions.

"What made you run away? Playing truant, eh?"

"I don't know."

"You oughtn't to do it, young fellow. Think how anxious your father and mother will be."

"They are away."

"Well, your nurse."

"I haven't got one."

"Who looks after you, then?" That question went home. Philip saw Mrs. Baines coming up the stairs at him, the heap of black cotton in the hall. He began to cry.

"Now, now, now," the sergeant said. He didn't know what to do; he wished his wife were with him; even a policewoman might have been useful.

"Don't you think it's funny," the constable said, "that there hasn't been an inquiry?"

"They think he's tucked up in bed."

"You are scared, aren't you?" the constable said. "What scared you?"

"I don't know."

"Somebody hurt you?"

"No."

"He's had bad dreams," the sergeant said. "Thought the house was on fire, I expect. I've brought up six of them. Rose is due back. She'll take him home."

"I want to go home with you," Philip said; he tried to smile at the constable, but the deceit was immature and unsuccessful.

"I'd better go," the constable said. "There may be something wrong."

"Nonsense," the sergeant said. "It's a woman's job. Tact is what you need. Here's Rose. Pull up your stockings, Rose. You're a disgrace to the Force. I've got a job of work for you." Rose shambled in· black cotton stockings drooping over her boots, a gawky Girl Guide manner, a hoarse hostile voice. "More tarts, I suppose."

"No, you've got to see this young man home." She looked at him owlishly.

"I won't go with her," Philip said. He began to cry again. "I don't like her."

"More of that womanly charm, Rose," the sergeant said. The telephone rang on his desk. He lifted the receiver. "What? What's that?" he said. "Number 48? You've got a doctor?" He put his hand over the telephone mouth. "No wonder this nipper wasn't reported," he said. "They've been too busy. An accident. Woman slipped on the stairs."

"Serious?" the constable asked. The sergeant mouthed at him; you didn't mention the word death before a child (didn't he know? he had six of them), you made noises in the throat, you grimaced, a complicated shorthand for a word of only five letters anyway.

"You'd better go, after all," he said, "and make a report. The doctor's there."

Rose shambled from the stove; pink apply-dapply cheeks, loose stockings. She stuck her hands behind her. Her large morgue-like mouth was full of blackened teeth. "You told me to take him and now just because something interesting . . . I don't expect justice from a man . . ."

"Who's at the house?" the constable asked.

"The butler."

"You don't think," the constable said, "he saw . . ."

"Trust me," the sergeant said. "I've brought up six. I know 'em through and through. You can't teach me anything about children."

"He seemed scared about something."

"Dreams," the sergeant said.

"What name?"

"Baines."

"This Mr. Baines," the constable said to Philip, "you like him, eh? He's good to you?" They were trying to get something out of him; he was suspicious of the whole roomful of them; he said "yes" without conviction because he was afraid at any moment of more responsibilities, more secrets.

"And Mrs. Baines?"

"Yes."

They consulted together by the desk: Rose was hoarsely aggrieved; she was like a female impersonator, she bore her womanhood with an unnatural emphasis even while she scorned it in her creased stockings and her weather-exposed face. The charcoal shifted in the stove; the room was overheated in the mild late summer evening. A notice on the wall described a body found in the Thames, or rather the body's clothes: wool vest, wool pants, wool shirt with blue stripes, size ten boots, blue serge suit worn at the elbows, fifteen and a half celluloid collar. They couldn't find anything to say about the body, except its measurements, it was just an ordinary body.

"Come along," the constable said. He was interested, he was glad to be going, but he couldn't help being embarrassed by his company, a small boy in pyjamas. His nose smelt something, he didn't know what, but he smarted at the sight of the amusement they caused: the pubs had closed and the streets were full again of men making as long a day of it as they could. He hurried through the less frequented streets, chose the darker pavements, wouldn't loiter, and Philip wanted more and more to loiter, pulling at his hand, dragging with his feet. He dreaded the sight of Mrs. Baines waiting in the hall: he knew now that she was dead. The sergeant's mouthings had conveyed that; but she wasn't buried, she wasn't out of sight; he was going to see a dead person in the hall when the door opened.

The light was on in the basement, and to his relief the constable made for the area steps. Perhaps he wouldn't have to see Mrs. Baines at all. The constable knocked on the door because it was too dark to see the bell, and Baines answered. He stood there in the doorway of the neat bright basement room and you could see the sad complacent plausible sentence he had prepared wither at the sight of Philip; he hadn't expected Philip to return like that in the policeman's company. He had to begin thinking all over again; he wasn't a deceptive man; if it hadn't been for Emmy he would have been quite ready to let the truth lead him where it would.

"Mr. Baines?" the constable asked.

He nodded; he hadn't found the right words; he was daunted by the shrewd knowing face, the sudden appearance of Philip there.

"This little boy from here?"

"Yes," Baines said. Philip could tell that there was a message he was trying to convey, but he shut his mind to it. He loved Baines, but Baines had involved him in secrets, in fears he didn't understand. The glowing morning thought, "This is life," had become under Baines's tuition the repugnant memory, "That was life": the musty hair across the mouth, the breathless cruel tortured inquiry, "Where are they," the heap of black cotton tipped into the hall. That was what happened when you loved: you got involved; and Philip extricated himself from life, from love, from Baines, with a merciless egotism.

There had been things between them, but he laid them low, as a retreating army cuts the wires, destroys the bridges. In the abandoned country you may leave much that is dear—a morning in the Park, an ice at a corner house, sausages for supper—but more is concerned in the retreat than temporary losses. There are old people who, as the tractors wheel away, implore to be taken, but you can't risk the rearguard for their sake: a whole prolonged retreat from life, from care, from human relationships is involved.

"The doctor's here," Baines said. He nodded at the door, moistened his mouth, kept his eyes on Philip, begging for something like a dog you can't understand. "There's nothing to be done. She slipped on these stone basement stairs. I was in here. I heard her fall." He wouldn't look at the notebook, at the constable's tiny spidery writing which got a terrible lot on one page.

"Did the boy see anything?"

"He can't have done. I thought he was in bed. Hadn't he better go up? It's a shocking thing. Oh," Baines said, losing control, "it's a shocking thing for a child."

"She's through there?" the constable asked.

"I haven't moved her an inch," Baines said.

"He'd better then—"

"Go up the area and through the hall," Baines said and again he begged dumbly like a dog: one more secret, keep this secret, do this for old Baines, he won't ask another.

"Come along," the constable said. "I'll see you up to bed. You're a gentleman; you must come in the proper way through the front door like the master should. Or will you go along with him, Mr. Baines, while I see the doctor?"

"Yes," Baines said, "I'll go." He came across the room to Philip, begging, begging, all the way with his soft old stupid expression: this is Baines, the old Coaster; what about a palm-oil chop, eh?; a man's life; forty niggers; never used a gun; I tell you I couldn't help loving them: it wasn't what we call love, nothing we could understand. The messages flickered out from the last posts at the border, imploring, beseeching, reminding: this is your old friend Baines; what about an eleven's; a glass of ginger pop won't do you any harm; sausages; a long day. But the wires were cut, the messages just faded out into the enormous vacancy of the neat scrubbed room in which there had never been a place where a man could hide his secrets.

"Come along, Phil, it's bedtime. We'll just go up the steps . . ." Tap, tap, tap, at the telegraph; you may get through, you can't tell, somebody may mend the right wire. "And in at the front door."

"No," Philip said, "no. I won't go. You can't make me go. I'll fight. I won't see her."

The constable turned on them quickly. "What's that? Why won't you go?"

"She's in the hall," Philip said. "I know she's in the hall. And she's dead. I won't see her."

"You moved her then?" the constable said to Baines. "All the way down here? You've been lying, eh? That means you had to tidy up. . . . Were you alone?"

"Emmy," Philip said, "Emmy." He wasn't going to keep any more secrets: he was going to finish once and for all with everything, with Baines and Mrs. Baines and the grown-up life beyond him; it wasn't his business and never, never again, he decided, would he share their confidences and companionship. "It was all Emmy's fault," he protested with a quaver which reminded Baines that after all he was only a child; it had been hopeless to expect help there; he was a child; he didn't understand what it all meant; he couldn't read this shorthand of terror; he'd had a long day and he was tired out. You could see him dropping asleep where he stood against the dresser, dropping back into the comfortable nursery peace. You couldn't blame him. When he woke in the morning, he'd hardly remember a thing.

"Out with it," the constable said, addressing Baines with professional ferocity, "who is she?" just as the old man sixty years later startled his secretary, his only watcher, asking, "Who is she? Who is she?" dropping lower and lower into death, passing on the way perhaps the image of Baines: Baines hopeless, Baines letting his head drop, Baines "coming clean."

Nathaniel Hawthorne

1804–1864

MY KINSMAN, MAJOR MOLINEUX

After the kings of Great Britain had assumed the right of appointing the colonial governors, the measures of the latter seldom met with the ready and generous approbation which had been paid to those of their predecessors, under the original charters. The people looked with most jealous scrutiny to the exercise of power which did not emanate from themselves, and they usually rewarded their rulers with slender gratitude for the compliances by which, in softening their instructions from beyond the sea, they had incurred the reprehension of those who gave them. The annals of Massachusetts Bay will inform us, that of six governors in the space of about forty years from the surrender of the old charter, under James II., two imprisoned by a popular insurrection; a third, as Hutchinson inclines to believe, was driven from the province by the whizzing of a musket-ball; a fourth, in the opinion of the same historian, was hastened to his grave by continual bickerings with the House of Representatives; and the remaining two, as well as their successors, till the Revolution, were favored with few and brief intervals of peaceful sway. The inferior members of the court party, in times of high political excitement, led scarcely a more desirable life. These remarks may serve as a preface to the following adventures, which chanced upon a summer night, not far from a hundred years ago. The reader, in order to avoid a long and dry detail of colonial affairs, is requested to dispense with an account of the train of circumstances that had caused much temporary inflammation of the popular mind.

It was near nine o'clock of a moonlight evening, when a boat crossed the ferry with a single passenger, who had obtained his conveyance at that unusual hour by the promise of an extra fare. While he stood on the landing-place, searching in either pocket for the means of fulfilling his agreement, the ferryman lifted a lantern, by the aid of which, and the newly risen moon, he took a very accurate survey of the stranger's figure. He was a youth of barely eighteen years, evidently country-bred, and now, as it should seem, upon his first visit to town. He was clad in a coarse gray coat, well worn, but in excellent repair; his under garments were durably constructed of leather, and fitted tight to a pair of serviceable and well-shaped limbs; his stockings of blue yarn were the incontrovertible work of a mother or a sister; and on his head was a three-cornered hat, which in its better days had perhaps sheltered the graver brow of the lad's father. Under his left arm was a heavy cudgel formed of an oak sapling, and retaining a part of the hardened root; and his equipment was completed by a wallet, not so abundantly stocked as to incommode the vigorous shoulders on which it hung. Brown, curly hair, well-shaped features, and bright, cheerful eyes were nature's gifts, and worth all that art could have done for his adornment.

The youth, one of whose names was Robin, finally drew from his pocket the half of a little province bill of five shillings, which, in the depreciation in that sort of currency, did but satisfy the ferryman's demand, with the surplus of a sexangular piece of parchment, valued at three pence. He then walked forward into the town, with as light a step as if his day's journey had not already exceeded thirty miles, and with as eager an eye as if he were entering London city, instead of the little metropolis of a New England colony. Before Robin had proceeded far, however, it occurred to him that he knew not whither to direct his steps; so he paused, and looked up and down the narrow street, scrutinizing the small and mean wooden buildings that were scattered on either side.

"This low hovel cannot be my kinsman's dwelling," thought he, "nor yonder old house, where the moonlight enters at the broken casement; and truly I see none hereabouts that might be worthy of him. It would have been wise to inquire my way of the ferryman, and doubtless he would have gone with me, and earned a shilling from the Major for his pains. But the next man I meet will do as well."

He resumed his walk, and was glad to perceive that the street now became wider, and the houses more respectable in their appearance. He soon discerned a figure moving on moderately in advance, and hastened his steps to overtake it. As Robin drew nigh, he saw that the passenger was a man in years, with a full periwig of gray hair, a wide-skirted coat of dark cloth, and silk stockings rolled above his knees. He carried a long and polished cane, which he struck down perpendicularly before him at every step; and at regular intervals he uttered two successive hems, of a peculiarly solemn and sepulchral intonation. Having made these observations, Robin laid hold of the skirt of the old man's coat, just when the light from the open door and windows of a barber's shop fell upon both their figures.

"Good evening to you, honored sir," said he, making a low bow, and still retaining his hold of the skirt. "I pray you tell me whereabouts is the dwelling of my kinsman, Major Molineux."

The youth's question was uttered very loudly; and one of the barbers, whose razor was descending on a well-soaped chin, and another who was dressing a Ramillies wig, left their occupations, and came to the door. The citizen, in the mean time, turned a long-favored countenance upon Robin, and answered him in a tone of excessive anger and annoyance. His two sepulchral hems, however, broke into the very centre of his rebuke, with most singular effect, like a thought of the cold grave obtruding among wrathful passions.

"Let go my garment, fellow! I tell you, I know not the man you speak of. What! I have authority, I have—hem, hem—authority; and if this be the respect you show for your betters, your feet shall be brought acquainted with the stocks by daylight, tomorrow morning!"

Robin released the old man's skirt, and hastened away, pursued by an ill-mannered roar of laughter from the barber's shop. He was at first considerably surprised by the result of his question, but, being a shrewd youth, soon thought himself able to account for the mystery.

"This is some country representative," was his conclusion, "who has never seen the inside of my kinsman's door, and lacks the breeding to answer a stranger civilly. The man is old, or verily—I might be tempted to turn back and smite him on the nose. Ah, Robin, Robin! even the barber's boys laugh at you for choosing such a guide! You will be wiser in time, friend Robin."

He now became entangled in a succession of crooked and narrow streets, which crossed each other, and meandered at no great distance from the water-side. The smell of tar was obvious to his nostrils, the masts of vessels pierced the moonlight above the tops of the buildings, and the numerous signs, which Robin paused to read, informed him that he was near the centre of business. But the streets were empty, the shops were closed, and lights were visible only in the second stories of a few dwelling-houses. At length, on the corner of a narrow lane, through which he was passing, he beheld the broad countenance of a British hero swinging before the door of an inn, whence proceeded the voices of many guests. The casement of one of the lower windows was thrown back, and a very thin curtain permitted Robin to distinguish a party at supper, round a well-furnished table. The fragrance of the good cheer steamed forth into the outer air, and the youth could not fail to recollect that the last remnant of his travelling stock of provision had yielded to his morning appetite, and that noon had found and left him dinnerless.

"Oh, that a parchment three-penny might give me a right to sit down at yonder table!" said Robin, with a sigh. "But the Major will make me welcome to the best of his victuals; so I will even step boldly in, and inquire my way to his dwelling."

He entered the tavern, and was guided by the murmur of voices and the fumes of tobacco to the public-room. It was a long and low apartment, with oaken walls, grown dark in the continual smoke, and a floor which was thickly sanded, but of no immaculate purity. A number of persons—

the larger part of whom appeared to be mariners, or in some way connected with the sea—occupied the wooden benches, or leather-bottomed chairs, conversing on various matters, and occasionally lending their attention to some topic of general interest. Three or four little groups were draining as many bowls of punch, which the West India trade had long since made a familiar drink in the colony. Others, who had the appearance of men who lived by regular and laborious handicraft, preferred the insulated bliss of an unshared potation, and became more taciturn under its influence. Nearly all, in short, evinced a predilection for the Good Creature in some of its various shapes, for this is a vice to which, as Fast Day sermons of a hundred years ago will testify, we have a long hereditary claim. The only guests to whom Robin's sympathies inclined him were two or three sheepish countrymen, who were using the inn somewhat after the fashion of a Turkish caravansary; they had gotten themselves into the darkest corner of the room, and heedless of the Nicotian atmosphere, were supping on the bread of their own ovens, and the bacon cured in their own chimney-smoke. But though Robin felt a sort of brotherhood with these strangers, his eyes were attracted from them to a person who stood near the door, holding whispered conversation with a group of ill-dressed associates. His features were separately striking almost to grotesqueness, and the whole face left a deep impression on the memory. The forehead bulged out into a double prominence, with a vale between; the nose came boldly forth in an irregular curve, and its bridge was of more than a finger's breadth; the eyebrows were deep and shaggy, and the eyes glowed beneath them like fire in a cave.

While Robin deliberated of whom to inquire respecting his kinsman's dwelling, he was accosted by the innkeeper, a little man in a stained white apron, who had come to pay his professional welcome to the stranger. Being in the second generation from a French Protestant, he seemed to have inherited the courtesy of his parent nation; but no variety of circumstances was ever known to change his voice from the one shrill note in which he now addressed Robin.

"From the country, I presume, sir?" said he, with a profound bow. "Beg leave to congratulate you on your arrival, and trust you intend a long stay with us. Fine town here, sir, beautiful buildings, and much that may interest a stranger. May I hope for the honor of your commands in respect to supper?"

"The man sees a family likeness! the rogue has guessed that I am related to the Major!" thought Robin, who had hitherto experienced little superfluous civility.

All eyes were now turned on the country lad, standing at the door, in his worn three-cornered hat, gray coat, leather breeches, and blue yarn stockings, leaning on an oaken cudgel, and bearing a wallet on his back.

Robin replied to the courteous innkeeper, with such an assumption of confidence as befitted the Major's relative. "My honest friend," he said,

"I shall make it a point to patronize your house on some occasion, when"—here he could not help lowering his voice—"when I may have more than a parchment three-pence in my pocket. My present business," continued he, speaking with lofty confidence, "is merely to inquire my way to the dwelling of my kinsman, Major Molineux."

There was a sudden and general movement in the room, which Robin interpreted as expressing the eagerness of each individual to become his guide. But the innkeeper turned his eyes to a written paper on the wall, which he read, or seemed to read, with occasional recurrences to the young man's figure.

"What have we here?" said he, breaking his speech into little dry fragments. " 'Left the house of the subscriber, bounden servant, Hezekiah Mudge,—had on, when he went away, gray coat, leather breeches, master's third-best hat. One pound currency reward to whosoever shall lodge him in any jail of the providence. Better trudge, boy; better trudge!"

Robin had begun to draw his hand towards the lighter end of the oak cudgel, but a strange hostility in every countenance induced him to relinquish his purpose of breaking the courteous innkeeper's head. As he turned to leave the room, he encountered a sneering glance from the bold-featured personage whom he had before noticed; and no sooner was he beyond the door, than he heard a general laugh, in which the innkeeper's voice might be distinguished, like the dropping of small stones into a kettle.

"Now, is it not strange," thought Robin, with his usual shrewdness,—"is it not strange that the confession of an empty pocket should outweigh the name of my kinsman, Major Molineux? Oh, if I had one of those grinning rascals in the woods, where ı and my oak sapling grew up together, I would teach him that my arm is heavy though my purse be light!"

On turning the corner of the narrow lane, Robin found himself in a spacious street, with an unbroken line of lofty houses on each side, and a steepled building at the upper end, whence the ringing of a bell announced the hour of nine. The light of the moon, and the lamps from the numerous shop-windows, discovered people promenading on the pavement, and amongst them Robin had hoped to recognize his hitherto inscrutable relative. The result of his former inquiries made him unwilling to hazard another, in a scene of such publicity, and he determined to walk slowly and silently up the street, thrusting his face close to that of every elderly gentleman, in search of the Major's lineaments. In his progress, Robin encountered many gay and gallant figures. Embroidered garments of showy colors, enormous periwigs, gold-laced hats, and silver-hilted swords glided past him and dazzled his optics. Travelled youths, imitators of the European fine gentlemen of the period, trod jauntily along, half dancing to the fashionable tunes which they hummed, and making poor Robin ashamed of his quiet and natural gait. At length, after many pauses to examine the gorgeous display of goods in the shop-windows, and after suffering some rebukes for the impertinence of his scrutiny into people's faces, the Major's kinsman found himself near the steepled building, still unsuccessful in his search. As yet, however, he had seen only one side of the thronged street; so Robin crossed, and continued the same sort of in-quisition down the opposite pavement, with stronger hopes than the phi-losopher seeking an honest man, but with no better fortune. He had arrived about midway towards the lower end, from which his course began, when he overheard the approach of some one who struck down a cane on the flag-stones at every step, uttering at regular intervals, two sepulchral hems.

"Mercy on us!" quoth Robin, recognizing the sound.

Turning a corner, which chanced to be close at his right hand, he hastened to pursue his researches in some other part of the town. His pa-tience now was wearing low, and he seemed to feel more fatigue from his rambles since he crossed the ferry, than from his journey of several days on the other side. Hunger also pleaded loudly within him, and Robin began to balance the propriety of demanding, violently, and with lifted cudgel, the necessary guidance from the first solitary passenger whom he should meet. While a resolution to this effect was gaining strength, he entered a street of mean appearance, on either side of which a row of ill-built houses was straggling towards the harbor. The moonlight fell upon no passenger along the whole extent, but in the third domicile which Robin passed there was a half-opened door, and his keen glance detected a woman's garment within.

"My luck may be better here," said he to himself.

Accordingly, he approached the door, and beheld it shut closer as he did so; yet an open space remained, sufficing for the fair occupant to ob-serve the stranger, without a corresponding display on her part. All that Robin could discern was a strip of scarlet petticoat, and the occasional sparkle of an eye, as if the moonbeams were trembling on some bright thing.

"Pretty mistress," for I may call her so with a good conscience, thought the shrewd youth, since I know nothing to the contrary,—"my sweet pretty mistress, will you be kind enough to tell me whereabouts I must seek the dwelling of my kinsman, Major Molineux?"

Robin's voice was plaintive and winning, and the female, seeing nothing to be shunned in the handsome country youth, thrust open the door, and came forth into the moonlight. She was a dainty little figure, with a white neck, round arms, and a slender waist, at the extremity of which her scar-let petticoat jutted out over a hoop, as if she were standing in a balloon. Moreover, her face was oval and pretty, her hair dark beneath the little cap, and her bright eyes possessed a sly freedom, which triumphed over those of Robin.

"Major Molineux dwells here," said this fair woman.

Now, her voice was the sweetest Robin had heard that night, yet he could not help doubting whether that sweet voice spoke Gospel truth. He looked up and down the mean street, and then surveyed the house before which they stood. It was a small, dark edifice of two stories, the second of which projected over the lower floor, and the front apartment had the aspect of a shop for petty commodities.

"Now, truly, I am in luck," replied Robin, cunningly, "and so indeed is my kinsman, the Major, in having so pretty a housekeeper. But I prithee trouble him to step to the door; I will deliver him a message from his friends in the country, and then go back to my lodgings at the inn."

"Nay, the Major has been abed this hour or more," said the lady of the scarlet petticoat; "and it would be to little purpose to disturb him to-night, seeing his evening draught was of the strongest. But he is a kind-hearted man, and it would be as much as my life's worth to let a kinsman of his turn away from the door. You are the good old gentleman's very picture, and I could swear that was his rainy-weather hat. Also he has garments very much resembling those leather small-clothes. But come in, I pray, for I bid you hearty welcome in his name."

So saying, the fair and hospitable dame took our hero by the hand; and the touch was light, and the force was gentleness, and though Robin read in her eyes what he did not hear in her words, yet the slender-waisted woman in the scarlet petticoat proved stronger than the athletic country youth. She had drawn his half-willing footsteps nearly to the threshold, when the opening of a door in the neighborhood startled the Major's housekeeper, and, leaving the Major's kinsman, she vanished speedily into her own domicile. A heavy yawn preceded the appearance of a man, who, like the Moonshine of Pyramus and Thisbe, carried a lantern, needlessly aiding his sister luminary in the heavens. As he walked sleepily up the street, he turned his broad, dull face on Robin, and displayed a long staff, spiked at the end.

"Home, vagabond, home!" said the watchman, in accents that seemed to fall asleep as soon as they were uttered. "Home, or we'll set you in the stocks by peep of day!"

"This is the second hint of the kind," thought Robin. "I wish they would end my difficulties, by setting me there to-night."

Nevertheless, the youth felt an instinctive antipathy towards the guardian of midnight order, which at first prevented him from asking his usual question. But just when the man was about to vanish behind the corner, Robin resolved not to lose the opportunity, and shouted lustily after him,—

"I say, friend! will you guide me to the house of my kinsman, Major Molineux?"

The watchman made no reply, but turned the corner and was gone; yet Robin seemed to hear the sound of drowsy laughter stealing along the solitary street. At that moment, also, a pleasant titter saluted him from the open window above his head; he looked up, and caught the sparkle of a saucy eye; a round arm beckoned to him, and next he heard light footsteps descending the staircase within. But Robin, being of the household of a

New England clergyman, was a good youth, as well as a shrewd one; so he resisted temptation, and fled away.

He now roamed desperately, and at random, through the town, almost ready to believe that a spell was on him, like that by which a wizard of his country had once kept three pursuers wandering, a whole winter night, within twenty paces of the cottage which they sought. The streets lay before him, strange and desolate, and the lights were extinguished in almost every house. Twice, however, little parties of men, among whom Robin distinguished individuals in outlandish attire, came hurrying along; but, though on both occasions, they paused to address him, such intercourse did not at all enlighten his perplexity. They did but utter a few words in some language of which Robin knew nothing, and perceiving his inability to answer, bestowed a curse upon him in plain English and hastened away. Finally, the lad determined to knock at the door of every mansion that might appear worthy to be occupied by his kinsman, trusting that perseverance would overcome the fatality that had hitherto thwarted him. Firm in this resolve, he was passing beneath the walls of a church, which formed the corner of two streets, when, as he turned into the shade of its steeple, he encountered a bulky stranger, muffled in a cloak. The man was proceeding with the speed of earnest business, but Robin planted himself full before him, holding the oak cudgel with both hands across his body as a bar to further passage.

"Halt, honest man, and answer me a question," said he, very resolutely. "Tell me, this instant, whereabouts is the dwelling of my kinsman, Major Molineux!"

"Keep your tongue between your teeth, fool, and let me pass!" said a deep, gruff voice, which Robin partly remembered. "Let me pass, or I'll strike you to the earth!"

"No, no, neighbor!" cried Robin, flourishing his cudgel, and then thrusting its larger end close to the man's muffled face. "No, no, I'm not the fool you take me for, nor do you pass till I have an answer to my question. Whereabouts is the dwelling of my kinsman, Major Molineux?"

The stranger, instead of attempting to force his passage, stepped back into the moonlight, unmuffled his face, and stared full into that of Robin.

"Watch here an hour, and Major Molineux will pass by," said he.

Robin gazed with dismay and astonishment on the unprecedented physiognomy of the speaker. The forehead with its double prominence, the broad hooked nose, the shaggy eyebrows, and fiery eyes were those which he had noticed at the inn, but the man's complexion had undergone a singular, or, more properly, a twofold change. One side of the face blazed an intense red, while the other was black as midnight, the division line being in the broad bridge of the nose; and a mouth which seemed to extend from ear to ear was black or red, in contrast to the color of the cheek. The effect was as if two individual devils, a fiend of fire and a fiend of darkness, had united themselves to form this infernal visage. The stranger grinned in Robin's face, muffled his party-colored features, and was out of sight in a moment.

"Strange things we travellers see!" ejaculated Robin.

He seated himself, however, upon the steps of the church-door, resolving to wait the appointed time for his kinsman. A few moments were consumed in philosophical speculations upon the species of man who had just left him; but having settled this point shrewdly, rationally, and satisfactorily, he was compelled to look elsewhere for his amusement. And first he threw his eyes along the street. It was of more respectable appearance than most of those into which he had wandered; and the moon, creating, like the imaginative power, a beautiful strangeness in familiar objects, gave something of romance to a scene that might not have possessed it in the light of day. The irregular and often quaint architecture of the houses, some of whose roofs were broken into numerous little peaks, while others ascended, steep and narrow, into a single point, and others again were square; the pure snow-white of some of their complexions, the aged darkness of others, and the thousand sparklings, reflected from bright substances in the walls of many; these matters engaged Robin's attention for a while, and then began to grow wearisome. Next he endeavored to define the forms of distant objects, starting away, with almost ghostly indistinctness, just as his eye appeared to grasp them; and finally he took a minute survey of an edifice which stood on the opposite side of the street, directly in front of the church-door, where he was stationed. It was a large, square mansion, distinguished from its neighbors by a balcony, which rested on tall pillars, and by an elaborate Gothic window, communicating therewith.

"Perhaps this is the very house I have been seeking," thought Robin.

Then he strove to speed away the time, by listening to a murmur which swept continually along the street, yet was scarcely audible, except to an unaccustomed ear like his; it was a low, dull, dreamy sound, compounded of many noises, each of which was at too great a distance to be separately heard. Robin marvelled at this snore of a sleeping town, and marvelled more whenever its continuity was broken by now and then a distant shout, apparently loud where it originated. But altogether it was a sleep-inspiring sound, and, to shake off its drowsy influence, Robin arose, and climbed a window-frame, that he might view the interior of the church. There the moonbeams came trembling in, and fell down upon the deserted pews, and extended along the quiet aisles. A fainter yet more awful radiance was hovering around the pulpit, and one solitary ray had dared to rest upon the open page of the great Bible. Had nature, in that deep hour, become a worshipper in the house which man had builded? Or was that heavenly light the visible sanctity of the place,—visible because no earthly and impure feet were within the walls? The scene made Robin's heart shiver with a sensation of loneliness stronger than he had ever felt in the remotest depths of his native woods; so he turned away and sat down again before the door. There were graves around the church, and now an uneasy thought obtruded into Robin's breast. What if the object of his search, which had been so often and so strangely thwarted, were all the time mouldering in his shroud? What if his kinsman should glide through yonder gate, and nod and smile to him in dimly passing by?

"Oh that any breathing thing were here with me!" said Robin.

Recalling his thoughts from this uncomfortable track, he sent them over forest, hill, and stream, and attempted to imagine how that evening of ambiguity and weariness had been spent by his father's household. He pictured them assembled at the door, beneath the tree, the great old tree, which had been spared for its huge twisted trunk and venerable shade, when a thousand leafy brethren fell. There, at the going down of the summer sun, it was his father's custom to perform domestic worship, that the neighbors might come and join with him like brothers of the family, and that the wayfaring man might pause to drink at that fountain, and keep his heart pure by freshening the memory of home. Robin distinguished the seat of every individual of the little audience; he saw the good man in the midst, holding the Scriptures in the golden light that fell from the western clouds; he beheld him close the book and all rise up to pray. He heard the old thanksgivings for daily mercies, the old supplications for their continuance, to which he had so often listened in weariness, but which were now among his dear remembrances. He perceived the slight inequality of his father's voice when he came to speak of the absent one; he noted how his mother turned her face to the broad and knotted trunk; how his elder brother scorned, because the beard was rough upon his upper lip, to permit his features to be moved; how the younger sister drew down a low hanging branch before her eyes; and how the little one of all, whose sports had hitherto broken the decorum of the scene, understood the prayer for her playmate, and burst into clamorous grief. Then he saw them go in at the door; and when Robin would have entered also, the latch tinkled into its place, and he was excluded from his home.

"Am I here, or there?" cried Robin, starting; for all at once, when his thoughts had become visible and audible in a dream, the long, wide, solitary street shone out before him.

He aroused himself, and endeavored to fix his attention steadily upon the large edifice which he had surveyed before. But still his mind kept vibrating between fancy and reality; by turns, the pillars of the balcony lengthened into the tall, bare stems of pines, dwindled down to human figures, settled again into their true shape and size, and then commenced a new succession of changes. For a single moment, when he deemed himself awake, he could have sworn that a visage—one which he seemed to remember, yet could not absolutely name as his kinsman's—was looking towards him from the Gothic window. A deeper sleep wrestled with and nearly overcame him, but fled at the sound of footsteps along the opposite pavement. Robin rubbed his eyes, discerned a man passing at the foot of the balcony, and addressed him in a loud, peevish, and lamentable cry.

"Hallo, friend! must I wait here all night for my kinsman, Major Molineux?"

The sleeping echoes awoke, and answered the voice; and the passenger, barely able to discern a figure sitting in the oblique shade of the steeple, traversed the street to obtain a nearer view. He was himself a gentleman in his prime, of open, intelligent, cheerful, and altogether prepossessing countenance. Perceiving a country youth, apparently homeless and without friends, he accosted him in a tone of real kindness, which had become strange to Robin's ears.

"Well, my good lad, why are you sitting here?" inquired he. "Can I be of service to you in any way?"

"I am afraid not, sir," replied Robin, despondingly; "yet I shall take it kindly, if you'll answer me a single question. I've been searching, half the night, for one Major Molineux; now, sir, is there really such a person in these parts, or am I dreaming?"

"Major Molineux! The name is not altogether strange to me," said the gentleman, smiling. "Have you any objection to telling me the nature of your business with him?"

Then Robin briefly related that his father was a clergyman, settled on a small salary, at a long distance back in the country, and that he and Major Molineux were brothers' children. The Major, having inherited riches, and acquired civil and military rank, had visited his cousin, in great pomp, a year or two before; had manifested much interest in Robin and an elder brother, and, being childless himself, had thrown out hints respecting the future establishment of one of them in life. The elder brother was destined to succeed to the farm which his father cultivated in the interval of sacred duties; it was therefore determined that Robin should profit by his kinsman's generous intentions, especially as he seemed to be rather the favorite, and was thought to possess other necessary endowments.

"For I have the name of being a shrewd youth," observed Robin, in this part of his story.

"I doubt not you deserve it," replied his new friend, good-naturedly; "but pray proceed."

"Well, sir, being nearly eighteen years old, and well grown, as you see," continued Robin, drawing himself up to his full height, "I thought it high time to begin in the world. So my mother and sister put me in handsome trim, and my father gave me half the remnant of his last year's salary, and five days ago I started for this place, to pay the Major a visit. But, would you believe it, sir! I crossed the ferry a little after dark, and have yet found nobody that would show me the way to his dwelling; only, an hour or two since, I was told to wait here, and Major Molineux would pass by."

"Can you describe the man who told you this?" inquired the gentleman.

"Oh, he was a very ill-favored fellow, sir," replied Robin, "with two great bumps on his forehead, a hook nose, fiery eyes; and, what struck me as the strangest, his face was of two different colors. Do you happen to know such a man, sir?"

"Not intimately," answered the stranger, "but I chanced to meet him a little time previous to your stopping me. I believe you may trust his word, and that the Major will very shortly pass through this street. In the mean time, as I have a singular curiosity to witness your meeting, I will sit down here upon the steps and bear you company."

He seated himself accordingly, and soon engaged his companion in animated discourse. It was but of brief continuance, however, for a noise of shouting, which had long been remotely audible, drew so much nearer that Robin inquired its cause.

"What may be the meaning of this uproar?" asked he. "Truly, if your town be always as noisy, I shall find little sleep while I am an inhabitant."

"Why, indeed, friend Robin, there do appear to be three or four riotous fellows abroad to-night," replied the gentleman. "You must not expect all the stillness of your native woods here in our streets. But the watch will shortly be at the heels of these lads and"—

"Ay, and set them in the stocks by peep of day," interrupted Robin, recollecting his own encounter with the drowsy lanternbearer. "But, dear sir, if I may trust my ears, an army of watchmen would never make head against such a multitude of rioters. There were at least a thousand voices went up to make that one shout."

"May not a man have several voices, Robin, as well as two complexions?" said his friend.

"Perhaps a man may; but Heaven forbid that a woman should!" responded the shrewd youth, thinking of the seductive tones of the Major's housekeeper.

The sounds of a trumpet in some neighboring street now became so evident and continual, that Robin's curiosity was strongly excited. In addition to the shouts, he heard frequent bursts from many instruments of discord, and a wild and confused laughter filled up the intervals. Robin rose from the steps, and looked wistfully towards a point whither people seemed to be hastening.

"Surely some prodigious merry-making is going on," exclaimed he. "I have laughed very little since I left home, sir, and should be sorry to lose an opportunity. Shall we step round the corner by that darkish house, and take our share of the fun?"

"Sit down again, sit down, good Robin," replied the gentleman, laying his hand on the skirt of the gray coat. "You forget that we must wait here for your kinsman; and there is reason to believe that he will pass by, in the course of a very few moments."

The near approach of the uproar had now disturbed the neighborhood; windows flew open on all sides; and many heads, in the attire of the pillow, and confused by sleep suddenly broken, were protruded to the gaze of whoever had leisure to observe them. Eager voices hailed each other from house to house, all demanding the explanation, which not a soul could give. Half-dressed men hurried towards the unknown commotion, stumbling as they went over the stone steps that thrust themselves into the narrow footwalk. The shouts, the laughter, and the tuneless bray, the antipodes of music, came onwards with increasing din, till scattered individuals, and then denser bodies, began to appear round a corner at the distance of a hundred yards.

"Will you recognize your kinsman, if he passes in this crowd?" inquired the gentleman.

"Indeed, I can't warrant it, sir; but I'll take my stand here, and keep a bright lookout," answered Robin, descending to the outer edge of the pavement.

A mighty stream of people now emptied into the street, and came rolling slowly towards the church. A single horseman wheeled the corner in the midst of them, and close behind him came a band of fearful wind-instruments, sending forth a fresher discord now that no intervening buildings kept it from the ear. Then a redder light disturbed the moonbeams, and a dense multitude of torches shone along the street, concealing, by their glare, whatever object they illuminated. The single horseman, clad in a military dress, and bearing a drawn sword, rode onward as the leader, and, by his fierce and variegated countenance, appeared like war personified; the red of one cheek was an emblem of fire and sword; the blackness of the other betokened the mourning that attends them. In his train were wild figures in the Indian dress, and many fantastic shapes without a model, giving the whole march a visionary air, as if a dream had broken forth from some feverish brain, and were sweeping visibly through the midnight streets. A mass of people, inactive, except as applauding spectators, hemmed the procession in; and several women ran along the sidewalk, piercing the confusion of heavier sounds with their shrill voices of mirth or terror.

"The double-faced fellow has his eye upon me," muttered Robin, with an indefinite but an uncomfortable idea that he was himself to bear a part in the pageantry.

The leader turned himself in the saddle, and fixed his glance full upon the country youth, as the steed went slowly by. When Robin had freed his eyes from those fiery ones, the musicians were passing before him, and the torches were close at hand; but the unsteady brightness of the latter formed a veil which he could not penetrate. The rattling of wheels over the stones sometimes found its way to his ear, and confused traces of a human form appeared at intervals, and then melted into the vivid light. A moment more, and the leader thundered a command to halt: the trumpets vomited a horrid breath, and then held their peace; the shouts and laughter of the people died away, and there remained only a universal hum, allied to silence. Right before Robin's eyes was an uncovered cart. There the torches

Ralph Ellison

b. 1914

FLYING HOME

When Todd came to, he saw two faces suspended above h[im], hot and blinding that he could not tell if they we[re] stirred, feeling a pain that burned as though h[e] open to the sun which glared into his eyes. Fo[r] being touched by white hands seized him. The[n] pain began slowly to clear his head. Sounds ca[me] come to. Who are they? he thought. Naw he ai[n't] white. Then he heard clearly:

"You hurt bad?"

Something within him uncoiled. It was a Negro so[und]

"He's still out," he heard.

"Give 'im time. . . . Say, son, you hurt bad?"

Was he? There was that awful pain. He lay rigid, h[ear]ing and trying to weave a meaning between them and painfully upon the ground. He watched them warily, h[is] back over a painful distance. Jagged scenes, swiftly u[nrolling as in a] movie trailer, reeled through his mind, and he saw himsel[f] spinning plane and landing and landing and falling fr[om] and trying to stand. Then, as in a great silence, he rememb[ered] of crunching bone, and now, looking up into the anxious fa[ce of the] Negro man and a boy from where he lay in the same field, [it] sickened him and he wanted to remember no more.

"How you feel, son?"

Todd hesitated, as though to answer would be to admit an in[tolerable] weakness. Then, "It's my ankle," he said.

"Which one?"

"The left."

With a sense of remoteness he watched the old man bend and r[emove] his boot, feeling the pressure ease.

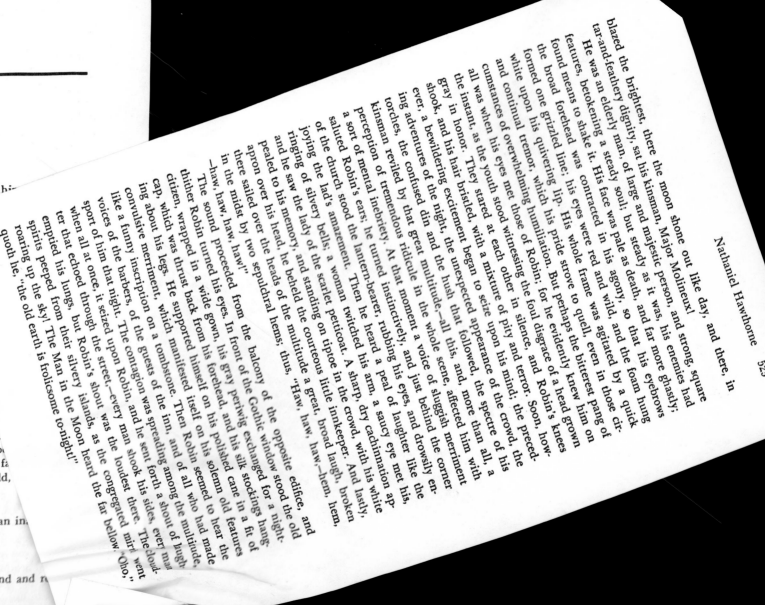

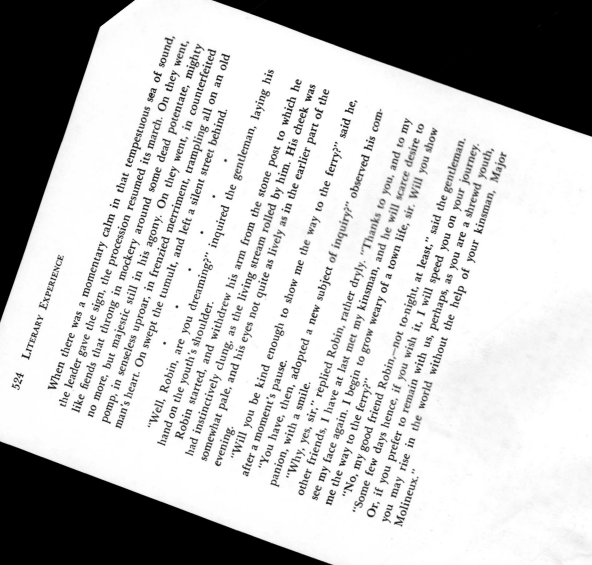

When there was a momentary calm in that tempestuous sea of sound, the leader gave the sign, the procession resumed its march. On they went, like fiends that throng in mockery around some dead potentate, mighty no more, but majestic still in his agony. On they went, in counterfeited pomp, in senseless uproar, in frenzied merriment, trampling all on an old man's heart. On swept the tumult, and left a silent street behind.

"Well, Robin, are you dreaming?" inquired the gentleman, laying his hand on the youth's shoulder.

Robin started, and withdrew his arm from the stone post to which he had instinctively clung, as the living stream rolled by him. His cheek was somewhat pale, and his eyes not quite as lively as in the earlier part of the evening.

"Will you be kind enough to show me the way to the ferry?" said he, after a moment's pause.

"You have, then, adopted a new subject of inquiry?" observed his companion, with a smile.

"Why, yes, sir," replied Robin, rather dryly. "Thanks to you, and to my other friends, I have at last met my kinsman, and he will scarce desire to see my face again. I begin to grow weary of a town life, sir. Will you show me the way to the ferry?"

"No, my good friend Robin,—not to-night, at least," said the gentleman. "Some few days hence, if you wish it, I will speed you on your journey. Or, if you prefer to remain with us, perhaps, as you are a shrewd youth, you may rise in the world without the help of your kinsman, Major Molineux."

"That any better?"

"A lot. Thank you."

He had the sensation of discussing someone else, that his concern was with some far more important thing, which for some reason escaped him.

"You done broke it bad," the old man said. "We have to get you to a doctor."

He felt that he had been thrown into a tailspin. He looked at his watch; how long had he been here? He knew there was but one important thing in the world, to get the plane back to the field before his officers were displeased.

"Help me up," he said. "Into the ship."

"But it's broke too bad. . . ."

"Give me your arm!"

"But, son . . ."

Clutching the old man's arm he pulled himself up, keeping his left leg clear, thinking, "I'd never make him understand," as the leather-smooth face came parallel with his own.

"Now, let's see."

He pushed the old man back, hearing a bird's insistent shrill. He swayed giddily. Blackness washed over him, like infinity.

"You best sit down."

"No, I'm O.K."

"But, son. You jus' gonna make it worse. . . ."

It was a fact that everything in him cried out to deny, even against the flaming pain in his ankle. He would have to try again.

"You mess with that ankle they have to cut your foot off," he heard.

Holding his breath, he started up again. It pained so badly that he had to bite his lips to keep from crying out and he allowed them to help him down with a pang of despair.

"It's best you take it easy. We gon' git you a doctor."

Of all the luck, he thought. Of all the rotten luck, now I have done it. The fumes of high-octane gasoline clung in the heat, taunting him.

"We kin ride him into town on old Ned," the boy said.

Ned? He turned, seeing the boy point toward an ox team browsing where the buried blade of a plow marked the end of a furrow. Thoughts of himself riding an ox through the town, past streets full of white faces, down the concrete runways of the airfield made swift images of humiliation in his mind. With a pang he remembered his girl's last letter. "Todd," she had written, "I don't need the papers to tell me you had the intelligence to fly. And I have always known you to be as brave as anyone else. The papers annoy me. Don't you be contented to prove over and over again that you're brave or skillful just because you're black, Todd. I think they keep beating that dead horse because they don't want to say why you boys are not yet fighting. I'm really disappointed, Todd. Anyone with brains can learn to fly, but then what? What about using it, and who will you use it for? I wish, dear, you'd write about this. I sometimes think they're playing a trick on us. It's very humiliating. . . ." He wiped cold sweat from his face, thinking, What does she know of humiliation? She's never been down South. Now the humiliation would come. When you must have them judge you, knowing that they never accept your mistakes as your own, but hold it against your whole race—that was humiliation. Yes, and humiliation was when you could never be simply yourself, when you were always a part of this old black ignorant man. Sure, he's all right. Nice and kind and helpful. But he's not you. Well, there's one humiliation I can spare myself.

"No," he said. "I have orders not to leave the ship. . . ."

"Aw," the old man said. Then turning to the boy, "Teddy, then you better hustle down to Mister Graves and get him to come. . . ."

"No, wait!" he protested before he was fully aware. Graves might be white. "Just have him get word to the field, please. They'll take care of the rest."

He saw the boy leave, running.

"How far does he have to go?"

"Might' nigh a mile."

He rested back, looking at the dusty face of his watch. But now they know something has happened, he thought. In the ship there was a perfectly good radio, but it was useless. The old fellow would never operate it. That buzzard knocked me back a hundred years, he thought. Irony danced within him like the gnats circling the old man's head. With all I've learned I'm dependent upon this "peasant's" sense of time and space. His leg throbbed. In the plane, instead of time being measured by the rhythms of pain and a kid's legs, the instruments would have told him at a glance. Twisting upon his elbows he saw where dust had powdered the plane's fuselage, feeling the lump form in his throat that was always there when he thought of flight. It's crouched there, he thought, like the abandoned shell of a locust. I'm naked without it. Not a machine, a suit of clothes you wear. And with a sudden embarrassment and wonder he whispered, "It's the only dignity I have. . . ."

He saw the old man watching, his torn overalls clinging limply to him in the heat. He felt a sharp need to tell the old man what he felt. But that would be meaningless. If I tried to explain why I need to fly back, he'd think I was simply afraid of white officers. But it's more than fear . . . a sense of anguish clung to him like the veil of sweat that hugged his face. He watched the old man, hearing him humming snatches of a tune as he admired the plane. He felt a furtive sense of resentment. Such old men often came to the field to watch the pilots with childish eyes. At first it had made him proud; they had been a meaningful part of a new experience. But soon he realized they did not understand his accomplishments and they came to shame and embarrass him, like the distasteful praise of an idiot. A part of the meaning of flying had gone then, and he had not been able to regain it. If I were a prizefighter I would be more human, he thought. Not a monkey doing tricks, but a man. They were pleased simply that he was a Negro who could fly, and that was not enough. He felt cut off from them by age, by understanding, by sensibility, by technology and by his need to measure himself against the mirror of) other men's appreciation. Somehow he felt betrayed, as he had when as a child he grew to discover that his father was dead. Now for him any real appreciation lay with his white officers; and with them he could never be sure. Between ignorant black men and condescending whites, his course of flight seemed mapped by the nature of things away from all needed and natural landmarks. Under some sealed orders, couched in ever more technical and mysterious terms, his path curved swiftly away from both the shame the old man symbolized and the cloudy terrain of white men's regard. Flying blind, he knew but one point of landing and there he would receive his wings. After that the enemy would appreciate his skill and he would assume his deepest meaning, he thought sadly, neither from those who condescended nor from those who praised without understanding, but from the enemy who would recognize his manhood and skill in terms of hate. . . .

He sighed, seeing the oxen making queer, prehistoric shadows against the dry brown earth.

"You just take it easy, son," the old man soothed. "That boy won't take long. Crazy as he is about airplanes."

"I can wait," he said.

"What kinda airplane you call this here'n?"

"An Advanced Trainer," he said, seeing the old man smile. His fingers were like gnarled dark wood against the metal as he touched the low-slung wing.

" 'Bout how fast can she fly?"

"Over two hundred an hour."

"Lawd! That's so fast I bet it don't seem like you moving!"

Holding himself rigid, Todd opened his flying suit. The shade had gone and he lay in a ball of fire.

"You mind if I take a look inside? I was always curious to see. . . ."

"Help yourself. Just don't touch anything."

He heard him climb upon the metal wing, grunting. Now the questions would start. Well, so you don't have to think to answer. . . .

He saw the old man looking over into the cockpit, his eyes bright as a child's.

"You must have to know a lot to work all these here things."

He was silent, seeing him step down and kneel beside him.

"Son, how come you want to fly way up there in the air?"

Because it's the most meaningful act in the world . . . because it makes me less like you, he thought.

But he said: "Because I like it, I guess. It's as good a way to fight and die as I know."

"Yeah? I guess you right," the old man said. "But how long you think before they gonna let you all fight?"

He tensed. This was the question all Negroes asked, put with the same timid hopefulness and longing that always opened a greater void within him than that he had felt beneath the plane the first time he had flown. He felt light-headed. It came to him suddenly that there was something sinister about the conversation, that he was flying unwillingly into unsafe and uncharted regions. If he could only be insulting and tell this old man who was trying to help him to shut up!

"I bet you one thing . . ."

"Yes?"

"That you was plenty scared coming down."

He did not answer. Like a dog on a trail the old man seemed to smell out his fears and he felt anger bubble within him.

"You sho' scared me. When I seen you coming down in that thing with it a-rollin' and a-jumpin' like a pitchin' hoss, I thought sho' you was a goner. I almost had me a stroke!"

He saw the old man grinning. "Ever'thin's been happening round here this morning, come to think of it."

"Like what?" he asked.

"Well, first thing I know, here come two white fellers looking for Mister Rudolph, that's Mister Graves's cousin. That got me worked up right away. . . ."

"Why?"

"Why? 'Cause he done broke outta the crazy house, that's why. He liable to kill somebody," he said. "They oughta have him by now though. Then here you come. First I think it's one of them white boys. Then doggone if you don't fall outta there. Lawd, I'd done heard about you boys but I haven't never seen one o' you-all. Cain't tell you how it felt to see somebody what look like me in a airplane!"

The old man talked on, the sound streaming around Todd's thoughts like air flowing over the fuselage of a flying plane. You were a fool, he thought, remembering how before the spin the sun had blazed bright against the billboard signs beyond the town, and how a boy's blue kite had bloomed beneath him, tugging gently in the wind like a strange, odd-shaped flower. He had once flown such kites himself and tried to find the boy at the end of the invisible cord. But he had been flying too high and too fast. He had climbed steeply away in exultation. Too steeply, he thought. And one of the first rules you learn is that if the angle of thrust is too steep the plane goes into a spin. And then, instead of pulling out of it and going into a dive you let a buzzard panic you. A lousy buzzard!

"Son, what made all that blood on the glass?"

"A buzzard," he said, remembering how the blood and feathers had sprayed back against the hatch. It had been as though he had flown into a storm of blood and blackness.

"Well, I declare! They's lots of 'em around here. They after dead things. Don't eat nothing what's alive."

"A little bit more and he would have made a meal out of me," Todd said grimly.

"They bad luck all right. Teddy's got a name for 'em, calls 'em jimcrows," the old man laughed.

"It's a damned good name."

"They the damnedest birds. Once I seen a hoss all stretched out like he was sick, you know. So I hollers, 'Gid up from there, suh!' Just to make sho! An' doggone, son, if I don't see two ole jimcrows come flying right up outa that hoss's insides! Yessuh! The sun was shinin' on 'em and they couldn't a been no greasier if they'd been eating barbecue."

Todd thought he would vomit, his stomach quivered.

"You made that up," he said.

"Nawsuh! Saw him just like I see you."

"Well, I'm glad it was you."

"You see lots a funny things down here, son."

"No, I'll let you see them," he said.

"By the way, the white folks round here don't like to see you boys up there in the sky. They ever bother you?"

"No."

"Well, they'd like to."

"Someone always wants to bother someone else," Todd said. "How do you know?"

"I just know."

"Well," he said defensively, "no one has bothered us."

Blood pounded in his ears as he looked away into space. He tensed, seeing a black spot in the sky, and strained to confirm what he could not clearly see.

"What does that look like to you?" he asked excitedly.

"Just another bad luck, son."

Then he saw the movement of wings with disappointment. It was gliding smoothly down, wings outspread, tail feathers gripping the air, down swiftly—gone behind the green screen of trees. It was like a bird he had imagined there, only the sloping branches of the pines remained, sharp against the pale stretch of sky. He lay barely breathing and stared at the point where it had disappeared, caught in a spell of loathing and admiration. Why did they make them so disgusting and yet teach them to fly so well? It's like when I was up in heaven, he heard, starting.

The old man was chuckling, rubbing his stubbled chin.

"What did you say?"

"Sho', I died and went to heaven . . . maybe by time I tell you about it they be done come after you."

"I hope so," he said wearily.

"You boys ever sit around and swap lies?"

"Not often. Is this going to be one?"

"Well, I ain't so sho', on account of it took place when I was dead."

The old man paused, "That wasn't no lie 'bout the buzzards, though."

"All right," he said.

"Sho' you want to hear 'bout heaven?"

"Please," he answered, resting his head upon his arm.

"Well, I went to heaven and right away started to sproutin' me some wings. Six good ones, they was. Just like them the white angels had. I couldn't hardly believe it. I was so glad that I went off on some clouds by myself and tried 'em out. You know, 'cause I didn't want to make a fool outta myself the first thing. . . ."

It's an old tale, Todd thought. Told me years ago. Had forgotten. But at least it will keep him from talking about buzzards.

He closed his eyes, listening.

". . . First thing I done was to git up on a low cloud and jump off. And doggone, boy, if them wings didn't work! First I tried the right; then I tried the left; then I tried 'em both together. Then Lawd, I started to move on out among the folks. I let 'em see me. . . ."

He saw the old man gesturing flight with his arms, his face full of mock pride as he indicated an imaginary crowd, thinking, It'll be in the newspapers, as he heard, ". . . so I went and found me some colored angels—somehow I didn't believe I was an angel till I seen a real black one, ha, yes! Then I was sho'—but they tole me I better come down 'cause us colored folks had to wear a special kin' a harness when we flew. That was how come they wasn't flyin'. Oh yes, an' you had to be extra strong for a black man even, to fly with one of them harnesses. . . ."

This is a new turn, Todd thought, what's he driving at?

"So I said to myself, I ain't gonna be bothered with no harness! Oh naw! 'Cause if God let you sprout wings you oughta have sense enough not to let nobody make you wear something what gits in the way of flyin'. So I starts to flyin'. Heck, son," he chuckled, his eyes twinkling, "you know I had to let eve'ybody know that old Jefferson could fly good as anybody else. And I could too, fly smooth as a bird! I could even loop-the-loop—only I had to make sho' to keep my long white robe down roun' my ankles. . . ."

Todd felt uneasy. He wanted to laugh at the joke, but his body refused, as of an independent will. He felt as he had as a child when after he had chewed a sugar-coated pill which his mother had given him, she had laughed at his efforts to remove the terrible taste.

". . . Well," he heard, "I was doing all right 'til I got to speeding.

Found out I could fan up a right strong breeze, I could fly so fast. I could do all kin'sa stunts too. I started flying up to the stars and divin' down and zooming roun' the moon. Man, I like to scare the devil outa some ole white angels. I was raisin' hell. Not that I meant any harm, son. But I was just feeling good. It was so good to know I was free at last. I accidentally knocked the tips offa some stars and they tell me I caused a storm and a coupla lynchings down here in Macon County—though I swear I believe them boys what said that was making up lies on me. . . ."

He's mocking me, Todd thought angrily. He thinks it's a joke. Grinning down at me . . . His throat was dry. He looked at his watch; why the hell didn't they come? Since they had to, why? One day I was flying down one of them heavenly streets. You got yourself into it, Todd thought. Like Jonah in the whale.

"Justa throwin' feathers in everybody's face. An' ole Saint Peter called me in. Said, 'Jefferson, tell me two things, what you doin' flyin' without a harness; an' how come you flyin' so fast?' So I tole him I was flyin' without a harness 'cause it got in my way, but I couldn'ta been flyin' so fast, 'cause I wasn't usin' but one wing. Saint Peter said, 'You wasn't flyin' with but one wing?' 'Yessuh,' I says, scared-like. So he says, 'Well, since you got sucha extra fine pair of wings you can leave off yo' harness awhile. But from now on none of that there one-wing flyin', 'cause you gittin' up too damn much speed!' "

And with one mouth full of bad teeth you're making too damned much talk, thought Todd. Why don't I send him after the boy? His body ached from the hard ground and seeking to shift his position he twisted his ankle and hated himself for crying out.

"It gittin' worse?"

"I . . . I twisted it," he groaned.

"Try not to think about it, son. That's what I do."

He bit his lip, fighting pain with counter-pain as the voice resumed its rhythmical droning. Jefferson seemed caught in his own creation.

". . . After all that trouble I just floated roun' heaven in slow motion. But I forgot, like colored folks will do, and got to flyin' with one wing again. This time I was restin' my old broken arm and got to flyin' fast enough to shame the devil. I was comin' so fast, Lawd, I got myself called befo' ole Saint Peter again. He said, 'Jeff, didn't I warn you 'bout that speedin'?' 'Yessuh,' I says, 'but it was an accident.' He looked at me sad-like and shook his head and I knowed I was gone. He said, 'Jeff, you and that speedin' is a danger to the heavenly community. If I was to let you keep on flyin', heaven wouldn't be nothin' but uproar. Jeff, you got to go!' Son, I argued and pleaded with that old white man, but it didn't do a bit of good. They rushed me straight to them pearly gates and gimme a para- chute and a map of the state of Alabama . . ."

Todd heard him laughing so that he could hardly speak, making a screen between them upon which his humiliation glowed like fire.

"Maybe you'd better stop awhile," he said, his voice unreal.

"Ain't much more," Jefferson laughed. "When they gimme the parachute ole Saint Peter ask me if I wanted to say a few words before I went. I felt so bad I couldn't hardly look at him, specially with all them white angels standin' around. Then somebody laughed and made me mad. So I tole him, 'Well, you done took my wings. And you puttin' me out. You got charge of things so's I can't do nothin' about it. But you got to admit just this: While I was up here I was the flyinest sonofabitch what ever hit heaven!' "

At the burst of laughter Todd felt such an intense humiliation that only great violence would wash it away. The laughter which shook the old man like a boiling purge set up vibrations of guilt within him which not even the intricate machinery of the plane would have been adequate to transform and he heard himself screaming, "Why do you laugh at me this way?"

He hated himself at that moment, but he had lost control. He saw Jefferson's mouth fall open, "What—?"

"Answer me!"

His blood pounded as though it would surely burst his temples and he tried to reach the old man and fell, screaming, "Can I help it because they won't let us actually fly? Maybe we are a bunch of buzzards feeding on a dead horse, but we can hope to be eagles, can't we? Can't we?"

He fell back, exhausted, his ankle pounding. The saliva was like straw in his mouth. If he had the strength he would strangle this old man. This grinning, gray-headed clown who made him feel as he felt when watched by the white officers at the field. And yet this old man had neither power, prestige, rank nor technique. Nothing that could rid him of this terrible feeling. He watched him, seeing his face struggle to express a turmoil of feeling.

"What you mean, son? What you talking 'bout . . . ?"

"Go away. Go tell your tales to the white folks."

"But I didn't mean nothing like that. . . . I . . . I wasn't tryin' to hurt your feelings. . . ."

"Please. Get the hell away from me!"

"But I didn't, son. I didn't mean all them things a-tall."

Todd shook as with a chill, searching Jefferson's face for a trace of the mockery he had seen there. But now the face was somber and tired and old. He was confused. He could not be sure that there had ever been laughter there, that Jefferson had ever really laughed in his whole life. He saw Jefferson reach out to touch him and shrank away, wondering if anything except the pain, now causing his vision to waver, was real. Perhaps he had imagined it all.

"Don't let it get you down, son," the voice said pensively.

He heard Jefferson sigh wearily, as though he felt more than he could say. His anger ebbed, leaving only the pain.

"I'm sorry," he mumbled.

"You just wore out with pain, was all. . . ."

He saw him through a blur, smiling. And for a second he felt the embarrassed silence of understanding flutter between them.

"What you was doin' flyin' over this section, son? Wasn't you scared they might shoot you for a cow?"

Todd tensed. Was he being laughed at again? But before he could decide, the pain shook him and a part of him was lying calmly behind the screen of pain that had fallen between them, recalling the first time he had ever seen a plane. It was as though an endless series of hangars had been shaken ajar in the air base of his memory and from each, like a young wasp emerging from its cell, arose the memory of a plane.

The first time I ever saw a plane I was very small and planes were new in the world. I was four-and-a-half and the only plane that I had ever seen was a model suspended from the ceiling of the automobile exhibit at the State Fair. But I did not know that it was only a model. I did not know how large a real plane was, nor how expensive. To me it was a fascinating toy, complete in itself, which my mother said could only be owned by rich little white boys. I stood rigid with admiration, my head straining backwards as I watched the gray little plane describing arcs above the gleaming tops of the automobiles. And I vowed that, rich or poor, someday I would own such a toy. My mother had to drag me out of the exhibit and not even the merry-go-round, the Ferris wheel, or the racing horses could hold my attention for the rest of the Fair. I was too busy imitating the tiny drone of the plane with my lips, and imitating with my hands the motion, swift and circling, that it made in flight.

After that I no longer used the pieces of lumber that lay about our back yard to construct wagons and autos . . . now it was used for airplanes. I built biplanes, using pieces of board for wings, a small box for the fuselage, another piece of wood for the rudder. The trip to the Fair had brought something new into my small world. I asked my mother repeatedly when the Fair would come back again. I'd lie in the grass and watch the sky, and each fighting bird became a soaring plane. I would have been good a year just to have seen a plane again. I became a nuisance to everyone with my questions about airplanes. But planes were new to the old folks, too, and there was little that they could tell me. Only my uncle knew some of the answers. And better still, he could carve propellers from pieces of wood that would whirl rapidly in the wind, wobbling noisily upon oiled nails.

I wanted a plane more than I'd wanted anything; more than I wanted the red wagon with rubber tires, more than the train that ran on a track with its train of cars. I asked my mother over and over again:

"Mamma?"

"What do you want, boy?" she'd say.

"Mamma, will you get mad if I ask you?" I'd say.

"What do you want now? I ain't got time to be answering a lot of fool questions. What you want?"

"Mamma, when you gonna get me one . . . ?" I'd ask.

"Get you one what?" she'd say.

"You know, Mamma; what I been asking you. . . ."

"Boy," she'd say, "if you don't want a spanking you better come on an' tell me what you talking about so I can get on with my work."

"Aw, Mamma, you know. . . ."

"What I just tell you?" she'd say.

"I mean when you gonna buy me a airplane."

"Airplane! Boy, is you crazy? How many times I have to tell you to stop that foolishness. I done told you them things cost too much. I bet I'm gon' wham the living daylight out of you if you don't quit worrying me 'bout them things!"

But this did not stop me, and a few days later I'd try all over again.

Then one day a strange thing happened. It was spring and for some reason I had been hot and irritable all morning. It was a beautiful spring. I could feel it as I played barefoot in the backyard. Blossoms hung from the thorny black locust trees like clusters of fragrant white grapes. Butterflies flickered in the sunlight above the short new dew-wet grass. I had gone in the house for bread and butter and coming out I heard a steady unfamiliar drone. It was unlike anything I had ever heard before. I tried to place the sound. It was no use. It was a sensation like that I had when searching for my father's watch, heard ticking unseen in a room. It made me feel as though I had forgotten to perform some task that my mother had ordered . . . then I located it, overhead. In the sky, flying quite low and about a hundred yards off was a plane! It came so slowly that it seemed barely to move. My mouth hung wide; my bread and butter fell into the dirt. I wanted to jump up and down and cheer. And when the idea struck I trembled with excitement: "Some little white boy's plane's done flew away and all I got to do is stretch out my hands and it'll be mine!" It was a little plane like that at the Fair, flying no higher than the eaves of our roof. Seeing it come steadily forward I felt the world grow warm with promise. I opened the screen and climbed over it and clung there, waiting. I would catch the plane as it came over and swing down fast and run into the house before anyone could see me. Then no one could come to claim the plane. It droned nearer. Then when it hung like a silver cross in the blue directly above me I stretched out my hand and grabbed. It was like sticking my finger through a soap bubble. The plane flew on, as though I had simply blown my breath after it. I grabbed again, frantically, trying to catch the tail. My fingers clutched the air and disappointment surged tight and hard in my throat. Giving one last desperate grasp, I strained forward. My fingers ripped against the screen.

I was falling. The ground burst hard against me. I drummed the earth with my heels and when my breath returned, I lay there bawling.

My mother rushed through the door.

"What's the matter, chile! What on earth is wrong with you?"

"It's gone! It's gone!"

"What gone?"

"The airplane . . ."

"Airplane?"

"Yessum, jus' like the one at the Fair. . . . I . . . I tried to stop it an it kep' right on going. . . ."

"When, boy?"

"Just now," I cried, through my tears.

"Where it go, boy, what way?"

"Yonder, there . . ."

She scanned the sky, her arms akimbo and her checkered apron flapping in the wind as I pointed to the fading plane. Finally she looked down at me, slowly shaking her head.

"It's gone! It's gone!" I cried.

"Boy, is you a fool?" she said. "Don't you see that there's a real airplane 'stead of one of them toy ones?"

"Real . . . ?" I forgot to cry, "Real?"

"Yass, real. Don't you know that thing you reaching for is bigger'n a auto? You here trying to reach for it and I bet it's flying 'bout two hundred miles higher'n this roof." She was disgusted with me. "You come on in this house before somebody else sees what a fool you done turned out to be. You must think these here lil ole arms of you'n is mighty long. . . ."

I was carried into the house and undressed for bed and the doctor was called. I cried bitterly, as much from the disappointment of finding the plane so far beyond my reach as from the pain.

When the doctor came I heard my mother telling him about the plane and asking if anything was wrong with my mind. He explained that I had had a fever for several hours. But I was kept in bed for a week and I constantly saw the plane in my sleep, flying just beyond my fingertips, sailing so slowly that it seemed barely to move. And each time I'd reach out to grab it I'd miss and through each dream I'd hear my grandma warning:

> Young man, young man,
> Yo' arms too short
> To box with God. . . .

"Hey, son!"

At first he did not know where he was and looked at the old man pointing, with blurred eyes.

"Ain't that one of you-all's airplanes coming after you?"

As his vision cleared he saw a small black shape above a distant field, soaring through waves of heat. But he could not be sure and with the pain he feared that somehow a horrible recurring fantasy of being split in twain by the whirling blades of a propeller had come true.

"You think he sees us?" he heard.

"See? I hope so."

"He's coming like a bat outa hell!"

Straining, he heard the faint sound of a motor and hoped it would soon be over.

"How you feeling?"

"Like a nightmare," he said.

"Hey, he's done curved back the other way!"

"Maybe he saw us," he said. "Maybe he's gone to send out the ambulance and ground crew." And, he thought with despair, maybe he didn't even see us.

"Where did you send the boy?"

"Down to Mister Graves," Jefferson said. "Man what owns this land."

"Do you think he phoned?"

Jefferson looked at him quickly.

"Aw sho'. Dabney Graves is got a bad name on accounta them killings but he'll call though. . . ."

"What killings?"

"Them five fellers . . . ain't you heard?" he asked with surprise.

"No."

"Everybody knows 'bout Dabney Graves, especially the colored. He done killed enough of us."

Todd had the sensation of being caught in a white neighborhood after dark.

"What did they do?" he asked.

"Thought they was men," Jefferson said. "An' some he owed money, like he do me. . . ."

"But why do you stay here?"

"You black, son."

"I know, but . . ."

"You have to come by the white folks, too."

He turned away from Jefferson's eyes, at once consoled and accused. And I'll have to come by them soon, he thought with despair. Closing his eyes, he heard Jefferson's voice as the sun burned blood-red upon his lips.

"I got nowhere to go," Jefferson said, "an' they'd come after me if I did. But Dabney Graves is a funny fellow. He's all the time making jokes. He can be mean as hell, then he's liable to turn right around and back the colored against the white folks. I seen him do it. But me, I hates him for that more'n anything else. 'Cause just as soon as he gits tired helping a man he don't care what happens to him. He just leaves him stone cold. And then the other white folks is double hard on anybody he done helped. For him it's just a joke. He don't give a hilla beans for nobody—but hisself. . . ."

Todd listened to the thread of detachment in the old man's voice. It was as though he held his words arm's length before him to avoid their destructive meaning.

"He'd just as soon do you a favor and then turn right around and have you strung up. Me, I stays outa his way 'cause down here that's what you gotta do."

If my ankle would only ease for a while, he thought. The closer I spin toward the earth the blacker I become, flashed through his mind. Sweat ran into his eyes and he was sure that he would never see the plane if his head continued whirling. He tried to see Jefferson, what it was that Jefferson held in his hand? It was a little black man, another Jefferson! A little black Jefferson that shook with fits of belly-laughter while the other Jefferson looked on with detachment. Then Jefferson looked up from the thing in his hand and turned to speak, but Todd was far away, searching the sky for a plane in a hot dry land on a day and age he had long forgotten. He was going mysteriously with his mother through empty streets where black faces peered from behind drawn shades and someone was rapping at a window and he was looking back to see a hand and a frightened face frantically beckoning from a cracked door and his mother was looking down the empty perspective of the street and shaking her head and hurrying him along and at first it was only a flash he saw and a motor was droning as through the sun-glare he saw it gleaming silver as it circled and he was seeing a burst like a puff of white smoke and hearing his mother yell, Come along, boy, I got no time for them fool airplanes, I got no time, and he saw it a second time, the plane flying high, and the burst appeared suddenly and fell slowly, billowing out and sparkling like fireworks and he was watching and being hurried along as the air filled with a flurry of white pinwheeling cards that caught in the wind and scattered over the rooftops and into the gutters and a woman was running and snatching a card and reading it and screaming and he darted into the shower, grabbing as in winter he grabbed for snowflakes and bounding away at his mother's, Come on here, boy! Come on, I say! and he was watching as she took the card away, seeing her face grow puzzled and turning taut as her voice quavered, "Niggers Stay From the Polls," and died to a moan of terror as he saw the eyeless sockets of a white hood staring at him from the card and above he saw the plane spiraling gracefully, agleam in the sun like a fiery sword. And seeing it soar he was caught, transfixed between a terrible horror and a horrible fascination.

The sun was not so high now, and Jefferson was calling and gradually he saw three figures moving across the curving roll of the field.

"Look like some doctors, all dressed in white," said Jefferson.

They're coming at last, Todd thought. And he felt such a release of tension within him that he thought he would faint. But no sooner did he close his eyes than he was seized and he was struggling with three white men who were forcing his arms into some kind of coat. It was too much for him, his arms were pinned to his sides and as the pain blazed in his eyes, he realized that it was a straitjacket. What filthy joke was this?

"That oughta hold him, Mister Graves," he heard.

His total energies seemed focused in his eyes as he searched their faces. That was Graves; the other two wore hospital uniforms. He was poised between two poles of fear and hate as he heard the one called Graves saying, "He looks kinda purty in that there suit, boys. I'm glad you dropped by."

"This boy ain't crazy, Mister Graves," one of the others said. "He needs a doctor, not us. Don't see how you led us way out here anyway. It might be a joke to you, but your cousin Rudolph liable to kill somebody. White folks or niggers, don't make no difference. . . ."

Todd saw the man turn red with anger. Graves looked down upon him, chuckling.

"This nigguh belongs in a straitjacket, too, boys. I knowed that the minit Jeff's kid said something 'bout a nigguh flyer. You all know you cain't let the nigguh git up that high without his going crazy. The nigguh brain ain't built right for high altitudes. . . ."

Todd watched the drawling red face, feeling that all the unnamed horror and obscenities that he had ever imagined stood materialized before him.

"Let's git outta here," one of the attendants said.

Todd saw the other reach toward him, realizing for the first time that he lay upon a stretcher as he yelled.

"Don't put your hands on me!"

They drew back, surprised.

"What's that you say, nigguh?" asked Graves.

He did not answer and thought that Graves's foot was aimed at his head. It landed on his chest and he could hardly breathe. He coughed helplessly, seeing Graves's lips stretch taut over his yellow teeth, and tried to shift his head. It was as though a half-dead fly was dragging slowly across his face and a bomb seemed to burst within him. Blasts of hot, hysterical laughter tore from his chest, causing his eyes to pop and he felt that the veins in his neck would surely burst. And then a part of him stood behind it all, watching the surprise in Graves's red face and his own hysteria. He thought he would never stop, he would laugh himself to death. It rang in his ears like Jefferson's laughter and he looked for him, centering his eyes desperately upon his face, as though somehow he had become his sole salvation in an insane world of outrage and humiliation. It brought a certain relief. He was suddenly aware that although his body was still contorted it was an echo that no longer rang in his ears. He heard Jefferson's voice with gratitude.

"Mister Graves, the Army done tole him not to leave his airplane."

"Nigguh, Army or no, you gittin' off my land! That airplane can stay cause it was paid for by taxpayers' money. But you gittin' off. An' dead or alive, it don't make no difference to me."

Todd was beyond it now, lost in a world of anguish.

"Jeff," Graves said, "you and Teddy come and grab holt. I want you to take this here black eagle over to that nigguh airfield and leave him."

Jefferson and the boy approached him silently. He looked away, realizing and doubting at once that only they could release him from his overpowering sense of isolation.

They bent for the stretcher. One of the attendants moved toward Teddy.

"Think you can manage it, boy?"

"I think I can, suh," Teddy said.

"Well, you better go behind then, and let yo' pa go ahead so's to keep that leg elevated."

He saw the white men walking ahead of Jefferson and the boy carried him along in silence. Then they were pausing and he felt a hand wiping his face; then he was moving again. And it was as though he had been lifted out of his isolation, back into the world of men. A new current of communication flowed between the man and boy and himself. They moved him gently. Far away he heard a mockingbird liquidly calling. He raised his eyes, seeing a buzzard poised unmoving in space. For a moment the whole afternoon seemed suspended and he waited for the horror to seize him again. Then like a song within his head he heard the boy's soft humming and saw the dark bird glide into the sun and glow like a bird of flaming gold.

Ernest Hemingway

1899–1961

SOLDIER'S HOME

Krebs went to the war from a Methodist college in Kansas. There is a picture which shows him among his fraternity brothers, all of them wearing exactly the same height and style collar. He enlisted in the Marines in 1917 and did not return to the United States until the second division returned from the Rhine in the summer of 1919.

There is a picture which shows him on the Rhine with two German girls and another corporal. Krebs and the corporal look too big for their uniforms. The German girls are not beautiful. The Rhine does not show in the picture.

By the time Krebs returned to his home town in Oklahoma the greeting of heroes was over. He came back much too late. The men from the town who had been drafted had all been welcomed elaborately on their return. There had been a great deal of hysteria. Now the reaction had set in. People seemed to think it was rather ridiculous for Krebs to be getting back so late, years after the war was over.

At first Krebs, who had been at Belleau Wood, Soissons, the Champagne, St. Mihiel and in the Argonne did not want to talk about the war at all. Later he felt the need to talk but no one wanted to hear about it. His town had heard too many atrocity stories to be thrilled by actualities. Krebs found that to be listened to at all he had to lie, and after he had done this twice he, too, had a reaction against the war and against talking about it. A distaste for everything that had happened to him in the war set in because of the lies he had told. All of the times that had been able to make him feel cool and clear inside himself when he thought of them; the times so long back when he had done the one thing, the only thing for a man to do, easily and naturally, when he might have done something else, now lost their cool, valuable quality and then were lost themselves.

His lies were quite unimportant lies and consisted in attributing to himself things other men had seen, done or heard of, and stating as facts certain apocryphal incidents familiar to all soldiers. Even his lies were not sensational at the pool room. His acquaintances, who had heard detailed accounts of German women found chained to machine guns in the Argonne forest and who could not comprehend, or were barred by their patriotism from interest in, any German machine gunners who were not chained, were not thrilled by his stories.

Krebs acquired the nausea in regard to experience that is the result of untruth or exaggeration, and when he occasionally met another man who had really been a soldier and they talked a few minutes in the dressing room at a dance he fell into the easy pose of the old soldier among other soldiers: that he had been badly, sickeningly frightened all the time. In this way he lost everything.

During this time, it was late summer, he was sleeping late in bed, getting up to walk down town to the library to get a book, eating lunch at home, reading on the front porch until he became bored and then walking down through the town to spend the hottest hours of the day in the cool dark of the pool room. He loved to play pool.

In the evening he practised on his clarinet, strolled down town, read and went to bed. He was still a hero to his two young sisters. His mother would have given him breakfast in bed if he had wanted it. She often came in when he was in bed and asked him to tell her about the war, but her attention always wandered. His father was non-committal.

Before Krebs went away to the war he had never been allowed to drive the family motor car. His father was in the real estate business and always wanted the car to be at his command when he required it to take clients out into the country to show them a piece of farm property. The car always stood outside the First National Bank building where his father had an office on the second floor. Now, after the war, it was still the same car.

Nothing was changed in the town except that the young girls had grown up. But they lived in such a complicated world of already defined alliances and shifting feuds that Krebs did not feel the energy or the courage to break into it. He liked to look at them, though. There were so many good-looking young girls. Most of them had their hair cut short. When he went away only little girls wore their hair like that or girls that were fast. They all wore sweaters and shirt waists with round Dutch collars. It was a pattern. He liked to look at them from the front porch as they walked on the other side of the street. He liked to watch them walking under the shade of the trees. He liked the round Dutch collars above their sweaters. He liked their silk stockings and flat shoes. He liked their bobbed hair and the way they walked.

When he was in town their appeal to him was not very strong. He did not like them when he saw them in the Greek's ice cream parlor. He did not want them themselves really. They were too complicated. There was something else. Vaguely he wanted a girl but he did not want to have to work to get her. He would have liked to have a girl but he did not want to have to spend a long time getting her. He did not want to get into the intrigue and the politics. He did not want to have to do any courting. He did not want to tell any more lies. It wasn't worth it.

He did not want any consequences. He did not want any consequences ever again. He wanted to live along without consequences. Besides he did not really need a girl. The army had taught him that. It was all right to pose as though you had to have a girl. Nearly everybody did that. But it wasn't true. You did not need a girl. That was the funny thing. First a fellow boasted how girls mean nothing to him, that he never thought of them, that they could not touch him. Then a fellow boasted that he could not get along without girls, that he had to have them all the time, that he could not go to sleep without them.

That was all a lie. It was all a lie both ways. You did not need a girl unless you thought about them. He learned that in the army. Then sooner or later you always got one. When you were really ripe for a girl you always got one. You did not have to think about it. Sooner or later it would come. He had learned that in the army.

Now he would have liked a girl if she had come to him and not wanted to talk. But here at home it was all too complicated. He knew he could never get through it all again. It was not worth the trouble. That was the thing about French girls and German girls. There was not all this talking. You couldn't talk much and you did not need to talk. It was simple and you were friends. He thought about France and then he began to think about Germany. On the whole he had liked Germany better. He did not want to leave Germany. He did not want to come home. Still, he had come home. He sat on the front porch.

He liked the girls that were walking along the other side of the street. He liked the look of them much better than the French girls or the German girls. But the world they were in was not the world he was in. He would like to have one of them. But it was not worth it. They were such a nice pattern. He liked the pattern. It was exciting. But he would not go through all the talking. He did not want one badly enough. He liked to look at them all, though. It was not worth it. Not now when things were getting good again.

He sat there on the porch reading a book on the war. It was a history and he was reading about all the engagements he had been in. It was the most interesting reading he had ever done. He wished there were more maps. He looked forward with a good feeling to reading all the really good histories when they would come out with good detail maps. Now he was really learning about the war. He had been a good soldier. That made a difference.

One morning after he had been home about a month his mother came into his bedroom and sat on the bed. She smoothed her apron.

"I had a talk with your father last night, Harold," she said, "and he is willing for you to take the car out in the evenings."

"Yeah?" said Krebs, who was not fully awake. "Take the car out? Yeah?"

"Yes. Your father has felt for some time that you should be able to take the car out in the evenings whenever you wished but we only talked it over last night."

"I'll bet you made him," Krebs said.

"No. It was your father's suggestion that we talk the matter over."

"Yeah. I'll bet you made him." Krebs sat up in bed.

"Will you come down to breakfast, Harold?" his mother said.

"As soon as I get my clothes on," Krebs said.

His mother went out of the room and he could hear her frying something downstairs while he washed, shaved and dressed to go down into the dining-room for breakfast. While he was eating breakfast his sister brought in the mail.

"Well, Hare," she said. "You old sleepy-head. What do you ever get up for?"

Krebs looked at her. He liked her. She was his best sister.

"Have you got the paper?" he asked.

She handed him *The Kansas City Star* and he shucked off its brown wrapper and opened it to the sporting page. He folded *The Star* open and propped it against the water pitcher with his cereal dish to steady it, so he could read while he ate.

"Harold," his mother stood in the kitchen doorway, "Harold, please don't muss up the paper. Your father can't read his *Star* if it's been mussed."

"I won't muss it," Krebs said.

His sister sat down at the table and watched him while he read.

"We're playing indoor over at school this afternoon," she said. "I'm going to pitch."

"Good," said Krebs. "How's the old wing?"

"I can pitch better than lots of the boys. I tell them all you taught me. The other girls aren't much good."

"Yeah?" said Krebs.

"I tell them all you're my beau. Aren't you my beau, Hare?"

"You bet."

"Couldn't your brother really be your beau just because he's your brother?"

"I don't know."

"Sure you know. Couldn't you be my beau, Hare, if I was old enough and if you wanted to?"

"Sure. You're my girl now."

"Am I really your girl?"

"Sure."

"Do you love me?"

"Uh, huh."

"Will you love me always?"

"Sure."

"Will you come over and watch me play indoor?"

"Maybe."

"Aw, Hare, you don't love me. If you loved me, you'd want to come over and watch me play indoor."

Krebs's mother came into the dining-room from the kitchen. She carried a plate with two fried eggs and some crisp bacon on it and a plate of buckwheat cakes.

"You run along, Helen," she said. "I want to talk to Harold."

She put the eggs and bacon down in front of him and brought in a jug of maple syrup for the buckwheat cakes. Then she sat down across the table from Krebs.

"I wish you'd put down the paper a minute, Harold," she said.

Krebs took down the paper and folded it.

"Have you decided what you are going to do yet, Harold?" his mother said, taking off her glasses.

"No," said Krebs.

"Don't you think it's about time?" His mother did not say this in a mean way. She seemed worried.

"I hadn't thought about it," Krebs said.

"God has some work for everyone to do," his mother said. "There can be no idle hands in His Kingdom."

"I'm not in His Kingdom," Krebs said.

"We are all of us in His Kingdom."

Krebs felt embarrassed and resentful as always.

"I've worried about you so much, Harold," his mother went on. "I know the temptations you must have been exposed to. I know how weak men are. I know what your own dear grandfather, my own father, told us about the Civil War and I have prayed for you. I pray for you all day long, Harold."

Krebs looked at the bacon fat hardening on his plate.

"Your father is worried, too," his mother went on. "He thinks you have lost your ambition, that you haven't got a definite aim in life. Charley Simmons, who is just your age, has a good job and is going to be married. The boys are all settling down; they're all determined to get somewhere; you can see that boys like Charley Simmons are on their way to being really a credit to the community."

Krebs said nothing.

"Don't look that way, Harold," his mother said. "You know we love you and I want to tell you for your own good how matters stand. Your father does not want to hamper your freedom. He thinks you should be allowed to drive the car. If you want to take some of the nice girls out riding with you, we are only too pleased. We want you to enjoy yourself. But you are going to have to settle down to work, Harold. Your father doesn't care what you start in at. All work is honorable as he says. But you've got to make a start at something. He asked me to speak to you this morning and then you can stop in and see him at his office."

"Is that all?" Krebs said.

"Yes. Don't you love your mother, dear boy?"

"No," Krebs said.

His mother looked at him across the table. Her eyes were shiny. She started crying.

"I don't love anybody," Krebs said.

It wasn't any good. He couldn't tell her, he couldn't make her see it. It was silly to have said it. He had only hurt her. He went over and took hold of her arm. She was crying with her head in her hands.

"I didn't mean it," he said. "I was just angry at something. I didn't mean I didn't love you."

His mother went on crying. Krebs put his arm on her shoulder.

"Can't you believe me, mother?"

His mother shook her head.

"Please, please, mother. Please believe me."

"All right," his mother said chokily. She looked up at him. "I believe you, Harold."

Krebs kissed her hair. She put her face up to him.

"I'm your mother," she said. "I held you next to my heart when you were a tiny baby."

Krebs felt sick and vaguely nauseated.

"I know, Mummy," he said. "I'll try and be a good boy for you."

"Would you kneel and pray with me, Harold?" his mother asked.

They knelt down beside the dining-room table and Krebs's mother prayed.

"Now, you pray, Harold," she said.

"I can't," Krebs said.

"Try, Harold."

"I can't."

"Do you want me to pray for you?"

"Yes."

So his mother prayed for him and then they stood up and Krebs kissed his mother and went out of the house. He had tried so to keep his life from being complicated. Still, none of it had touched him. He had felt sorry for his mother and she had made him lie. He would go to Kansas City and get a job and she would feel all right about it. There would be one more scene maybe before he got away. He would not go down to his father's office. He would miss that one. He wanted his life to go smoothly. It had just gotten going that way. Well, that was all over now, anyway. He would go over to the schoolyard and watch Helen play indoor baseball.

James Baldwin

b. 1924

SONNY'S BLUES

I read about it in the paper, in the subway, on my way to work. I read it, and I couldn't believe it, and I read it again. Then perhaps I just stared at it, at the newsprint spelling out his name, spelling out the story. I stared at it in the swinging lights of the subway car, and in the faces and bodies of the people, and in my own face, trapped in the darkness which roared outside.

It was not to be believed, and I kept telling myself that as I walked from the subway station to the high school. And at the same time I couldn't doubt it. I was scared, scared for Sonny. He became real to me again. A great block of ice got settled in my belly and kept melting there slowly all day long, while I taught my classes algebra. It was a special kind of ice. It kept melting, sending trickles of ice water all up and down my veins, but it never got less. Sometimes it hardened and seemed to expand until I felt my guts were going to come spilling out or that I was going to choke or scream. This would always be at a moment when I was remembering some specific thing Sonny had once said or done.

When he was about as old as the boys in my classes, his face had been bright and open, there was a lot of copper in it; and he'd had wonderfully direct brown eyes, and great gentleness and privacy. I wondered what he looked like now. He had been picked up, the evening before, in a raid on an apartment downtown, for peddling and using heroin.

I couldn't believe it: but what I mean by that is that I couldn't find any room for it anywhere inside me. I had kept it outside me for a long time. I hadn't wanted to know. I had had suspicions, but I didn't name them, I kept putting them away. I told myself that Sonny was wild, but he wasn't crazy. And he'd always been a good boy, he hadn't ever turned hard or evil or disrespectful, the way kids can, so quick, so quick, especially in Harlem. I didn't want to believe that I'd ever see my brother going down, coming to nothing, all that light in his face gone out, in the condition I'd already seen so many others. Yet it had happened and here I was, talking about algebra to a lot of boys who might, every one of them for all I knew, be popping off needles every time they went to the head. Maybe it did more for them than algebra could.

I was sure that the first time Sonny had ever had horse, he couldn't have been much older than these boys were now. These boys, now, were living as we'd been living then, they were growing up with a rush and their heads bumped abruptly against the low ceiling of their actual possibilities. They were filled with rage. All they really knew were two darknesses, the darkness of their lives, which was now closing in on them, and the darkness of the movies, which had blinded them to that other darkness, and in which they now, vindictively, dreamed, at once more together than they were at any other time, and more alone.

When the last bell rang, the last class ended, I let out my breath. It seemed I'd been holding it for all that time. My clothes were set—I may have looked as though I'd been sitting in a steam bath, all dressed up, all afternoon. I sat alone in the classroom a long time. I listened to the boys outside, downstairs, shouting and cursing and laughing. Their laughter struck me for perhaps the first time. It was not the joyous laughter which —God knows why—one associates with children. It was mocking and insular, its intent was to denigrate. It was disenchanted, and in this, also, lay the authority of their curses. Perhaps I was listening to them because I was thinking about my brother and in them I heard my brother. And myself.

One boy was whistling a tune, at once very complicated and very simple, it seemed to be pouring out of him as though he were a bird, and it sounded very cool and moving through all that harsh, bright air, only just holding its own through all those other sounds.

I stood and walked over to the window and looked down into the courtyard. It was the beginning of the spring, and the sap was rising in the boys. A teacher passed through them every now and again, quickly, as though he or she couldn't wait to get out of that courtyard, to get those boys out of their sight and off their minds. I started collecting my stuff. I thought I'd better get home and talk to Isabel.

The courtyard was almost deserted by the time I got downstairs. I saw this boy standing in the shadow of a doorway, looking just like Sonny. I almost called his name. Then I saw that it wasn't Sonny, but somebody we used to know, a boy from around our block. He'd been Sonny's friend. He'd never been mine, having been too young for me, and, anyway, I'd never liked him. And now, even though he was a grown-up man, he still hung around that block, still spent hours on the street corner, was always high and raggy. I used to run into him from time to time, and he'd often work around to asking me for a quarter or fifty cents. He always had some real good excuse, too, and I always gave it to him, I don't know why.

But now, abruptly, I hated him. I couldn't stand the way he looked at me, partly like a dog, partly like a cunning child. I wanted to ask him what the hell he was doing in the school courtyard.

He sort of shuffled over to me, and he said, "I see you got the papers. So you already know about it."

"You mean about Sonny? Yes, I already know about it. How come they didn't get you?"

He grinned. It made him repulsive and it also brought to mind what he'd looked like as a kid. "I wasn't there. I stay away from them people."

"Good for you." I offered him a cigarette and I watched him through the smoke. "You come all the way down here just to tell me about Sonny?"

"That's right." He was sort of shaking his head and his eyes looked strange, as though they were about to cross. The bright sun deadened his damp dark brown skin and it made his eyes look yellow and showed up the dirt in his conked hair. He smelled funky. I moved a little away from him and I said, "Well, thanks. But I already know about it and I got to get home."

"I'll walk you a little ways," he said. We started walking. There were a couple of kids still loitering in the courtyard and one of them said good night to me and looked strangely at the boy beside me.

"What're you going to do?" he asked me. "I mean, about Sonny?"

"Look. I haven't seen Sonny for over a year, I'm not sure I'm going to do anything. Anyway, what the hell can I do?"

"That's right," he said quickly, "ain't nothing you can do. Can't much help old Sonny no more, I guess."

It was what I was thinking and so it seemed to me he had no right to say it.

"I'm surprised at Sonny, though," he went on—he had a funny way of talking, he looked straight ahead as though he were talking to himself— "I thought Sonny was a smart boy, I thought he was too smart to get hung."

"I guess he thought so, too," I said sharply, "and that's how he got hung. And how about you? You're pretty goddamn smart, I bet."

Then he looked directly at me, just for a minute. "I ain't smart," he said. "If I was smart, I'd have reached for a pistol a long time ago."

"Look. Don't tell me your sad story, if it was up to me, I'd give you one." Then I felt guilty—guilty probably, for never having supposed that the poor bastard had a story of his own, much less a sad one, and I asked, quickly, "What's going to happen to him now?"

He didn't answer this. He was off by himself someplace. "Funny thing," he said, and from his tone we might have been discussing the quickest way to get to Brooklyn, "when I saw the papers this morning, the first thing I asked myself was if I had anything to do with it. I felt sort of responsible."

I began to listen more carefully. The subway station was on the corner, just before us, and I stopped. He stopped, too. We were in front of a bar and he ducked slightly, peering in, but whoever he was looking for didn't seem to be there. The juke box was blasting away with something black and bouncy, and I half watched the barmaid as she danced her way from the juke box to her place behind the bar. And I watched her face as she laughingly responded to something someone said to her, still keeping time to the music. When she smiled one saw the little girl, one sensed the doomed, still-struggling woman beneath the battered face of the semi-whore.

"I never *give* Sonny nothing," the boy said finally, "but a long time ago I come to school high and Sonny asked me how it felt." He paused, I couldn't bear to watch him, I watched the barmaid, and I listened to the music which seemed to be causing the pavement to shake. "I told him it felt great." The music stopped, the barmaid paused and watched the juke box until the music began again. "It did."

All this was carrying me someplace I didn't want to go. I certainly didn't want to know how it felt. It filled everything, the people, the houses, the music, the dark, quicksilver barmaid, with menace; and this menace was their reality.

"What's going to happen to him now?" I asked again.

"They'll send him away someplace and they'll try to cure him." He shook his head. "Maybe he'll even think he's kicked the habit. Then they'll turn him loose"—He gestured, throwing his cigarette into the gutter. "That's all."

"What do you mean, that's *all?*"

But I knew what he meant.

"I *mean,* that's *all.*" He turned his head and looked at me, pulling down the corners of his mouth. "Don't you know what I mean?" he asked softly.

"How the hell *would* I know what you mean?" I almost whispered it, I don't know why.

"That's right," he said to the air, "how would *he* know what I mean?" He turned toward me again, patient and calm, and yet I somehow felt him shaking, shaking as though he were going to fall apart. I felt that ice in my guts again, the dread I'd felt all afternoon; and again I watched the barmaid, moving about the bar, washing glasses, and singing. "Listen. They'll let him out and then it'll just start over again. That's what I mean."

"You mean—they'll let him out. And then he'll just start working his way back in again. You mean he'll never kick the habit. Is that what you mean?"

"That's right," he said, cheerfully. "*You* see what I mean."

"Tell me," I said at last, "why does he want to die? He must want to die, he's killing himself, why does he want to die?"

He looked at me in surprise. He licked his lips. "He don't want to die. He wants to live. Don't nobody want to die, ever."

Then I wanted to ask him—too many things. He could not have

answered, or if he had, I could not have borne the answers. I started walking. "Well, I guess it's none of my business."

"It's going to be rough on old Sonny," he said. We reached the subway station. "This is your station?" he asked. I nodded. I took one step down. "Damn!" he said, suddenly. I looked up at him. He grinned again. "Damn if I didn't leave all my money home. You ain't got a dollar on you, have you? Just for a couple of days, is all."

All at once something inside gave and threatened to come pouring out of me. I didn't hate him any more. I felt that in another moment I'd start crying like a child.

"Sure," I said. "Don't sweat." I looked in my wallet and didn't have a dollar, I only had a five. "Here," I said. "That hold you?"

He didn't look at it—he didn't want to look at it. A terrible, closed look came over his face, as though he were keeping the number on the bill a secret from him and me. "Thanks," he said, and now he was dying to see me go. "Don't worry about Sonny. Maybe I'll write him or something."

"Sure," I said. "You do that. So long."

"Be seeing you," he said. I went on down the steps.

And I didn't write Sonny or send him anything for a long time. When I finally did, it was just after my little girl died, he wrote me back a letter which made me feel like a bastard.

Here's what he said:

Dear brother,

You don't know how much I needed to hear from you. I wanted to write you many a time but I dug how much I must have hurt you and so I didn't write. But now I feel like a man who's been trying to climb up out of some deep, real deep and funky hole and just saw the sun up there, outside. I got to get outside.

I can't tell you much about how I got here. I mean I don't know how to tell you. I guess I was afraid of something or I was trying to escape from something and you know I have never been very strong in the head (smile). I'm glad Mama and Daddy are dead and can't see what's happened to their son and I swear if I'd known what I was doing I would never have hurt you so, you and a lot of other fine people who were nice to me and who believed in me.

I don't want you to think it had anything to do with me being a musician. It's more than that. Or maybe less than that. I can't get anything straight in my head down here and I try not to think about what's going to happen to me when I get outside again. Sometime I think I'm going to flip and *never* get outside and sometime I think I'll come straight back. I tell you one thing, though, I'd rather blow my brains out than go through this again. But that's what they all say, so they tell me. If I tell you when I'm coming to New York and if you could meet me, I sure would appreciate it. Give my love to Isabel and the kids and I was sure sorry to hear about little Gracie. I wish I could be like Mama and say the Lord's will be done, but I don't know it seems to me that trouble is the one thing that never does get stopped and I don't know what good it does to blame it on the Lord. But maybe it does some good if you believe it.

Your brother,
SONNY

Then I kept in constant touch with him and I sent him whatever I could and I went to meet him when he came back to New York. When I saw him, many things I thought I had forgotten came flooding back to me. This was because I had begun, finally, to wonder about Sonny, about the life that Sonny lived inside. This life, whatever it was, had made him older and thinner and it had deepened the distant stillness in which he had always moved. He looked very unlike my baby brother. Yet, when he smiled, when we shook hands, the baby brother I'd never known looked out from the depths of his private life, like an animal waiting to be coaxed into the light.

"How you been keeping?" he asked me.

"All right. And you?"

"Just fine." He was smiling all over his face. "It's good to see you again."

"It's good to see you."

The seven years' difference in our ages lay between us like a chasm: I wondered if these years would ever operate between us as a bridge. I was remembering, and it made it hard to catch my breath, that I had been there when he was born; and I had heard the first words he had ever spoken. When he started to walk, he walked from our mother straight to me. I caught him just before he fell when he took the first steps he ever took in this world.

"How's Isabel?"

"Just fine. She's dying to see you."

"And the boys?"

"They're fine, too. They're anxious to see their uncle."

"Oh, come on. You know they don't remember me."

"Are you kidding? Of course they remember you."

He grinned again. We got into a taxi. We had a lot to say to each other, far too much to know how to begin.

As the taxi began to move, I asked, "You still want to go to India?"

He laughed. "You still remember that. Hell, no. This place is Indian enough for me."

"It used to belong to them," I said.

And he laughed again. "They damn sure knew what they were doing when they got rid of it."

Years ago, when he was around fourteen, he'd been all hipped on the idea of going to India. He read books about people sitting on rocks, naked, in all kinds of weather, but mostly bad, naturally, and walking barefoot through hot coals and arriving at wisdom. I used to say that it sounded to me as though they were getting away from wisdom as fast as they could. I think he sort of looked down on me for that.

"Do you mind," he asked, "if we have the driver drive alongside the park? On the west side—I haven't seen the city in so long."

"Of course not," I said. I was afraid that I might sound as though I were humoring him, but I hoped he wouldn't take it that way.

So we drove along, between the green of the park and the stony, lifeless elegance of hotels and apartment buildings, toward the vivid, killing streets of our childhood. These streets hadn't changed, though housing projects jutted up out of them now like rocks in the middle of a boiling sea. Most of the houses in which we had grown up had vanished, as had the stores from which we had stolen, the basements in which we had first tried sex, the rooftops from which we had hurled tin cans and bricks. But houses exactly like the houses of our past yet dominated the landscape, boys exactly like the boys we once had been found themselves smothering in these houses, came down into the streets for light and air and found themselves encircled by disaster. Some escaped the trap, most didn't. Those who got out always left something of themselves behind, as some animals amputate a leg and leave it in the trap. It might be said, perhaps, that I had escaped, after all, I was a schoolteacher; or that Sonny had, he hadn't lived in Harlem for years. Yet, as the cab moved uptown through streets which seemed, with a rush, to darken with dark people, and as I covertly studied Sonny's face, it came to me that what we both were seeking through our separate cab windows was that part of ourselves which had been left behind. It's always at the hour of trouble and confrontation that the missing member aches.

We hit 110th Street and started rolling up Lenox Avenue. And I'd known this avenue all my life, but it seemed to me again, as it had seemed on the day I'd first heard about Sonny's trouble, filled with a hidden menace which was its very breath of life.

"We almost there," said Sonny.

"Almost." We were both too nervous to say anything more.

We live in a housing project. It hasn't been up long. A few days after it was up it seemed uninhabitably new, now, of course, it's already run-down. It looked like a parody of the good, clean, faceless life—God knows the people who live in it do their best to make it a parody. The beat-looking grass lying around isn't enough to make their lives green, the hedges will never hold out the streets, and they know it. The big windows fool no one, they aren't big enough to make space out of no space. They don't bother with the windows, they watch the TV screen instead. The playground is most popular with the children who don't play at jacks, or skip rope, or roller skate, or swing, and they can be found in it after dark. We moved in partly because it's not too far from where I teach, and partly for the kids; but it's really just like the houses in which Sonny and I grew up. The same things happen, they'll have the same things to remember. The moment Sonny and I started into the house I had the feeling that I was simply bringing him back into the danger he had almost died trying to escape.

Sonny has never been talkative. So I don't know why I was sure he'd be dying to talk to me when supper was over the first night. Everything went fine, the oldest boy remembered him, and the youngest boy liked him, and Sonny had remembered to bring something for each of them; and Isabel, who is really much nicer than I am, more open and giving, had gone to a lot of trouble about dinner and was genuinely glad to see him. And she'd always been able to tease Sonny in a way that I haven't. It was nice to see her face so vivid again and to hear her laugh and watch her make Sonny laugh. She wasn't, or, anyway, she didn't seem to be, at all uneasy or embarrassed. She chatted as though there were no subject which had to be avoided and she got Sonny past his first, faint stiffness. And thank God she was there, for I was filled with that icy dread again. Everything I did seemed awkward to me, and everything I said sounded freighted with hidden meaning. I was trying to remember everything I'd heard about dope addiction and I couldn't help watching Sonny for signs. I wasn't doing it out of malice. I was trying to find out something about my brother. I was dying to hear him tell me he was safe.

"Safe!" my father grunted, whenever Mama suggested trying to move to a neighborhood which might be safer for children. "Safe, hell! Ain't no place safe for kids, nor nobody."

He always went on like this, but he wasn't, ever, really as bad as he sounded, not even on weekends, when he got drunk. As a matter of fact, he was always on the lookout for "something a little better," but he died before he found it. He died suddenly, during a drunken weekend in the middle of the war, when Sonny was fifteen. He and Sonny hadn't ever got on too well. And this was partly because Sonny was the apple of his father's eye. It was because he loved Sonny so much and was frightened for him, that he was always fighting with him. It doesn't do any good to fight with Sonny. Sonny just moves back, inside himself, where he can't be reached. But the principal reason that they never hit it off is that they were so much alike. Daddy was big and rough and loud-talking, just the opposite of Sonny, but they both had—that same privacy.

Mama tried to tell me something about this, just after Daddy died. I was home on leave from the army.

This was the last time I ever saw my mother alive. Just the same, this picture gets all mixed up in my mind with pictures I had of her when she was younger. The way I always see her is the way she used to be on a Sunday afternoon, say, when the old folks were talking after the big

Sunday dinner. I always see her wearing pale blue. She'd be sitting on the sofa. And my father would be sitting in the easy chair, not far from her. And the living room would be full of church folks and relatives. There they sit, in chairs all around the living room, and the night is creeping up outside, but nobody knows it yet. You can see the darkness growing against the windowpanes and you hear the street noises every now and again, or maybe the jangling beat of a tambourine from one of the churches close by, but it's real quiet in the room. For a moment nobody's talking, but every face looks darkening, like the sky outside. And my mother rocks a little from the waist, and my father's eyes are closed. Everyone is looking at something a child can't see. For a minute they've forgotten the children. Maybe a kid is lying on the rug, half asleep. Maybe somebody's got a kid in his lap and is absent-mindedly stroking the kid's head. Maybe there's a kid, quiet and big-eyed, curled up in a big chair in the corner. The silence, the darkness coming, and the darkness in the faces frighten the child obscurely. He hopes that the hand which strokes his forehead will never stop—will never die. He hopes that there will never come a time when the old folks won't be sitting around the living room, talking about where they've come from, and what they've seen, and what's happened to them and their kinfolk.

But something deep and watchful in the child knows that this is bound to end, is already ending. In a moment someone will get up and turn on the light. Then the old folks will remember the children and they won't talk any more that day. And when light fills the room, the child is filled with darkness. He knows that every time this happens he's moved just a little closer to that darkness outside. The darkness outside is what the old folks have been talking about. It's what they've come from. It's what they endure. The child knows that they won't talk any more because if he knows too much about what's happened to *them*, he'll know too much too soon, about what's going to happen to *him*.

The last time I talked to my mother, I remember I was restless. I wanted to get out and see Isabel. We weren't married then and we had a lot to straighten out between us.

There Mama sat, in black, by the window. She was humming an old church song, *Lord, you brought me from a long ways off*. Sonny was out somewhere. Mama kept watching the streets.

"I don't know," she said, "if I'll ever see you again, after you go off from here. But I hope you'll remember the things I tried to teach you."

"Don't talk like that," I said, and smiled. "You'll be here a long time yet."

She smiled, too, but she said nothing. She was quiet for a long time. And I said, "Mama, don't you worry about nothing. I'll be writing all the time, and you be getting the checks. . . ."

"I want to talk to you about your brother," she said, suddenly. "If anything happens to me, he ain't going to have nobody to look out for him."

"Mama," I said, "ain't nothing going to happen to you *or* Sonny. Sonny's all right. He's a good boy and he's got good sense."

"It ain't a question of his being a good boy," Mama said, "nor of his having good sense. It ain't only the bad ones, nor yet the dumb ones that gets sucked under." She stopped, looking at me. "Your Daddy once had a brother," she said, and smiled in a way that made me feel she was in pain. "You didn't never know that, did you?"

"No," I said. "I never knew that," and I watched her face.

"Oh, yes," she said, "your Daddy had a brother." She looked out of the window again. "I know you never saw your Daddy cry. But *I* did—many a time, through all these years."

I asked her, "What happened to his brother? How come nobody's ever talked about him?"

This was the first time I ever saw my mother look old.

"His brother got killed," she said, "when he was just a little younger than you are now. I knew him. He was a fine boy. He was maybe a little full of the devil, but he didn't mean nobody no harm."

Then she stopped, and the room was silent, exactly as it had sometimes been on those Sunday afternoons. Mama kept looking out into the streets.

"He used to have a job in the mill," she said, "and, like all young folks, he just liked to perform on Saturday nights. Saturday nights, him and your father would drift around to different places, go to dances and things like that, or just sit around with people they knew, and your father's brother would sing, he had a fine voice, and play along with himself on his guitar. Well, this particular Saturday night, him and your father was coming home from some place, and they were both a little drunk and there was a moon that night, it was bright like day. Your father's brother was feeling kind of good, and he was whistling to himself, and he had his guitar slung over his shoulder. They was coming down a hill, and beneath them was a road that turned off from the highway. Well, your father's brother, being always kind of frisky, decided to run down this hill, and he did, with that guitar banging and clanging behind him, and he ran across the road, and he was making water behind a tree. And your father was sort of amused at him and he was still coming down the hill, kind of slow. Then he heard a car motor and that same minute his brother stepped from behind the tree, into the road, in the moonlight. And he started to cross the road. And your father started to run down the hill, he says he don't know why. This car was full of white men. They was all drunk, and when they seen your father's brother they let out a great whoop and holler and they aimed the car straight at him. They was having fun, they just wanted to scare him, the way they do sometimes, you know. But they was drunk. And I guess the boy, being drunk, too, and scared, kind of lost his head. By the time he jumped it was too late. Your father says he heard his brother scream when the car rolled over him, and he heard the wood of that guitar when it give, and he heard them strings go flying, and he heard them white men shouting, and the car kept on a-going and it ain't stopped till this day. And, time your father got down the hill, his brother weren't nothing but blood and pulp."

Tears were gleaming on my mother's face. There wasn't anything I could say.

"He never mentioned it," she said, "because I never let him mention it before you children. Your Daddy was like a crazy man that night and for many a night thereafter. He says he never in his life seen anything as dark as that road after the lights of that car had gone away. Weren't nothing, weren't nobody on that road, just your Daddy and his brother and that busted guitar. Oh, yes. Your Daddy never did really get right again. Till the day he died he weren't sure but that every white man he saw was the man that killed his brother."

She stopped and took out her handkerchief and dried her eyes and looked at me.

"I ain't telling you all this," she said, "to make you scared or bitter or to make you hate nobody. I'm telling you this because you got a brother. And the world ain't changed."

I guess I didn't want to believe this. I guess she saw this in my face. She turned away from me, toward the window again, searching those streets.

"But I praise my Redeemer," she said at last, "that he called your Daddy home before me. I ain't saying it to throw no flowers at myself, but, I declare, it keeps me from feeling too cast down to know I helped your father get safely through this world. Your father always acted like he was the roughest, strongest man on earth. And everybody took him to be like that. But if he hadn't had *me* there—to see his tears!"

She was crying again. Still, I couldn't move. I said, "Lord, Lord, Mama, I didn't know it was like that."

"Oh, honey," she said, "there's a lot that you don't know. But you are going to find it out." She stood up from the window and came over to me. "You got to hold on to your brother," she said, "and don't let him fall, no matter what it looks like is happening to him and no matter how evil you gets with him. You going to be evil with him many a time. But don't you forget what I told you, you hear?"

"I won't forget," I said. "Don't you worry, I won't forget. I won't let nothing happen to Sonny."

My mother smiled as though she were amused at something she saw in my face. Then, "You may not be able to stop nothing from happening. But you got to let him know you's *there*."

Two days later I was married, and then I was gone. And I had a lot of things on my mind and I pretty well forgot my promise to Mama until I got shipped home on a special furlough for her funeral.

And, after the funeral, with just Sonny and me alone in the empty kitchen, I tried to find out something about him.

"What do you want to do?" I asked him.

"I'm going to be a musician," he said.

For he had graduated, in the time I had been away, from dancing to the juke box to finding out who was playing what, and what they were doing with it, and he had bought himself a set of drums.

"You mean, you want to be a drummer?" I somehow had the feeling that being a drummer might be all right for other people but not for my brother Sonny.

"I don't think," he said, looking at me very gravely, "that I'll ever be a good drummer. But I think I can play a piano."

I frowned. I'd never played the role of the older brother quite so seriously before, had scarcely ever, in fact, asked Sonny a damn thing. I sensed myself in the presence of something I didn't really know how to handle, didn't understand. So I made my frown a little deeper as I asked: "What kind of musician do you want to be?"

He grinned. "How many kinds do you think there are?"

"Be serious," I said.

He laughed, throwing his head back, and then looked at me. "I am serious."

"Well, then, for Christ's sake, stop kidding around and answer a serious question. I mean, do you want to be a concert pianist, you want to play classical music and all that, or—or, what?" Long before I finished he was laughing again. "For Christ's sake, Sonny!"

He sobered, but with difficulty. "I'm sorry. But you sound so—scared!" And he was off again.

"Well, you may think it's funny now, baby, but it's not going to be so funny when you have to make your living at it, let me tell you that." I was furious because I knew he was laughing at me and I didn't know why.

"No," he said, very sober now, and afraid, perhaps, that he'd hurt me, "I don't want to be a classical pianist. That isn't what interests me. I mean"—he paused, looking hard at me, as though his eyes would help me to understand, and then gestured helplessly, as though perhaps his hand would help—"I mean, I'll have a lot of studying to do, and I'll have to study everything, but, I mean, I want to play with—jazz musicians." He stopped. "I want to play jazz," he said.

Well, the word had never before sounded as heavy, as real, as it sounded that afternoon in Sonny's mouth. I just looked at him and I was probably frowning a real frown by this time. I simply couldn't see why on earth he'd want to spend his time hanging around night clubs, clowning around on bandstands, while people pushed each other around a dance floor. It seemed—beneath him, somehow. I had never thought about it before, had never been forced to, but I suppose I had always put jazz musicians in a class with what Daddy called "good-time people."

"Are you *serious?*"

"Hell, *yes*, I'm serious."

He looked more helpless than ever, and annoyed, and deeply hurt.

I suggested, helpfully: "You mean—like Louis Armstrong?"

His face closed as though I'd struck him. "No. I'm not talking about none of that old-time, down home crap."

"Well, look, Sonny, I'm sorry, don't get mad. I just don't altogether get it, that's all. Name somebody—you know, a jazz musician you admire."

"Bird."

"Who?"

"Bird! Charlie Parker! Don't they teach you nothing in the goddamn army?"

I lit a cigarette. I was surprised and then a little amused to discover that I was trembling. "I've been out of touch," I said. "You'll have to be patient with me. Now. Who's this Parker character?"

"He's just one of the greatest jazz musicians alive," said Sonny, sullenly, his hands in his pockets, his back to me. "Maybe *the* greatest," he added bitterly, "that's probably why *you* never heard of him."

"All right," I said, "I'm ignorant. I'm sorry. I'll go out and buy all the cat's records right away, all right?"

"It don't," said Sonny, with dignity, "make any difference to me. I don't care what you listen to. Don't do me no favors."

I was beginning to realize that I'd never seen him so upset before. With another part of my mind I was thinking that this would probably turn out to be one of those things kids go through and that I shouldn't make it seem important by pushing it too hard. Still, I didn't think it would do any harm to ask: "Doesn't all this take a lot of time? Can you make a living at it?"

He turned back to me and half leaned, half sat, on the kitchen table. "Everything takes time," he said, "and—well, yes, sure, I can make a living at it. But what I don't seem to be able to make you understand is that it's the only thing I want to do."

"Well, Sonny," I said gently, "you know people can't always do exactly what they want to do—"

"*No*, I don't know that," said Sonny, surprising me. "I think people *ought* to do what they want to do, what else are they alive for?"

"You getting to be a big boy," I said desperately, "it's time you started thinking about your future."

"I'm thinking about my future," said Sonny, grimly. "I think about it all the time."

I gave up. I decided, if he didn't change his mind, that we could always talk about it later. "In the meantime," I said, "you got to finish school."

We had already decided that he'd have to move in with Isabel and her folks. I knew this wasn't the ideal arrangement because Isabel's folks are inclined to be dicty and they hadn't especially wanted Isabel to marry me. But I didn't know what else to do. "And we have to get you fixed up at Isabel's."

There was a long silence. He moved from the kitchen table to the window. "That's a terrible idea. You know it yourself."

"Do you have a *better* idea?"

He just walked up and down the kitchen for a minute. He was as tall as I was. He had started to shave. I suddenly had the feeling that I didn't know him at all.

He stopped at the kitchen table and picked up my cigarettes. Looking at me with a kind of mocking, amused defiance, he put one between his lips. "You mind?"

"You smoking already?"

He lit the cigarette and nodded, watching me through the smoke. "I just wanted to see if I'd have the courage to smoke in front of you." He grinned and blew a great cloud of smoke to the ceiling. "It was easy." He looked at my face. "Come on, now. I bet you was smoking at my age, tell the truth."

I didn't say anything but the truth was on my face, and he laughed. But now there was something very strained in his laugh. "Sure. And I bet that ain't all you was doing."

He was frightening me a little. "Cut the crap," I said. "We already decided that you was going to go and live at Isabel's. Now what's got into you all of a sudden?"

"*You* decided it," he pointed out. "*I* didn't decide nothing." He stopped in front of me, leaning against the stove, arms loosely folded. "Look, brother. I don't want to stay in Harlem no more, I really don't." He was very earnest. He looked at me, then over toward the kitchen window. There was something in his eyes I'd never seen before, some thoughtfulness, some worry all his own. He rubbed the muscle of one arm. "It's time I was getting out of here."

"Where do you want to *go*, Sonny?"

"I want to join the army. Or the navy, I don't care. If I say I'm old enough, they'll believe me."

Then I got mad. It was because I was so scared. "You must be crazy. You goddamn fool, what the hell do you want to go and join the *army* for?"

"I just told you. To get out of Harlem."

"Sonny, you haven't even finished *school*. And if you really want to be a musician, how do you expect to study if you're in the *army*."

He looked at me, trapped, and in anguish. "There's ways. I might be able to work out some kind of deal. Anyway, I'll have the G.I. Bill when I come out."

"*If* you come out." We stared at each other. "Sonny, please. Be reasonable. I know the setup is far from perfect. But we got to do the best we can."

"I ain't learning nothing in school," he said. "Even when I go." He turned away from me and opened the window and threw his cigarette out into the narrow alley. I watched his back. "At least, I ain't learning nothing you'd want me to learn." He slammed the window so hard I thought the glass would fly out, and turned back to me. "And I'm sick of the stink of these garbage cans!"

"Sonny," I said, "I know how you feel. But if you don't finish school now, you're going to be sorry later that you didn't." I grabbed him by the shoulders. "And you only got another year. It ain't so bad. And I'll come back and I swear I'll help you do *whatever* you want to do. Just try to put up with it till I come back. Will you please do that? For me?"

He didn't answer and he wouldn't look at me.

"Sonny. You hear me?"

He pulled away. "I hear you. But you never hear anything *I* say."

I didn't know what to say to that. He looked out of the window and then back at me. "OK," he said, and sighed. "I'll try."

Then I said, trying to cheer him up a little, "They got a piano at Isabel's. You can practice on it."

And as a matter of fact, it did cheer him up for a minute. "That's right," he said to himself. "I forgot that." His face relaxed a little. But the worry, the thoughtfulness, played on it still, the way shadows play on a face which is staring into the fire.

But I thought I'd never hear the end of that piano. At first, Isabel would write me, saying how nice it was that Sonny was so serious about his music and how, as soon as he came in from school, or wherever he had been when he was supposed to be at school, he went straight to that piano and stayed there until suppertime. And, after supper, he went back to that piano and stayed there until everybody went to bed. He was at that piano all day Saturday and all day Sunday. Then he bought a record player and started playing records. He'd play one record over and over again, all day long sometimes, and he'd improvise along with it on the piano. Or he'd play one section of the record, one chord, one change, one progression, then he'd do it on the piano. Then back to the record. Then back to the piano.

Well, I really don't know how they stood it. Isabel finally confessed that it wasn't like living with a person at all, it was like living with sound. And the sound didn't make any sense to her, didn't make any sense to any of them—naturally. They began, in a way, to be afflicted by this presence that was living in their home. It was as though Sonny were some sort of god, or monster. He moved in an atmosphere which wasn't like theirs at all. They fed him and he ate, he washed himself, he walked in and out of their door; he certainly wasn't nasty or unpleasant or rude, Sonny isn't any of those things; but it was as though he were all wrapped up in some cloud, some fire, some vision all his own; and there wasn't any way to reach him.

At the same time, he wasn't really a man yet, he was still a child, and they had to watch out for him in all kinds of ways. They certainly couldn't throw him out. Neither did they dare to make a great scene about that piano because even they dimly sensed, as I sensed, from so many thousands of miles away, that Sonny was at that piano playing for his life.

But he hadn't been going to school. One day a letter came from the school board, and Isabel's mother got it—there had, apparently, been other letters but Sonny had torn them up. This day, when Sonny came in, Isabel's mother showed him the letter and asked where he'd been spending his time. And she finally got it out of him that he'd been down in Greenwich Village, with musicians and other characters, in a white girl's apartment. And this scared her and she started to scream at him, and what came up, once she began—though she denies it to this day—was what sacrifices they were making to give Sonny a decent home and how little he appreciated it.

Sonny didn't play the piano that day. By evening, Isabel's mother had calmed down but then there was the old man to deal with, and Isabel herself. Isabel says she did her best to be calm but she broke down and started crying. She says she just watched Sonny's face. She could tell, by watching him, what was happening with him. And what was happening was that they penetrated his cloud, they had reached him. Even if their fingers had been a thousand times more gentle than human fingers ever are, he could hardly help feeling that they had stripped him naked and were spitting on that nakedness. For he also had to see that his presence, that music, which was life or death to him, had been torture for them and that they had endured it, not at all for his sake, but only for mine. And Sonny couldn't take that. He can take it a little better today than he could then but he's still not very good at it and, frankly, I don't know anybody who is.

The silence of the next few days must have been louder than the sound of all the music ever played since time began. One morning, before she went to work, Isabel was in his room for something and she suddenly realized that all of his records were gone. And she knew for certain that he was gone. And he was. He went as far as the navy would carry him. He finally sent me a postcard from someplace in Greece, and that was the first I knew that Sonny was still alive. I didn't see him any more until we were both back in New York and the war had long been over.

He was a man by then, of course, but I wasn't willing to see it. He came by the house from time to time, but we fought almost every time we met. I didn't like the way he carried himself, loose and dreamlike all the time, and I didn't like his friends, and his music seemed to be merely an excuse for the life he led. It sounded just that weird and disordered.

Then we had a fight, a pretty awful fight, and I didn't see him for months. By and by I looked him up, where he was living, in a furnished room in the Village, and I tried to make it up. But there were lots of other people in the room, and Sonny just lay on his bed, and he wouldn't come downstairs with me, and he treated these other people as though they were his family and I weren't. So I got mad and then he got mad, and then I told him that he might just as well be dead as live the way he was living. Then he stood up and he told me not to worry about him any more in life, that he *was* dead as far as I was concerned. Then he pushed me to the door, and the other people looked on as though nothing were happening, and he slammed the door behind me. I stood in the hallway, staring at the door. I heard somebody laugh in the room and then the tears came to my eyes. I started down the steps, whistling to keep from crying, I kept whistling to myself, *You going to need me, baby, one of these cold, rainy days.*

I read about Sonny's trouble in the spring. Little Grace died in the fall. She was a beautiful little girl. But she only lived a little over two years. She died of polio and she suffered. She had a slight fever for a couple of days, but it didn't seem like anything and we just kept her in bed. And we would certainly have called the doctor, but the fever dropped, she seemed to be all right. So we thought it had just been a cold. Then, one day, she was up, playing, Isabel was in the kitchen fixing lunch for the two boys when they'd come in from school, and she heard Grace fall down in the living room. When you have a lot of children you don't always start running when one of them falls, unless they start screaming or something. And, this time, Grace was quiet. Yet, Isabel says that when she heard that *thump* and then that silence, something happened in her to make her afraid. And she ran to the living room and there was little Grace on the floor, all twisted up, and the reason she hadn't screamed was that she couldn't get her breath. And when she did scream, it was the worst sound, Isabel says, that she'd ever heard in all her life, and she still hears it sometimes in her dreams. Isabel will sometimes wake me up with a low, moaning, strangled sound, and I have to be quick to awaken her and hold her to me and where Isabel is weeping against me seems a mortal wound.

I think I may have written Sonny the very day that little Grace was buried. I was sitting in the living room in the dark, by myself, and I suddenly thought of Sonny. My trouble made his real.

One Saturday afternoon, when Sonny had been living with us, or, anyway, been in our house, for nearly two weeks, I found myself wandering aimlessly about the living room, drinking from a can of beer, and trying to work up the courage to search Sonny's room. He was out, he was usually out whenever I was home, and Isabel had taken the children to see their grandparents. Suddenly I was standing still in front of the living-room window, watching Seventh Avenue. The idea of searching Sonny's room made me still. I scarcely dared to admit to myself what I'd be searching for. I didn't know what I'd do if I found it. Or if I didn't.

On the sidewalk across from me, near the entrance to a barbecue joint, some people were holding an old-fashioned revival meeting. The barbecue cook, wearing a dirty white apron, his conked hair reddish and metallic in the pale sun, and a cigarette between his lips, stood in the doorway, watching them. Kids and older people paused in their errands and stood there, along with some older men and a couple of very tough-looking women who watched everything that happened on the avenue, as though they owned it, or were maybe owned by it. Well, they were watching this, too. The revival was being carried on by three sisters in black, and a brother. All they had were their voices and their Bibles and a tambourine. The brother was testifying and while he testified two of the sisters stood together, seeming to say, Amen, and the third sister walked around with the tambourine outstretched and a couple of people dropped coins into it. Then the brother's testimony ended, and the sister who had been taking up the collection dumped the coins into her palm and transferred them to the pocket of her long black robe. Then she raised both hands, striking the tambourine against the air, and then against one hand, and she started to sing. And the two other sisters and the brother joined in.

It was strange, suddenly, to watch, though I had been seeing these street meetings all my life. So, of course, had everybody else down there. Yet, they paused and watched and listened and I stood still at the window. "'Tis the old ship of Zion," they sang, and the sister with the tambourine kept a steady, jangling beat, "it has rescued many a thousand!" Not a soul under the sound of their voices was hearing this song for the first time, not one of them had been rescued. Nor had they seen much in the way of rescue work being done around them. Neither did they especially believe in the holiness of the three sisters and the brother, they knew too much about them, knew where they lived, and how. The woman with the tambourine, whose voice dominated the air, whose face was bright with joy, was divided by very little from the woman who stood watching her, a cigarette between her heavy, chapped lips, her hair a cuckoo's nest, her face scarred and swollen from many beatings, and her black eyes glittering like coal. Perhaps they both knew this, which was why, when, as rarely, they addressed each other, they addressed each other as Sister. As the singing filled the air, the watching, listening faces underwent a change, the eyes focusing on something within; the music seemed to soothe a poison out of them; and time seemed, nearly, to fall away from the sullen, belligerent, battered faces, as though they were fleeing back to their first condition, while dreaming of their last. The barbecue cook half shook his head and smiled, and dropped his cigarette and disappeared into his joint. A man fumbled in his pockets for change and stood holding it in his hand impatiently, as though he had just remembered a pressing appointment further up the avenue. He looked furious. Then I saw Sonny, standing on the edge of the crowd. He was carrying a wide, flat notebook with a green cover, and it made him look, from where I was standing, almost like a schoolboy. The coppery sun brought out the copper in his skin, he was very faintly smiling, standing very still. Then the singing stopped, the tambourine turned into a collection plate again. The furious man dropped in his coins and vanished, so did a couple of the women, and Sonny dropped some change in the plate, looking directly at the woman with a little smile. He started across the avenue, toward the house. He has a slow, loping walk, something like the way Harlem hipsters walk, only he's imposed on this his own half-beat. I had never really noticed it before.

I stayed at the window, both relieved and apprehensive. As Sonny disappeared from my sight, they began singing again. And they were still singing when his key turned in the lock.

"Hey," he said.

"Hey, yourself. You want some beer?"

"No. Well, maybe." But he came up to the window and stood beside me, looking out. "What a warm voice," he said.

They were singing *If I could only hear my mother pray again!*

"Yes," I said, "and she can sure beat that tambourine."

"But what a terrible song," he said, and laughed. He dropped his notebook on the sofa and disappeared into the kitchen. "Where's Isabel and the kids?"

"I think they went to see their grandparents. You hungry?"

"No." He came back into the living room with his can of beer. "You want to come someplace with me tonight?"

I sensed, I don't know how, that I couldn't possibly say no. "Sure. Where?"

He sat down on the sofa and picked up his notebook and started leafing through it. "I'm going to sit in with some fellows in a joint in the Village."

"You mean, you're going to play, tonight?"

"That's right." He took a swallow of his beer and moved back to the window. He gave me a sidelong look. "If you can stand it."

"I'll try," I said.

He smiled to himself, and we both watched as the meeting across the way broke up. The three sisters and the brother, heads bowed, were singing *God be with you till we meet again.* The faces around them were very quiet. Then the song ended. The small crowd dispersed. We watched the three women and the lone man walk slowly up the avenue.

"When she was singing before," said Sonny, abruptly, "her voice reminded me for a minute of what heroin feels like sometimes—when it's in your veins. It makes you feel sort of warm and cool at the same time. And distant. And—and sure." He sipped his beer, very deliberately not looking at me. I watched his face. "It makes you feel—in control. Sometimes you've got to have that feeling."

"Do you?" I sat down slowly in the easy chair.

"Sometimes." He went to the sofa and picked up his notebook again. "Some people do."

"In order," I asked, "to play?" And my voice was very ugly, full of contempt and anger.

"Well"—he looked at me with great, troubled eyes, as though, in fact, he hoped his eyes would tell me things he could never otherwise say— "they *think* so. And *if* they think so—!"

"And what do *you* think?" I asked.

He sat on the sofa and put his can of beer on the floor. "I don't know," he said, and I couldn't be sure if he were answering my question or pursuing his thoughts. His face didn't tell me. "It's not so much to *play*. It's to *stand* it, to be able to make it at all. On any level." He frowned and smiled: "In order to keep from shaking to pieces."

"But these friends of yours," I said, "they seem to shake themselves to pieces pretty goddamn fast."

"Maybe." He played with the notebook. And something told me that I should curb my tongue, that Sonny was doing his best to talk, that I should listen. "But of course you only know the ones that've gone to pieces. Some don't—or at least they haven't *yet* and that's just about all *any* of us can say." He paused. "And then there are some who just live, really, in hell, and they know it and they see what's happening and they go right on. I don't know." He sighed, dropped the notebook, folded his arms. "Some guys, you can tell from the way they play, they on something *all* the time. And you can see that, well, it makes something real for them. But of course," he picked up his beer from the floor and sipped it and put the can down again, "they *want* to, too, you've got to see that. Even some of them that say they don't—*some*, not all."

"And what about you?" I asked—I couldn't help it. "What about you? Do *you* want to?"

He stood up and walked to the window and remained silent for a long time. Then he sighed. "Me," he said. Then: "While I was downstairs before, on my way here, listening to that woman sing, it struck me all of a sudden how much suffering she must have had to go through—to sing like that. It's *repulsive* to think you have to suffer that much."

I said: "But there's no way not to suffer—is there, Sonny?"

"I believe not," he said, and smiled, "but that's never stopped anyone from trying." He looked at me. "Has it?" I realized, with this mocking look, that there stood between us, forever, beyond the power of time or forgiveness, the fact that I had held silence—so long!—when he had needed human speech to help him. He turned back to the window. "No, there's no way not to suffer. But you try all kinds of ways to keep from drowning in it, to keep on top of it, and to make it seem—well, like *you*. Like you did something, all right, and now you're suffering for it. You know?" I said nothing. "Well you know," he said, impatiently, "why *do* people suffer?

Maybe it's better to do something to give it a reason, *any* reason."

"But we just agreed," I said, "that there's no way not to suffer. Isn't it better, then, just to—take it?"

"But nobody just takes it," Sonny cried, "that's what I'm telling you! *Everybody* tries not to. You're just hung up on the *way* some people try— it's not *your* way!"

The hair on my face began to itch, my face felt wet. "That's not true," I said, "that's not true. I don't give a damn what other people do, I don't even care how they suffer. I just care how *you* suffer." And he looked at me. "Please believe me," I said, "I don't want to see you—die—trying not to suffer."

"I won't," he said, flatly, "die trying not to suffer. At least, not any faster than anybody else."

"But there's no need," I said, trying to laugh, "is there, in killing yourself?"

I wanted to say more, but I couldn't. I wanted to talk about will power and how life could be—well, beautiful. I wanted to say that it was all within; but was it? Or, rather, wasn't that exactly the trouble? And I wanted to promise that I would never fail him again. But it would all have sounded—empty words and lies.

So I made the promise to myself and prayed that I would keep it.

"It's terrible sometimes, inside," he said, "that's what's the trouble. You walk these streets, black and funky and cold, and there's not really a living ass to talk to, and there's nothing shaking, and there's no way of getting it out—that storm inside. You can't talk it and you can't make love with it, and when you finally try to get with it and play it, you realize *nobody's* listening. So *you've* got to listen. You got to find a way to listen."

And then he walked away from the window and sat on the sofa again, as though all the wind had suddenly been knocked out of him. "Sometimes you'll do *anything* to play, even cut your mother's throat." He laughed and looked at me. "Or your brother's." Then he sobered. "Or your own." Then: "Don't worry. I'm all right now and I think I'll *be* all right. But I can't forget—where I've been. I don't mean just the physical place I've been, I mean where I've *been*. And *what* I've been."

"What have you been, Sonny?" I asked.

He smiled—but sat sideways on the sofa, his elbow resting on the back, his fingers playing with his mouth and chin, not looking at me. "I've been something I didn't recognize, didn't know I could be. Didn't know anybody could be." He stopped, looking inward, looking helplessly young, looking old. "I'm not talking about it now because I feel *guilty* or anything like that—maybe it would be better if I did, I don't know. Anyway, I can't really talk about it. Not to you, not to anybody." And now he turned and faced me. "Sometimes, you know, and it was actually when I was most out of the world, I felt that I was in it, that I was *with* it, really, and I could play or I didn't really have to *play*, it just came out of me, it was there. And I don't know how I played, thinking about it now, but I know I did awful things, those times, sometimes, to people. Or it wasn't that I *did* anything to them—it was that they weren't real." He picked up the beer can; it was empty; he rolled it between his palms: "And other times—well, I needed a fix, I needed to find a place to lean, I needed to clear a space to *listen*—and I couldn't find it, and I—went crazy, I did terrible things to *me*, I was terrible *for* me." He began pressing the beer can between his hands, I watched the metal begin to give. It glittered, as he played with it, like a knife, and I was afraid he would cut himself, but I said nothing. "Oh well. I can never tell you. I was all by myself at the bottom of something, stinking and sweating and crying and shaking, and I smelled it, you know? *My* stink, and I thought I'd die if I couldn't get away from it and yet, all the same, I knew that everything I was doing was just locking me in with it. And I didn't know," he paused, still flattening the beer can, "I didn't know, I still *don't* know, something kept telling me that maybe it was good to smell your own stink, but I didn't think *that* was what I'd been trying to do—and—who can stand it?" And he abruptly dropped the ruined beer can, looking at me with a small, still smile, and then rose, walking to the window as though it were the lodestone rock. I watched his face, he watched the avenue. "I couldn't tell you when Mama died—but the reason I wanted to leave Harlem so bad was to get away from drugs. And then, when I ran away, that's what I was running from—really. When I came back, nothing had changed, *I* hadn't changed, I was just—older." And he stopped, drumming with his fingers on the windowpane. The sun had vanished, soon darkness would fall. I watched his face. "It can come again," he said, almost as though speaking to himself. Then he turned to me. "It can come again," he repeated. "I just want you to know that."

"All right," I said at last. "So it can come again. All right."

He smiled, but the smile was sorrowful. "I had to try to tell you," he said.

"Yes," I said. "I understand that."

"You're my brother," he said, looking straight at me, and not smiling at all.

"Yes," I repeated, "yes. I understand that."

He turned back to the window, looking out. "All that hatred down there," he said, "all that hatred and misery and love. It's a wonder it doesn't blow the avenue apart."

We went to the only night club on a short, dark street, downtown. We squeezed through the narrow, chattering, jam-packed bar to the entrance of the big room, where the bandstand was. And we stood there for a moment, for the lights were very dim in this room and we couldn't see. Then, "Hello, boy," said a voice, and an enormous black man, much older than Sonny or myself, erupted out of all that atmospheric lighting and put an arm around Sonny's shoulder. "I been sitting right here," he said, "waiting for you."

He had a big voice, too, and heads in the darkness turned toward us.

Sonny grinned and pulled a little away, and said, "Creole, this is my brother. I told you about him."

Creole shook my hand. "I'm glad to meet you, son," he said, and it was clear that he was glad to meet me *there,* for Sonny's sake. And he smiled. "You got a real musician in *your* family," and he took his arm from Sonny's shoulder and slapped him, lightly, affectionately, with the back of his hand.

"Well. Now I've heard it all," said a voice behind us. This was another musician, and a friend of Sonny's, a coal-black, cheerful-looking man, built close to the ground. He immediately began confiding to me, at the top of his lungs, the most terrible things about Sonny, his teeth gleaming like a lighthouse and his laugh coming up out of him like the beginning of an earthquake. And it turned out that everyone at the bar knew Sonny, or almost everyone; some were musicians, working there, or nearby, or not working, some were simply hangers-on, and some were there to hear Sonny play. I was introduced to all of them and they were all very polite to me. Yet, it was clear that, for them, I was only Sonny's brother. Here, I was in Sonny's world. Or, rather: his kingdom. Here, it was not even a question that his veins bore royal blood.

They were going to play soon, and Creole installed me, by myself, at a table in a dark corner. Then I watched them, Creole, and the little black man, and Sonny, and the others, while they horsed around, standing just below the bandstand. The light from the bandstand spilled just a little short of them and, watching them laughing and gesturing and moving about, I had the feeling that they, nevertheless, were being most careful not to step into that circle of light too suddenly: that if they moved into the light too suddenly, without thinking, they would perish in flame. Then, while I watched, one of them, the small, black man, moved into the light and crossed the bandstand and started fooling around with his drums. Then—being funny and being, also, extremely ceremonious—Creole took Sonny by the arm and led him to the piano. A woman's voice called Sonny's name, and a few hands started clapping. And Sonny, also being funny and being ceremonious, and so touched, I think, that he could have cried, but neither hiding it nor showing it, riding it like a man, grinned, and put both hands to his heart and bowed from the waist.

Creole then went to the bass fiddle and a lean, very bright-skinned brown man jumped up on the bandstand and picked up his horn. So there they were, and the atmosphere on the bandstand and in the room began to change and tighten. Someone stepped up to the microphone and announced them. Then there were all kinds of murmurs. Some people at the bar shushed others. The waitress ran around, frantically getting in the last orders, guys and chicks got closer to each other, and the lights on the bandstand, on the quartet, turned to a kind of indigo. Then they all looked different there. Creole looked about him for the last time, as though he were making certain that all his chickens were in the coop, and then he—jumped and struck the fiddle. And there they were.

All I know about music is that not many people ever really hear it. And even then, on the rare occasions when something opens within, and the music enters, what we mainly hear, or hear corroborated, are personal, private, vanishing evocations. But the man who creates the music is hearing something else, is dealing with the roar rising from the void and imposing order on it as it hits the air. What is evoked in him, then, is of another order, more terrible because it has no words, and triumphant, too, for that same reason. And his triumph, when he triumphs, is ours. I just watched Sonny's face. His face was troubled, he was working hard, but he wasn't with it. And I had the feeling that, in a way, everyone on the bandstand was waiting for him, both waiting for him and pushing him along. But as I began to watch Creole, I realized that it was Creole who held them all back. He had them on a short rein. Up there, keeping the beat with his whole body, wailing on the fiddle, with his eyes half closed, he was listening to everything, but he was listening to Sonny. He was having a dialogue with Sonny. He wanted Sonny to leave the shore line and strike out for the deep water. He was Sonny's witness that deep water and drowning were not the same thing—he had been there, and he knew. And he wanted Sonny to know. He was waiting for Sonny to do the things on the keys which would let Creole know that Sonny was in the water.

And, while Creole listened, Sonny moved, deep within, exactly like someone in torment. I had never before thought of how awful the relationship must be between the musician and his instrument. He has to fill it, this instrument, with the breath of life, his own. He has to make it do what he wants it to do. And a piano is just a piano. It's made out of so much wood and wires and little hammers and big ones, and ivory. While there's only so much you can do with it, the only way to find this out is to try and make it do everything.

And Sonny hadn't been near a piano for over a year. And he wasn't on much better terms with his life, not the life that stretched before him now. He and the piano stammered, started one way, got scared, stopped; started another way, panicked, marked time, started again; then seemed to have found a direction, panicked again, got stuck. And the face I saw on Sonny I'd never seen before. Everything had been burned out of it, and, at the same time, things usually hidden were being burned in, by the fire and fury of the battle which was occurring in him up there.

Yet, watching Creole's face as they neared the end of the first set, I had the feeling that something had happened, something I hadn't heard. Then they finished, there was scattered applause, and then, without an instant's warning, Creole started into something else, it was almost sardonic, it was

Am I Blue. And, as though he commanded, Sonny began to play. Something began to happen. And Creole let out the reins. The dry, low, black man said something awful on the drums, Creole answered, and the drums talked back. Then the horn insisted, sweet and high, slightly detached perhaps, and Creole listened, commenting now and then, dry, and driving, beautiful and calm and old. Then they all came together again, and Sonny was part of the family again. I could tell this from his face. He seemed to have found, right there beneath his fingers, a damn brand-new piano. It seemed that he couldn't get over it. Then, for a while, just being happy with Sonny, they seemed to be agreeing with him that brand-new pianos certainly were a gas.

Then Creole stepped forward to remind them that what they were playing was the blues. He hit something in all of them, he hit something in me, myself, and the music tightened and deepened, apprehension began to beat the air. Creole began to tell us what the blues were all about. They were not about anything very new. He and his boys up there were keeping it new, at the risk of ruin, destruction, madness, and death, in order to find new ways to make us listen. For, while the tale of how we suffer, and how we are delighted, and how we may triumph is never new, it always must be heard. There isn't any other tale to tell, it's the only light we've got in all this darkness.

And this tale, according to that face, that body, those strong hands on those strings, has another aspect in every country, and a new depth in every generation. Listen, Creole seemed to be saying, listen. Now these are Sonny's blues. He made the little black man on the drums know it, and the bright, brown man on the horn. Creole wasn't trying any longer to get Sonny in the water. He was wishing him Godspeed. Then he stepped back, very slowly, filling the air with the immense suggestion that Sonny speak for himself.

Then they all gathered around Sonny, and Sonny played. Every now and again one of them seemed to say, Amen. Sonny's fingers filled the air with life, his life. But that life contained so many others. And Sonny went all the way back, he really began with the spare, flat statement of the opening phrase of the song. Then he began to make it his. It was very beautiful because it wasn't hurried and it was no longer a lament. I seemed to hear with what burning he had made it his, with what burning we had yet to make it ours, how we could cease lamenting. Freedom lurked around us and I understood, at last, that he could help us to be free if we would listen, that he would never be free until we did. Yet, there was no battle in his face now. I heard what he had gone through, and would continue to go through until he came to rest in earth. He had made it his: that long line, of which we knew only Mama and Daddy. And he was giving it back, as everything must be given back, so that, passing through death, it can live forever. I saw my mother's face again, and felt, for the first time, how the stones of the road she had walked on must have bruised her feet. I saw the moonlit road where my father's brother died. And it brought something else back to me, and carried me past it. I saw my little girl again and felt Isabel's tears again, and I felt my own tears begin to rise. And I was yet aware that this was only a moment, that the world waited outside, as hungry as a tiger, and that trouble stretched above us, longer than the sky.

Then it was over. Creole and Sonny let out their breath, both soaking wet, and grinning. There was a lot of applause and some of it was real. In the dark, the girl came by and I asked her to take drinks to the bandstand. There was a long pause, while they talked up there in the indigo light and after a while I saw the girl put a Scotch and milk on top of the piano for Sonny. He didn't seem to notice it, but just before they started playing again, he sipped from it and looked toward me, and nodded. Then he put it back on top of the piano. For me, then, as they began to play again, it glowed and shook above my brother's head like the very cup of trembling.

Mary McCarthy

b. 1912

"CRUEL AND BARBAROUS TREATMENT"

She could not bear to hurt her husband. She impressed this on the Young Man, on her confidantes, and finally on her husband himself. The thought of Telling Him actually made her heart turn over in a sudden and sickening way, she said. This was true, and yet she knew that being a potential divorcee was deeply pleasurable in somewhat the same way that being an engaged girl had been. In both cases, there was at first a subterranean courtship, whose significance it was necessary to conceal from outside observers. The concealment of the original, premarital courtship had, however, been a mere superstitious gesture, briefly sustained. It had also been, on the whole, a private secretiveness, not a partnership of silence. One put one's family and one's friends off the track because one was still afraid that the affair might not come out right, might not lead in a clean, direct line to the altar. To confess one's aspirations might be, in the end, to publicize one's failure. Once a solid understanding had been reached, there followed a short intermission of ritual bashfulness, in which both parties awkwardly participated, and then came the Announcement.

But with the extramarital courtship, the deception was prolonged where it had been ephemeral, necessary where it had been frivolous, conspiratorial where it had been lonely. It was, in short, serious where it had been dilettantish. That it was accompanied by feelings of guilt, by sharp and genuine revulsions, only complicated and deepened its delights, by abrading the sensibilities, and by imposing a sense of outlawry and consequent mutual dependence upon the lovers. But what this interlude of deception gave her, above all, she recognized, was an opportunity, unparalleled in her experience, for exercising feelings of superiority over others. For her husband she had, she believed, only sympathy and compunction. She got no fun, she told the Young Man, out of putting horns on her darling's head, and never for a moment, she said, did he appear to her as the comic figure of the cuckolded husband that one saw on the stage.

(The Young Man assured her that his own sentiments were equally delicate, that for the wronged man he felt the most profound respect, tinged
with consideration.) It was as if by the mere act of betraying her husband,
she had adequately bested him; it was supererogatory for her to gloat, and,
if she gloated at all, it was over her fine restraint in not-gloating, over the
integrity of her moral sense, which allowed her to preserve even while
engaged in sinfulness the acute realization of sin and shame. Her overt
superiority feelings she reserved for her friends. Lunches and teas, which
had been time-killers, matters of routine, now became perilous and dramatic adventures. The Young Man's name was a bright, highly explosive
ball which she bounced casually back and forth in these feminine tête-à-
têtes. She would discuss him in his status of friend of the family, speculate
on what girls he might have, attack him or defend him, anatomize him,
keeping her eyes clear and impersonal, her voice empty of special emphasis, her manner humorously detached. *While all the time . . . !*

Three times a week or oftener, at lunch or tea, she would let herself
tremble thus on the exquisite edge of self-betrayal, involving her companions in a momentous game whose rules and whose risks only she herself
knew. The Public Appearances were even more satisfactory. To meet at a
friend's house by design and to register surprise, to strike just the right
note of young-matronly affection at cocktail parties, to treat him formally
as "my escort" at the theater during intermissions—these were triumphs of
stage management, more difficult of execution, more nerveracking than the
lunches and teas, because *two* actors were involved. His overardent glance
must be hastily deflected; his too-self-conscious reading of his lines must
be entered in the debit side of her ledger of love, in anticipation of an
indulgent accounting in private.

The imperfections of his performance were, indeed, pleasing to her.
Not, she thought, because his impetuosities, his gaucheries, demonstrated
the sincerity of his passion for her, nor because they proved him a new
hand at this game of intrigue, but rather because the high finish of her
own acting showed off well in comparison. "I should have gone on the
stage," she could tell him gaily, "or been a diplomat's wife or an interna-
tional spy," while he would admiringly agree. Actually, she doubted
whether she could ever have been an actress, acknowledging that she
found it more amusing and more gratifying to play herself than to interpret any character conceived by a dramatist. In these private theatricals
it was her own many-faceted nature that she put on exhibit, and the audience, in this case unfortunately limited to two, could applaud both her
skill of projection and her intrinsic variety. Furthermore, this was a play
in which the donnée was real, and the penalty for a missed cue or an
inopportune entrance was, at first anyway, unthinkable.

She loved him, she knew, for being a bad actor, for his docility in accepting her tender, mock-impatient instruction. Those superiority feelings
were fattening not only on the gullibility of her friends, but also on the

comic flaws of her lover's character, and on the vulnerability of her lover's position. In this particular hive she was undoubtedly queen bee.

The Public Appearances were not exclusively duets. They sometimes took the form of a trio. On these occasions the studied and benevolent carefulness which she always showed for her husband's feelings served a double purpose. She would affect a conspicuous domesticity, an affectionate conjugal demonstrativeness, would sprinkle her conversation with "Darlings," and punctuate it with pats and squeezes till her husband would visibly expand and her lover plainly and painfully shrink. For the Young Man no retaliation was possible. These endearments of hers were sanctioned by law, usage, and habit; they belonged to her rôle of wife and could not be condemned or paralleled by a young man who was himself unmarried. They were clear provocations, but they could not be called so, and the Young Man preferred not to speak of them. *But she knew. . . .* Though she was aware of the sadistic intention of these displays, she was not ashamed of them, as she was sometimes twistingly ashamed of the hurt she was preparing to inflict on her husband. Partly she felt that they were punishments which the Young Man richly deserved for the wrong he was doing her husband, and that she herself in contriving them was acting, quite fittingly, both as judge and accused. Partly, too, she believed herself justified in playing the fond wife, whatever the damage to her lover's ego, because, in a sense, she actually was a fond wife. She *did* have these feelings, she insisted, whether she was exploiting them or not.

Eventually, however, her reluctance to wound her husband and her solicitude for his pride were overcome by an inner conviction that her love affair must move on to its next preordained stage. The possibilities of the subterranean courtship had been exhausted; it was time for the Announcement. She and the Young Man began to tell each other in a rather breathless and literary style that the Situation Was Impossible, and Things Couldn't Go On This Way Any Longer. The ostensible meaning of these flurried laments was that, under present conditions, they were not seeing enough of each other, that their hours together were too short and their periods of separation too dismal, that the whole business of deception had become morally distasteful to them. Perhaps the Young Man really believed these things; she did not. For the first time, she saw that the virtue of marriage as an institution lay in its public character. Private cohabitation, long continued, was, she concluded, a bore. Whatever the coziness of isolation, the warm delights of having a secret, a love affair finally reached the point where it needed the glare of publicity to revive the interest of its protagonists. Hence, she thought, the engagement parties, the showers, the big church weddings, the presents, the receptions. These were simply socially approved devices by which the lovers got themselves talked about. The gossip-value of a divorce and remarriage was obviously far greater than the gossip-value of a mere engagement, and she was now ready, indeed hungry, to hear What People Would Say.

The lunches, the teas, the Public Appearances were getting a little flat. It was not, in the end, enough to be a Woman With A Secret, if to one's friends one appeared to be a woman without a secret. The bliss of having a secret required, in short, the consummation of telling it, and she looked forward to the My-dear-I-had-no-idea's, the I-thought-you-and-Bill-were-so-happy-together's, the How-did-you-keep-it-so-dark's with which her intimates would greet her announcement. The audience of two no longer sufficed her; she required a larger stage. She tried it first, a little nervously, on two or three of her closest friends, swearing them to secrecy. "Bill must hear it first from me," she declared. "It would be too terrible for his pride if he found out afterwards that the whole town knew it before he did. So you mustn't tell, even later on, that I told you about this today. I felt I had to talk to someone." After these lunches she would hurry to a phone booth to give the Young Man the gist of the conversation, just as a reporter, sent to cover a fire, telephones in to the city desk. "She certainly was surprised," she could always say with a little gush of triumph. "But she thinks it's fine." *But did they actually?* She could not be sure. Was it possible that she sensed in these luncheon companions, her dearest friends, a certain reserve, a certain unexpressed judgment?

It was a pity, she reflected, that she was so sensitive to public opinion. "I couldn't really love a man," she murmured to herself once, "if everybody didn't think he was wonderful." Everyone seemed to like the Young Man, of course. *But still.* . . . She was getting panicky, she thought. Surely it was only common sense that nobody is admired by everybody. And even if a man were universally despised, would there not be a kind of defiant nobility in loving him in the teeth of the whole world? There would, certainly, but it was a type of heroism that she would scarcely be called upon to practice, for the Young Man was popular, he was invited everywhere, he danced well, his manners were ingratiating, he kept up intellectually. But was he not perhaps *too* amiable, *too* accommodating? Was it for this that her friends seemed silently to criticize him?

At this time a touch of acridity entered into her relations with the Young Man. Her indulgent scoldings had an edge to them now, and it grew increasingly difficult for her to keep her make-believe impatience from becoming real. She would look for dark spots in his character and drill away at them as relentlessly as a dentist at a cavity. A compulsive didacticism possessed her: no truism of his, no cliché, no ineffectual joke could pass the rigidity of her censorship. And, hard as she tried to maintain the character of charming schoolmistress, the Young Man, she saw, was taking alarm. She suspected that, frightened and puzzled, he contemplated flight. She found herself watching him with scientific interest, speculating as to what course he would take, and she was relieved but faintly disappointed when it became clear that he ascribed her sharpness to the tension of the situation and had decided to stick it out.

The moment had come for her to tell her husband. By this single, cathartic act, she would, she believed, rid herself of the doubts and anxieties that beset her. If her husband were to impugn the Young Man's character, she could answer his accusations and at the same time discount them as arising from jealousy. From her husband, at least, she might expect the favor of an open attack to which she could respond with the prepared defense that she carried, unspoken, about with her. Further, she had an intense, childlike curiosity as to How Her Husband Would Take It, a curiosity which she disguised for decency's sake as justifiable apprehension. The confidences already imparted to her friends seemed like pale dress rehearsals of the supreme confidence she was about to make. Perhaps it was toward this moment that the whole affair had been tending, for this moment that the whole affair had been designed. This would be the ultimate testing of her husband's love, its final, rounded, quintessential expression. Never, she thought, when you live with a man do you feel the full force of his love. It is gradually rationed out to you in an impure state, compounded with all the other elements of daily existence, so that you are hardly sensible of receiving it. There is no single point at which it is concentrated; it spreads out into the past and the future until it appears as a nearly imperceptible film over the surface of your life. Only face to face with its own annihilation could it show itself wholly, and, once shown, drop into the category of completed experiences.

She was not disappointed. She told him at breakfast in a fashionable restaurant, because, she said, he would be better able to control his feelings in public. When he called at once for the check, she had a spasm of alarm lest in an access of brutality or grief he leave her there alone, conspicuous, and, as it were, unfulfilled. But they walked out of the restaurant together and through the streets, hand in hand, tears streaming, "unchecked," she whispered to herself, down their faces. Later they were in the Park, by an artificial lake, watching the ducks swim. The sun was very bright, and she felt a kind of superb pathos in the careful and irrelevant attention they gave to the pastoral scene. This was, she knew, the most profound, the most subtle, the most idyllic experience of her life. All the strings of her nature were, at last, vibrant. She was both doer and sufferer: she inflicted pain and participated in it. And she was, at the same time, physician, for, as she was the weapon that dealt the wound, she was also the balm that could assuage it. Only she could know the hurt that engrossed him, and it was to her that he turned for the sympathy she had ready for him. Finally, though she offered him his discharge slip with one hand, with the other she beckoned him to approach. She was wooing him all over again, but wooing him to a deeper attachment than he had previously experienced, to an unconditional surrender. She was demanding his total understanding of her, his compassion, and his forgiveness. When at last he answered her repeated and agonized I-love-you's by grasping her hand more tightly and saying gently, "I know," she saw that she had won him over. She had drawn him into a truly mystical union. Their marriage was complete.

Afterwards everything was more prosaic. The Young Man had to be telephoned and summoned to a conference à trois, a conference, she said, of civilized, intelligent people. The Young Man was a little awkward, even dropped a tear or two, which embarrassed everyone else, but what after all, she thought, could you expect? He was in a difficult position; his was a thankless part. With her husband behaving so well, indeed, so gallantly, the Young Man could not fail to look a trifle inadequate. The Young Man would have preferred it, of course, if her husband had made a scene, had bullied or threatened her, so that he himself might have acted the chivalrous protector. She, however, did not hold her husband's heroic courtesy against him: in some way, it reflected credit on herself. The Young Man, apparently, was expecting to Carry Her Off, but this she would not allow. "It would be too heartless," she whispered when they were alone for a moment. "We must all go somewhere together."

So the three went out for a drink, and she watched with a sort of desperation her husband's growing abstraction, the more and more per-functory attention he accorded the conversation she was so bravely sus-taining. "He is bored," she thought. "He is going to leave." The prospect of being left alone with the Young Man seemed suddenly unendurable. If her husband were to go now, he would take with him the third dimension that had given the affair depth, and abandon her to a flat and vulgar love scene. Terrified, she wondered whether she had not already prolonged the drama beyond its natural limits, whether the confession in the restaurant and the absolution in the Park had not rounded off the artistic whole, whether the sequel of divorce and remarriage would not, in fact, consti-tute an anticlimax. Already she sensed that behind her husband's good manners an ironical attitude toward herself had sprung up. Was it possible that he had believed that they would return from the Park and all would continue as before? It was conceivable that her protestations of love had been misleading, and that his enormous tenderness toward her had been based, not on the idea that he was giving her up, but rather on the idea that he was taking her back—with no questions asked. If that were the case, the telephone call, the conference, and the excursion had in his eyes been a monstrous gaffe, a breach of sensibility and good taste, for which he would never forgive her. She blushed violently. Looking at him again, she thought he was watching her with an expression which declared: I have found you out: now I know what you are like. For the first time, she felt him utterly alienated.

When he left them she experienced the let-down she had feared but also a kind of relief. She told herself that it was as well that he had cut himself off from her: it made her decision simpler. There was now noth-ing for her to do but to push the love affair to its conclusion, whatever that might be, and this was probably what she most deeply desired. Had the poignant intimacy of the Park persisted, she might have been tempted to drop the adventure she had begun and return to her routine. But that was, looked at coldly, unthinkable. For if the adventure would seem a little flat after the scene in the Park, the resumption of her marriage would seem even flatter. If the drama of the triangle had been amputated by her confession, the curtain had been brought down with a smack on the drama of wedlock.

And, as it turned out, the drama of the triangle was not quite ended by the superficial rupture of her marriage. Though she had left her husband's apartment and been offered shelter by a confidante, it was still necessary for her to see him every day. There were clothes to be packed, and possessions to be divided, love letters to be reread and mementos to be wept over in common. There were occasional passionate, unconsummated embraces; there were endearments and promises. And though her husband's irony remained, it was frequently vulnerable. It was not, as she had at first thought, an armor against her, but merely a sword, out of *Tristan and Isolde,* which lay permanently between them and enforced discretion.

They met often, also, at the houses of friends, for, as she said, "What can I do? I know it's not tactful, but we all know the same people. You can't expect me to give up my friends." These Public Appearances were heightened in interest by the fact that these audiences, unlike the earlier ones, had, as it were, purchased librettos, and were in full possession of the intricacies of the plot. She preferred, she decided, the evening parties to the cocktail parties, for there she could dance alternately with her lover and her husband to the accompaniment of subdued gasps on the part of the bystanders.

This interlude was at the same time festive and heartrending: her only dull moments were the evenings she spent alone with the Young Man. Unfortunately, the Post-Announcement period was only too plainly an interlude and its very nature demanded that it be followed by something else. She could not preserve her anomalous status indefinitely. It was not decent, and, besides, people would be bored. From the point of view of one's friends, it was all very well to entertain a Triangle as a novelty; to cope with it as a permanent problem was a different matter. Once they had all three gotten drunk, and there was a scene, and, though everyone talked about it afterwards, her friends were, she thought, a little colder, a little more critical. People began to ask her when she was going to Reno. Furthermore, she noticed that her husband was getting a slight edge in popularity over the Young Man. It was natural, of course, that everyone should feel sorry for him, and be especially nice. *But yet. . . .*

When she learned from her husband that he was receiving invitations from members of her own circle, invitations in which she and the Young Man were unaccountably not included, she went at once to the station and bought her ticket. Her good-bye to her husband, which she had privately allocated to her last hours in town, took place prematurely, two days before she was to leave. He was rushing off to what she inwardly feared was a Gay Weekend in the country; he had only a few minutes; he wished her a pleasant trip; and he would write, of course. His highball was drained while her glass still stood half full; he sat forward nervously on his chair; and she knew herself to be acting the Ancient Mariner, but her dignity would not allow her to hurry. She hoped that he would miss his train for her, but he did not. He left her sitting in the bar, and that night the Young Man could not, as he put it, do a thing with her. There was nowhere, absolutely nowhere, she said passionately, that she wanted to go, nobody she wanted to see, nothing she wanted to do. "You need a drink," he said with the air of a diagnostician. "A drink," she answered bitterly. "I'm sick of the drinks we've been having. Gin, whiskey, rum, what else is there?" He took her into a bar, and she cried, but he bought her a fancy mixed drink, something called a Ramos gin fizz, and she was a little appeased because she had never had one before. Then some friends came in, and they all had another drink together, and she felt better. "There," said the Young Man, on the way home, "don't I know what's good for you? Don't I know how to handle you?" "Yes," she answered in her most humble and feminine tones, but she knew that they had suddenly dropped into a new pattern, that they were no longer the cynosure of a social group, but merely another young couple with an evening to pass, another young couple looking desperately for entertainment, wondering whether to call on a married couple or to drop in somewhere for a drink. This time the Young Man's prescription had worked, but it was pure luck that they had chanced to meet someone they knew. A second or a third time they would scan the faces of the other drinkers in vain, would order a second drink and surreptitiously watch the door, and finally go out alone, with a quite detectable air of being unwanted.

When, a day and a half later, the Young Man came late to take her to the train, and they had to run down the platform to catch it, she found him all at once detestable. He would ride to 125th Street with her, he declared in a burst of gallantry, but she was angry all the way because she was afraid there would be trouble with the conductor. At 125th Street, he stood on the platform blowing kisses to her and shouting something that she could not hear through the glass. She made a gesture of repugnance, but, seeing him flinch, seeing him weak and charming and incompetent, she brought her hand reluctantly to her lips and blew a kiss back. The other passengers were watching, she was aware, and though their looks were doting and not derisive, she felt herself to be humiliated and somehow vulgarized. When the train began to move, and the Young Man began to run down the platform after it, still blowing kisses and shouting alternately, she got up, turned sharply away from the window and walked back to the club car. There she sat down and ordered a whiskey and soda.

There were a number of men in the car, who looked up in unison as she gave her order, but, observing that they were all the middle-aged, small-business-men who "belonged" as inevitably to the club car as the white-coated porter and the leather-bound *Saturday Evening Post,* she paid them no heed. She was now suddenly overcome by a sense of depression and loss that was unprecedented for being in no way dramatic or pleasurable. In the last half hour she had seen clearly that she would never marry the Young Man, and she found herself looking into an insubstantial future with no signpost to guide her. Almost all women, she thought, when they are girls never believe that they will get married. The terror of spinsterhood hangs over them from adolescence on. Even if they are popular they think that no one really interesting will want them enough to marry them. Even if they get engaged they are afraid that something will go wrong, something will intervene. When they do get married it seems to them a sort of miracle, and, after they have been married for a time, though in retrospect the whole process looks perfectly natural and inevitable, they retain a certain unarticulated pride in the wonder they have performed. Finally, however, the terror of spinsterhood has been so thoroughly exorcised that they forget ever having been haunted by it, and it is at this stage that they contemplate divorce. "How could I have forgotten?" she said to herself and began to wonder what she would do.

She could take an apartment by herself in the Village. She would meet new people. She would entertain. But, she thought, if I have people in for cocktails, there will always come the moment when they have to leave, and I will be alone and have to pretend to have another engagement in order to save embarrassment. If I have them to dinner, it will be the same thing, but at least I will not have to pretend to have an engagement. I shall give dinners. Then, she thought, there will be the cocktail parties, and, if I go alone, I shall always stay a little too late, hoping that a young man or even a party of people will ask me to dinner. And if I fail, if no one asks me, I shall have the ignominy of walking out alone, trying to look as if I had somewhere to go. Then there will be the evenings at home with a good book when there will be no reason at all for going to bed, and I shall perhaps sit up all night. And the mornings when there will be no point in getting up, and I shall perhaps stay in bed till dinnertime. There will be the dinners in tea rooms with other unmarried women, tea rooms because women alone look conspicuous and forlorn in good restaurants. And then, she thought, I shall get older.

She would never, she reflected angrily, have taken this step, had she felt that she was burning her bridges behind her. She would never have left one man unless she had had another to take his place. But the Young Man, she now saw, was merely a sort of mirage which she had allowed herself to mistake for an oasis. "If the Man," she muttered, "did not exist, the Moment would create him." This was what had happened to her. She had made herself the victim of an imposture. But, she argued, with an access of cheerfulness, if this were true, if out of the need of a second, a new, husband she had conjured up the figure of one, she had possibly been impelled by unconscious forces to behave more intelligently than appearances would indicate. She was perhaps acting out in a sort of hypnotic trance a ritual whose meaning had not yet been revealed to her, a ritual which required that, first of all, the Husband be eliminated from the cast of characters. Conceivably, she was designed for the rôle of *femme fatale*, and for such a personage considerations of safety, provisions against loneliness and old age, were not only Philistine but irrelevant. She might marry a second, a third, a fourth time, or she might never marry again. But, in any case, for the thrifty bourgeois love-insurance, with its daily payments of patience, forbearance, and resignation, she was no longer eligible. She would be, she told herself delightedly, a bad risk.

She was, or soon would be, a Young Divorcee, and the term still carried glamor. Her divorce decree would be a passport conferring on her the status of citizeness of the world. She felt gratitude toward the Young Man for having unwittingly effected her transit into a new life. She looked about her at the other passengers. Later she would talk to them. They would ask, of course, where she was bound for; that was the regulation opening move of train conversations. But it was a delicate question what her reply should be. To say "Reno" straight out would be vulgar; it would smack of confidences too cheaply given. Yet to lie, to say "San Francisco" for instance, would be to cheat herself, to minimize her importance, to mislead her interlocutor into believing her an ordinary traveler with a commonplace destination. There must be some middle course which would give information without appearing to do so, which would hint at a *vie galante* yet indicate a barrier of impeccable reserve. It would probably be best, she decided, to say "West" at first, with an air of vagueness and hesitation. Then, when pressed, she might go so far as to say "Nevada." But no farther.

William Faulkner

1897–1962

DRY SEPTEMBER

1

Through the bloody September twilight, aftermath of sixty-two rainless days, it had gone like a fire in dry grass—the rumor, the story, whatever it was. Something about Miss Minnie Cooper and a Negro. Attacked, insulted, frightened: none of them, gathered in the barber shop on that Saturday evening where the ceiling fan stirred, without freshening it, the vitiated air, sending back upon them, in recurrent surges of stale pomade and lotion, their own stale breath and odors, knew exactly what had happened.

"Except it wasn't Will Mayes," a barber said. He was a man of middle age; a thin, sand-colored man with a mild face, who was shaving a client. "I know Will Mayes. He's a good nigger. And I know Miss Minnie Cooper, too."

"What do you know about her?" a second barber said.

"Who is she?" the client said. "A young girl?"

"No," the barber said. "She's about forty, I reckon. She aint married. That's why I dont believe—"

"Believe, hell!" a hulking youth in a sweat-stained silk shirt said. "Wont you take a white woman's word before a nigger's?"

"I dont believe Will Mayes did it," the barber said. "I know Will Mayes."

"Maybe you know who did it, then. Maybe you already got him out of town, you damn niggerlover."

"I dont believe anybody did anything. I dont believe anything happened. I leave it to you fellows if them ladies that get old without getting married dont have notions that a man cant—"

"Then you are a hell of a white man," the client said. He moved under the cloth. The youth had sprung to his feet.

"You dont?" he said. "Do you accuse a white woman of lying?"

The barber held the razor poised above the half-risen client. He did not look around.

"It's this durn weather," another said. "It's enough to make a man do anything. Even to her."

Nobody laughed. The barber said in his mild, stubborn tone: "I aint accusing nobody of nothing. I just know and you fellows know how a woman that never—"

"You damn niggerlover!" the youth said.

"Shut up, Butch," another said. "We'll get the facts in plenty of time to act."

"Who is? Who's getting them?" the youth said. "Facts, hell! I—"

"You're a fine white man," the client said. "Aint you?" In his frothy beard he looked like a desert rat in the moving pictures. "You tell them, Jack," he said to the youth. "If there aint any white men in this town, you can count on me, even if I aint only a drummer and a stranger."

"That's right, boys," the barber said. "Find out the truth first. I know Will Mayes."

"Well, by God!" the youth shouted. "To think that a white man in this town—"

"Shut up, Butch," the second speaker said. "We got plenty of time."

The client sat up. He looked at the speaker. "Do you claim that anything excuses a nigger attacking a white woman? Do you mean to tell me you are a white man and you'll stand for it? You better go back North where you came from. The South dont want your kind here."

"North what?" the second said. "I was born and raised in this town."

"Well, by God!" the youth said. He looked about with a strained, baffled gaze, as if he was trying to remember what it was he wanted to say or to do. He drew his sleeve across his sweating face. "Damn if I'm going to let a white woman—"

"You tell them, Jack," the drummer said. "By God, if they—"

The screen door crashed open. A man stood in the floor, his feet apart and his heavy-set body poised easily. His white shirt was open at the throat; he wore a felt hat. His hot, bold glance swept the group. His name was McLendon. He had commanded troops at the front in France and had been decorated for valor.

"Well," he said, "are you going to sit there and let a black son rape a white woman on the streets of Jefferson?"

Butch sprang up again. The silk of his shirt clung flat to his heavy shoulders. At each armpit was a dark halfmoon. "That's what I been telling them! That's what I—"

"Did it really happen?" a third said. "This aint the first man scare she ever had, like Hawkshaw says. Wasn't there something about a man on the kitchen roof, watching her undress, about a year ago?"

"What?" the client said. "What's that?" The barber had been slowly forcing him back into the chair; he arrested himself reclining, his head lifted, the barber still pressing him down.

McLendon whirled on the third speaker. "Happen? What the hell difference does it make? Are you going to let the black sons get away with it until one really does it?"

"That's what I'm telling them!" Butch shouted. He cursed, long and steady, pointless.

"Here, here," a fourth said. "Not so loud. Dont talk so loud."

"Sure," McLendon said; "no talking necessary at all. I've done my talking. Who's with me?" He poised on the balls of his feet, roving his gaze.

The barber held the drummer's face down, the razor poised. "Find out the facts first, boys. I know Willy Mayes. It wasn't him. Let's get the sheriff and do this thing right."

McLendon whirled upon him his furious, rigid face. The barber did not look away. They looked like men of different races. The other barbers had ceased also above their prone clients. "You mean to tell me," McLendon said, "that you'd take a nigger's word before a white woman's? Why, you damn niggerloving—"

The third speaker rose and grasped McLendon's arm; he too had been a soldier. "Now, now. Let's figure this thing out. Who knows anything about what really happened?"

"Figure out hell!" McLendon jerked his arm free. "All that're with me get up from there. The ones that aint—" He roved his gaze, dragging his sleeve across his face.

Three men rose. The drummer in the chair sat up. "Here," he said, jerking at the cloth about his neck; "get this rag off me. I'm with him. I dont live here, but by God, if our mothers and wives and sisters—" He smeared the cloth over his face and flung it to the floor. McLendon stood in the floor and cursed the others. Another rose and moved toward him. The remainder sat uncomfortable, not looking at one another, then one by one they rose and joined him.

The barber picked the cloth from the floor. He began to fold it neatly. "Boys, dont do that. Will Mayes never done it. I know."

"Come on," McLendon said. He whirled. From his hip pocket protruded the butt of a heavy automatic pistol. They went out. The screen door crashed behind them reverberant in the dead air.

The barber wiped the razor carefully and swiftly, and put it away, and ran to the rear, and took his hat from the wall. "I'll be back as soon as I can," he said to the other barbers. "I cant let—" He went out, running. The two other barbers followed him to the door and caught it on the rebound, leaning out and looking up the street after him. The air was flat and dead. It had a metallic taste at the base of the tongue.

"What can he do?" the first said. The second one was saying "Jees Christ, Jees Christ" under his breath. "I'd just as lief be Will Mayes as Hawk, if he gets McLendon riled."

"Jees Christ, Jees Christ," the second whispered.

"You reckon he really done it to her?" the first said.

2

She was thirty-eight or thirty-nine. She lived in a small frame house with her invalid mother and a thin, sallow, unflagging aunt, where each morning between ten and eleven she would appear on the porch in a lace-trimmed boudoir cap, to sit swinging in the porch swing until noon. After dinner she lay down for a while, until the afternoon began to cool. Then, in one of the three or four new voile dresses which she had each summer, she would go downtown to spend the afternoon in the stores with the other ladies, where they would handle the goods and haggle over the prices in cold, immediate voices, without any intention of buying.

She was of comfortable people—not the best in Jefferson, but good people enough—and she was still on the slender side of ordinary looking, with a bright, faintly haggard manner and dress. When she was young she had had a slender, nervous body and a sort of hard vivacity which had enabled her for a time to ride upon the crest of the town's social life as exemplified by the high school party and church social period of her contemporaries while still children enough to be unclass-conscious.

She was the last to realize that she was losing ground; that those among whom she had been a little brighter and louder flame than any other were beginning to learn the pleasure of snobbery—male—and retaliation—female. That was when her face began to wear that bright, haggard look. She still carried it to parties on shadowy porticoes and summer lawns, like a mask or a flag, with that bafflement of furious repudiation of truth in her eyes. One evening at a party she heard a boy and two girls, all school-mates, talking. She never accepted another invitation.

She watched the girls with whom she had grown up as they married and got homes and children, but no man ever called on her steadily until the children of the other girls had been calling her "aunty" for several years, the while their mothers told them in bright voices about how popular Aunt Minnie had been as a girl. Then the town began to see her driving on Sunday afternoons with the cashier in the bank. He was a widower of about forty—a high-colored man, smelling always faintly of the barber shop or of whisky. He owned the first automobile in town, a red runabout; Minnie had the first motoring bonnet and veil the town ever saw. Then the town began to say: "Poor Minnie." "But she is old enough to take care of herself," others said. That was when she began to ask her old schoolmates that their children call her "cousin" instead of "aunty."

It was twelve years now since she had been relegated into adultery by public opinion, and eight years since the cashier had gone to a Memphis bank, returning for one day each Christmas, which he spent at an annual bachelors' party at a hunting club on the river. From behind their curtains the neighbors would see the party pass, and during the over-the-way Christmas day visiting they would tell her about him, about how well he looked, and how they heard that he was prospering in the city, watching with bright, secret eyes her haggard, bright face. Usually by that hour there would be the scent of whisky on her breath. It was supplied her by a youth, a clerk at the soda fountain: "Sure; I buy it for the old gal. I reckon she's entitled to a little fun."

Her mother kept to her room altogether now; the gaunt aunt ran the house. Against that background Minnie's bright dresses, her idle and empty days, had a quality of furious unreality. She went out in the evenings only with women now, neighbors, to the moving pictures. Each afternoon she dressed in one of the new dresses and went downtown alone, where her young "cousins" were already strolling in the late afternoons with their delicate, silken heads and thin, awkward arms and conscious hips, clinging to one another or shrieking and giggling with paired boys in the soda fountain when she passed and went on along the serried store fronts, in the doors of which the sitting and lounging men did not even follow her with their eyes any more.

3

The barber went swiftly up the street where the sparse lights, insect-swirled, glared in rigid and violent suspension in the lifeless air. The day had died in a pall of dust; above the darkened square, shrouded by the spent dust, the sky was as clear as the inside of a brass bell. Below the east was a rumor of the twice-waxed moon.

When he overtook them McLendon and three others were getting into a car parked in an alley. McLendon stooped his thick head, peering out beneath the top. "Changed your mind, did you?" he said. "Damn good thing; by God, tomorrow when this town hears about how you talked tonight—"

"Now, now," the other ex-soldier said. "Hawkshaw's all right. Come on, Hawk; jump in."

"Will Mayes never done it, boys," the barber said. "If anybody done it. Why, you all know well as I do there aint any town where they got better niggers than us. And you know how a lady will kind of think things about men when there aint any reason to, and Miss Minnie anyway—"

"Sure, sure," the soldier said. "We're just going to talk to him a little; that's all."

"Talk hell!" Butch said. "When we're through with the—"

"Shut up, for God's sake!" the soldier said. "Do you want everybody in town—"

"Tell them, by God!" McLendon said. "Tell everyone of the sons that'll let a white woman—"

"Let's go; let's go: here's the other car." The second car slid squealing out of a cloud of dust at the alley mouth. McLendon started his car and took the lead. Dust lay like fog in the street. The street lights hung nimbused as in water. They drove on out of town.

A rutted lane turned at right angles. Dust hung above it too, and above all the land. The dark bulk of the ice plant, where the Negro Mayes was night watchman, rose against the sky. "Better stop here, hadn't we?" the soldier said. McLendon did not reply. He hurled the car up and slammed to a stop, the headlights glaring on the blank wall.

"Listen here, boys," the barber said; "if he's here, dont that prove he never done it? Dont it? If it was him, he would run. Dont you see he would?" The second car came up and stopped. McLendon got down; Butch sprang down beside him. "Listen, boys," the barber said.

"Cut the lights off!" McLendon said. The breathless dark rushed down. There was no sound in it save their lungs as they sought air in the parched dust in which for two months they had lived; then the diminishing crunch of McLendon's and Butch's feet, and a moment later McLendon's voice:

"Will! . . . Will!"

Below the east the wan hemorrhage of the moon increased. It heaved above the ridge, silvering the air, the dust, so that they seemed to breathe, live, in a bowl of molten lead. There was no sound of night-bird nor insect, no sound save their breathing and a faint ticking of contracting metal about the cars. Where their bodies touched one another they seemed to sweat dryly, for no more moisture came. "Christ!" a voice said; "let's get out of here."

But they didn't move until vague noises began to grow out of the darkness ahead; then they got out and waited tensely in the breathless dark. There was another sound: a blow, a hissing expulsion of breath and McLendon cursing in undertone. They stood a moment longer, then they ran forward. They ran in a stumbling clump, as though they were fleeing something. "Kill him, kill the son," a voice whispered. McLendon flung them back.

"Not here," he said. "Get him into the car." "Kill him, kill the black son!" the voice murmured. They dragged the Negro to the car. The barber had waited beside the car. He could feel himself sweating and he knew he was going to be sick at the stomach.

"What is it, captains?" the Negro said. "I aint done nothing. 'Fore God, Mr John." Someone produced handcuffs. They worked busily about the Negro as though he were a post, quiet, intent, getting in one another's way. He submitted to the handcuffs, looking swiftly and constantly from dim face to dim face. "Who's here, captains?" he said, leaning to peer into the faces until they could feel his breath and smell his sweaty reek. He spoke a name or two. "What you all say I done, Mr John?"

McLendon jerked the car door open. "Get in!" he said.

The Negro did not move. "What you all going to do with me, Mr John? I aint done nothing. White folks, captains, I aint done nothing: I swear 'fore God." He called another name.

"Get in!" McLendon said. He struck the Negro. The others expelled their breath in a dry hissing and struck him with random blows and he whirled and cursed them, and swept his manacled hands across their faces and slashed the barber upon the mouth, and the barber struck him also. "Get him in there," McLendon said. They pushed at him. He ceased struggling and got in and sat quietly as the others took their places. He sat between the barber and the soldier, drawing his limbs in so as not to touch them, his eyes going swiftly and constantly from face to face. Butch clung to the running board. The car moved on. The barber nursed his mouth with his handkerchief.

"What's the matter, Hawk?" the soldier said.

"Nothing," the barber said. They regained the highroad and turned away from town. The second car dropped back out of the dust. They went on, gaining speed; the final fringe of houses dropped behind.

"Goddamn, he stinks!" the soldier said.

"We'll fix that," the drummer in front beside McLendon said. On the running board Butch cursed into the hot rush of air. The barber leaned suddenly forward and touched McLendon's arm.

"Let me out, John," he said.

"Jump out, niggerlover," McLendon said without turning his head. He drove swiftly. Behind them the sourceless lights of the second car glared in the dust. Presently McLendon turned into a narrow road. It was rutted with disuse. It led back to an abandoned brick kiln—a series of reddish mounds and weed- and vine-choked vats without bottom. It had been used for pasture once, until one day the owner missed one of his mules. Although he prodded carefully in the vats with a long pole, he could not even find the bottom of them.

"John," the barber said.

"Jump out, then," McLendon said, hurling the car along the ruts. Beside the barber the Negro spoke:

"Mr Henry."

The barber sat forward. The narrow tunnel of the road rushed up and past. Their motion was like an extinct furnace blast: cooler, but utterly dead. The car bounded from rut to rut.

"Mr Henry," the Negro said.

The barber begain to tug furiously at the door. "Look out, there!" the soldier said, but the barber had already kicked the door open and swung onto the running board. The soldier leaned across the Negro and grasped at him, but he had already jumped. The car went on without checking speed.

The impetus hurled him crashing through dust-sheathed weeds, into the ditch. Dust puffed about him, and in a thin, vicious crackling of sapless stems he lay choking and retching until the second car passed and died away. Then he rose and limped on until he reached the highroad and turned toward town, brushing at his clothes with his hands. The moon was higher, riding high and clear of the dust at last, and after a while the town began to glare beneath the dust. He went on, limping. Presently he heard cars and the glow of them grew in the dust behind him and he left the road and crouched again in the weeds until they passed. McLendon's car came last now. There were four people in it and Butch was not on the running board.

They went on; the dust swallowed them; the glare and the sound died away. The dust of them hung for a while, but soon the eternal dust absorbed it again. The barber climbed back onto the road and limped on toward town.

4

As she dressed for supper on that Saturday evening, her own flesh felt like fever. Her hands trembled among the hooks and eyes, and her eyes had a feverish look, and her hair swirled crisp and crackling under the comb. While she was still dressing the friends called for her and sat while she donned her sheerest underthings and stockings and a new voile dress. "Do you feel strong enough to go out?" they said, their eyes bright too, with a dark glitter. "When you have had time to get over the shock, you must tell us what happened. What he said and did; everything."

In the leafed darkness, as they walked toward the square, she began to breathe deeply, something like a swimmer preparing to dive, until she ceased trembling, the four of them walking slowly because of the terrible heat and out of solicitude for her. But as they neared the square she began to tremble again, walking with her head up, her hands clenched at her sides, their voices about her murmurous, also with that feverish, glittering quality of their eyes.

They entered the square, she in the center of the group, fragile in her fresh dress. She was trembling worse. She walked slower and slower, as children eat ice cream, her head up and her eyes bright in the haggard banner of her face, passing the hotel and the coatless drummers in chairs along the curb looking around at her: "That's the one: see? The one in pink in the middle." "Is that her? What did they do with the nigger? Did they—?" "Sure. He's all right." "All right, is he?" "Sure. He went on a little trip." Then the drug store, where even the young men lounging in the doorway tipped their hats and followed with their eyes the motion of her hips and legs when she passed.

They went on, passing the lifted hats of the gentlemen, the suddenly ceased voices, deferent, protective. "Do you see?" the friends said. Their voices sounded like long, hovering sighs of hissing exultation. "There's not a Negro on the square. Not one."

They reached the picture show. It was like a miniature fairyland with its lighted lobby and colored lithographs of life caught in its terrible and beautiful mutations. Her lips began to tingle. In the dark, when the picture began, it would be all right; she could hold back the laughing so it would not waste away so fast and so soon. So she hurried on before the turning faces, the undertones of low astonishment, and they took their accustomed places where she could see the aisle against the silver glare and the young men and girls coming in two and two against it.

The lights flicked away; the screen glowed silver, and soon life began to unfold, beautiful and passionate and sad, while still the young men and girls entered, scented and sibilant in the half dark, their paired backs in silhouette delicate and sleek, their slim, quick bodies awkward, divinely young, while beyond them the silver dream accumulated inevitably on and on. She began to laugh. In trying to suppress it, it made more noise than ever; heads began to turn. Still laughing, her friends raised her and led her out, and she stood at the curb, laughing on a high, sustained note, until the taxi came up and they helped her in.

They removed the pink voile and the sheer underthings and the stockings, and put her to bed, and cracked ice for her temples, and sent for the doctor. He was hard to locate, so they ministered to her with hushed ejaculations, renewing the ice and fanning her. While the ice was fresh and cold she stopped laughing and lay still for a time, moaning only a little. But soon the laughing welled again and her voice rose screaming.

"Shhhhhhhhhhh! Shhhhhhhhhhhhhh!" they said, freshening the icepack, smoothing her hair, examining it for gray; "poor girl!" Then to one another: "Do you suppose anything really happened?" their eyes darkly aglitter, secret and passionate. "Shhhhhhhhhh! Poor girl! Poor Minnie!"

5

It was midnight when McLendon drove up to his neat new house. It was trim and fresh as a birdcage and almost as small, with its clean, green-and-white paint. He locked the car and mounted the porch and entered. His wife rose from a chair beside the reading lamp. McLendon stopped in the floor and stared at her until she looked down.

"Look at that clock," he said, lifting his arm, pointing. She stood before him, her face lowered, a magazine in her hands. Her face was pale, strained, and weary-looking. "Haven't I told you about sitting up like this, waiting to see when I come in?"

"John," she said. She laid the magazine down. Poised on the balls of his feet, he glared at her with his hot eyes, his sweating face.

"Didn't I tell you?" He went toward her. She looked up then. He caught her shoulder. She stood passive, looking at him.

"Don't, John. I couldn't sleep . . . The heat; something. Please, John. You're hurting me."

"Didn't I tell you?" He released her and half struck, half flung her across the chair, and she lay there and watched him quietly as he left the room.

He went on through the house, ripping off his shirt, and on the dark, screened porch at the rear he stood and mopped his head and shoulders with the shirt and flung it away. He took the pistol from his hip and laid it on the table beside the bed, and sat on the bed and removed his shoes, and rose and slipped his trousers off. He was sweating again already, and he stooped and hunted furiously for the shirt. At last he found it and wiped his body again, and, with his body pressed against the dusty screen, he stood panting. There was no movement, no sound, not even an insect. The dark world seemed to lie stricken beneath the cold moon and the lidless stars.

John Cheever

b. 1912

TORCH SONG

After Jack Lorey had known Joan Harris in New York for a few years, he began to think of her as The Widow. She always wore black, and he was always given the feeling, by a curious disorder in her apartment, that the undertakers had just left. This impression did not stem from malice on his part, for he was fond of Joan. They came from the same city in Ohio and had reached New York at about the same time in the middle thirties. They were the same age, and during their first summer in the city they used to meet after work and drink Martinis in places like the Brevoort and Charles', and have dinner and play checkers at the Lafayette.

Joan went to a school for models when she settled in the city, but it turned out that she photographed badly, so after spending six weeks learning how to walk with a book on her head she got a job as a hostess in a Longchamps. For the rest of the summer she stood by the hatrack, bathed in an intense pink light and the string music of heartbreak, swinging her mane of dark hair and her black skirt as she moved forward to greet the customers. She was then a big, handsome girl with a wonderful voice, and her face, her whole presence, always seemed infused with a gentle and healthy pleasure at her surroundings, whatever they were. She was innocently and incorrigibly convivial, and would get out of bed and dress at three in the morning if someone called her and asked her to come out for a drink, as Jack often did. In the fall, she got some kind of freshman executive job in a department store. They saw less and less of each other and then for quite a while stopped seeing each other altogether. Jack was living with a girl he had met at a party, and it never occurred to him to wonder what had become of Joan.

Jack's girl had some friends in Pennsylvania, and in the spring and summer of his second year in town he often went there with her for weekends. All of this—the shared apartment in the Village, the illicit relationship, the Friday-night train to a country house—were what he had imagined life in New York to be, and he was intensely happy. He was returning to New York with his girl one Sunday night on the Lehigh line. It was one of those trains that move slowly across the face of New Jersey, bringing back to the city hundreds of people, like the victims of an immense and strenuous picnic, whose faces are blazing and whose muscles are lame. Jack and his girl, like most of the other passengers, were overburdened with vegetables and flowers. When the train stopped in Pennsylvania Station, they moved with the crowd along the platform, toward the escalator. As they were passing the wide, lighted windows of the diner, Jack turned his head and saw Joan. It was the first time he had seen her since Thanksgiving, or since Christmas. He couldn't remember.

Joan was with a man who had obviously passed out. His head was in his arms on the table, and an overturned highball glass was near one of his elbows. Joan was shaking his shoulders gently and speaking to him. She seemed to be vaguely troubled, vaguely amused. The waiters had cleared off all the other tables and were standing around Joan, waiting for her to resurrect her escort. It troubled Jack to see in these straits a girl who reminded him of the trees and the lawns of his home town, but there was nothing he could do to help. Joan continued to shake the man's shoulders, and the crowd pressed Jack past one after another of the diner's windows, past the malodorous kitchen, and up the escalator.

He saw Joan again, later that summer, when he was having dinner in a Village restaurant. He was with a new girl, a Southerner. There were many Southern girls in the city that year. Jack and his belle had wandered into the restaurant because it was convenient, but the food was terrible and the place was lighted with candles. Halfway through dinner, Jack noticed Joan on the other side of the room, and when he had finished eating, he crossed the room and spoke to her. She was with a tall man who was wearing a monocle. He stood, bowed stiffly from the waist, and said to Jack, "We are very pleased to meet you." Then he excused himself and headed for the toilet. "He's a count, he's a Swedish count," Joan said. "He's on the radio, Friday afternoons at four-fifteen. Isn't it exciting?" She seemed to be delighted with the count and the terrible restaurant.

Sometime the next winter, Jack moved from the Village to an apartment in the East Thirties. He was crossing Park Avenue one cold morning on his way to the office when he noticed, in the crowd, a woman he had met a few times at Joan's apartment. He spoke to her and asked about his friend. "Haven't you heard?" she said. She pulled a long face. "Perhaps I'd better tell you. Perhaps you can help." She and Jack had breakfast in a drugstore on Madison Avenue and she unburdened herself of the story.

The count had a program called "The Song of the Fiords," or something like that, and he sang Swedish folk songs. Everyone suspected him of being a fake, but that didn't bother Joan. He had met her at a party and, sensing a soft touch, had moved in with her the following night. About a week later, he complained of pains in his back and said he must have some morphine. Then he needed morphine all the time. If he didn't get morphine, he was abusive and violent. Joan began to deal with those doctors and druggists who peddle dope, and when they wouldn't supply her, she went down to the bottom of the city. Her friends were afraid she would be found some morning stuffed in a drain. She got pregnant. She had an abortion. The count left her and moved to a flea bag near Times Square, but she was so impressed by then with his helplessness, so afraid that he would die without her, that she followed him there and shared his room and continued to buy his narcotics. He abandoned her again, and Joan waited a week for him to return before she went back to her place and her friends in the Village.

It shocked Jack to think of the innocent girl from Ohio having lived with a brutal dope addict and traded with criminals, and when he got to his office that morning, he telephoned her and made a date for dinner that night. He met her at Charles'. When she came into the bar, she seemed as wholesome and calm as ever. Her voice was sweet, and reminded him of elms, of lawns, of those glass arrangements that used to be hung from porch ceilings to tinkle in the summer wind. She told him about the count. She spoke of him charitably and with no trace of bitterness, as if her voice, her disposition, were incapable of registering anything beyond simple affection and pleasure. Her walk, when she moved ahead of him toward their table, was light and graceful. She ate a large dinner and talked enthusiastically about her job. They went to a movie and said goodbye in front of her apartment house.

That winter, Jack met a girl he decided to marry. Their engagement was announced in January and they planned to marry in July. In the spring, he received, in his office mail, an invitation to cocktails at Joan's. It was for a Saturday when his fiancée was going to Massachusetts to visit her parents, and when the time came and he had nothing better to do, he took a bus to the Village. Joan had the same apartment. It was a walkup. You rang the bell above the mailbox in the vestibule and were answered with a death rattle in the lock. Joan lived on the third floor. Her calling card was in a slot on the mailbox, and above her name was written the name Hugh Bascomb.

Jack climbed the two flights of carpeted stairs, and when he reached Joan's apartment, she was standing by the open door in a black dress. After she greeted Jack, she took his arm and guided him across the room. "I want you to meet Hugh, Jack," she said.

Hugh was a big man with a red face and pale-blue eyes. His manner was courtly and his eyes were inflamed with drink. Jack talked with him for a little while and then went over to speak to someone he knew, who was standing by the mantelpiece. He noticed then, for the first time, the indescribable disorder of Joan's apartment. The books were in their shelves and the furniture was reasonably good, but the place was all wrong, somehow. It was as if things had been put in place without thought or real interest, and for the first time, too, he had the impression that there had been a death there recently.

As Jack moved around the room, he felt that he had met the ten or twelve guests at other parties. There was a woman executive with a fancy hat, a man who could imitate Roosevelt, a grim couple whose play was in rehearsal, and a newspaperman who kept turning on the radio for news of the Spanish Civil War. Jack drank Martinis and talked with the woman in the fancy hat. He looked out of the window at the back yards and the ailanthus trees and heard, in the distance, thunder exploding off the cliffs of the Hudson.

Hugh Bascomb got very drunk. He began to spill liquor, as if drinking, for him, were a kind of jolly slaughter and he enjoyed the bloodshed and the mess. He spilled whiskey from a bottle. He spilled a drink on his shirt and then tipped over someone else's drink. The party was not quiet, but Hugh's hoarse voice began to dominate the others. He attacked a photographer who was sitting in a corner explaining camera techniques to a homely woman. "What did you come to the party for if all you wanted to do was to sit there and stare at your shoes?" Hugh shouted. "What did you come for? Why don't you stay at home?"

The photographer didn't know what to say. He was not staring at his shoes. Joan moved lightly to Hugh's side. "Please don't get into a fight now, darling," she said. "Not this afternoon."

"Shut up," he said. "Let me alone. Mind your own business." He lost his balance, and in struggling to steady himself he tipped over a lamp.

"Oh, your lovely lamp, Joan," a woman sighed.

"Lamps!" Hugh roared. He threw his arms into the air and worked them around his head as if he were bludgeoning himself. "Lamps. Glasses. Cigarette boxes. Dishes. They're killing me. They're killing me, for Christ's sake. Let's all go up to the mountains, for Christ's sake. Let's all go up to the mountains and hunt and fish and live like men, for Christ's sake."

People were scattering as if a rain had begun to fall in the room. It had, as a matter of fact, begun to rain outside. Someone offered Jack a ride uptown, and he jumped at the chance. Joan stood at the door, saying goodbye to her routed friends. Her voice remained soft, and her manner, unlike that of those Christian women who in the face of disaster can summon new and formidable sources of composure, seemed genuinely simple. She appeared to be oblivious of the raging drunk at her back, who was pacing up and down, grinding glass into the rug, and haranguing one of the survivors of the party with a story of how he, Hugh, had once gone without food for three weeks.

In July, Jack was married in an orchard in Duxbury, and he and his wife went to West Chop for a few weeks. When they returned to town, their apartment was cluttered with presents, including a dozen after-dinner coffee cups from Joan. His wife sent her the required note, but they did nothing else.

Later in the summer, Joan telephoned Jack at his office and asked if he wouldn't bring his wife to see her; she named an evening the following week. He felt guilty about not having called her, and accepted the invitation. This made his wife angry. She was an ambitious girl who liked a social life that offered rewards, and she went unwillingly to Joan's Village apartment with him.

Written above Joan's name on the mailbox was the name Franz Denzel. Jack and his wife climbed the stairs and were met by Joan at the open door. They went into her apartment and found themselves among a group of people for whom Jack, at least, was unable to find any bearings.

Franz Denzel was a middle-aged German. His face was pinched with bitterness or illness. He greeted Jack and his wife with that elaborate and clever politeness that is intended to make guests feel that they have come too early or too late. He insisted sharply upon Jack's sitting in the chair in which he himself had been sitting, and then went and sat on a radiator. There were five other Germans sitting around the room, drinking coffee. In a corner was another American couple, who looked uncomfortable. Joan passed Jack and his wife small cups of coffee with whipped cream. "These cups belonged to Franz's mother," she said. "Aren't they lovely? They were the only things he took from Germany when he escaped from the Nazis."

Franz turned to Jack and said, "Perhaps you will give us your opinion on the American educational system. That is what we were discussing when you arrived."

Before Jack could speak, one of the German guests opened an attack on the American educational system. The other Germans joined in, and went on from there to describe every vulgarity that had impressed them in American life and to contrast German and American culture generally. Where, they asked one another passionately, could you find in America anything like the Mitropa dining cars, the Black Forest, the pictures in Munich, the music in Bayreuth? Franz and his friends began speaking in German. Neither Jack nor his wife nor Joan could understand German, and the other American couple had not opened their mouths since they were introduced. Joan went happily around the room, filling everyone's cup with coffee, as if the music of a foreign language were enough to make an evening for her.

Jack drank five cups of coffee. He was desperately uncomfortable. Joan went into the kitchen while the Germans were laughing at their German jokes, and he hoped she would return with some drinks, but when she came back, it was with a tray of ice cream and mulberries.

"Isn't this pleasant?" Franz asked, speaking in English again.

Joan collected the coffee cups, and as she was about to take them back to the kitchen, Franz stopped her.

"Isn't one of those cups chipped?"

"No, darling," Joan said. "I never let the maid touch them. I wash them myself."

"What's that?" he asked, pointing at the rim of one of the cups.

"That's the cup that's always been chipped, darling. It was chipped when you unpacked it. You noticed it then."

"These things were perfect when they arrived in this country," he said. Joan went into the kitchen and he followed her.

Jack tried to make conversation with the Germans. From the kitchen there was the sound of a blow and a cry. Franz returned and began to eat his mulberries greedily. Joan came back with her dish of ice cream. Her voice was gentle. Her tears, if she had been crying, had dried as quickly as the tears of a child. Jack and his wife finished their ice cream and made their escape. The wasted and unnerving evening enraged Jack's wife, and he supposed that he would never see Joan again.

Jack's wife got pregnant early in the fall, and she seized on all the prerogatives of an expectant mother. She took long naps, ate canned peaches in the middle of the night, and talked about the rudimentary kidney. She chose to see only other couples who were expecting children, and the parties that she and Jack gave were temperate. The baby, a boy, was born in May, and Jack was very proud and happy. The first party he and his wife went to after her convalescence was the wedding of a girl whose family Jack had known in Ohio.

The wedding was at St. James', and afterward there was a big reception at the River Club. There was an orchestra dressed like Hungarians, and a lot of champagne and Scotch. Toward the end of the afternoon, Jack was walking down a dim corridor when he heard Joan's voice. "Please don't, darling," she was saying. "You'll break my arm. *Please* don't, darling." She was being pressed against the wall by a man who seemed to be twisting her arm. As soon as they saw Jack, the struggle stopped. All three of them were intensely embarrassed. Joan's face was wet and she made an effort to smile through her tears at Jack. He said hello and went on without stopping. When he returned, she and the man had disappeared.

When Jack's son was less than two years old, his wife flew with the baby to Nevada to get a divorce. Jack gave her the apartment and all its furnishings and took a room in a hotel near Grand Central. His wife got her decree in due course, and the story was in the newspapers. Jack had a telephone call from Joan a few days later.

"I'm awfully sorry to hear about your divorce, Jack," she said. "She seemed like *such* a nice girl. But that wasn't what I called you about. I want your help, and I wondered if you could come down to my place tonight around six. It's something I don't want to talk about over the phone."

He went obediently to the Village that night and climbed the stairs. Her apartment was a mess. The pictures and the curtains were down and the books were in boxes. "You moving, Joan?" he asked.

"That's what I wanted to see you about, Jack. First, I'll give you a drink." She made two Old-Fashioneds. "I'm being evicted, Jack," she said. "I'm being evicted because I'm an immoral woman. The couple who have the apartment downstairs—they're charming people, I've always thought—have told the real-estate agent that I'm a drunk and a prostitute and all kinds of things. Isn't that fantastic? This real-estate agent has always been so nice to me that I didn't think he'd believe them, but he's cancelled my lease, and if I make any trouble, he's threatened to take the matter up with the store, and I don't want to lose my job. This nice real-estate agent won't even talk with me any more. When I go over to the office, the receptionist leers at me as if I were some kind of dreadful woman. Of course, there have been a lot of men here and we sometimes are noisy, but I can't be expected to go to bed at ten every night. Can I? Well, the agent who manages this building has apparently told all the other agents in the neighborhood that I'm an immoral and drunken woman, and none of them will give me an apartment. I went in to talk with one man—he seemed to be such a nice old gentleman—and he made me an indecent proposal. Isn't it fantastic? I have to be out of here on Thursday and I'm literally being turned out into the street."

Joan seemed as serene and innocent as ever while she described this scourge of agents and neighbors. Jack listened carefully for some sign of indignation or bitterness or even urgency in her recital, but there was none. He was reminded of a torch song, of one of those forlorn and touching ballads that had been sung neither for him nor for her but for their older brothers and sisters by Marion Harris. Joan seemed to be singing her wrongs.

"They've made my life miserable," she went on quietly. "If I keep the radio on after ten o'clock, they telephone the agent in the morning and tell him I had some kind of orgy here. One night when Phillip—I don't think you've met Phillip; he's in the Royal Air Force; he's gone back to England—one night when Phillip and some other people were here, they called the police. The police came bursting in the door and talked to me as if I were I don't know what and then looked in the bedroom. If they think there's a man up here after midnight, they call me on the telephone and say all kinds of disgusting things. Of course, I can put my furniture into storage and go to a hotel, I guess. I guess a hotel will take a woman with my kind of reputation, but I thought perhaps you might know of an apartment. I thought—"

It angered Jack to think of this big, splendid girl's being persecuted by her neighbors, and he said he would do what he could. He asked her to have dinner with him, but she said she was busy.

Having nothing better to do, Jack decided to walk uptown to his hotel.

It was a hot night. The sky was overcast. On his way, he saw a parade in a dark side street off Broadway near Madison Square. All the buildings in the neighborhood were dark. It was so dark that he could not see the placards the marchers carried until he came to a street light. Their signs urged the entry of the United States into the war, and each platoon represented a nation that had been subjugated by the Axis powers. They marched up Broadway, as he watched, to no music, to no sound but their own steps on the rough cobbles. It was for the most part an army of elderly men and women—Poles, Norwegians, Danes, Jews, Chinese. A few idle people like himself lined the sidewalks, and the marchers passed between them with all the self-consciousness of enemy prisoners. There were children among them dressed in the costumes in which they had, for the newsreels, presented the Mayor with a package of tea, a petition, a protest, a constitution, a check, or a pair of tickets. They hobbled through the darkness of the loft neighborhood like a mortified and destroyed people, toward Greeley Square.

In the morning, Jack put the problem of finding an apartment for Joan up to his secretary. She started phoning real-estate agents, and by afternoon she had found a couple of available apartments in the West Twenties. Joan called Jack the next day to say that she had taken one of the apartments and to thank him.

Jack didn't see Joan again until the following summer. It was a Sunday evening; he had left a cocktail party in a Washington Square apartment and had decided to walk a few blocks up Fifth Avenue before he took a bus. As he was passing the Brevoort, Joan called to him. She was with a man at one of the tables on the sidewalk. She looked cool and fresh, and the man appeared to be respectable. His name, it turned out, was Pete Bristol. He invited Jack to sit down and join in a celebration. Germany had invaded Russia that weekend, and Joan and Pete were drinking champagne to celebrate Russia's changed position in the war. The three of them drank champagne until it got dark. They had dinner and drank champagne with their dinner. They drank more champagne afterward and then went over to the Lafayette and then to two or three other places. Joan had always been tireless in her gentle way. She hated to see the night end, and it was after three o'clock when Jack stumbled into his apartment. The following morning he woke up haggard and sick, and with no recollection of the last hour or so of the previous evening. His suit was soiled and he had lost his hat. He didn't get to his office until eleven. Joan had already called him twice, and she called him again soon after he got in. There was no hoarseness at all in her voice. She said that she had to see him, and he agreed to meet her for lunch in a seafood restaurant in the Fifties.

He was standing at the bar when she breezed in, looking as though she had taken no part in that calamitous night. The advice she wanted concerned selling her jewelry. Her grandmother had left her some jewelry, and she wanted to raise money on it but didn't know where to go. She took some rings and bracelets out of her purse and showed them to Jack. He said that he didn't know anything about jewelry but that he could lend her some money. "Oh, I couldn't borrow money from you, Jack," she said. "You see, I want to get the money for Pete. I want to help him. He wants to open an advertising agency, and he needs quite a lot to begin with." Jack didn't press her to accept his offer of a loan after that, and the project wasn't mentioned again during lunch.

He next heard about Joan from a young doctor who was a friend of theirs. "Have you seen Joan recently?" the doctor asked Jack one evening when they were having dinner together. He said no. "I gave her a checkup last week," the doctor said, "and while she's been through enough to kill the average mortal—and you'll never know what she's been through—she still has the constitution of a virtuous and healthy woman. Did you hear about the last one? She sold her jewelry to put him into some kind of a business, and as soon as he got the money, he left her for another girl, who had a car—a convertible."

Jack was drafted into the Army in the spring of 1942. He was kept at Fort Dix for nearly a month, and during this time he came to New York in the evening whenever he could get permission. Those nights had for him the intense keenness of a reprieve, a sensation that was heightened by the fact that on the train in from Trenton women would often press upon him dog-eared copies of *Life* and half-eaten boxes of candy, as though the brown clothes he wore were surely cerements. He telephoned Joan from Pennsylvania Station one night. "Come right over, Jack," she said. "Come right over. I want you to meet Ralph."

She was living in that place in the West Twenties that Jack had found for her. The neighborhood was a slum. Ash cans stood in front of her house, and an old woman was there picking out bits of refuse and garbage and stuffing them into a perambulator. The house in which Joan's apartment was located was shabby, but the apartment itself seemed familiar. The furniture was the same. Joan was the same big, easy-going girl. "I'm so glad you called me," she said. "It's so good to see you. I'll make you a drink. I was having one myself. Ralph ought to be here by now. He promised to take me to dinner." Jack offered to take her to Cavanagh's, but she said that Ralph might come while she was out. "If he doesn't come by nine, I'm going to make myself a sandwich. I'm not really hungry."

Jack talked about the Army. She talked about the store. She had been working in the same place for—how long was it? He didn't know. He had never seen her at her desk and he couldn't imagine what she did. "I'm terribly sorry Ralph isn't here," she said. "I'm sure you'd like him. He's not a young man. He's a heart specialist who loves to play the viola." She turned on some lights, for the summer sky had got dark. "He has this dreadful wife on Riverside Drive and four ungrateful children. He—"

The noise of an air-raid siren, lugubrious and seeming to spring from

pain, as if all the misery and indecision in the city had been given a voice, cut her off. Other sirens, in distant neighborhoods, sounded, until the dark air was full of their noise. "Let me fix you another drink before I have to turn out the lights," Joan said, and took his glass. She brought the drink back to him and snapped off the lights. They went to the windows, and, as children watch a thunderstorm, they watched the city darken. All the lights nearby went out but one. Air-raid wardens had begun to sound their whistles in the street. From a distant yard came a hoarse shriek of anger. "Put out your lights, you Fascists!" a woman screamed. "Put out your lights, you Nazi Fascist Germans. Turn out your lights. Turn out your lights." The last light went off. They went away from the window and sat in the lightless room.

In the darkness, Joan began to talk about her departed lovers, and from what she said Jack gathered that they had all had a hard time. Nils, the suspect count, was dead. Hugh Bascomb, the drunk, had joined the Merchant Marine and was missing in the North Atlantic. Franz, the German, had taken poison the night the Nazis bombed Warsaw. "We listened to the news on the radio," Joan said, "and then he went back to his hotel and took poison. The maid found him dead in the bathroom the next morning." When Jack asked her about the one who was going to open an advertising agency, she seemed at first to have forgotten him. "Oh, Pete," she said after a pause. "Well, he was always very sick, you know. He was supposed to go to Saranac, but he kept putting it off and putting it off and—" She stopped talking when she heard steps on the stairs, hoping, he supposed, that it was Ralph, but whoever it was turned at the landing and continued to the top of the house. "I wish Ralph would come," she said, with a sigh. "I want you to meet him." Jack asked her again to go out, but she refused, and when the all-clear sounded, he said goodbye.

Jack was shipped from Dix to an infantry training camp in the Carolinas and from there to an infantry division stationed in Georgia. He had been in Georgia three months when he married a girl from the Augusta boarding-house aristocracy. A year or so later, he crossed the continent in a day coach and thought sententiously that the last he might see of the country he loved was the desert towns like Barstow, that the last he might hear of it was the ringing of the trolleys on the Bay Bridge. He was sent into the Pacific and returned to the United States twenty months later, uninjured and apparently unchanged. As soon as he received his furlough, he went to Augusta. He presented his wife with the souvenirs he had brought from the islands, quarrelled violently with her and all her family, and, after making arrangements for her to get an Arkansas divorce, left for New York.

Jack was discharged from the Army at a camp in the East a few months later. He took a vacation and then went back to the job he had left in 1942. He seemed to have picked up his life at approximately the moment when it had been interrupted by the war. In time, everything came to look and feel the same. He saw most of his old friends. Only two of the men he knew had been killed in the war. He didn't call Joan, but he met her one winter afternoon on a crosstown bus.

Her fresh face, her black clothes, and her soft voice instantly destroyed the sense—if he had ever had such a sense—that anything had changed or intervened since their last meeting, three or four years ago. She asked him up for cocktails and he went to her apartment the next Saturday afternoon. Her room and her guests reminded him of the parties she had given when she had first come to New York. There was a woman with a fancy hat, an elderly doctor, and a man who stayed close to the radio, listening for news from the Balkans. Jack wondered which of the men belonged to Joan and decided on an Englishman who kept coughing into a handkerchief that he pulled out of his sleeve. Jack was right. "Isn't Stephen brilliant?" Joan asked him a little later, when they were alone in a corner. "He knows more about the Polynesians than anyone else in the world."

Jack had returned not only to his old job but to his old salary. Since living costs had doubled and since he was paying alimony to two wives, he had to draw on his savings. He took another job, which promised more money, but it didn't last long and he found himself out of work. This didn't bother him at all. He still had money in the bank, and anyhow it was easy to borrow from friends. His indifference was the consequence not of lassitude or despair but rather of an excess of hope. He had the feeling that he had only recently come to New York from Ohio. The sense that he was very young and that the best years of his life still lay before him was an illusion that he could not seem to escape. There was all the time in the world. He was living in hotels then, moving from one to another every five days.

In the spring, Jack moved to a furnished room in the badlands west of Central Park. He was running out of money. Then, when he began to feel that a job was a desperate necessity, he got sick. At first, he seemed to have only a bad cold, but he was unable to shake it and he began to run a fever and to cough blood. The fever kept him drowsy most of the time, but he roused himself occasionally and went out to a cafeteria for a meal. He felt sure that none of his friends knew where he was, and he was glad of this. He hadn't counted on Joan.

Late one morning, he heard her speaking in the hall with his landlady. A few moments later, she knocked on his door. He was lying on the bed in a pair of pants and a soiled pajama top, and he didn't answer. She knocked again and walked in. "I've been looking everywhere for you, Jack," she said. She spoke softly. "When I found out that you were in a place like this I thought you must be broke or sick. I stopped at the bank and got some money, in case you're broke. I've brought you some Scotch. I thought a little drink wouldn't do you any harm. Want a little drink?"

Joan's dress was black. Her voice was low and serene. She sat in a chair beside his bed as if she had been coming there every day to nurse him. Her features had coarsened, he thought, but there were still very few lines in her face. She was heavier. She was nearly fat. She was wearing black cotton gloves. She got two glasses and poured Scotch into them. He drank his whiskey greedily. "I didn't get to bed until three last night," she said. Her voice had once before reminded him of a gentle and despairing song, but now, perhaps because he was sick, her mildness, the mourning she wore, her stealthy grace, made him uneasy. "It was one of those nights," she said. "We went to the theatre. Afterward, someone asked us up to his place. I don't know who he was. It was one of those places. They're so strange. There were some meat-eating plants and a collection of Chinese snuff bottles. Why do people collect Chinese snuff bottles? We all autographed a lampshade, as I remember, but I can't remember much."

Jack tried to sit up in bed, as if there were some need to defend himself, and then fell back again, against the pillows. "How did you find me, Joan?" he asked.

"It was simple," she said. "I called that hotel. The one you were staying in. They gave me this address. My secretary got the telephone number. Have another little drink."

"You know you've never come to a place of mine before—never," he said. "Why did you come now?"

"Why did I come, darling?" she asked. "What a question! I've known you for thirty years. You're the oldest friend I have in New York. Remember that night in the Village when it snowed and we stayed up until morning and drank whiskey sours for breakfast? That doesn't seem like twelve years ago. And that night—"

"I don't like to have you see me in a place like this," he said earnestly. He touched his face and felt his beard.

"And all the people who used to imitate Roosevelt," she said, as if she had not heard him, as if she were deaf. "And that place on Staten Island where we all used to go for dinner when Henry had a car. Poor Henry. He bought a place in Connecticut and went out there by himself, one weekend. He fell asleep with a lighted cigarette and the house, the barn, everything burned. Ethel took the children out to California." She poured more Scotch into his glass and handed it to him. She lighted a cigarette and put it between his lips. The intimacy of this gesture, which made it seem not only as if he were deathly ill but as if he were her lover, troubled him.

"As soon as I'm better," he said, "I'll take a room at a good hotel. I'll call you then. It was nice of you to come."

"Oh, don't be ashamed of this room, Jack," she said. "Rooms never bother me. It doesn't seem to matter to me where I am. Stanley had a filthy room in Chelsea. At least, other people told me it was filthy. I never noticed it. Rats used to eat the food I brought him. He used to have to hang the food from the ceiling, from the light chain."

"I'll call you as soon as I'm better," Jack said. "I think I can sleep now if I'm left alone. I seem to need a lot of sleep."

"You really *are* sick, darling," she said. "You must have a fever." She sat on the edge of his bed and put a hand on his forehead.

"How is that Englishman, Joan?" he asked. "Do you still see him?"

"What Englishman?" she said.

"You know. I met him at your house. He kept a handkerchief up his sleeve. He coughed all the time. You know the one I mean."

"You must be thinking of someone else," she said. "I haven't had an Englishman at my place since the war. Of course, I can't remember everyone." She turned and, taking one of his hands, linked her fingers in his.

"He's dead, isn't he?" Jack said. "That Englishman's dead." He pushed her off the bed, and got up himself. "Get out," he said.

"You're sick, darling," she said. "I can't leave you alone here."

"Get out," he said again, and when she didn't move, he shouted, "What kind of an obscenity are you that you can smell sickness and death the way you do?"

"You poor darling."

"Does it make you feel young to watch the dying?" he shouted. "Is that the lewdness that keeps you young? Is that why you dress like a crow? Oh, I know there's nothing I can say that will hurt you. I know there's nothing filthy or corrupt or depraved or brutish or base that the others haven't tried, but this time you're wrong. I'm not ready My life isn't ending. My life's beginning There are wonderful years ahead of me. There are, there are wonderful, wonderful, wonderful years ahead of me, and when they're over, when it's time, then I'll call you. Then, as an old friend, I'll call you and give you whatever dirty pleasure you take in watching the dying, but until then, you and your ugly and misshapen forms will leave me alone."

She finished her drink and looked at her watch. "I guess I'd better show up at the office," she said. "I'll see you later. I'll come back tonight. You'll feel better then, you poor darling." She closed the door after her, and he heard her light step on the stairs.

Jack emptied the whiskey bottle into the sink. He began to dress. He stuffed his dirty clothes into a bag. He was trembling and crying with sickness and fear. He could see the blue sky from his window, and in his fear it seemed miraculous that the sky would be blue, that the white clouds should remind him of snow, that from the sidewalk he could hear the shrill voices of children shrieking, "I'm the king of the mountain, I'm the king of the mountain, I'm the king of the mountain." He emptied the ashtray containing his nail parings and cigarette butts into the toilet, and swept the floor with a shirt, so that there would be no trace of his life, of his body, when that lewd and searching shape of death came there to find him in the evening.

Anton Chekhov

1860–1904

GOOSEBERRIES

Translated by Constance Garnett

The whole sky had been overcast with rain-clouds from early morning; it was a still day, not hot, but heavy, as it is in gray dull weather when the clouds have been hanging over the country for a long while, when one expects rain and it does not come. Ivan Ivanovich, the veterinary surgeon, and Burkin, the high school teacher, were already tired from walking, and the fields seemed to them endless. Far ahead of them they could just see the windmills of the village of Mironositskoe; on the right stretched a row of hillocks which disappeared in the distance behind the village, and they both knew that this was the bank of the river, that there were meadows, green willows, homesteads there, and that if one stood on one of the hillocks one could see from it the same vast plain, telegraph-wires, and a train which in the distance looked like a crawling caterpillar, and that in clear weather one could even see the town. Now, in still weather, when all nature seemed mild and dreamy, Ivan Ivanovich and Burkin were filled with love of the countryside, and both thought how great, how beautiful a land it was.

"Last time we were in Prokofy's barn," said Burkin, "you were about to tell me a story."

"Yes; I meant to tell you about my brother."

Ivan Ivanovich heaved a deep sigh and lighted a pipe to begin to tell his story, but just at that moment the rain began. And five minutes later heavy rain came down, covering the sky, and it was hard to tell when it would be over. Ivan Ivanovich and Burkin stopped in hesitation; the dogs, already drenched, stood with their tails between their legs gazing at them feelingly.

"We must take shelter somewhere," said Burkin. "Let us go to Alehin's; it's close by."

"Come along."

They turned aside and walked through mown fields, sometimes going straight forward, sometimes turning to the right, till they came out on the road. Soon they saw poplars, a garden, then the red roofs of barns; there was a gleam of the river, and the view opened onto a broad expanse of water with a windmill and a white bathhouse: this was Sofino, where Alehin lived.

The watermill was at work, drowning the sound of the rain; the dam was shaking. Here wet horses with drooping heads were standing near their carts, and men were walking about covered with sacks. It was damp, muddy, and desolate; the water looked cold and malignant. Ivan Ivanovich and Burkin were already conscious of a feeling of wetness, messiness, and discomfort all over; their feet were heavy with mud, and when, crossing the dam, they went up to the barns, they were silent, as though they were angry with one another.

In one of the barns there was the sound of a winnowing machine, the door was open, and clouds of dust were coming from it. In the doorway was standing Alehin himself, a man of forty, tall and stout, with long hair, more like a professor or an artist than a landowner. He had on a white shirt that badly needed washing, a rope for a belt, drawers instead of trousers, and his boots, too, were plastered up with mud and straw. His eyes and nose were black with dust. He recognized Ivan Ivanovich and Burkin, and was apparently much delighted to see them.

"Go into the house, gentlemen," he said, smiling; "I'll come directly, this minute."

It was a big two-storied house. Alehin lived in the lower story, with arched ceilings and little windows, where the bailiffs had once lived; here everything was plain, and there was a smell of rye bread, cheap vodka, and harness. He went upstairs into the best rooms only on rare occasions, when visitors came. Ivan Ivanovich and Burkin were met in the house by a maidservant, a young woman so beautiful that they both stood still and looked at one another.

"You can't imagine how delighted I am to see you, my friends," said Alehin, going into the hall with them. "It is a surprise! Pelageya," he said, addressing the girl, "give our visitors something to change into. And, by the way, I will change too. Only I must first go and wash, for I almost think I have not washed since spring. Wouldn't you like to come into the bathhouse? And meanwhile they will get things ready here."

Beautiful Pelageya, looking so refined and soft, brought them towels and soap, and Alehin went to the bathhouse with his guests.

"It's a long time since I had a wash," he said, undressing. "I have got a nice bathhouse, as you see—my father built it—but I somehow never have time to wash."

He sat down on the steps and soaped his long hair and his neck, and the water round him turned brown.

"Yes, I must say," said Ivan Ivanovich meaningly, looking at his head.

"It's a long time since I washed . . ." said Alehin with embarrassment, giving himself a second soaping, and the water near him turned dark blue, like ink.

Ivan Ivanovich went outside, plunged into the water with a loud splash, and swam in the rain, flinging his arms out wide. He stirred the water into waves which set the white lilies bobbing up and down; he swam to the very middle of the millpond and dived, and came up a minute later in another place, and swam on, and kept on diving, trying to touch bottom.

"Oh, my goodness!" he repeated continually, enjoying himself thoroughly. "Oh, my goodness!" He swam to the mill, talked to the peasants there, then returned and lay on his back in the middle of the pond, turning his face to the rain. Burkin and Alehin were dressed and ready to go, but he still went on swimming and diving. "Oh, my goodness! . . ." he said. "Oh, Lord, have mercy on me! . . ."

"That's enough!" Burkin shouted to him.

They went back to the house. And only when the lamp was lighted in the big drawing-room upstairs, and Burkin and Ivan Ivanovich, attired in silk dressing-gowns and warm slippers, were sitting in armchairs; and Alehin, washed and combed, in a new coat, was walking about the drawing-room, evidently enjoying the feeling of warmth, cleanliness, dry clothes, and light shoes; and when lovely Pelageya, stepping noiselessly on the carpet and smiling softly, handed tea and jam on a tray—only then Ivan Ivanovich began on his story, and it seemed as though not only Burkin and Alehin were listening, but also the ladies, young and old, and the officers who looked down upon them sternly and calmly from their gold frames.

"There are two of us brothers," he began—"I, Ivan Ivanovich, and my brother, Nikolay Ivanovich, two years younger. I went in for a learned profession and became a veterinary surgeon, while Nikolay sat in a government office from the time he was nineteen. Our father, Chimsha-Himalaisky, was the son of a private, but he himself rose to be an officer and left us a little estate and the rank of nobility. After his death the little estate went in debts and legal expenses; but, anyway, we had spent our childhood running wild in the country. Like peasant children, we passed our days and nights in the fields and the woods, looked after horses, stripped the bark off the trees, fished and so on. . . . And, you know, whoever has once in his life caught perch or has seen the migrating of the thrushes in autumn, watched how they float in flocks over the village on bright, cool days, he will never be a real townsman, and will have a yearning for freedom to the day of his death. My brother was miserable in the government office. Years passed by, and he went on sitting in the same place, went on writing the same papers and thinking of one and the same thing—how to get into the country. And this yearning by degrees passed

into a definite desire, into a dream of buying himself a little farm somewhere on the banks of a river or a lake.

"He was a gentle, good-natured fellow, and I was fond of him, but I
never sympathized with his desire to shut himself up for the rest of his
life in a little farm of his own. It's the correct thing to say that a man
needs no more than six feet of earth. But six feet is what a corpse needs,
not a man. And they say, too, now, that if our intellectual classes are attracted to the land and yearn for a farm, it's a good thing. But these
farms are just the same as six feet of earth. To retreat from town, from
the struggle, from the bustle of life, to retreat and bury oneself in one's
farm—it's not life, it's egoism, laziness, it's monasticism of a sort, but
monasticism without good works. A man does not need six feet of earth
or a farm, but the whole globe, all nature, where he can have room to
display all the qualities and peculiarities of his free spirit.

"My brother Nikolay, sitting in his government office, dreamed of how
he would eat his own cabbages, which would fill the whole yard with such
a savory smell, take his meals on the green grass, sleep in the sun, sit for
whole hours on the seat by the gate gazing at the fields and the forest.
Gardening books and the agricultural hints in calendars were his delight,
his favorite spiritual sustenance; he enjoyed reading newspapers, too, but
the only things he read in them were the advertisements of so many acres
of arable land and a grass meadow with farmhouses and buildings, a river,
a garden, a mill and millponds, for sale. And his imagination pictured the
garden-paths, flowers and fruit, starling cotes, the carp in the pond, and
all that sort of thing, you know. These imaginary pictures were of different
kinds according to the advertisements which he came across, but for some
reason in every one of them he always had to have gooseberries. He could
not imagine a homestead, he could not picture an idyllic nook, without
gooseberries.

" 'Country life has its conveniences,' he would sometimes say. 'You sit
on the veranda and you drink tea, while your ducks swim on the pond,
there is a delicious smell everywhere, and . . . and the gooseberries are
growing.'

"He used to draw a map of his property, and in every map there were
the same things—(a) house for the family, (b) servants' quarters, (c) kitchen-
garden, (d) gooseberry-bushes. He lived parsimoniously, was frugal in food
and drink, his clothes were beyond description; he looked like a beggar,
but kept on saving and putting money in the bank. He grew fearfully
avaricious. I did not like to look at him, and I used to give him something and send him presents for Christmas and Easter, but he used to save
that too. Once a man is absorbed by an idea there is no doing anything
with him.

"Years passed: he was transferred to another province. He was over
forty, and he was still reading the advertisements in the papers and saving

up. Then I heard he was married. Still with the same object of buying a farm and having gooseberries, he married an elderly and ugly widow without a trace of feeling for her, simply because she had filthy lucre. He went on living frugally after marrying her, and kept her short of food, while he put her money in the bank in his name.

"Her first husband had been a postmaster, and with him she was accustomed to pies and homemade wines, while with her second husband she did not get enough black bread; she began to pine away with this sort of life, and three years later she gave up her soul to God. And I need hardly say that my brother never for one moment imagined that he was responsible for her death. Money, like vodka, makes a man queer. In our town there was a merchant who, before he died, ordered a plateful of honey and ate up all his money and lottery tickets with the honey, so that no one might get the benefit of it. While I was inspecting cattle at a railway-station a cattle-dealer fell under an engine and had his leg cut off. We carried him into the waiting-room, the blood was flowing—it was a horrible thing—and he kept asking them to look for his leg and was very much worried about it; there were twenty roubles in the boot on the leg that had been cut off, and he was afraid they would be lost."

"That's a story from a different opera," said Burkin.

"After his wife's death," Ivan Ivanovich went on, after thinking for half a minute, "my brother began looking out for an estate for himself. Of course, you may look about for five years and yet end by making a mistake, and buying something quite different from what you have dreamed of. My brother Nikolay bought through an agent a mortgaged estate of three hundred and thirty acres, with a house for the family, with servants' quarters, with a park, but with no orchard, no gooseberry-bushes, and no duck-pond; there was a river, but the water in it was the color of coffee, because on one side of the estate there was a brickyard and on the other a factory for burning bones. But Nikolay Ivanovich did not grieve much; he ordered twenty gooseberry-bushes, planted them, and began living as a country gentleman.

"Last year I went to pay him a visit. I thought I would go and see what it was like. In his letters my brother called his estate 'Chumbaroklov Waste, alias Himalaiskoe.' I reached 'alias Himalaiskoe' in the afternoon. It was hot. Everywhere there were ditches, fences, hedges, fir-trees planted in rows, and there was no knowing how to get to the yard, where to put one's horse. I went up to the house, and was met by a fat red dog that looked like a pig. It wanted to bark, but was too lazy. The cook, a fat, barefooted woman, came out of the kitchen, and she, too, looked like a pig, and said that her master was resting. I went in to see my brother. He was sitting up in bed with a quilt over his legs; he had grown older, fatter, wrinkled; his cheeks, his nose, and his mouth all stuck out—he looked as though he might begin grunting into the quilt at any moment.

"We embraced each other, and shed tears of joy and of sadness at the thought that we had once been young and now were both gray-headed and near the grave. He dressed, and led me out to show me the estate.

" 'Well, how are you getting on here?' I asked.

" 'Oh, all right, thank God; I am getting on very well.'

"He was no more a poor timid clerk, but a real landowner, a gentleman. He was already accustomed to it, had grown used to it, and liked it. He ate a great deal, went to the bathhouse, was growing stout, was already at law with the village commune and both factories, and was very much offended when the peasants did not call him 'your Honor.' And he concerned himself with the salvation of his soul in a substantial, gentlemanly manner, and performed deeds of charity, not simply, but with an air of consequence. And what deeds of charity! He treated the peasants for every sort of disease with soda and castor oil, and on his name-day had a thanksgiving service in the middle of the village, and then treated the peasants to a gallon of vodka—he thought that was the thing to do. Oh, those horrible gallons of vodka! One day the fat landowner hauls the peasants up before the district captain for trespass, and next day, in honor of a holiday, treats them to a gallon of vodka, and they drink and shout 'Hurrah!' and when they are drunk bow down to his feet. A change of life for the better and being well fed and idle develop in a Russian the most insolent self-conceit. Nikolay Ivanovich, who at one time in the government office was afraid to have any views of his own, now could say nothing that was not gospel truth, and uttered such truths in the tone of a prime minister. 'Education is essential, but for the peasants it is premature.' 'Corporal punishment is harmful as a rule, but in some cases it is necessary and there is nothing to take its place.'

" 'I know the peasants and understand how to treat them,' he would say. 'The peasants like me. I need only to hold up my little finger and the peasants will do anything I like.'

"And all this, observe, was uttered with a wise, benevolent smile. He repeated twenty times over 'We noblemen,' 'I as a noble'; obviously he did not remember that our grandfather was a peasant, and our father a soldier. Even our surname Chimsha-Himalaisky, in reality so incongruous, seemed to him now melodious, distinguished, and very agreeable.

"But the point just now is not he, but myself. I want to tell you about the change that took place in me during the brief hours I spent at his country place. In the evening, when we were drinking tea, the cook put on the table a plateful of gooseberries. They were not bought, but his own gooseberries, gathered for the first time since the bushes were planted. Nikolay Ivanovich laughed and looked for a minute in silence at the gooseberries, with tears in his eyes; he could not speak for excitement. Then he put one gooseberry in his mouth, looked at me with the triumph of a child who has at last received his favorite toy, and said:

" 'How delicious!'

"And he ate them greedily, continually repeating, 'Ah, how delicious! Do taste them!'

"They were sour and unripe, but, as Pushkin says:

> *Dearer to us the falsehood that exalts*
> *Than hosts of baser truths.*

"I saw a happy man whose cherished dream was so obviously fulfilled, who had attained his object in life, who had gained what he wanted, who was satisfied with his fate and himself. There is always, for some reason, an element of sadness mingled with my thoughts of human happiness, and, on this occasion, at the sight of a happy man I was overcome by an oppressive feeling that was close upon despair. It was particularly oppressive at night. A bed was made up for me in the room next to my brother's bedroom, and I could hear that he was awake, and that he kept getting up and going to the plate of gooseberries and taking one. I reflected how many satisfied, happy people there really are! What an overwhelming force it is! You look at life: the insolence and idleness of the strong, the ignorance and brutishness of the weak, incredible poverty all about us, overcrowding, degeneration, drunkenness, hypocrisy, lying. . . . Yet all is calm and stillness in the houses and in the streets; of the fifty thousand living in a town, there is not one who would cry out, who would give vent to his indignation aloud. We see the people going to market for provisions, eating by day, sleeping by night, talking their silly nonsense, getting married, growing old, serenely escorting their dead to the cemetery; but we do not see and we do not hear those who suffer, and what is terrible in life goes on somewhere behind the scenes. . . . Everything is quiet and peaceful, and nothing protests but mute statistics: so many people gone out of their minds, so many gallons of vodka drunk, so many children dead from malnutrition. . . . And this order of things is evidently necessary; evidently the happy man only feels at ease because the unhappy bear their burden in silence, and without that silence happiness would be impossible. It's a case of general hypnotism. There ought to be behind the door of every happy, contented man someone standing with a hammer continually reminding him with a tap that there are unhappy people; that however happy he may be, life will show him her jaws sooner or later, trouble will come for him—disease, poverty, losses, and no one will see or hear, just as now he neither sees nor hears others. But there is no man with a hammer; the happy man lives at his ease, the trivial daily cares faintly agitate him like the wind in the aspen-tree—and all goes well.

"That night I realized that I, too, was happy and contented," Ivan Ivanovich went on, getting up. "I, too, at dinner and at the hunt liked to lay down the law on life and religion, and the way to manage the peasantry. I, too, used to say that science was light, that culture was essential, but for the simple people reading and writing was enough for the time.

Freedom is a blessing, I used to say; we can no more do without it than without air, but we must wait a little. Yes, I used to talk like that, and now I ask, 'For what reason are we to wait?' " asked Ivan Ivanovich, looking angrily at Burkin. "Why wait, I ask you? What grounds have we for waiting? I shall be told, it can't be done all at once; every idea takes shape in life gradually, in its due time. But who is it says that? Where is the proof that it's right? You will fall back upon the natural order of things, the uniformity of phenomena; but is there order and uniformity in the fact that I, a living, thinking man, stand over a chasm and wait for it to close of itself, or to fill up with mud at the very time when perhaps I might leap over it or build a bridge across it? And again, wait for the sake of what? Wait till there's no strength to live? And meanwhile one must live, and one wants to live!

"I went away from my brother's early in the morning, and ever since then it has been unbearable for me to be among people. I am oppressed by peace and quiet; I am afraid to look at the windows, for there is no spectacle more painful to me now than the sight of a happy family sitting round the table drinking tea. I am old and am not fit for the struggle; I am not even capable of hatred; I can only grieve inwardly, feel irritated and vexed; but at night my head is hot from the rush of ideas, and I cannot sleep. . . . Ah, if I were young!"

Ivan Ivanovich walked backwards and forwards in excitement, and repeated: "If I were young!"

He suddenly went up to Alehin and began pressing first one of his hands and then the other.

"Pavel Konstantinovich," he said in an imploring voice, "don't be calm and contented, don't let yourself be put to sleep! While you are young, strong, confident, be not weary in well-doing! There is no happiness, and there ought not to be; but if there is a meaning and an object in life, that meaning and object is not our happiness, but something greater and more rational. Do good!"

And all this Ivan Ivanovich said with a pitiful, imploring smile, as though he were asking him a personal favor.

Then all three sat in armchairs at different ends of the drawing-room and were silent. Ivan Ivanovich's story had not satisfied either Burkin or Alehin. When the generals and ladies gazed down from their gilt frames, looking in the dusk as though they were alive, it was dreary to listen to the story of the poor clerk who ate gooseberries. They felt inclined for some reason to talk about elegant people, about women. And their sitting in the drawing-room where everything—the chandeliers in their covers, the armchairs, and the carpet under their feet—reminded them that those very people who were now looking down from their frames had once moved about, sat, drunk tea in this room, and the fact that lovely Pelageya was moving noiselessly about was better than any story.

Alehin was fearfully sleepy; he had got up early, before three o'clock in the morning, to look after his work, and now his eyes were closing; but he was afraid his visitors might tell some interesting story after he had gone, and he lingered on. He did not go into the question whether what Ivan Ivanovich had just said was right and true. His visitors did not talk of groats, nor of hay, nor of tar, but of something that had no direct bearing on his life, and he was glad and wanted them to go on.

"It's bedtime, though," said Burkin, getting up. "Allow me to wish you good night."

Alehin said good night and went downstairs to his own domain, while the visitors remained upstairs. They were both taken for the night to a big room where there stood two old wooden beds decorated with carvings, and in the corner was an ivory crucifix. The big cool beds, which had been made by the lovely Pelageya, smelt agreeably of clean linen.

Ivan Ivanovich undressed in silence and got into bed.

"Lord forgive us sinners!" he said, and put his head under the quilt.

His pipe lying on the table smelt strongly of stale tobacco, and Burkin could not sleep for a long while, and kept wondering where the oppressive smell came from.

The rain was pattering on the windowpanes all night.

Flannery O'Connor

1915–1964

A GOOD MAN IS HARD TO FIND

The grandmother didn't want to go to Florida. She wanted to visit some of her connections in east Tennessee and she was seizing at every chance to change Bailey's mind. Bailey was the son she lived with, her only boy. He was sitting on the edge of his chair at the table, bent over the orange sports section of the *Journal*. "Now look here, Bailey," she said, "see here, read this," and she stood with one hand on her thin hip and the other rattling the newspaper at his bald head. "Here this fellow that calls himself The Misfit is aloose from the Federal Pen and headed toward Florida and you read here what it says he did to these people. Just you read it. I wouldn't take my children in any direction with a criminal like that aloose in it. I couldn't answer to my conscience if I did."

Bailey didn't look up from his reading so she wheeled around then and faced the children's mother; a young woman in slacks, whose face was as broad and innocent as a cabbage and was tied around with a green headkerchief that had two points on the top like rabbit's ears. She was sitting on the sofa, feeding the baby his apricots out of a jar. "The children have been to Florida before," the old lady said. "You all ought to take them somewhere else for a change so they would see different parts of the world and be broad. They never have been to east Tennessee."

The children's mother didn't seem to hear her, but the eight-year-old boy, John Wesley, a stocky child with glasses, said, "If you don't want to go to Florida, why dontcha stay at home?" He and the little girl, June Star, were reading the funny papers on the floor.

"She wouldn't stay at home to be queen for a day," June Star said without raising her yellow head.

"Yes, and what would you do if this fellow, The Misfit, caught you?" the grandmother asked.

"I'd smack his face," John Wesley said.

"She wouldn't stay at home for a million bucks," June Star said. "Afraid she'd miss something. She has to go everywhere we go."

"All right, Miss," the grandmother said. "Just remember that the next time you want me to curl your hair."

June Star said her hair was naturally curly.

The next morning the grandmother was the first one in the car, ready to go. She had her big black valise that looked like the head of a hippopotamus in one corner, and underneath it she was hiding a basket with Pitty Sing, the cat, in it. She didn't intend for the cat to be left alone in the house for three days because he would miss her too much and she was afraid he might brush against one of the gas burners and accidentally asphyxiate himself. Her son, Bailey, didn't like to arrive at a motel with a cat.

She sat in the middle of the back seat with John Wesley and June Star on either side of her. Bailey and the children's mother and the baby sat in the front and they left Atlanta at eight forty-five with the mileage on the car at 55890. The grandmother wrote this down because she thought it would be interesting to say how many miles they had been when they got back. It took them twenty minutes to reach the outskirts of the city.

The old lady settled herself comfortably, removing her white cotton gloves and putting them up with her purse on the shelf in front of the back window. The children's mother still had on slacks and still had her head tied up in a green kerchief, but the grandmother had on a navy blue straw sailor hat with a bunch of white violets on the brim and a navy blue dress with a small white dot in the print. Her collar and cuffs were white organdy trimmed with lace and at her neckline she had pinned a purple spray of cloth violets containing a sachet. In case of an accident, anyone seeing her dead on the highway would know at once that she was a lady.

She said she thought it was going to be a good day for driving, neither too hot nor too cold, and she cautioned Bailey that the speed limit was fifty-five miles an hour and that the patrolmen hid themselves behind billboards and small clumps of trees and sped out after you before you had a chance to slow down. She pointed out interesting details of the scenery: Stone Mountain; the blue granite that in some places came up to both sides of the highway; the brilliant red clay banks slightly streaked with purple; and the various crops that made rows of green lace-work on the ground. The trees were full of silver-white sunlights and the meanest of them sparkled. The children were reading comic magazines and their mother had gone back to sleep.

"Let's go through Georgia fast so we won't have to look at it much,' John Wesley said.

"If I were a little boy," said the grandmother, "I wouldn't talk about my native state that way. Tennessee has the mountains and Georgia has the hills."

"Tennessee is just a hillbilly dumping ground," John Wesley said, "and Georgia is a lousy state too."

"You said it," June Star said.

"In my time," said the grandmother, folding her thin veined fingers, "children were more respectful of their native states and their parents and everything else. People did right then. Oh look at the cute little pickaninny!" she said and pointed to a Negro child standing in the door of a shack. "Wouldn't that make a picture, now?" she asked and they all turned and looked at the little Negro out of the back window. He waved.

"He didn't have any britches on," June Star said.

"He probably didn't have any," the grandmother explained. "Little niggers in the country don't have things like we do. If I could paint, I'd paint that picture," she said.

The children exchanged comic books

The grandmother offered to hold the baby and the children's mother passed him over the front seat to her. She set him on her knee and bounced him and told him about the things they were passing. She rolled her eyes and screwed up her mouth and stuck her leathery thin face into his smooth bland one. Occasionally he gave her a faraway smile. They passed a large cotton field with five or six graves fenced in the middle of it, like a small island. "Look at the graveyard!" the grandmother said, pointing it out. "That was the old family burying ground. That belonged to the plantation."

"Where's the plantation?" John Wesley asked.

"Gone With the Wind," said the grandmother. "Ha. Ha."

When the children finished all the comic books they had brought, they opened the lunch and ate it. The grandmother ate a peanut butter sandwich and an olive and would not let the children throw the box and the paper napkins out the window. When there was nothing else to do they played a game by choosing a cloud and making the other two guess what shape it suggested. John Wesley took one the shape of a cow and June Star guessed a cow and John Wesley said, no, an automobile, and June Star said he didn't play fair, and they began to slap each other over the grandmother.

The grandmother said she would tell them a story if they would keep quiet. When she told a story, she rolled her eyes and waved her head and was very dramatic. She said once when she was a maiden lady she had been courted by a Mr. Edgar Atkins Teagarden from Jasper, Georgia. She said he was a very good-looking man and a gentleman and that he brought her a watermelon every Saturday afternoon with his initials cut in it, E.A.T. Well, one Saturday, she said, Mr. Teagarden brought the watermelon and there was nobody at home and he left it on the front porch and returned in his buggy to Jasper, but she never got the watermelon, she said, because a nigger boy ate it when he saw the initials, E.A.T.! This story tickled John Wesley's funny bone and he giggled and giggled but

June Star didn't think it was any good. She said she wouldn't marry a man that just brought her a watermelon on Saturday. The grandmother said she would have done well to marry Mr. Teagarden because he was a gentleman and had bought Coca-Cola stock when it first came out and that he had died only a few years ago, a very wealthy man.

They stopped at The Tower for barbecued sandwiches. The Tower was a part-stucco and part-wood filling station and dance hall set in a clearing outside of Timothy. A fat man named Red Sammy Butts ran it and there were signs stuck here and there on the building and for miles up and down the highway saying, TRY RED SAMMY'S FAMOUS BARBECUE. NONE LIKE FAMOUS RED SAMMY'S! RED SAM! THE FAT BOY WITH THE HAPPY LAUGH. A VETERAN! RED SAMMY'S YOUR MAN!

Red Sammy was lying on the bare ground outside The Tower with his head under a truck while a gray monkey about a foot high, chained to a small chinaberry tree, chattered nearby. The monkey sprang back into the tree and got on the highest limb as soon as he saw the children jump out of the car and run toward him.

Inside, The Tower was a long dark room with a counter at one end and tables at the other and dancing space in the middle. They all sat down at a broad table next to the nickelodeon and Red Sam's wife, a tall burnt-brown woman with hair and eyes lighter than her skin, came and took their order. The children's mother put a dime in the machine and played "The Tennessee Waltz," and the grandmother said that tune always made her want to dance. She asked Bailey if he would like to dance but he only glared at her. He didn't have a naturally sunny disposition like she did and trips made him nervous. The grandmother's brown eyes were very bright. She swayed her head from side to side and pretended she was dancing in her chair. June Star said play something she could tap to so the children's mother put in another dime and played a fast number and June Star stepped out onto the dance floor and did her tap routine.

"Ain't she cute?" Red Sam's wife said, leaning over the counter. "Would you like to come be my little girl?"

"No, I certainly wouldn't," June Star said. "I wouldn't live in a broken-down place like this for a million bucks!" and she ran back to the table.

"Ain't she cute?" the woman repeated, stretching her mouth politely.

"Aren't you ashamed?" hissed the grandmother.

Red Sam came in and told his wife to quit lounging on the counter and hurry up with these people's order. His khaki trousers reached just to his hip bones and his stomach hung over them like a sack of meal swaying under his shirt. He came over and sat down at a table nearby and let out a combination sigh and yodel. "You can't win," he said. "You can't win," and he wiped his sweating red face off with a gray handkerchief. "These days you don't know who to trust," he said. "Ain't that the truth?"

"People are certainly not nice like they used to be," said the grandmother.

"Two fellers come in here last week," Red Sammy said, "driving a Chrysler. It was a old beat-up car but it was a good one and these boys looked all right to me. Said they worked at the mill and you know I let them fellers charge the gas they bought? Now why did I do that?"

"Because you're a good man!" the grandmother said at once.

"Yes'm, I suppose so," Red Sam said as if he were struck with this answer.

His wife brought the orders, carrying the five plates all at once without a tray, two in each hand and one balanced on her arm. "It isn't a soul in this green world of God's that you can trust," she said. "And I don't count nobody out of that, not nobody," she repeated, looking at Red Sammy.

"Did you read about that criminal, The Misfit, that's escaped?" asked the grandmother.

"I wouldn't be a bit surprised if he didn't attact this place right here," said the woman. "If he hears about it being here, I wouldn't be none surprised to see him. If he hears it's two cent in the cash register, I wouldn't be a tall surprised if he. . . ."

"That'll do," Red Sam said. "Go bring these people their Co'Colas," and the woman went off to get the rest of the order.

"A good man is hard to find," Red Sammy said. "Everything is getting terrible. I remember the day you could go off and leave your screen door unlatched. Not no more."

He and the grandmother discussed better times. The old lady said that in her opinion Europe was entirely to blame for the way things were now. She said the way Europe acted you would think we were made of money and Red Sam said it was no use talking about it, she was exactly right. The children ran outside into the white sunlight and looked at the monkey in the lacy chinaberry tree. He was busy catching fleas on himself and biting each one carefully between his teeth as if it were a delicacy.

They drove off again into the hot afternoon. The grandmother took cat naps and woke up every few minutes with her own snoring. Outside of Toombsboro she woke up and recalled an old plantation that she had visited in this neighborhood once when she was a young lady. She said the house had six white columns across the front and that there was an avenue of oaks leading up to it and two little wooden trellis arbors on either side in front where you sat down with your suitor after a stroll in the garden. She recalled exactly which road to turn off to get to it. She knew that Bailey would not be willing to lose any time looking at an old house, but the more she talked about it, the more she wanted to see it once again and find out if the little twin arbors were still standing. "There was a secret panel in this house," she said craftily, not telling the truth but wishing that she were, "and the story went that all the family silver was hidden in it when Sherman came through but it was never found. . . ."

"Hey!" John Wesley said. "Let's go see it! We'll find it! We'll poke all the woodwork and find it! Who lives there? Where do you turn off at? Hey Pop, can't we turn off there?"

"We never have seen a house with a secret panel!" June Star shrieked. "Let's go to the house with the secret panel! Hey, Pop, can't we go see the house with the secret panel!"

"It's not far from here, I know," the grandmother said. "It wouldn't take over twenty minutes."

Bailey was looking straight ahead. His jaw was as rigid as a horseshoe. "No," he said.

The children began to yell and scream that they wanted to see the house with the secret panel. John Wesley kicked the back of the front seat and June Star hung over her mother's shoulder and whined desperately into her ear that they never had any fun even on their vacation, that they could never do what THEY wanted to do. The baby began to scream and John Wesley kicked the back of the seat so hard that his father could feel the blows in his kidney.

"All right!" he shouted and drew the car to a stop at the side of the road. "Will you all shut up? Will you all just shut up for one second? If you don't shut up, we won't go anywhere."

"It would be very educational for them," the grandmother murmured.

"All right," Bailey said, "but get this. This is the only time we're going to stop for anything like this. This is the one and only time."

"The dirt road that you have to turn down is about a mile back," the grandmother directed. "I marked it when we passed."

"A dirt road," Bailey groaned.

After they had turned around and were headed toward the dirt road, the grandmother recalled other points about the house, the beautiful glass over the front doorway and the candle lamp in the hall. John Wesley said that the secret panel was probably in the fireplace.

"You can't go inside this house," Bailey said. "You don't know who lives there."

"While you all talk to the people in front, I'll run around behind and get in a window," John Wesley suggested.

"We'll all stay in the car," his mother said.

They turned onto the dirt road and the car raced roughly along in a swirl of pink dust. The grandmother recalled the times when there were no paved roads and thirty miles was a day's journey. The dirt road was hilly and there were sudden washes in it and sharp curves on dangerous embankments. All at once they would be on a hill, looking down over the blue tops of trees for miles around, then the next minute, they would be in a red depression with the dust-coated trees looking down on them.

"This place had better turn up in a minute," Bailey said, "or I'm going to turn around."

The road looked as if no one had traveled on it in months.

"It's not much farther," the grandmother said and just as she said it, a horrible thought came to her. The thought was so embarrassing that she turned red in the face and her eyes dilated and her feet jumped up, upsetting her valise in the corner. The instant the valise moved, the newspaper top she had over the basket under it rose with a snarl and Pitty Sing, the cat, sprang onto Bailey's shoulder.

The children were thrown to the floor and their mother, clutching the baby, was thrown out the door onto the ground; the old lady was thrown into the front seat. The car turned over once and landed right-side-up in a gulch on the side of the road. Bailey remained in the driver's seat with the cat—gray-striped with a broad white face and an orange nose—clinging to his neck like a caterpillar.

As soon as the children saw they could move their arms and legs, they scrambled out of the car, shouting, "We've had an ACCIDENT!" The grandmother was curled up under the dashboard, hoping she was injured so that Bailey's wrath would not come down on her all at once. The horrible thought she had had before the accident was that the house she had remembered so vividly was not in Georgia but in Tennessee.

Bailey removed the cat from his neck with both hands and flung it out the window against the side of a pine tree. Then he got out of the car and started looking for the children's mother. She was sitting against the side of the red gutted ditch, holding the screaming baby, but she only had a cut down her face and a broken shoulder. "We've had an ACCIDENT!" the children screamed in a frenzy of delight.

"But nobody's killed," June Star said with disappointment as the grandmother limped out of the car, her hat still pinned to her head but the broken front brim standing up at a jaunty angle and the violet spray hanging off the side. They all sat down in the ditch, except the children, to recover from the shock. They were all shaking.

"Maybe a car will come along," said the children's mother hoarsely.

"I believe I have injured an organ," said the grandmother, pressing her side, but no one answered her. Bailey's teeth were clattering. He had on a yellow sport shirt with bright blue parrots designed in it and his face was as yellow as the shirt. The grandmother decided that she would not mention that the house was in Tennessee.

The road was about ten feet above and they could see only the tops of the trees on the other side of it. Behind the ditch they were sitting in there were more woods, tall and dark and deep. In a few minutes they saw a car some distance away on top of a hill, coming slowly as if the occupants were watching them. The grandmother stood up and waved both arms dramatically to attract their attention. The car continued to come on slowly, disappeared around a bend and appeared again, moving even slower, on top of the hill they had gone over. It was a big black battered hearselike automobile. There were three men in it.

It came to a stop just over them and for some minutes, the driver looked down with a steady expressionless gaze to where they were sitting, and didn't speak. Then he turned his head and muttered something to the other two and they got out. One was a fat boy in black trousers and a red sweat shirt with a silver stallion embossed on the front of it. He moved around on the right side of them and stood staring, his mouth partly open in a kind of loose grin. The other had on khaki pants and a blue striped coat and a gray hat pulled down very low, hiding most of his face. He came around slowly on the left side. Neither spoke.

The driver got out of the car and stood by the side of it, looking down at them. He was an older man than the other two. His hair was just beginning to gray and he wore silver-rimmed spectacles that gave him a scholarly look. He had a long creased face and didn't have on any shirt or undershirt. He had on blue jeans that were too tight for him and was holding a black hat and a gun. The two boys also had guns.

"We've had an ACCIDENT!" the children screamed.

The grandmother had the peculiar feeling that the bespectacled man was someone she knew. His face was as familiar to her as if she had known him all her life but she could not recall who he was. He moved away from the car and began to come down the embankment, placing his feet carefully so that he wouldn't slip. He had on tan and white shoes and no socks, and his ankles were red and thin. "Good afternoon," he said. "I see you all had you a little spill."

"We turned over twice!" said the grandmother.

"Oncet," he corrected. "We seen it happen. Try their car and see will it run, Hiram," he said quietly to the boy with the gray hat.

"What you got that gun for?" John Wesley asked. "Whatcha gonna do with that gun?"

"Lady," the man said to the children's mother, "would you mind calling them children to sit down by you? Children make me nervous. I want all you all to sit down right together there where you're at."

"What are you telling US what to do for?" June Star asked.

Behind them the line of woods gaped like a dark open mouth. "Come here," said their mother.

"Look here now," Bailey began suddenly, "we're in a predicament! We're in. . . ."

The grandmother shrieked. She scrambled to her feet and stood staring. "You're The Misfit!" she said. "I recognized you at once!"

"Yes'm," the man said, smiling slightly as if he were pleased in spite of himself to be known, "but it would have been better for all of you, lady, if you hadn't of reckernized me."

Bailey turned his head sharply and said something to his mother that shocked even the children. The old lady began to cry and The Misfit reddened.

"Lady," he said, "don't you get upset. Sometimes a man says things he don't mean. I don't reckon he meant to talk to you thataway."

"You wouldn't shoot a lady, would you?" the grandmother said and removed a clean handkerchief from her cuff and began to slap at her eyes with it.

The Misfit pointed the toe of his shoe into the ground and made a little hole and then covered it up again. "I would hate to have to," he said.

"Listen," the grandmother almost screamed, "I know you're a good man. You don't look a bit like you have common blood. I know you must come from nice people!"

"Yes mam," he said, "finest people in the world." When he smiled he showed a row of strong white teeth. "God never made a finer woman than my mother and my daddy's heart was pure gold," he said. The boy with the red sweat shirt had come around behind them and was standing with his gun at his hip. The Misfit squatted down on the ground. "Watch them children, Bobby Lee," he said. "You know they make me nervous." He looked at the six of them huddled together in front of him and he seemed to be embarrassed as if he couldn't think of anything to say. "Ain't a cloud in the sky," he remarked, looking up at it. "Don't see no sun but don't see no cloud neither."

"Yes, it's beautiful day," said the grandmother. "Listen," she said, "you shouldn't call yourself The Misfit because I know you're a good man at heart. I can just look at you and tell."

"Hush!" Bailey yelled. "Hush! Everybody shut up and let me handle this!" He was squatting in the position of a runner about to sprint forward but he didn't move.

"I pre-chate that, lady," The Misfit said and drew a little circle in the ground with the butt of his gun.

"It'll take a half a hour to fix this here car," Hiram called, looking over the raised hood of it.

"Well, first you and Bobby Lee get him and that little boy to step over yonder with you," The Misfit said, pointing to Bailey and John Wesley. "The boys want to ast you something," he said to Bailey. "Would you mind stepping back in them woods there with them?"

"Listen," Bailey began, "we're in a terrible predicament! Nobody realizes what this is," and his voice cracked. His eyes were as blue and intense as the parrots in his shirt and he remained perfectly still.

The grandmother reached up to adjust her hat brim as if she were going to the woods with him but it came off in her hand. She stood staring at it and after a second she let it fall on the ground. Hiram pulled Bailey up by the arm as if he were assisting an old man. John Wesley caught hold of his father's hand and Bobby Lee followed. They went off toward the woods and just as they reached the dark edge, Bailey turned and supporting himself against a gray naked pine trunk, he shouted, "I'll be back in a minute, Mamma, wait on me!"

"Come back this instant!" his mother shrilled but they all disappeared into the woods.

"Bailey Boy!" the grandmother called in a tragic voice but she found she was looking at The Misfit squatting on the ground in front of her. "I just know you're a good man," she said desperately. "You're not a bit common!"

"Nome, I ain't a good man," The Misfit said after a second as if he had considered her statement carefully, "but I ain't the worst in the world neither. My daddy said I was different breed of dog from my brothers and sisters. 'You know,' Daddy said, 'it's some that can live their whole life out without asking about it and it's others has to know why it is, and this boy is one of the latters. He's going to be into everything!'" He put on his black hat and looked up suddenly and then away deep into the woods as if he were embarrassed again. "I'm sorry I don't have on a shirt before you ladies," he said, hunching his shoulders slightly. "We buried our clothes that we had on when we escaped and we're just making do until we can get better. We borrowed these from some folks we met," he explained.

"That's perfectly all right," the grandmother said. "Maybe Bailey has an extra shirt in his suitcase."

"I'll look and see terrectly," The Misfit said.

"Where are they taking him?" the children's mother screamed.

"Daddy was a card himself," The Misfit said. "You couldn't put anything over on him. He never got in trouble with the Authorities though. Just had the knack of handling them."

"You could be honest too if you'd only try," said the grandmother. "Think how wonderful it would be to settle down and live a comfortable life and not have to think about somebody chasing you all the time."

The Misfit kept scratching in the ground with the butt of his gun as if he were thinking about it. "Yes'm, somebody is always after you," he murmured.

The grandmother noticed how thin his shoulder blades were just behind his hat because she was standing up looking down on him. "Do you ever pray?" she asked.

He shook his head. All she saw was the black hat wiggle between his shoulder blades. "Nome," he said.

There was a pistol shot from the woods, followed closely by another. Then silence. The old lady's head jerked around. She could hear the wind move through the tree tops like a long satisfied insuck of breath. "Bailey Boy!" she called.

"I was a gospel singer for a while," The Misfit said. "I been most everything. Been in the arm service, both land and sea, at home and abroad, been twict married, been an undertaker, been with the railroads, plowed Mother Earth, been in a tornado, seen a man burnt alive oncet," and he looked up at the children's mother and the little girl who were sitting close together, their faces white and their eyes glassy; "I even seen a woman flogged," he said.

"Pray, pray," the grandmother began, "pray, pray. . . ."

"I never was a bad boy that I remember of," The Misfit said in an almost dreamy voice, "but somewheres along the line I done something wrong and got sent to the penitentiary. I was buried alive," and he looked up and held her attention to him by a steady stare.

"That's when you should have started to pray," she said. "What did you do to get sent to the penitentiary that first time?"

"Turn to the right, it was a wall," The Misfit said, looking up again at the cloudless sky. "Turn to the left, it was a wall. Look up it was a ceiling, look down it was a floor. I forget what I done, lady. I set there and set there, trying to remember what it was I done and I ain't recalled it to this day. Oncet in a while, I would think it was coming to me, but it never come."

"Maybe they put you in by mistake," the old lady said vaguely.

"Nome," he said. "It wasn't no mistake. They had the papers on me."

"You must have stolen something," she said.

The Misfit sneered slightly. "Nobody had nothing I wanted," he said. "It was a head-doctor at the penitentiary said what I had done was kill my daddy but I known that for a lie. My daddy died in nineteen ought nineteen of the epidemic flu and I never had a thing to do with it. He was buried in the Mount Hopewell Baptist churchyard and you can go there and see for yourself."

"If you would pray," the old lady said, "Jesus would help you."

"That's right," The Misfit said.

"Well then, why don't you pray?" she asked trembling with delight suddenly.

"I don't want no hep," he said. "I'm doing all right by myself."

Bobby Lee and Hiram came ambling back from the woods. Bobby Lee was dragging a yellow shirt with bright blue parrots in it.

"Throw me that shirt, Bobby Lee," The Misfit said. The shirt came flying at him and landed on his shoulder and he put it on. The grandmother couldn't name what the shirt reminded her of. "No, lady," The Misfit said while he was buttoning it up, "I found out the crime don't matter. You can do one thing or you can do another, kill a man or take a tire off his car, because sooner or later you're going to forget what it was you done and just be punished for it."

The children's mother had begun to make heaving noises as if she couldn't get her breath. "Lady," he asked, "would you and that little girl like to step off yonder with Bobby Lee and Hiram and join your husband?"

"Yes, thank you," the mother said faintly. Her left arm dangled helplessly and she was holding the baby, who had gone to sleep, in the other. "Hep that lady up, Hiram," The Misfit said as she struggled to climb out of the ditch, "and Bobby Lee, you hold onto that little girl's hand."

"I don't want to hold hands with him," June Star said. "He reminds me of a pig."

The fat boy blushed and laughed and caught her by the arm and pulled her off into the woods after Hiram and her mother.

Alone with The Misfit, the grandmother found that she had lost her voice. There was not a cloud in the sky nor any sun. There was nothing around her but woods. She wanted to tell him that he must pray. She opened and closed her mouth several times before anything came out. Finally she found herself saying, "Jesus. Jesus," meaning, Jesus will help you, but the way she was saying it, it sounded as if she might be cursing.

"Yes'm," The Misfit said as if he agreed. "Jesus thrown everything off balance. It was the same case with Him as with me except He hadn't committed any crime and they could prove I had committed one because they had the papers on me. Of course," he said, "they never shown me my papers. That's why I sign myself now. I said long ago, you get you a signature and sign everything you do and keep a copy of it. Then you'll know what you done and you can hold up the crime to the punishment and see do they match and in the end you'll have something to prove you ain't been treated right. I call myself The Misfit," he said, "because I can't make what all I done wrong fit what all I gone through in punishment."

There was a piercing scream from the woods, followed closely by a pistol report. "Does it seem right to you, lady, that one is punished a heap and another ain't punished at all?"

"Jesus!" the old lady cried. "You've got good blood! I know you wouldn't shoot a lady! I know you come from nice people! Pray! Jesus, you ought not to shoot a lady. I'll give you all the money I've got!"

"Lady," The Misfit said, looking beyond her far into the woods, "there never was a body that give the undertaker a tip."

There were two more pistol reports and the grandmother raised her head like a parched old turkey hen crying for water and called, "Bailey Boy, Bailey Boy!" as if her heart would break.

"Jesus was the only One that ever raised the dead," The Misfit continued, "and He shouldn't have done it. He thrown everything off balance. If He did what He said, then it's nothing for you to do but throw away everything and follow Him, and if He didn't then it's nothing for you to do but enjoy the few minutes you got left the best way you can—by killing somebody or burning down his house or doing some other meanness to him. No pleasure but meanness," he said and his voice had become almost a snarl.

"Maybe He didn't raise the dead," the old lady mumbled, not knowing what she was saying and feeling so dizzy that she sank down in the ditch with her legs twisted under her.

"I wasn't there so I can't say He didn't," The Misfit said. "I wisht I had of been there," he said, hitting the ground with his fist. "It ain't right I wasn't there because if I had of been there I would of known. Listen lady," he said in a high voice, "if I had of been there I would of known and I wouldn't be like I am now." His voice seemed about to crack and the grandmother's head cleared for an instant. She saw the man's face twisted close to her own as if he were going to cry and she murmured, "Why, you're one of my babies. You're one of my own children!" She reached out and touched him on the shoulder. The Misfit sprang back as if a snake had bitten him and shot her three times through the chest. Then he put his gun down on the ground and took off his glasses and began to clean them.

Hiram and Bobby Lee returned from the woods and stood over the ditch, looking down at the grandmother who half sat and half lay in a puddle of blood with her legs crossed under her like a child's and her face smiling up at the cloudless sky.

Without his glasses, The Misfit's eyes were red-rimmed and pale and defenseless-looking. "Take her off and thow her where you thown the others," he said, picking up the cat that was rubbing itself against his leg.

"She was a talker, wasn't she?" Bobby Lee said, sliding down the ditch with a yodel.

"She would of been a good woman," The Misfit said, "if it had been somebody there to shoot her every minute of her life."

"Some fun!" Bobby Lee said.

"Shut up, Bobby Lee," The Misfit said. "It's no real pleasure in life."

Leo Tolstoy

1828–1910

THE DEATH OF IVAN ILYCH

Translated by Louise and Aylmer Maude

I

During an interval in the Melvinski trial in the large building of the Law Courts, the members and public prosecutor met in Ivan Egorovich Shebek's private room, where the conversation turned on the celebrated Krasovski case. Fëdor Vasilievich warmly maintained that it was not subject to their jurisdiction, Ivan Egorovich maintained the contrary, while Peter Ivanovich, not having entered the discussion at the start, took no part in it but looked through the *Gazette* which had just been handed in.

"Gentlemen," he said, "Ivan Ilych has died!"

"You don't say so!"

"Here, read it yourself," replied Peter Ivanovich, handing Fëdor Vasilievich the paper still damp from the press. Surrounded by a black border were the words: "Praskovya Fëdorovna Golovina, with profound sorrow, informs relatives and friends of the demise of her beloved husband Ivan Ilych Golovin, Member of the Court of Justice, which occurred on February the 4th of this year 1882. The funeral will take place on Friday at one o'clock in the afternoon."

Ivan Ilych had been a colleague of the gentlemen present and was liked by them all. He had been ill for some weeks with an illness said to be incurable. His post had been kept open for him, but there had been conjectures that in case of his death Alexeev might receive his appointment, and that either Vinnikov or Shtabel would succeed Alexeev. So on receiving the news of Ivan Ilych's death the first thought of each of the gentlemen in that private room was of the changes and promotions it might occasion among themselves or their acquaintances.

"I shall be sure to get Shtabel's place or Vinnikov's," thought Fëdor

Vasilievich. "I was promised that long ago, and the promotion means an extra eight hundred rubles a year for me besides the allowance."

"Now I must apply for my brother-in-law's transfer from Kaluga," thought Peter Ivanovich. "My wife will be very glad, and then she won't be able to say that I never do anything for her relations."

"I thought he would never leave his bed again," said Peter Ivanovich aloud. "It's very sad."

"But what really was the matter with him?"

"The doctors couldn't say—at least they could, but each of them said something different. When last I saw him I thought he was getting better."

"And I haven't been to see him since the holidays. I always meant to go."

"Had he any property?"

"I think his wife had a little—but something quite trifling."

"We shall have to go to see her, but they live so terribly far away."

"Far away from you, you mean. Everything's far away from your place."

"You see, he never can forgive my living on the other side of the river," said Peter Ivanovich, smiling at Shebek. Then, still talking of the distances between different parts of the city, they returned to the Court.

Besides considerations as to the possible transfers and promotions likely to result from Ivan Ilych's death, the mere fact of the death of a near acquaintance aroused, as usual, in all who heard of it the complacent feeling that, "it is he who is dead and not I."

Each one thought or felt, "Well, he's dead but I'm alive!" But the more intimate of Ivan Ilych's acquaintances, his so-called friends, could not help thinking also that they would now have to fulfil the very tiresome demands of propriety by attending the funeral service and paying a visit of condolence to the widow.

Fëdor Vasilievich and Peter Ivanovich had been his nearest acquaintances. Peter Ivanovich had studied law with Ivan Ilych and had considered himself to be under obligations to him.

Having told his wife at dinner-time of Ivan Ilych's death and of his conjecture that it might be possible to get her brother transferred to their circuit, Peter Ivanovich sacrificed his usual nap, put on his evening clothes, and drove to Ivan Ilych's house.

At the entrance stood a carriage and two cabs. Leaning against the wall in the hall downstairs near the cloak-stand was a coffin-lid covered with cloth of gold, ornamented with gold cord and tassels, that had been polished up with metal powder. Two ladies in black were taking off their fur cloaks. Peter Ivanovich recognized one of them as Ivan Ilych's sister, but the other was a stranger to him. His colleague Schwartz was just coming downstairs, but on seeing Peter Ivanovich enter he stopped and winked at him, as if to say: "Ivan Ilych has made a mess of things—not like you and me."

Schwartz's face with his Piccadilly whiskers and his slim figure in evening dress had as usual an air of elegant solemnity which contrasted with the playfulness of his character and had a special piquancy here, or so it seemed to Peter Ivanovich.

Peter Ivanovich allowed the ladies to precede him and slowly followed them upstairs. Schwartz did not come down but remained where he was, and Peter Ivanovich understood that he wanted to arrange where they should play bridge that evening. The ladies went upstairs to the widow's room, and Schwartz with seriously compressed lips but a playful look in his eyes, indicated by a twist of his eyebrows the room to the right where the body lay.

Peter Ivanovich, like everyone else on such occasions, entered feeling uncertain what he would have to do. All he knew was that at such times it is always safe to cross oneself. But he was not quite sure whether one should make obeisances while doing so. He therefore adopted a middle course. On entering the room he began crossing himself and made a slight movement resembling a bow. At the same time, as far as the motion of his head and arm allowed, he surveyed the room. Two young men—apparently nephews, one of whom was a high-school pupil—were leaving the room, crossing themselves as they did so. An old woman was standing motionless, and a lady with strangely arched eyebrows was saying something to her in a whisper. A vigorous, resolute Church Reader, in a frock-coat, was reading something in a loud voice with an expression that precluded any contradiction. The butler's assistant, Gerasim, stepping lightly in front of Peter Ivanovich, was strewing something on the floor. Noticing this, Peter Ivanovich was immediately aware of a faint odour of a decomposing body.

The last time he had called on Ivan Ilych, Peter Ivanovich had seen Gerasim in the study. Ivan Ilych had been particularly fond of him and he was performing the duty of a sick nurse.

Peter Ivanovich continued to make the sign of the cross, slightly inclining his head in an intermediate direction between the coffin, the Reader, and the icons on the table in a corner of the room. Afterwards, when it seemed to him that this movement of his arm in crossing himself had gone on too long, he stopped and began to look at the corpse.

The dead man lay, as dead men always lie, in a specially heavy way, his rigid limbs sunk in the soft cushions of the coffin, with the head forever bowed on the pillow. His yellow waxen brow with bald patches over his sunken temples, was thrust up in the way peculiar to the dead, the protruding nose seemed to press on the upper lip. He was much changed and had grown even thinner since Peter Ivanovich had last seen him, but, as is always the case with the dead, his face was handsomer and above all more dignified than when he was alive. The expression on the face said that what was necessary had been accomplished, and accomplished rightly. Besides this there was in that expression a reproach and a warning to the living. This warning seemed to Peter Ivanovich out of place, or at least not applicable to him. He felt a certain discomfort and so he hurriedly crossed himself once more and turned and went out of the door—too hurriedly and too regardless of propriety, as he himself was aware.

Schwartz was waiting for him in the adjoining room with legs spread wide apart and both hands toying with his top-hat behind his back. The mere sight of that playful, well-groomed, and elegant figure refreshed Peter Ivanovich. He felt that Schwartz was above all these happenings and would not surrender to any depressing influences. His very look said that this incident of a church service for Ivan Ilych could not be a sufficient reason for infringing the order of the session—in other words, that it would certainly not prevent his unwrapping a new pack of cards and shuffling them that evening while a footman placed four fresh candles on the table: in fact, that there was no reason for supposing that this incident would hinder their spending the evening agreeably. Indeed he said this in a whisper as Peter Ivanovich passed him, proposing that they should meet for a game at Fëdor Vasilievich's. But apparently Peter Ivanovich was not destined to play bridge that evening. Praskovya Fëdorovna (a short, fat woman who despite all efforts to the contrary had continued to broaden steadily from her shoulders downwards and who had the same extraordinarily arched eyebrows as the lady who had been standing by the coffin), dressed all in black, her head covered with lace, came out of her own room with some other ladies, conducted them to the room where the dead body lay, and said: "The service will begin immediately. Please go in."

Schwartz, making an indefinite bow, stood still, evidently neither accepting nor declining this invitation. Praskovya Fëdorovna, recognizing Peter Ivanovich, sighed, went close up to him, took his hand, and said: "I know you were a true friend of Ivan Ilych . . ." and looked at him awaiting some suitable response. And Peter Ivanovich knew that, just as it had been the right thing to cross himself in that room, so what he had to do here was to press her hand, sigh, and say, "Believe me. . . ." So he did all this and as he did it felt that the desired results had been achieved: that both he and she were touched.

"Come with me. I want to speak to you before it begins," said the widow. "Give me your arm."

Peter Ivanovich gave her his arm and they went to the inner rooms, passing Schwartz, who winked at Peter Ivanovich compassionately.

"That does for our bridge! Don't object if we find another player. Perhaps you can cut in when you do escape," said his playful look.

Peter Ivanovich sighed still more deeply and despondently, and Praskovya Fëdorovna pressed his arm gratefully. When they reached the drawing-room, upholstered in pink cretonne and lighted by a dim lamp, they sat down at the table—she on a sofa and Peter Ivanovich on a low pouffe, the springs of which yielded spasmodically under his weight. Praskovya Fëdorovna had been on the point of warning him to take another seat, but felt that such a warning was out of keeping with her present condition and so changed her mind. As he sat down on the pouffe Peter Ivanovich recalled how Ivan Ilych had arranged this room and had consulted him regarding this pink cretonne with green leaves. The whole room was full of furniture and knick-knacks, and on her way to the sofa the lace of the widow's black shawl caught on the carved edge of the table. Peter Ivanovich rose to detach it, and the springs of the pouffe, relieved of his weight, rose also and gave him a push. The widow began detaching her shawl herself, and Peter Ivanovich again sat down, suppressing the rebellious springs of the pouffe under him. But the widow had not quite freed herself and Peter Ivanovich got up again, and again the pouffe rebelled and even creaked. When this was all over she took out a clean cambric handkerchief and began to weep. The episode with the shawl and the struggle with the pouffe had cooled Peter Ivanovich's emotions and he sat there with a sullen look on his face. This awkward situation was interrupted by Sokolov, Ivan Ilych's butler, who came to report that the plot in the cemetery that Praskovya Fëdorovna had chosen would cost two hundred rubles. She stopped weeping and, looking at Peter Ivanovich with the air of a victim, remarked in French that it was very hard for her. Peter Ivanovich made a silent gesture signifying his full conviction that it must indeed be so.

"Please smoke," she said in a magnanimous yet crushed voice, and turned to discuss with Sokolov the price of the plot for the grave.

Peter Ivanovich while lighting his cigarette heard her inquiring very circumstantially into the prices of different plots in the cemetery and finally decide which she would take. When that was done she gave instructions about engaging the choir. Sokolov then left the room.

"I look after everything myself," she told Peter Ivanovich, shifting the albums that lay on the table; and noticing that the table was endangered by his cigarette-ash, she immediately passed him an ash-tray, saying as she did so: "I consider it an affectation to say that my grief prevents my attending to practical affairs. On the contrary, if anything can—I won't say console me, but—distract me, it is seeing to everything concerning him." She again took out her handkerchief as if preparing to cry, but suddenly, as if mastering her feeling, she shook herself and began to speak calmly. "But there is something I want to talk to you about."

Peter Ivanovich bowed, keeping control of the springs of the pouffe, which immediately began quivering under him.

"He suffered terribly the last few days."

"Did he?" said Peter Ivanovich.

"Oh, terribly! He screamed unceasingly, not for minutes but for hours. For the last three days he screamed incessantly. It was unendurable. I cannot understand how I bore it; you could hear him three rooms off. Oh, what I have suffered!"

"Is it possible that he was conscious all that time?" asked Peter Ivanovich.

"Yes," she whispered. "To the last moment. He took leave of us a quarter of an hour before he died, and asked us to take Volodya away."

The thought of the sufferings of this man he had known so intimately, first as a merry little boy, then as a school-mate, and later as a grown-up colleague, suddenly struck Peter Ivanovich with horror, despite an unpleasant consciousness of his own and this woman's dissimulation. He again saw that brow, and that nose pressing down on the lip, and felt afraid for himself.

Three days of frightful suffering and then death! Why, that might suddenly, at any time, happen to me, he thought, and for a moment felt terrified. But—he did not himself know how—the customary reflection at once occurred to him that this had happened to Ivan Ilych and not to him, and that it should not and could not happen to him, and that to think that it could would be yielding to depression which he ought not to do, as Schwartz's expression plainly showed. After which reflection Peter Ivanovich felt reassured, and began to ask with interest about the details of Ivan Ilych's death, as though death was an accident natural to Ivan Ilych but certainly not to himself.

After many details of the really dreadful physical sufferings Ivan Ilych had endured (which details he learnt only from the effect those sufferings had produced on Praskovya Fëdorovna's nerves) the widow apparently found it necessary to get to business.

"Oh, Peter Ivanovich, how hard it is! How terribly, terribly hard!" and she again began to weep.

Peter Ivanovich sighed and waited for her to finish blowing her nose. When she had done so he said, "Believe me . . ." and she again began talking and brought out what was evidently her chief concern with him—namely, to question him as to how she could obtain a grant of money from the government on the occasion of her husband's death. She made it appear that she was asking Peter Ivanovich's advice about her pension, but he soon saw that she already knew about that to the minutest detail, more even than he did himself. She knew how much could be got out of the government in consequence of her husband's death, but wanted to find out whether she could not possibly extract something more. Peter Ivanovich tried to think of some means of doing so, but after reflecting for a while and, out of propriety, condemning the government for its niggardliness, he said he thought that nothing more could be got. Then she sighed and evidently began to devise means of getting rid of her visitor. Noticing this, he put out his cigarette, rose, pressed her hand, and went out into the anteroom.

In the dining-room where the clock stood that Ivan Ilych had liked so much and had bought at an antique shop, Peter Ivanovich met a priest and a few acquaintances who had come to attend the service, and he recognized Ivan Ilych's daughter, a handsome young woman. She was in black and her slim figure appeared slimmer than ever. She had a gloomy, determined, almost angry expression, and bowed to Peter Ivanovich as though he were in some way to blame. Behind her, with the same offended look, stood a wealthy young man, an examining magistrate, whom Peter Ivanovich also knew and who was her fiancé, as he had heard. He bowed mournfully to them and was about to pass into the death-chamber, when from under the stairs appeared the figure of Ivan Ilych's schoolboy son, who was extremely like his father. He seemed a little Ivan Ilych, such as Peter Ivanovich remembered when they studied law together. His tear-stained eyes had in them the look that is seen in the eyes of boys of thirteen or fourteen who are not pure-minded. When he saw Peter Ivanovich he scowled morosely and shamefacedly. Peter Ivanovich nodded to him and entered the death-chamber. The service began: candles, groans, incense, tears, and sobs. Peter Ivanovich stood looking gloomily down at his feet. He did not look once at the dead man, did not yield to any depressing influence, and was one of the first to leave the room. There was no one in the anteroom, but Gerasim darted out of the dead man's room, rummaged with his strong hands among the fur coats to find Peter Ivanovich's, and helped him on with it.

"Well, friend Gerasim," said Peter Ivanovich, so as to say something. "It's a sad affair, isn't it?"

"It's God's will. We shall all come to it some day," said Gerasim, displaying his teeth—the even, white teeth of a healthy peasant—and, like a man in the thick of urgent work, he briskly opened the front door, called the coachman, helped Peter Ivanovich into the sledge, and sprang back to the porch as if in readiness for what he had to do next.

Peter Ivanovich found the fresh air particularly pleasant after the smell of incense, the dead body, and carbolic acid.

"Where to, sir?" asked the coachman.

"It's not too late even now. . . . I'll call round on Fëdor Vasilievich."

He accordingly drove there and found them just finishing the first rubber, so that it was quite convenient for him to cut in.

II

Ivan Ilych's life had been most simple and most ordinary and therefore most terrible.

He had been a member of the Court of Justice, and died at the age of forty-five. His father had been an official who after serving in various ministries and departments in Petersburg had made the sort of career which brings men to positions from which by reason of their long service they cannot be dismissed, though they are obviously unfit to hold any responsible position, and for whom therefore posts are specially created, which though fictitious carry salaries of from six to ten thousand rubles that are not fictitious, and in receipt of which they live on to a great age.

Such was the Privy Councillor and superfluous member of various superfluous institutions, Ilya Epimovich Golovin.

He had three sons, of whom Ivan Ilych was the second. The eldest son was following in his father's footsteps only in another department, and was already approaching that stage in the service at which a similar sinecure would be reached. The third son was a failure. He had ruined his prospects in a number of positions and was now serving in the railway department. His father and brothers, and still more their wives, not merely disliked meeting him, but avoided remembering his existence unless compelled to do so. His sister had married Baron Greff, a Petersburg official of her father's type. Ivan Ilych was *le phénix de la famille* as people said. He was neither as cold and formal as his elder brother nor as wild as the younger, but was a happy mean between them—an intelligent, polished, lively, and agreeable man. He had studied with his younger brother at the School of Law, but the latter had failed to complete the course and was expelled when he was in the fifth class. Ivan Ilych finished the course well. Even when he was at the School of Law he was just what he remained for the rest of his life: a capable, cheerful, good-natured, and sociable man, though strict in the fulfilment of what he considered to be his duty: and he considered his duty to be what was so considered by those in authority. Neither as a boy nor as a man was he a toady, but from early youth was by nature attracted to people of high station as a fly is drawn to the light, assimilating their ways and views of life and establishing friendly relations with them. All the enthusiasms of childhood and youth passed without leaving much trace on him; he succumbed to sensuality, to vanity, and latterly among the highest classes to liberalism, but always within limits which his instinct unfailingly indicated to him as correct.

At school he had done things which had formerly seemed to him very horrid and made him feel disgusted with himself when he did them; but when later on he saw that such actions were done by people of good position and that they did not regard them as wrong, he was able not exactly to regard them as right, but to forget about them entirely or not be at all troubled at remembering them.

Having graduated from the School of Law and qualified for the tenth rank of the civil service, and having received money from his father for his equipment, Ivan Ilych ordered himself clothes at Scharmer's, the fashionable tailor, hung a medallion inscribed *respice finem* on his watch-chain, took leave of his professor and the prince who was patron of the school, had a farewell dinner with his comrades at Donon's first-class restaurant, and with his new and fashionable portmanteau, linen, clothes, shaving and other toilet appliances, and a travelling rug, all purchased at the best shops, he set off for one of the provinces where, through his father's influence, he had been attached to the Governor as an official for special service.

In the province Ivan Ilych soon arranged as easy and agreeable a position for himself as he had had at the School of Law. He performed his official tasks, made his career, and at the same time amused himself pleasantly and decorously. Occasionally he paid official visits to country districts, where he behaved with dignity both to his superiors and inferiors, and performed the duties entrusted to him, which related chiefly to the sectarians, with an exactness and incorruptible honesty of which he could not but feel proud.

In official matters, despite his youth and taste for frivolous gaiety, he was exceedingly reserved, punctilious, and even severe; but in society he was often amusing and witty, and always good-natured, correct in his manner, and *bon enfant*, as the Governor and his wife—with whom he was like one of the family—used to say of him.

In the province he had an affair with a lady who made advances to the elegant young lawyer, and there was also a milliner; and there were carousals with aides-de-camp who visited the district, and after-supper visits to a certain outlying street of doubtful reputation; and there was too some obsequiousness to his chief and even to his chief's wife, but all this was done with such a tone of good breeding that no hard names could be applied to it. It all came under the heading of the French saying: *"Il faut que jeunesse se passe."*[1] It was done with clean hands, in clean linen, with French phrases, and above all among people of the best society and consequently with the approval of people of rank.

So Ivan Ilych served for five years and then came a change in his official life. The new and reformed judicial institutions were introduced, and new men were needed. Ivan Ilych became such a new man. He was offered the post of examining magistrate, and he accepted it though the post was in another province and obliged him to give up the connexions he had formed and to make new ones. His friends met to give him a send-off; they had a group-photograph taken and presented him with a silver cigarette-case, and he set off to his new post.

As examining magistrate Ivan Ilych was just as *comme il faut* and decorous a man, inspiring general respect and capable of separating his official duties from his private life, as he had been when acting as an official on special service. His duties now as examining magistrate were far more interesting and attractive than before. In his former position it had been pleasant to wear an undress uniform made by Scharmer, and to pass through the crowd of petitioners and officials who were timorously awaiting an audience with the Governor, and who envied him as with free and easy gait he went straight into his chief's private room to have a cup of tea and a cigarette with him. But not many people had been directly dependent on him—only police officials and the sectarians when he went on special missions—and he liked to treat them politely, almost as comrades, as if he were letting them feel that he who had the power to crush them was treating them in this simple, friendly way. There were then but few such people. But now, as an examining magistrate, Ivan Ilych felt that everyone

[1] Youth must have its fling.

without exception, even the most important and self-satisfied, was in his power, and that he need only write a few words on a sheet of paper with a certain heading, and this or that important, self-satisfied person would be brought before him in the role of an accused person or a witness, and if he did not choose to allow him to sit down, would have to stand before him and answer his questions. Ivan Ilych never abused his power; he tried on the contrary to soften its expression, but the consciousness of it and of the possibility of softening its effect, supplied the chief interest and attraction of his office. In his work itself, especially in his examinations, he very soon acquired a method of eliminating all considerations irrelevant to the legal aspect of the case, and reducing even the most complicated case to a form in which it would be presented on paper only in its externals, completely excluding his personal opinion of the matter, while above all observing every prescribed formality. The work was new and Ivan Ilych was one of the first men to apply the new Code of 1864.[2]

On taking up the post of examining magistrate in a new town, he made new acquaintances and connexions, placed himself on a new footing, and assumed a somewhat different tone. He took up an attitude of rather dignified aloofness towards the provincial authorities, but picked out the best circle of legal gentlemen and wealthy gentry living in the town and assumed a tone of slight dissatisfaction with the government, of moderate liberalism, and of enlightened citizenship. At the same time, without at all altering the elegance of his toilet, he ceased shaving his chin and allowed his beard to grow as it pleased.

Ivan Ilych settled down very pleasantly in this new town. The society there, which inclined towards opposition to the Governor, was friendly, his salary was larger, and he began to play *vint* [a form of bridge], which he found added not a little to the pleasure of life, for he had a capacity for cards, played good-humouredly, and calculated rapidly and astutely, so that he usually won.

After living there for two years he met his future wife, Praskovya Fëdorovna Mikhel, who was the most attractive, clever, and brilliant girl of the set in which he moved, and among other amusements and relaxations from his labours as examining magistrate, Ivan Ilych established light and playful relations with her.

While he had been an official on special service he had been accustomed to dance, but now as an examining magistrate it was exceptional for him to do so. If he danced now, he did it as if to show that though he served under the reformed order of things, and had reached the fifth official rank, yet when it came to dancing he could do it better than most people. So at the end of an evening he sometimes danced with Praskovya Fëdorovna, and it was chiefly during these dances that he captivated her. She fell in

---

2 The emancipation of the serfs in 1861 was followed by a thorough all-round reform of judicial proceedings.—A.M. [TRANSLATOR'S NOTE.]

love with him. Ivan Ilych had at first no definite intention of marrying, but when the girl fell in love with him he said to himself: "Really, why shouldn't I marry?"

Praskovya Fëdorovna came of a good family, was not bad-looking, and had some little property. Ivan Ilych might have aspired to a more brilliant match, but even this was good. He had his salary, and she, he hoped, would have an equal income. She was well connected, and was a sweet, pretty, and thoroughly correct young woman. To say that Ivan Ilych married because he fell in love with Praskovya Fëdorovna and found that she sympathized with his views of life would be as incorrect as to say that he married because his social circle approved of the match. He was swayed by both these considerations: the marriage gave him personal satisfaction, and at the same time it was considered the right thing by the most highly placed of his associates.

So Ivan Ilych got married.

The preparations for marriage and the beginning of married life, with its conjugal caresses, the new furniture, new crockery, and new linen, were very pleasant until his wife became pregnant—so that Ivan Ilych had begun to think that marriage would not impair the easy, agreeable, gay, and always decorous character of his life, approved of by society and re-garded by himself as natural, but would even improve it. But from the first months of his wife's pregnancy, something new, unpleasant, depressing, and unseemly, and from which there was no way of escape, unexpectedly showed itself.

His wife, without any reason—de gaieté de cœur as Ivan Ilych expressed it to himself—began to disturb the pleasure and propriety of their life. She began to be jealous without any cause, expected him to devote his whole attention to her, found fault with everything, and made coarse and ill-mannered scenes.

At first Ivan Ilych hoped to escape from the unpleasantness of this state of affairs by the same easy and decorous relation to life that had served him heretofore: he tried to ignore his wife's disagreeable moods, continued to live in his usual easy and pleasant way, invited friends to his house for a game of cards, and also tried going out to his club or spending his evenings with friends. But one day his wife began upbraiding him so vigorously, using such coarse words, and continued to abuse him every time he did not fulfil her demands, so resolutely and with such evident determi-nation not to give way till he submitted—that is, till he stayed at home and was bored just as she was—that he became alarmed. He now realized that matrimony—at any rate with Praskovya Fëdorovna—was not always condu-cive to the pleasures and amenities of life, but on the contrary often in-fringed both comfort and propriety, and that he must therefore entrench himself against such infringement. And Ivan Ilych began to seek for means of doing so. His official duties were the one thing that imposed upon Praskovya Fëdorovna, and by means of his official work and the duties attached to it he began struggling with his wife to secure his own independence.

With the birth of their child, the attempts to feed it and the various failures in doing so, and with the real and imaginary illnesses of mother and child, in which Ivan Ilych's sympathy was demanded but about which he understood nothing, the need of securing for himself an existence outside his family life became still more imperative.

As his wife grew more irritable and exacting and Ivan Ilych transferred the center of gravity of his life more and more to his official work, so did he grow to like his work better and become more ambitious than before.

Very soon, within a year of his wedding, Ivan Ilych had realized that marriage, though it may add some comforts to life, is in fact a very intricate and difficult affair towards which in order to perform one's duty, that is, to lead a decorous life approved of by society, one must adopt a definite attitude just as towards one's official duties.

And Ivan Ilych evolved such an attitude towards married life. He only required of it those conveniences—dinner at home, housewife, and bed—which it could give him, and above all that propriety of external forms required by public opinion. For the rest he looked for light-hearted pleasure and propriety, and was very thankful when he found them, but if he met with antagonism and querulousness he at once retired into his separate fenced-off world of official duties, where he found satisfaction.

Ivan Ilych was esteemed a good official, and after three years was made Assistant Public Prosecutor. His new duties, their importance, the possibility of indicting and imprisoning anyone he chose, the publicity his speeches received, and the success he had in all these things, made his work still more attractive.

More children came. His wife became more and more querulous and ill-tempered, but the attitude Ivan Ilych had adopted towards his home life rendered him almost impervious to her grumbling.

After seven years' service in that town he was transferred to another province as Public Prosecutor. They moved, but were short of money and his wife did not like the place they moved to. Though the salary was higher the cost of living was greater, besides which two of their children died and family life became still more unpleasant for him.

Praskovya Fëdorovna blamed her husband for every inconvenience they encountered in their new home. Most of the conversations between husband and wife, especially as to the children's education, led to topics which recalled former disputes, and those disputes were apt to flare up again at any moment. There remained only those rare periods of amorousness which still came to them at times but did not last long. These were islets at which they anchored for a while and then again set out upon that ocean of veiled hostility which showed itself in their aloofness from one another. This aloofness might have grieved Ivan Ilych had he considered that it ought not to exist, but he now regarded the position as normal, and even made it the goal at which he aimed in family life. His aim was to free himself more and more from those unpleasantnesses and to give them a semblance of harmlessness and propriety. He attained this by spending less and less time with his family, and when obliged to be at home he tried to safeguard his position by the presence of outsiders. The chief thing however was that he had his official duties. The whole interest of his life now centered in the official world and that interest absorbed him. The consciousness of his power, being able to ruin anybody he wished to ruin, the importance, even the external dignity of his entry into court, or meetings with his subordinates, his success with superiors and inferiors, and above all his masterly handling of cases, of which he was conscious—all this gave him pleasure and filled his life, together with chats with his colleagues, dinners, and bridge. So that on the whole Ivan Ilych's life continued to flow as he considered it should do—pleasantly and properly.

So things continued for another seven years. His eldest daughter was already sixteen, another child had died, and only one son was left, a schoolboy and a subject of dissension. Ivan Ilych wanted to put him in the School of Law, but to spite him Praskovya Fëdorovna entered him at the High School. The daughter had been educated at home and had turned out well: the boy did not learn badly either.

III

So Ivan Ilych lived for seventeen years after his marriage. He was already a Public Prosecutor of long standing, and had declined several proposed transfers while awaiting a more desirable post, when an unanticipated and unpleasant occurrence quite upset the peaceful course of his life. He was expecting to be offered the post of presiding judge in a University town, but Happe somehow came to the front and obtained the appointment instead. Ivan Ilych became irritable, reproached Happe, and quarrelled both with him and with his immediate superiors—who became colder to him and again passed him over when other appointments were made.

This was in 1880, the hardest year of Ivan Ilych's life. It was then that it became evident on the one hand that his salary was insufficient for them to live on, and on the other that he had been forgotten, and not only this, but that what was for him the greatest and most cruel injustice appeared to others a quite ordinary occurrence. Even his father did not consider it his duty to help him. Ivan Ilych felt himself abandoned by everyone, and that they regarded his position with a salary of 3,500 rubles as quite normal and even fortunate. He alone knew that with the consciousness of the injustices done him, with his wife's incessant nagging, and with the debts he had contracted by living beyond his means, his position was far from normal.

In order to save money that summer he obtained leave of absence and went with his wife to live in the country at her brother's place. In the country, without his work, he experienced *ennui* for the first time in his life, and not only *ennui* but intolerable depression, and he decided that it was impossible to go on living like that, and that it was necessary to take energetic measures.

Having passed a sleepless night pacing up and down the veranda, he decided to go to Petersburg and bestir himself, in order to punish those who had failed to appreciate him and to get transferred to another ministry.

Next day, despite many protests from his wife and her brother, he started for Petersburg with the sole object of obtaining a post with a salary of five thousand rubles a year. He was no longer bent on any particular department, or tendency, or kind of activity. All he now wanted was an appointment to another post with a salary of five thousand rubles, either in the administration, in the banks, with the railways, in one of the Empress Marya's Institutions, or even in the customs—but it had to carry with it a salary of five thousand rubles and be in a ministry other than that in which they had failed to appreciate him.

And this quest of Ivan Ilych's was crowned with remarkable and unexpected success. At Kursk an acquaintance of his, F. I. Ilyin, got into the first-class carriage, sat down beside Ivan Ilych, and told him of a telegram just received by the Governor of Kursk announcing that a change was about to take place in the ministry: Peter Ivanovich was to be superseded by Ivan Semënovich.

The proposed change, apart from its significance for Russia, had a special significance for Ivan Ilych, because by bringing forward a new man, Peter Petrovich, and consequently his friend Zachar Ivanovich, it was highly favourable for Ivan Ilych, since Zachar Ivanovich was a friend and colleague of his.

In Moscow this news was confirmed, and on reaching Petersburg Ivan Ilych found Zachar Ivanovich and received a definite promise of an appointment in his former department of Justice.

A week later he telegraphed to his wife: "Zachar in Miller's place. I shall receive appointment on presentation of report."

Thanks to this change of personnel, Ivan Ilych had unexpectedly obtained an appointment in his former ministry which placed him two stages above his former colleagues besides giving him five thousand rubles salary and three thousand five hundred rubles for expenses connected with his removal. All his ill humour towards his former enemies and the whole department vanished, and Ivan Ilych was completely happy.

He returned to the country more cheerful and contented than he had been for a long time. Praskovya Fëdorovna also cheered up and a truce was arranged between them. Ivan Ilych told of how he had been fêted by everybody in Petersburg, how all those who had been his enemies were put to shame and now fawned on him, how envious they were of his appointment, and how much everybody in Petersburg had liked him.

Praskovya Fëdorovna listened to all this and appeared to believe it. She did not contradict anything, but only made plans for their life in the town to which they were going. Ivan Ilych saw with delight that these plans were his plans, that he and his wife agreed, and that, after a stumble, his life was regaining its due and natural character of pleasant lightheartedness and decorum.

Ivan Ilych had come back for a short time only, for he had to take up his new duties on the 10th of September. Moreover, he needed time to settle into the new place, to move all his belongings from the province, and to buy and order many additional things: in a word, to make such arrangements as he had resolved on, which were almost exactly what Praskovya Fëdorovna too had decided on.

Now that everything had happened so fortunately, and that he and his wife were at one in their aims and moreover saw so little of one another, they got on together better than they had done since the first years of marriage. Ivan Ilych had thought of taking his family away with him at once, but the insistence of his wife's brother and her sister-in-law, who had suddenly become particularly amiable and friendly to him and his family, induced him to depart alone.

So he departed, and the cheerful state of mind induced by his success and by the harmony between his wife and himself, the one intensifying the other, did not leave him. He found a delightful house, just the thing both he and his wife had dreamt of. Spacious, lofty reception rooms in the old style, a convenient and dignified study, rooms for his wife and daughter, a study for his son—it might have been specially built for them. Ivan Ilych himself superintended the arrangements, chose the wallpapers, supplemented the furniture (preferably with antiques which he considered particularly *comme il faut*), and supervised the upholstering. Everything progressed and progressed and approached the ideal he had set himself: even when things were only half completed they exceeded his expectations. He saw what a refined and elegant character, free from vulgarity, it would all have when it was ready. On falling asleep he pictured to himself how the reception-room would look. Looking at the yet unfinished drawing-room he could see the fireplace, the screen, the what-not, the little chairs dotted here and there, the dishes and plates on the walls, and the bronzes, as they would be when everything was in place. He was pleased by the thought of how his wife and daughter, who shared his taste in this matter, would be impressed by it. They were certainly not expecting as much. He had been particularly successful in finding, and buying cheaply, antiques which gave a particularly aristocratic character to the whole place. But in his letters he intentionally understated everything in order to be able to surprise them. All this so absorbed him that his new duties —though he liked his official work—interested him less than he had expected. Sometimes he even had moments of absent-mindedness during the

Court Sessions, and would consider whether he should have straight or curved cornices for his curtains. He was so interested in it all that he often did things himself, rearranging the furniture, or rehanging the curtains. Once when mounting a step-ladder to show the upholsterer, who did not understand, how he wanted the hangings draped, he made a false step and slipped, but being a strong and agile man he clung on and only knocked his side against the knob of the window frame. The bruised place was painful but the pain soon passed, and he felt particularly bright and well just then. He wrote: "I feel fifteen years younger." He thought he would have everything ready by September, but it dragged on till mid-October. But the result was charming not only in his eyes but to everyone who saw it.

In reality it was just what is usually seen in the houses of people of moderate means who want to appear rich, and therefore succeed only in resembling others like themselves: there were damasks, dark wood, plants, rugs, and dull and polished bronzes—all the things people of a certain class have in order to resemble other people of that class. His house was so like the others that it would never have been noticed, but to him it all seemed to be quite exceptional. He was very happy when he met his family at the station and brought them to the newly furnished house all lit up, where a footman in a white tie opened the door into the hall decorated with plants, and when they went on into the drawing-room, and the study uttering exclamations of delight. He conducted them everywhere, drank in their praises eagerly, and beamed with pleasure. At tea that evening, when Praskovya Fëdorovna among other things asked him about his fall, he laughed and showed them how he had gone flying and had frightened the upholsterer.

"It's a good thing I'm a bit of an athlete. Another man might have been killed, but I merely knocked myself, just here; it hurts when it's touched, but it's passing off already—it's only a bruise."

So they began living in their new home—in which, as always happens, when they got thoroughly settled in they found they were just one room short—and with the increased income, which as always was just a little (some five hundred rubles) too little, but it was all very nice.

Things went particularly well at first, before everything was finally arranged and while something had still to be done: this thing bought, that thing ordered, another thing moved, and something else adjusted. Though there were some disputes between husband and wife, they were both so well satisfied and had so much to do that it all passed off without any serious quarrels. When nothing was left to arrange it became rather dull and something seemed to be lacking, but they were then making acquaintances, forming habits, and life was growing fuller.

Ivan Ilych spent his mornings at the law courts and came home to dinner, and at first he was generally in a good humour, though he occasionally became irritable just on account of his house. (Every spot on the

tablecloth or the upholstery, and every broken windowblind string, irritated him. He had devoted so much trouble to arranging it all that every
disturbance of it distressed him.) But on the whole his life ran its course
as he believed life should do: easily, pleasantly, and decorously.

He got up at nine, drank his coffee, read the paper, and then put on his
undress uniform and went to the law courts. There the harness in which
he worked had already been stretched to fit him and he donned it without
a hitch: petitioners, inquiries at the chancery, the chancery itself, and the
sittings public and administrative. In all this the thing was to exclude
everything fresh and vital, which always disturbs the regular course of
official business, and to admit only official relations with people, and then
only on official grounds. A man would come, for instance, wanting some
information. Ivan Ilych, as one in whose sphere the matter did not lie,
would have nothing to do with him: but if the man had some business
with him in his official capacity, something that could be expressed on
officially stamped paper, he would do everything, positively everything he
could within the limits of such relations, and in doing so would maintain
the semblance of friendly human relations, that is, would observe the
courtesies of life. As soon as the official relations ended, so did everything
else. Ivan Ilych possessed this capacity to separate his real life from the
official side of affairs and not mix the two, in the highest degree, and by
long practice and natural aptitude had brought it to such a pitch that
sometimes, in the manner of a virtuoso, he would even allow himself to let
the human and official relations mingle. He let himself do this just because he felt that he could at any time he chose resume the strictly official
attitude again and drop the human relation. And he did it all easily,
pleasantly, correctly, and even artistically. In the intervals between the
sessions he smoked, drank tea, chatted a little about politics, a little about
general topics, a little about cards, but most of all about official appointments. Tired, but with the feelings of a virtuoso—one of the first violins
who has played his part in an orchestra with precision—he would return
home to find that his wife and daughter had been out paying calls, or had
a visitor, and that his son had been to school, had done his homework
with his tutor, and was duly learning what is taught at High Schools.
Everything was as it should be. After dinner, if they had no visitors, Ivan
Ilych sometimes read a book that was being much discussed at the time,
and in the evening settled down to work, that is, read official papers, compared the depositions of witnesses, and noted paragraphs of the Code
applying to them. This was neither dull nor amusing. It was dull when he
might have been playing bridge, but if no bridge was available it was at
any rate better than doing nothing or sitting with his wife. Ivan Ilych's
chief pleasure was giving little dinners to which he invited men and
women of good social position, and just as his drawing-room resembled all
other drawing-rooms so did his enjoyable little parties resemble all other
such parties.

Once they even gave a dance. Ivan Ilych enjoyed it and everything went off well, except that it led to a violent quarrel with his wife about the cakes and sweets. Praskovya Fëdorovna had made her own plans, but Ivan Ilych insisted on getting everything from an expensive confectioner and ordered too many cakes, and the quarrel occurred because some of those cakes were left over and the confectioner's bill came to forty-five rubles. It was a great and disagreeable quarrel. Praskovya Fëdorovna called him "a fool and an imbecile," and he clutched at his head and made angry allusions to divorce.

But the dance itself had been enjoyable. The best people were there, and Ivan Ilych had danced with Princess Trufonova, a sister of the distinguished founder of the Society "Bear my Burden."

The pleasures connected with his work were pleasures of ambition; his social pleasures were those of vanity; but Ivan Ilych's greatest pleasure was playing bridge. He acknowledged that whatever disagreeable incident happened in his life, the pleasure that beamed like a ray of light above everything else was to sit down to bridge with good players, not noisy partners, and of course to four-handed bridge (with five players it was annoying to have to stand out, though one pretended not to mind), to play a clever and serious game (when the cards allowed it), and then to have supper and drink a glass of wine. After a game of bridge, especially if he had won a little (to win a large sum was unpleasant), Ivan Ilych went to bed in specially good humour.

So they lived. They formed a circle of acquaintances among the best people and were visited by people of importance and by young folk. In their views as to their acquaintances, husband, wife, and daughter were entirely agreed, and tacitly and unanimously kept at arm's length and shook off the various shabby friends and relations who, with much show of affection, gushed into the drawing-room with its Japanese plates on the walls. Soon these shabby friends ceased to obtrude themselves and only the best people remained in the Golovins' set.

Young men made up to Lisa, and Petrishchev, an examining magistrate and Dmitri Ivanovich Petrishchev's son and sole heir, began to be so attentive to her that Ivan Ilych had already spoken to Praskovya Fëdorovna about it, and considered whether they should not arrange a party for them, or get up some private theatricals.

So they lived, and all went well, without change, and life flowed pleasantly.

IV

They were all in good health. It could not be called ill health if Ivan Ilych sometimes said that he had a queer taste in his mouth and felt some discomfort in his left side.

But this discomfort increased and, though not exactly painful, grew into a sense of pressure in his side accompanied by ill humour. And his irritability became worse and worse and began to mar the agreeable, easy, and correct life that had established itself in the Golovin family. Quarrels between husband and wife became more and more frequent, and soon the ease and amenity disappeared and even the decorum was barely maintained. Scenes again became frequent, and very few of those islets remained on which husband and wife could meet without an explosion. Praskovya Fëdorovna now had good reason to say that her husband's temper was trying. With characteristic exaggeration she said he had always had a dreadful temper, and that it had needed all her good nature to put up with it for twenty years. It was true that now the quarrels were started by him. His bursts of temper always came just before dinner, often just as he began to eat his soup. Sometimes he noticed that a plate or dish was chipped, or the food was not right, or his son put his elbow on the table, or his daughter's hair was not done as he liked it, and for all this he blamed Praskovya Fëdorovna. At first she retorted and said disagreeable things to him, but once or twice he fell into such a rage at the beginning of dinner that she realized it was due to some physical derangement brought on by taking food, and so she restrained herself and did not answer, but only hurried to get the dinner over. She regarded this self-restraint as highly praiseworthy. Having come to the conclusion that her husband had a dreadful temper and made her life miserable, she began to feel sorry for herself, and the more she pitied herself the more she hated her husband. She began to wish he would die; yet she did not want him to die because then his salary would cease. And this irritated her against him still more. She considered herself dreadfully unhappy just because not even his death could save her, and though she concealed her exasperation, that hidden exasperation of hers increased his irritation also.

After one scene in which Ivan Ilych had been particularly unfair and after which he had said in explanation that he certainly was irritable but that it was due to his not being well, she said that if he was ill it should be attended to, and insisted on his going to see a celebrated doctor.

He went. Everything took place as he had expected and as it always does. There was the usual waiting and the important air assumed by the doctor, with which he was so familiar (resembling that which he himself assumed in court), and the sounding and listening, and the questions which called for answers that were foregone conclusions and were evidently unnecessary, and the look of importance which implied that "if only you put yourself in our hands we will arrange everything—we know indubitably how it has to be done, always in the same way for everybody alike." It was all just as it was in the law courts. The doctor put on just the same air towards him as he himself put on towards an accused person.

The doctor said that so-and-so indicated that there was so-and-so inside the patient, but if the investigation of so-and-so did not confirm this, then he must assume that and that. If he assumed that and that, then . . . and so on. To Ivan Ilych only one question was important: was his case serious or not? But the doctor ignored that inappropriate question. From his point of view it was not the one under consideration, the real question was to decide between a floating kidney, chronic catarrh, or appendicitis. It was not a question of Ivan Ilych's life or death, but one between a floating kidney and appendicitis. And that question the doctor solved brilliantly, as it seemed to Ivan Ilych, in favour of the appendix, with the reservation that should an examination of the urine give fresh indications the matter would be reconsidered. All this was just what Ivan Ilych had himself brilliantly accomplished a thousand times in dealing with men on trial. The doctor summed up just as brilliantly, looking over his spectacles triumphantly and even gaily at the accused. From the doctor's summing up Ivan Ilych concluded that things were bad, but that for the doctor, and perhaps for everybody else, it was a matter of indifference, though for him it was bad. And this conclusion struck him painfully, arousing in him a great feeling of pity for himself and of bitterness towards the doctor's indifference to a matter of such importance.

He said nothing of this, but rose, placed the doctor's fee on the table, and remarked with a sigh: "We sick people probably often put inappropriate questions. But tell me, in general, is this complaint dangerous, or not? . . ."

The doctor looked at him sternly over his spectacles with one eye, as if to say: "Prisoner, if you will not keep to the questions put to you, I shall be obliged to have you removed from the court."

"I have already told you what I consider necessary and proper. The analysis may show something more." And the doctor bowed.

Ivan Ilych went out slowly, seated himself disconsolately in his sledge, and drove home. All the way home he was going over what the doctor had said, trying to translate those complicated, obscure, scientific phrases into plain language and find in them an answer to the question: "Is my condition bad? Is it very bad? Or is there as yet nothing much wrong?" And it seemed to him that the meaning of what the doctor had said was that it was very bad. Everything in the streets seemed depressing. The cabmen, the houses, the passers-by, and the shops, were dismal. His ache, this dull gnawing ache that never ceased for a moment, seemed to have acquired a new and more serious significance from the doctor's dubious remarks. Ivan Ilych now watched it with a new and oppressive feeling.

He reached home and began to tell his wife about it. She listened, but in the middle of his account his daughter came in with her hat on, ready to go out with her mother. She sat down reluctantly to listen to this tedious story, but could not stand it long, and her mother too did not hear him to the end.

"Well, I am very glad," she said. "Mind now to take your medicine
regularly. Give me the prescription and I'll send Gerasim to the chemist's."
And she went to get ready to go out.

While she was in the room Ivan Ilych had hardly taken time to breathe,
but he sighed deeply when she left it.

"Well," he thought, "perhaps it isn't so bad after all."

He began taking his medicine and following the doctor's directions, which
had been altered after the examination of the urine. But then it happened that there was a contradiction between the indications drawn from
the examination of the urine and the symptoms that showed themselves.
It turned out that what was happening differed from what the doctor had
told him, and that he had either forgotten, or blundered, or hidden something from him. He could not, however, be blamed for that, and Ivan
Ilych still obeyed his orders implicitly and at first derived some comfort
from doing so.

From the time of his visit to the doctor, Ivan Ilych's chief occupation
was the exact fulfilment of the doctor's instructions regarding hygiene
and the taking of medicine, and the observation of his pain and his excretions. His chief interests came to be people's ailments and people's
health. When sickness, deaths, or recoveries were mentioned in his presence, especially when the illness resembled his own, he listened with agitation which he tried to hide, asked questions, and applied what he heard
to his own case.

The pain did not grow less, but Ivan Ilych made efforts to force himself
to think that he was better. And he could do this so long as nothing
agitated him. But as soon as he had any unpleasantness with his wife, any
lack of success in his official work, or held bad cards at bridge, he was at
once acutely sensible of his disease. He had formerly borne such mis-
chances, hoping soon to adjust what was wrong, to master it and attain
success, or make a grand slam. But now every mischance upset him and
plunged him into despair. He would say to himself: "There now, just as
I was beginning to get better and the medicine had begun to take effect,
comes this accursed misfortune, or unpleasantness. . . ." And he was furious with the mishap, or with the people who were causing the unpleasantness and killing him, for he felt that this fury was killing him but could
not restrain it. One would have thought that it should have been clear
to him that this exasperation with circumstances and people aggravated
his illness, and that he ought therefore to ignore unpleasant occurrences.
But he drew the very opposite conclusion: he said that he needed peace,
and he watched for everything that might disturb it and became irritable
at the slightest infringement of it. His condition was rendered worse by
the fact that he read medical books and consulted doctors. The progress
of his disease was so gradual that he could deceive himself when comparing one day with another—the difference was so slight. But when he

consulted the doctors it seemed to him that he was getting worse, and even very rapidly. Yet despite this he was continually consulting them.

That month he went to see another celebrity, who told him almost the same as the first had done but put his questions rather differently, and the interview with this celebrity only increased Ivan Ilych's doubts and fears. A friend of a friend of his, a very good doctor, diagnosed his illness again quite differently from the others, and though he predicted recovery, his questions and suppositions bewildered Ivan Ilych still more and increased his doubts. A homœopathist diagnosed the disease in yet another way, and prescribed medicine which Ivan Ilych took secretly for a week. But after a week, not feeling any improvement and having lost confidence both in the former doctor's treatment and in this one's, he became still more despondent. One day a lady acquaintance mentioned a cure effected by a wonder-working icon. Ivan Ilych caught himself listening attentively and beginning to believe that it had occurred. This incident alarmed him. "Has my mind really weakened to such an extent?" he asked himself. "Nonsense! It's all rubbish. I mustn't give way to nervous fears but having chosen a doctor must keep strictly to his treatment. That is what I will do. Now it's all settled. I won't think about it, but will follow the treatment seriously till summer, and then we shall see. From now there must be no more of this wavering!" This was easy to say but impossible to carry out. The pain in his side oppressed him and seemed to grow worse and more incessant, while the taste in his mouth grew stranger and stranger. It seemed to him that his breath had a disgusting smell, and he was conscious of a loss of appetite and strength. There was no deceiving himself: something terrible, new, and more important than anything before in his life, was taking place within him of which he alone was aware. Those about him did not understand or would not understand it, but thought everything in the world was going on as usual. That tormented Ivan Ilych more than anything. He saw that his household, especially his wife and daughter who were in a perfect whirl of visiting, did not understand anything of it and were annoyed that he was so depressed and so exacting, as if he were to blame for it. Though they tried to disguise it he saw that he was an obstacle in their path, and that his wife had adopted a definite line in regard to his illness and kept to it regardless of anything he said or did. Her attitude was this: "You know," she would say to her friends, "Ivan Ilych can't do as other people do, and keep to the treatment prescribed for him. One day he'll take his drops and keep strictly to his diet and go to bed in good time, but the next day unless I watch him he'll suddenly forget his medicine, eat sturgeon—which is forbidden—and sit up playing cards till one o'clock in the morning."

"Oh, come, when was that?" Ivan Ilych would ask in vexation. "Only once at Peter Ivanovich's."

"And yesterday with Shebek."

"Well, even if I hadn't stayed up, this pain would have kept me awake."
"Be that as it may you'll never get well like that, but will always make
us wretched."

Praskovya Fëdorovna's attitude to Ivan Ilych's illness, as she expressed
it both to others and to him, was that it was his own fault and was another of the annoyances he caused her. Ivan Ilych felt that this opinion
escaped her involuntarily—but that did not make it easier for him.

At the law courts too, Ivan Ilych noticed, or thought he noticed, a
strange attitude towards himself. It sometimes seemed to him that people
were watching him inquisitively as a man whose place might soon be
vacant. Then again, his friends would suddenly begin to chaff him in a
friendly way about his low spirits, as if the awful, horrible, and unheard-of
thing that was going on within him, incessantly gnawing at him and irre-
sistibly drawing him away, was a very agreeable subject for jests. Schwartz
in particular irritated him by his jocularity, vivacity, and *savoir-faire,*
which reminded him of what he himself had been ten years ago.

Friends came to make up a set and they sat down to cards. They dealt,
bending the new cards to soften them, and he sorted the diamonds in his
hand and found he had seven. His partner said "No trumps" and supported him with two diamonds. What more could be wished for? It ought
to be jolly and lively. They would make a grand slam. But suddenly Ivan
Ilych was conscious of that gnawing pain, that taste in his mouth, and it
seemed ridiculous that in such circumstances he should be pleased to make
a grand slam.

He looked at his partner Mikhail Mikhaylovich, who rapped the table
with his strong hand and instead of snatching up the tricks pushed the
cards courteously and indulgently towards Ivan Ilych that he might have
the pleasure of gathering them up without the trouble of stretching out
his hand for them. "Does he think I am too weak to stretch out my arm?"
thought Ivan Ilych, and forgetting what he was doing he over-trumped
his partner, missing the grand slam by three tricks. And what was most
awful of all was that he saw how upset Mikhail Mikhaylovich was about
it but did not himself care. And it was dreadful to realize why he did
not care.

They all saw that he was suffering, and said: "We can stop if you are
tired. Take a rest." Lie down? No, he was not at all tired, and he finished
the rubber. All were gloomy and silent. Ivan Ilych felt that he had dif-
fused this gloom over them and could not dispel it. They had supper and
went away, and Ivan Ilych was left alone with the consciousness that his
life was poisoned and was poisoning the lives of others, and that this
poison did not weaken but penetrated more and more deeply into his
whole being.

With this consciousness, and with physical pain besides the terror, he
must go to bed, often to lie awake the greater part of the night. Next
morning he had to get up again, dress, go to the law courts, speak and

write; or if he did not go out, spend at home those twenty-four hours a day each of which was a torture. And he had to live thus alone on the brink of an abyss, with no one who understood or pitied him.

V

So one month passed and then another. Just before the New Year his brother-in-law came to town and stayed at their house. Ivan Ilych was at the law courts and Praskovya Fëdorovna had gone shopping. When Ivan Ilych came home and entered his study he found his brother-in-law there— a healthy, florid man—unpacking his portmanteau himself. He raised his head on hearing Ivan Ilych's footsteps and looked up at him for a moment without a word. That stare told Ivan Ilych everything. His brother-in-law opened his mouth to utter an explanation of surprise but checked himself, and that action confirmed it all.

"I have changed, eh?"

"Yes, there is a change."

And after that, try as he would to get his brother-in-law to return to the subjects of his looks, the latter would say nothing about it. Praskovya Fëdorovna came home and her brother went out to her. Ivan Ilych locked the door and began to examine himself in the glass, first full face, then in profile. He took up a portrait of himself taken with his wife, and compared it with what he saw in the glass. The change in him was immense. Then he bared his arms to the elbow, looked at them, drew the sleeves down again, sat down on an ottoman, and grew blacker than night.

"No, no, this won't do!" he said to himself, and jumped up, went to the table, took up some law papers, and began to read them, but could not continue. He unlocked the door and went into the reception-room. The door leading to the drawing-room was shut. He approached it on tiptoe and listened.

"No, you are exaggerating!" Praskovya Fëdorovna was saying.

"Exaggerating! Don't you see it? Why, he's a dead man! Look at his eyes—there's no light in them. But what is it that is wrong with him?"

"No one knows. Nikolaevich [that was another doctor] said something, but I don't know what. And Leshchetitsky [this was the celebrated specialist] said quite the contrary. . . ."

Ivan Ilych walked away, went to his own room, lay down, and began musing: "The kidney, a floating kidney." He recalled all the doctors had told him of how it detached itself and swayed about. And by an effort of imagination he tried to catch that kidney and arrest it and support it. So little was needed for this, it seemed to him. "No, I'll go to see Peter Ivanovich again." [That was the friend whose friend was a doctor.] He rang, ordered the carriage, and got ready to go.

652   Literary Experience

"Where are you going, Jean?" asked his wife, with a specially sad and exceptionally kind look.

This exceptionally kind look irritated him. He looked morosely at her. "I must go to see Peter Ivanovich."

He went to see Peter Ivanovich, and together they went to see his friend, the doctor. He was in, and Ivan Ilych had a long talk with him.

Reviewing the anatomical and physiological details of what in the doctor's opinion was going on inside him, he understood it all.

There was something, a small thing, in the vermiform appendix. It might all come right. Only stimulate the energy of one organ and check the activity of another, then absorption would take place and everything would come right. He got home rather late for dinner, ate his dinner, and conversed cheerfully, but could not for a long time bring himself to go back to work in his room. At last, however, he went to his study and did what was necessary, but the consciousness that he had put something aside —an important, intimate matter which he would revert to when his work was done—never left him. When he had finished his work he remembered that this intimate matter was the thought of his vermiform appendix. But he did not give himself up to it, and went to the drawing-room for tea. There were callers there, including the examining magistrate who was a desirable match for his daughter, and they were conversing, playing the piano, and singing. Ivan Ilych, as Praskovya Fëdorovna remarked, spent that evening more cheerfully than usual, but he never for a moment forgot that he had postponed the important matter of the appendix. At eleven o'clock he said good-night and went to his bedroom. Since his illness he had slept alone in a small room next to his study. He undressed and took up a novel by Zola, but instead of reading it he fell into thought, and in his imagination that desired improvement in the vermiform appendix occurred. There was the absorption and evacuation and the reestablishment of normal activity. "Yes, that's it!" he said to himself. "One need only assist nature, that's all." He remembered his medicine, rose, took it, and lay down on his back watching for the beneficent action of the medicine and for it to lessen the pain. "I need only take it regularly and avoid all injurious influences. I am already feeling better, much better." He began touching his side: it was not painful to the touch. "There, I really don't feel it. It's much better already." He put out the light and turned on his side. . . . "The appendix is getting better, absorption is occurring." Suddenly he felt the old, familiar, dull, gnawing pain, stubborn and serious. There was the same familiar loathsome taste in his mouth. His heart sank and he felt dazed. "My God! My God!" he muttered. "Again, again! and it will never cease." And suddenly the matter presented itself in a quite different aspect. "Vermiform appendix! Kidney!" he said to himself. "It's not a question of appendix or kidney, but of life and . . . death. Yes, life was there and now it is going, going and

I cannot stop it. Yes. Why deceive myself? Isn't it obvious to everyone but me that I'm dying, and that it's only a question of weeks, days . . . it may happen this moment. There was light and now there is darkness. I was here and now I'm going there! Where?" A chill came over him, his breathing ceased, and he felt only the throbbing of his heart.

"When I am not, what will there be? There will be nothing. Then where shall I be when I am no more? Can this be dying? No, I don't want to!" He jumped up and tried to light the candle, felt for it with trembling hands, dropped candle and candlestick on the floor, and fell back on his pillow.

"What's the use? It makes no difference," he said to himself, staring with wide-open eyes into the darkness. "Death. Yes, death. And none of them know or wish to know it, and they have no pity for me. Now they are playing." (He heard through the door the distant sound of a song and its accompaniment.) "It's all the same to them, but they will die too! Fools! I first, and they later, but it will be the same for them. And now they are merry . . . the beasts!"

Anger choked him and he was agonizingly, unbearably miserable. "It is impossible that all men have been doomed to suffer this awful horror!" He raised himself.

"Something must be wrong. I must calm myself—must think it all over from the beginning." And he again began thinking. "Yes, the beginning of my illness: I knocked my side, but I was still quite well that day and the next. It hurt a little, then rather more. I saw the doctors, then followed despondency and anguish, more doctors, and I drew nearer to the abyss. My strength grew less and I kept coming nearer and nearer, and now I have wasted away and there is no light in my eyes. I think of the appendix—but this is death! I think of mending the appendix, and all the while here is death! Can it really be death?" Again terror seized him and he gasped for breath. He leant down and began feeling for the matches, pressing with his elbow on the stand beside the bed. It was in his way and hurt him, he grew furious with it, pressed on it still harder, and upset it. Breathless and in despair he fell on his back, expecting death to come immediately.

Meanwhile the visitors were leaving. Praskovya Fëdorovna was seeing them off. She heard something fall and came in.

"What has happened?"

"Nothing. I knocked it over accidentally."

She went out and returned with a candle. He lay there panting heavily, like a man who has run a thousand yards, and stared upwards at her with a fixed look.

"What is it, Jean?"

"No . . . o . . . thing. I upset it." ("Why speak of it? She won't understand," he thought.)

And in truth she did not understand. She picked up the stand, lit his candle, and hurried away to see another visitor off. When she came back he still lay on his back, looking upwards.

"What is it? Do you feel worse?"

"Yes."

She shook her head and sat down.

"Do you know, Jean, I think we must ask Leshchetitsky to come and see you here."

This meant calling in the famous specialist, regardless of expense. He smiled malignantly and said "No." She remained a little longer and then went up to him and kissed his forehead.

While she was kissing him he hated her from the bottom of his soul and with difficulty refrained from pushing her away.

"Good-night. Please God you'll sleep."

"Yes."

VI

Ivan Ilych saw that he was dying, and he was in continual despair.

In the depth of his heart he knew he was dying, but not only was he not accustomed to the thought, he simply did not and could not grasp it.

The syllogism he had learnt from Kiezewetter's Logic: "Caius is a man, men are mortal, therefore Caius is mortal," had always seemed to him correct as applied to Caius, but certainly not as applied to himself. That Caius—man in the abstract—was mortal, was perfectly correct, but he was not Caius, not an abstract man, but a creature quite, quite separate from all others. He had been little Vanya, with a mamma and a papa, with Mitya and Volodya, with the toys, a coachman and a nurse, afterwards with Katenka and with all the joys, griefs, and delights of childhood, boyhood, and youth. What did Caius know of the smell of that striped leather ball Vanya had been so fond of? Had Caius kissed his mother's hand like that, and did the silk of her dress rustle so for Caius? Had he rioted like that at school when the pastry was bad? Had Caius been in love like that? Could Caius preside at a session as he did? "Caius really was mortal, and it was right for him to die; but for me, little Vanya, Ivan Ilych, with all my thoughts and emotions, it's altogether a different matter. It cannot be that I ought to die. That would be too terrible."

Such was his feeling.

"If I had to die like Caius I should have known it was so. An inner voice would have told me so, but there was nothing of the sort in me and I and all my friends felt that our case was quite different from that of Caius. And now here it is!" he said to himself. "It can't be. It's impossible! But here it is. How is this? How is one to understand it?"

He could not understand it, and tried to drive this false, incorrect, morbid thought away and to replace it by other proper and healthy thoughts. But that thought, and not the thought only but the reality itself, seemed to come and confront him.

And to replace that thought he called up a succession of others, hoping to find in them some support. He tried to get back into the former current of thoughts that had once screened the thought of death from him. But strange to say, all that had formerly shut off, hidden, and destroyed his consciousness of death, no longer had that effect. Ivan Ilych now spent most of his time in attempting to re-establish that old current. He would say to himself: "I will take up my duties again—after all I used to live by them." And banishing all doubts he would go to the law courts, enter into conversation with his colleagues, and sit carelessly as was his wont, scanning the crowd with a thoughtful look and leaning both his emaciated arms on the arms of his oak chair; bending over as usual to a colleague and drawing his papers nearer he would interchange whispers with him, and then suddenly raising his eyes and sitting erect would pronounce certain words and open the proceedings. But suddenly in the midst of those proceedings the pain in his side, regardless of the stage the proceedings had reached, would begin its own gnawing work. Ivan Ilych would turn his attention to it and try to drive the thought of it away, but without success. *It* would come and stand before him and look at him, and he would be petrified and the light would die out of his eyes, and he would again begin asking himself whether *It* alone was true. And his colleagues and subordinates would see with surprise and distress that he, the brilliant and subtle judge, was becoming confused and making mistakes. He would shake himself, try to pull himself together, manage somehow to bring the sitting to a close, and return home with the sorrowful consciousness that his judicial labours could not as formerly hide from him what he wanted them to hide, and could not deliver him from *It*. And what was worst of all was that *It* drew his attention to itself not in order to make him take some action but only that he should look at *It*, look it straight in the face: look at it and, without doing anything, suffer inexpressibly.

And to save himself from this condition Ivan Ilych looked for consolations—new screens—and new screens were found and for a while seemed to save him, but then they immediately fell to pieces or rather became transparent, as if *It* penetrated them and nothing could veil *It*.

In these latter days he would go into the drawing-room he had arranged —that drawing-room where he had fallen and for the sake of which (how bitterly ridiculous it seemed) he had sacrificed his life—for he knew that his illness originated with that knock. He would enter and see that something had scratched the polished table. He would look for the cause of this and find that it was the bronze ornamentation of an album, that had got bent. He would take up the expensive album which he had lovingly arranged, and feel vexed with his daughter and her friends for their untidiness—for the album was torn here and there and some of the photographs turned upside down. He would put it carefully in order and bend the ornamentation back into position. Then it would occur to him to place all those things in another corner of the room, near the plants. He could call the footman, but his daughter or wife would come to help him. They would not agree, and his wife would contradict him, and he would dispute and grow angry. But that was all right, for then he did not think about *It*. *It* was invisible.

But then, when he was moving something himself, his wife would say: "Let the servants do it. You will hurt yourself again." And suddenly *It* would flash through the screen and he would see it. It was just a flash, and he hoped it would disappear, but he would involuntarily pay attention to his side. "It sits there as before, gnawing just the same!" And he could no longer forget *It*, but could distinctly see it looking at him from behind the flowers. "What is it all for?"

"It really is so! I lost my life over that curtain as I might have done when storming a fort. Is that possible? How terrible and how stupid. It can't be true! It can't, but it is."

He would go to his study, lie down, and again be alone with *It*: face to face with *It*. And nothing could be done with *It* except to look at it and shudder.

VII

How it happened it is impossible to say because it came about step by step, unnoticed, but in the third month of Ivan Ilych's illness, his wife, his daughter, his son, his acquaintances, the doctors, the servants, and above all he himself, were aware that the whole interest he had for other people was whether he would soon vacate his place, and at last release the living from the discomfort caused by his presence and be himself released from his sufferings.

He slept less and less. He was given opium and hypodermic injections of morphine, but this did not relieve him. The dull depression he experienced in a somnolent condition at first gave him a little relief, but only as something new, afterwards it became as distressing as the pain itself or even more so.

Special foods were prepared for him by the doctors' orders, but all those foods became increasingly distasteful and disgusting to him.

For his excretions also special arrangements had to be made, and this was a torment to him every time—a torment from the uncleanliness, the unseemliness, and the smell, and from knowing that another person had to take part in it.

But just through this most unpleasant matter, Ivan Ilych obtained comfort. Gerasim, the butler's young assistant, always came in to carry the things out. Gerasim was a clean, fresh peasant lad, grown stout on town food and always cheerful and bright. At first the sight of him, in his clean Russian peasant costume, engaged on that disgusting task embarrassed Ivan Ilych.

Once when he got up from the commode too weak to draw up his trousers, he dropped into a soft armchair and looked with horror at his bare, enfeebled thighs with the muscles so sharply marked on them.

Gerasim with a firm light tread, his heavy boots emitting a pleasant smell of tar and fresh winter air, came in wearing a clean Hessian apron, the sleeves of his print shirt tucked up over his strong, bare young arms; and refraining from looking at his sick master out of consideration for his feelings, and restraining the joy of life that beamed from his face, he went up to the commode.

"Gerasim!" said Ivan Ilych in a weak voice.

Gerasim started, evidently afraid he might have committed some blunder, and with a rapid movement turned his fresh, kind, simple young face which just showed the first downy signs of a beard.

"Yes, sir?"

"That must be very unpleasant for you. You must forgive me. I am helpless."

"Oh, why, sir," and Gerasim's eyes beamed and he showed his glistening white teeth, "what's a little trouble? It's a case of illness with you sir."

And his deft strong hands did their accustomed task, and he went out of the room stepping lightly. Five minutes later he as lightly returned.

Ivan Ilych was still sitting in the same position in the armchair.

"Gerasim," he said when the latter had replaced the freshly-washed utensil. "Please come here and help me." Gerasim went up to him. "Lift me up. It is hard for me to get up, and I have sent Dmitri away."

Gerasim went up to him, grasped his master with his strong arms deftly but gently, in the same way that he stepped—lifted him, supported him with one hand, and with the other drew up his trousers and would have set him down again, but Ivan Ilych asked to be led to the sofa. Gerasim, without an effort and without apparent pressure, led him, almost lifting him, to the sofa and placed him on it.

"Thank you. How easily and well you do it all!"

Gerasim smiled again and turned to leave the room. But Ivan Ilych felt his presence such a comfort that he did not want to let him go.

"One thing more, please move up that chair. No, the other one—under my feet. It is easier for me when my feet are raised."

Gerasim brought the chair, set it down gently in place, and raised Ivan Ilych's legs on to it. It seemed to Ivan Ilych that he felt better while Gerasim was holding up his legs.

"It's better when my legs are higher," he said. "Place that cushion under them."

Gerasim did so. He again lifted the legs and placed them, and again Ivan Ilych felt better while Gerasim held his legs. When he set them down Ivan Ilych fancied he felt worse.

"Gerasim," he said. "Are you busy now?"

"Not at all, sir," said Gerasim, who had learnt from the townsfolk how to speak to gentlefolk.

"What have you still to do?"

"What have I to do? I've done everything except chopping the logs for tomorrow."

"Then hold my legs up a bit higher, can you?"

"Of course I can. Why not?" And Gerasim raised his master's legs higher and Ivan Ilych thought that in that position he did not feel any pain at all.

"And how about the logs?"

"Don't trouble about that, sir. There's plenty of time."

Ivan Ilych told Gerasim to sit down and hold his leg, and began to talk to him. And strange to say it seemed to him that he felt better while Gerasim held his legs up.

After that Ivan Ilych would sometimes call Gerasim and get him to hold his legs on his shoulders, and he liked talking to him. Gerasim did it all easily, willingly, simply, and with a good nature that touched Ivan Ilych. Health, strength, and vitality in other people were offensive to him, but Gerasim's strength and vitality did not mortify but soothed him.

What tormented Ivan Ilych most was the deception, the lie, which for some reason they all accepted, that he was not dying but was simply ill, and that he only need keep quiet and undergo a treatment and then something very good would result. He however knew that do what they would nothing would come of it, only still more agonizing suffering and death. This deception tortured him—their not wishing to admit what they all knew and what he knew, but wanting to lie to him concerning his terrible condition, and wishing and forcing him to participate in that lie. Those lies—lies enacted over him on the eve of his death and destined to degrade this awful, solemn act to the level of their visitings, their curtains, their sturgeon for dinner—were a terrible agony for Ivan Ilych. And strangely enough, many times when they were going through their antics over him he had been within a hairbreadth of calling out to them: "Stop lying! You know and I know that I am dying. Then at least stop lying about it." But he had never had the spirit to do it. The awful, terrible act of his dying was, he could see, reduced by those about him to the level of a casual, unpleasant, and almost indecorous incident (as if someone entered a drawing-room diffusing an unpleasant odour) and this was done by that very decorum which he had served all his life long. He saw that no one felt for him, because no one even wished to grasp his position. Only Gerasim recognized it and pitied him. And so Ivan Ilych felt at ease only with him. He felt comforted when Gerasim supported his legs (sometimes all night long) and refused to go to bed, saying: "Don't you worry, Ivan Ilych. I'll get sleep enough later on," or when he suddenly became familiar and exclaimed: "If you weren't sick it would be another matter, but as it is, why should I grudge a little trouble?" Gerasim alone did not lie; everything showed that he alone understood the facts of the case and did not consider it necessary to disguise them, but simply felt sorry for his emaciated and enfeebled master. Once when Ivan Ilych was sending him away he even said straight out: "We shall all of us die, so why should I grudge a little trouble?"—expressing the fact that he did not think his work burdensome, because he was doing it for a dying man and hoped someone would do the same for him when his time came.

Apart from this lying, or because of it, what most tormented Ivan Ilych was that no one pitied him as he wished to be pitied. At certain moments after prolonged suffering he wished most of all (though he would have been ashamed to confess it) for someone to pity him as a sick child is pitied. He longed to be petted and comforted. He knew he was an important functionary, that he had a beard turning grey, and that therefore what he longed for was impossible, but still he longed for it. And in Gerasim's attitude towards him there was something akin to what he wished for, and so that attitude comforted him. Ivan Ilych wanted to weep, wanted to be petted and cried over, and then his colleague Shebek would come, and instead of weeping and being petted, Ivan Ilych would assume a serious, severe, and profound air, and by force of habit would express his opinion on a decision of the Court of Cassation and would stubbornly insist on that view. This falsity around him and within him did more than anything else to poison his last days.

VIII

It was morning. He knew it was morning because Gerasim had gone, and Peter the footman had come and put out the candles, drawn back one of the curtains, and begun quietly to tidy up. Whether it was morning or evening, Friday or Sunday, made no difference, it was all just the same: the gnawing, unmitigated, agonizing pain, never ceasing for an instant, the consciousness of life inexorably waning but not yet extinguished, the approach of that ever dreaded and hateful Death which was the only reality, and always the same falsity. What were days, weeks, hours, in such a case?

"Will you have some tea, sir?"

"He wants things to be regular, and wishes the gentlefolk to drink tea in the morning," thought Ivan Ilych, and only said "No."

"Wouldn't you like to move onto the sofa, sir?"

"He wants to tidy up the room, and I'm in the way. I am uncleanliness and disorder," he thought, and said only:

"No, leave me alone."

The man went on bustling about. Ivan Ilych stretched out his hand. Peter came up, ready to help.

"What is it, sir?"

"My watch."

Peter took the watch which was close at hand and gave it to his master.

"Half-past eight. Are they up?"

"No, sir, except Vladimir Ivanovich" (the son) "who has gone to school. Praskovya Fëdorovna ordered me to wake her if you asked for her. Shall I do so?"

"No, there's no need to." "Perhaps I'd better have some tea," he thought, and added aloud: "Yes, bring me some tea."

Peter went to the door, but Ivan Ilych dreaded being left alone. "How can I keep him here? Oh yes, my medicine." "Peter, give me my medicine." "Why not? Perhaps it may still do me some good." He took a spoonful and swallowed it. "No, it won't help. It's all tomfoolery, all deception," he decided as soon as he became aware of the familiar, sickly, hopeless taste. "No, I can't believe in it any longer. But the pain, why this pain? If it would only cease just for a moment!" And he moaned. Peter turned towards him. "It's all right. Go and fetch me some tea."

Peter went out. Left alone Ivan Ilych groaned not so much with pain, terrible though that was, as from mental anguish. Always and forever the same, always these endless days and nights. If only it would come quicker! If only *what* would come quicker? Death, darkness? . . . No, no! Anything rather than death!

When Peter returned with the tea on a tray, Ivan Ilych stared at him for a time in perplexity, not realizing who and what he was. Peter was disconcerted by that look and his embarrassment brought Ivan Ilych to himself.

"Oh, tea! All right, put it down. Only help me to wash and put on a clean shirt."

And Ivan Ilych began to wash. With pauses for rest, he washed his hands and then his face, cleaned his teeth, brushed his hair, and looked in the glass. He was terrified by what he saw, especially by the limp way in which his hair clung to his pallid forehead.

While his shirt was being changed he knew that he would be still more frightened at the sight of his body, so he avoided looking at it. Finally he was ready. He drew on a dressing-gown, wrapped himself in a plaid, and sat down in the armchair to take his tea. For a moment he felt refreshed, but soon as he began to drink the tea he was again aware of the same taste, and the pain also returned. He finished it with an effort, and then lay down stretching out his legs, and dismissed Peter.

Always the same. Now a spark of hope flashes up, then a sea of despair rages, and always pain; always pain, always despair, and always the same. When alone he had a dreadful and distressing desire to call someone, but he knew beforehand that with others present it would be still worse. "Another dose of morphine—to lose consciousness. I will tell him, the doctor, that he must think of something else. It's impossible, impossible, to go on like this."

An hour and another pass like that. But now there is a ring at the door bell. Perhaps it's the doctor? It is. He comes in fresh, hearty, plump, and cheerful, with that look on his face that seems to say: "There now, you're in a panic about something, but we'll arrange it all for you directly!" The doctor knows this expression is out of place here, but he has put it on once for all and can't take it off—like a man who has put on a frock-coat in the morning to pay a round of calls.

The doctor rubs his hands vigorously and reassuringly.

"Brr! How cold it is! There's such a sharp frost; just let me warm myself!" he says, as if it were only a matter of waiting till he was warm, and then he would put everything right.

"Well now, how are you?"

Ivan Ilych feels that the doctor would like to say: "Well, how are our affairs?" but that even he feels that this would not do, and says instead: "What sort of a night have you had?"

Ivan Ilych looks at him as much as to say: "Are you really never ashamed of lying?" But the doctor does not wish to understand this question, and Ivan Ilych says: "Just as terrible as ever. The pain never leaves me and never subsides. If only something . . ."

"Yes, you sick people are always like that. . . . There, now I think I am warm enough. Even Praskovya Fëdorovna, who is so particular, could find no fault with my temperature. Well, now I can say good-morning," and the doctor presses his patient's hand.

Then, dropping his former playfulness, he begins with a most serious face to examine the patient, feeling his pulse and taking his temperature, and then begins the sounding and auscultation.

Ivan Ilych knows quite well and definitely that all this is nonsense and pure deception, but when the doctor, getting down on his knee, leans over him, putting his ear first higher then lower, and performs various gymnastic movements over him with a significant expression on his face, Ivan Ilych submits to it all as he used to submit to the speeches of the lawyers, though he knew very well that they were all lying and why they were lying.

The doctor, kneeling on the sofa, is still sounding him when Praskovya Fëdorovna's silk dress rustles at the door and she is heard scolding Peter for not having let her know of the doctor's arrival.

She comes in, kisses her husband, and at once proceeds to prove that she has been up a long time already, and only owing to a misunderstanding failed to be there when the doctor arrived.

Ivan Ilych looks at her, scans her all over, sets against her the whiteness and plumpness and cleanness of her hands and neck, the gloss of her hair, and the sparkle of her vivacious eyes. He hates her with his whole soul. And the thrill of hatred he feels for her makes him suffer from her touch.

Her attitude towards him and his disease is still the same. Just as the doctor had adopted a certain relation to his patient which he could not abandon, so had she formed one towards him—that he was not doing something he ought to do and was himself to blame, and that she reproached him lovingly for this—and she could not now change that attitude.

"You see he doesn't listen to me and doesn't take his medicine at the proper time. And above all he lies in a position that is no doubt bad for him—with his legs up."

She described how he made Gerasim hold his legs up.

The doctor smiled with a contemptuous affability that said: "What's to be done? These sick people do have foolish fancies of that kind, but we must forgive them."

When the examination was over the doctor looked at his watch, and then Praskovya Fëdorovna announced to Ivan Ilych that it was of course as he pleased, but she had sent today for a celebrated specialist who would examine him and have a consultation with Michael Danilovich (their regular doctor).

"Please don't raise any objections. I am doing this for my own sake," she said ironically, letting it be felt that she was doing it all for his sake and only said this to leave him no right to refuse. He remained silent, knitting his brows. He felt that he was so surrounded and involved in a mesh of falsity that it was hard to unravel anything.

Everything she did for him was entirely for her own sake, and she told him she was doing for herself what she actually was doing for herself, as if that was so incredible that he must understand the opposite.

At half-past eleven the celebrated specialist arrived. Again the sounding began and the significant conversations in his presence and in another room, about the kidneys and the appendix, and the questions and answers, with such an air of importance that again, instead of the real question of life and death which now alone confronted him, the question arose of the kidney and appendix which were not behaving as they ought to and would now be attacked by Michael Danilovich and the specialist and forced to amend their ways.

The celebrated specialist took leave of him with a serious though not hopeless look, and in reply to the timid question Ivan Ilych, with eyes glistening with fear and hope, put to him as to whether there was a chance of recovery, said that he could not vouch for it but there was a possibility. The look of hope with which Ivan Ilych watched the doctor out was so pathetic that Praskovya Fëdorovna, seeing it, even wept as she left the room to hand the doctor his fee.

The gleam of hope kindled by the doctor's encouragement did not last long. The same room, the same pictures, curtains, wallpaper, medicine bottles, were all there, and the same aching suffering body, and Ivan Ilych began to moan. They gave him a subcutaneous injection and he sank into oblivion.

It was twilight when he came to. They brought him his dinner and he swallowed some beef tea with difficulty, and then everything was the same again and night was coming on.

After dinner, at seven o'clock, Praskovya Fёdorovna came into the room in evening dress, her full bosom pushed up by her corset, and with traces of powder on her face. She had reminded him in the morning that they were going to the theatre. Sarah Bernhardt was visiting the town and they had a box, which he had insisted on their taking. Now he had forgotten about it and her toilet offended him, but he concealed his vexation when he remembered that he had himself insisted on their securing a box and going because it would be an instructive and aesthetic pleasure for the children.

Praskovya Fёdorovna came in, self-satisfied but yet with a rather guilty air. She sat down and asked how he was, but, as he saw, only for the sake of asking and not in order to learn about it, knowing that there was nothing to learn—and then went on to what she really wanted to say: that she would not on any account have gone but that the box had been taken and Helen and their daughter were going, as well as Petrishchev (the examining magistrate, their daughter's fiancé), and that it was out of the question to let them go alone; but that she would have much preferred to sit with him for a while; and he must be sure to follow the doctor's orders while she was away.

"Oh, and Fёdor Petrovich" (the fiancé) "would like to come in. May he? And Lisa?"

"All right."

Their daughter came in in full evening dress, her fresh young flesh exposed (making a show of that very flesh which in his own case caused so much suffering), strong, healthy, evidently in love, and impatient with illness, suffering, and death, because they interfered with her happiness.

Fёdor Petrovich came in too, in evening dress, his hair curled à la Capoul, a tight stiff collar round his long sinewy neck, an enormous white shirt-front, and narrow black trousers tightly stretched over his strong thighs. He had one white glove tightly drawn on, and was holding his opera hat in his hand.

Following him the schoolboy crept in unnoticed, in a new uniform, poor little fellow, and wearing gloves. Terribly dark shadows showed under his eyes, the meaning of which Ivan Ilych knew well.

His son had always seemed pathetic to him, and now it was dreadful to see the boy's frightened look of pity. It seemed to Ivan Ilych that Vasya was the only one besides Gerasim who understood and pitied him.

They all sat down and again asked how he was. A silence followed. Lisa asked her mother about the opera-glasses, and there was an altercation between mother and daughter as to who had taken them and where they had been put. This occasioned some unpleasantness.

Fëdor Petrovich inquired of Ivan Ilych whether he had ever seen Sarah Bernhardt. Ivan Ilych did not at first catch the question, but then replied: "No, have you seen her before?"

"Yes, in *Adrienne Lecouvreur*."

Praskovya Fëdorovna mentioned some rôles in which Sarah Bernhardt was particularly good. Her daughter disagreed. Conversation sprang up as to the elegance and realism of her acting—the sort of conversation that is always repeated and is always the same.

In the midst of the conversation Fëdor Petrovich glanced at Ivan Ilych and became silent. The others also looked at him and grew silent. Ivan Ilych was staring with glittering eyes straight before him, evidently indignant with them. This had to be rectified, but it was impossible to do so. The silence had to be broken, but for a time no one dared to break it and they all became afraid that the conventional deception would suddenly become obvious and the truth become plain to all. Lisa was the first to pluck up courage and break that silence, but by trying to hide what everybody was feeling, she betrayed it.

"Well, if we are going it's time to start," she said, looking at her watch, a present from her father, and with a faint and significant smile at Fëdor Petrovich relating to something known only to them. She got up with a rustle of her dress.

They all rose, said good-night, and went away.

When they had gone it seemed to Ivan Ilych that he felt better; the falsity had gone with them. But the pain remained—that same pain and that same fear that made everything monotonously alike, nothing harder and nothing easier. Everything was worse.

Again minute followed minute and hour followed hour. Everything remained the same and there was no cessation. And the inevitable end of it all became more and more terrible.

"Yes, send Gerasim here," he replied to a question Peter asked.

IX

His wife returned late at night. She came in on tiptoe, but he heard her, opened his eyes, and made haste to close them again. She wished to send Gerasim away and to sit with him herself, but he opened his eyes and said: "No, go away."

"Are you in great pain?"

"Always the same."

"Take some opium."

He agreed and took some. She went away.

Till about three in the morning he was in a state of stupefied misery. It seemed to him that he and his pain were being thrust into a narrow, deep black sack, but though they were pushed further and further in they could not be pushed to the bottom. And this, terrible enough in itself, was accompanied by suffering. He was frightened yet wanted to fall through the sack, he struggled but yet co-operated. And suddenly he broke through, fell, and regained consciousness. Gerasim was sitting at the foot of the bed dozing quietly and patiently, while he himself lay with his emaciated stockinged legs resting on Gerasim's shoulders; the same shaded candle was there and the same unceasing pain.

"Go away, Gerasim," he whispered.

"It's all right, sir. I'll stay a while."

"No. Go away."

He removed his legs from Gerasim's shoulders, turned sideways onto his arm, and felt sorry for himself. He only waited till Gerasim had gone into the next room and then restrained himself no longer but wept like a child. He wept on account of his helplessness, his terrible loneliness, the cruelty of man, the cruelty of God, and the absence of God.

"Why hast Thou done all this? Why hast Thou brought me here? Why, why dost Thou torment me so terribly?"

He did not expect an answer and yet wept because there was no answer and could be none. The pain again grew more acute, but he did not stir and did not call. He said to himself: "Go on! Strike me! But what is it for? What have I done to Thee? What is it for?"

Then he grew quiet and not only ceased weeping but even held his breath and became all attention. It was as though he were listening not to an audible voice but to the voice of his soul, to the current of thoughts arising within him.

"What is it you want?" was the first clear conception capable of expression in words, that he heard.

"What do you want? What do you want?" he repeated to himself.

"What do I want? To live and not to suffer," he answered.

And again he listened with such concentrated attention that even his pain did not distract him.

"To live? How?" asked his inner voice.

"Why, to live as I used to—well and pleasantly."

"As you lived before, well and pleasantly?" the voice repeated.

And in imagination he began to recall the best moments of his pleasant life. But strange to say none of those best moments of his pleasant life now seemed at all what they had then seemed—none of them except the first recollections of childhood. There, in childhood, there had been something really pleasant with which it would be possible to live if it could return. But the child who had experienced that happiness existed no longer, it was like a reminiscence of somebody else.

As soon as the period began which had produced the present Ivan Ilych, all that had then seemed joys now melted before his sight and turned into something trivial and often nasty.

And the further he departed from childhood and the nearer he came to the present the more worthless and doubtful were the joys. This began with the School of Law. A little that was really good was still found there —there was lightheartedness, friendship, and hope. But in the upper classes there had already been fewer of such good moments. Then during the first years of his official career, when he was in the service of the Governor, some pleasant moments again occurred; they were the memories of love for a woman. Then all became confused and there was still less of what was good; later on again there was still less that was good, and the further he went the less there was. His marriage, a mere accident, then the disenchantment that followed it, his wife's bad breath and the sensuality and hypocrisy: then that deadly official life and those preoccupations about money, a year of it, and two, and ten, and twenty, and always the same thing. And the longer it lasted the more deadly it became. "It is as if I had been going downhill while I imagined I was going up. And that is really what it was. I was going up in public opinion, but to the same extent life was ebbing away from me. And now it is all done and there is only death."

"Then what does it mean? Why? It can't be that life is so senseless and horrible. But if it really has been so horrible and senseless, why must I die and die in agony? There is something wrong!"

"Maybe I did not live as I ought to have done," it suddenly occurred to him. "But how could that be, when I did everything properly?" he replied, and immediately dismissed from his mind this, the sole solution of all the riddles of life and death, as something quite impossible.

"Then what do you want now? To live? Live how? Live as you lived in the law courts when the usher proclaimed 'The judge is coming!' The judge is coming, the judge!" he repeated to himself. "Here he is, the judge. But I am not guilty!" he exclaimed angrily. "What is it for?" And he ceased crying, but turning his face to the wall continued to ponder on the same question: Why, and for what purpose, is there all this horror? But however much he pondered he found no answer. And whenever the thought occurred to him, as it often did, that it all resulted from his not having lived as he ought to have done, he at once recalled the correctness of his whole life and dismissed so strange an idea.

X

Another fortnight passed. Ivan Ilych now no longer left his sofa. He would not lie in bed but lay on the sofa, facing the wall nearly all the time. He suffered ever the same unceasing agonies and in his loneliness pondered always on the same insoluble question: "What is this? Can it be that it Death?" And the inner voice answered: "Yes, it is Death."

"Why these sufferings?" And the voice answered, "For no reason—they just are so." Beyond and besides this there was nothing.

From the very beginning of his illness, ever since he had first been to see the doctor, Ivan Ilych's life had been divided between two contrary and alternating moods: now it was despair and the expectation of this uncomprehended and terrible death, and now hope and an intently interested observation of the functioning of his organs. Now before his eyes there was only a kidney or an intestine that temporarily evaded its duty, and now only that incomprehensible and dreadful death from which it was impossible to escape.

These two states of mind had alternated from the very beginning of his illness, but the further it progressed the more doubtful and fantastic became the conception of the kidney, and the more real the sense of impending death.

He had but to call to mind what he had been three months before and what he was now, to call to mind with what regularity he had been going downhill, for every possibility of hope to be shattered.

Latterly during that loneliness in which he found himself as he lay facing the back of the sofa, a loneliness in the midst of a populous town and surrounded by numerous acquaintances and relations but that yet could not have been more complete anywhere—either at the bottom of the sea or under the earth—during that terrible loneliness Ivan Ilych had lived only in memories of the past. Pictures of his past rose before him one after another. They always began with what was nearest in time and then went back to what was most remote—to his childhood—and rested there. If he thought of the stewed prunes that had been offered him that day, his mind went back to the raw shrivelled French plums of his childhood, their peculiar flavour and the flow of saliva when he sucked their stones, and along with the memory of that taste came a whole series of memories of those days: his nurse, his brother, and their toys. "No, I mustn't think of that. . . . It is too painful," Ivan Ilych said to himself, and brought himself back to the present—to the button on the back of the sofa and the creases in its morocco. "Morocco is expensive, but it does not wear well: there had been a quarrel about it. It was a different kind of quarrel and a different kind of morocco that time when we tore father's portfolio and were punished, and mamma brought us some tarts. . . ." And again his thoughts dwelt on his childhood, and again it was painful and he tried to banish them and fix his mind on something else.

Then again together with that chain of memories another series passed through his mind—of how his illness had progressed and grown worse. There also the further back he looked the more life there had been. There had been more of what was good in life and more of life itself. The two

Just as the pain went on getting worse and worse, so . . . rse and worse," he thought. "There is one bright spot . . . ack, at the beginning of life, and afterwards all becomes . . . olacker and proceeds more and more rapidly—in inverse ratio . . . are of the distance from death," thought Ivan Ilych. And the . . . of a stone falling downwards with increasing velocity entered his min . . . Life, a series of increasing sufferings, flies further and further towards its end—the most terrible suffering. "I am flying. . . ." He shuddered, shifted himself, and tried to resist, but was already aware that resistance was impossible, and again, with eyes weary of gazing but unable to cease seeing what was before them, he stared at the back of the sofa and waited—awaiting that dreadful fall and shock and destruction.

"Resistance is impossible!" he said to himself. "If I could only understand what it is all for! But that too is impossible. An explanation would be possible if it could be said that I have not lived as I ought to. But it is impossible to say that," and he remembered all the legality, correctitude, and propriety of his life. "That at any rate can certainly not be admitted," he thought, and his lips smiled ironically as if someone could see that smile and be taken in by it. "There is no explanation! Agony, death. . . . What for?"

XI

Another two weeks went by in this way and during that fortnight an event occurred that Ivan Ilych and his wife had desired. Petrishchev formally proposed. It happened in the evening. The next day Praskovya Fëdorovna came into her husband's room considering how best to inform him of it, but that very night there had been a fresh change for the worse in his condition. She found him still lying on the sofa but in a different position. He lay on his back, groaning and staring fixedly straight in front of him.

She began to remind him of his medicines, but he turned his eyes towards her with such a look that she did not finish what she was saying; so great an animosity, to her in particular, did that look express.

"For Christ's sake let me die in peace!" he said.

She would have gone away, but just then their daughter came in and went up to say good morning. He looked at her as he had done at his wife, and in reply to her inquiry about his health said dryly that he would soon free them all of himself. They were both silent and after sitting with him for a while went away.

"Is it our fault?" Lisa said to her mother. "It's as if we were to blame! I am sorry for papa, but why should we be tortured?"

The doctor came at his usual time. Ivan Ilych answered "Yes" and

"No," never taking his angry eyes from him, and at last said: "You know you can do nothing for me, so leave me alone."

"We can ease your sufferings."

"You can't even do that. Let me be."

The doctor went into the drawing-room and told Praskovya Fëdorovna that the case was very serious and that the only resource left was opium to allay her husband's sufferings, which must be terrible.

It was true, as the doctor said, that Ivan Ilych's physical sufferings were terrible, but worse than the physical sufferings were his mental sufferings, which were his chief torture.

His mental sufferings were due to the fact that that night, as he looked at Gerasim's sleepy, good-natured face with its prominent cheekbones, the question suddenly occurred to him: "What if my whole life has really been wrong?"

It occurred to him that what had appeared perfectly impossible before, namely that he had not spent his life as he should have done, might after all be true. It occurred to him that his scarcely perceptible attempts to struggle against what was considered good by the most highly placed people, those scarcely noticeable impulses which he had immediately suppressed, might have been the real thing, and all the rest false. And his professional duties and the whole arrangement of his life and of his family, and all his social and official interests, might all have been false. He tried to defend all those things to himself and suddenly felt the weakness of what he was defending. There was nothing to defend.

"But if that is so," he said to himself, "and I am leaving this life with the consciousness that I have lost all that was given me and it is impossible to rectify it—what then?"

He lay on his back and began to pass his life in review in quite a new way. In the morning when he saw first his footman, then his wife, then his daughter, and then the doctor, their every word and movement confirmed to him the awful truth that had been revealed to him during the night. In them he saw himself—all that for which he had lived—and saw clearly that it was not real at all, but a terrible and huge deception which had hidden both life and death. This consciousness intensified his physical suffering tenfold. He groaned and tossed about, and pulled at his clothing which choked and stifled him. And he hated them on that account.

He was given a large dose of opium and became unconscious, but at noon his sufferings began again. He drove everybody away and tossed from side to side.

His wife came to him and said:

"Jean, my dear, do this for me. It can't do any harm and often helps. Healthy people often do it."

He opened his eyes wide.

"What? Take communion? Why? It's unnecessary! However . . ."

She began to cry.

"Yes, do, my dear. I'll send for our priest. He is such a nice man."

"All right. Very well," he muttered.

When the priest came and heard his confession, Ivan Ilych was softened and seemed to feel a relief from his doubts and consequently from his sufferings, and for a moment there came a ray of hope. He again began to think of the vermiform appendix and the possibility of correcting it. He received the sacrament with tears in his eyes.

When they laid him down again afterwards he felt a moment's ease, and the hope that he might live awoke in him again. He began to think of the operation that had been suggested to him. "To live! I want to live!" he said to himself.

His wife came in to congratulate him after his communion, and when uttering the usual conventional words she added:

"You feel better, don't you?"

Without looking at her he said "Yes."

Her dress, her figure, the expression of her face, the tone of her voice, all revealed the same thing. "This is wrong, it is not as it should be. All you have lived for and still live for is falsehood and deception, hiding life and death from you." And as soon as he admitted that thought, his hatred and his agonizing physical suffering again sprang up, and with that suffering a consciousness of the unavoidable, approaching end. And to this was added a new sensation of grinding shooting pain and a feeling of suffocation.

The expression of his face when he uttered that "yes" was dreadful. Having uttered it, he looked her straight in the eyes, turned on his face with a rapidity extraordinary in his weak state and shouted:

"Go away! Go away and leave me alone!"

XII

From that moment the screaming began that continued for three days, and was so terrible that one could not hear it through two closed doors without horror. At the moment he answered his wife he realized that he was lost, that there was no return, that the end had come, the very end, and his doubts were still unsolved and remained doubts.

"Oh! Oh! Oh!" he cried in various intonations. He had begun by screaming "I won't!" and continued screaming on the letter O.

For three whole days, during which time did not exist for him, he struggled in that black sack into which he was being thrust by an invisible, resistless force. He struggled as a man condemned to death struggles in the hands of the executioner, knowing that he cannot save himself. And every moment he felt that despite all his efforts he was drawing nearer and nearer to what terrified him. He felt that his agony was due to his being thrust into that black hole and still more to his not being able to get right into it. He was hindered from getting into it by his conviction that his life had been a good one. That very justification of his life held him fast and prevented his moving forward, and it caused him most torment of all.

Suddenly some force struck him in the chest and side, making it still harder to breathe, and he fell through the hole and there at the bottom was a light. What had happened to him was like the sensation one sometimes experiences in a railway carriage when one thinks one is going backwards while one is really going forwards and suddenly becomes aware of the real direction.

"Yes, it was all not the right thing," he said to himself, "but that's no matter. It can be done. But what *is* the right thing?" he asked himself, and suddenly grew quiet.

This occurred at the end of the third day, two hours before his death. Just then his schoolboy son had crept softly in and gone up to the bedside. The dying man was still screaming desperately and waving his arms. His hand fell on the boy's head, and the boy caught it, pressed it to his lips, and began to cry.

At that very moment Ivan Ilych fell through and caught sight of the light, and it was revealed to him that though his life had not been what it should have been, this could still be rectified. He asked himself, "What *is* the right thing?" and grew still, listening. Then he felt that someone was kissing his hand. He opened his eyes, looked at his son, and felt sorry for him. His wife came up to him and he glanced at her. She was gazing at him open-mouthed, with undried tears on her nose and cheek and a despairing look on her face. He felt sorry for her too.

"Yes, I am making them wretched," he thought. "They are sorry, but it will be better for them when I die." He wished to say this but had not the strength to utter it. "Besides, why speak? I must act," he thought. With a look at his wife he indicated his son and said: "Take him away . . . sorry for him . . . sorry for you too. . . ." He tried to add, "Forgive me," but said "forgo" and waved his hand, knowing that He whose understanding mattered would understand.

And suddenly it grew clear to him that what had been oppressing him and would not leave him was all dropping away at once from two sides, from ten sides, and from all sides. He was sorry for them, he must act so as not to hurt them: release them and free himself from these sufferings. "How good and how simple!" he thought. "And the pain?" he asked himself. "What has become of it? Where are you, pain?"

He turned his attention to it.

"Yes, here it is. Well, what of it? Let the pain be."

"And death . . . where is it?"

He sought his former accustomed fear of death and did not find it. "Where is it? What death?" There was no fear because there was no death.

In place of death there was light.

"So that's what it is!" he suddenly exclaimed aloud. "What joy!"

To him all this happened in a single instant, and the meaning of that instant did not change. For those present his agony continued for another two hours. Something rattled in his throat, his emaciated body twitched, then the gasping and rattle became less and less frequent.

"It is finished!" said someone near him.

He heard these words and repeated them in his soul.

"Death is finished," he said to himself. "It is no more!"

He drew in a breath, stopped in the midst of a sigh, stretched out, and died.

Dramatic: Alternate Contents

SETTING AND STRUCTURE
>Hedda Gabler   118

CHARACTER
>The Glass Menagerie   228

LANGUAGE
>Romeo and Juliet   35

TRAGEDY
>Antigone   3

COMEDY
>The Playboy of the Western World   184

Poetic: Alternate Contents

I. THE NARRATIVE POEM: *Dramatized Experience*

Sir Patrick Spens	297	The Song of Wandering	
Ulysses	379	Aengus	426
Porphyria's Lover	382	The River-Merchant's Wife:	
My Last Duchess	383	A Letter	446
A Bird came down the Walk	405	The Love Song of J. Alfred	
The Convergence of the		Prufrock	437
Twain	410	*See also* the works of John Donne	

II. THE DIDACTIC POEM: *Contemplative Experience*

The Nymph's Reply to the		Tell all the Truth but tell it	
Shepherd	301	slant	403
The expense of spirit in a		Terence, This Is Stupid Stuff	412
waste of shame	314	The Second Coming	430
To His Coy Mistress	336	Mundus et Infans	460
from An Essay on Man	340	#4: First fight. Then fiddle. Ply	
Elegy Written in a Country		the slipping string	470
Churchyard	346		
The World Is Too Much			
with Us	366		

III. THE LYRIC POEM: *Song of Experience*

Song (Go and catch a		Down by the Salley Gardens	418
falling star)	319	Siege	450
Still to Be Neat	331	if i have made, my lady,	
Upon Julia's Clothes	333	intricate	453
The Tyger	356	O Where Are You Going	460
She Walks in Beauty	370	O When I Take My Love Out	
Ode to the West Wind	372	Walking	465
To Autumn (Keats)	376	The Pennycandystore	471
Out of the Cradle Endlessly		*See also* the works of Shakespeare,	
Rocking	388	Blake, and Yeats	
God's Grandeur	407		

IV. THE IMAGISTIC POEM: *Construction of Experience—*
Statues in the Mind

Kubla Khan	368	In a Station of the Metro	446
Meeting at Night	385	Hymn	448
I heard a Fly buzz—when I		The Diver	466
died	398	Fall's Girl	475
Lapis Lazuli	432	*See also* the works of Dickinson	
Birches	434	and Yeats	
The Red Wheelbarrow	445		

Narrative:　Alternate Contents

PLOT

    Dry September　583
    The Death of Ivan Ilych　628

SETTING

    Flying Home　525
    A Good Man Is Hard to Find　615

SCENES

    My Kinsman, Major Molineux　570
    Torch Song　593

CHARACTER

    Sonny's Blues　547
    Gooseberries　606

POINT OF VIEW

    The Basement Room　490
    "Cruel and Barbarous Treatment"　573

LANGUAGE AND SYMBOLISM

    Araby　485
    Soldier's Home　541

Index of Authors and Titles

A

Adam's Curse 418
After great pain, a formal feeling comes 401
Agony. As Now., An 480
Ah! Sun-flower 354
Ah! why hath Nature to so hard a heart 302
America 449
Ancient Music 447
Antigone 3
anyone lived in a pretty how town 452
Apparition, The 320
Araby 485
Are Not the Joys of Morning Sweeter 363
Arnold, Matthew 386
At the round earth's imagined corners, blow 328
Auden, W. H. 460
Auld Lang Syne 351

B

Baldwin, James 547
Basement Room, The 490
Batter my heart, three-personed God; for You 330
Because I could not stop for Death 398
Birches 434
Bird came down the Walk, A 405
Blake, William 353
Blossom, The 354
Brooke, Rupert 415
Brooks, Gwendolyn 470
Browning, Robert 350
Burns, Robert 350
Byron, George Noel Gordon, Lord 370

C

Cannery, The 476
Canonization, The 327
Channel Firing 409
Cheever, John 593
Chekhov, Anton 606
Chimney Sweeper, The 359, 360
Clod and the Pebble, The 362
Coleridge, Samuel Taylor 368
Come, My Celia 331
Community 318
Composed upon Westminster Bridge 366
Convergence of the Twain, The 410
Corinna's Going A-Maying 334
Crazy Jane Talks with the Bishop 422
"Cruel and Barbarous Treatment" 473
Cummings, E. E. 452

D

Death be not proud, though some have called thee 329
Death of Ivan Ilych, The 628
Delight in Disorder 333
Devouring Time, blunt thou the lion's paws 306
Dialogue of Self and Soul, A 420
Dickey, James 473
Dickinson, Emily 394
Diver, The 466
Divine Image, The 358
Do Not Go Gentle into That Good Night 469
Donne, John 318
Dover Beach 386
Down by the Salley Gardens 418
Dry September 583
Dugan, Alan 472
Dulce et Decorum Est 417

E

Eagle: A Fragment, The 381
Easter, 1916 428
Ecstasy, The 324
Edward 296
Elegy Written in a Country Churchyard 346
Eliot, T. S. 437
Ellison, Ralph 525
Epistle I. Of the Nature and State of Man, With Respect to the Universe 340
Epistle II. Of the Nature and State of Man, With Respect to Himself, as an Individual 345
Essential Oils — are wrung 403
expense of spirit in a waste of shame, The 314

F

Fall's Girl 475
Fascination of What's Difficult, The 420
Faulkner, William 583
Ferlinghetti, Lawrence 471
First fight. Then fiddle. Ply the slipping string 470
Flea, The 321
Fly, The 357
Flying Home 525
Force That through the Green Fuse Drives the Flower, The 468
From fairest creatures we desire increase 304
Frost, Robert 434
Further in Summer than the Birds 396

G

Garden of Love, The   360
Glass Menagerie, The   228
God's Grandeur   407
Good Man Is Hard to Find, A   615
Gooseberries   606
Gray, Thomas   346
Greene, Graham   490

H

Hardy, Thomas   409
Hawthorne, Nathaniel   510
Hayden, Robert E.   466
H. D. (Hilda Doolittle)   448
Heaven   515
Hedda Gabler   118
Hemingway, Ernest   541
Herrick, Robert   333
Hopkins, Gerard Manley   407
Housman, A. E.   412
How sweet and lovely dost thou make the shame   312
Hymn   448

I

I Asked a Thief to Steal Me a Peach   360
I cannot dance upon my Toes   402
I felt a Funeral, in my Brain   400
I heard a Fly buzz—when I died   398
Ibsen, Henrik   118
if i have made, my lady, intricate   453
I'm ceded—I've stopped being Theirs   402
In a Station of the Metro   446
In loving thee know'st I am forsworn   317
In the old age black was not counted fair   313
I've seen a Dying Eye   397

J

Jones, LeRoi   480
Jonson, Ben   331
Journey of the Magi   441
Joyce, James   485

K

Keats, John   376
Kubla Khan   368

L

Lake Isle of Innisfree, The   423
Lamb, The   355
Lapis Lazuli   432
Leda and the Swan   431
Let me not to the marriage of true minds   313
London   361
Love Song of J. Alfred Prufrock, The   437

M

Mad Song   363
Marlowe, Christopher   300
Marvell, Andrew   336
McCarthy, Mary   473
McKay, Claude   449
Meeting at Night   385
Men call you fair, and you do credit it   302
Millay, Edna St. Vincent   450
Milton, John   338
Mundus et Infans   460
My Kinsman, Major Molineux   510
My Last Duchess   383
My love is as a fever, longing still   316
My mistress' eyes are nothing like the sun   314
My Papa's Waltz   463

N

Nathan, Leonard E.   475
No more be grieved at that which thou hast done   308
Not marble, nor the gilded monuments   309
Nymph's Reply to the Shepherd, The   301

O

O Lapwing, Thou Fliest Around the Heath   364
O When I Take My Love Out Walking   465
O Where Are You Going   460
O'Connor, Flannery   615
Ode on a Grecian Urn   377
Ode to the West Wind   372
Of Bronze—and Blaze   404
On His Blindness   338
On His Having Arrived at the Age of Twenty-Three   338
Once by the Pacific   435
One need not be a Chamber—to be Haunted   399
Out of the Cradle Endlessly Rocking   388
Outer—from the Inner, The   405
Owen, Wilfred   417

P

Passionate Shepherd to His Love, The   300
Patchen, Kenneth   465
Pennycandystore, The   471
Perception of an object costs   404
Performance, The   473
Pied Beauty   407
Pit, The   476
Playboy of the Western World, The   184
Poison Tree, A   362
Poor soul, the centre of my sinful earth   316
Pope, Alexander   340
Porphyria's Lover   382
Pound, Ezra   446
Preface to Milton   364

R

Raleigh, Sir Walter   301
Red Wheelbarrow, The   445
River-Merchant's Wife: A Letter, The   446
Roethke, Theodore   463
Romeo and Juliet   35

S

Sailing to Byzantium   426
Second Coming, The   430
Shakespeare, William   35, 304
Shall I compare thee to a summer's day?   306
She Walks in Beauty   370
Shelley, Percy Bysshe   372
Sick Rose, The   355
Siege   450
Since brass, nor stone, nor earth, nor boundless sea   309
Sir Patrick Spens   297
Snyder, Gary   478
Soldier's Home   541
Song (Go and catch a falling star)   319
Song (My silks and fine array)   357
Song of the Wandering Aengus, The   426
Sonny's Blues   547
Sophocles   3
Spenser, Edmund   302
Spring   450
Spring and All   444
Spring and Fall   408
Stevens, Wallace   454
Still to Be Neat   331
Stryk, Lucien   476
Sun Rising, The   322
Sunday Morning   456
Synge, John Millington   184

T

Tell all the Truth but tell it slant   403
Tennyson, Alfred, Lord   379
Terence, This Is Stupid Stuff   412
That thou hast her, it is not all grief   308
That time of year thou mayst in me behold   310
There came a Wind like a Bugle   396
There's a certain Slant of light   400
They shut me up in Prose   394
They that have power to hurt and will do none   311
Thirteen Ways of Looking at a Blackbird   454
This Consciousness that is aware   401
"this poem is for deer"   478
This World is not Conclusion   394

Thomas, Dylan   468
Thou Hast a Lap Full of Seed   364
Thus is his cheek the map of days outworn   310
To a Mouse   350
To Autumn   353, 376
To His Coy Mistress   336
To Spring   353
Tolstoy, Leo   628
Torch Song   593
Tribute to Kafka for Someone Taken   472
Twa Corbies, The   295
'Twas warm — at first — like Us   397
Two loves I have of comfort and despair   315
Tyger, The   356

U

Ulysses   379
Upon Julia's Clothes   333

V

Valediction: Forbidding Mourning, A   323
Valediction: Of Weeping, A   320

W

Waking, The   463
Was it the proud full sail of his great verse   310
What if this present were the world's last night?   329
What mystery pervades a well!   395
When a Man Hath No Freedom   370
When forty winters shall besiege thy brow   305
When I do count the clock that tells the time   305
When I Heard the Learn'd Astronomer   393
When, in disgrace with fortune and men's eyes   307
When in the chronicle of wasted time   312
When my love swears that she is made of t·uth   315
When to the sessions of sweet silent thought   307
Whitman, Walt   388
Why Should Not Old Men Be Mad?   425
Wild Old Wicked Man, The   423
Williams, Tennessee   228
Williams, William Carlos   443
word dropped careless on a Page, A   406
Word made Flesh is seldom, A   406
Wordsworth, William   366
World Is Too Much with Us, The   366

Y

Yachts, The   443
Yeats, William Butler   418

Index of First Lines

A

A bird came down the Walk   405
A cold coming we had of it   441
A little black thing among the snow   360
A sudden blow: the great wings beating still 431
A sweet disorder in the dress   333
A Word dropped careless on a Page   406
A Word made Flesh is seldom   406
After great pain, a formal feeling comes   401
Against the wind, she took the field – long hair 475
Ah, Sun-flower! weary of time   354
Ah! why hath Nature to so hard a heart   302
Although she feeds me bread of bitterness 449
Among twenty snowy mountains   454
And did those feet in ancient time   364
anyone lived in a pretty how town   452
apparition of these faces in the crowd, The 446
Are not the joys of morning sweeter   363
As I was walking all alane   295
As virtuous men pass mildly away   323
At the round earth's imagined corners, blow 328
Awake, my St. John! leave all meaner things 340

B

Batter my heart, three-personed God; for You 330
"Because I am mad about women   423
Because I could not stop for Death   398
Bent double, like old beggars under sacks 417
Busy old fool, unruly sun   322
By the road to the contagious hospital   444

C

Come live with me and be my love   300
Come, my Celia, let us prove   331
Complacencies of the peignoir, and late   456
contend in a sea which the land partly encloses 443
curfew tolls the knell of parting day, The 346

D

Death be not proud, though some have called thee   329
Devouring Time, blunt thou the lion's paws 306
Do not go gentle into that good night   469
Down by the salley gardens my love and I did meet   418

E

Earth has not anything to show more fair 366
Essential oils – are wrung   403
expense of spirit in a waste of shame, The 314

F

fascination of what's difficult, The   420
First fight. Then fiddle. Ply the slipping string 470
Fish (fly-replete, in depth of June   415
For God's sake, hold your tongue, and let me love   327
force that through the green fuse drives the flower, The   468
From fairest creatures we desire increase 304
Further in Summer than the Birds   396

G

Get up, get up for shame, the blooming morn 334
Glory be to God for dappled things   407
Go and catch a falling star   319
Good we must love, and must hate ill   318
gray sea and the long black land, The   385

H

Had we but world enough, and time   336
He clasps the crag with crooked hands   381
How soon hath Time, the subtle thief of youth   338
How sweet and lovely dost thou make the shame   312

I

I am inside someone   480
I asked a thief to steal me a peach   360
I cannot dance upon my Toes   402
"I dance on all the mountains   478
I felt a Funeral, in my Brain   400
I have heard that hysterical women say   432
I have met them at close of day   428
I heard a Fly buzz – when I died   398
I met a traveler from an antique land   375
I met the Bishop on the road   422
I wake to sleep, and take my waking slow   463
I wander thro' each charter'd street   361
I was angry with my friend   362
I went out to the hazel wood   426
I went to the Garden of Love   360
I will arise and go now, and go to Innisfree   423
If all the world and love were young   301
if i have made, my lady, intricate   453
I'm ceded – I've stopped being Theirs   402
In a solitude of the sea   410
In loving thee thou know'st I am forsworn   317
In summer this town is full of rebels   476
In the old age black was not counted fair   313
In Xanadu did Kubla Khan   368
It little profits that an idle king   379
I've seen a Dying Eye   397

K

Kicking his mother until she let go of his soul   460
king sits in Dunfermline toune, The   296
Know then thyself, presume not God to scan   345

L

last time I saw Donald Armstrong, The   473
Let me not to the marriage of true minds   313
Let me pour forth   320
Let us go then, you and I   437
Little Fly   357
Little Lamb, who made thee?   355
"Love seeketh not Itself to please   362

M

Márgarét, are you gríeving   408
Mark but this flea, and mark in this   321
Men call you fair, and you do credit it   302
Merry, Merry Sparrow   354
My love is as a fever, longing still   316
My mistress' eyes are nothing like the sun   314

My silks and fine array   357
My Soul. I summon to the winding ancient stair   420

N

No more be grieved at that which thou hast done   308
Not marble, nor the gilded monuments   309

O

O Autumn, laden with fruit, and stained   353
O lapwing, thou fliest around the heath   364
O Rose, thou art sick!   355
O thou with dewy locks, who lookest down   353
O when I take my love out walking   465
"O where are you going?" said reader to rider   460
O wild West Wind, thou breath of Autumn's being   372
Of Bronze – and Blaze   404
Of unguent in a jar   448
One need not be a Chamber – to be Haunted   399
Out of the cradle endlessly rocking   388
Outer – from the Inner, The   405

P

Party is going strong, The   472
pennycandystore beyond the El, The   471
Perception of an object costs   404
Poor soul, the centre of my sinful earth   316

R

rain set early in tonight, The   382

S

Sank through easeful   466
sea is calm tonight, The   386
Season of mists and mellow fruitfulness   376
Shall I compare thee to a summer's day?   306
shattered water made a misty din, The   435
She walks in beauty, like the night   370
Should auld acquaintance be forgot   351
Since brass, nor stone, nor earth, nor boundless sea   309
so much depends   445
Still to be neat, still to be dressed   331

T

Tell all the Truth but tell it slant   403
"Terence, this is stupid stuff   412

That is no country for old men. The young 426

That night your great guns, unawares 409

That thou hast her, it is not all my grief 308

That time of year thou mayst in me behold 310

That's my last Duchess painted on the wall 383

There came a Wind like a Bugle 396

There's a certain Slant of light 400

They shut me up in Prose— 394

They that have power to hurt and will do none 311

This Consciousness that is aware 401

This I do, being mad 450

This World is not Conclusion 394

Thou hast a lap full of seed 364

Thou still unravished bride of quietness 377

Thus is his cheek the map of days outworn 310

To Mercy, Pity, Peace, and Love 358

To what purpose, April, do you return again 450

Turning and turning in the widening gyre 430

'Twas warm—at first—like Us 397

Twenty years. I still remember 476

Two loves I have of comfort and despair 315

Tyger! Tyger! burning bright 356

W

Was it the proud full sail of his great verse 310

We sat together at one summer's end 418

Wee, sleekit, cowrin, tim'rous beastie 350

What if this present were the world's last night 329

What mystery pervades a well! 395

When a man hath no freedom to fight for at home 370

When by thy scorn, O murd'ress, I am dead 320

When forty winters shall besiege thy brow 305

When I consider how my light is spent 338

When I do count the clock that tells the time 305

When I heard the learn'd astronomer 393

When I see birches bend to left and right 434

When, in disgrace with fortune and men's eyes 307

When in the chronicle of wasted time 312

When my love swears that she is made of truth 315

When my mother died I was very young 359

When to the sessions of sweet silent thought 307

Whenas in silks my Julia goes 333

Where, like a pillow on a bed 324

While my hair was still cut straight across my forehead 446

whiskey on your breath, The 463

"Why dois your brand sae drap wi bluid 296

Why should not old men be mad? 425

wild winds weep, The 363

Winter is icumen in 447

world is charged with the grandeur of God, The 407

world is too much with us; late and soon, The 366